Lecture Notes in Computer Science

Commenced Publication in 1973
Founding and Former Series Editors:
Gerhard Goos, Juris Hartmanis, and Jan van Leeuwen

Editorial Board

Boualem Benatallah   Fabio Casati
Paolo Traverso (Eds.)

Service-Oriented Computing – ICSOC 2005

Third International Conference
Amsterdam, The Netherlands, December 12-15, 2005
Proceedings

 Springer

Volume Editors

Boualem Benatallah
The University of New South Wales, School of Computer Science and Engineering
Sydney, NSW 2052, Australia
E-mail: boualem@cse.unsw.edu.au

Fabio Casati
Hewlett-Packard
1501 Page Mill Rd, MS 1142, Palo Alto, CA, 94304, USA
E-mail: fabio.casati@hp.com

Paolo Traverso
ITC-IRST
Via Sommarive 18, Povo, 38050 Trento, Italy
E-mail: traverso@itc.it

Library of Congress Control Number: 2005936810

CR Subject Classification (1998): C.2, D.2, D.4, H.4, H.3, K.4.4

ISSN   0302-9743
ISBN-10   3-540-30817-2 Springer Berlin Heidelberg New York
ISBN-13   978-3-540-30817-1 Springer Berlin Heidelberg New York

Springer is a part of Springer Science+Business Media

springeronline.com

© Springer-Verlag Berlin Heidelberg 2005
Printed in Germany

Typesetting: Camera-ready by author, data conversion by Scientific Publishing Services, Chennai, India
Printed on acid-free paper   SPIN: 11596141   06/3142   5 4 3 2 1 0

Preface

This volume contains the proceedings of the Third International Conference on Service-Oriented Computing (ICSOC 2005), that took place in Amsterdam, The Netherlands, December 12-15, 2005.

The 2005 edition had the important and ambitious goal of bringing together the different communities working in Web services and service-oriented computing. By attracting excellent contributions from different scientific communities, ICSOC aims at creating a scientific venue where participants can share ideas and compare their approaches to tackling the many still-open common research challenges. The commitment to cross-area fertilization was put into practice by having a very diversified Program Committee and by the presence of several *area coordinators*, leaders in the respective communities who encouraged and supervised submissions in each area. This is also the first edition to feature a successful workshop and demo program, with selected demos also presented in a paper-like fashion so that they get the attention they deserve.

In addition, ICSOC 2005 inherited from previous editions a strong industrial presence, both in the conference organization and in the program. This is very important due to the industrial relevance and the many challenges of service oriented technologies.

The paper selection process was very thorough. This year, ICSOC introduced a two-phase review process where authors were invited to provide their own feedback, which the Program Committee took into account in the discussion and final decision on paper acceptance. ICSOC 2005 received over 200 contributions, accepting 32 full papers (3 of which are industrial papers) and 14 short papers. In addition to the regular, industry, and short presentations, the conference featured tutorials, panels, a vision session to discuss the evolution of service-oriented computing, and – as customary in ICSOC – top-notch keynotes, given by leaders in the industrial and academic community.

The excellent program that was assembled for presentation at this conference is a reflection of the hard and dedicated work of numerous people. We thank the members of the Program Committee and the reviewers for their great efforts in selecting the papers, even more so this year as the two-phase review process posed an additional burden on the reviewers. We also acknowledge the great contribution of Willem Jan van den Heuvel and Kees Leune in the local organization, of Shonali Krishnaswamy, Helen Paik, and Michael Sheng in handling the publicity, and of Frans Laurijssen, who maintained the website. Special thanks go to Piergiorgio Bertoli and Maurizio Napolitano for the tremendous job and their impressive and continuous assistance with the review process logistics and for handling the camera-ready contributions. We also thank Christoph Bussler and Meichun Hsu (Panel Chairs), Schahram Dustdar (Demo Program Chair), Asit Dan and Vincenzo D'Andrea (Tutorial Chairs), Frank Leymann and Winfried Lamersdorf (Workshop Chairs), and Maurizio Marchese

(Financial Chair). Last but not least, we thank our sponsors, which include IBM, Hewlett-Packard, the Universities of Tilburg and Trento along with the Vrijie Universiteit Amsterdam, NICTA, ITC-irst, and our partners ACM SIGWeb and SIGSoft.

We hope you find the papers in this volume interesting and stimulating.

Paco Curbera and Mike Papazoglou (ICSOC 2005 Conference Chairs)

Boualem Benatallah, Fabio Casati, and Paolo Traverso (ICSOC 2005 Program Chairs)

Jean Jaques Dubray (ICSOC 2005 Industrial Chair)

Organization

ICSOC 2005 Conference Chairs

Conference Chairs	Francisco Curbera, IBM Research, USA Mike Papazoglou, Tilburg University, Netherlands
Program Chairs	Boualem Benatallah, UNSW, Australia Fabio Casati, Hewlett-Packard, USA Paolo Traverso, ITC-irst, Italy
Industrial Track Chair	Jean Jacques Dubray, Attachmate, USA
Demo Chair	Schahram Dustdar, Vienna University of Technology, Austria
Panel Chairs	Christoph Bussler, DERI, Ireland Mei Hsu, USA
Tutorial Chairs	Asit Dan, IBM Research, USA Vincenzo D'Andrea, Univ. of Trento, Italy
Workshop Chairs	Frank Leymann, Univ. of Stuttgart, Germany Winfried Lamersdorf, Hamburg University, Germany
Financial Chair	Maurizio Marchese, Univ. of Trento, Italy
Publicity Chairs	Helen Paik, QUT, Australia Shonali Krishnaswamy, Monash Univ., Australia Michael Sheng, UNSW, Australia
Area Coordinators	Roger Barga, Microsoft
	Elisa Bertino, Purdue
	Jim Blythe, ISI/USC
	Stefano Ceri, Politecnico di Milano
	Boi Faltings, EPFL
	Ian Foster - ANL & University of Chicago
	Carlo Ghezzi, Politecnico di Milano
	Richard Hull, Bell Labs Research, Lucent Tech.
	Hui Lei, IBM
	Ugo Montanari, University of Pisa

	John Mylopolous, University of Toronto
	Colette Roland, University of Paris
Local Organization Chairs	Willem Jan van den Heuvel, Tilburg University, Netherlands
	Kees Leune, Tilburg University, Netherlands

Program Committee

Wil van der Aalst	Eindhoven University of Technology, Netherlands
Marco Aiello	University of Trento, Italy
Jose Luis Ambite	ISI, USA
Mikio Aoyama	Nanzan University, Japan
Carlo Batini	Univ. Milano – Bicocca, Italy
Luciano Baresi	Politecnico di Milano, Italy
Walter Binder	EPFL, Switzerland
Susanne Biundo	Univ. of Ulm, Germany
Sjaak Brinkkemper	Univ. of Utrecht, Netherlands
Athman Bouguettaya	Virginia Tech, USA
Marco Brambilla	Politecnico di Milano, Italy
Tevfik Bultan	University of California, USA
Malu Castellanos	Hewlett-Packard, USA
Jen-Yao Chung	IBM T. J. Watson Research center, USA
Bruno Crispo	Free University Amsterdam, Netherlands
Ernesto Damiani	University of Milano, Italy
Umesh Dayal	Hewlett-Packard, USA
Jens-Peter Dittrich	ETH Zurich, Switzerland
Alex Delis	University of Athens, Greece
Asuman Dogac	METU, Turkey
John Domingue	Open University, UK
Schahram Dustdar	Vienna University of Technology, Austria
Kim Elms	SAP, Australia
Dieter Fensel	DERI, Ireland
Ioannis Fikouras	BIBA, Germany
Gianluigi Ferrari	University of Pisa, Italy
Daniela Florescu	Oracle, USA
Dimitrios Georgakopoulos	Telcordia, USA
Enrico Giunchiglia	University of Genoa, Italy
Claude Godart	INRIA, France
Andrew D. Gordon	Microsoft Research, Cambridge, UK
Jaap Gordijn	Free Univ. Amsterdam, Netherlands

Paul Grefen	Eindhoven Univ. of Technology, Netherlands
John Grundy	University of Auckland, New Zealand
Mohand-Said Hacid	Université Claude Bernard Lyon, France
Jos van Hillegersberg	Erasmus Univ., Netherlands
Meichun Hsu	HP, USA
Subbarao Kambhampati	Arizona State University, USA
Alfons Kemper	TU München, Germany
Matthias Klusch	DFKI, Germany
Jana Koehler	IBM Zurich, Switzerland
Bernd Kraemer	University of Hagen, Germany
Ruben Lara	Tecnologia, Informacion y Finanzas, Spain
Ninghui Li	Purdue University, USA
Ling Liu	Georgia Tech, USA
Brian LaMacchia	Microsoft, USA
Frank Leymann	University of Stuttgart, Germany
Heiko Ludwig	IBM Research, USA
Pierluigi Lucchese	ITC-irst, Italy
Ioana Manolescu	INRIA, France
Neil Maiden	City University, London, UK
David Martin	SRI International, USA
Massimo Mecella	University "La Sapienza" Rome, Italy
Aad Van Moorsel	Newcastle Univ., UK
Brahim Medjahed	University of Michigan, USA
Anne Ngu	Southwest Texas State University, USA
Tommaso Di Noia	Politecnico di Bari, Italy
Aris M. Ouksel	University of Illinois at Chicago, USA
Beng Chin Ooi	National University of Singapore, Singapore
Maria Orlowska	UQ, Australia
Flavio De Paoli	Univ. Milano – Bicocca, Italy
Barbara Pernici	Politecnico di Milano, Italy
Marco Pistore	Università di Trento, Italy
Dimitris Plexousakis	FORTH, Greece
Bijan Parsia	University of Maryland at College Park, USA
Axel Polleres	Digital Enterprise Research Institute InnsbrAustria
Omer Rana	Cardiff Univ., UK
Calton Pu	Georgia Tech, USA
Rainer Ruggaber	SAP, Germany
Vladimiro Sassone	University of Sussex, UK
Akhil Sahai	Hewlett-Packard, USA
Rizos Sakellariou	University of Manchester, UK

Ming-Chien Shan	Hewlett-Packard, USA
Amit Sheth	University of Georgia, USA
John Shepherd	UNSW, Australia
Biplav Srivastava	IBM, India
Ian Sommerville	Lancaster University, UK
Maarten Steen	Telematica Institute, Netherlands
Jianwen Su	UCSB, USA
Katia Sycara	Carnegie Mellon University, USA
Kian-Lee Tan	National University of Singapore, Singapore
Paolo Tonella	ITC-irst, Italy
Farouk Toumani	LIMOS, France
Vijay Varadharajan	Macquarie Univ. and Microsoft, Australia
Athena Vakali	Aristotle University, Greece
Raymond Wong	University of New South Wales, Australia
Michael Wooldridge	University of Liverpool, UK
Martin Wirsing	Ludwig Maximilians University Munich, Germany
Roel Wieringa	University of Twente, Netherlands
Jian Yang	Macquarie University, Australia
Arkady Zaslavsky	Monash University, Australia
Gianluigi Zavattaro	University of Bologna, Italy
Yanchun Zhang	Victoria University, Australia

Additional Referees

D. Ardagna	G. Elia
C. Ardagna	F. Eruysal
R. Batenburg	D. Florescu
D. Berardi	P. Fournogerakis
P. Bertoli	G. Frankova
C. Braghin	F. Frati
F. Cabitza	E. Freiter
C. Cappiello	C. Fugazza
P. Ceravolo	G.R. Gangadharan
G. Chafle	G. Gianini
G. Conforti	D. Gorla
A. Corallo	R. Helms
V. D'Andrea	W. Hordijk
M. Daneva	K. Hribernik
S. De Capitani di Vimercati	S. Jansen
F. De Rosa	R. Kazhamiakin
E. Di Sciascio	N. Kokash
F. Donini	J. Kopecky

K. Kuladinithi
A. Kumar
M. Lankhorst
H. Lausen
A. Lazovik
R. Levenshteyn
L. Liang
T. Liebig
X. Liu
M. Loregian
D. Lundquist
J. Ma
L. Maesano
A. Marconi
L. Mariani
S. Marrara
A. Maurino
N. Mehandjiev
C. Mentrup
P. Missier
S. Mittal
S. Modafferi
E. Mussi

P. Philipopoulos
P. Plebani
S. Pokraev
Y. Qi
B. Schattenberg
M. Sheng
P. Strating
D. Teller
C. Tziviskou
A. Udugama
J. van der Spek
P. van Eck
J. Versendaal
M. Viviani
G. Vizzari
J. Vonk
T. Wang
K. Windt
A. Wombacher
D. Wong
L. Xu
X. Yang
G. Zheng

Sponsoring Institutions

Tilburg University, Netherlands
University of Trento, Italy
Vrije Universiteit Amsterdam, Netherlands
ITC-irst, Italy
NICTA, Australia
ACM SIGWeb, USA
ACM SIGSoft, USA
Hewlett-Packard , USA
IBM, USA

Table of Contents

Vision Papers

Autonomic Web Processes
Kunal Verma, Amit P. Sheth 1

The (Service) Bus: Services Penetrate Everyday Life
Frank Leymann 12

Service Oriented Architectures for Science Gateways on Grid Systems
Dennis Gannon, Beth Plale, Marcus Christie, Liang Fang,
Yi Huang, Scott Jensen, Gopi Kandaswamy, Suresh Marru,
Sangmi Lee Pallickara, Satoshi Shirasuna, Yogesh Simmhan,
Aleksander Slominski, Yiming Sun 21

Service Specification and Modelling

Toward a Programming Model for Service-Oriented Computing
Francisco Curbera, Donald Ferguson, Martin Nally,
Marcia L. Stockton 33

Speaking a Common Language: A Conceptual Model for Describing
Service-Oriented Systems
Massimiliano Colombo, Elisabetta Di Nitto, Massimiliano Di Penta,
Damiano Distante, Maurilio Zuccalà 48

A Rule Driven Approach for Developing Adaptive Service Oriented
Business Collaboration
Bart Orriens, Jian Yang, Mike Papazoglou 61

Service Design and Validation

Pattern-Based Specification and Validation of Web Services Interaction
Properties
Zheng Li, Jun Han, Yan Jin 73

Using Test Cases as Contract to Ensure Service Compliance Across
Releases
Marcello Bruno, Gerardo Canfora, Massimiliano Di Penta,
Gianpiero Esposito, Valentina Mazza 87

Towards a Classification of Web Service Feature
Interactions
Michael Weiss, Babak Esfandiari, Yun Luo 101

Service Selection and Discovery

A High-Level Functional Matching for Semantic Web Services
Islam Elgedawy, Zahir Tari, James A. Thom 115

Service Selection Algorithms for Composing Complex Services with
Multiple QoS Constraints
Tao Yu, Kwei-Jay Lin 130

On Service Discovery Process Types
Peer Hasselmeyer 144

SPiDeR: P2P-Based Web Service Discovery
*Ozgur D. Sahin, Cagdas E. Gerede, Divyakant Agrawal,
Amr El Abbadi, Oscar Ibarra, Jianwen Su* 157

An Approach to Temporal-Aware Procurement of Web Services
*Octavio Martín-Díaz, Antonio Ruiz-Cortés, Amador Durán,
Carlos Müller* 170

Service Composition and Aggregation

Approaching Web Service Coordination and Composition by Means of
Petri Nets. The Case of the Nets-within-Nets Paradigm
P. Álvarez, J.A. Bañares, J. Ezpeleta 185

Modeling and Analyzing Context-Aware Composition of Services
Enzo Colombo, John Mylopoulos, Paola Spoletini 198

Towards Semi-automated Workflow-Based Aggregation of Web
Services
Antonio Brogi, Razvan Popescu 214

Choreography and Orchestration: A Synergic Approach for System
Design
*Nadia Busi, Roberto Gorrieri, Claudio Guidi, Roberto Lucchi,
Gianluigi Zavattaro* 228

Service Monitoring

PerfSONAR: A Service Oriented Architecture for Multi-domain
Network Monitoring
*Andreas Hanemann, Jeff W. Boote, Eric L. Boyd, Jérôme Durand,
Loukik Kudarimoti, Roman Lapacz, D. Martin Swany,
Szymon Trocha, Jason Zurawski* 241

DySOA: Making Service Systems Self-adaptive
Johanneke Siljee, Ivor Bosloper, Jos Nijhuis, Dieter Hammer 255

Towards Dynamic Monitoring of WS-BPEL Processes
Luciano Baresi, Sam Guinea 269

Service Management

Template-Based Automated Service Provisioning – Supporting the
Agreement-Driven Service Life-Cycle
Heiko Ludwig, Henner Gimpel, Asit Dan, Bob Kearney 283

Proactive Management of Service Instance Pools for Meeting Service
Level Agreements
Kavitha Ranganathan, Asit Dan 296

Adaptive Component Management Service in ScudWare Middleware
for Smart Vehicle Space
Qing Wu, Zhaohui Wu 310

Semantic Web and Grid Services

Semantic Caching for Web Services
Stefan Seltzsam, Roland Holzhauser, Alfons Kemper 324

ODEGSG Framework, Knowledge-Based Annotation and Design of
Grid Services
*Carole Goble, Asunción Gómez-Pérez, Rafael González-Cabero,
María S. Pérez-Hernández* 341

Implicit Service Calls in ActiveXML Through OWL-S
Salima Benbernou, Xiaojun He, Mohand-Said Hacid 353

Semantic Tuplespace
Liangzhao Zeng, Hui Lei, Badrish Chandramouli 366

Security, Exception Handling, and SLAs

Trust-Based Secure Workflow Path Construction
  M. Altunay, D. Brown, G. Byrd, R. Dean 382

Reputation-Based Service Level Agreements for Web Services
  Radu Jurca, Boi Faltings 396

Handling Faults in Decentralized Orchestration of Composite Web
Services
  Girish Chafle, Sunil Chandra, Pankaj Kankar, Vijay Mann 410

What's in an Agreement? An Analysis and an Extension of
WS-Agreement
  Marco Aiello, Ganna Frankova, Daniela Malfatti 424

Industrial and Application Papers

SOA in the Real World – Experiences
  Manoj Acharya, Abhijit Kulkarni, Rajesh Kuppili,
  Rohit Mani, Nitin More, Srinivas Narayanan, Parthiv Patel,
  Kenneth W. Schuelke, Subbu N. Subramanian 437

Service-Oriented Design: The Roots
  Tiziana Margaria, Bernhard Steffen, Manfred Reitenspieß 450

A Service Oriented Architecture for Deploying and Managing Network
Services
  Victor A.S.M. de Souza, Eleri Cardozo 465

Demo Papers

Dynamo: Dynamic Monitoring of WS-BPEL Processes
  Luciano Baresi, Sam Guinea 478

WofBPEL: A Tool for Automated Analysis of BPEL Processes
  Chun Ouyang, Eric Verbeek, Wil M.P. van der Aalst,
  Stephan Breutel, Marlon Dumas, Arthur H.M. ter Hofstede 484

OpenWS-Transaction: Enabling Reliable Web Service Transactions
  Ivan Vasquez, John Miller, Kunal Verma, Amit Sheth 490

ASTRO: Supporting Composition and Execution of Web Services
Michele Trainotti, Marco Pistore, Gaetano Calabrese,
Gabriele Zacco, Gigi Lucchese, Fabio Barbon, Piergiorgio Bertoli,
Paolo Traverso 495

Demonstrating Dynamic Configuration and Execution of Web Processes
Karthik Gomadam, Kunal Verma, Amit P. Sheth,
John A. Miller 502

Short Papers

Programming and Compiling Web Services in GPSL
Dominic Cooney, Marlon Dumas, Paul Roe 508

Semantic Management of Web Services
Daniel Oberle, Steffen Lamparter, Andreas Eberhart,
Steffen Staab 514

Composition of Services with Nondeterministic Observable Behavior
Daniela Berardi, Diego Calvanese, Giuseppe De Giacomo,
Massimo Mecella 520

Efficient and Transparent Web-Services Selection
Nicolas Gibelin, Mesaac Makpangou 527

An Approach to Parameterizing Web Service Flows
Dimka Karastoyanova, Frank Leymann, Alejandro Buchmann 533

Dynamic Policy Management on Business Performance Management
Architecture
Teruo Koyanagi, Mari Abe, Gaku Yamamoto, Jun Jang Jeng 539

A Lightweight Formal Framework for Service-Oriented Applications
Design
Aliaksei Yanchuk, Alexander Ivanyukovich, Maurizio Marchese 545

A MDE Approach for Power Distribution Service Development
Cristina Marin, Philippe Lalanda, Didier Donsez 552

Semantic Web Services for Activity-Based Computing
E. Michael Maximilien, Alex Cozzi, Thomas P. Moran 558

The Price of Services
Justin O'Sullivan, David Edmond, Arthur H.M. ter Hofstede 564

Managing End-to-End Lifecycle of Global Service Policies
Daniela Rosu, Asit Dan 570

Applying a Web Engineering Method to Design Web Services
Marta Ruiz, Pedro Valderas, Vicente Pelechano 576

An Architecture for Unifying Web Services Authentication and
Authorization
Robert Steele, Will Tao 582

Specifying Web Service Compositions on the Basis of Natural Language
Requests
Alessio Bosca, Giuseppe Valetto, Roberta Maglione, Fulvio Corno 588

Author Index 595

Autonomic Web Processes

Kunal Verma and Amit P. Sheth

LSDIS Lab, Dept. of Computer Science, University of Georgia, Athens, GA 30605, USA
{verma, amit@cs.uga.edu}

Abstract. We seek to elevate autonomic computing from infrastructure to process level. Different aspects of autonomic computing – self configuring, self healing, self optimizing and self aware are studied for Autonomic Web Processes (AWPs) with the help of a supply chain process scenario. Existing technologies and steps needed to shorten the gap from current process management systems to AWPs are studied in this paper. The behavior of AWPs is controlled by policies defined by users. Sympathetic and parasympathetic policies are introduced to model short and long term policies. A key advantage for elevating autonomic computing to a process level is that the trade-offs can be more evident because the process components map more readily to business functions.

1 Introduction

The increasing complexity in computing models, as well as massive growth in computing resources has made efficient interaction of humans and information technology increasingly difficult [10]. The vision of autonomic computing [14] proposes a computing model analogous to the autonomic functioning of the human nervous system which regulates various human functions without conscious control of the human mind. Autonomic computing is characterized by systems with capabilities of self management of their resources based on policies. The field of autonomic computing has addressed some very important research issues like self adaptive middleware [16], autonomic server monitoring [20] and policy driven data centers [15]. In this paper, we propose to elevate autonomic computing from infrastructure level to the process level to create Autonomic Web Processes (AWPs).

We present AWPs as a natural evolution of autonomic computing from individual information technology resources to the business processes that govern the functioning of various businesses activities. Essentially, AWPs are self aware, self configuring, self optimizing and self healing processes that interact with the environment based on user specified policies. AWPs may be a more appealing way to benefit from autonomic computing. This is because it is inherently more difficult to define and measure tangible ROI for an infrastructure, but it can be more possible to do so since business functions that can be directly supported by AWPs or mapped to its components.

In this paper, we will build upon previous research on semantic Web processes [18], workflows and autonomic computing to create a framework for AWPs. One of the three process architectures presented in [22] termed "dynamic trading processes" shared the characteristics of AWPs such as self configuration and dynamism. We use

B. Benatallah, F. Casati, and P. Traverso (Eds.): ICSOC 2005, LNCS 3826, pp. 1–11, 2005.
© Springer-Verlag Berlin Heidelberg 2005

a motivating scenario to discuss the potential advantages of supporting autonomic properties at the process level. We also briefly survey the current research and technological expertise for supporting each of the properties and try to outline enhancements to current state of the art to create AWPs.

Consider following examples:

- When there is a change in supplier's capabilities in highly reactive part procurement process of a computer manufacturer such as Dell. Currently delays in part deliveries lead to huge losses [13]. This is largely due to non responsive business processes that take time to react to the environment. Using an AWP would help the process to react to the situation with the help of declaratively specified policies. It is important to be able to model both the short term and the long term policies. A short term policy may want to re-order the part from some other supplier to reduce the immediate loss, but a long term policy might consider the previous order fulfillment history of the supplier, as well as, the relationship with the supplier. In order to capture such policies, we introduce the concept of sympathetic (short term) and parasympathetic (long term) policies.

- Where the manufacturer has already decided the suppliers, but a sudden change in foreign currency exchange rate (modeled as an external/environmental constraint/parameter), may make another set of suppliers more optimal. For example, Indian textiles became cheaper and the need to distribute risks became more important when China announced 2.5% devaluation of its currency and stopped linking it solely to US$.

- When market demands and buyer needs change suddenly. Consider the case of iPOD component manufacturers, before and after the announcement of iPOD Nano. Based on the popularity of iPOD Mini, a manufacturer of its component mini-drive could raise the cost or even be tempted to invest into new production lines to increase capacity. However, if the manufacturer does not very quickly react to the announcement and sudden popularity of the iPOD Nano which uses flash memory, it could face substantial losses.

An AWP must continuously try to self optimize and must have the ability to reconfigure the process. The rest of the paper is organized as follows. Section 2 provides some background information about the autonomic nervous system and autonomic computing. AWPs are defined in Section 3. The motivating scenario is presented in Section 4. Section 5 presents AWP Properties in detail. Finally, Section 6 outlines the conclusions and future work.

2 Background – Autonomous Nervous System and Autonomic Computing

In this section, we provide a brief background of the autonomic nervous system (ANS) and autonomic computing. The ANS is responsible for maintaining constant internal environment of the human body by controlling involuntary functions like digestion, respiration, perspiration, and metabolism, and modulating blood pressure [6]. All these functions are not voluntarily controlled by us (e.g., a person does not have direct control over blood pressure). At a high level of granularity, the ANS has four main functions [12]: 1) Sensory function – It gathers information from the outside world and inside the human body, 2) Transmit function – transmits the information to the processing area, 3) Integrative Function – processes the information and decides the best response and 4) Motor function – sends information to the muscles, glands and organs so that they can respond properly. It is divided into two subsystems- sympathetic and parasympathetic. The sympathetic nervous systems deals with providing responses and energy needed to cope with stressful situations such as fear or extremes of physical activity. It increases blood pressure, heart rate, and the blood supply to the skeletal muscles at the expense of the gastrointestinal tract, kidneys, and skin. On the other hand, the parasympathetic nervous systems brings normalcy in between stressful periods. It lowers the heart rate and blood pressure, diverts blood back to the skin and the gastrointestinal tract.

The vision of autonomic computing aims to make systems that simulate the autonomic nervous system by being more self managing. The objective is to let user specify high level policies and then the system should be able to manage itself, based on those policies. The following properties have been defined for autonomic systems [10] – self aware, self configuring and reconfiguring, self optimizing, self healing, policy based interaction with other components and self protecting.

A blueprint for autonomic architectures [30] was presented in [11]. It identifies the main entities in an autonomic system as – resources, touchpoints and autonomic managers. The resources are the entities that are managed by managers. Touchpoints are the interfaces by which the entities interact with the autonomic managers or other resources. A touchpoint has two sub components – sensors and effectors. Sensors are used to disseminate information about the resource by providing an interface for accessing the state of the resources. They also support event generation for sending events to the autonomic managers. Effectors provide interfaces which are used by autonomic managers to change state of resources. Another crucial aspect of autonomic computing is the representation and reasoning based on policies.

3 Autonomic Web Processes

AWPs are Web service based processes that support the autonomic computing properties of being self configuring, self healing, self optimizing, self aware, self protecting and self healing. The underlying backbone of AWPs will be based on autonomic infrastructure proposed by various autonomic computing researchers. Our aim is elevate these properties to the business process level, as the business processes are the backbone of the businesses and key to their competitiveness. Fig. 1 shows the benefits of autonomic computing at the infrastructure level and the process level. The benefits of autonomic computing at the infrastructure level are manifold. Human involvement is reduced in configuring infrastructure and recovering from failures. In addition, businesses are able to guarantee SLAs based on autonomic resources. We believe that these benefits can be leveraged in an even more efficient manner if the business processes that control the infrastructure were also autonomic. Hence, the benefits of autonomic computing would be magnified by reducing human involvement in configuring the processes and recovering from failures. In addition, the processes would be self optimizing and highly reactive to changes in the environment.

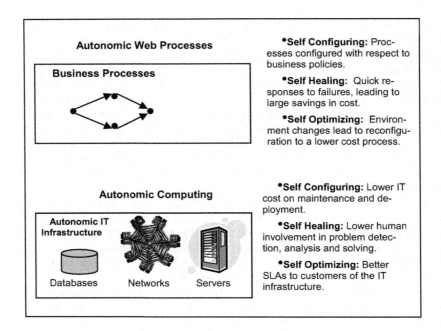

Fig. 1. Autonomic Web Processes and Autonomic Computing

4   Motivating Scenario

Consider the part procurement process of a computer manufacturer. The inventory management software (IMS) sends an order of a number of parts to the procurement module (PM). It is the IMS's job to decide the quantities and number of parts to be ordered. It is also responsible for deciding the amount of money to be spent on the whole process and/or for each individual part and setting required times for delivery. In addition, it may specify some compatibility issues between some quantities of the parts (e.g. ordering a certain quantity of a type motherboard requires ordering matching quantities of compatible memory, video cards, etc.). In other words, the IMS is responsible for setting the configuration parameters for the part procurement process.

We now introduce the part procurement process of the PM, which is responsible for actually procuring the parts from suppliers without violating the constraints set by the IMS. The PM has some more factors to consider like whether to order only from preferred suppliers, or to choose cyclically among its bag of suppliers [13]. Ideally, it should be able to optimally configure the part procurement process and then place the orders. Then it should monitor the orders for physical and logical failures and have the ability to deal with them. Physical failures are based on the supplier service going off-line, while logical failures might include delay in delivery or partial order fulfillment by suppliers.

In this paper, we will explore the autonomic aspects of the process shown in Fig. 2. The AWP properties that we will consider are as follows.

- *Self Configuring:* How can the process be self-configured without violating the constraints (policies) of the IMS and PM?
- *Self Healing:* Can the process use the policies to recover from physical and logical failures?
- *Self Optimizing:* Identifying points for the process to be notified of more optimal suppliers or currency exchange rates.
- *Self Aware:* Creating a comprehensive semantic model expressive enough to support the above mentioned AWP properties.

In order to support these properties, we propose four AWP components, the autonomic execution engine and three autonomic managers that support self configuring, self healing and self optimizing functionalities.

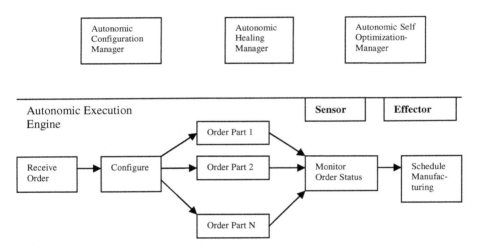

Fig. 2. Autonomic Part Procurement Process

5   Defining Autonomic Computing Properties for AWPs

In this section, we describe different properties for AWPs. We start by explaining each property with the help of motivating scenario presented in Section 4 and then survey some of the research work relevant for supporting the property.

5.1   Self Configuring

An AWP must be able to configure itself on the basis on the user policies. For an AWP, configuration may include the following functions- discovery of partners, querying partners for quotes, negotiation with the partners, constraint analysis (non quantitative analysis, optimization using integer linear programming/genetic algorithms, etc.) and dynamic/runtime binding. For the motivating scenario in Section 4, self configuration refers to the optimal selection of suppliers of the process on the basis of the computer manufacturer's policies. The AWP configuration manager must be able to configure the process with respect to the policies. The policy language must be able to specify the goals of the configuration. In this case the goals of configuration are the following:

1. Identify supplier(s) for each part (discovery)
2. Retrieve quote from database/ Query suppliers for quotes (cost estimation)
3. Negotiate better prices if possible (negotiation)
4. Find optimal suppliers and quantities based on the policies (constraint analysis)
5. Configure the process with the optimal suppliers (dynamic binding)

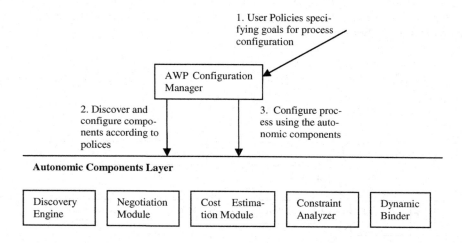

Fig. 3. AWP Configuration Manager

A high level overview of the AWP configuration manager is shown in Fig. 3. There are three steps to the configuration. The AWP sends the configuration module the goals for configuring it. Then the configuration module finds the required components for the tasks needed and configures them. (e.g., a certain protocol may be loaded for negotiation to configure the negotiation module). Finally, the process must be configured using the different components.

There has been noteworthy research in all modules mentioned for configuration. Semantic Web service which enhances the querying capabilities of UDDI has been discussed [19] [26] [24]. The process of requesting quote from suppliers in the electronics domain has been standardized by RosettaNet. Negotiation using game theory was discussed in [7] [9]. Constraint analysis has been discussed using integer linear programming [2], genetic algorithms and SWRL [28]. Dynamic binding capabilities for Web processes have been discussed in [25]. For creating an infrastructure for self configuration AWPs all the modules must be created as autonomic components and the interactions between them should be policy driven.

5.2 Self Healing

An AWP must be able to recover from failures. There could be two types of failures – system level failures and logical level failures. An example of a physical level failure is a supplier Web service failing during order placement. Logical failures include delay in delivery or the supplier fulfilling only part of the order. For either kind of failure, the AWP must be able to make an optimal choice based on existing alternatives. The choices could include replacing the supplier or canceling the order as a whole. Replacing the supplier could be costly, as there may be a long term relationship or some other parts' orders may have to be cancelled and re-ordered because of part dependencies.

The self healing behavior of an AWP should be governed by policies. In order to preserve the long term business policies, we propose to model the recovery policies as sympathetic policies (e.g., replace supplier after 5 retries or short term profit maximization) and the long term policies as parasympathetic policies (e.g., preferred supplier order cancellation should be avoided). The AWP framework should be able to reason on the policies and choose the most appropriate plan for healing. The self healing aspect of an AWP can borrow from the rich work on workflow transactions [21], compensation [4] and recovery [17]. Ideally, a cost based healing mechanism must be created for AWPs, which combines all the three models (transaction, compensation, recovery) with some optimization model.

5.3 Self Optimizing

An AWP must be able to optimize itself with changes in the environment. It must have the ability to monitor the changes in the environment and reconfigure itself, if there exists a more optimal configuration. As an example of change of the environment, consider the case where some of the suppliers are in different countries and the change in currency conversion rates can render an optimal process sub-optimal. In that case, the AWP must be able to change the suppliers by reconfiguring the process. Other changes in the environments include a supplier announcing a discount, the most favorable clause of a contract getting activated because the supplied offered a better deal to another buyer or a new supplier registering itself with the manufacturer.

As shown in Fig. 4, the self optimization manager has a number of listeners, which monitor the environment of the AWP. The entities and variables to be monitored are selected according to the user specified policies. In this case, there are two entities being monitored – currency exchange rates and supplier discounts. Fig. 4 shows a currency change event above the user specified threshold which is detected by a listener and sent to the self optimization manager. The self optimization manager generates a reconfigure event for the configuration manager, which performs analysis using different reasoning engines at its disposal. If a more optimal solution is found, it uses the effector of the execution engine to change the process configuration. The self optimization property creates a need for a new generation of process coordination (workflow) engines that are not only guided by control flow constructs but also by optimal execution based on the changing environment.

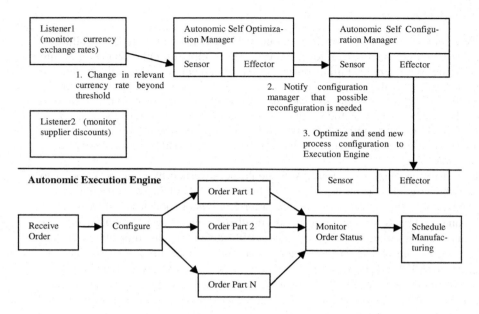

Fig. 4. Self Optimization of AWP due to change in Environment

5.4 Self Aware

In order to achieve the autonomic computing properties in this section, an AWP must be aware of itself and its environment. This implies that there must be a comprehensive model of the AWP, the Web services, the environment and the policies that guide its operation. Given the already entrenched position of the WSDL and related standards, a truly extensible and upwardly compatible approach that preserves current investment in tools, techniques and training must be used to create model. Based on our experience with the METEOR-S [18] project, which deals with modeling the complete lifecycle of Web processes, we have concluded that no one approach is enough to capture all the intricacies of AWPs. We will build upon our broad classification of the semantics [23] required for this – data, functional, execution and non-functional semantics to outline the model.

The emerging field of the Semantic Web [29] proposes using description logics based ontologies (with the W3C recommended OWL language) to capture the semantics of data on the Web. While, this seems adequate to capture the necessary data semantics (inputs/outputs) of Web services, it is not adequate to capture the functional semantics of Web services (what the Web service does), where a different representation like horn logic based SWRL may be more adequate. The execution semantics focus on the behavioral aspects of Web services, the current state of Web processes and different approaches like task skeletons [5], Petri nets based YAWL [1] or different variants of temporal logic can be considered to represent the behavior of Web services.

The non-functional semantics include the policies, business rules, constraints, and configuration/reconfiguration parameters. While the logic based modeling languages are good for capturing qualitative aspects of business rules, and process constraints, they are not effective in capturing the quantitative constraints for process optimization, which can be represented using an operations research based technique like integer linear programming (ILP). For goal or utility based reconfiguration of processes [15] or decision theoretic planning models like Markov decision processes may be more adequate. Another important issue in non functional semantics is the ability to represent the policies at different levels - Business Level Policies, Process Level Policies, Instance Level Policies, and Individual Component Level Policies and have the ability to resolve conflicts between them.

For self configuration, the discovery phase would require functional, data and non functional semantics. All other phases – negotiation, constraint analysis and binding will be guided by policies (i.e. non functional semantics). For self healing the execution semantics which includes the state of process and transactional traits on the Web services will be required. In addition, the best plan for healing will be decided using the policies. For self optimizing, the entities in the environment to be monitored will be specified using policies. Both, self optimizing and self healing involve reconfiguration.

An important aspect of our approach is the ability to map our model to existing service oriented architecture standards [8] using the extensibility features, provided by the standards. This has been illustrated in our previous work in WSDL-S [3] [24], which adds data and functional semantics to WSDL and semantic extensions to WS-Policy [27], which proposes using OWL ontologies and SWRL rules to represent non-functional semantics of Web services using the WS-Policy framework.

6 Conclusions and Future Work

In this paper, we have a presented an approach for elevating autonomic computing to the process level. We have provided a brief outline of how an AWP can support self configuration, self healing and self optimizing properties. The contributions of this paper include:

- Defining and creating a framework for AWPs.
- Studying the applicability of current research for creating AWPs.

As we discussed earlier, there has been significant work done on autonomic computing, semantic and dynamic Web processes and workflows. AWPs are the logical next step in the evolution of all these fields, as it builds upon the work done in these vast and rich areas. As a first step towards creating AWPs, a comprehensive semantic model of all aspects of AWPs will have to be created. In future, we will demonstrate explicit need and use of the four types of semantics we have identified: data semantics, functional semantics, non-functional semantics and execution semantics [23].

We have also tried to outline some of the initial steps which will be needed to support the other AWP properties. We have provided initial discussions on how to model the first two examples mentioned in the introduction – autonomic supply chain recovery from failure with the sympathetic and parasympathetic policies and self optimization due to changes in environment with the help of the sensors, effectors and autonomic managers. We plan to implement these scenarios and test our hypotheses about the benefits of AWPs.

As the benefits from creating AWPs are manifold for both business and scientific processes, we aim to collaborate with our research partners in the industry and the academia to realize this vision. Our future work includes creating a research prototype that supports AWPs and creating a theoretical model to represent all aspects of AWPs.

Acknowledgements

We would to thank members of the LSDIS Lab and the METEOR-S project whose valuable insights and ideas helped us in writing this paper. In particular, special thanks go to John A. Miller, Karthik Gomadam and Prashant Doshi.

References

[1] Wil M. P. van der Aalst, A.r H. M. ter Hofstede: YAWL: yet another workflow language. Inf. Syst. 30(4): 245-275 (2005)

[2] R. Aggarwal, K. Verma, J. Miller and W. Milnor, "Constraint Driven Web Service Composition in METEORS," Proc. of the 2004 IEEE International Conference on Services Computing (SCC 2004), 2004, pp. 23-30

[3] R. Akkiraju, J. Farrell, J. Miller, M. Nagarajan, M. Schmidt, A. Sheth, K. Verma, Web Service Semantics - WSDL-S, A joint UGA-IBM Technical Note, version 1.0, http://www.alphaworks.ibm.com/g/g.nsf/img/semanticsdocs/$file/wssemantic_annotation.pdf

[4] G. Alonso, D. Agrawal, A. Abbadi, M. Kamath, R. Günthör, C. Mohan: Advanced Transaction Models in Workflow Contexts. ICDE 1996: 574-581

[5] P. Attie, M.. Singh, E. A. Emerson, A. P. Sheth, M. Rusinkiewicz: Scheduling workflows by enforcing intertask dependencies. Distributed Systems Engineering 3(4): 222-238 (1996)

[6] S. Bakewell, The Autonomic Nervous System, available at http://www.nda.ox.ac.uk/wfsa/html/u05/u05_010.htm

[7] M. Burstein, C. Bussler, T. Finin, M. Huhns, M. Paolucci, A. Sheth, S. Williams, M. Zaremba, A Semantic Web Services Architecture, To appear in IEEE Internet Computing, 2006.

[8] F. Curbera, R. Khalaf, N. Mukhi, S. Tai, S. Weerawarana: The next step in Web services. Communication of the ACM 46(10): 29-34 (2003)

[9] H. Davulcu, M. Kifer, I. V. Ramakrishnan: CTR-S: a logic for specifying contracts in semantic web services. WWW (Alternate Track Papers & Posters) 2004: 144-153

[10] IBM Autonomic Computing Website, http://researchweb.watson.ibm.com/autonomic/

[11] IBM Autonomic Computing Blueprint Website, http://www-03.ibm.com/autonomic/blueprint.shtml

[12] J. Johnson, Autonomic Nervous System, http://www.sirinet.net/~jgjohnso/nervous.html

[13] R. Kapuscinski, R.. Zhang, P. Carbonneau, Robert Moore, Bill Reeves, Inventory Decisions in Dell's Supply Chain, Interfaces, Vol. 34, No. 3, May–June 2004, pp. 191–205

[14] Jeffrey O. Kephart, David M. Chess: The Vision of Autonomic Computing. IEEE Computer 36(1): 41-50 (2003)

[15] J. Kephart, W.. Walsh: An Artificial Intelligence Perspective on Autonomic Computing Policies. POLICY 2004: 3-12

[16] V. Kumar, B. Cooper, K. Schwan, Distributed Stream Management using Utility-Driven Self-Adaptive Middleware, The Proceedings of the 2nd IEEE International Conference on Autonomic Computing, 2005.

[17] F. Leymann: Supporting Business Transactions Via Partial Backward Recovery In Work-flow Management Systems. BTW 1995: 51-70

[18] METEOR-S: Semantic Web Services and Processes, http://lsdis.cs.uga.edu/projects/meteor-s/

[19] M. Paolucci, T. Kawamura, T. Payne and K. Sycara, Semantic Matching of Web Services Capabilities, Proc. of the 1st International Semantic Web Conference, 2002.

[20] C. Roblee V. B. George Cybenko, Large-Scale Autonomic Server Monitoring Using Process Query Systems, The Proceedings of the 2nd IEEE International Conference on Autonomic Computing, 2005.

[21] M. Rusinkiewicz, A. P. Sheth: Specification and Execution of Transactional Workflows. Modern Database Systems 1995: 592-620

[22] A. P. Sheth, W. M. P. Aalst, I. B. Arpinar: Processes Driving the Networked Economy. IEEE Concurrency 7(3): 18-31, 1999

[23] A. P. Sheth, "Semantic Web Process Lifecycle: Role of Semantics in Annotation, Dis-covery, Composition and Orchestration," Invited Talk, Workshop on E-Services and the Semantic Web, WWW, 2003.

[24] K. Sivashanmugam, K. Verma, A. P. Sheth, J. A. Miller, Adding Semantics to Web Ser-vices Standards, Proc. of the 1st International Conference on Web Services, 2003.

[25] K. Verma, R. Akkiraju, R. Goodwin, P. Doshi, J. Lee, On Accommodating Inter Service Dependencies in Web Process Flow Composition, Proc. of the AAAI Spring Symposium on Semantic Web Services, March, 2004.

[26] K. Verma, K. Sivashanmugam, A. Sheth, A. Patil, S. Oundhakar and J. Miller, METEOR-S WSDI: A Scalable Infrastructure of Registries for Semantic Publication and Discovery of Web Services, Journal of Information Technology and Management, 6 (1), pp. 17-39, 2005.

[27] K. Verma, R. Akkiraju, R. Goodwin, Semantic matching of Web service policies, The Proceedings of the Second Workshop on Semantic and Dynamic Web Processes (SDWP), (in conjunction with ICWS), Orlando, Fl, 2005.

[28] K. Verma, K. Gomadam, A. P. Sheth, J. A. Miller, Z. Wu, "The METEOR-S Approach for Configuring and Executing Dynamic Web Processes", LSDIS Lab Technical Report , University of Georgia, June 24, 2005

[29] W3C Semantic Web Activity, http://www.w3.org/2001/sw/

[30] S. White, J. Hanson, I. Whalley, D. Chess, J. Kephart: An Architectural Approach to Autonomic Computing. ICAC 2004: 2-9

The (Service) Bus: Services Penetrate Everyday Life

Frank Leymann

Institute of Architecture of Application Systems,
University of Stuttgart, Universitätsstr. 38,
70569 Stuttgart, Germany

Frank.Leymann@informatik.uni-stuttgart.de

Abstract: We sketch the vision of a ubiquitous service bus that will be the base for hosting and accessing services everywhere. The utility model for using IT artifacts is implied. Applications on top of the service bus will be centered on business processes and will be adaptive in multiple dimensions. The ubiquitous service bus will change the way we think about information technology.

1 Introduction

Service oriented computing and service oriented architectures are accepted as the next step in building distribute applications. Especially, Web services ([1], [16]) as particular incarnation of service oriented technology has broad acceptance in the industry and is supported by products of many vendors.

In this paper we sketch the vision of a globally available infrastructure for hosting and accessing services everywhere. Services in our context are not only software functions usually thought of when talking about services but also hardware artifacts. The latter is brought to the area of service orientation by recent movements of Grid computing towards Web service technology [4].

Section 2 describes the basic component of this infrastructure, namely the service bus, and its key capabilities supporting our vision. The new model of using IT in a manner we are familiar with from traditional utilities is sketched in Section 3. Application structures fostered by the envisioned infrastructure and envisioned exploitation model are portrayed in Section 4.

2 The Bus

The architecture of a middleware platform for realizing service oriented computing based on Web service standards is outlined in [16]. We refer to this middleware simply as service bus. Complying to Web service standards a particular implementation of a service bus interoperates by definition with all other implementations of a service bus – at least when ignoring all the interoperability issues addressed by initiatives like WS-I, which we take the liberty to do in sketching our vision. In this sense, the collection of

B. Benatallah, F. Casati, and P. Traverso (Eds.): ICSOC 2005, LNCS 3826, pp. 12–20, 2005.
© Springer-Verlag Berlin Heidelberg 2005

interacting service bus implementations can be viewed as one single piece of middleware referred to as *the* *service bus* (or even just *the* *bus*) – similar to the Web being realized by a collection of interacting components like HTTP origin servers, proxies, browsers, etc.

2.1 Virtualization

The main functionality of the service bus is *virtualization* (see Fig. 1): Since all services accessible via the service bus are described by WSDL the service bus hides from a user of a service the implementation details of a service like the programming language used for its implementation, the hosting application server, the underlying operating system platform, and so on. When making a request, a user of a service simply refers to the (WSDL) interface an implementation of which is needed and passes the data to be processed by an implementation, and the service bus will select one of the available corresponding implementations of this interface to perform the user's request [11].

To further support proper selection done by the service bus, both, requests as well as services may be annotated by policies. Policies describe non-functional properties like transactional capabilities, security features, costs etc. Basically, services publish the non-functional properties they support, and requests specify the non-functional properties expected. The service bus uses the policies associated with a request to further reduce the number of matching services. In doing so, the service bus determines based on both policies an "effective policy" that will govern the actual interaction between the requestor and the service chosen.

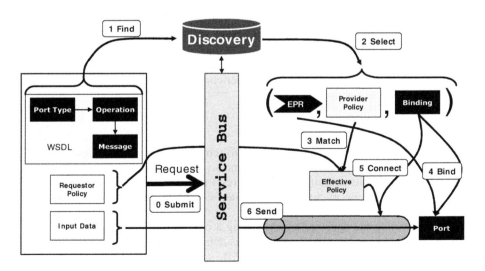

Fig. 1. Executing Requests within the Bus

The service bus may even support requests without requestors having to specify the interface a service has to implement. Services may be annotated with semantics describing the business meaning of the functions provided. In turn, requestors have to provide semantic descriptions of the function requested instead of explicitly naming a corresponding interface. The service bus locates and selects a matching service based on these semantic descriptions. Web services describing the functions they offer semantically are referred to as "semantic Web services" [6].

2.2 Optimization

Thus, the service bus virtualizes services based on interface descriptions or semantic descriptions as well as based on non-functional properties: All service implementations supporting the interface or semantic description as well as the non-functional properties of a request are interchangeable from the requestor's point of view. The corresponding services can be jointly viewed as a pool of services being able to satisfy the request. The members of such a pool can be distributed over the network, they can be implemented in very different environments, they can be accessible over very different protocols etc. In case more than one service qualifies the service bus will use additional criteria to select a particular member from that pool.

When selecting such an implementation on behalf of a user the service bus has all liberties as long as the service chosen matches the functional and non-functional properties of the request of the user. Consequently, the spectrum of possible mechanisms for choosing a member from the pool of all qualifying services reaches from very simply mechanisms like random selections up to sophisticated optimization mechanisms.

Optimization may be done according to various sets of criteria. For example, the service bus may consider the workload of the overall environment (evenly distributing work), the cost of mediating the request (preferring local implementations of a service over remotely available implementations) etc. Optimization may favor implementations of the provider of the local service bus used by the requestor, may strive towards reducing costs for the requestor, or may strive towards maximizing profit across all requests served by a certain provider considering a set of service level agreements, and so on (see Section 3.3 below).

2.3 Management

To enable optimization the service bus must able to retrieve information required for the various kinds of optimizations like state data and so on. Similarly, the service bus must be able to influence the state of services like restarting a certain service. For this purpose, services have to support corresponding interfaces in addition to the interface providing the proper (application) functions.

Data that is providing the context for performing a request offered by a service is referred to as a "WS-Resource". An element of this data context is called a "resource property". The resource framework ([24], [25]) specifies certain requests to manipulate resource properties and to manage the lifecycle of WS-Resources (see [18] for more details). Changes of resource properties may influence optimization decisions or may require actions on the corresponding services to change their state.

For this purpose, a topic-based notification or publish/subscribe infrastructure has been defined that is part of the service bus itself ([26], [27]) and allows to register for changes of resource properties.

The corresponding infrastructure can be used in a much broader sense: Any data required to decide about proper management of a resource may be specified as a collection of corresponding resource properties. Here, a *resource* is any software or hardware artifact made available as a (manageable) service. Resources of different types support specific operations to enable management of its instances. The publish/subscribe features of the service bus may then be used by systems management components to monitor resources and properly react by using the resource specific interfaces. In this sense, the service bus itself becomes the basis for managing an overall environment in a service-oriented manner [28].

The publish/subscribe features can also be used as the basis for realizing feedback loops to control resources in an autonomic manner [13]: The monitoring component of such a feedback loop filters and aggregates notification events from the resources, the analysis component correlates the remaining events and predicts potential critical situations, the planning component decides on actions needed to prevent such situations by generating a corresponding plan, and the execution component performs this plan (see [20] for more details). After executing the plan, the predicted situation is unlikely to occur. Furnishing the service bus with such feedback loops results in an infrastructure that can protect, optimize, and heal itself [5].

For example, a critical situation may indicate that a certain application needs more resources to meet its goals in terms of the number of users to be supported with a certain response time. The plan for preventing not meeting this goal is a flow with activities that use the interfaces of the resource types required (like CPUs, storage, installation services). After executing such a "provisioning flow" [8] additional resource are available to the application such that it will not miss its goal [2].

3 Utility Computing

The service bus is the basis for sharing resources. For example, resources owned by one company can be made available to other parties – and this can be done on a fee base enabling a business for outsourcing IT artifacts.

3.1 Traditional ASP Model

Abstracting from technology, this is the "traditional" service provider model. Within the application service provider (ASP) model, the provider hosts, runs, maintains an application on behalf of another company for a fee. When the ASP model came up fees had been determined upfront based on an estimation of the resources needed to satisfy the non-functional requirements (response time, availability, number of users etc.) of a customer. Typically, these estimations were based on expected peak loads and as a consequence, customers had to pay for resources that they seldom need. This is often seen as an obstruction to the broad acceptance of the ASP model – despite the fact that companies ask for the ability to outsource parts of their IT infrastructure to be able to focus on their core business competencies.

3.2 Dynamic Provisioning

Dynamic provisioning technology and autonomic technology will remove this hurdle: Customers specify service levels objectives for outsourced resources with their provider and will only pay for the actual resources used. At the provider side this is based on the kind of feedback loops sketched above that ensure to meet the service levels agreed, with provisioning flows being performed when service level objectives are jeopardized. When dynamically provisioned resources are no longer needed they will be automatically de-provisioned. Thus, over-provisioning will no longer take place as in the original ASP model resulting in an economy of scale that reduces fees for outsourced resources.

The corresponding model is referred to as "utility model" [14]: Paying only for what has been actually used is the model of classical utilities (power, gas, water...). Using compute resources (both, software and hardware) in such a manner will create a new kind of utility called "computing utility". Making compute resources available when needed and for the time needed is also called "computing on demand".

3.3 Software as a Service

Using software in the utility model implies that the provider does also provide the hardware and middleware required to actually run the software. Thus, using software in the utility model typically means for a customer to outsource the corresponding complete infrastructure to the provider. The customer uses "software as a service" (aka SaaS).

If critical functions are used based on this model customers negotiate service level objectives such as average response time, availability etc. with the service provider. The agreed too set of objectives together with fees to be paid by the customer if the objectives are met and penalties to be paid by the provider if objectives are not met result in a service level agreement (SLA) [3]. The service provider strives to optimize profits based on the set of SLAs negotiated with his customers: This is one kind of optimization mentioned above (see Section 2.2) that the service bus must support (either directly or by some component extending its functionality).

4 Applications

Often, services are composed of other services. Business processes are the most widespread example for such a composition. The term *orchestration* got established in the meantime for supporting the composition of services into a business process. Since the services offered by an orchestration may be used in other orchestrations a recursive composition model for services results. BPEL ([21], [22]) is the established language for specifying orchestrations in the Web service area.

When specifying an orchestration it is opaque whether or not a service used is also an orchestration. If a service used in an orchestration is again structured as an orchestration and both of the structures are considered for composition more precise interaction details can be specified. Such a specification is referred to as *choreography* in the meantime. WS-CDL [23] has been proposed as language for specifying choreographies.

4.1 Structure

Applications based on services thus consist of orchestrations and services they use, i.e. applications in a service environment are based on a two-level programming model ([9], [17]). To be precise, an orchestration specifies the types of services used, and during deployment of an orchestration additional information must be provided that allows the service bus to select appropriate services at runtime of the orchestration (see [12], [13]).

The overall infrastructure, thus, includes an orchestration engine as an integral part which is typically based on workflow systems [10] that support BPEL. Even business processes that include interactions with human beings may be supported [19]. The orchestration engine navigates through the underlying process model and determines the kind of service needed. The underlying service bus selects a matching service on behalf of the orchestration engine and returns the response of the service chosen to it.

In doing so, quality of services are folded in based on policies that describe the requirements of the business process and polices that are associated with the candidates considered by the service bus (see Section 2.1). For example, a business process may specify that messages exchanged between the orchestration and the service chosen must be encrypted and transported reliably, or that an invocation of a service must be done transactional. Thus, non-functional requirements of an application can be specified that will be enforced at runtime by the service bus.

4.2 Adaptability

The service bus may choose for different instances of the same business process model different services for one and the same activity of the business process model. Thus, the overall orchestration is adaptive in terms of services used, i.e. the underlying services available to an orchestration may change in terms of different providers, different implementation etc. This is similar to adaptability in terms of people performing a certain activity which is supported since long in workflow systems [10]. Adaptability in terms of services chosen may even go further by supporting the selection of services that deviate from the type of service prescribed by the business process model [7]. Adaptability in terms of the logic (i.e. control and data flow) of an orchestration may be supported too [15]. Finally, based on dynamic provisioning technology the environment hosting an application is adaptive too as described in Section 2.3.

Additional flexibility can be supported based on providing "skeletons" of process models (Fig. 2). Being characterized as a skeleton has various aspects, represented to the outside via "points of variability" (see $v_1,...,v_4$ in the figure below). For example: A business process model may only specify that certain kind of activities have to be performed and the type of messages exchanged with each of such an activity, but the type of services to be used is not specified – the type has to be detailed by the organization deploying the process model (point of variability v_1 below). Or a business process model may define some of its structure as fixed while other parts of the model may be changed by the deploying organization; point of variability v_2 below allows to change transition condition q, for instance, and point of variability v_4 allows to omit

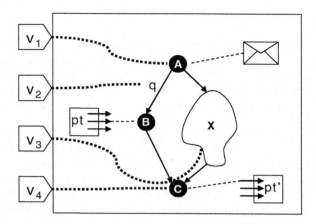

Fig. 2. Variable Applications

activity C at all in the business process model. Or a business process model vaguely specifies that some sort of actions must happen in course of the business process but the whole corresponding fragment of the model must be provided by the deploying organization (point of variability v_3 below). Or a business process model may only specify its externally observable behavior while its internal implementation is "arbitrary" (and possibly hidden) as long as the specified behavior results.

This spectrum of adaptability is important for reasons like customization of applications, representing best practices, or specifying constraints for using collections of services. Applications will externalize their points of variability, and tools will present them allowing to modify the applications accordingly. Not only will application logic be represented as points of variability but also environment aspects of an application; these aspects correspond to service level objectives, for example, which influence the selection of underlying hardware, middleware etc. to satisfy the objectives. Dynamic provisioning (Section 3.2) and using software as a service (Section 3.3) will make use of these kinds of points of variability to negotiate SLAs and set up the overall environment appropriately (see [8] and [13] for more details).

4.3 Outsourcing

Since BPEL itself is portable across environments customers can specify their business processes in BPEL and run them anywhere in the environment. The services needed by the orchestration are selected by the bus based on deployment information specified for the orchestration. This selection can be influenced by preferences of the provider of the hosting infrastructure of the orchestration, i.e. the provider may itself offer the corresponding services or may have special contracts with other providers of those services. Thus, a customer may outsource a business process completely, even without taking care about the providers of the services composed by the corresponding orchestration. I.e. the utility computing model applies to complete business processes and applications.

5 Conclusion

The current Web is an infrastructure for accessing content everywhere ("content Web"). Web service technology will likely provide an infrastructure for accessing services everywhere ("service Web"). Since Web service technology is not restricted to Web protocols access to services over any kind of suitable protocols, across heterogeneous environments will be supported. Quality of services used from today's application servers will be supported by the service bus. Composition of services from other services available on the bus will be the way of building new applications. These applications can be hosted anywhere on the bus resulting in a utility model for IT artifacts. As a consequence, outsourcing and off-shoring of IT will become ubiquitous allowing companies to focus on their core business.

References

1. G. Alonso, F. Casati, H. Kuno, V. Machiraju. Web Services, Springer 2004.
2. K. Appleby, S.B. Calo, J.R.Giles, K.-W.Lee. Policy-based automated provisioning, IBM Systems Journal 43(1) (2004).
3. A. Dan, D. Davis, R. Kearney, A. Keller, R. King, D. Kuebler, H. Ludwig, M. Polan, M. Spreitzer, A. Yousse. Web services on demand: WSLA-driven automated management, IBM Systems Journal 43(1) (2004).
4. I. Foster, C. Kesselmann. The Grid 2, Morgan Kaufmann 2004.
5. A.G. Ganek, T.A. Corbi. The dawning of the autonomic computing area, IBM Systems Journal 42(1) (2003).
6. M. Hepp, F. Leymann, J. Domingue, A. Wahler, D. Fensel. Semantic Business Process Management: Using Semantic Web Services for Business Process Management, Proc. IEEE ICEBE 2005 (Beijing, China, October 18-20, 2005).
7. D. Karastoyanova, A. Houspanossian, M. Cilia, F. Leymann, A. Buchmann. Extending BPEL for Run Time Adaptability, Proc. EDOC'2005, (Enschede, The Netherlands, September 19 – 23, 2005).
8. A. Keller, R. Badonnel. Automating the Provisioning of Application Services with the BPEL4WS Workflow Language, Proc. DSOM 2004 (Nancy, France, November 2004).
9. F. Leymann, D. Roller. Workflow based applications, IBM Systems Journal 36(1) (1997) 102-123.
10. F. Leymann, D. Roller. Production Workflow: Concepts and Techniques, Prentice Hall 2000.
11. F. Leymann. Web Services: Distributed applications without limits, Proc. BTW'03 (Leipzig, Germany, February 2003), Springer 2003.
12. F. Leymann. The Influence of Web Services on Software: Potentials and Tasks, Proc. 34th Annual Meeting of the German Computer Society (Ulm, Germany, September 20 – 24, 2004), Springer 2004.
13. F. Leymann, Combining Web Services and the Grid: Towards Adaptive Enterprise Applications, Proc. CAiSE/ASMEA'05 (Porto, Portugal, June 2005).
14. M.A. Rappa. The utility business model and the future of computing services, IBM Systems Journal 43(1) (2004).
15. M. Reichert, P. Dadam. ADEPTflex - Supporting Dynamic Changes of Workflows Without Losing Control, Journal of Intelligent Information Systems 10(2) (1998).

16. S. Weerawarana, F. Curbera, F. Leymann, T. Storey, D.F. Ferguson. Web Services Platform Architecture, Prentice Hall 2005.
17. G. Wiederhold, P. Wegner, S. Ceri. Towards Megaprogramming: A paradigm for component-based programming, Comm. ACM 35(22) 1992, 89 – 99.

Links: (followed on September 17, 2005)

18. K. Czajkowski, D. Ferguson, I. Foster, J. Frey, F. Leymann, M. Nally, T. Storey, S. Tuecke, S.Weerawarana. Modeling stateful resources with Web services, Globus Alliance & IBM, 2004, http://www.ibm.com/developerworks/library/ws-resource/ws-modelingresources.pdf
19. M. Kloppmann, D. Koenig, F. Leymann, G. Pfau, A. Rickayzen, C. von Riegen, P. Schmidt, I. Trickovic, WS-BPEL Extension for People (BPEL4People), IBM, SAP 2005 http://www-128.ibm.com/developerworks/webservices/library/specification/ws-bpel4people/
20. D. H. Steinberg. What you need to know now about autonomic computing, Part 2: The infrastructure, IBM Developerworks, 2003. ftp://www6.software.ibm.com/software/developer/library/i-autonom2.pdf
21. Business Process Execution Language For Web Services V1.1, BEA, IBM, Microsoft, SAP & Siebel, 2003, http://www-128.ibm.com/developerworks/library/specification/ws-bpel/
22. OASIS BPEL Technical Committee, http://www.oasis-open.org/committees/tc_home.php?wg_abbrev=wsbpel
23. Web Services Choreography Description Language, W3C Working Draft, 2004, http://www.w3.org/TR/ws-cdl-10/
24. Web Services Resource Framework, IBM, Globus, Computer Associates, Fujitsu, Hewlett-Packard http://www-106.ibm.com/developerworks/library/ws-resource/
25. OASIS Resource Framework Technical Committee, http://www.oasis-open.org/committees/tc_home.php?wg_abbrev=wsrf
26. Web Services Notification, Akamai, Computer Associates, Fujitsu, Globus, Hewlett-Packard, IBM, SAP, Sonic Software, TIBCO Software 2004, http://www-106.ibm.com/developerworks/library/specification/ws-notification/
27. OASIS WS-Notification Technical Committee, http://www.oasis-open.org/committees/tc_home.php?wg_abbrev=wsn
28. OASIS Web Services Distributed Management (WSDM) http://www.oasis-open.org/committees/tc_home.php?wg_abbrev=wsdm

Service Oriented Architectures
for Science Gateways on Grid Systems

Dennis Gannon, Beth Plale, Marcus Christie, Liang Fang,
Yi Huang, Scott Jensen, Gopi Kandaswamy, Suresh Marru,
Sangmi Lee Pallickara, Satoshi Shirasuna, Yogesh Simmhan,
Aleksander Slominski, and Yiming Sun

Department of Computer Science, Indiana University,
Bloomington Indiana, USA
gannon@cs.indiana.edu

Abstract. Grid computing is about allocating distributed collections of resources including computers, storage systems, networks and instruments to form a coherent system devoted to a "virtual organization" of users who share a common interest in solving a complex problem or building an efficient agile enterprise. Service oriented architectures have emerged as the standard way to build Grids. This paper provides a brief look at the Open Grid Service Architecture, a standard being proposed by the Global Grid Forum, which provides the foundational concepts of most Grid systems. Above this Grid foundation is a layer of application-oriented services that are managed by workflow tools and "science gateway" portals that provide users transparent access to the applications that use the resources of a Grid. In this paper we will also describe these Gateway framework services and discuss how they relate to and use Grid services.

1 Introduction

A Grid is a network of compute and data resources that has been supplemented with a layer of services that provide uniform and secure access to a set of applications of interest to a distributed community of users. The most significant examples of Grid systems have come from communities engaged in distributed scientific collaborations. For example, NEESGrid [1] is a set of shared resources used by earthquake engineers. The Particle Physics Data Grid [2] is a collaboration based on sharing data and analysis tools used in the hunt for subatomic particles. There are many more examples. There is also now a very active industrial community that is defining Grid technology in terms of the requirements of data center management and application service provisioning.

In the early days, Grid systems were built with ad hoc collections of software, but the emergence of Web Services has galvanized the community around Service Oriented Architectures (SOAs). Two organizations have emerged to help organize standard for these groups. The Enterprise Grid Alliance [3], let by Oracle is defining use cases for service frameworks for the data center. The Global Grid Forum (GGF) [4] is the older and larger organization that represents both the scientific and industrial community in defining the standards for Grid technology. GGF is organized along a standards track and a community track. The focus of the standards track is the Open

B. Benatallah, F. Casati, and P. Traverso (Eds.): ICSOC 2005, LNCS 3826, pp. 21 – 32, 2005.

Grid Services Architecture (OGSA), which is being promoted by GGF as the future SOA for Grid systems. The community track is a forum of research groups that are looking at the role of new technologies in both the scientific and vertical market domains such as telecommunications, biotechnology and media.

In this paper we will provide a very brief, high level overview of OGSA and then turn to a discussion of the service architecture that is used by virtual organizations centered around scientific applications of Grid systems. Within the Teragrid project [5] these are referred to as "Science Gateways". The goal of a science gateway is to provide a community of users access to scientific tools and applications that execute on the back-end compute and data resources. The users should be able to use the applications as an extension of their desktop without ever knowing that there may be a massive Grid framework in the background supplying the computing power. Typically these gateways are organized around a web portal and a family of desktop tools. The portal server authenticates the user and establishes the user's authorization to access data resources and applications. The applications often take the form of workflow templates that are instantiated and executed on the user's behalf. As illustrated in Figure 1, the workflow engine must interact with application metadata and data services, application registries and data directories and Grid resource brokers. Notification services are used to log and monitor application progress and to create the provenance documentation needed to make computational experiments repeatable.

There are many examples of gateway systems in use today and each has a slightly different version of the service architecture that supports it. In many cases the gateway services are built directly on top of an OGSA-like SOA, and in other cases the true Grid layer is very thin or even non-existent. In this paper we will describe examples of each and we will consider one in detail that does build upon a solid Grid foundation.

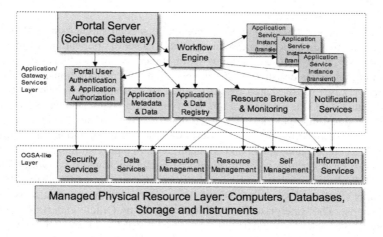

Fig. 1. Service Architecture for a Science Gateway

2 The Open Grid Service Architecture

The Open Grid Service Architecture (OGSA) is a product of the Global Grid Forum OGSA-WG led by Hiro Kishimoto. The first specification of OGSA [6] can be viewed as a profile for the organization of a standard Grid. OGSA contains six families of services which, when properly integrated, deliver a functioning Grid system. It must be noted that, at the time of this writing, there are no official implementations of OGSA, because the details of a basic service profile is still being developed. However, understanding the six core components can be a useful way to understand how Grid systems differ from other SOAs. We describe each of these service classes below.

2.1 Execution Management Services

Most Grid systems must manage the execution of computing tasks on the resources that comprise the Grid. OGSA models execution management in terms of three classes of services: Resources, Job Management and Monitoring, and Resource selection. The Resource services describe service containers and persistent state handlers. The Job Manager handles the full lifecycle of the execution of a set of jobs. It interacts with task queues on each computation resource as well as the other services involved in resource brokering and resource monitoring. The resource selection services consist of execution planning, which build schedules of jobs and resources, candidate set generation services, which produce the likely resources for running a particular job or set of jobs, and reservation services which interact with accounting and authorization systems. One interesting outcome of this work has been the Job Submission Description Language that is a schema for describing jobs. JSDL [7] is being used by a variety of Grid projects including the large Japanese Grid project NARAGI [9] and GridSAM [8] from the London e-Science Centre and the Open Middleware Infrastructure Institute [10].

2.2 Data Services

OGSA data services are intended to address the movement and management of a number of different data resources. These include the standards such as flat files, data streams and relational, object and XML databases. But they are also concerned with derivations, i.e. data that is derived by queries or transformations on other data, and Data services such as sensors. The types of activities that must be supported by the data services include remote access, staging, replication, federation, derivation and metadata generation and management. In addition, these capabilities are to be presented to the user in the form of virtualized services that hide the different implementations that are required to support different media and low-level data types. Virtualized services are a way to realize in practice the distributed systems notion of "access transparency".

The OGSA working groups involved with defining the specific data services are still hard at work. However, there are important pieces that are currently in use. One important component is OGSA Data Access and Integration [11], which establishes the definition and development of generic Grid data services providing access to and integration of data held in relational database management systems, as well as semi-structured data held in XML repositories. Another important contribution is the replica location service provided by the Globus toolkit GT4.

2.3 Resource Management Services

There are three categories of resource management that are of concern to OGSA. First there are the actual physical resources: computers, networks, storage systems and instruments. At the lowest level this management is done through standard protocols and frameworks like CIM and SNMP. But OGSA stipulates that there is another intermediate level where a common interface and approach is needed. This is where the Web Service Resource Framework (WSRF), a proposed standard, is most appropriate because it gives a standard way to discover and interrogate services that interact with the management interface of each resource. WSDM, Web Services Distributed Management, is an additional tool that OGSA envisions using for this activity.

The second class of resource management involves resources of a Grid such as resource reservation and monitoring. The third class is the management of the OGSA infrastructure itself. There are two type of interfaces to these management services: functional interfaces, which accomplish tasks such as creating or destroying a job, and manageability interfaces, which provide the mechanisms to manage a capability, such as monitoring a job manager. In general, these services provide resource reservation, monitoring and control of resources, virtual organization management, problem determination and fault management, metering and policy management.

2.4 Security Services

The OGSA security services are designed to make it possible to enforce the security policies of a particular Grid and its member organizations. OGSA postulates the existence of six services: a credential validation service, a trust service, an authorization service, an attribute service, an audit service and a bridge translation service. Though OGSA does not give the precise definition of these services they observe that the services must support the following capabilities:

- Authentication. The credential validation and trust service should be able to verify an identity assertion.
- Identity Mapping. The trust, attribute and bridge translation service should enable the translation of an identity that is valid in one domain within the Grid into an identity that is valid in another domain within the same Grid.

Authorization should be provided by the authorization service. The audit service tracks security-relevant events and is policy driven.

2.5 Self-management Services

An important concept in OGSA is that interactions between users and services are largely based on Service Level Agreement (SLA), which are documents that govern the way transactions are carried out. For example, when submitting a job, a user negotiates the jobs priority, a guaranteed completion time and required resources with a service level manager to arrive at a working SLA. Self-management services automate the tasks of configuration, healing and optimization needed to keep the Grid operating correctly and meeting its SLAs.   The service level management services operate by monitoring load and utilization of resources and the running state of the other services.   Based on the monitoring data, the management services must do an analysis to make sure that all the SLAs can be satisfied.   If not, the management services must adjust priorities or provision additional resources.

2.6 Information Services

Information services provide the mechanisms for the other Grid services to learn about dynamic events used for status monitoring and directory information that is used to discover services and logged data.   The information services are typically based on a web service publish-subscribe event notification system such as WS-Eventing or WS-Notification. But dynamic directory and query services also play a critical role.

A closely related and important concept is that of naming. OGSA assumes a three level naming systems in which the top-level is a human readable name. The middle level is a persistent abstract unique identifier. The lowest level is the actual address (or addresses) of the object being named. For example, a Grid notification may state that a new resource exists identified by its abstract unique name.   A user or another service can use a name resolver service or directory to obtain an address for this object. A human user can use the directory services to discover entities that correspond to a particular human readable name.

3 Actual Grid Systems

OGSA is still a work in progress, so there are no certified implementations. However there are a number of software stacks that are available that are used in different Grid deployments and many of these contain many of the features of OGSA. Several of these are available as open source systems and are used extensively in the scientific community. The Globus Toolkit GT4 [12] is the most frequently used. It contains elements of all of the OGSA core service areas except for self-management. It will be used as the core service layer for the National Science Foundation TeraGrid project [5]. It is also used in the bioinformatics Grid GeneGrid [13], and GridCast [14], a Grid to support the delivery of multi-media for the BBC.   The Laser Interferometer Gravitational Wave Observatory (LIGO) [15] uses GT3, the previous version of Globus. GT3 is also used in the Network for Earthquake Engineering [1] and Cancer Biomedical Informatics Grid caGrid [16].

Another SOA for Grids, gLite [17], coming out of CERN, supports research in high-energy physics. gLite is used in the "Enabling Grids for E-SciencE" EGEE project [18] and the LHC Computing Grid [19].   Another large Physics project is the Open Science Grid OSG [20], which uses elements of GT4 and gLite. The Legion system, which is one of the oldest software platforms for Grid computing is being redeveloped as a web SOA by the University of Virginia and is being used in the Global Bio Grid [21]. Another early OGSA-like Grid is Discovery Net [22]. In addition to these OGSA-like SOAs used in large science Grids, there are several commercial products that are available and in use in the enterprise computing sector. We expect that many of these will evolve into close compliance with OGSA.

4 The Application Service Layer: Scientific Gateways

There are really two types of Science Gateways. One type is a service gateway that bridges two Grids. An example of this is a proposed Gateway between TeraGrid and the Open Science Grid (OSG) that will allow OSG users access to TeraGrid resources. The second type of Gateway is a collection of tools that allow a large number of users transparent access to remotely deployed application and database services. Typically these systems use a web portal and desktop tools such as a workflow composer and visualization tools. There are many excellent examples of this type of service organization. Some projects use an extensive Grid infrastructure similar to OGSA as the underlying foundation, while others are relatively lightweight and self-contained. For example, the Taverna [23] system, which is widely used in biomedical applications, does not rely on an underlying Grid. Rather it directly orchestrates web service and other services available on the Internet. Another powerful tool to help scientists orchestrate web services and other applications is Kepler [24]. While Kepler can be used as a desktop tool to orchestrate simple services, it can also be used in a large grid-based gateway, such as the Biomedical Informatics Research Network BIRN [25]. Finally, Triana [26] is a workflow composition tool that can be used by scientists either as a desktop application, or as a component to a larger Grid Gateway, such as used with the GridLab project [27]. Another excellent Gateway that does not require extensive backend OGSA-style Grid support is ServoGrid [28], a portal for computation geophysics. On a closely related topic, the Earth Systems Grid [29] provides an excellent portal that provides access to tools for climate research. Unlike some of the others, it is based on a substantial Globus-based Grid foundation.

To provide a better idea of what a Grid based Gateway architecture looks like, we will look at one project in detail. The Linked Environments for Atmospheric Discovery (LEAD) project is an National Science Foundation sponsored effort to vastly improve our ability to predict tornadoes, hurricanes and other mesoscale weather events. The project, led by Kelvin Drogemeier at the University of Oklahoma involves seven other primary institutions[1]. The use-case for LEAD can be described as follows. Vast arrays of instruments are constantly collecting data about the weather. This includes ground sensors measuring pressure, humidity, lighting strikes as well as Doppler radars and airborne detectors such as balloons and commercial aircraft, and satellites. There are also substantial data about previous weather events. In LEAD, data-mining agents will monitor the instrument data streams looking for interesting emerging severe storm conditions. When something significant is detected, the agent will broadcast notification events to a workflow engine. These events will trigger one or more waiting workflows to begin executing. The job of the workflows is to interact with resource broker services to invoke a series of data "ingest" analysis services and start up an "ensemble" of weather forecast simulations each representing a

---

[1] Indiana University, the University of Alabama Huntsville, the National Center for Supercomputing Applications (NCSA), UNIDATA/UCAR, Millersville University, Howard University and the University of North Carolina.

slightly different scenario. (An ensemble may be a few dozen simulations or hundreds, depending on resource availability.) As these simulations proceed other data analysis services will compare the output of each with the evolving state of the real weather. Those simulations that fail to track reality will be terminated and those that are doing well will be given more resources. As the simulations predict a developing area of trouble, the workflows will be able to direct some of the instruments, such as the newest generation of Doppler radars, to gather more detailed information in the region of concern. This improved data can be used to increase the resolution of the simulation. When the simulations begin to converge on a serious severe storm in the making, the scientific team will be alerted. At this point the scientists may choose to interact with the workflow to cause additional scenarios to be explored or to generate visualizations.

In addition to this real-time adaptive storm prediction scenario, LEAD must also support a workbench for researchers, teachers and students of all age groups. This diverse user base has vastly different requirements. The LEAD Gateway service architecture has components that support two primary activities:

- Data discovery, data and metadata management, and data storage.
- Workflow management for simulation and data analysis services.

To support these activities there are six persistent services as illustrated in Figure 2. The portal server is user's primary access point. When the user authenticates with the server (via standard https protocols), the portal server fetches the user's Proxy X.509 certificate and a set of SAML based authorization tokens. The authorization tokens determine which other services the user has access to. The portal server presents the user with a series of JSR-168 portlets that provide the interfaces to the other core services.

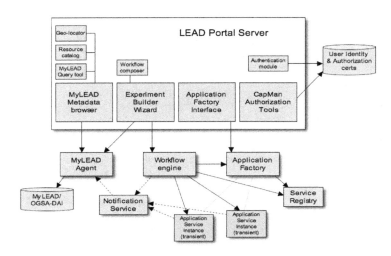

Fig. 2. LEAD Gateway Services

For most users, the primary portlet is the MyLEAD service [30] and associated tools. MyLEAD is a metadata catalog of each users experimental data and results. The tools associated with MyLEAD include an interactive query tool that allows a user to search for data based on a variety of experimental attributes, a Geo-query tool that allows a user to define data in terms of geospatial (*i.e.,* map coordinates), temporal and data attributes, and a resource catalog, that allows the user to select data from public weather services such as UNIDATA Local Data Manager (LDM) servers. The portal components of MyLEAD talk to the MyLEAD agent web service which is the front end for the MyLEAD catalog which is built on the OGSA-DAI service [11].

The "high-end" experimental users of LEAD need the ability to integrate large scale simulation and data analysis codes into experimental workflows. The way they do this is through an Application Factory service. They begin by deploying their application on some host in the back-end Grid. A description of the deployment and how it is invoked (including the types of input files it needs and output files it generates) is encoded by the scientist into a "service map document". This document can then be uploaded into the portal application factory interface, which passes it to the application factory service. The application factory is now able to create a web service component that can launch the application as part of a workflow or directly from the portal. The WSDL for the generated application service is loaded into a service registry, which uses soft-state concept of "leases" to keep track of the state of the service. These application service instances are not assumed to be persistent because they run on remote hosts as user processes. The application factory is capable of restarting an application service that is no longer running if it is needed by a workflow.

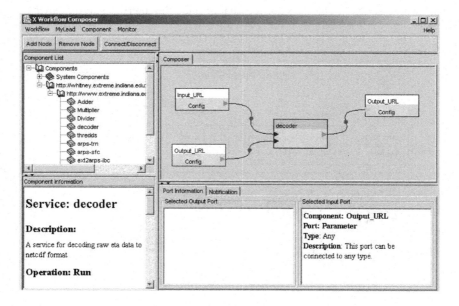

Fig. 3. The workflow composer tool

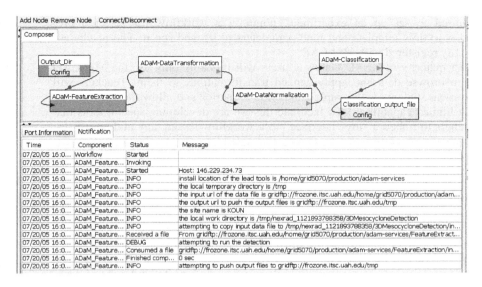

Fig. 4. The workflow composer can be used to monitor events published by a data mining workflow

The workflow service is based on a limited version of BPEL we call GPEL. It has been designed specifically to host long-running workflows that interact with application and data management services. Because BPEL is not a language that atmospheric scientists find very friendly, we have built a graphical user interface along the lines of Kepler and Triana. As shown in Figure 3, this interface allows the user to compose application components from a pallet of known application components. The composer tool compiles the graphical description into a BPEL document which is stored in the user's persistent space (i.e., MyLEAD) and in the workflow engine. Because the application services typically work by consuming and producing large files, the input and output components allow the user to specify these files by the persistent abstract unique identifier which can be used by a Grid name resolver to locate and stage a copy of the desired object.

The final service is Notification. The LEAD notification system is based on a service that implements both the WS-Eventing and an early version of the WS-Notification standards. This critical service ties together many of the components of the LEAD gateway. Every application service publishes events about its current state for each invocation of that service. Collectively, the event histories for each service invoked as part of a workflow form a record of each computational experiment. The entire event history is logged in the user's MyLEAD space as part of the record for that experiment. This gives the user the ability to examine each step of the process and also provides provenance information for every data product generated along the way. As shown in Figure 4, it is possible for the workflow composer to subscribe to the experiment event stream and monitor it as it progresses. This has proven to be an essential tool for debugging. The anticipated number of users who will actually compose and debug new workflows is expected very small. But to simplify their task, the portal contains an Experiment wizard which is able to guide a user through all the steps required to set up an experiment, compose a workflow (or select a pre-composed workflow template and bind parameters to it), and run it. The results are automatically registered with MyLEAD.

The vast majority of LEAD Gateway users will probably only use the MyLEAD interface to browse data and apply canned transformations to them. Teachers will want to present students with simple simulation scenarios and allow them to execute them with limited capabilities. To facilitate this we are developing special tools that allow teachers to imbed a "user interface" to a workflow so that any authorized student can enact it. The user interface can be embedded into the xhtml text of an educational module.

5 Conclusions

It should now be clear that a service-oriented architecture is both an elegant and a practical way in which to provide scientific communities shared access to tools and resources. SOAs are the basis for both OGSA-style Grids and science gateways. These gateway frameworks are usually built around a web portal and a set of desktop clients that access backend application services. The OGSA group has done an excellent job of characterizing the families of services required for different classes of computing and data Grids. What remains unclear is the degree to which a gateway framework needs the full power of an OGSA-style Grid. In many communities, it is sufficient to provide a portal and tools that allow users unfettered access to public web services. These communities resist installing complex grid infrastructures because of the management overhead it requires. They want lightweight, simple solutions that can be dropped into any user's environment with little or no effort.

In other cases, such as the LEAD example described here, a full-blown Grid infrastructure is needed to handle the task of doing state-of-the-art predictions of storms. Yet LEAD must also serve a community of educators and scientists that demand lightweight solutions. The dividing line between these two extremes involves the size of the data and the scale of computing required to satisfy the users needs. The high-end of LEAD tasks require massive data management and supercomputing support, while the educational environment requires modest data access and analysis and very limited simulation capability. In the majority of life science applications, the work is data analysis and transformation based on relatively small data sets available from public web services. Consequently, large Grid deployment is not always necessary in many bioinformatics applications.

A flexible service oriented architecture for Science Gateways is one that allows application services to be installed as simple components on any platform, yet they must be able to connect and interoperate with the larger, more secure back-end Grid services in a manner that is transparent to the user. By building the gateway service architecture as a modular component framework where one can deploy application services as needed, it is possible to create a system that works in a local environment but also exploits the power of large Grids.

References

1. Network for Earthquake Engineering http://it.nees.org/
2. The Particle Physics Data Grid. http://ppdg.net
3. The Enterprise Grid Alliance. http://www.gridalliance.org/en/index.asp
4. The Global Grid Forum. http://www.ggf.org
5. NSF Teragrid Project, http://www.teragrid.org/
6. Foster, I., Berry, D., Djaoui, A., Grimshaw, A., Horn, B., Kishimoto, H., Maciel, F., Savva, A., Seibenlist, F., Subramaniam, R., Treadwell, J., Von Reich, J.: The Open Grid Service Architecture, V. 1.0, www.ggf.org/ggf_docs_final.htm, GFD.30. July 2004.
7. Global Grid Forum, Job Submission Description Language. Draft specification available at http://forge.gridforum.org/projects/jsdl-wg
8. GridSAM – Grid Job Submission and Monitoring Web Service, http://www.lesc.ic.ac.uk/gridsam/
9. Matsuoka, S., Shimojo, S, Aoyagi, M., Sekiguchi, S., Usami, H., Mura, K., Japanese Computational Grid Project: NAREGI. Proc. IEEE vol. 93, no. 510, 2005.
10. Open Middleware Infrastructure Institute, http://www.omii.ac.uk
11. Antonioletti, M., Atkinson, M., Baxter, R., Borley, A., Chue Hong, N., Collins, B., Hardman, N., Hume, A., Knox, A., Jackson, M., Krause, A., Laws, S., Magowan, J., Paton, N., Pearson, D., Sugden, T., Watson, P., and Westhead, M.: Design and implementation of Grid database services in OGSA-DAI, *Concurrency and Computation: Practice and Experience*, Vol. 17, No. 2-4, Feb-Apr 2005, pp. 357-376.
12. The Globus Project: GT4. http://www.globus.org/toolkit/.
13. Jithesh, P., Kelly, N., Donachy, P., Harmer, T., Perrott, R., McCurley, M., Townsley, M., Johnston, J., McKee, S.: GeneGrid: Grid Based Solution for Bioinformatics Application Integration and Experiment Execution. *CBMS* 2005: 523-528
14. Belfast e-Science Center, http://www.qub.ac.uk/escience/projects/gridcast.
15. Laser Interferometer Gravitational Wave Observatory, http://www.ligo.caltech.edu
16. William Sanchez, Brian Gilman, Manav Kher, Steven Lagou, Peter Covitz, caGRID White Paper, https://cabig.nci.nih.gov/guidelines_documentation/caGRIDWhitepaper.pdf
17. Light Weight Middleware for Grid Computing, http://glite.web.cern.ch/glite/
18. Enabling Grids for E-SciencE, http://public.eu-egee.org
19. LHC Computing Grid, http://lcg.web.cern.ch/lcg/
20. Open Science Grid, http://www.opensciencegrid.org/gt4
21. The University of Virginia, The Global Bio Grid http://www.cs.virginia.edu/~gbg
22. Al Sairafi, S., Emmanouil, S., Ghanem, M., Giannadakis, N., Guo, Y., Kalaitzopolous, D., Osmond, M., Rowe, A., Syed I., and Wendel P.: The Design of Discovery Net: Towards Open Grid Services for Knowledge Discovery. I*International Journal of High Performance Computing Applications*. Vol 17 Issue 3. 2003.
23. Oinn, T., Greenwood, M., Addis, M., Ferris, J., Glover, K., Goble C., Hull, D., Marvin, D., Li,, P., Lord, P., Pocock, M., Senger, M., Wipat, A. and Wroe, C.: Taverna: Lessons in creating a workflow environment for the life sciences. *Concurrency and Computation: Practice & Experience, Special Issue on Scientific Workflows*, to appear 2005.
24. Ludaescher, B., Altintas, I., Berkley, C., Higgins, D., Jaeger-Frank, E., Jones, M., Lee, E., Tao, Zhao, J.: Scientific Workflow Management and the Kepler System. *CC:P&E, Special Issue on Scientific Workflows*, to be published 2005.
25. Grethe JS, Baru C, Gupta A, James M, Ludaescher B, Martone ME, Papadopoulos PM, Peltier ST, Rajasekar A, Santini S, Zaslavsky IN, Ellisman MH. : Biomedical informatics research network: building a national collaboratory to hasten the derivation of new understanding and treatment of disease. *Stud Health Technol Inform.* 2005;112:100-9.

26. Churches, D., Gombas, G., Harrison, A., Maassen, J., Robinson, C., Shields, M., Taylor, I., Wang, I.: Programming Scientific and Distributed Workflow with Triana Services. *CC:P&E, Special Issue on Scientific Workflows*, to appear 2005.
27. The GridLab Project. http://www.gridlab.org/
28. Aktas, M., Aydin, G., Donnellan, A., Fox, G., Granat, R., Lyzenga, G., McLeod, D., Pallickara, S., Parker, J., Pierce, M., Rundle, J., and Sayar, A.: Implementing Geographical Information System Grid Services to Support Computational Geophysics in a Service-Oriented Environment. *NASA Earth-Sun System Technology Conf.*, June 2005
29. Bernholdt, D., Bharathi, S., Brown, D., Chanchio, K., Chen, M., Chervenak, A., Cinquini, L., Drach, B., Foster, I., Fox, P., Garcia, J., Kesselman, C., Middleton, M. VNefedova, V., Pouchard, L., Shoshani, A., Sim, A., Strand, G., and Williams, D.: The Earth System Grid: Supporting the Next Generation of Climate Modeling Research. *Proc. IEEE*, vol. 93, no. 485, 2005
30. Plale, B., Gannon, D., Huang, Y., Kandaswamy, G., Lee Pallickara, S., Slominski, A.: Cooperating Services for Data-Driven Computational Experimentation, Computing in Science & Engineering, *IEEE Computing in Science and Engineering*, vol 7, no. 5, pp. 24-33, 2005.

Toward a Programming Model
for Service-Oriented Computing

Francisco Curbera, Donald Ferguson, Martin Nally, and Marcia L. Stockton

IBM Corp.
{curbera, dff, nally, mls}@us.ibm.com

Abstract. The service oriented paradigm is, at its core, a model of distributed software components, built around the idea of multi-protocol interoperability and standardized component contracts. The Web Services Interoperability (WS-I) profiles provide standards for runtime interoperability, and the Web Services Description Language (WSDL) and WS-Policy define service contracts that support interoperability between developer tools. A major goal of Service Oriented Architectures (SOAs) is to enable an abstraction layer that integrates and bridges over platform and implementation technology differences, effectively providing a universal business software component and integration framework. Achieving a complete solution requires a portable component model and well-defined patterns for components types. This paper examines the main requirements for a SOA programming model and identifies its most relevant characteristics. In line with SOA's goals, such model must allow a broad community of users (including non-programmers) to create service-oriented applications by *instantiating*, using, *assembling* and *customizing* different *component types* that match the user's goals, skills, and conceptual framework. Moreover, these component types must be portable and interoperable between multiple different vendors' runtimes.

1 Introduction: Service Oriented Architectures

This paper deals with the problem of defining a service-oriented programming model (component model). At its core, a programming model defines

1. A set of *roles,* and skills for each role.
2. A set of *tasks* and an associated role.
3. A set of *part types* or *component types* that the roles create and use.
4. A set of interfaces that a role uses when implementing a specific component type.

As an example, in Java 2 Enterprise Edition™ (J2EE) [1], "dynamic Web page developer" might be a role. A programmer in this role produces Java Server Pages (JSPs) [2] and Servlets [3], and may use JavaBeans™ [4] that encapsulate access to business logic and back-end systems. Programmers in other roles provide the JavaBeans, isolating the dynamic Web page developers from the details of relational database access or integration with non-J2EE applications through connectors and adaptors.

Roles are not necessarily programmer roles, and we use the terms "implement" and "interface" in a loose sense. Defining a programming model has many benefits, most noticeably a reduction in complexity. No single role needs to understand all of the

B. Benatallah, F. Casati, and P. Traverso (Eds.): ICSOC 2005, LNCS 3826, pp. 33–47, 2005.

possible ways of implementing a function, or all the interfaces a system exports. There are well defined bounds on the breadth of complexity exposed to each role, and well-defined hand-offs between differently skilled developers (different roles). Finally, a programming model enables vendors to provide role and task based tools. The visual metaphors a tool should surface to a programmer implementing a workflow process are significantly different from the metaphors for WYSIWYG Web page design.

This paper focuses primarily on the part types or components of a programming model for Service Oriented Architectures (SOAs). The goals of the service-oriented architecture approach to building enterprise applications include enabling faster integration of business applications inside and between organizations, fostering reuse of application logic, and supporting flexible transformation of enterprise business processes. Taking their cue from the success of the Web in the realm of human-to-application interactions, some say that eventually SOAs should be able to provide support for a new global, fully networked, and dynamic economy.

A precise characterization of SOA may at this point still be a matter of debate. Some key aspects, however, seem to have been widely accepted by now:

1. SOA is a "distributed component" architecture. SOA components are transparently located inside or outside the enterprise and universally accessible as services through a stack of universally supported, interoperable remote procedure call (RPC) and messaging protocols. Standards for defining interfaces provide interoperability between developer tools. "On the wire" protocol interoperability, as opposed to code portability, is the centerpiece of SOA component interactions because it supports the principle of universal access and platform independence. Today, SOA only provides platform independence from the caller's perspective; the service implementer, however, is linked to a specific platform and development tool.
2. Like other component models before it, SOA components encapsulate functionality and enable reuse. However, well-defined SOA components do so at a level granularity and abstraction much closer to the business functions and requirements that are meaningful at the business modeling level (as opposed to the information technology level).
3. SOA components offer declarative, machine processable contracts that enable third parties to access the services that the components provide. SOA contracts explicitly state functional characteristics as well as non-functional (quality of service - QoS) capabilities and requirements. SOA components may document their operations using the Web Services Description Language WSDL [5], and extend this definition to document valid sequences of operations using Business Process Execution Language for Web Services (BPEL4WS) [6] abstract processes.
4. Based on their explicit contracts, components can be automatically and dynamically found, selected and bound by means of their declarative properties, and integrated using composition mechanisms.

The purpose of this paper is to discuss requirements and characteristics of a SOA programming model. Current standards and specifications imply much about the design of the programming model. Four important aspects of a SOA programming model may be derived from the preceding summary characterization of SOA:

1. Platform independence and virtualization.
2. Centrality of composition mechanisms.
3. Flexibility in the component configuration.
4. Loose coupling between components.

We discuss these aspects below.

Virtualization
The central role of universal interoperability in SOA naturally leads to the notion of *virtualization*. From an interoperability standpoint, all applications are accessed as services regardless of their underlying implementation differences and their location in the network (co-resident, inside an enterprise, over the Internet). Likewise, from a *SOA programming model* perspective, applications are (potentially) *SOA components,* despite being implemented in a variety of different underlying technologies.

A SOA programming model in this sense is fundamentally different from other programming models in that it is "virtual" and maps over and into a variety of platform-specific concrete programming models.

Consider two examples:

1. Programmers can use the XSL Transformations (XSLT) language [7] to implement a service that converts the messages used by a "legacy" application to the XML schema defined by an industry standard. The abstraction is portable (XSLT, service invocation). Concrete infrastructures may choose to "compile" the XSLT in Java, C, stored procedure languages, or use an XSLT interpreter.
2. BPEL4WS provides support for defining a service implementation that choreographs and aggregates other services. BPEL4WS *invoke* activity and *partnerLinks* provide a virtual calling mechanism. Other activity types provide support for implementing the service. The programming model is virtual, and specific infrastructures may interpret or compile BPEL4WS as needed.

Although SOA components are not native to any particular platform (.NET, J2EE), applications developed for any platform are potentially SOA components. If the J2EE, .NET, etc. components implement the SOA component model externals (protocols, contracts), other SOA component implementations and solutions can call them.

The preceding examples reveal three aspects of a SOA virtual component and programming model:

1. An abstract primitive for defining requirements on other services (e.g. BPEL4WS partnerLink).
2. An abstraction for calling an operation on a service.
3. A portable abstraction for defining implementation logic (e.g. BPEL4WS, XSLT).

A SOA component model is introduced in Section 2. A virtual component model also requires an abstraction for access to "data" or "information" from within a component's implementation. In the XSLT example, some of the transformations may require table look-ups. The component is inextricably linked to a specific data access model for data format without such an abstraction. Section 6 describes how Service Data Objects (SDOs) provide this data virtualization layer.

Component Composition

The development of individual (or atomic [1]) service components may rely on platform-specific programming models and languages, or may use an atomic SOA component type like a transform component. Programmers may choose to implement base components using J2EE, PHP [8], etc. A core concern of SOA as a programming model is the interaction of those components and their integration into new composite components or applications. SOA composition may be achieved using platform-specific models, such as a J2EE session bean that accesses back-end services to provide a new service.

SOA-centric composition models, however, can also build directly on top of a SOA component model without mapping into another programming model. BPEL4WS is probably the best known SOA composition language, but different composition models are possible. Most successful composition models will naturally derive from current practice, incorporating proven integration approaches into a SOA programming model.

There are two main perspectives on composition. *Behavioral composition* describes the implementation of the composite; process-oriented composition (derived from workflow models), and a state machine metaphor (such as UML State Diagrams [9]) are good examples of this type of composition. A *structural composition,* on the other hand, defines the assembly of a set of existing components into larger solutions. We discuss composition paradigms in Section 3.

Flexibility and Customization

SOA aims to enable the wide reuse of service components. The composition model allows programmers to find services having the desired interfaces and infrastructure (QoS) policies, and aggregate them into new services and solutions. These new services can themselves be composed. It is unlikely, however, that a service can be always be reused "as is", without configuration, customization or tailoring. When change is needed, the current state of the art is source code modification. However, the ability to deliver wide reuse of components depends heavily on the capability to adapt components to the environment in which they are used. A SOA programming model should enable building services and modules that "programmers" can customize without source code modification. This is especially important when the programmer is in a different organization than the programmers who built the components.

In Section 4 we discuss two possible mechanisms for supporting component customization: *adaptation* though *points of variability* (POV) on the component's behavior, and *mediation* which focuses on processing in-flight messages.

Loose Coupling

Another benefit of a SOA programming model is the ability to substitute one component for another at various times during the software lifecycle. This is enabled by the late binding of declared interfaces to implementations supporting them. There are many business reasons why substituting units of functionality is desirable. Most important of these, perhaps, is to reduce the difficulty of managing change in a large

---

[1] This use of the term atomic is different from the use in transaction processing. In this context, we use atomic to mean a service that is not a composite or aggregate of other components.

enterprise. Being able to introduce change gradually, and limiting the impact of change by adhering to defined interfaces, confers increased flexibility. It also matches the loose coupling that is often characteristic of large human organizations. This feature of a SOA programming model enables groups with different skills, needs and timetables to work collaboratively in a way that maximizes the efficiency of resources, and allows the business to respond more rapidly to change.

There are several elements to loose coupling:

1. Describing messages (operation parameters) using XML Schema makes services less fragile in the face of message evolution. Messages can evolve, for example, through reordering or by adding elements, without breaking existing service implementations. Operation addition or reordering in WSDL does not break existing callers.
2. Dynamic binding is inherently more flexible than existing approaches based on program linking or class paths.
3. The mediation model allows message (request) routing and processing, expanding on the flexibility of dynamic binding. Using routing mediations allows for addition of new or alternate implementations of services, which can be selected during operation invocation based on business logic or rules.

Paper Overview
The rest of this paper examines these aspects of the service oriented architecture from a programming model point of view. Section 2 introduces the notion of SOA components and component types, and discusses some of these component types. Section 3 presents SOA composition models, focusing on structural and behavioral composition paradigms. Section 4 discusses component customization, and in Section 5 we show how data access virtualization is supported by Service Data Objects. Section 6 provides an architectural perspective to the concepts of this paper. In Section 7 we discuss related work and the Service Component Architecture, a recently released SOA programming model. Finally, Section 8 summarizes the results of this paper.

2 SOA Components

Most literature on Web services, especially standards, focuses on the interoperability protocols and service interfaces, and their use. This paper instead focuses on the programming model for *implementing* services and assembling them into solutions. A *component model* simplifies the process of building and assembling services. Here we outline the design of a SOA component model. First, an important distinction between a SOA component and a service must be made. A service is a visible access point to a component. A component can offer multiple services, while at the same time require, as part of its implementation, access to a number or external services. With this distinction in mind, we distinguish three main elements in a SOA component model: service specifications, the service component implementation, and the service component.

A "*service specification*" defines an access channel to a SOA component. It is defined by the following 3 groups of specifications.

- Interfaces, which are typically WSDL portTypes.
- Policies that document QoS properties like transactional behavior, security, etc.
- Behavioral descriptions, for example a BPEL4WS abstract process, or a UML2 state model. Callers can compute valid sequences of operations from the abstract process or state model.

A service specification is different form a Web service in that it is not bound to a network address. An address is assigned to the services provided by a specific component instance, not to the service specifications.

A *service component implementation* is the definition of a particular kind of component, which will in turn admit multiple realizations or instantiations as actual service components. It is defined by 5 groups of specifications.

- Provided "service specifications" define the characteristics of the services that components exposes to potential users.
- Required "service specifications" define the services that the component requires from other service providers to function.
- Properties that may be set on the component to tailor or customize the behavior of each instance of the implementation.
- "Container directives" (policies) that are invariant for all instances of the implementation, including information of the kind typically encoded in J2EE deployment descriptors.
- An implementation artifact (Java class, BPEL document, set of XSLT rules, etc) that defines the implementation of the component.

Finally, a *service component* (instance) represents a component actually deployed and accessible to other applications. It defined by the following.

- A component name.
- A service component implementation
- The values of any properties of the implementation that are being set to tailor the instance
- The specification of any services that resolve the "required" service specifications of the implementation. These may be "wires" that connect component instances or a "query" that executes to find a component at runtime that implements an interface, and has the right QoS policies and the required behavior (abstract process, etc.).

There are two basic approaches to defining a SOA component. The first is a *control file*: a document that, by reference, associates or joins all the parts of the component. For example, the control file may reference the WSDL definition (*interface provided*), the Java class that implements the component (*implementation artifact*), the associated policy documents (*policy assertions*), etc. The control file format gathers several individually-developed artifacts into a collection that, together, comprises the component. Application development tools aid in defining the control file.

The second format uses *pragmas:* structured comments (e.g. XDoclet tags [10]) or metadata language elements (as in JSR 175 [11]) specifying the same information, but contained within the body of a single source file. There is evolving support in Java [11] to make these annotations part of the language, but this approach does not support other models like a set of SQL or XQuery statements. For example, structured comments in a Java source file indicate which Java methods will become Web service operations on the generated WSDL defining the component's service interfaces. We will illustrate this concept further in the discussion of individual component types.

2.1 Component Types

Because of the virtual nature of the SOA component model, many SOA components naturally support multiple implementation technologies. On the other hand, different implementation technologies are better suited for different tasks. To improve transparency, we introduced the notion of *service component types*, each suited for a developer with a given set of skills, performing a specific task, and using a certain tool. For queries, the programmer implements a .SQL file and a file containing a set of XQuery statements; for document conversion, XSLT style sheets, and so forth, using tools optimized for that task. There is no need to know that a Web service, Enterprise JavaBean (EJB) or other artifact is generated upon deployment, just that the overall result will be exposed and made available as a generic SOA component.

Programmers build a specific type of component adapted to the task, concentrating on the problem to be solved and the tool for doing so, not on the resulting artifacts. SOA development tools should focus on the skills of the developer and the concepts they understand. In the remainder of this section we take a brief look as some component types. When necessary, references are made to IBM products supporting the function being described.

Plain Old Java Object and Stateless SessionBeans
The most basic type of service component implementation is a "plain old Java object" (a "POJO"). JSR 109 defines the model and architecture for implementing Web services in J2EE [13, 14]. Tools like WebSphere Studio [15] can publish a Java class through a Web service abstraction. The Java class runs in the Web container, and has full access to the J2EE programming model's facilities. The WebSphere tools and runtime automate the conversion from SOA-encoded XML to the Java interface and operations of the POJO, and vice versa. Programmers may also use Stateless SessionBeans to implement services. WebSphere Studio tools automate publishing a Stateless SessionBean through a WSDL/SOA abstraction.

WebSphere Rapid Deployment [12] is a tool that simplifies defining a service in Java using the *pragma* format described previously. Using an editor, a programmer annotates the Java source file with control tags derived from the XDoclet model [10]. These tags specify whether the component is a POJO or Stateless SessionBean, the values for deployment descriptors (e.g. the transaction model), and the operations that must become part of the remote interface and WSDL.

IMS Transactions
The IMS SOAP Gateway [17] adds the ability to seamlessly expose existing and newly-created IMS application assets as Web services, in conjunction with the IMS Connect capabilities in IMS version 9. The gateway supports synchronous SOAP interactions over HTTP and HTTPS to enable the IMS application to receive inbound service requests. Additional functions such as SOAP client outbound support and

additional Web service protocols such as WS-Security, WS-Atomic Transaction, and WS-Addressing support are expected to be available in the near future.

The mapping of an IMS transaction to a Web service operation is defined by several files: an XML-COBOL converter, a WSDL Web service interface definition, and an XML correlator that relates the name of the application to the name of the XML-COBOL converter and provides protocol details for the connection between the SOAP runtime and IMS Connect. An XML Enablement utility in WebSphere Studio Enterprise Developer generates these artifacts to repurpose IMS COBOL applications as Web services.

SQL Statements
Products like the Websphere Information Integrator (WII) [18] enable databases to consume Web services. WII can make data sources described by XML schema accessible through standard SQL queries, the form familiar to DB2 programmers. The tools and runtime convert XML data sources to relational tables. A set of adapters provide a common WSDL-described interface for accessing XML information from WII. The basic SQL SELECT, UPDATE, and INSERT commands are integrated with compatible Web service operations. The DB2 database can invoke operations on Web services, both in queries and stored procedures, from SQL. Likewise, to publish enterprise information as Web services without programming, it is possible to expose SQL queries, database stored procedures, and other database artifacts as Web services.

3 Component Assembly and Customization

As has been mentioned before, composition is the core development task in a SOA programming model. We focus in this section on two forms of component composition that can be used to compose new services from existing ones. Each one derives from well established models of application integration and assembly.

1. *Structural composition* is the assembly of modules and solutions from existing components. Structural composition reflects the current practice of deploying solutions by assembling and connecting (logically "wiring" together) a set of existing components.
2. *Behavioral or process-oriented composition* describes the implementation of the composite service, called a *process*, via a classic procedural programming metaphor: what services to call, in what order, and how to aggregate the results. Process-oriented composition, directly derived from the legacy of workflow-oriented integration of applications [20] and human tasks, is one approach. Many programmers will also approach behavior composition through a state machine or {event, state, action} metaphor using, for example, UML State Diagrams [9].

Structural Composition
As we have seen, SOA components document the interfaces they need from other services (*imports*), and the interfaces they offer (*exports*). In structural composition,

programmers wire the required interfaces of a component to interfaces that other components or services provide. This *wiring* metaphor is similar to defining UML collaboration diagrams. The "wires" represent the flow of messages from one component's required interface to an interface that another component implements. Service composition can also connect a service's exported interfaces to event driven architecture (EDA) environments, allowing services' operations to be driven by subscriptions to events. Wiring can also connect imported interfaces, the interfaces the service calls, to topics to generate events that drive other services or software. The WS-Notification [31] family of specifications provides a model for integrate EDA with SOA.

A collection of services wired together into a bundle is called a *module*. A module can likewise declare imports and exports and be wired into a larger assembly, thus supporting a *recursive composition* model, so modules can aggregate other modules. Wires defined at assembly time are not satisfied until, at runtime, they are bound to deployed component instances.

An important concept in structural composition is that of *mediation* services. A mediation service defines the "behavior" of a wire, and is invoked by the SOA infrastructure (such as an Enterprise Service Bus (ESB) [21, 22]) whenever a message traverses the wire. Mediations typically do one of the following:

- Content based routing – Route the message to one or more alternative destinations based on content.
- Transformation – Transform messages and map operations, adapting the required interface to the implemented interface.
- Augmentation – Retrieve additional information to put the message into the form expected by the target service.
- Side effect – Perform an extra operation needed by the infrastructure or by an enterprise policy, beyond that specified in the data payload. For example, log financial messages.

Mediations are first class services, with supporting tools. WebSphere Business Integration Message Broker [23] for example supports powerful, complex mediations including augmentation, transformation and routing mediations.

Behavioral Composition
BPEL4WS provides Web services centric process composition. A BPEL4WS *process* is a directed graph[2] of *activity nodes* representing a single business activity—for example, a "quick loan" service in a banking business. Processes are classified as short- or long-running. Short-running processes have a single transaction per process and can be defined using basic process choreography. Long-running processes persist their execution state in a database. They require advanced process choreography and support transactionality at the activity level. They may include *compensations* to roll back partially completed work in the event of a failure, for long lived processes that

---

[2] BPEL4WS also supports other compound activities in addition to the directed graph model. For example, there is a language construct for a sequence of more basic activities.

cannot rely on the resource locking mechanisms of transaction managers, or for operations that lack transaction support.

A *business state machine* (BSM) is a service that aggregates other services and business logic relying on state based behavior. Consider the example of a purchase order processing service. The implementation of the *cancelPurchaseOrder* operation may depend on the "state" of the purchase order. If the purchase order has been entered, but not processed, there is one implementation of cancel. If, however, purchase ordering processing is complete and the PO is shipping, there may be a different implementation. A business state machine has one or more interfaces, which in turn have operations. The business state machine instance has a current state, and the state determines which operations are enabled.

4 Component Customization

A *customizable* component is one that can be tailored for reuse in a new context or within an assembly, or adapted to evolving business policies, without changing the source code.   Our SOA programming model introduces two approaches to customization: adaptation, and mediation. *Adaptation* is achieved by providing *points of variability* (POV) on the component's behavior and its contract, which allow flexibility in the use of the component while not requiring any modification to the component's intrinsic implementation. The component provider declares points of variability by documenting a required interface. Other programmers configure or customize the component by providing a companion service that implements the POVs. The documentation of POVs is a generalization of the Strategy Pattern [24].

Mediation (selection) is a model in which the infrastructure or new customization logic processes in-flight messages. Processing can include routing to one of multiple implementations.

Consider an example of a commerce (shopping) component.

1. Discount algorithms change over time, and change from one organization to another. By declaring a POV *computeDiscount(shoppingCart)*, the commerce component provider role allows another programmer to tailor the component's behavior over time, changing the discount computation without affecting the component's intrinsic behavior or source code.
2. A commerce component may require access to an inventory management service. The component provider cannot know which of several inventory systems a particular enterprise will use. By mediating the interaction between the commerce component's required interface and implementing services, it is possible to route and transform the messages for the proper inventory system.

5 Virtualization of Data Access

Service Data Objects (SDOs) [25] replace diverse data access models with a uniform abstraction for creating, retrieving, updating, iterating through and deleting business data used by service implementations.   A SDOs *data graph* is a collection of tree-structured objects that may be disconnected from the data source. Programmers use the single data graph abstraction to access data available through heterogeneous sources and technologies such as JDBC, the Java Messaging Service, Web services, Java 2 Connectors, RMI/IIOP, etc.

To maintain this abstraction, applications don't connect to a data source directly. Instead, they access an intermediary called a *data access service* (DAS) and receive a data graph in response. A DAS is an adapter that handles the technical details for a particular kind of data source. It transforms the data into a SDO graph for the client. To apply an update to the original data source, the application returns the updated graph to the DAS, which in turn interacts with the data source.

SDO sidesteps technology churn -- the rewriting of applications to keep up with shifting technology -- by encapsulating data access details to insulate business applications from technology changes. For example, consider a Java web application designed to read product descriptions from a database and display them as web pages. To access product descriptions in the database, the application might use JDBC heavily. Suppose that later the application topology changes, placing a web service between the application and the database. Now the application can no longer use JDBC to access the data and needs substantial rework to substitute a Web service data access application programming interface (API) such as DOM or JAX-RPC. SDO avoids this problem; an application written with SDO need not change.

6 Architectural Perspective

A runtime architecture supporting SOA and a SOA centric programming model comprises two broad categories of artifacts: service endpoints and the message transport fabric interconnecting them. A general architecture as provided by the IBM family of runtimes (none of which individually is the sole delivery vehicle for SOA) is illustrated in Figure 1.

At the core is an *enterprise service bus* (ESB) supplying connectivity among services. The ESB is multi-protocol, and supports point-to-point and publish-subscribe style communication between services, as well as being the container for *mediation services* that process messages in flight.

There are three key insights into the ESB concept:

1. WSDL and WS-I protocols provide the conceptual model. A specific deployed service may support additional optimized bindings, for example local calls or IIOP. Service implementers and callers are isolated from the optimizations.
2. There is a point-to-point, wire model for connecting component instances, but interfaces may also be connected to "topics" in a publish/subscribe infrastructure.
3. All calls may be mediated – The ESB is a logical concept, and may reside in endpoints when services are co-resident in a container.

A SOA component resides in an abstract hosting environment known as a *container* and provides a specific programming metaphor. The container loads the service's implementation code, provides connectivity to the ESB, and manages service instances. Figure 1 shows how different component types typically reside in different containers.

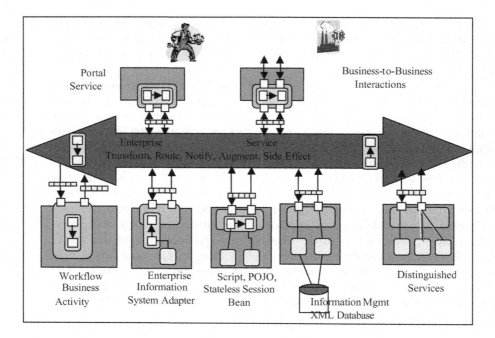

Fig. 1. A general service-oriented architecture

7 Related and Previous Work

Service Oriented Architectures are a paradigm or model which many enterprises have exploited for many years. The new concepts resonate with customers and have rapid adoption because they map to existing enterprise scenarios.

A key aspect of SOA is well-defined interfaces decoupled from implementation. There have been many previous systems employing this concept, most notably CORBA [26] and COM [27]. These approaches typically implemented an RPC model for connecting a caller to a component implementation, and supported a naming service for binding to a component by "name." J2EE [1] introduced a component model tightly linked with the Java language. J2EE uses Java interfaces for the IDL, supports declaring required interfaces through "ejbRefs" and "serviceRefs" and uses a naming service to bind required interfaces to implemented interfaces. An explicit role, the application assembler, manually connects the requested interfaces to deployed components that implement the interface. J2EE also supports component "policies" (deployment descriptors) for annotating a component with infrastructure requirements like security or transactions. Many of these concepts derive from IBM's Component Broker [29].

The SOA component model and SOA/Web services in general introduce several extensions or improvements to CORBA, J2EE, COM and other interface definition models:

- Contract languages (XML Schema, WSDL) are programming language agnostic. Even CORBA and COM IDL favored the C type space, while J2EE focuses on Java.
- XSD and WSDL are more tolerant of interface evolution. Element and operation reordering and addition typically do not affect implementations using prior versions.
- SOA and Web services inherently support both a call-return model and an asynchronous, one way messaging model. Previous systems either started with message driven processing and added an RPC model, or started with an RPC model and added asynchronous messaging. These approaches did not work well over complex, multi-hop, fire-walled Internet scenarios.
- SOA components support richer contracts that include quality of service properties and behavioral descriptions (using abstract processes) in addition to interface definitions. The SOA components model also introduces mediations and intermediaries.

Both J2EE and COM, and its evolution to .NET, provide some support for virtual access to data. J2EE introduced the concept of *container managed persistence* (CMP) for EntityBeans. COM and .NET also introduced the concept of ADOs [28], an abstraction for data that can map to multiple back-ends systems. SOA component models build on these approaches. The most noticeable improvement is linking the "data object" concept with the SOA model. There are two well-defined contracts in the SOA data object model: the contract between the component implementation and the data object (similar to ADOs and CMP EntityBeans), and a well-defined, data delivery and access service interface.

Finally, a key element of the SOA component model is the concept of "component types." J2EE introduced this concept with SessionBeans that implement the task model, and EntityBeans that represent the "data" model. The SOA component model we describe in this paper builds on this initial approach to introduce component kinds that more closely match the intent or tasks that programmers have when implementing a component/solution.

7.1 The Service Component Architecture

The Service Component Architecture (SCA) [30] is a common model for logic dealing with business data. SCA and Web Services together provide a framework for delivering SOA: SCA provides the common abstraction of implementation concerns and Web Services provides the common abstraction of interoperability concerns. SCA provides an implementation and assembly model for service oriented business applications. Here we briefly review the main concepts of the SCA programming model.

An SCA "implementation" provides the business logic for one or more services. Implementations can be written in many languages, such as Java, BPEL4WS, PHP, C, COBOL, etc. Implementations define their requirement on other services in form of "references". Further, an implementation can define "properties" that allow for configuration of its behavior. Both the services and references of an implementation are typed by interfaces. SCA is open with respect to the interface type system used (Java interfaces, WSDL portTypes, etc.) to type the services and references of the implementation, but favors the simple single-input single-output pattern standardized by WS-I [WSI] to promote interoperability among Web services.

Services, references, and properties define the configurable aspects of an SCA implementation, and together determine the "component type" of the implementation. An "SCA component" is defined in terms of a configured SCA implementation, by setting the values of the implementation properties and resolving its references to other SCA components via a "component wiring" specification. Finally, an "SCA module" is the packaging mechanism for implementations and components. Components are contained in the module assembly file that is part of the module package.

An SCA module can provide for the interaction between internal components and external applications by defining "external services" and "entry points". An external service allows components inside the module to access services outside of it; entry points are used to publish services of the module to external clients (outside of the module). External services and entry points use "SCA bindings" to configure the possible interaction mechanisms (Web services binding, stateless session EJB, etc.). SCA supports quality of service policies at the binding level and implementation level. Binding level policies are based on WS-Policy and define the quality of service (e.g. security, transactions, reliability, and so on) of the interaction across module boundaries. Implementation level policies are quality of service directives to the container hosting the implementation.

8 Conclusion

To support SOA requirements, a SOA programming model should support virtualization, multiple composition mechanisms, flexible component configuration, and loose coupling. The discussion of SOA programming models rises above the debate on the merits of different platform-specific technologies to a higher level of abstraction, integration and synthesis that is only achievable through the use of platform- and language-neutral standards. Standards are vital not only to insulate individual developers (who may not be IT professionals) from technology churn and enable them to utilize IT assets to perform their business duties. They are also vital to enable conceptual simplification by abstracting the alarming proliferation of software technologies, practices, tools, and platforms.

This article has described features of a new SOA programming model that can enable persons with different skill levels and different roles in the enterprise, not necessarily IT professionals, to create and use IT assets throughout every stage of the software development lifecycle. The result can be dramatically improved business agility for the on-demand enterprise.

References

1. Sun Microsystems, "Java 2 Platform, Enterprise Edition (J2EE)," java.sun.com/j2ee/1.4/download.html#platformspec.
2. Sun Microsystems, "Java Server Pages", http://java.sun.com/products/jsp/.
3. Sun Microsystems, "Java Servlets", http://java.sun.com/products/servlet/.
4. Sun Microsystems, "JavaBeans", http://java.sun.com/products/javabeans/.
5. "Web Services Description Language (WSDL) 1.1", http://www.w3.org/TR/wsdl, March 2001.

6. "Business Process Execution Language for Web Services (BPEL4WS) v1.1," http://www. ibm.com/developerworks/library/ws-bpel/, May 2003.
7. "XSL Transformations (XSLT) Version 1.0", http://www.w3.org/TR/xslt, November 1999.
8. R. Lerdorf and K. Tatroe, "Programming PHP", O'Reilly, March 2002.
9. Object Management Group, "Universal Modeling Language 2.0 Superstructure FTF convenience document", http://omg.org/cgi-bin/doc?ptc/2004-10-02, Oct 2004.
10. R. Hightower, "Enhance J2EE Component Reuse With XDoclets," http://www-106.ibm. com/developerworks/edu/ws-dw-ws-j2x-i.html.
11. Sun Microsystems, "JSR 175: A Metadata Facility for the Java™ Programming Language", http://www.jcp.org/en/jsr/detail?id=175.
12. IBM Corp., "WebSphere Application Server", http://www-306.ibm.com/software/ webservers/appserv/was/.
13. IBM Corp., "Build Interoperable Web Services with JSR-109", http://www-106.ibm.com/ developerworks/li brary/ws-jsrart/?ca=dnt-431, Aug 2003.
14. Sun Microsystems, "Java 2 Platform, Enterprise Edition (J2EE)," java.sun.com/j2ee/1.4/ download.html#platformspec.
15. IBM Corp., "Websphere Studio", http://www-306.ibm.com/software/info1/websphere/ index.jsp?tab=products/studio.
16. S. Kim, "Java Web Start: Developing and Distributing Java Applications for the Client Side," http://www-106.ibm.com/developerworks/java/library/j-webstart/.
17. IBM Corp., "IMS SOAP Gateway", http://www-306.ibm.com/software/data/ims/soap/.
18. IBM Corp., "IBM DB2 Information Integrator Application Developer's Guide v8.2".
19. "XQuery 1.0: An XML Query Language," W3C working draft, http://www.w3.org/ TR/xquery/, February 2005.
20. F. Leymann and D. Roller, "Production Workflow. Concepts and Techniques", Prentice Hall, September 1999.
21. R. Robinson, "Understand Enterprise Service Bus scenarios and solutions in Service-Oriented Architecture", http://www-128.ibm.com/developerworks/webservices/library/ws-esbscen/index.html.
22. D. Chappell, "Enterprise Service Bus", O'Reilly, June 2004.
23. IBM Corp. "WebSphere Business Integration Message Broker", http://www-306.ibm.com/ software/integration/wbimessagebroker/.
24. E. Gamma, R. Helm, R. Johnson, and J. Vlissides, "Design Patterns: Elements of Reusable Object-Oriented Software", Addison-Wesley, January 1995.
25. B. Portier and F. Budinsky, "Introduction to Service Data Objects: Next-generation data programming in the Java environment", http://www-106.ibm.com/developerworks/java/ library/j-sdo/, September 2004.
26. M. Henning and S. Vinoski, "Advanced CORBA(R) Programming with C++", Addison Wesley, February 1999.
27. D. Box, "Essential COM", Addison Wesley, December 1997.
28. D. Sceppa, "Microsoft ADO.NET (Core Reference)", Microsoft Press, May 2002.
29. O. Gample, A. Gregor, S. B. Hassen, D. Johnson, W. Jonsson, D. Racioppo, H. Stöllinger, K. Washida, and L. Widengren, "Component Broker Connector Overview", IBM ITSC, May 1997.
30. IBM Corp., "Websphere Integration Developer 6.0. Technical Product Overview", available at http://publib.boulder.ibm.com/infocenter/dmndhelp/v6rxmx/topic/com.ibm. wbit.help.prodovr.doc/pdf/prodovr.pdf.
31. WS-Notification", http://www.ibm.com/developerworks/library/specification/ws-pubsub.

Speaking a Common Language: A Conceptual Model for Describing Service-Oriented Systems

Massimiliano Colombo[1], Elisabetta Di Nitto[1], Massimiliano Di Penta[2],
Damiano Distante[2], and Maurilio Zuccalà[1]

[1] CEFRIEL – Politecnico di Milano,
Via Fucini 2, 20133 Milano, Italy
dinitto@elet.polimi.it, {mcolombo, zuccala}@cefriel.it
http://www.cefriel.it
[2] RCOST – Research Centre on Software Technology,
University of Sannio, Department of Engineering,
Palazzo ex Poste, Viale Traiano, 82100 Benevento, Italy
{dipenta, distante}@unisannio.it
http://www.rcost.unisannio.it

Abstract. The diffusion of service-oriented computing is today heavily influencing many software development and research activities. Despite this, service-oriented computing is a relatively new field, where many aspects still suffer from a lack of standardization. Also, the service-oriented approach is bringing together researchers from different communities or from organizations having developed their own solutions. This introduces the need for letting all these people communicate with each other using a common language and a common understanding of the technologies they are using or building.

This paper proposes a conceptual model that describes actors, activities and entities involved in a service-oriented scenario and the relationships between them. While being created for a European project, the model is easily adaptable to address the needs of any other service-oriented initiative.

1 Introduction

Service-oriented computing represents a conceptual approach and a set of technologies that are greatly contributing to radically change the perspective of today's software development. Services are an effective solution to let software systems, developed by different organizations and spread across the world, interoperate. One typical example is, for sure, the one of bioinformatics [1], where services allow an easier integration of solutions developed by different research groups, each one having different skills and using various development technologies. Also, services permit to parallelize computational-intensive tasks: Grid Computing is probably the most relevant example in which parallel computing can benefit from services.

Lately, interesting challenges such as automatic service discovery, composition, or verification, have pushed several researchers, coming from different fields

B. Benatallah, F. Casati, and P. Traverso (Eds.): ICSOC 2005, LNCS 3826, pp. 48–60, 2005.

and communities, to put together their efforts. However, service-oriented computing is still a relatively new field. There are too many different issues that are not yet mature, lacking standardization or even full comprehension by researchers. A significant example of these problems is ensuring trustworthiness [2] between interacting parties. There are attempts to identify approaches solving the issue under specific constraints, which usually imply the preliminary establishment of a service level agreement (SLA). However, the issue of offering mechanisms to enable trust in a dynamically changing set of services is still open.

More in general, there is no common terminology nor common understanding on the basic concepts of the service domain. For example, in some cases services are assimilated to components, while in some others they appear to be a distinct even if related concept. This introduces the need for a rationalization of activities, entities, and stakeholders involved in the service-oriented scenario, clearly indicating their meaning and their relationships.

Working within the SeCSE European project [3] – which aims at developing processes, methods and tools to develop service-oriented systems – we faced the urgent need to provide a clear definition of the concept of service and of the related concepts concerning service publication, discovery, composition, execution, and monitoring, as a common reference for partners involved in the project. As we discuss in Sect. 5, although other conceptualization attempts have been proposed in the literature, they focus on aspects that are different or complementary to our goals.

This paper presents our conceptual model for service-oriented systems. Even if it has been originally created to deal with the needs of the SeCSE project, its main principles should fit any service-oriented scenario. The model describes actors, entities, and activities relevant to the service domain, and the relationships existing between them. The model is specified using UML class diagrams complemented with a data dictionary. To properly ensure the model understanding, we have instantiated it on a simple scenario. The remainder of the paper is organized as follows. Sect. 2 presents the requirements for our conceptual model. Sect. 3 presents the model itself describing the diagrams it is composed of. Sect. 4 introduces the scenario we use to exemplify the conceptual model. Sect. 5 summarizes other attempts to conceptualize the world of service-oriented systems and relates them to our approach. Sect. 6 concludes the paper.

2   Requirements for the Conceptual Model

The definition of our conceptual model has been driven by the need to provide a common conceptual framework within the SeCSE project. The first two (meta) requirements we faced were compactness – thus avoiding the redundancies and inconsistencies we found in other models (see Sect. 5) – and extensibility – thus enabling the possibility to add new concepts, relationships, and activities to the model itself. Moreover, for the sake of generality, we decided to keep the model independent of any technological choice or standard, even if the SeCSE project is currently focusing on Web services as its main technology.

Such overall needs led to the following more specific requirements:

- *To clarify the meaning of 'service'.* We have noticed that this term is being used in quite different ways in various domains. For example, in the technical domain it is usually considered as a particular software system that can be published, located, and invoked across the Internet. In the business domain it has a much broader and abstract meaning, and it is defined as the non-material equivalent of a good, while service provision is defined as an economic activity that does not result in ownership; this is what differentiates it from providing physical goods.
- *To clarify the difference between a service and its public description.* A service is really available if information on how to access it is made public. In some cases services are confused with their public descriptions. While this is understandable from the service consumer viewpoint, we think that for service developers and integrators it is beneficial to highlight differences and relationships between those concepts.
- *To clarify the distinction between 'simple' vs. 'stateless', and 'composite' vs. 'stateful' services.* While in [4] there is no clear distinction between the elements of these two pairs, we think that they are distinct if not orthogonal. In particular, we argue that the term 'stateful' refers to the possibility for a service to maintain a state between two consecutive operation requests, while the term 'stateless' has the opposite meaning. Moreover, we feel that the terms 'simple' and 'composite' are better used to mean, respectively, services that do not rely on the execution of others, and services that do so.
- *To identify the various stakeholders that exploit, offer, and manage services.* Various actors are involved in a service-oriented system. Besides the usual roles of service consumers and providers, we have noticed that other important roles are the different mediators who compose or certify services, support service discovery, etc. Indeed, we have also noticed that such roles are increasingly played by automated agents, not only by human beings.
- *To capture the relevant aspects concerning service discovery, composition, publication, execution, and monitoring.* These, in fact, are the main research areas of the SeCSE project. More in detail, the project is structured in the following research activities:
  - *Service engineering:* extending the existing approaches to service and system specification in order to include requirements capable of modeling, from a service perspective, quality of service (QoS) specifications, and to provide support for using these specifications within service discovery and binding mechanisms. The project is also developing approaches and tools for service testing.
  - *Service discovery:* providing means to discover services in different phases of the service life-cycle, from requirement analysis to run-time execution.
  - *Service delivery:* focusing, at deployment and operation level, on tools and techniques for the validation, testing and run-time monitoring of services and service-centric systems.

- *System engineering:* focusing on the analysis and development of architectural models for service-centric systems that accommodate services, components, and their dynamic composition.

3 Conceptual Model Overview

The SeCSE conceptual model aims at providing a common terminology across the project. It has been designed as a compact and extensible model that takes into account all the service-related concepts that have been identified inside the project. The model is specified using UML and is described by means of different diagrams, each offering a view on a specific aspect of the service-oriented system engineering process. Namely these diagrams are: *Agent-Actors*, *Core*, *Service Description*, *Service Discovery*, *Service Composition*, *Service Monitoring* and *Service Publication*. In the remainder of this section we briefly describe each diagram (conceptual model items are capitalized and formatted in *italic* the first time they appear). We only show the most interesting ones due to the limited space available. The interested reader can find all the diagrams in the extended technical report [5]. It is worth pointing out that any ontology-based language could be used instead of UML for describing the model.

3.1 Agents and Actors

A very important aspect concerning the development and operation of any application is to identify the stakeholders and the roles they play. This is particularly important for service-oriented systems since in this case, as we have highlighted in Sect. 2, the number of different stakeholders and roles can be quite high. We use the term *Agents* to mean entities of the real-world, and *Actors* to indicate roles that Agents may play. Agents include *Person* or *Organization*, *Software System*, *Service* and *Legacy System*. Actors include *Service Provider*, *Service Developer*, *Service Integrator*, *Service Broker*, *Service Consumer*, *Service Monitor*, *Service Certifier* and *System Engineer*. In principle, an Agent can take any of the roles identified by Actors (e.g., a Person can act as an Operation Provider), and vice versa a role can be taken by any Agent (e.g., a Service Consumer can either be a Person or a Service). Some of the identified Actors are represented in the Core model in Fig. 1, while a complete diagram showing the hierarchy of Agents and Actors can be found in [5].

3.2 Core Model

Fig. 1 depicts the main concepts that are part of the conceptual model, and highlights the main Actors that interact with them. A Service is a particular concrete *Resource* which is offered by a Software System.

A Service has a *Service Description*. In order to discover a Service, a Service Consumer can express a *Service Request* that may match with zero or more

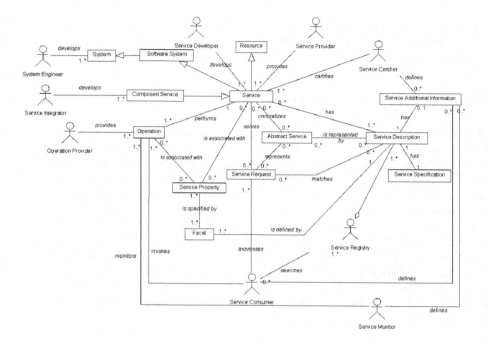

Fig. 1. Core model

Service Descriptions. After being discovered, a Service will serve the Service Request, i.e., it will be used by the Service Consumer that invokes its *Operations*. Either a Service Request or a Service Description by itself can represent an *Abstract Service*, i.e., the 'idea' of a service, a service that does not have a concrete implementation (yet). An Abstract Service can be published, discovered, and then concretized when needed in a (concrete) Service. A *Composed Service* is a particular kind of Service, developed by a Service Integrator, which makes use of other Services.

3.3   Service Description

An important aspect of services is their Service Description. In fact, it is through such a description that they are known by the potential consumers. In our model both aspects of a Service Description, i.e., Service Specification and Service Additional Information, are expressed by means of *Facets*. Each Facet is the expression of one or more *Service Properties* in some specification language. A Service Specification is usually provided by the Service Provider and may include both functional and non-functional information such as the service interface, service behavior, information on service exceptions, test suites, or service QoS attributes. The Service Additional Information is usually provided by actors different from the Service Provider (e.g., by Service Consumers, or by Service

Certifiers) and may include information such as user Ratings, Measured QoS, Usage History, some measure of trustworthiness, etc.

3.4 Service Discovery

Service discovery can be performed in various phases of a service–oriented system life cycle. It can be done when the requirements for a new system are gathered (within the SeCSE project this is called 'early discovery'), when the system is being designed and new specific needs for services are identified (in SeCSE this is called 'Architecture-time discovery'), or when the system is running. Run-time discovery has the goal of finding Services that can replace the ones that the system is currently using or, also, part of the internal logic of the system itself. Consistently with this classification, the conceptual model includes three types of queries that are executed in the three cases described above.

3.5 Service Composition

Fig. 2 presents the classification of a Service with respect to its state (i.e., stateless vs. stateful) and its compositeness (i.e., simple vs. composed), already discussed in Sect. 2. The diagram also shows the relationships existing between a Composed Service and the adopted *Composition Architectural Styles*, the Roles a Service can accordingly play, etc. In addition, the diagram links the concept

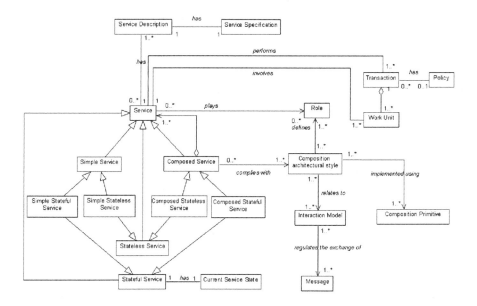

Fig. 2. Service composition

of *Transaction* and *Work Unit* with a Service: a Service performs Transactions, which are composed of Work Units (these are atomic steps for which some property applies, e.g., ACID). A *Policy* associated with a Transaction is a collection of assertions that declare the semantics of the Transaction itself (e.g., ACID or long-running, participants, coordination protocol, transaction faults and corresponding actions to be performed, etc.).

3.6   Service Monitoring

Monitoring is very important in a service-oriented scenario where the services being used within a system are not under the control of the system itself. Fig. 3 depicts the main concepts and the relationships involved in monitoring. A Service can be monitored if the software system that features it offers some appropriate monitoring mechanisms, i.e. the *Monitoring Sockets*. A Monitoring Socket is able to produce some *Monitoring Data* that are then checked by some *Monitoring Rule*, to verify some *Monitored Constraints* expressed over one or more *Quality Metrics*. These, in turn, express some measure of some Service Property (see Sect. 3.3). Service Properties can refer either to an entire Service (e.g., Mean Time Between Failure (MTBF) of 1 hour per week) or to one or more Operations offered by the Service itself (e.g., operation 'X' has to feature some transactional property). Monitoring Data can be collected in a *History*. In some cases the Monitored Constraints check an entire History rather than a single datum. Service monitoring is performed by a Service Monitor. The kind of prop-

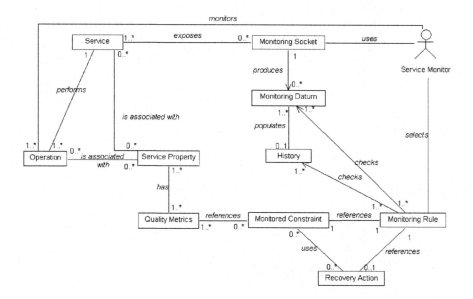

Fig. 3. Service monitoring

erties involved in a Monitored Constraint usually depends on the actual agent that performs the monitoring and on its visibility on the service execution.

3.7   Service Publication

The service publication model addresses the fact that a Service Provider can publish one or more Service Descriptions on a *Service Registry*. Service Registries can be organized in *Federations* resulting from an agreement made by organizations running Service Registries to achieve a joint aim (e.g., being focused on a similar topic, having some trust relationship, etc.). Federations can be used to propagate information (e.g., Service Requests or Service Descriptions) among different Service Registries.

4   An Example Scenario: The Pizza Delivery System

In this section we exemplify the concepts composing the conceptual model presented in Sect. 3 by describing an example scenario. We firstly describe the scenario from a service consumer viewpoint. Then, we provide a description of the scenario from a behind-the-scenes perspective. Finally, we explicitly map the conceptual model component elements over the scenario. Services are formatted in `typewriter` style, while in Sect. 4.3 conceptual model items are again capitalized and formatted in *italic* the first time they appear.

4.1   Pizza Delivery System: The Service Consumer Viewpoint

James and his wife Sarah want to have pizza for dinner at home. Through his PDA, James connects to the service directory of his Internet Service Provider (ISP) and searches for 'pizza'. He gets assorted results (pizza restaurants, pizza parlors offering delivery or takeaway, supermarkets selling frozen pizzas, recipes to prepare and bake pizza at home, etc.).

James refines his request searching for 'pizza parlor and delivery'. Then he selects one of the available parlors, taking into account criteria such as oven type, price range, maximum delivery time and rating expressed by previous clients of that service. The selected service is `PizzaOverall`.

James accesses the `PizzaOverall` service interface and orders two pizzas providing his and Sarah's preferences as for topping and baking options (with pepperoni and crusty for James, with mushrooms and soft for Sarah) together with other required information such as delivery address and time. He invokes the proper service operations providing necessary input data.

James is also requested to select a payment method to complete the order. He chooses to pay by credit card, so he has to provide further details such as card company, card number, expiration date, etc. After this, the service invocation is finished and James receives a receipt via e-mail with a detailed summary.

At 8 p.m., perfectly on time, a delivery boy knocks at James and Sarah's door and delivers their pizzas. James signs a delivery receipt on the delivery boy's PDA which records the delivery time and completes the payment transaction.

James and Sarah have a very nice dinner and at the end, since they are very satisfied of the service received, they decide to recommend the service to other Internet users.

4.2 Pizza Delivery System: Behind the Scenes

PizzaOverall, the service chosen by James, is a 'virtual' pizza parlor: it represents a service capable of dynamically discovering and combining actual services in order to accomplish its task. In particular, PizzaOverall has to discover and compose services such as an actual pizza parlor, a delivery service, and a payment gateway service.

In order to discover other services, PizzaOverall relies on the 'local' registry made available by its service provider. Through the discovery phase, PizzaOverall can find services that, once properly composed, can satisfy James's request and meet the related criteria (price range, delivery time, etc.).

PizzaOverall finds PizzaExpress, a pizza parlor which also offers delivery. The credit card transaction will be handled through PayBridge, as most of PizzaOverall payment transactions. In this case there was no need to dynamically discover a payment gateway since PayBridge is a well-known service, which, in addition, offers to its clients a price per transaction decreasing with the number of processed transactions.

PizzaOverall forwards James's order to PizzaExpress. PizzaExpress starts to bake two pizzas as requested, but then it encounters a problem: its drivers unexpectedly go on strike. PizzaOverall recognizes that PizzaExpress will not be able to perform the delivery task, so a substitutive service has to be found not to loose James' order.

PizzaOverall searches the registry again, this time broadening the search scope: this is possible because the local registry links to other external registries, so service requests can be properly propagated to other registries (e.g., following a topic-based approach). PizzaOverall discovers a delivery service, named PizzaWherever, which is likely to solve the delivery issue. A delivery is booked in order to pick up the pizzas baked by PizzaExpress and bring them to James's place all the same.

PizzaWherever has tens of delivery boys spread all over the city, driving bikes or mopeds equipped with wireless devices that they use to receive delivery orders, directions, and to communicate delivery status information to PizzaWherever's central logistic system.

One delivery boy is thus notified to pick up two pizzas at PizzaExpress's parlor at 7.45 p.m., and to promptly deliver them to James's place. He reaches James's apartment at 8 p.m. sharp. PizzaWherever, and then PizzaOverall in turn, are notified of the final delivery, as James signs the delivery receipt. All the pending payment transactions are finalized as well.

Another service, named DeliveryMonitor, transparently to James and Sarah, has followed the pizza order and delivery process, and is also notified of the time of delivery, then stored in the service history.

4.3 Explaining the Mapping Between the Example and the Conceptual Model

James is a *Person* acting as a *Service Consumer*. He uses his PDA to query his ISP *Service Registry* in order to discover *Services* and then invoke the *Operations* they expose. James's ISP is an *Organization* acting as a *Service Provider*.

James's *Service Requests* (e.g., 'have pizza for dinner') can be considered as *Abstract Services*, i.e., they represent the description (more or less detailed) of Services.

Through the discovery phase, James finds one or more *Service Descriptions* of one or more abstract or concrete Services that match or are relevant to his Service Requests. In particular, Service Requests are matched up with the *Service Properties*. Service Properties may belong to the *Service Specification* (i.e., type of oven, price range) or to the *Service Additional Information* (e.g., ratings expressed by previous customers) stored in the Service Registry by means of *Facet* structures. The Service Specification and Service Additional Information form the *Service Description*.

`PizzaOverall`, the Service James has chosen, is actually an *Abstract Service*, i.e., it describes a Service which does not correspond to any fixed concrete implementation. Such an Abstract Service has been published by the ISP itself on its own Service Registry, in order to globally represent a possible way to compose some of the available concrete Services.

James's choice to invoke `PizzaOverall` leads to the concretization of the Service which will actually satisfy his request. `PizzaOverall` is concretized by means of a *Service Integrator*, that is able to perform dynamic Composition of Services, based on the goals to be achieved (i.e., pizza baking, delivery, and payment), and according to one or more specific *Composition Architectural Styles* (e.g., peer to peer). The resulting process is annotated with assertions which enable run-time monitoring. For example, the fact that `PizzaExpress` could not perform the delivery corresponds to a violation of the postcondition of its Operation 'bake and delivery', thus triggering a proper *Recovery Action* (i.e., federated discovery of a delivery service) leading to run-time discovery of a substitute Service. This time the discovery phase involves external Service Registries which are linked by the local registry and form with this a *Federation* of Registries.

`PizzaWherever`'s central logistic system can be seen as a *Legacy System*, which has been enabled to communicate with delivery boy's wireless devices. `PayBridge` is a *Stateful Service*, i.e., the results of its invocation depend also on its inner *Current Service State* (e.g., number of previous invocations by the same consumer).

The feedback provided by James and Sarah enriches the Service Additional Information available for `PizzaOverall`. `DeliveryMonitor`, finally, is a *Service Monitor* that tracks James's order till the pizzas are delivered, and uses proper *Metrics* to measure `PizzaOverall` service properties, such as delivery time, then storing the *Monitoring Data* in the service *History*.

5 Related Work

Several attempts to conceptualize the world of services can be found in the literature, and our work was initially inspired by some of them. In particular, our core model is rooted in the Web Service Architecture (WSA) [6] drafted by the W3C. The WSA conceptual model is structured in four parts each focusing on a specific aspect, namely the service (*Service Model*), messages (*Message Oriented Model*), resources (*Resource Oriented Model*), and policies that can constrain resources and behaviors (*Policy Model*).

In general, the WSA model and our model can be seen as complementary since we do not fully address the message oriented, resource oriented, and policy models of the WSA, but we try to clarify and detail more than the WSA does the concept of service, as well as all the concepts relevant to the service-related activities (i.e., publication, discovery, composition, and monitoring). Also, we try to clarify the relationships between the concepts of service description, semantics, and service interface, while the distinction among these concepts is not evident in the WSA. Moreover, we have choosen a different approach to characterize agents and actors which allows us to express the fact that roles can be covered, in principle, by any agent and vice versa.

Our model also has similarities with the Service-Oriented Solutions Approach (SOSA) [7] proposed by Computer Associates International, Inc. technology services department. The SOSA conceptual model is part of a method that aims to maximize the potential of Web services and SOA within medium and large enterprises. Such method is based on best practices (e.g., tracks, techniques, work packages, and deliverables) for service-oriented development [7]. The SOSA model has a complementary relationship to our model since it focuses more on service interfaces and business oriented issues, while it is less detailed with respect to other aspects related, e.g., to the publication, discovery, and execution of services.

Our model is quite different in objectives and scopes to other works such as OWL-S [4] and the Web Services Modeling Ontology (WSMO) [8]. A first difference between our model and OWL-S stands in their different objectives. Our model provides a common understanding for human readers about the main actors, entities and artifacts that are somehow involved in the creation of a service-centric system. On the contrary, the OWL-S ontology was created to provide a computer-interpretable description of a service (particularly, web-based services), to allow software agents to discover, invoke, compose, and monitor Web resources offering services having particular properties. As a consequence, the OWL-S ontology pursues a very detailed service description suitable for the needs of software agents. On the other hand, our model tries to embrace a larger application domain than OWL-S, i.e., the overall set of main actors and concepts involved in the various steps of the service-centric system creation process.

The WSMO, in line with the Web Services Modeling Framework (WSMF) [9], aims at providing a conceptual model for developing and describing Web services and their composition by means of a language (Web Services Modeling Language, WSML) and an execution environment (Web Services Modeling eXecution Environment, WSMX). The WSMF consists of four different main elements: ontologies that provide the terminology used by other elements, goal repositories that define the problems that should be solved by Web services, Web services descriptions that define various aspects of a Web service, and mediators which bypass interoperability problems. The WSMO extends these main elements by defining a set of cross-wise non-functional properties named core-properties. WSMO mainly focuses on service descriptions, i.e., pre and post-conditions, non-functional properties, etc. Differently from our model, it does not provide a conceptual model of some key activities of a service-centric scenario, such as discovery, delivery, and monitoring.

6 Conclusions

The aim of this work is to provide a conceptual model that is complementary to the ones already presented in the literature, and is focused on the main issues concerning the development and operation of service-oriented systems.

We are currently enacting the adoption of the model within the SeCSE project as a unique reference for definitions and main concepts for the whole consortium. We experimented the first release of the model by having the other project partners check if their main ideas, requirements, and technical solutions fit into it. All partners provided comments and inputs that will be included in the next releases.

The model now plays a key role in the project, since it is used as a means for exchanging ideas and results in a coherent framework, thus helping every partner to better achieve the project goals (e.g., the development of a platform supporting the life cycle of SOA-based solutions).

The interest of the project partners, their willingness to participate in our discussions, and the number of debates we are still triggering convince us that the model can evolve to become a good common language, not necessarily limited to the SeCSE project.

Our model is already being exploited by the European Commission (Directorate D – Network and Communication Technologies, Software Technologies) as a framework to classify and explain the European projects related to service development [10].

Acknowledgements

This work is framed within the IST European Integrated Project *SeCSE (Service Centric Systems Engineering)* [3], 6th Framework Programme, Contract No. 511680. We thank all our partners in the project for their valuable comments and proposals aiming at improving the conceptual model.

References

1. Hong Gao, T., Huffman Hayes, J., Cai, H.: Integrating Biological Research through Web Services. IEEE Computer **38** (2005) 26–31
2. de Mes, A., Rongen, E.: Technical note: Web service credentials. IBM Systems Journal **42** (2003) 532–537

 3. SeCSE Website: *http://secse.eng.it/* (2005)
 4. Martin, D., Burstein, M., Hobbs, J., Lassila, O., McDermott, D., McIlraith, S., Narayanan, S., Paolucci, M., Parsia, B., Payne, T., Sirin, E., Srinivasan, N., Sycara, K.: OWL-S: Semantic Markup for Web Services. W3C Member Submission (2004)
 5. Colombo, M., Di Nitto, E., Di Penta, M., Distante, D., Zuccalà, M.: Speaking a Common Language: A Conceptual Model for Describing Service-Oriented Systems. Technical report, RCOST (2005) *http://www.rcost.unisannio.it/mdipenta/cm.pdf.*
 6. W3C: Web Services Architecture (WSA). W3C Working Group Note 11 February 2004. (2004)
 7. Lefever, B.: Service-Oriented Solutions Approach (SOSA). Technical report, Computer Associates International, Inc. (2005) *http://www.ca.com/be/english/past-events/lunch-s3/041209-sosa-lb-final-lefever.pdf.*
 8. de Bruijn, J., Bussler, C., Domingue, J., Fensel, D., Hepp, M., Kifer, M., König-Ries, B., Kopecky, J., Rubén, L., Oren, E., Polleres, A., Scicluna, J., Stollberg, M.: Web Service Modeling Ontology WSMO (2005)
 9. Fensel, D., Bussler, C.: The Web Service Modeling Framework WSMF. Electronic Commerce: Research and Applications (2002) 113–137
10. Sassen, A.M., Macmillan, C.: The service engineering area: An overview of its current state and a vision of its future. European Commission, Directorate D – Network and Communication Technologies, Software Technologies (2005) *ftp://ftp.cordis.lu/pub/ist/docs/directorate_d/st-ds/sota_v1-0.pdf.*

A Rule Driven Approach for Developing Adaptive Service Oriented Business Collaboration

Bart Orriens[1], Jian Yang[2], and Mike Papazoglou[1]

[1] Infolab, Tilburg University,
PO Box 90153, 5000 LE Tilburg, The Netherlands
{b.orriens, mikep}@uvt.nl
[2] Department of Computing, Macquarie University,
Sydney, NSW, 2109, Australia
jian@comp.mq.edu.au

Abstract. Current composite web service development and management solutions, e.g. BPEL, do not cater for flexible and adaptive business collaborations due to their pre-defined and inflexible nature that precludes them accommodating business dynamics. In this paper we propose a rule driven approach for adaptive business collaboration development in which rules drive and govern the development process. We introduce the Business Collaboration Development Framework (BCDF), which provides enterprizes with the context to define their capabilities and business collaboration agreements. Subsequently, we explain how rules can drive and control the business collaboration development process to develop complete, correct and consistent business collaboration agreements that are conform the conditions under which parties wish to cooperate.

1 Introduction

Nowadays enterprizes need to be dynamic and adaptive in order to stay competitive. This has led to an increasing demand for providing business services that can adapt to changes. Recently there has been increasing focus on service oriented computing to deliver flexible and adaptable corporate business services by utilizing existing business services cross organizational boundaries, i.e. via business collaboration. Business collaboration here refers to a cooperation between multiple enterprizes working together to achieve some common business-related goal.

In order to realize this vision enterprizes require an environment in which they can: 1) easily define their business collaboration potential both from a business and technical point of view; and 2) quickly establish the possibility to cooperate with each other. If collaboration is possible, a business collaboration agreement can eventually be negotiated. This type of negotiation also requires that enterprizes can foresee how future changes like new legislative requirements may influence their ability to cooperate with each other. In addition, enterprizes need to be able to assess how such changes may affect existing collaborations,

B. Benatallah, F. Casati, and P. Traverso (Eds.): ICSOC 2005, LNCS 3826, pp. 61–72, 2005.

which moreover need be managed properly (i.e., defined, verified and versioned) and deliver consistent results when executed [30].

Unfortunately, current composite web service development and management solutions including the defacto standard BPEL4WS [11] are too narrowly focused and not capable of addressing the requirements of business collaboration, which relies on agile and dynamic processes. As a result existing technologies and standards to development business collaborations and agreements is very difficult to manage. To address this problem, we propose a rule-based approach where business rules are used to drive and constrain business collaborations. Flexibility then comes from the fact that development of business collaborations is governed by business rules, which further more can be chained and used for making complex decisions and diagnoses. Adaptability can be achieved as changes can be managed with minimum disruption to existing collaborations.

The ideas presented are illustrated using a complex multi-party, insurance claim handling scenario [18]. The example outlines the manner in which a car damage claim is handled by an insurance company (AGFIL). AGFIL cooperates with several contract parties to provide a service that enables efficient claim settlement. The parties involved are Europ Assist, Lee Consulting Services, Garages and Assessors. Europ Assist offers a 24-hour emergency call answering service to policyholders. Lee C.S. coordinates and manages the operation of the emergency service on a day-to-day level on behalf of AGFIL. Garages are responsible for car repair. Assessors conduct the physical inspections of damaged vehicles and agree repair upon figures with the garages.

2   Business Collaboration Development Framework

Before we discuss how enterprizes can use rules to drive the process of coming to a business collaboration agreement, we shall first explore the context of business collaboration to determine the requirements for our approach. In order to capture the context in which business collaboration development takes place, we have developed the Business Collaboration Development Framework (BCDF). This framework provides context by adopting a three dimensional view in order to achieve separation of concern and modularization in the definition of business collaborations. An overview is shown in Fig. 1.

The first dimension is *collaboration aspects* which place emphasis on the different behaviors of an enterprize in business collaboration; where the purpose and target of development varies [15, 24, 29]: 1) before seeking partners to cooperate with an enterprize will first need to capture its **private behavior** in the *internal business process aspect* (like e.g. [1, 8]); 2) Based on its internal behavior the enterprize can then specify its capabilities in its **exposed behavior** (i.e. its externally visible behavior) in the *participant public behavior aspect* (similar to e.g. WSDL [10] and ebXML CPP [16]); 3) Subsequently, the enterprize can start negotiating with other parties to establish a cooperation. If negotiation is successful, the result will be the definition of an **agreed upon behavior** (i.e. the externally observable behavior in a business collaboration) captured in the

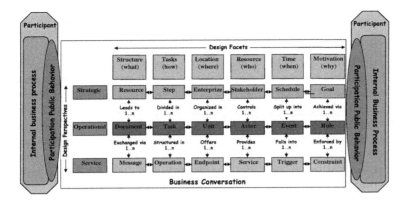

Fig. 1. Business Collaboration Development Framework (BCDF)

business conversation aspect; where the agreement is based on the participant public behavior aspects of the parties involved (somewhat akin as the merging of two CPPs to form a CPA in the ebXML architecture [16]). Note: the temporal order implied above is illustrative for developing customized, complex business collaborations like the AGFIL scenario. The order may be different when dealing with standardized, simple collaborations (as defined e.g. by RosettaNet [25]).

When enterprizes try to cooperate they must take into consideration both business and technical requirements as well as dependencies between them. This is addressed in the second dimension *levels*, which identifies three different layers of abstraction to allow separation of concern [20, 31]: 1) *strategic level*: at which enterprizes describe their purpose and high level requirements for a business collaboration, with the development process resulting in a strategic agreement expressing shared objectives (like [6, 29]); 2) *operational level*: at which enterprizes depict the operational conditions under which they can cooperate, where the result of development is an operational agreement capturing how set out objectives will be realized in terms of concrete business activities (similar to e.g. RosettaNet [25]); 3) *service level*: at which enterprizes define the technical realization of their business activities, where negotiation amounts to an agreement describing the interactions among the services from the different parties (comparable to e.g. [7], [11]).

At each level of abstraction enterprizes need to consider many issues, for example scheduling, resource usage and logistic optimization at the strategic level. To reduce the complexity resulting from covering all these different issues, the third dimension of *facets* achieves modularization in the definition of business collaborations. This helps enterprizes describe the different contexts from which a business collaboration can be observed at the different levels. The identified facets are [12, 28, 31]: *what* facet emphasizing the structural view, *how* facet taking functional standpoint, *where* facet expressing geographical facet, *who* facet concerning participants, *when* facet covering temporal aspect, and *why* facet concentrating on rationale. The facets provide a complete coverage for each individual level, where their semantics are dependent on the level that they modularize.

Facet interactions reflect the relationships that exist among the different contexts, such as the interaction between the temporal context of a collaboration and its control flow.

In summary, the main conclusion is that business collaboration is highly complex; which in turn makes their development a very complex affair. An important factor that contributes to this complication is that enterprizes must be able to handle a diverse range of changes. In the current business environment changes can occur anywhere, ranging from technological innovation to adoption of new business strategies. Enterprizes need to be able to assess the effect of such changes, both in terms of their potential to collaborate with others as well as regards the consistency of their own behavior. Only in this way, can enterprizes effectively and adequately deal with change in the business collaboration context.

3   Modeling in the BCDF

To capture the three dimensions of collaborations aspects, levels and facets BCDF uses two types of model: meta models and models, both of which are defined for individual levels. Meta models provide design guidelines in terms of classes and their relationships, where depending on the collaboration aspect being modeled additional constraints are placed on the meta-model. Models represent a particular application design, and are derived by populating a meta model's *classes*. Every meta model consists of six classes, where each class captures a particular facet; i.e. for *what, how, where, who, when* and *why* facet. Every class constitutes a set of logically related *attributes*. *Associations* connect the classes expressing dependencies among facets. *Mappings* define dependencies among levels by providing links between classes that describe the same facet at different perspectives (illustrated by the arrows between facets at different perspectives in Fig. 1). Dependencies among collaboration aspects are expressed using *connections*, which link the same meta model classes as they are applied in different aspects.

Snippets of exemplary models for the AGFIL application are illustrated in Fig. 2, showing its strategic, operational and service model respectively; where the models are represented based on UML conventions. In order to distinguish different development facets, we represent them in different shapes in their UML models (see also legend in Fig. 2): *what* facet is shown as folded corners, *how* facet as rounded rectangles, *where* facet as plaques, *who* facet as octagons, *when* facet as hectagons, and *why* facet as diamonds. In the following we briefly discuss the purpose of these models in relation to existing work (see [21] for more details).

At strategic level, strategic models like the AGFIL-BM in Fig. 2 capture purpose and high level requirements of business collaborations, akin to requirements analysis [6, 29]. Participant public behavior aspect (all elements at border of stakeholder like Lee C.S) specifies strategic capabilities of individual enterprizes such as consume car, whereas internal business process aspect (inside particular stakeholders) identifies the private enterprize processes (e.g. handle car) to realize these capabilities. When a strategic agreement is made, business

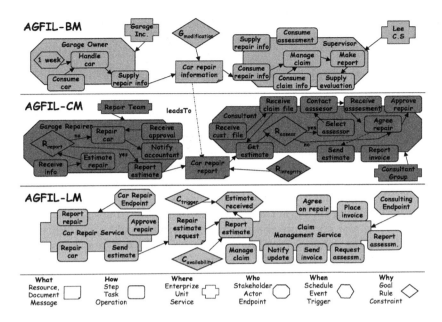

Fig. 2. AGFIL Application Models

conversation aspect (all modeling elements external to or on boundary of stakeholders like **garage owner**) defines the exchange of resources like **car repair information** between enterprizes to achieve shared strategic objectives.

At operational level, strategic models are concretized in operational models via mappings; where for example **car repair information** in AGFIL-BM **leads to car repair report** in AGFIL-CM (see the dotted arrow in Fig. 2 labeled 'leadsTo'). Note that due to space limitations other mappings are not discussed here. In terms of aspects, in participant public behavior aspect (e.g. elements on border of **garage repairer**) the tasks an actor can perform are depicted e.g. **get estimate** (like ebCPP [16]); whereas internal business process aspect (elements within actor) is similar to e.g. BPML [8] or workflow [1], specifying how and when activities such as **estimate repair** are conducted. Business conversation aspect (all elements on or outside actor borders e.g. **consultant**) captures operational agreements between enterprizes by defining the flow of information between actors; like specified by RosettaNet [25] or BPSS [16].

At service level, operational models are translated in service models where specified activities are realized by services and their operations. Resembling interface behavior in [15], the public participant behavior aspect is captured in models formed by elements placed on the border of individual services like **car repair service** depicting offered operations (akin to e.g. WSDL [10]). Within a service the modeling elements depict internal business process aspect akin to orchestration; where a service internally engages other services to realize its functionality (not shown in Fig. 2). Finally, business conversation aspect (the el-

ements on or outside the border of services) is akin to the notion of choreography
[24] defining the agreed upon exchange of messages among services.

4   Using Rules to Drive Business Collaboration Development

We believe that business collaboration development and management is too complex and dynamic to handle manually. We therefore submit that enterprizes need
a mechanism which assists them in the flexible development and adaptive management of business collaboration. We adopt a rule driven mechanism for this
purpose where the central notion is to let enterprizes explicitly specify the rules
under which 1) they conduct their private behavior, 2) are willing to cooperate and 3) are observing in factual business collaborations. These rules can
then be used to drive and constrain the process of defining and/or changing a
business collaboration agreement. Flexibility comes from the fact that business
collaboration development is governed by the rules, which are used for appropriately chaining complex decisions and diagnoses; while adaptability is achieved
as changes can be managed with minimum disruption to existing collaborations.

4.1   Types of Rules

Rules in our approach are defined as "precise statements that describe, constrain
and control the structure, operations and strategies of a business" [26]. Three
main types of rules are employed: development, management and derivation
rules. **Development rules** are employed to drive development expressing the
peculiarities, originality and values of individual enterprizes. Classified along collaboration aspect in *internal business process aspect* they depict internal guidelines and policies, in *participant public behavior aspect* stipulate cooperations,
whereas in *business conversation aspect*, they reflect the conditions agreed upon
by the parties involved.

Development rules are also classified along level and facet. Along level they are
sub-categorized to enable their usage at different levels of abstraction resulting
in a) *strategic rules* expressed in terms of **goals**, b) *operational rules* defined in
terms of **business rules**, and c) *service rules* specified in terms of **constraints**.
In order to achieve alignment of the different levels in BCDF the strategic,
operational and service rules of an enterprize must not contradict each other.
Along facet development rules are grouped in relation to the context in which
they are applied, resulting in a) *structural rules* in *what* facet, b) *functional rules*
in *how* facet, c) *geographical rules* in *where* facet, d) *participant rules* in *who*
facet; and e) *temporal rules* in *when* facet. As the different contexts interact with
one another, consistency among these five types of rules is required to define
coherent models.

Assurance of outlined forms of consistency is facilitated via **management
rules**, serving two purposes: firstly, *consistency rules* ensure semantical soundness of models, i.e. that their meaning is consistent. Consistency rules are sub-
categorized in: a) *individual rules* dealing with consistency of individual models

(e.g. agreement at strategic perspective), b) *alignment rules* dealing with consistency between models at different levels; and c) *compatibility rules* dealing with consistency between models describing different collaboration aspects. Secondly, *completeness rules* and *correctness rules* enforce syntactical soundness; where the former ensure that models and relationships among models are complete, and the latter ensure the correctness of these models and dependencies.

To partially automate the development process we employ so-called *derivation rules*. These rules assist enterprizes by automatically deriving (parts of) models, where they fall in three categories: a) *individual level* enabling derivation of links between elements (i.e. interactions between facets) in strategic, operational and service model, b) *between levels* facilitating derivation of mappings between elements from models at different levels, and c) *between aspects* facilitating derivation of (skeleton) exposed behavior from private behavior as well as (skeleton) agreements from exposed behavior of two parties.

4.2 Rule Specification

Specification of discussed types of development, management and derivation rule is done in the context provided by the meta models and models introduced in Sect. 3. Concretely, rules are grounded on the modeling description atoms (i.e. elements, attributes, links, mappings and connections) that constitute the different BCDF models constraining their existence and/or value. To express rules we adopt RuleML [27], an XML based standard for rule specification currently under development. For conciseness we use its shorthand counterpart POSL [4] (Positional-Slotted Language) here to express rules; whereas RuleML can be used for communication with other parties and execution purposes.

To exemplify, suppose `Garage Inc` has a strategic security rule with regard to `car repair information` in Fig. 2. Let us assume here that for high repair cost estimates `Garage Inc` will want the estimate to be communicated without it being modifiable. For this purpose `Garage Inc` includes the following goal $G_{modification}$ (where the label 'G' reflects the fact that it is a goal) in its public participant behavior aspect model:

$G_{modification}$: property(?ModProp modification,true,carRepairInformation) :- element(carRepairInformation,resource)

In this Prolog like notation $G_{modification}$ states that if there is an element named `carRepairInformation` its property 'modification' must be set to 'true'.

Goals, business rules and constraints are all expressed in an uniform manner. For example, operational rule $BR_{integrity}$ ('BR' indicating that it is a business rule) states that for all `car repair report` files that contain a car repair value greater than $1000, integrity must be guaranteed:

$R_{garageintegrity}$: property(?IntProp integrity,true,carRepairReport) :- element(?Element carRepairReport,document), link(?Link has,carRepairReport,carRepairReportValuePart), property(?ValueProp value,?X,carRepairReportValuePart), greaterThan(?X,1000)

We can define the different kinds of management rule in a similar manner. For example, $\text{MAP}_{modification}$ states that for all resources that require modification protections, all documents communicated to realize exchange of these resources must use some form of integrity mechanism:

$\text{MR}_{modificationMapping}$: mappingConflict(leadsTo,?X,?Y) :- property(integrity,true,?Y) $\wedge$ element(?X,resource) $\wedge$ property(modification,true,?X) $\wedge$ element(?Y,document) $\wedge$ mapping(leadsTo,?X,?Y)

which states that if a resource X is mapped to a document Y, 'modification' is set to true for the resource and 'integrity' to 'false' for the document, a mapping conflict exists. To conclude our discussion on rule specification the derivation rule $\text{CDR}_{matchinteractions}$ exemplifies that the rule language can express all types of rule in a singular manner:

element(?Element document, ?ConversationModel) :- conversation(?Conversation-Model), element(?Element document, ?ParticipantModelOne), link(?MyLink receives, ?Source, ?Element, ?ParticipantModelOne), link(?MyLink sends, ?Source, ?Element, ?ParticipantModelTwo), Naf(equal(?ParticipantModelOne,?ParticipantModelTwo)), Naf(equal(?ConversationModel,?ParticipantModel)).

where the intuitive purpose behind this rule is to find all matching receive/send pairs concerning communication of documents in the exposed behaviors of two parties in order to derive a skeleton business collaboration agreement.

4.3   Developing Business Collaboration Agreements

In the previous subsections we introduced the different kinds of rule in our approach, and discussed their specification in context of BCDF. Here we shall explain how the development of business collaboration agreements is driven by combining the development, management and derivation rules introduced in Sect. 4. The development of such agreements constitutes the following: 1) take the exposed behaviors of both parties and merge them into a business conversation aspect model using derivation rules; 2) verify the model using consistency rules; and 3) any detected inconsistencies can then be resolved, where changes are verified against the exposed behaviors of both parties using *compatibility rules*.

To illustrate, let us look at development of operational agreement between garage repairer and consultant, where their exposed behavior is as depicted in Fig. 2. That is, garage repairer can perform report estimate and receive approval, whereas consultant can carry out get estimate and approve repair. We merge these two behaviors using *compatibility derivation rules* such as $\text{CDR}_{matchinteractions}$ in subsection 4.2 to generate an initial, skeleton-like agreement. Taking document `car repair report` in Fig. 2 as an example, `garage repairer` has a link between this document and task `report estimate` of type 'send'; whereas `consultant` has a link with its task `get estimate`. Application of $CDR_{matchinteractions}$ will result in finding a matching receive/send pair, i.e. a feasible interaction between the two.

Once the initial model has been established, the development rules of both parties are applied and checked. Assume that $BR_{garageintegrity}$ from subsection 4.2 is part of `Garage Inc`'s exposed behavior at operational level stating that `Garage Inc.` will send `car repair report` containing a car repair value greater than \$1000 using some integrity mechanism. Also assume that `Lee C.S` has adopted a similar rule $BR_{leecsintegrity}$, however, it expects `car repair report` to be tamper proof if car repair value greater than \$500. To detect such inconsistencies *rule consistency checking* is performed using consistency rules like $CR_{propertyConsistency}$, which states that if there are two properties of the same type belonging to the same element but with different values, they are in conflict:

$CR_{propertyConsistency}$: propertyValueConflict(?Type, ?Element) :- property(?Prop1 ?Type, ?Value1, ?Element), property(?Prop2 ?Type, ?Value2, ?Element), notEqual (?Value1, ?Value2)

Through negotiation `Garage Inc.` and `Lee C.S.` agree to observe $R_{leecsintegrity}$. `Garage Inc.` can ensure that it can accommodate this change as follows: firstly, `Garage Inc.` updates its exposed behavior, where affected areas are identified through compatibility rules like $COR_{propertyCompatibility}$:

$COR_{propertyCompatibility}$: propertyValueConflict(?Type, ?Element) :- property(?Prop ?Type, ?Value, ?Element, ?Exposed), property(?Prop1 ?Type, ?Value1, ?Element, ?AgreedUpon), notEqual(?Value, ?Value1)

Then, by using similar compatibility rules governing the relation between its private and exposed behavior, `Garage Inc.` can assess the affect and feasibility of the change on its internal business process activities.

One type of rule not discussed so far concerns the alignment of agreements at different levels. To illustrate their usage, suppose that at strategic level `Lee C.S.` has goal $G_{modification}$ in its exposed behavior, stating that for all elements of type 'resource' named `car repair information`, their property 'modification' must be set to 'true':

$G_{modification}$: property(modification,true,carRepairInformation) :- element(carRepairInformation,resource)

Now, `car repair information` at strategic level `leads to car repair report` at operational level. Let us assume that earlier defined $R_{leecsintegrity}$ applies to `car repair report`. Now goal $G_{carRepairInformation}$ requires modification protection for all claims, whereas $R_{leecsintegrity}$ does not mandate integrity until claim value exceeds \$1000). To detect the described inconsistency $MR_{modificationMapping}$ in subsection 4.2 can be used.

This works as follows: suppose we have `car repair information` with value \$750. Consequently we also have `car repair report` with document part 'value' equal to \$750. According to $G_{modification}$ we can conclude that 'modification' is set to 'true'; whereas from $R_{integrity}$ we can conclude that 'integrity' is set to 'false'. Based on these conclusions and the fact that `car repair information` leads to `car repair report`, $M_{modificationMapping}$ results in the conclusion of a mapping conflict; as it states that when 'modification' is 'true', 'integrity' must be true for a mapped resource and document.

In the above we have briefly illustrated how rules can assist enterprizes during the development of business collaboration agreements. Whereas the exact types of rules used depend on the behavior being modeled (i.e. private, exposed or agreed upon behavior) the combined usage of development, management and derivation rules remains principally the same; where development rules ensure that models are conform organizational policies, legislations, etceteras, management rules enforce that they are semantically and syntactically correct, and derivation rules partially automate the development process.

5   Related Work

When it comes to service composition and business collaboration in general, most work has focused on development without taking adaptability into too much consideration. Current solutions like BPEL [11] and ebXML BPSS [16] are pre-determined and pre-specified, have narrow applicability and are almost impossible to reuse and manage. The same applies to works from academia like from workflow [1, 5], system development [6, 29] and enterprize modeling [31].

Relevant work in [3] and [19] describe a generic mechanism for defining WS-Policy based policies (e.g. in [14]), but only web service based rule specification is supported. Also, only rules in participant public behavior aspect are considered. [2] describes a way to establish WS-Agreements between service providers and requesters, but business and technical details are mixed. [9] presents a web service management architecture, however, its metrics cannot capture high level business requirements. [32] describes the rule inference framework DYflow, but there is no clear separation between technical and business rules.

In comparison our work provides a systematic way of specifying development rules for business collaboration in the BCDF context. The business collaboration development process is driven by these development rules to capture the different behaviors of enterprizes; where it is constrained by management rules in terms of 1) conformance and consistency of models, 2) alignment of strategic, operational and service models, and 3) compatibility among different models describing private, exposed and agreed upon behavior; and where it is partially automated by derivation rules.

6   Conclusions

Current standards in business collaboration design, due to their pre-defined and inflexible nature, are precluded from accommodating business dynamics. The challenge is thus to provide a solution in which business collaboration development can be done in an flexible and adaptive manner.

In this paper we presented a rule driven approach for business collaboration development. We introduced the Business Collaboration Design Framework (BCDF), which gives context for business collaboration modeling. Subsequently we explained how rules drive, control and further the design process to facilitate flexible and adaptive business collaboration development.

Work for future research will foremost be focused on incorporation of payment, quality of service and security details. A prototype for presented approach is currently under development; where an early, partial implementation has been reported in [22].

References

1. W. van der Aalst et al, Business Process Management: A Survey, *Proceedings of the International Conference on Business Process Management, 2003.*
2. A. Andrieux et al, Web Services Agreement Specification (WS-Agreement), *http://www.gridforum.org/Meetings/GGF11/Documents/draft-ggf-graap-agreement.pdf, June 2004*
3. S. Bajaj et al, Web Services Policy Framework (WS-Policy), *http://www-106.ibm.com/developerworks/library/specification/ws-polfram/, September 2004*
4. Harold Boley, Integrating Positional and Slotted Knowledge on the Semantic Web?, *http://www.cs.unb.ca/ bspencer/cs6795swt/poslintweb-talk-pp4.pdf, September 2004*
5. J. Bowers et al, Workflow from within and without, *Proceedings of the 4th European Conference on CSCW, 1995*
6. P. Bresciani et al, Tropos: An Agent-Oriented Software Development Methodology, *Autonomous Agents and Multi-Agent Sytems, Vol. 8, No. 3, pp. 203-236, 2004*
7. D. Burdett et al, Web Service Conversation Language *http://www.w3.org/TR/ws-chor-model/, March 24, 2004*
8. Business Process Modeling Initiative, Business Process Modeling Language, *http://www.bpmi.org, June 24, 2002*
9. F. Casati et al, Business-Oriented Management of Web Services, *Communications of the ACM, Vol. 46, No. 10, pp. 55-60, 2003*
10. E. Christensen et al, Web Service Description Language, *http://www.w3.org/TR/wsdl, March 15, 2001*
11. F. Curbera et al, Business Process Execution Language for Web Services, *http://www-106.ibm.com/developerworks/webservices/library/ws-bpel/, July 31, 2002*
12. B. Curtis et al, Process Modeling, *Communications of the ACM, Vol. 35, No. 9, pp. 75-90, 1992*
13. W. Deiters et al, Flexibility in Workflow Management: Dimensions and Solutions, *International Journal of Computer Systems Science and Engineering, Vol. 15, No. 5, pp. 303-313, September 2000*

14. G. Della-Libera et al, Web Services Security Policy, *http://www-106.ibm.com/ developers/library/ws-secpol/, 2002*
15. R. Dijkman et al, Service-oriented Design: A Multi-viewpoint Approach, *International Journal of Cooperative Information Systems, Vol. 13, No. 4, pp. 337-368, 2004*
16. ebXML, *http://www.ebxml.org*
17. D. Fensel et al, The Web Service Modeling Framework WSMF, *Electronic Commerce Research and Applications, Vol. 1, No. 2, pp. 113-137, 2002*
18. P. Grefen et al, CrossFlow: Cross-Organizational Workflow Management in Dynamic Virtual Enterprises, *International Journal of Computer Systems Science & Engineering, Vol. 15, No. 5, pp. 277-290, 2000*
19. P. Nolan, Understand WS-Policy processing, *http://www-106.ibm.com/ developerworks/webservices/library/ws-policy.html, 2004*
20. Object Management Group, Model Driven Architecture, *http://www.omg.org/ docs/ormsc/01-07-01.pdf, July 2001*
21. B. Orriens et al, Establishing and Maintaining Compatibility in Service Oriented Business Collaboration, *Proceedings of the 7th International Conference on Electronic Commerce, Xi'an, China, August 2005*
22. B. Orriens et al, ServiceCom: A Tool for Service Composition Reuse and Specialization, *Proceedings of the 4th International Conference on Web Information Systems Engineering, Rome, Italy, 2003*
23. M. Papazoglou et al, Service-Oriented Computing, *Communications of the ACM, Vol. 46, No. 10, pp. 25-28, October 2003*
24. C. Peltz, Web services orchestration: a review of emerging technologies, tools, and standards, *Hewlett Packard White Paper, January 2003*
25. RosettaNet, *http://www.rosettanet.org*
26. R. Ross, Principles of the Business Rule Approach, *Addison-Wesley, 2003*
27. RuleML, *http://www.ruleml.org*
28. A. Scheer, Architecture for Integrated Information Systems - Foundations of Enterprise Modeling, *Springer-Verlag New York, Secaucus, NJ, USA, 1992*
29. P. Traverso et al, Supporting the Negotiation between Global and Local Business Requirements in Service Oriented Development, *Proceedings of the 2d International Conference on Service Oriented Computing, New York, USA, 2004*
30. J. Yang, Web Service Componentization: Towards Service Reuse and Specialization, *Communications of ACM, Vol. 46, No. 10, pp. 35-40, October 2003*
31. J.A. Zachman, A framework for information systems architecture, *IBM Systems Journal, Vol. 26, no. 3, pp. 276-292, 1987*
32. L. Zeng et al, Flexible Composition of Enterprise Web Services, *Electronic Markets - The International Journal of Electronic Commerce and Business Media, Vol. 13, No. 2, pp. 141-152, 2003*

Pattern-Based Specification and Validation of Web Services Interaction Properties

Zheng Li, Jun Han, and Yan Jin

Faculty of ICT, Swinburne University of Technology,
John Street, Hawthorn, Melbourne, Victoria 3122, Australia
{zli, jhan, yjin}@ict.swin.edu.au

Abstract. There have been significant efforts in providing semantic descriptions for Web services, including the approach as exemplified by OWL-S. Part of the semantic description in OWL-S is about the interaction process of the service concerned, and adopts a procedural programming style. We argue that this style of description for service interactions is not natural to publishing service behavior properties from the viewpoint of facilitating third-party service composition and analysis. In this paper, we introduce a declarative approach that better supports the specification and use of service interaction properties in the service description and composition process. This approach uses patterns to describe the interaction behavior of a service as a set of constraints. As such, it supports the incremental description of a service's interaction behavior from the service developer's perspective, and the easy understanding and analysis of the interaction properties from the service user's perspective. We also introduce a framework and tool support for monitoring and checking the conformance of the service's run-time interactions against its specified interaction properties, to test whether the service is used properly and whether the service fulfils its behavioral obligations.

1 Introduction

Service-Oriented Computing (SOC) is emerging as an important paradigm for IT architectures and applications. A service provider publishes the interface description of the service in a registry, through which a user may search and access the description to locate the required services. The interface description of a Web service serves as the contract of interaction with its consumers and is the place where a consumer can find information about the service. In general, such a contract should cover issues beyond interface signatures, including functionality, quality and interaction behavior of the service. The more information about the service is provided, the more likely the service will be properly understood and utilized. However, the current Web service description standard - WSDL, only specifies the location and operation signatures of a service, but lacks the mechanisms for capturing its behavioral properties. This may cause significant problems regarding behavioral interoperability when the service is used. Without the behavioral properties or knowledge of a service, the consumer may make incorrect assumptions about the service, which may lead to interaction failure. As such, a rich

B. Benatallah, F. Casati, and P. Traverso (Eds.): ICSOC 2005, LNCS 3826, pp. 73–86, 2005.

service description model is needed to publish the observable behavior of Web services in general and its interaction protocols in particular, so that the consumer can have a better understanding of the service execution semantics and know how to interact with the service in a proper manner [12].

OWL-S is a prevailing rich description model for Web services. Its service model describes the interaction behavior of a service by viewing the service as a process. It provides a set of control constructs such as sequence, split, split+join etc. to specify the possible execution flow of a service's operations. The service model employs a procedural/imperative programming approach, and specifies step by step the process that the service will perform to reach a particular result. Although this procedural approach is suitable to certain situations, it has obvious limitations in characterizing services with diverse behaviors because the resulting process model will become too complex as part of the interface description. A complex interface description is difficult to comprehend, process and therefore use.

We argue that a rule-based declarative approach provides a better choice as it requires much simpler description, needing only one-third to one-sixth of the statements required by the procedural approach, when representing the same behavior [10]. In fact, a declarative style conveys the "what" rather than the "how" of the procedural style, and is consistent with the intention of service (interaction) description, i.e., "what" the service (interaction) behavior is. In addition, describing a service in a declarative manner enables the consumer to use the service in ways that the service designer does not foresee [11]. It also gives better support to automatic reasoning-based validation of the composition of multiple services with diverse behaviors [18]. For frequently changing services, adding and removing rules require much less effort than modifying existing procedural definitions. This is a very useful feature in the service design process, which always involves many iterations of modification and revision on the service behavior definition.

In this paper, we introduce a declarative approach to specifying the interaction behavior of Web services as interaction constraints. Each constraint states an occurrence or sequencing properties of a service's operation invocations, representing a partial view of the service protocol on the invocations. As such, this approach allows incremental specification of a service's interaction protocol.

This approach is based on our previous research on interaction constraint specification for software components [14, 15], which advocates the use of the property specification pattern system proposed by Dwyer *et al.* in [9] in order to give software practitioners easy access to the specification approach. As the basis for the interaction constraint specification for Web services, we develop an OWL-based ontology for the property patterns in this paper. We add this ontology to OWL-S as an enhancement and an alternative to its procedural style definition of service interaction behaviors.

We further introduce a framework and tool to monitor and check the conformance of a service's run-time behavior against the specified service interaction constraints. The framework employs finite state automata (FSA) to represent semantically an interaction constraint, utilizes a SOAP message monitor to track the run-time interactions of the service, and includes a validation module that checks the interactions against the FSAs (*i.e.* interaction constraints) for error detection.

The remainder of the paper is structured as follows. In section 2, we give a reference example as a basis for further discussion. Section 3 presents our constraint-based approach to specifying service behavioral properties together with the ontology for the interaction property patterns. Section 4 introduces the validation framework and its implementation. We then discuss the related work in section 5 before drawing some conclusions in section 6.

2   A Reference Example

Let us consider an auctioneer service that provides auction services on the Web. The auctioneer publishes its interface description in WSDL and communicates with a number of bidders and sellers by exchanging SOAP messages. The service is able to accept registrations from new bidders/sellers and hold auctions among registered bidders. It provides several operations to allow users to query the information of auction items, register and un-register themselves to the service, login and logout the service, bid or sell an item. The service also provides an operation allowing bidders to retract their previous bids. Figure 1 shows an excerpt of the WSDL description for the auctioneer.

```
<wsdl:definitions targetNamespace="http://localhost:8080/axis/services/Auctioneer"
  ......
  <wsdl:portType name="Auctioneer">
    <wsdl:operation name="opRegister" parameterOrder="userInfo">
      <wsdl:input message="impl:opRegisterRequest" name="opRegisterRequest"/>
      <wsdl:output message="impl:opRegisterResponse" name="opRegisterResponse"/>
    </wsdl:operation>

    <wsdl:operation name="opUnRegister" parameterOrder="userInfo">
      <wsdl:input message="impl:opUnRegisterRequest" name="opUnRegisterRequest"/>
      <wsdl:output message="impl:opUnRegisterResponse" name="opUnRegisterResponse"/>
    </wsdl:operation>

    <wsdl:operation name="opLogin" parameterOrder="userInfo">
      <wsdl:input message="impl:opLoginRequest" name="opLoginRequest"/>
      <wsdl:output message="impl:opLoginResponse" name="opLoginResponse"/>
    </wsdl:operation>

    <wsdl:operation name="opLogout" parameterOrder="userInfo">
      <wsdl:input message="impl:opLogoutRequest" name="opLogoutRequest"/>
      <wsdl:output message="impl:opLogoutResponse" name="opLogoutResponse"/>
    </wsdl:operation>

    <wsdl:operation name="opBid" parameterOrder="userInfo itemNo price">
      <wsdl:input message="impl:opBidRequest" name="opBidRequest"/>
      <wsdl:output message="impl:opBidResponse" name="opBidResponse"/>
    </wsdl:operation>

    <wsdl:operation name="opRetract" parameterOrder="userInfo bidRefNo">
      <wsdl:input message="impl:opRetractRequest" name="opRetractRequest"/>
      <wsdl:output message="impl:opRetractResponse" name="opRetractResponse"/>
    </wsdl:operation>

    <wsdl:operation name="opSell" parameterOrder="userInfo itemInfo">
      <wsdl:input message="impl:opSellRequest" name="opSellRequest"/>
      <wsdl:output message="impl:opSellResponse" name="opSellResponse"/>
    </wsdl:operation>
  </wsdl:portType>
  ......
</wsdl:definitions>
```

Fig. 1. Excerpt of the Auctioneer Web Service Description in WSDL 1.1

3 Pattern-Based Interaction Property Specification

In this section, we first introduce our pattern-based approach to specifying the interaction behavior of Web services. We then define an ontology for the pattern system to provide the semantic basis for such service behavior description. An example is given to illustrate how the ontology is used to define service interaction constraints.

3.1 Property Specification Patterns

Our approach to defining interaction constraints for Web services builds on the property Specification Pattern System (SPS) proposed by Dywer *et al.* in [9]. The SPS patterns were originally developed as "high-level specification abstractions" to assist practitioners to formally specify system properties. The authors showed in [9] that SPS is able to cater for a majority of system properties.

In our approach, the SPS patterns and scopes are used to define basic and higher-level operators used to specify the occurrence and sequencing rules about invocations to a Web service. The introduction of SPS is aimed to facilitate the use of formal methods by Web service developers in describing the service interaction constraints or protocol. Precisely defined constraints are essential to ensure the proper use of the services when composing business applications or processes. In Figure 2, we list the basic pattern and scope operators used in our work as well as their usage, where op_1, ..., and op_4 are distinct operations and n is a natural.

Fig. 2. Pattern and Scope Operators

Specifically, for a Web service, we provide SPS patterns for specifying the restrictions on both the occurrence of individual operations' invocations and the order (or sequencing) between different operation invocations. The occurrence patterns include *absence*, *existence*, and *bounded existence*. In particular, the absence pattern requires that invocations to the given operation not occur (within the given scope). The existence pattern states that invocations to the given operation must appear. The bounded existence pattern extends it with lower and upper bounds on the number of invocations. For example, to control the overall system performance, the auction service provider may want to set a limit on the number of bids that a bidder can make during each session. This can be stated as:

opBid **exists at most 3 times after** *opLogin* **until** *opLogout;*

where the upper bound is 3 (see below for explanations of the "after-until" scope).

The sequencing patterns include *precedence*, *response*, *precedence chain*, and *response chain*. For instance, a precedence property of the auctioneer service "*opRegister* **precedes** *opUnRegister*" states that there must be at least one *opRegister* invocation before any *opUnRegister* invocation. One may think *opRegister* enables *opUnRegister*. A response property *"opLogin* **leads to** *opLogout"* states that an *opLogin* invocation must eventually be followed by an *opLogout* invocation. In essence, this specifies a cause-effect relationship between *opLogin* and *opLogout*.

To handle more complex properties, SPS patterns can be associated with various scopes such as *global, before, after, between-and,* and *after-until*. Each scope specifies a portion(s) of a service's interaction history, in which the given pattern takes effect. More specifically, the *global* scope refers to the entire history. The *before* scope refers to the initial portion of the history up to the first occurrence of an call message of the given operation. The *after* scope however states the inverse, *i.e.* the portion after the first occurrence of a reply message of the given operation. In the *between-and* scope, each portion is marked between consecutive occurrences of two messages. The starting message is the reply message of the first given operation, while the ending message is the call message of the second given operation. The *after-until* scope is similar but allows the portion to be open ended. That is, the given pattern continues to take effect after a reply to the first operation, even if the second operation will never be invoked afterwards. In contrast, in the *between-and* scope, the second operation has to be invoked in order for the given pattern to be applicable.

In the above, we have assumed operations be the atomic unit of concern. To cope with realistic services, however, one needs to consider the effect of different parameter values on the service interaction logic. Therefore, we allow conditions to be associated with each constraint specification to fine-tune the specified relationship. For example, the earlier constraint on the upper bound of bids by *each bidder* can be elaborated as:

> *opBid* **exists at most 3 times after** *opLogin* **until** *opLogout*
>   **where** *opBid.userInfo = opLogin.userInfo = opLogout.userInfo;*

As detailed later, we make use of the Semantic Web Rule Language (SWRL) to state such conditions.

Note that, in general, SPS patterns can be nested to describe complex constraints [9]. For simplicity, we do not explicitly deal with pattern nesting in this paper. It is however easy to accommodate them in our specification approach.

The following are two further example constraints for the auctioneer service:

> *opBid* **precedes** *opRetract* **after** *opLogin* **until** *opLogout*
>   **where** *opBid.userInfo = opRetract.userInfo = opLogin.userInfo = opLogout.userInfo*
>   and *opBid.bidRefNo = opRetract.bidRefNo;*
>
> *opSell* **precedes** *opBid* **where** *opSell.itemNo = opBid.itemNo;*

The first constraint states that if a bidder is to retract a valid bid (*opRetract*), there must be a preceding successful bid (*opBid*) by the same bidder in the same session. The second constraint says that a bidder can only bid for items on sale.

3.2 An Ontology for Interaction Property Patterns

The patterns and scopes used to specify service interaction constraints are defined in the ontology for Interaction Property Patterns (IPPs). It provides a common terminology for service developers to specify the interaction constraints of Web services in a standard and formal way.

The IPP ontology is defined using OWL and is designed as an add-on to OWL-S as a complement to the Service Model. More specifically, the topmost class defined in this ontology, *InteractionContract*, serves as an alternative to OWL-S *CompositeProcess* class. Figure 3 depicts the relationship between the IPP ontology and OWL-S. As shown, *InteractionContract* is embedded in the Service Model and uses the *AtomicProcess* class as the basic entities to define the interaction constraints of Web services in a rule-based/declarative manner. Note that the Service Profile and Service Grounding are not affected.

Figure 4 presents all the classes and their relationships as defined in the IPP ontology, where classes are drawn as ovals and properties are depicted as arc labels. Note that the shaded classes are not part of the IPP ontology, but are defined in OWL-S or XML Schema.

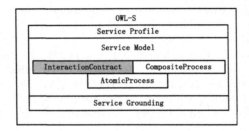

Fig. 3. Relationship between the IPP ontology and OWL-S

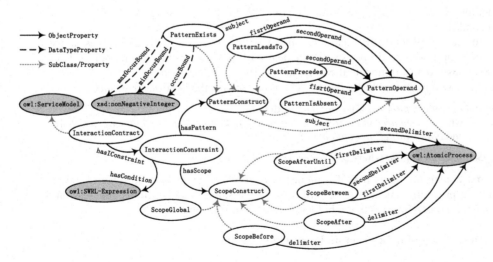

Fig. 4. Classes in the IPP Ontology

Class *InteractionContract*. In the IPP ontology, *InteractionContract* is the topmost concept denoting all the interaction constraints for a service. *InteractionContract* is defined as a subclass of OWL-S *ServiceModel*. It has a *hasIConstraint* property, specifying an *InteractionConstraint* instance.

Class *InteractionConstraint*. The *InteractionConstraint* class has three properties, *hasPattern, hasScope* and *hasCondition*. The *hasPattern* property ranges over the class *PatternConstruct*. Its value specifies an occurrence or sequencing rule over some operations' invocations. The *hasScope* property ranges over the class *ScopeConstruct*. Its value indicates the scope over which the specified rule applies. The *hasCondition* property specifies an *SWRL-Expression* (defined in the OWL-S) for the condition governing operation parameter values.

Class *PatternConstruct*. *PatternConstruct* is the superclass of four pattern classes: *PatternIsAbsent, PatternExists, PatternPrecedes* and *PatternLeadsTo*. Each of them is used to express one specific type of the service behavior. *PatternIsAbsent* has one property *subject* that names the operation of concern. The value of *subject* is an instance of *PatternOperand* that can be of either type OWL-S *AtomicProcess*, or *PatternConstruct*. The latter enables potential pattern nesting. The *subject* property of *PatternExists* is similar. In addition, *PatternExists* has three cardinality properties: *maxOccurBound, minOccurBound* and *occurBound* used to restrict the number of invocations to the operation of interest. All these properties are of the XML schema data type: *xsd:nonNegativeInteger*. Well-formedness rules about their occurrences are straightforward and thus omitted here. Both *PatternPrecedes* and *PatternLeadsTo* have two properties, *firstOperand* and *secondOperand,* ranging over *PatternOperand*.

Class *ScopeConstruct*. As noted earlier, the *ScopeConstruct* class is used to indicate a portion of the interaction history over which the constraint must be satisfied. There are five *ScopeConstruct* subclasses: *ScopeGlobal, ScopeBefore, ScopeAfter, ScopeBetween, ScopeAfterUntil*. Each of these classes defines zero, one or two delimiters, specifying the starting and ending operation invocations or replies. It is worth noting that the scope within which the constraint is evaluated starts, if applicable, after the reply message of the first operation is received, and finishes, if applicable, before the call message of the second operation is received.

Class*SWRL-Expression*. As noted above, we use the *SWRL-Expression* class to specify conditions for interaction constraints. The detail of this class can be found in OWL-S and is thus not repeated here.

3.3 Example

To illustrate the use of the IPP ontology, consider the auctioneer Web service. As discussed earlier, assume that a user can only bid at most 3 times within each of his logins. This means the *opBid* operation can only be invoked at most 3 times after the user successfully invokes *opLogin* and before he invokes *opLogOut*. Figure 5 shows the definition of this constraint according to the IPP ontology.

```
<ipp:InteractionConstraint>
    <ipp:hasPattern>
        <ipp:PatternExists>
            <ipp:subject>
                <process:process rdf:resource="#opBid"/>
            </ipp:subject>
            <ipp:maxOccurBound rdf:datatype="&xsd;#nonNegativeInteger">3</ipp:maxOccurBound>
        </ipp:PatternExists>
    </ipp:hasPattern>

    <ipp:hasScope>
        <ipp:ScopeAfterUntil>
            <ipp:firstDelimiter>
                <process:process rdf:resource="#opLogin"/>
            </ipp:firstDelimiter>
            <ipp:secondDelimiter>
                <process:process rdf:resource="#opLogOut"/>
            </ipp:secondDelimiter>
        </ipp:ScopeAfterUntil>
    </ipp:hasScope>

    <ipp:hasCondition>
        <expr:SWRL-Expression>
            <expr:expressionBody rdf:parseType="Literal">
            <swrl:AtomList>
                <rdf:first>
                    <swrl:sameIndividualAtom>
                        <swrl:argument1 rdf:resource="#opBidUserInfo"/>
                        <swrl:argument2 rdf:resource="#opLoginUserInfo"/>
                        <swrl:argument3 rdf:resource="#opLogOutUserInfo"/>
                    </swrl:sameIndividualAtom>
                </rdf:first>
                <rdf:rest rdf:resource="&rdf;#nil"/>
            </swrl:AtomList>
            </expr:expressionBody>
        </expr:SWRL-Expression>
    </ipp:hasCondition>
</ipp:InteractionConstraint>
```

Fig. 5. An Example Interaction Constraint Definition

4   Runtime Validation of Interaction Constraints

Explicit specification of Web service interaction constraints helps the service designer and the service client to implement and use a service properly. Whether or not a service is actually used correctly at run-time is a different question. Validation or testing is often required. In this section, we introduce a framework and a tool that allows us to validate the interactions with a Web service at run-time against its pre-defined interaction constraints.

4.1   Validation Framework

Our validation framework and tool monitor and validate the messages received and sent by a service against its interaction constraint specifications. Its message monitoring and interception builds on Web service platforms and tools. Its validation mainly makes use of the tool implementation of [14]. The monitoring and validation process is fully automated at run time. Figure 6 shows the overall validation architecture. The key techniques used include:

- Translating the constraint specifications into finite state automata (FSAs) that serve as the constraints' internal representation for easy processing;
- Identifying and intercepting the run-time messages exchanged with a Web service;

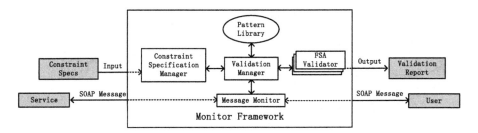

Fig. 6. Validation Framework

– Advancing the effective constraint FSAs using the intercepted message, and reporting violations, if any.

The monitoring framework consists of five components: Validation Manager (VM), Constraint Specification Manager (CSM), FSA Validators (FVs), Message Monitor (MM) and Pattern Library (PL), with VM coordinating all the other four components. PL maintains all the patterns and scopes and their FSA semantics. CSM reads the interaction constraint specifications embedded in the OWL-S service description file, translates them into an internal format. MM observes the incoming and outgoing SOAP messages of the Web service and intercepts the run-time operation invocations. All the SOAP messages exchanged between the service and the user are logged and forwarded to VM. Upon receiving a message, VM queries CSM to get all relevant constraint specifications. If the corresponding FVs have not been created, VM initialize them based on the used patterns and their FSA semantics stored in PL. It then asks all the relevant FVs to check the intercepted operation invocation message against their internal FSAs. If the message is not acceptable to any FSA, a violation report is issued.

4.2 Constraint Representation

The semantics of interaction constraints is informally given in section 3. To enable tool support, their semantics needs to be precisely defined. To do so, we choose FSAs as their formal semantic representations. When involving no condition about parameter values, in general, each interaction constraint has a corresponding FSA representation where arc labels are sets of operation call or reply messages. Such a FSA can be constructed prior to the first relevant message being identified. When a "where" condition is stated, an interaction constraint corresponds to a number of FSAs, each for a possible value combination of the parameters. Such an FSA is dynamically instantiated only when a parameter value of interest is observed. Further details about the FSA representation can be found in [13, 14]. We illustrate below the FSA representation of constraints using the earlier example on the bounded existence of bids (Figure 5).

Figure 7 shows the FSA corresponding to this example constraint, where opBid_{b_1} denotes the set of all *opBid* call and reply messages exchanged with bidder b_1 (i.e., *opBid.userInfo* refers to b_1 as the ID). $\text{opLogin}_{b_1}^{\text{reply}}$ is the set of *opLogin* reply messages

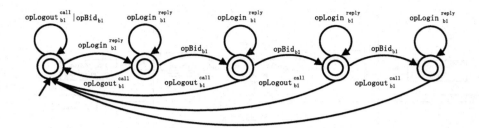

Fig. 7. FSA for the Example Interaction Constraint of Figure 5

to b_1. opLogout$_{b1}^{call}$ is the set of *opLogout* call messages from b1. Note that we have omitted all the other messages that can be received at every state for brevity. As shown, *opBid* cannot be invoked when the FSA enters the rightmost state until b_1 logs out and re-logs in.

4.3 Validation Process

The validation process starts when the Message Monitor detects a SOAP request/response message and forwards the message to the Validation Manager. Then VM finds out from CSM all the interaction constraint specifications in which such a message is of interest, and creates a FSA validator for each constraint using the message's parameter values, if such a FV does not already exist. VM then tries to advance the state of each of these relevant FVs using the observed message. An error or violation will be reported if the intercepted message is inhibited at the current state of any FSA. That is, the message does not appear in any labeling set of any outgoing arc of the current state. For example, an *opBid* call message received at the rightmost state of Figure 7 represents a constraint violation. If there is no interaction constraint in which an observed message is of interest, the message will be ignored by the Validation Manager.

4.4 Implementation

Our implementation of the run-time monitoring framework is based on open source platforms and tools. The reason behind this decision is that the source code is available and new features can be added if required. For our implementation, Tomcat 5 and Apache Axis 1.2 are used to set up a web server to run Web services. Tomcat is a lightweight HTTP server with all the features we need to run Web services. Axis provides an implementation of the W3C SOAP standard. They constitute a reliable and stable platform on which to implement Java Web Services.

In implementing the validation framework, we have reused the architecture of a runtime validation tool developed in [14] for CORBA-based systems, including the Pattern Library, Validation Manager and FSA Validator. However, these modules have been enhanced to better deal with the full range of interaction property patterns. We have also modified the Constraint Specification Manager module for processing the XML-based specifications of service interaction constraints. A new addition in this work is the Message Monitor that captures the SOAP messages (calls and returns) exchanged between a service and its user(s), and analyzes them at run-time as to their types, corresponding operations, etc. Part of it is a tool in the Axis package called SOAP Monitor, providing a way to intercept the SOAP messages. The SOAP Monitor utility adds one new handler to the global handler chain in the Axis architecture. As SOAP requests and responses go in and out of the service, the SOAP messages are forwarded to the SOAP Monitor service where it can be displayed using a web browser interface.

It is worth noting that our validation framework is not centralized. The Message Monitor (MM) resides on each server hosting services. The other parts of the framework can be deployed on the server, with the client or elsewhere. As long as the MM on the server side is working, one or more validation applications can be connected to MM, which enables multiple parties, such as service owner and users, to monitor and validate service behavior simultaneously.

5 Related Work and Discussion

Some proposed Web service standards, such as BPEL [3] and WSCDL [16], are composition languages in nature and specify service behavior from the service composition or business process point of view [6].What they specify is the required behavior for services rather than the behavior services actually provide.

Some ongoing research efforts recognize the needs for describing the behavior properties of individual services, but use rather abstract notations that are not suitable for service developers or users. [6-8] use a single finite state machine (FSM) to describe the overall observable behavior of a service. [8] focuses on protocol compatibility checking and [6, 7] extend FSMs by associating more properties to transitions. Such a FSM-based approach is good at describing services with simple behavior. However, when dealing with services with diverse behavior, this approach does not scale well with the increase in the number of states and transitions. The resultant FSMs can become difficult to understand and process. In contrast, our divide-and-conquer specification approach scales well with the number of constraints. On the other hand, [6, 7] deal with time-based service protocols. This can be potentially integrated with our work emphasizing inter-message relationships, resulting in more comprehensive service protocol descriptions.

[4, 19, 20] employ an ontological approach to specify interaction protocols. [4, 20] define ontologies for FSMs. Like [6-8], they use a single FSM to model each service behavior. Therefore, their approaches are subject to the same scalability limitation. Whereas in our approach, the FSA is only used for run-time validation and we use interaction property patterns for service behavior specification. Furthermore, we use multiple constraints/FSAs to cover the full behavior of services, which offers modularity and better scalability. [19] uses ontologies to represent service operation, input, conditional/unconditional output, precondition, and conditional/unconditional effect as the behavior constraint of a service. This approach is not capable of expressing temporal sequencing interaction constraints.

A body of work on Web service monitoring has been reported. [17] proposes an approach to specifying and monitoring Service Level Agreements. It focuses on Quality of Service, and monitors such properties as performance and costs instead of interaction behavior. [5] aims to monitor service compositions at run-time to see whether services satisfy the assertions specified in the service composition defined by BPEL. The assertions are the requirements from the service consumer, rather than services' properties. In contrast, our monitoring framework intends to assess whether a service's behavior conforms to its designer's intent. In addition, our monitor attaches to the service itself rather than to a service consumer such as the BPEL process.

Also related to our approach is the work based on patterns. [1] provides a rich set to patterns that can be used to model workflow. The workflow patterns follow the procedural approach to interaction specification and are very similar to the ControlConstructs defined in OWL-S's Service Model. The approach we propose is declarative in nature and is aimed at addressing the limitations of procedural approach employed by OWL-S. The "Service Interaction Patterns" in [2] describes how an individual message or a request/response message pair is transferred between two or more parties, whereas our patterns describe the sequential order in which multiple messages or operation invocations may occur. They mainly look at message exchanges from a system point of view, while we primarily study message exchanges from an individual service's point of view. As such, these two approaches have different focuses.

When putting our approach into practical use, the service designer needs to ensure the consistency of all the interaction constraints of a service. Inconsistency among constraints will leads to a situation where calls to an operation will always violate some rules. This issue is discussed in [13] where consistency checking is done by testing the non-emptiness of the language intersection of the interaction constraints and proving that each operation has its role in the intersection.

6   Conclusion

In this paper, we have introduced a declarative constraint-based approach to specifying the observable behavioral properties of Web services. The approach employs intuitive patterns to help practitioners describe the interaction constraints of a Web service. The constraints conjunctively determine the behavioral properties of the service. We have defined an ontology for these patterns and embed it into the OWL-S framework, enabling pattern-based interaction behavior description for Web services.

We have also presented a framework that supports the monitoring and validation of the runtime interactions with Web services against their specified interaction constraints. This provides a useful tool for adjudicating whether a service's behavior conforms to its design and whether the service is being used properly. The tool is able to identify and report any violations of such nature.

Our future work will include considering required operations of services and static checking of interaction compatibility between services or between individual services and the service composition specification.

Acknowledgement. This work is partially supported by the Department of Education, Science and Training (DEST) grant (AU-DEST-CG060081) from the Innovation Access Programme - International Science and Technology established under the Australian Government's innovation statement, Backing Australia's Ability.

References

1. Workflow Patterns. www.workflowpatterns.com (2005)
2. Alistair Barros, M.D., Arthur ter Hofstede: Service Interaction Patterns. In Proc. 3rd International Conference on Business Process Management (2005) 302-318, Eindhoven, The Netherlands
3. Andrews, T., Curbera, F., Dholakia, H., Goland, Y., Klein, J., Leymann, F., Liu, K., Roller, D., Smith, D., Thatte, S., Trickovic, I., Weerawarana, S.: Business Process Execution Language for Web Services version 1.1. http://www-128.ibm.com/developerworks/library/specification/ws-bpel/ (2003)
4. Ashri, R., Denker, G., Marvin, D., Surridge, M., Payne, T.R.: Semantic Web Service Interaction Protocols: An Ontological Approach. In Proc. Third International Semantic Web Conference, Vol. 3298 (2004) 304-319, Hiroshima, Japan
5. Baresi, L., Ghezzi, C., Guinea, S.: Smart Monitors for Composed Services. In Proc. International Conference on Service-Oriented Computing (2004) 193-202, New York City, NY, USA
6. Benatallah, B., Casati, F., Skogsrud, H., Toumani, F.: Abstracting and Enforcing Web Service Protocols. International Journal of Cooperative Information Systems Vol. 13 (4) (2004) 413-440
7. Benatallah, B., Casati, F., Toumani, F., Hamadi, R.: Conceptual Modeling of Web Service Conversations. In Proc. Advanced Information Systems Engineering (CAiSE), Vol. 2681 (2003) 449-467, Klagenfurt/Velden, Austria
8. Berardi, D., Calvanese, D., Giacomo, G.D., Lenzerini, M., Mecella, M.: Automatic Composition of e-Services that Export their Behavior. In Proc. International Conference on Service-Oriented Computing (2003) 43-58, Trento, Italy
9. Dwyer, M.B., Avrunin, G.S., Corbett, J.C.: Patterns in Property Specifications for Finite-state Verification. In Proc. International Conference on Software Engineering (1999) 411-420, Los Angeles, CA, USA
10. Gottesdiener, E.: Procedural versus declarative. Application Development Trends Magazine (1997)
11. Guillaume, D., Plante, R.: Declarative Metadata Processing with XML and Java. In Proc. Astronomical Society of the Pacific Conference Series, Vol. 238 (2001)
12. Han, J.: Interaction Compatibility: An Essential Ingredient for Service Composition. In Proc. International Workshop on Grid and Cooperative Computing (2003) 59-66, Shanghai, China
13. Jin, Y., Han, J.: Consistency and Interoperability Checking for Component Interaction Rules. In Proc. Twelfth Asia-Pacific Software Engineering Conference (2005), Taipei, Taiwan
14. Jin, Y., Han, J.: Runtime Validation of Behavioural Contracts for Component Software. In Proc. Fifth International Conference On Quality Software (2005) 177-184, Melbourne, Australia
15. Jin, Y., Han, J.: Specifying Interaction Constraints of Software Components for Better Understandability and Interoperability. In Proc. International Conference on COTS-Based Software Systems, Vol. 3412 (2005) 54-64, Orlando, Florida, USA
16. Kavantzas, N., Burdett, D., Ritzinger, G.: Web Services Choreography Description Language Version 1.0. http://www.w3.org/TR/2004/WD-ws-cdl-10-20040427/ (2004)
17. Keller, A., Ludwig, H.: Defining and Monitoring Service-Level Agreements for Dynamic e-Business. In Proc. Conference on Systems Administration (2002) 189-204, Philadelphia, PA, USA

18. Lara, R., Lausen, H., Arroyo, S., Bruijn, J.d., Fensel, D.: Semantic web services: description requirements and current technologies. In Proc. International Workshop on Electronic Commerce, Agents, and Semantic Web Services, In conjunction with the Fifth International Conference on Electronic Commerce (ICEC) (2003), Pittsburgh, PA, USA
19. Sriharee, N., Senivongse, T.: Discovering Web Services Using Behavioural Constraints and Ontology. In Proc. International Conference on Distributed Applications and Interoperable Systems, Vol. 2893 (2003) 248-259, Paris, France
20. Toivonen, S., Helin, H.: Representing Interaction Protocols in DAML. In Proc. International Symposium on Agent Mediated Knowledge Management, Vol. 2926 (2003) 310-321, Stanford, CA, USA

Using Test Cases as Contract to Ensure Service Compliance Across Releases

Marcello Bruno, Gerardo Canfora, Massimiliano Di Penta,
Gianpiero Esposito, and Valentina Mazza

RCOST - Research Centre on Software Technology,
University of Sannio, Palazzo ex Poste,
Via Traiano 82100, Benevento, Italy
{marcello.bruno, canfora, dipenta, gianpiero.esposito,
valentina.mazza}@unisannio.it

Abstract. Web Services are entailing a major shift of perspective in software engineering: software is used and not owned, and operation happens on machines that are out of the user control. This means that the user cannot decide the strategy to migrate to a new version of a service, as it happens with COTS. Therefore, a key issue is to provide users with means to build confidence that a service i) delivers over the time the desired function and ii) at the same time it is able to meet Quality of Service requirements.

This paper proposes the use of test cases as a form of contract between the provider and the users of a service, and describes an approach and a tool to allow users running a test suite against a service, to discover if functional or non-functional expectations are maintained over the time. The approach has been evaluated by applying it to two case studies.

Keywords: Service Testing, Evolution of Service–Oriented Systems, Regression Testing, Service Level Agreements.

1 Introduction

Service–oriented architectures are having a relevant impact on the development of today's software systems, and promise to become a major technology to even enable the development of business–critical applications. This, however, requires highly reliable and robust services. To this aim, it is necessary to perform service testing. All in all, a service can be considered very similar to a component, and thus testing approaches developed in Component–Based Software Engineering (CBSE) can be adapted to services. Much in the same way, a complex service–oriented system is a distributed system, thus, again, existing techniques can be reused.

However, service–oriented architectures introduce some important issues that need to be considered when performing software testing. In a service–oriented scenario, users just invoke a service, instead of physically integrating it (as it happens for components). The service provider can decide to maintain the service, and the user could not be aware of that. For example:

B. Benatallah, F. Casati, and P. Traverso (Eds.): ICSOC 2005, LNCS 3826, pp. 87–100, 2005.

– *new features can be added:* despite that, the service provider could decide
  not to advertise in the service interface the change performed, because the
  input and output parameters are not affected. However, the change made
  alters the service behavior, and alters the service non-functional properties
  (e.g., the *response time*) as well;
– *optimizations (e.g., changes in algorithmic solutions) can be performed:* this
  will, for sure, cause a variation in the service non-functional properties. As
  a result, the Service Level Agreement (SLA) stipulated between the user
  and the provider may or may not be violated. In fact, an optimization could
  improve a non-functional property while worsening another, or even an improvement of some Quality of Service (QoS) attributes (e.g., the *response
  time*) may not be desirable since it may cause unwanted effects in the whole
  system behavior. Last but not least, any optimization could introduce faults,
  thus varying the service functional behavior as well.

To deal with the aforementioned issues, this paper proposes the use of test
cases as a way to stipulate contracts between a service provider and service
users[1]. This calls for empowering users to perform regression testing [1] with
the aim of discovering if a new version of a given service is still in line with the
expectations and assumptions that led to the inclusion of the service in a system.

Test suites are published by the service provider as a part (*facet*) of the service
description. When a user acquires a service, s/he can use such test suites to check
whether the service behaves as desired. In addition, the user can add a further
test suite (this can be particularly important since the user may not completely
trust test cases delivered by the provider). If no deviation from the expected
behavior is noticed, the contract is stipulated, and the test suite specifies the
service behavior required to fulfill the contract. Then, the user can periodically
run the test suite to discover if changes made to the service implementation
entail the violation of any of the initial assumptions and expectations, either
functional or related to QoS.

This paper makes the following contribution:

– it proposes to support service consistency verification through evolution by
  executing test suites contained in a XML–encoded facet attached to the
  service;
– it presents a toolkit that allows to generate testing facets from JUnit test
  suites, combining static and dynamic analysis, and to run them against the
  service; and
– it discusses empirical data demonstrating the effectiveness of using test cases
  as a contract between service providers and users.

The rest of the paper is organized as follows. Section 2 describes the proposed
approach and tool. Section 3 presents and discusses results from empirical studies

---

[1] According to service–oriented architecture terminology, the term user is used here
to refer to the organization or individual engineer that integrates a service into a
service–oriented system, and not to the end user of the system itself, that is not
expected to test a service.

performed to assess the approach. Finally, after a discussion of the related work, Section 5 concludes.

2   The Approach

The basic idea behind our approach is to provide a service with i) a set of test cases and ii) a set of QoS assertions. This idea comes from component–based software testing, where some authors proposed the idea of providing a test suite together with the component [2, 3]. However, the fact that a service is executed on the server machine and evolves independently from the systems using it, and the need for a service to meet non-functional requirements established in the SLA, introduce new issues that the approach has to fulfill.

When the user acquires a service, s/he is able to access the XML–encoded test cases and QoS assertions hyperlinked to the service WSDL. These test cases and assertions constitute a kind of "contract" between the user and the service provider. By executing the test cases, the user can observe the service functional and non-functional behavior. If satisfied, the user stipulates the contract. The provider, on his/her own, agrees to guarantee such a behavior over a specified period of time, regardless of any change that will be made to the service implementation. If, during that period, the service evolves (i.e., a new release is deployed), deviations from the agreed behavior would cause a contract violation.

Fig. 1 provides an overview of the whole test case generation and regression testing process. The light gray area indicates what happens when the service

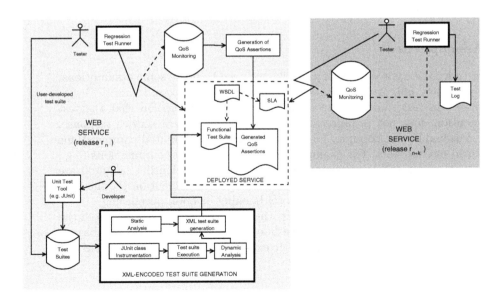

Fig. 1. Test generation and execution

is acquired (release r_n). The dark gray area indicates what happens when the service evolves (to release r_{n+k}) and the user re-tests the service. When the developer implements the service, s/he also provides for it a unit test suite. By proper analysis and transformations, the test suite is XML-encoded and attached to the service interface. The service is therefore published together with the testing facet, comprising test cases (and, eventually, QoS assertions). Subsequently, the service user can periodically re-execute the test suite against the service to verify whether the service still exhibits the functional and non-functional properties held when the service was acquired. The whole approach is supported by a toolkit, developed in Java, composed of two modules:

- the *testing facet generator* that, as described in Section 2.2 supports the generation of the XML-encoded testing facet. In the current implementation, the tool accepts JUnit[2] test suites, although we plan to extend our tool so to be able to accept as input test suites developed using other tools (and for services written using different languages). JUnit supports the development of a unit test suite as a Java class, containing a series of methods that constitute the test cases. Each test case is composed of a sequence of assertions checking properties of the class under test. The tool relies on JavaCC[3] to perform Java source code analysis and transformation, on the Axis web services framework[4] on the Xerces[5] XML parser.
- the *test suite runner* that permits the service consumer to execute the test suite against the service and produces the test log.

After describing the approach's assumptions, the next subsections thoroughly describe the different phases of the test case generation and execution process.

2.1 Assumptions

In order to let the approach work properly, we need to make some assumptions, and, in case they fail, proper countermeasures should be taken.

An user can test someone else's service with the assumption that the test case execution does not produce any side effect, but only a service response. This is reasonable, for example, for services used for distributed computations or in a grid environment. For example, services performing computations (e.g., image compressing, DNA microarray processing, or any scientific calculus) are suitable. This is not the case, however, of services whose execution produces an irreversible effect, such as services for hotel booking or book purchasing.

In the case of services with side effects, the approach is still feasible from the provider's side, after isolating the service from its environment (e.g., databases), or even from the user side if the provider exports operations to allow users to test the service in isolation.

---

[2] *http://www.junit.org/*
[3] *https://javacc.dev.java.net/*
[4] *http://xml.apache.org/axis/*
[5] *http://xml.apache.org/xerces2-j/*

Testing may become problematic for the provider if it is highly resource–demanding or, for the user, if the service has not a fixed fee (e.g., a monthly–usage fee) but the cost depends on the number of its invocations. These issues are discussed in Section 5.

Finally, as explained in Section 2.2, the approach is able to generate assertions for testing service non-functional properties. However, this is based on monitoring data that can depend on the current configuration (server machine and load, network bandwidth and load, etc.). While averaging on several measures can mitigate the influence of network/server load at a given time, changes in network or machines may lead to completely different QoS values.

2.2   Step 1: Generating the XML–Encoded Test Suite

The *testing facet generator* XML–encodes a unit test suite provided with the service. First, the service provider indicates to the tool the service class and the JUnit class containing the test suite for the service–under–test. Then, the tool starts analyzing both the service and the JUnit class. The translation of the JUnit test suite into the facet is not straightforward: in general, any JUnit assertion involves expressions of variables containing references to local objects, and method invocations related to these objects. However, the XML–encoded test suite needs to be executed from user–side. The service user can only access to service operations. Any other expression needs therefore to be evaluated on server side and thus XML–encoded as a literal. Expression evaluation is performed

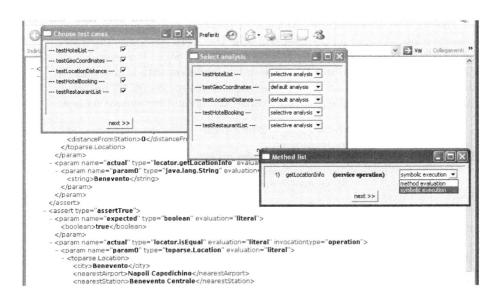

Fig. 2. Test case generation tool

by executing an instrumented version of the JUnit test class from server–side. The obtained dynamic information is then complemented with test suite static analysis to generate the XML testing facet.

The tool shows to the user the list of test cases contained in the test suite ("Choose test case" window in Fig. 2). The user can decide which JUnit test cases should be encoded in XML. For the selected test cases, the user can select (from the "Select analysis" window) two options:

1. *automatic test case transformation:* the tool automatically translates any expression, but service operation invocations, in literals and generates the XML–encoded test suite;
2. *selective translation:* the user can select which method invocations, corresponding to service operations (see the "Method list" window) should be evaluated and which should be left symbolic in the testing facet.

Finally, the service needs to be complemented with QoS assertions, that can be used to verify whether the service is able to preserve its non-functional behavior over the evolution. These assertions can be automatically generated by executing all test cases against the deployed service and measuring each time the QoS attributes by means of a monitoring system. Supposing that each test case contains an assertion involving a service operation, when the test case is executed (and thus the operation invoked) QoS values can be measured. In the current implementation, we are able to measure *response time* and *throughput*; however, with the aid of external monitoring systems, even more complex QoS measures can be used.

The measured values will constitute constraints that should hold in future releases of the service. After obtained this set of constraints and encoded them in XML (see Section 2.2), the service user will send the XML file to the provider. Under some extents, these constraints can be part of the SLA. For example, if the user acquires a service and, invoking one of its operation with a given set of parameters (contained in the test case), observes a *response time* of 20 ms (over a large number of runs), then the generated constraint should be something like:

$$ResponseTime < 20ms + \Delta \tag{1}$$

where Δ represents a tolerance threshold for the expected *response time*, or

$$ResponseTime < p_i \tag{2}$$

where p_i is the i_{th} percentile of the *response time* distribution as measured when acquiring the service.

As an alternative of using QoS assertions, the service non-functional behavior can be checked against any SLA document attached to the service. However, while the assertions allow to check the QoS achieved for each test case, SLA can only be used to check the average QoS values.

XML–Encoding of Test Suites. The *testing facet generator* produces a facet organized in two levels:

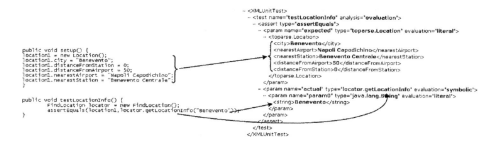

Fig. 3. XML-encoding of a JUnit assertion

1. A **first level**, containing a *Facet Description* and a *Test Specification*. The
   Facet Description contains general information such as the facet owner or
   the creation date. The *Test Specification Overview* contains, for each test
   suite enclosed in the facet, information such as the testing strategy adopted
   (e.g., Functional or Structural) and the tool used to develop the test suite
   (e.g., JUnit). Then, the *Data* section contains links to XML files containing
   the test suite itself and QoS assertions.
2. A **second level**, comprising files containing XML–encoded test suites and
   QoS–assertions.

Fig. 3 shows an example of how a JUnit test case can be mapped to a XML
file. The example is related to a service returning travel information for a given
location (i.e., closest airport and train station, plus distance to get to the airport and to the station). The left–side of the figure shows a portion of the JUnit
test case. The method `setUp()` creates an instance variable containing a *Location* object (`location1`), while the `testLocationInfo()` method asserts that
`location1` must match the result of the *getLocationInfo* operation when the
passed parameter is "Benevento".

The right–side of Fig. 3 shows the XML mapping. In particular, it is worth
noting that:

- objects are serialized in XML (using the XStream[6] serializer);
- the *param* tag has an attribute (*evaluation*) indicating whether the parameter
  is a literal serialized in the XML, or whether it is symbolic (i.e., it is a service
  operation that needs to be invoked). For the latter, actual parameters are
  specified.

QoS assertions are XML–encoded using the WSLA schema [4]. While the
SLA poses general QoS constraints[7] (e.g., *"Throughput > 1 Mbps"* or *"Average
response time < 1 ms."*), QoS assertions indicate which will be the expected
service performance in correspondence of a given set of inputs (specified in the
test case). For example, when the input (as specified in the test case) of a MP3

---

[6] *http://xstream.codehaus.org/*
[7] That must hold for any service usage.

compression service is a 5 MBytes file, the QoS assertion may indicate a *response time* of 30 s (that will clearly be different in case the input file is smaller or bigger).

2.3   Step 2: Running the Test Suite

Once the test suite has been published together with the service, the tester (either a user, a third-party or the provider) can:

1. *download the test suite and the QoS assertions*, hyperlinked to the service WSDL interface;
2. *run the test suite and get the test log:* service operations contained in the test suite are invoked, and assertions evaluated. A test log is generated, indicating, for each test case, i) whether the test case has passed or failed and ii) the differences between the expected and actual QoS values. Also in this case, the QoS monitoring is used to measure actual QoS values, thus permitting the evaluation of QoS assertions.

The service user can also provide, on his/her side, further test cases. This is particularly important: the user might not trust the developer's test suite; on the contrary, s/he wants to develop an additional test suite as a contract reflecting the intended service usage (that might have not been contemplated by the provider). In a semi–structured environment (e.g., a service registry of a big organization) the user can therefore publish this new test suite to the service, and other users can eventually reuse it. On the contrary, this may not

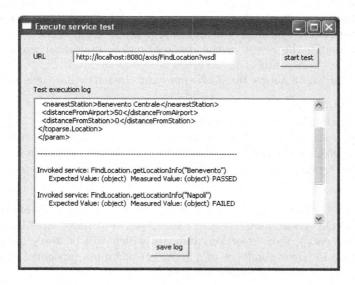

Fig. 4. Test suite runner

be possible in an open environment, where the additional test suite is stored by the user, and only serves to check whether future service releases still satisfy the user requirements.

The decision on whether the user has to add further test case may be based on the analysis of the provider's test suite (e.g., characterizing the range of inputs covered), and from the test strategy used by the provider to generate such a test suite – e.g., the functional coverage criterion used – also advertised in the test facet.

The trustability level of the provider's test suite can be assessed, for instance, by analyzing the domain in which the service inputs varies, and the functional coverage criteria adopted.

Fig. 4 shows a screenshot of the *test suite runner*. As shown, after specifying the service URL, it is possible to run the test cases against the service. The window reports the log indicating whether the different assertions passed or failed, and, each time an assertion uses a XML-serialized object, such an object is shown in the window as well.

3   Empirical Study

To validate the proposed approach, we need to generate test cases and related QoS assertions on a service release. Then, test cases need to be run again against subsequent releases, to check whether the service "violates the contract".

We published as web services five releases of two open source systems, *dns-java* and *InetAddressLocator*. *dnsjava*[8] is a Domain Name System (DNS) client and server; in particular, for this study's purpose, the *dig* (domain information groper) utility has been wrapped with a web service. *dig* is used to gather information from DNS servers, while *InetAddressLocator*[9] is a utility that, given an IP address, returns its geographical location.

The *dig* web service has five parameters: the domain to be solved (compulsory), the server used to solve the domain, the query type, the query class and an option switch. The service answers with two strings: the query sent to the DNS, and the DNS answer. The *InetAddressLocator* service interface is quite simple: the input parameter is just the IP address to be located, while the output is a string specifying the geographic location. For both services, we carefully checked whether the response message contained values such as timestamps, increasing id, etc., that could have biased the result, i.e., causing a failure for any test case execution. Test case generation was guided by determining, for each input parameter, equivalence classes. The number of test cases was large enough (1000 for *dnsjava* and 2500 for *InetAddressLocator*) to cover any combination of the equivalence classes. After services have been deployed, test cases are run against all the releases of each system. For *dnsjava*, two different analyses of the test execution logs have been performed:

---

[8] *http://www.dnsjava.org/*
[9] *http://javainetlocator.sourceforge.net/*

Table 1. dnsjava: % of failed test cases

	strong check				soft check			
	1.3.0	1.4.0	1.5.0	1.6.1	1.3.0	1.4.0	1.5.0	1.6.1
1.2.0	3%	74%	74%	74%	1%	7%	7%	7%
1.3.0		74%	74%	74%		9%	9%	9%
1.4.0			0%	0%			0%	0%
1.5.0				0%				0%

1. *strong check*, comparing both *dnsjava* response messages (i.e., the DNS query and answer). This is somewhat representative of a "stronger" functional–contract between the service user and the provider, that guarantees an exact match of the whole service response over a set of releases;
2. *soft check*, comparing only the DNS answer, i.e., the information that often a user needs from a DNS client. This is somewhat representative of a "weaker" functional contract.

For *InetAddressLocator*, we simply compared the (single) response message. Finally, for *dnsjava* we also measured two QoS attributes, i.e., the *response time* and the *throughput*. To mitigate the randomness of these measures, the test case execution was replicated 10 times, and average values considered[10].

This section reports and discusses the results obtained analyzing test case executions. The following subsections will discuss results related to functional and non-functional testing.

Functional Testing. Table 1 reports the percentage of test cases that failed when comparing different *dnsjava* releases, considering the *strong check* contract. Rows represent the releases when the user could have acquired the service, while columns represent the service evolution. It clearly appears that a large percentage of failures (corresponding to contract violations) is reported in correspondence of release 1.4. This is mostly explained by changes in the set of DNS types supported by *dnsjava*.

All the users who bought the service before could have reported problems in the service usage. User–side testing would have therefore noticed the user of the change, while provider–side testing would have suggested to advertise (e.g., updating the service description, although leaving the service interface unaltered) the change made. Vice–versa, users who bought the services at release 1.4 experienced no problem when the service evolved towards releases 1.5 and 1.6.

Let us now consider the case in which the comparison is limited to the DNS answer (*soft check*). As shown in Table 1, in this case the percentage of violations in correspondence of release 1.4 is lower (it decreases from 74% to 7–9%). This large difference is due to the fact that only the DNS query (compared with the strong check) reports DNS types: here the comparison of just resolved IP addresses did not produce a large percentage of failures. Where present, failures

---

[10] According to what we verified, the standard deviation was below 10% of the average value.

Table 2. InetAddressLocator: % of failed test cases

	2.12	2.14	2.16	2.18
2.10	0%	1%	1%	5%
2.12		1%	1%	5%
2.14			0%	4%
2.16				4%

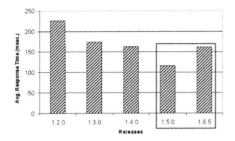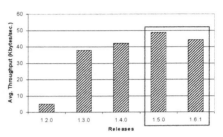

Fig. 5. dnsjava measured QoS over different releases

are mainly due to the different way subsequent releases handle exceptions. While this happens in a few cases, it represents a situation to which both provider and service users should pay careful attention.

Finally, Table 2 shows results for the *InetAddressLocator* software system. Here the differences, mainly appearing in the last release (2.18) are mainly due to updates in the location database. While in this case a different behavior may be considered as a service improvement, it is worth noticing that this could still lead to undesired behaviors from user's side. For example, if the user expects that the *InetAddressLocator* replies with the string *Europe* to a given set of IP addresses, while the new release (more precise) returns the string *Italy*, then the behavior of the system using the service may be affected.

Non-functional Testing. Fig. 5 reports average *response time* and *throughput* values measured over the different *dnsjava* releases. A *response time* increase (or a *throughput* decrease) may cause a violation in the SLA stipulated between the provider and the user. Basically, the figure indicates that:

- except for release 1.6, the performance always improved;
- users who acquired the service at release 1.5 could have noticed a SLA violation, in case the provider guaranteed, for future releases, at least the same performances exhibited by release 1.5;
- users who acquired the service at release 1.4 could have noticed, in correspondence of release 1.6, a (slight) decrease of the *response time*, even if a (slight) improvement in terms of *throughput*; and
- finally, all users who acquired the service before release 1.4 were fully satisfied.

Overall, we thus noticed that the QoS always improved over its evolution, but for release 1.6.5, where developers decided to add new features at the cost of worsening the performances.

4   Related Work

As stated in Section 2, the idea of complementing web services with a support for testing comes from the testing of component–based systems. As described by Weyuker [3], Bertolino *et al.* [2] and Orso *et al.* [5, 6], components can be complemented with a high–level specification, a built-in test suite, and also a traceability map able to relate specifications to component interfaces and to test cases. Weyuker [3] indicates that, especially for components developed outside the user organization, the provider might not be able to effectively perform component unit testing, because s/he is not aware of the target usage scenarios. As a consequence, the component user is required to perform a more careful re-test inside his/her own scenario. As discussed in Section 5, this is particularly true for services. For this reason, developer's test cases need to be complemented with user's test cases.

In literature there are plenty of approaches for regression testing. The state of the art is presented by Harrold [7], explaining the different techniques and issues related to coverage identification, test–suite minimization and prioritization, testability etc. Regression test selection [8, 9, 10] constitutes an important aspect aiming to reduce the cost of regression testing, that largely affects the overall software maintenance cost [1]. Much in the same way, it is important to prioritize test cases that better contribute to achieve a given goal, such as code coverage or the number of faults revealed [11, 12].

Cost–benefits models for regression testing have also been developed [13, 14, 15]. Although this is out of scope of the present paper, the issue of modeling, predicting and trying to reduce the testing cost is particularly important for web service testing. Even when test cases are available, service testing consumes network resources, and the provider might want to limit it (see Section 5).

5   Concluding Remarks

Regression testing, performed to ensure that an evolving service maintains the functional and QoS assumptions and expectations valid at the time of integration into a system, is a key issue to achieve highly–reliable service–oriented systems. We have proposed the idea of test cases as a form of contract between a service provider and a service user, and have shown an approach to publish test cases as a facet of the service description, and using such a facet to regression test a service over the time. Whilst the focus of the paper is on the user-side testing, the approach proposed can also be useful for third-party-side testing and provider-side testing, which, similarly to what happens for components [16], constitute the three main perspectives when testing a service–oriented system:

1. *provider/developer perspective:* the service developer would periodically check whether the service, after its maintenance/evolution, is still compliant to the contract stipulated with the customers. To avoid affecting service performance, testing can be performed off–line, possibly on a separate instance (i.e., not the one deployed) of the service and on a separate machine;
2. *user perspective:* on his/her side, the user may periodically want to re-test the service to ensure that its evolution, or even changes in the underlying software/hardware do not affect the functional and non-functional behavior. Particular attention needs to be paid from the provider's side: service invocation is supposed to have a cost and to consume resources. High–frequency, massive testing of the service from many users would lead to a denial–of–service. Proper countermeasures need therefore to be set from provider's side, limiting the number of service invocations per period of time, and maybe allowing access during periods when the service workload is low;
3. *certifier perspective:* a certifier acts similarly to a user, with the aim of repeatedly testing the service, possibly on behalf of a user, to check whether it is compliant to some functional and non-functional behavior specified in the test suite.

Work–in–progress is devoted to enhance the tool and to integrate it in a complex service–oriented development environment. We are also tackling issues such as the automatic generation of test cases, starting from a service specification or interface, with the aim of violating functional or non-functional contracts. Also, supporting test case reuse and performing cost–benefits analysis are important issues to be considered. Finally, the preliminary empirical studies performed need to be replicated with larger, industrial service–oriented systems.

Acknowledgments

This work is framed within the IST European Integrated Project *SeCSE (Service Centric Systems Engineering) – http://secse.eng.it*, 6th Framework Programme, Contract No. 511680. Authors would like to thank Alberto Troisi for his work the service regression testing tool.

References

1. Leung, H.K.N., White, L.: Insights into regression testing. In: Proceedings of IEEE International Conference on Software Maintenance. (1989) 60–69
2. Bertolino, A., Marchetti, E., Polini, A.: Integration of "components" to test software components. ENTCS **82** (2003)
3. Weyuker, E.: Testing component-based software: A cautionary tale. IEEE Softw. **15** (1998) 54–59
4. Ludwig, H., Keller, A., Dan, A., King, R., Franck, R.: Web Service Level Agreement (WSLA) language specification (2005) *http://www.research.ibm.com/wsla/WSLASpecV1-20030128.pdf.*

5. Orso, A., Harrold, M., Rosenblum, D., Rothermel, G., Soffa, M., Do, H.: Using component metacontent to support the regression testing of component-based software. In: Proceedings of IEEE International Conference on Software Maintenance. (2001) 716–725
6. Orso, A. Harrold, M., Rosenblum, D.: Component metadata for software engineering tasks. In: EDO2000. (2000) 129–144
7. Harrold, M.J.: Testing evolving software. J. Syst. Softw. **47** (1999) 173–181
8. Graves, T.L., Harrold, M.J., Kim, J.M., Porter, A., Rothermel, G.: An empirical study of regression test selection techniques. ACM Trans. Softw. Eng. Methodol. **10** (2001) 184–208
9. Harrold, M.J., Rosenblum, D., Rothermel, G., Weyuker, E.: Empirical studies of a prediction model for regression test selection. IEEE Trans. Softw. Eng. **27** (2001) 248–263
10. Rothermel, G., Harrold, M.J.: Empirical studies of a safe regression test selection technique. IEEE Trans. Softw. Eng. **24** (1998) 401–419
11. Elbaum, S., Malishevsky, A.G., Rothermel, G.: Test case prioritization: A family of empirical studies. IEEE Trans. Softw. Eng. **28** (2002) 159–182
12. Rothermel, G., Untch, R.J., Chu, C.: Prioritizing test cases for regression testing. IEEE Trans. Softw. Eng. **27** (2001) 929–948
13. Leung, H.K.N., White, L.: A cost model to compare regression testing strategies. In: Proceedings of IEEE International Conference on Software Maintenance. (1991) 201–208
14. Malishevsky, A., Rothermel, G., Elbaum, S.: Modeling the cost-benefits tradeoffs for regression testing techniques. In: Proceedings of IEEE International Conference on Software Maintenance, IEEE Computer Society (2002) 204
15. Rosenblum, D.S., Weyuker, E.J.: Using coverage information to predict the cost-effectiveness of regression testing strategies. IEEE Trans. Softw. Eng. **23** (1997) 146–156
16. Harrold, M.J., Liang, D., Sinha, S.: An approach to analyzing and testing component-based systems. In: First International ICSE Workshop on Testing Distributed Component-Based Systems, Los Angeles, CA (1999) 333–347

Towards a Classification of Web Service Feature Interactions

Michael Weiss[1], Babak Esfandiari[2], and Yun Luo[1]

[1] School of Computer Science, Carleton University, Ottawa, Canada
{weiss, yluo}@scs.carleton.ca
[2] Department of Systems and Computer Engineering, Carleton University
babak@sce.carleton.ca

Abstract. Web services promise to allow businesses to adapt rapidly to changes in the business environment, and the needs of different customers. The rapid introduction of new web services into a dynamic business environment can lead to undesirable interactions that negatively impact service quality and user satisfaction. In previous work, we have shown how to model such interactions between web services as feature interactions, and reason about undesirable side-effects of web service composition. In this paper we present the results of subsequent research on a classification of feature interactions among web services. Such a classification is beneficial as we can then search for ways of detecting and resolving each class of feature interaction in a generic manner. To illustrate the interactions we use a fictitious e-commerce scenario.

1 Introduction

Feature interactions are interactions between independently developed features, which can be either intended, or unintended and result in undesirable side-effects. In previous work [9], we have shown how to model undesirable side-effects of web service composition as feature interactions. The formal study of feature interactions is known as the feature interaction problem. This problem has first been investigated in the telecommunications domain [4]. It concerns the coordination of features such that they cooperate towards a desired result at the application level. However, the feature interaction problem is not limited to telecommunications. The phenomenon of undesirable interactions between components of a system can occur in *any* software system that is subject to changes.

Interaction is certainly the very foundation of service-oriented architectures. Web services *must* interact, and useful web services will "emerge" from the interaction of more specialized services. As the number of web services available increases, their interactions will also become more complex. Systems we build will use third-party services, over whose implementation we have little control. Many of the web service interactions will be intended, but others may be unintended and undesirable, and we need to prevent their consequences from occurring. As noted by [7], many of the side-effects are related to security and privacy.

B. Benatallah, F. Casati, and P. Traverso (Eds.): ICSOC 2005, LNCS 3826, pp. 101–114, 2005.

This paper builds on our previous work [9, 11] by providing a categorization of feature interactions in web services by cause, following similar work in the telecommunications domain [2]. We also now propose a unified, realistic, and quite generic case study (the "Amazin" virtual bookstore) that illustrates all the discussed causes while remaining technology-agnostic and easily translatable to other domains. We believe that the case study can be used as a benchmark for future studies in feature interactions in web services.

While in our previous work we had hand-crafted our examples in order to highlight the potential for feature interaction, in this work we used a candid approach in which features were described individually, and without consideration as to their possible participation in feature interactions. The feature interactions that we can observe only arose from composing the services for the scenario in the case study. We believe that this approach strengthens our claims with respect to the pervasiveness of the feature interaction problem in web services.

The paper is organized as follows. We first provide more background on the feature interaction problem as it applies to web services, and on modeling web services as features. We then present our classification of web service feature interactions. To illustrate the interactions we present our case study of a fictitious virtual bookstore. This classification is followed a summary of related work. We conclude with a discussion and an outlook on future research.

2   Feature Interaction Problem

The first generation of web services did not exploit the benefits of a web *of* services. They were either of a simple, non-composite nature (often information services, such as a stock quote lookup service), or provided access to application functionality over pre-existing business relationships. By contrast, the current generation of web services are typically composite (i.e., they are constructed from other, more primitive web services), and offered by third-party service providers, and thus not grounded in existing relationships.

Web services of the first generation were predicated on two implicit assumptions: (1) that services developed in isolation would either be used in isolation, or, if part of a composite service, would not interact in inadvertent ways, and (2) that users had full control over the services they used, or there was a common understanding of the operation, and side-effects of these services. We argue that those assumptions are no longer valid for current web services.

Consider the example of a word-processing service that uses two third-party services, spell-checking and formatting [9]. Assume that the user has set her language preference for the word-processing service to UK English. However, let us also assume that, hidden to the word-processing service, the formatting service itself incorporates a spell-checking service. This time, the formatting service does not specify a language preference to the spell checking service. Suppose that the spell checking service uses a US English dictionary by default. The result of the service composition is that the incorrect language option will be applied.

This is a case of an undesirable feature interaction. The concepts of feature and feature interaction originated in the telecommunication domain. A *feature* is the minimum user-visible service unit in this domain [4]. Features are often independently developed and deployed. A *feature interaction* occurs when a feature invokes or influences another feature directly or indirectly. Although many of these interactions are, indeed, intended, undesirable side-effects as a result of the interaction of features are referred to as *feature interaction problem.*

3   Modeling Web Services as Features

Our approach is to model features at the early requirements stage using the User Requirements Notation (URN) [1]. These models allow us to reason about feature interactions, and document detection and resolution strategies. In this approach, the intent and side-effects of a feature are modeled as goals, and their operation in the form of scenarios. The interaction of features is captured in the form of links between goals. Finally, we can represent the allocation of features to subsystems (known as actors or components in URN), and the relationships between these actors. This section provides a brief overview of the approach.

3.1   User Requirements Notation

URN contains two complementary notations: Goal-oriented Requirements Language (GRL) [3], and Use Case Maps (UCM) [8]. In GRL requirements are modeled as goals to be achieved by the design of a system. The main elements of the notation are summarized in Fig. 1. During the analysis, a set of initial goals is iteratively refined into subgoals. These goals and their refinement relationships form a goal graph that shows the influence of goals on each other, and can be analyzed for goal conflicts. The perspectives of different stakeholders

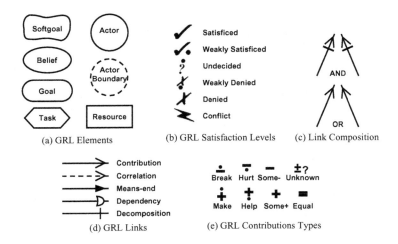

Fig. 1. Summary of the Goal-oriented Requirements Language (GRL)

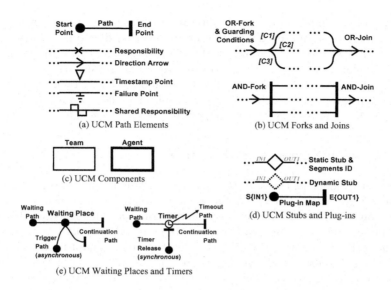

Fig. 2. Summary of the Use Case Map (UCM) notation

can also be described in GRL. For each stakeholder we model their goals, as well as their dependencies on one another to achieve those goals. These goals of one stakeholder can now also compromise the goals of other stakeholders. The objective of the analysis is to determine the design alternative that resolves the goal conflicts in a way that best satisfies all stakeholder's initial goals.

The UCM notation provides a way of describing scenarios without the need to commit to system components. The main elements of the notation are summarized in Fig. 2. A scenario is a causally ordered set of responsibilities that a system performs. Responsibilities can be allocated to components by placing them within the boundaries of that component. This is how we will be modeling feature deployment. With UCMs, different structures suggested by alternatives that were identified in a GRL model can be expressed and evaluated by moving responsibilities from one component (which is the UCM equivalent of a GRL actor) to another, or by restructuring components. This perspective allows us to refine the goals identified in a GRL model into greater detail, as necessary. Generally, when creating these models we would iterate between both views. That is, we cannot decide on the allocation of goals to actors simply within, eg, a GRL model, but only after repeatedly refining both perspectives.

3.2   Feature Interaction Analysis

In our adoption of URN, we model features as goals, and service providers as actors/components. The methodology proposed in [9] includes three steps:

1. Model the features to be analyzed as a GRL goal graph. Goal graphs allow us to represent features, and to reason about conflicts between them.

2. Analyze the goal graph for conflicts. Conflicts point to possible feature interactions, in particular, if a conflict "breaks" expected functionality.
3. Resolve the interactions. During this step, UCM models allow us to explore the different alternatives suggested by the GRL models.

Examples of applying steps 1 and 2 will be provided in Section 5.

4   Classification of Feature Interactions

We propose to classify feature interactions among web services by their type, and their cause. We thus position our classification in the tradition of existing classifications of feature interactions for the telecommuncations domain [2], while emphasizing web service-specific aspects. A classification of web service feature interactions is beneficial as it allows their avoidance, detection, and resolution in a *generic* manner for each type of interaction. Solutions for specific feature interactions can then be generalized to other interactions of the same category.

Our classification is an extension of the work by [2] for the telecommunications domain. That work was based on the premise, even more important now with web services, that service creation is no longer governed by a single organization. It also discusses a categorization by *nature* of the interactions, which depended on the nature of the features involved ,the number of users, and the number of components in the network. However, some causes of feature interactions do not carry over to the web services domain. So we have dropped "Limitations on Network Support" as a cause, since explicit service invocation in web services possibly avoids all signaling ambiguity.

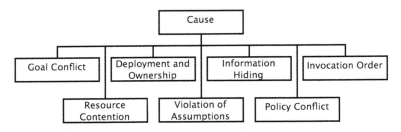

Fig. 3. Classification by cause

In our classification, a first distinction is made between functional and non-functional interactions with [9]. This distinction reflects that many of the side-effects are, in fact, of a non-functional nature, that is, they affect service properties such security, privacy, or availability. What this paper adds is a classification by cause shown in Fig. 3. It introduces two causes of interactions that we consider specific to web services, and are not encountered in closed, centralized telecommunications systems: deployment and ownership, and information hiding.

Goal conflicts take the shape of conflicting (non-functional) goals. They often occur as a result of unanticipated side effects, where in trying to achieve one goal, we inadvertently negatively impact another goal. We can indicate side effects in a GRL diagram by using a positive contribution link for the first, and a negative correlation link for the second goal. *Resource contention* is the fact that the use of some resource by a service makes it unavailable to another. It may result in service availability issues. *Deployment and ownership* decisions (where services are deployed, and who provides them) lead to performance, scalability and quality assurance issues, as well as conflicts of interest.

Assumption violations are caused by services that make incorrect assumptions about how another service works, and can, for example, be due to semantic ambiguity (use of the same concepts in different ways), or the presence of different versions of the same service. A result of *information hiding* is that service users cannot control how a service is implemented. This can lead to duplication of effort, inconsistencies, and even incorrect execution. *Policy conflicts* arise over contradictory policies that govern the behavior of services. Finally, *invocation order* is about features being invoked in a incorrect order, which may cause features to become ineffective, or timing glitches causing intermittent errors.

5   Selected Examples of Interactions

In this section, we provide examples of interactions to illustrate the classification. The context is a fictitious virtual bookstore, described in two parts:

1. We first describe the individual web services that will be used by the application. These services are developed without knowledge of how they will be composed later. Often they include third-party services that provide certain supplementary functionality such as identity management or payment.
2. We then create a composite service for an virtual bookstore from these services. We analyze the feature interactions that can occur as a result. As the services have been implemented independently they may embody assumptions that cause unexpected behavior as the services are composed.

This purpose of this division is to reproduce the problems that can result in the actual development of service-based applications. Each web service/feature is implemented with developers making assumptions that are individually valid, that is they faithfully implement the service interfaces. Feature interactions only result when these services are composed, often in unanticipated ways.

5.1   Examples of Features

The following features have one aspect in common: they all focus on one narrow type of service, and are usually employed in a supporting role. Examples of such supplementary services are identity management, payment processing, or shipping. In principle, any of these services could be provided by the requesting actor, but usually at a significant development cost, or risk of poor quality.

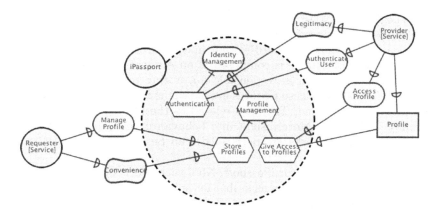

Fig. 4. GRL model of the iPassport feature

iPassport. The first example is an identity management feature. Identity management simplifies authentication with multiple service providers. It allows service requesters to authenticate themselves once with one service provider, and to access other service providers related to the initial service provider through a circle of trust. It simplifies the implementation of service providers, as well, because they no longer need to provide their own authentication component.

Fig. 4 is a GRL model of the iPassport feature. It models the service as well as each type of client as an actor (circle). As the diagram shows, iPassport mediates between Requesters [Service] and Providers [Service], and acts thus as a kind of broker. Requesters [Service] use iPassport to manage their profiles through the Manage Profile service, while Providers [Service] can authenticate users and access their profiles through the Authenticate and Access Profile services. Service provisioning relationships are modeled as functional dependencies. Functional requirements are represented as goals (rounded rectangle) that an actor wants to achieve. As shown, the dependencies are not restricted to interfaces. They also include non-functional and resource dependencies, for example, iPassport ensures

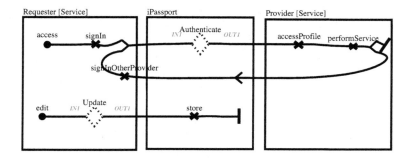

Fig. 5. UCM model of the iPassport feature

the requester's **Legitimacy**. Non-functional requirements are specified as softgoals (clouds) that cannot be achieved in an absolute manner. Resources (rectangles) represent physical or informational entities that must be available.

Internally, the **iPassport** feature is composed of an **Authentication** and a **Profile Management** features, which is responsible for storing profiles, and giving access to profile information. These features are shown as tasks (hexagons) that specify ways of achieving a goal. They are related to the **Identity Management** goal via decomposition links. More insight into behavioral and deployment aspects of a feature (how the tasks are performed) can be gained from a UCM model.

Fig. 5 shows the UCM model for **iPassport**. Note that this is only a top-level model with placeholders (also known as stubs) for submaps that define the **Authenticate** and **Update** behaviors (not shown). For example, the diagram captures (in the feedback loop with **signInOtherProvider**) that one **Provider [Service]** can link to another outside of the user's control. In the diagram crosses represent responsibilities, filled circles start points, and bars end points of paths.

PayMe. Payment processing allows payers to make secure payments online, and simplifies credit card processing for payees, while contributing to increased sales for them. As shown in Fig. 6, the payment processing feature **PayMe** provides two service interfaces: one to the **Payer [Order]** to **Manage Accounts**, and one to the **Payee [Order]** to receive payment for an order. The **Process Payment** service includes functionality to submit order details, as well as to cancel payments.

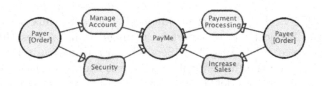

Fig. 6. GRL model of the PayMe service

Other Features. For reasons of space, we will sketch out the descriptions of the other features. The **ShipEx** feature provides a **Delivery** service to the **Shipper [Order]** with functionality for initiating shipment of an order, and canceling shipments, as well as a **Tracking** service for the **Shippee [Order]** to check on the status of a shipment. The **EvilAds** feature is an advertisement placement service, which provides a **ClickAds** service to any **Host [Ad]** that chooses to embed ads into its services. Finally, the **Shark** proxy service provides a **Caching** service through which a **Provider [Service]** can cache the results of popular service requests.

We implemented prototypes of these features, and tested them independently. However, space does not permit us to provide details of the implementation here, and we limit ourselves to describing the analysis of the observed interactions. Then we combined them into composite services, and analyzed the result for feature interactions. The largest of these case studies is described next.

5.2   Composite Service: Virtual Bookstore

The actor diagram for the composite service is shown in Fig. 7. The diagram models the Amazin virtual bookstore that gives Customers access to its virtual catalog, and the option to order books from the catalog through its Order Processing service. This service is composed from the features described above.

Amazin relies on a number of Suppliers to fulfill customer orders. Customer logins are handled through the iPassport identity management service, which provides an Authenticate User and an Access Profile service. On receiving a customer order, Amazin authenticates the customer, and accesses the customer's profile. It then selects a Supplier which stocks the ordered book and invokes its Order Processing service, passing along the customer's identity.

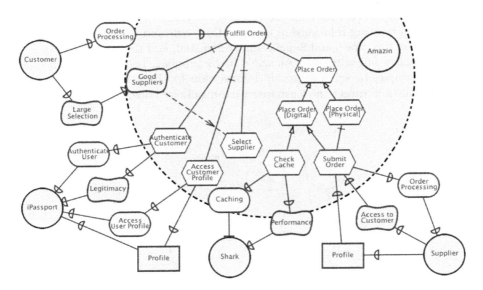

Fig. 7. GRL model of virtual bookstore Amazin

An internal structure of the Amazin service that fits this description is also shown in Fig. 7. This design makes assumptions that, while in agreement with service interfaces, may cause feature interactions. One potential source of interactions is the following optimization: in addition to physical books, Amazin also offers digital books for download, and it caches copies of popular orders.

The Supplier determines the availability of the ordered book, and, if successful, obtains the customer's payment and shipping preferences from the iPassport service. It then invokes the Payment Processing service provided by the PayMe financial service provider, and the Delivery service of Amazin's ShipEx fulfillment partner. Customers can track the progress of their orders via the Tracking service. They can also manage their online profiles, and accounts through services.

If a Supplier cannot fulfill an order, it will attempt to satisfy it from its network of Other Suppliers. Although omitted from the diagram, the chosen Other Supplier will use the same payment and delivery services as Supplier. Finally, some Suppliers choose to share selected customer information to an EvilAds advertisement agency via its ClickAds service as an additional source of revenue.

In the following we use this application to provide examples of the different causes of interactions identified in Fig. 3, as well as their types.

5.3   Goal Conflict

One conflict arises between Manage Profile and Access Profile, and is of type non-functional. As refined GRL model of the interaction is given in Fig. 8. The Convenience and Privacy goals of the Customer conflict with one another, since any iPassport member organization can access the profile, including those organizations with whom the customer has no trusting relationship.

While there is a trusting relationship between Customer and Amazin, the relationships between Customers and Suppliers are untrusted, and there is no guarantee that a Supplier will adhere to Amazin's privacy policy. Instead, it could decide, as an example, to sell the profile information to the target marketer EvilAds, which will then target the Customer with unsolicited ads.

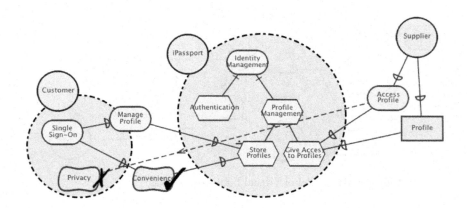

Fig. 8. Goal conflict between Manage Profile and Access Profile

This interaction is an example of a goal conflict, but it can also be classified as caused by deployment and ownership, information hiding, or a policy conflict. Deployment and ownership because at the root of the problem is one and the same entity (iPassport) authenticates the Customer and controls access to its profile. Profile information is shared between Amazin and its Suppliers without involvement of the Customer (as the UCM model in Fig. 5 clearly shows). Information hiding since the Manage Profile interface does not declare that profiles will be shared with parties the customer does not trust directly. Policy conflict because Suppliers are not bound to the same privacy policy as Amazin, whose policy is the only one the Customer has accepted explicitly.

5.4   Resource Contention

When Amazin invokes the Order Processing service of one of its Suppliers, this supplier will, in turn, place an order with one of its network of Other Suppliers, if it does not have the requested book in stock. However, this can lead to a situation where the order is sent back to Amazin itself, which is just an Other Supplier. Fig. 9 shows a scenario where Amazin is both a client, as well as a supplier to a given Supplier. If undetected, this can lead to an infinite loop of order requests, which could cause all actors linked via the loop to become unavailable. The dependencies at the source of the issue have been highlighted for emphasis.

This is a feature interaction between two implementations of the same feature, Order Processing, as implemented by multiple actors.

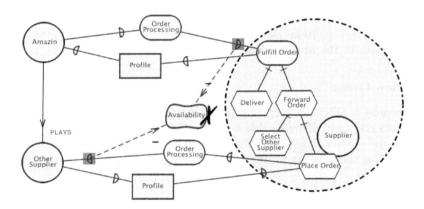

Fig. 9. Resource contention between OrderProcessing and OrderProcessing

5.5   Violation of Assumptions

The Caching service used by the Amazin service to keep local copies of digital content, and the Payment Processing service interact as result of a violation of assumptions. Caching digital content (in Shark, or another proxy) has the potential of preventing that access to the content will be properly billed. The Amazin service works correctly without caching, and thus an assumption may have been built in that for every order, a respective order will be placed with a supplier, and thus no internal accounting is required. If caching is added to improve the performance of the service, there is a potential that the implications of this change (breaking this assumption) are not fully understood by the designers.

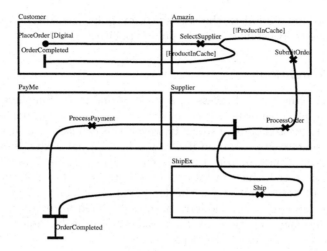

Fig. 10. Interaction between between Caching and Payment Processing–Delivery

The UCM model in Fig. 10 helps explain the situation. If ProductInCache is true, the return path in the upper left of the diagram will be taken.

5.6   Invocation Order

There is a potential conflict between Payment Processing and Order Processing, or Payment Processing and Delivery due to timing errors. The interaction can result in either the customer getting charged without the product shipped, or the customer getting the product for free. Both errors exploit timing glitches, for

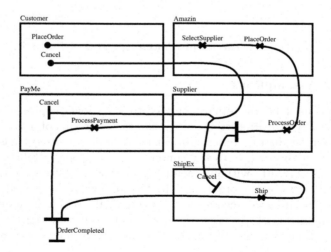

Fig. 11. Interaction between between Payment Processing and Order Processing

example, when the customer cancels their order, it could be that payment still gets processed (because Payment Processing was started before the order was canceled) but Delivery is aborted. The cancellation request was sent just before payment started, but arrived after Payment Processing has proceeded.

The UCM model in Fig. 11 provides the basis for understanding the cause of the interaction. The ProcessPayment and Ship responsibilities are initiated in parallel (the vertical bar after ProcessOrder indicates concurrency), and can execute in any order of one another. The Cancel requests to a component only take effect, if the ProcessPayment and Ship requests have not been started yet. This means that there are two successful cancellation scenarios, and two unsuccessful ones (where one of these requests has already been performed).

6 Related Work

In our earlier work [9] we have provided additional examples of interactions, as well as approaches for resolving them. By contrast this paper does not consider resolution. The goal conflict scenario is based on our work on assessing privacy technologies [10]. This paper also describes other privacy-caused interactions.

Liu und Yu [5] describe work on discovering privacy and security problems in P2P networks using GRL/i*. Although they do not refer to feature interactions, they introduce a concept of conflict, and an extension to the GRL notation to indicate sources of conflict, as well as potential threats in a GRL model. In future work, we will integrate their results into our approach.

7 Conclusion

In this work we have presented work towards a classification of web service feature interactions. Our goal was to identify potential feature interactions in a composite web service. While some of these interactions can clearly be anticipated by service designers from past experience, it is impossible to plan for all circumstances during which interactions may occur, including interactions with services that do not even exist when a service is developed.

In our example, we therefore did not try to anticipate possible interactions, but focused on implementing the specified service interfaces. We can liken the development of web services to an iceberg. When we view a web service through its interface we only see the tip of the iceberg. While we can make the interface more specific, there will always be elements of its operation that escape the interface specification, just as the tip of the iceberg is no indication of its size.

More work on the classification is required. Our vision is that once a stable classification is in place we will be able to describe in a generic manner how interactions of services that fit a certain type and cause can be detected and resolved. Identifying and describing such patterns for detecting and resolving different kinds of interactions will set the agenda for our future work.

References

1. Amyot, D., Introduction to the User Requirements Notation: Learning by Example. Computer Networks, 42(3), 285–301, 2003.
2. Cameron, J., Griffeth, N., et al, A Feature Interaction Benchmark for IN and Beyond, Feature Interaction Workshop, 1–23, 1994.
3. GRL, http://www.cs.toronto.edu/km/GRL, last accessed in June 2005.
4. Keck, D, and Kuehn, P., The Feature and Service Interaction Problem in Telecommunications Systems, IEEE Trans. on Software Engineering, 779–796, 1998.
5. Liu, L., Yu, E., and Mylopoulos, J., Analyzing Security Requirements as Relationships among Strategic Actors, Symposium on Requirements Engineering for Information Security (SREIS), 2002.
6. O'Sullivan, J., Edmond, D., and ter Hofstede, A., What's in a Service? Towards Accurate Description of Non-Functional Service Properties, Distributed and Parallel Databases, 12, 117–133, Kluwer, 2002.
7. Ryman, A., Understanding Web Services, http://www.software.ibm.com/wsdd/techarticles/0307_ryman/ryman.html, 2003.
8. UCM, http://www.usecasemaps.org, last accessed in June 2005.
9. Weiss, M. and Esfandiari, B., On Feature Interactions among Web Services, International Conference on Web Services (ICWS), 88–95, IEEE, 2004.
10. Weiss, M., and Esfandiari, B., Modeling Method for Assessing Privacy Technologies, in: Yee, G., Privacy in e-Services, Idea Books, 2006 (to appear).
11. Weiss, M., and Esfandiari, B., On Feature Interactions among Web Services, International Journal on Web Services Research, 2(4), 21-45, October-December, 2005.

A High-Level Functional Matching
for Semantic Web Services

Islam Elgedawy, Zahir Tari, and James A. Thom

School of Computer Science and Information Technology,
RMIT University, Melbourne, Australia
{elgedawy, zahirt, jat}@cs.rmit.edu.au

Abstract. Existing service matching techniques such as keyword-based and ontology-based, do not guarantee the correctness of the matching results (i.e. do not guarantee fulfilling user goals). This paper deals with this problem by capturing the high-level functional aspects (namely goals, contexts, and expected external behaviors) for both web services and users in a machine-processable format, then matching these aspects using the proposed functional substitutability matching scheme (FSMS). Based on FSMS, this paper describes a direct matching technique in which a user request is examined against one service description at a time, such that web services match users requests when they have substitutable goals, contexts and expected external behaviors. The substitutability semantics between the elements of application domains are captured via the proposed substitutability graphs, which are used during the matching process to mediate between users requests and web services descriptions. Simulation results show that the proposed matching approach succeeds in retrieving only the correct answers, while keyword-based and ontology-based retrieval techniques could not eliminate the appearance of false negatives and false positives.

1   Introduction

Existing matching techniques used in web service discovery, such as keyword-based techniques and ontology-based techniques, fail to provide high matching precision [4]. These techniques can be classified as "generic" as they are supposed to work in all contexts and for all application domains. In a nutshell, generic matching techniques examine the descriptions of web services by eliciting the various concepts, including inputs, outputs and entities, from the descriptions. Later, such concepts are matched using a keyword-based approach ([3]), a more precise approach (which uses generic subsumption rules given via domain taxonomies [8]), a form of Logic ([1, 9]), or a combination of approaches. Generic matching techniques are not suitable for web services as they do not take into consideration additional semantics related to web services and users[1], such as goals, contexts and expected external behaviors, that are needed to obtain correct results [4, 6, 7], as they provide information about (what a service

---

[1] The term "user" is used to refer to humans and machines.

B. Benatallah, F. Casati, and P. Traverso (Eds.): ICSOC 2005, LNCS 3826, pp. 115–129, 2005.

does/what a user wants) [4], the adopted constraints [6] and how the required goal is going to be achieved[7]. To guarantee the correctness of the matching results, we have identified the following requirements:

- User goals, contexts and expected external behavior should be semantically captured in a machine understandable format so that the matchmaker can understand them and later use them to find the correct answers.
- The high level functional aspects of web services, such as goals, contexts and expected external behavior should be explicitly captured in a machine understandable format so that the matchmaker can understand them and use them to find the correct answers.
- The functional semantics of the application domain should be explicitly captured in a machine understandable format such that the matchmaker can use them to mediate between the user request and web services descriptions.
- A formal matching scheme should use all these captured semantics (user semantics, web service semantics, and application domain semantics) and should guarantee the correctness of the matching results.

The G^+ model we previously proposed in [4, 6] captures high-level functional aspects (such as goals, functional contexts[2], and expected external behaviors) for both web services and users. Existing solutions for describing web services (such as OWL-S[2]) do not have explicit representations for these high-level functional aspects as they are described via text descriptions in the service profile. Recently, WSMO [9] followed a similar approach to ours by providing an explicit semantic representation for the high-level functional aspects such as goals, however it lacks explicit representation for web services behaviors (both internal and external).

The matching scheme indicates what comparison aspect between the involved elements is used, what matching rule is used, and how to judge the correctness of the matching results. Therefore, this paper introduces the functional substitutability matching scheme (FSMS) that uses high-level functionality as the comparison aspect, substitutability as the matching rule, and goal achievement as the correctness criterion.

The proposed direct matching approach starts by filtering services that correspond to different application domains and supports different domain roles. Then checks the substitutability of the G^+ models against user G^+ model to find the suitable set of services that fulfill user request. Substitutability between two G^+ models is determined according to the substitutability status between the functional contexts and the operation sequences of the corresponding scenarios. Functional context substitutability is determined according to the substitutability of their pre, post and describing sets of constraints. Substitutability status between two sets of constraints is determined by finding a sequence of consistent transformations that transform the elements of the source set into the elements of the target set using the proposed substitutability graphs. Substitutability of

---

[2] A functional context describes the requirements for correct goal achievement, as indicated in later sections.

operation sequences is determined according to the substitutability of their corresponding behavior models. A behavior model is a sequence of states elicited by tracing the transition points between the operations in the corresponding operation sequence, such that a state is represented by the active constraints at the corresponding transition point. Two states are matched according to the substitutability status between their constraints.

This paper is organized as follows. Section 2 provides an overview of the G^+ model used to capture the high-level functional aspects. An overview of the meta-ontology used is also provided. Section 3 introduces the functional substitutability matching scheme. Section 4 provides details related to the proposed direct matching approach between two given G^+ models. Experiment results are described in Section 5, and Section 6 concludes the paper.

2   The G^+ Model

The G^+ model [4, 6] is an extended goal model that provides an integration of various concepts, including operational goals[3], the corresponding functional contexts[4], and the corresponding realization scenarios[5]. A functional context is represented by three sets of constraints[6]: pre-constraints (goal pre-conditions), post-constraints (goal post-conditions), and describing-constraints. Table 1 provides an example of a G^+ instance, describing HotelReservationService, where Hotel-Reservation, Submit-Room-Details, Submit-Payment-Details, Send-Confirmation are tourism domain operations defined in the used domain ontology.

Table 1. A G^+ Example

Goal= "Hotel-Reservation"
FunctionalContext = ⟨ {CreditCard.Type = VISA, Hotel.Country = Australia},
  {Payment.Status = OK, Confirmation.Status = Sent},
  {Hotel.Function ∈ (Casino, Bank, Baby Setting, SPA, GYM)}⟩
RealizationScenario=SubmitRoomDetails: SubmitPaymentDetails: SendConfirmation

As an application domain can be described by multiple ontologies, our approach uses a meta-ontology that acts as a schema for domain ontologies that indicate what should be captured in an ontology and how. Hence during the matching process, specific types of application domains' elements and their semantics will be used. The proposed meta-ontology consists of two layers: schematic layer and a semantic layer. At the schematic layer, the types of the domain elements are defined. At the semantic layer, the relations between the domain elements are

---

[3] A goal that is represented by an application domain operation.
[4] The requirements for correct goal achievements.
[5] A scenario represents a sequence of application domain operations that tells one story about how to achieve the goal.
[6] Any constraint is formulated as Entity.Attribute Operator Value.

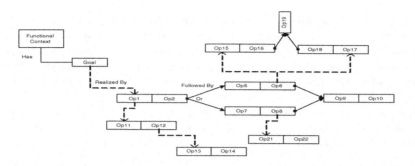

Fig. 1. An Example of a Scenario Network

captured. The proposed approach, however, restricts these relations to only one
type, namely the functional substitution relation, as FSMS uses substitutability
as the matching rule. The components of the schematic layer are concepts, operations and roles. Concepts represent the domain entities, which are described
by a set of features. A feature is an attribute with its corresponding value. Operations represent the domain legitimate transaction types. Every operation is
described by a set of features. Every operation has a set of input concepts and
a set of conditions over these concepts. Every operation has a set of output
concepts and a set of conditions over these concepts. Roles represent domain
legitimate actors. Every role is described by a set of features.

As many different scenarios can describe the achievement of a given goal, a
more complex G^+ model can be defined by a scenario network allowing multiple
abstraction levels, showing how such a goal could be achieved. An example is
given in Figure 1. Tracing a goal scenario network from the goal node until a leaf
operation node represents one of the expected paths for achieving the goal. Such
a path is called *Goal Achievement Pattern* (GAP). A GAP describes a global
(end-to-end) snapshot of how a service goal is expected to be accomplished. This
snapshot provides information that helps the matchmaker to anticipate the external behavior of a service in a given context. In a nutshell, a GAP consists
of the following information: a functional context, a goal, and an operation sequence. A functional context represents the context of the corresponding service
defined in conjunction with any existing sub-contexts (that is the value cases of
the branching conditions along the path). Sub-contexts are added to the set of
pre-constraints that belongs to the functional context. An operation sequence is
a result of the tracing of a scenario network from the goal node till a leaf opera-
tion node. Formally, $\mathsf{GAP} = \langle \mathsf{Cntxt}, \mathsf{G}, \mathsf{OpSeq} \rangle$, where Cntxt is the GAP functional
context, G represents the GAP goal, and OpSeq is the GAP operation sequence.

A scenario network provides multiple abstraction levels for describing the
achievement of a given service goal (that is, an operation in a given scenario
could be described by another scenario network). So, we can extract multiple
abstraction level GAPs such that a group of GAPs will describe the same story
but at different levels of detail. This provides great flexibility to the matchmaker
to choose a suitable abstraction level to work on.

3   The FSMS Matching Scheme

The following factors are used to judge the correctness of the results produced by a the proposed matching approach. (i) A comparison aspect that indicates which facts (about the involved entities) will be considered. (ii) A matching rule that indicates how the comparison aspect will be examined. Finally, (iii) a correctness criterion that validates the obtained results after applying the matching rule. Any matching scheme should define its own comparison aspect, matching rule and correctness criterion. This section describes a new matching scheme, called *Functional Substitutability Matching Scheme* (FSMS), which uses *functionality* as the comparison aspect, *substitutability* as the matching rule, and *goal achievement* as the matching correctness criterion. A service's functionality is the service's capability for achieving a given goal. This is captured using the G^+ model. In general, a goal G is considered achieved when transforming a set of constraints W_i into another set of constraints W_j. This is denoted as $(W_i \longmapsto_G W_j)$, and its reads as "the goal G is achieved when transforming W_1 into W_2 using S", where $\longmapsto$ is the achievement operator. Adopting the G^+ model, a goal is considered achieved when transforming the pre-constraint set into the post-constraint set of the functional context using the defined GAP (that is invoking the corresponding sequence of operations).

A user specifies both the request (in the G^+ format) and the G^+ models to be published. The matchmaker succeeds in the matching of a service with the user's request when the service can achieve the request goal. For example, if the request's goal G is achieved when $(W_1 \longmapsto_G W_2)$, and a service S achieves G by transforming W_3 into W_4 $(W_3 \longmapsto_G W_4)$, then S is considered a match for the request when $W_1 \Rightarrow W_3$ (W_1 can substitute W_3) and $W_4 \Rightarrow W_2$ (W_4 can substitute W_2). This enables the transformation of W_1 into W_2 by invoking S, which means G is achieved. Constraint substitution via implication is restrictive as it leads to the appearance of false negatives. For example, the constraint (City.Name=Cairo) implies the constraint (Country.Name= Egypt). However this cannot be derived using implication as the two constraints have two different scopes. To overcome this problem, we propose the concept of "constraints semantics subsumption" that adopts the substitution semantics of application domains; to find a transformation that transforms the source constraints into the target constraints to determine the substitutability status between these constraints. We propose to extend the meta-ontology to support use of substitutability graphs.

Definition 1. *(Substitutability Graph) A substitutability graph is a directed graph, where a node is in the form of entity.attribute and an edge indicates the substitutability direction. Every edge has the corresponding substitutability conditions that must be satisfied in order to substitute a given entity's attribute with another entity's attribute **with respect to** a given domain operation. Also every edge has the corresponding conversion function between the attributes' values.*

As an entity could be a concept or a role, this implies for every domain two substitutability graphs will be defined: a concept substitutability graph and a

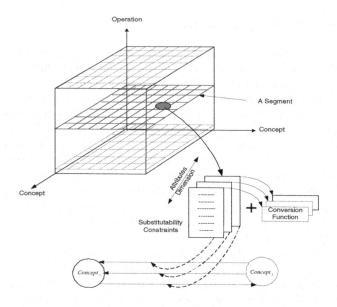

Fig. 2. Concepts Substitutability Graph

role substitutability graph. Figure 2 shows how a concept substitutability graph has been introduced: for every domain operation, and for every pair of concepts, substitutability conditions are defined.

If no attributes are explicitly defined; this means all the concepts' attributes with the same name are substitutable with respect to such domain operation. Their corresponding conversion functions will be a simple equality between the attributes values. However if only specific attributes are substitutable, for every pair of substitutable attributes an edge should be created such that the corresponding substitutability constraints and conversion functions are defined. For example, the attribute Rank of the concept Hotel can have the values in the set {5,4,3,2,1}, which corresponds to the number of stars of the hotel, while the attribute Class of the concept Accommodation can have values in {Business,Economy}. For a hotel-reservation operation in the tourism domain, the concept Accommodation could be substituted with the concept Hotel if the accommodation type is temporary. Hence, the attribute Class could be substituted by the attribute Rank using a specific conversion function, as indicated in Table 2.

Table 2. An Example of a Substitutability Graph Entry

Source	Target	Conversion Function	Substitutability Conditions

Hotel.Rank	Accommodation.Class	If Hotel.Rank $\geq$ 3
		 Then Accommodation.Class = Business
		 Else
		 Accommodation.Class = Economy
		 End IF
			Accommodation.Type=
			 Temporary

For instance (Hotel.Rank=4) and a service description (that indicates that the service can book temporary business class accommodations), the match-maker can return the service as a correct one if the other constraints in the request are fulfilled. Formally, we introduce **concepts substitutability graph** SG_c as a directed graph such that $SG_c = \bigcup_{i=1}^{n}\{\langle Op_i, V_c, E_c\rangle\}$, where Op_i is a domain operation, n is the number of operations in the domain, V_c is a set of graph nodes such that $V_c \subseteq \Delta_c \bigotimes \Delta_A$ that Δ_c is the set of all concepts Δ_A is the set of all attributes. E_c represents a set of graph edges such that $\forall E_i \in E_c, E_i = \langle V_a, V_b, \Pi_{ab}, \Psi_{ab}\rangle$. Π_{ab} is the set of substitution conditions that must be satisfied in order for the concept.attribute represented by the node V_a (source node) to be substituted with the concept.attribute represented by the node V_b (target node)[7]. Ψ_{ab} is the conversion function that maps the value of the source node into a value for the attribute in the target node. In a similar way, we define **role substitutability graph** SG_r. A substitutability graph is used to determine if there exists a direct substitution (DS) between constraints' scopes.

Definition 2. *(Direct Substitution) Given two constraints Cn_i and Cn_j and two scopes A and B, such that A is the scope of Cn_i and B is the scope of Cn_j, a goal G, and a set of constraints W such that $Cn_j \in W$, there exists a direct substitution (DS) between A and B with respect to G and W iff there exists a valid path $P = L_1, L_2, ..., L_n$ between A and B in the corresponding substitutability graph such that $W \Rightarrow \wedge_{i=1}^{i=n}\Pi_{L_i}$ where L_i is an edge between two scopes, and Π_{L_i} is the substitution constraints of edge L_i[8].*

When a matchmaker attempts to transform a constraint Cn_i (the source constraint) into another constraint Cn_j (the target constraint) with respect to a given goal, first it checks if there exists a DS between their scopes. If so, it uses the conversion function(s) to transform the source constraint Cn_i into another constraint Cn_k such that $Cn_k \Rightarrow Cn_j$[9]. Otherwise the transformation is considered not valid and the constraints cannot be substituted.

Two scopes are considered *reachable* if there exists a DS, or a sequence of DSs between them. This sequence of DSs is the **required transformation** in order to substitute the target constraint with the source one. When such a transformation exists, the source constraint is considered to semantically subsume the target constraint with respect to the involved goal.

Definition 3. *(Constraints Semantic Subsumption) Given two constraints Cn_i, Cn_j and a goal G, Cn_i semantically subsumes Cn_j with respect to G (denoted as $Cn_i \mapsto_G Cn_j$) iff Cn_i and Cn_j scopes are reachable with respect to G using a transformation β, and Cn_i is transformed to Cn_q using β such that $Cn_q \Rightarrow Cn_j$.*

---

[7] The correctness of the substitution conditions is the responsibility of the ontology engineer.

[8] A set of constraints is treated in implication as one constraint that is a conjunction of the set elements.

[9] It is important to note that Cn_k and Cn_j have the same scope.

Adopting Definition 3, Cn_i matches Cn_j when the involved transformation does not violate the set of active constraints existed at the substitution time.

4   The Direct Matching Approach

Matching two web services based on their high-level functional aspects using FSMS is determined according to the substitutability of their corresponding G^+ models. We will first show how simple G^+ models (represented by only one GAP) are matched. Later we will show the same process on complex G^+ models (represented by a GAP forest).

Definition 4. *(Direct G^+ Matching) Given two simple G^+ models G_i^+ and G_j^+, G_j^+ can be substituted by G_i^+, denoted as $(G_i^+ \unrhd G_j^+)$, iff $(Op_i = Op_j) \wedge (Ctxt_i \unrhd_{Op_j} Ctxt_j) \wedge (GAP_i \unrhd_{Op_j} GAP_j)$, where Op_i and Op_j are the operations representing the goals of G_i^+ and G_j^+ respectively. $Ctxt_i$ and $Ctxt_j$ are the functional contexts of G_i^+ and G_j^+ respectively. GAP_i and GAP_j are the goal achievement patterns of G_i^+ and G_j^+ respectively.*

Definition 4 indicates that G_j^+ matches G_i^+ when they are represented by the same domain operation and the achievement requirements of G_j^+ (captured by its functional context) are substitutable by the achievement requirements of G_i^+. So, the goal achievement pattern of G_j^+ is substitutable by the goal achievement pattern of G_i^+. The first step to realize Definition 4 is to illustrate how two functional contexts are going to be matched in FSMS; later we will show how two GAPs will be matched in FSMS.

Definition 5. *(Functional Context Matching) Given two contexts $Ctxt_i$, $Ctxt_j$ and a given goal G, $Ctxt_j$ can be substituted by $Ctxt_i$ with respect to G (denoted as $Ctxt_i \unrhd_G Ctxt_j$) iff $((Ctxt_i^{Pre} \unrhd_G Ctxt_j^{Pre}) \wedge (Ctxt_i^{Post} \unrhd_G Ctxt_j^{Post}) \wedge (Ctxt_i^{Desc} \unrhd_G Ctxt_j^{Desc}))$.*

Definition 5 indicates that a functional context $Ctxt_j$ matches $Ctxt_i$ when its constraints sets (pre, post and describing) are substitutable by the corresponding constraints sets of $Ctxt_i$. More details about context matching can be found in [6]. So, two GAPs are matched in FSMS as indicated in Definition 6.

Definition 6. *(GAP Matching) Given two goal achievement patterns GAP_i and GAP_j such that $GAP_i = \langle\ Cntxt_i,\ G_i,\ OpSeq_i\ \rangle$ and $GAP_j = \langle\ Cntxt_j,\ G_j, OpSeq_j\ \rangle$. GAP_j can be substituted by (matches) GAP_i denoted as $(GAP_i \unrhd GAP_j)$ iff $(G_i = G_j) \wedge (Cntxt_i \unrhd_{G_j} Cntxt_j) \wedge (OpSeq_i \unrhd_{G_j} OpSeq_j)$.*

Definition 6 indicates that matched GAPs will be realizing the same goal and will be having substitutable contexts and substitutable operation sequences. Operation sequences could be matched syntactically, semi-semantically (adopts 1-to-1 state matching) or semantically (adopts many-to-many state matching).

The semantic approach takes into consideration the effect of a group of operations on the external behavior of the service. The effect of invoking a sequence of operations on (the external behavior of) a service resembles a sequence of state transitions, where a state represents the (active) constraints at the corresponding transition point. Every state corresponds to a specific set of user interactions with the service (the external behavior). These user interactions are reflected by the active constraints captured in the state. The state model corresponds to the transition point between two operations (Op_x and Op_{x+1}) and differentiates between the active and idle constraints, as the idle constraints do not have any effects over the successor operation so they will be discarded during state matching.

Definition 7. *(State Definition) Given an operation sequence $OpSeq = Op_0$, $Op_1, \ldots, Op_n$, a state S_x between the operations Op_{x-1} and Op_x is defined as $\langle f_x^e, f_x^i \rangle$ such that $f_x = f_x^e + f_x^i$, where f_x is the set of active constraints at transition point x, f_x^e is the set of effective constraints, f_x^i is the set of idle constraints and $+$ represents the union operator between two sets. f_x, f_x^e, and f_x^i are computed as follows:(1) $f_0 = Ctxt^{Pre}$. (2)$f_x = f_{x-1}^i + Op_x^{Post}$, where $1 \leq x \leq n+1$. (3) $f_x^i = f_x \diamond_G Op_x^{Pre}$, where $\diamond_G$ is the semantic difference between two sets of constraints with respect to G.[10] (4)$f_{n+1}^e = f_{n+1}$. (5) $f_{n+1}^i = \{\}$.*

Every state has a corresponding scope that is defined as the set of element.attribute appearing as scopes in f_x^e of the state. The following example indicates how a state is automatically created.

Example 1. *(State Creation) Let us consider two consecutive operations Submit-Payment(Payment):Payment and Confirm-Order (Order, Payment): Order in a given purchase online transaction. The pre-conditions of "Submit-Payment" operations are { Payment.method = Null , Payment.details = Null }, while its post-conditions are { Payment.method $\neq$ Null, Payment.details $\neq$ Null, Payment.status = valid }. The pre-conditions of "Confirm-Order" are {Payment.status = valid, Order.status = created }, while its post-conditions are { Order.status = confirmed }. According to Definition 7, the state that represents the transition point between "Submit-Payment" and "Confirm-Order" will be as follows: Assuming the independent set $f_{x-1}^i = \{Order.status = created\}$, hence f_x is equal to { Order.status =created , Payment.method $\neq$ Null, Payment.details $\neq$ Null, Payment.status = valid }, the effective constraints are the ones that imply the pre-conditions of "Confirm-Order" operation and the rest of the constraints will be the independent idle constraints as follows:*

f_x^e	f_x^i
{Order.status = created, Payment.status = valid}	{Payment.method $\neq$ Null, Payment.details $\neq$ Null}

---

[10] A semantic difference between f_x and Op_x^{Pre} is a subset of f_x that has no reachable scopes to elements of Op_x^{Pre}.

The corresponding state sequence is created by applying Definition 7 at every transition point, by tracing all the transition points in a given operation sequence. After automatically constructing the state sequences from the involved operation sequences, they are going to be matched using FSMS such that when the two state sequences are matched, the corresponding operation sequences will be considered matched. State sequences will be matched adopting many-to-many manner, in which a group of states will be examined against another group of states.

Definition 8. *(State Matching) Given two states $S_x = \langle S_x^e, S_x^i \rangle$, $S_y = \langle S_y^e, S_y^i \rangle$ and a goal G, S_y can be substituted by S_x with respect to G (denoted as $S_x \trianglerighteq_G S_y$) iff $(S_x^e \trianglerighteq_G S_y^e)$.*

As the many-to-many approach is adopted, state merging is required to realize such an approach. A state is represented by a set of constraints at a given transition point. Merging two states means generating a new state that represents the set of constraints resulted after forming a virtual composite operation, that is resulted from merging the operations following the transition points of the merged states, as indicated in Figure 3.

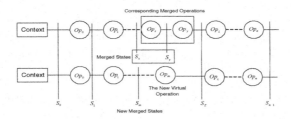

Fig. 3. Merging States

Op_m should not affect any other state in the corresponding sequence. To maintain this principle, both the pre/post conditions of Op_m are defined as follows: $Op_m^{Pre} = Op_x^{Pre} + (Op_{x+1}^{Pre} \diamond_G Op_x^{Post})$, and $Op_m^{Post} = Op_{x+1}^{Post} + (Op_x^{Post} \diamond_G Op_{x+1}^{Pre})$ [5]. The new state resulting from the merge S_m will be created according to the operator defined in Definition 7, adopting the values of Op_m's pre/post conditions (see Definition 9).

Definition 9. *(State Merge) Given two consecutive states $S_x = \langle f_x^e, f_x^i \rangle$, $S_{x+1} = \langle f_{x+1}^e, f_{x+1}^i \rangle$ and a goal G, the state $S_m = \langle f_m^e, f_m^i \rangle$ resulting from merging S_x and S_{x+1} with respect to G (denoted as $S_m = S_x \oplus_G S_{x+1}$) is defined as follows: $f_m^i = (f_x^i \diamond_G f_{x+1}^e)$. $f_m^e = (f_x^i + f_x^e) \diamond_G (f_x^i \diamond_G f_{x+1}^e)$.*

Definition 10. *(Expandable State) Given states S_x and S_y belonging to $StatSeq_i$ and $StatSeq_j$ respectively and a goal G, S_x is expandable with respect to S_y and G iff there exists a state S_q belonging to $StatSeq_i$, $x \leq q$, such that $(S_w \trianglerighteq_G S_y)$, where S_w is a new state resulting from merging the states from S_x to S_q.*

Definition 10 implies the expansion direction is "down", however a state could be expanded in "up" direction, meaning that this will be merged with its predecessors. In order to realize the many-to-many matching approach, we need to determine both the states in a given sequence that should be expanded as well as the direction for the matching. We propose a transformation procedure, called

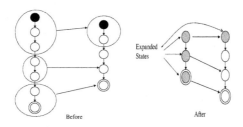

Fig. 4. Before and After Invoking SEQA

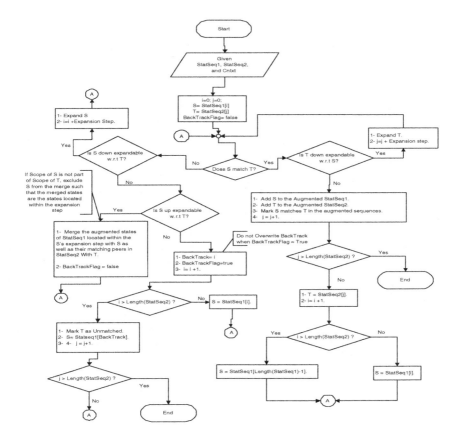

Fig. 5. SEQA Flow Chart

sequence augmenter (SEQA), to decide which and when states will be merged and the direction of merging. SEQA accepts two state sequences, a source sequence and a target sequence and the involved goal as its input, then returns two augmented state sequences and their corresponding matching peers. Figure 4 shows how the sequence augmenter works.

Figure 5 depicts the flow chart of SEQA. *StatSeq*1 is the source sequence and *StatSeq*2 is the target sequence. Let T represent the current target state to be matched in *StatSeq*2 and S represent the current proposed matching state in *StatSeq*1 that will be examined against T. Using Definition 8, SEQA checks whether or not S matches T. If this holds, this will mean that $Scope(S) \supseteq Scope(T)$, which gives an opportunity to check whether S also matches T's successor when merged with T. If this is true, T will be down expanded, and this process will be repeated until T is not down expandable. The current S is added to the augmented source sequence and the current T (the expanded T if so) is added to the augmented target sequence. Also, S and T are marked as a matching peer. S may not match T, meaning either they have different scopes or they have the same scope but the states' conditions contradict, meaning they will never match. However, having different scopes implies either (Scope(S) $\subset$ Scope(T)) or (Scope(S) $\cap$ Scope(T) = $\emptyset$).

When Scope(S) $\subset$ Scope(T), there is a chance for S to match T by down expanding S. Even for the case of (Scope(S) $\cap$ Scope(T)= $\emptyset$) by down expanding S, there may be a chance for the successors of S to match T. Hence, SEQA will try to down expand S, marked as backtracking point. If S down expansion fails, there is an opportunity for S to be up expandable with respect to T. If up expansion succeeds, then the augmented sequences (source and target) should be restructured. This happens by both merging all the states that lie within the expansion step and merging their matching peers in the other augmented sequence. If the up expansion procedure fails, this means the current S cannot match the current state T. Therefore SEQA will try the S's successor to match it with T and also will check all the previous scenarios. If one of the previous scenarios works and S matches T, SEQA prepares the next state in the target sequence to be matched. But if all the previous scenarios did not work for all the successors of S, this implies that T cannot be matched with the given source state sequence. Therefore T will be marked as unmatched, and SEQA prepares the successor of T to be matched. It backtracks to the S's state that first tested with the unmatched T so as to give a chance for the successor of T to be checked against this backtracked S. SEQA considers a source state sequence is a match for a target state sequence, when every state in the target augmented sequence must be substituted by an augmented state in the source in an order-preserving manner. Complexity of SEQA is $O(n^3)$. The complexity of SEQA is high as the worst case is every state in the target sequence must be examined against the states of the source sequence for up and down state expansion, which costs $O(n^2)$.

5   Validation

The correctness of matching results can be judged through the F-measure metric [11], as when having its value equal to one implies the matching results are totally correct. Unfortunately, there are neither benchmarks nor standard data sets for matching semantic web services. Hence we opted to use a random approach, where a random data set and queries are generated so as to validate the devised matching techniques, following the same simulation experiments indicated in [6] used for testing context matching. This section will therefore focus on the evaluation of devised GAP matching techniques and compare them to the semantic, semi-semantic and syntactic approaches.

Work-Load Generation. The proposed technique requires the existence of a domain ontology that adopts the meta-ontology structure. The elements of the conducted experiments are: a domain ontology (that includes concepts, operations, roles and the substitutability graphs); a data set of generic GAPs; and a query set and its correct answers. We have generated a random number of concepts, a random number of operations and a random number of roles to represent the domain elements. To make sure there are no contradicting conditions when a new operation is generated, the following restrictions are followed when generating the domain operations: (i) every operation has one distinct concept as input parameter and it will be the operation output concept as well. (2) Every operation has one pre condition over an attribute of the input concept, such that the value of this attribute equals to its lower limit. (3) Every operation has one post condition over the same attribute used in the pre conditions such that the value of this attribute is less than its upper limit. Operation sequences are generated by selecting a random number of operations from the generated operations; in order to form our data set of generic GAPs.

Experiment Logic. We have generated a random data set of generic GAPs. Then a query set is constructed by randomly selecting 10% of the data set. Experiments are performed as follows. First, data and query sets are generated. Second, ten mutated query sets are produced such that the first mutated query set has the first 10% of the query set being mutated, the second mutated query set has the first 20% of the query set being mutated, and so on until the tenth mutated query set has 100% mutated queries. Third, all query sets are applied to the semantic matching approach, the semi-semantic matching approach and the syntactic approach. Fourth, the retrieval precision is calculated as indicated before for all approaches. Finally, the above procedure is repeated 1000 times and the final average result is computed.

Without a loss of generality, the mutation process is performed by merging all the operations of a given GAP into one operation such that the new mutated GAP will have only one operation. This operation is constructed as follows: (1) Its input is a collection of the GAP operations' inputs. (2) Its output is a collection of the GAP operations' outputs. (3) Its pre condition is a conjunction of

---

[11] F-measure $= \frac{2 \times Precision \times Recall}{Precision + Recall}$.

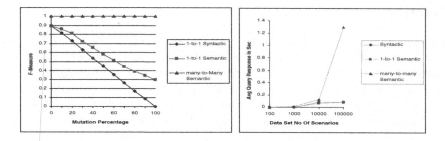

Fig. 6. A Comparison of GAP Matching Techniques

the GAP operations' pre conditions. (4) Its post condition is a conjunction of the GAP operations' post conditions. The pre/post conditions of the new constructed operation are deliberately mutated to generate new sets of conditions, so that the scopes of the original conditions are reachable from the scopes of the mutated conditions using a randomly generated substitutability graphs. For example, constraint (x>12) will be mutated into constraint (y>12) such that x is reachable from y. Experiment results are shown in Figure 6.

As the original query set and the mutated query sets have the same answers, the syntactic approach fails to answer the mutated queries. This is reflected by the decrease of retrieval precision, as the percentage of mutated queries increases. Also the semi-semantic approach fails to answer the mutated queries, except for the cases that its GAP has only one operation. Therefore, the semi-semantic approach could have the same behavior of the syntactic approach against the mutated queries. This indicates that many-to-many matching approach should be used instead of one-to-one approach when semantic matching is adopted. However, precision is expensive as indicated in the figure but we believe there is a good potential for performance enhancement as basic retrieval techniques are used in these experiments.

6   Conclusion

This paper demonstrates that capturing the semantics of web services, users and application domain in a machine-processable format is crucial for obtaining correct matching results. This paper proposed an advanced matching scheme for semantic web services, called *Functional Substitutability Matching Scheme* (FSMS), which uses high-level functionality (as a comparison aspect), substitutability (as a matching rule), and goal achievement (as a correctness criterion). The application domain functional substitutability semantics are captured via concept and role substitutability graphs. Adopting FSMS, we devised a direct matching technique for semantic web services that is shown to provide correct matching results (more details about other approaches are in [10]). Aggregate service matching adopting FSMS is the future extension of this work (more details in [5]).

Acknowledgment

This project is proudly supported by the ARC (Australian Research Council), under the ARC Linkage project no. LP0347217.

References

1. J. Castillo, D. Trastour, and C. Bartolini. Description logics for matchmaking of services. In *Proceedings of Workshop on Application of Description Logics*, Austria, September 2001.
2. OWL Services Coalition. Owl_S : Semantic markup for web services. http://www.daml.org/services/owl-s/1.0/owl-s.pdf, 2003.
3. X. Dong, A. Halevy, J. Madhavan, E. Nemes, and J. Zhang. Similarity search for web services. In *Proceedings of the 30th International Conference on Very Large Data Bases (VLDB)*, pages 132–143. Morgan Kaufmann, 2004.
4. I. Elgedawy. A conceptual framework for web services semantic discovery. In *Proceedings of On The Move (OTM) to meaningful internet systems*, pages 1004–1016, Italy, 2003. Springer Verlag.
5. I. Elgedawy and Z. Tari. Aggregate high-level functional matching for semantic web services. Technical Report TR-05-3, RMIT University, Australia, 2005.
6. I. Elgedawy, Z. Tari, and M. Winikoff. Exact functional context matching for web services,. In *International Conference on Service Oriented Computing (ICSOC)*, November 2004.
7. I. Elgedawy, Z. Tari, and M. Winikoff. Scenario matching using functional substitutability in web services. In *Proceedings of the International Conference on Web Information Systems Engineering (WISE)*, 2004.
8. P. Ganesan, H. Garcia Molina, and J. Widom. Exploiting hierarchical domain structure to compute similarity. *ACM Transactions on Information Systems*, 21(1):64–93, January 2003.
9. U. Keller, R. Lara, A. Polleres, I. Toma, M. Kifer, and Dieter Fensel. Wsmo web service discovery. http://www.wsmo.org/2004/d5/d5.1/v0.1/20041112, 2004.
10. I. Elgedawy, Z. Tari, and M. Winikoff. Functional context matching for web services. Technical Report TR-04-3, RMIT University, Australia, 2004.

Service Selection Algorithms for Composing Complex Services with Multiple QoS Constraints

Tao Yu and Kwei-Jay Lin

Dept. of Electrical Engineering and Computer Science,
University of California, Irvine, California 92697-2625, USA

Abstract. One of the promises of the service-oriented architecture
(SOA) is that complex services can be composed using individual services. Individual services can be selected and integrated either statically
or dynamically based on the service functionalities and performance constraints. For many distributed applications, the runtime performance
(e.g. end-to-end delay, cost, reliability and availability) of complex services are very important. In our earlier work, we have studied the service
selection problem for complex services with only one QoS constraint. This
paper extends the service selection problem to multiple QoS constraints.
The problem can be modelled in two ways: the combinatorial model and
the graph model. The combinatorial model defines the problem as the
multi-dimension multi-choice 0-1 knapsack problem (MMKP). The graph
model defines the problem as the multi-constraint optimal path (MCOP)
problem. We propose algorithms for both models and study their performances by test cases. We also compare the pros & cons between the
two models.

1 Introduction

Web services present a promising technology to compose complex service applications from individual (atomic) services. Using Web services, distributed
applications and enterprise business processes can be integrated by individual
service components developed independently. The service components may also
be upgraded or replaced dynamically at run time as system conditions change
or applications' needs evolve. The enhanced service composability provides a
desirable flexibility and reusability in building distributed enterprise or grid solutions. This is important for enterprise computing since the fast and dynamic
construction of business processes (for supply chain or service network) is essential for companies in order to adapt their operations to dynamic market conditions. Similar needs exist in global transaction systems, health care and travel
industry.

However, the composition flexibility comes at the price of increased system
engineering complexity. The complexity of Web service composition includes
three main factors: (1) the large number of atomic services that may be available;
(2) the different possibilities of integrating atomic service components into a
complex service; (3) various performance requirements (e.g. end-to-end delay,

B. Benatallah, F. Casati, and P. Traverso (Eds.): ICSOC 2005, LNCS 3826, pp. 130–143, 2005.

service cost, server capability) of a complex service. Web service composition thus creates a QoS engineering problem since the service selection must select the best services to compose an efficient complex service.

In recent years, it has become a common practice for service providers to offer different service levels so as to meet the needs of different customers. Companies have offered different service qualities (e.g. first class vs. coach class, gold card member vs. regular member) based on user qualifications or service costs. Similarly, although many atomic services have a similar functionality (e.g. checking market condition, making reservations, planning meetings, etc.), they differ from each other by non-functional qualities, such as service time, transaction cost, and system availability. The QoS of a Web service may be offered by different service level agreements (SLA) between service providers and clients [5].

In our study, we have proposed a broker-based framework (QCWS) for QoS-aware Web service composition [16]. In QCWS, Web service composition with QoS assurance includes two steps: *service planning* and *service selection*, which are are performed by the *Composition Manager (CM)* and *Selection Manager (SM)* in the QoS broker, respectively. In [15], we study the service selection problem for complex service with one QoS requirement. In this paper, we extend the system model to handle multiple QoS requirements. We study this problem using two different models: *the combinatorial model*, by defining the problem as a multi-dimension multi-choice 0-1 knapsack problem (MMKP) and *the graph model*, by defining the problem as a multi-constraint optimal path problem (MCOP). The objective of service selection is to maximize a user-defined utility function under the overall QoS constraints. The utility function definition may include an extended set of system parameters to achieve some user specific objective. We propose several service selection algorithms and report simulation results to compare their performances.

The rest of this paper is organized as follows. Section 2 reviews some related work. Section 3 presents the system model and assumptions for the Web service composition with QoS assurance in our study. Section 4 discusses various algorithms in both combinatorial and graph approaches, including heuristic and optimal ones. Section 5 shows the performance evaluation and comparison of different algorithms. The paper is concluded in Section 6.

2   Related Work

Web service composition has received much interest for supporting enterprise application integration. Many industry standards have been developed, such as BPEL4WS (Business Process Execution Language for Web Services) [4] and BPML (Business Process Modelling Language) [2]. Many projects have studied the Web service composition problem. The SWORD project [13] gives a simple and efficient mechanism for offline Web service composition using a rule-based expert system. SWORD is more focused on the service interoperability and no QoS issue has been addressed. The eFlow project [3] provides a dynamic and adaptive service composition mechanism for e-business process management. In eFlow, each service node contains a search recipe, which defines the service selection rule to select a specific service for this node. The selection rule is based on local criteria and does not address the overall QoS assurance problem of the business process.

QoS guarantee for Web services is one of the main concerns of the SLA framework [5]. The framework proposes differentiated levels of Web services using automated management and service level agreements (SLAs). The service levels are differentiated based on many variables such as responsiveness, availability and performance. An initial version of the framework was released as part of the IBM Emerging Technologies Toolkit (ETTK) version 1.0 in April 2003. Although it included several SLA monitoring services to ensure a maximum level of objectivity, no end-to-end QoS management capability was implemented.

There are projects studying QoS-empowered service selection, such as [17] and [1]. In [17], authors propose a quality driven approach to select component services during execution of a composite service. They consider multiple QoS criteria such as price, duration, reliability and take into account of global constraints. [1] has studied a similar approach. Both of them use the integer linear programming method to solve the service selection problem, which is too complex for run time decisions.

3   System Model and Assumptions

We assume that the same service interface definition is used by all atomic service candidates for a specific service component. So we are not concerned about the compatibility issue among services and focus on the QoS service selection problem. In this study, we define the concept of *service class*. A *service class* (denoted as S) is a collection of atomic Web services with a common functionality but different non-functional properties (e.g. time, quality). A class interface parameter set (S_{in}, S_{out}) is defined for each service class. We also assume each atomic Web service (denoted as s) in the service class can provide a service according to the class interface.

Each atomic service may provide $\mathcal{L}$ different service levels; each level is associated with a QoS vector $q(s, l) = [q^1(s, l), .., q^n(s, l)]$ $(1 \leq l \leq \mathcal{L})$ which contains n application-level QoS parameters such as service time, cost, reliability, availability [5]. Each service level is a candidate in the service class for service selection. Each service level also has an associated utility function $\mathcal{F}$. The utility function is defined by a set of system parameters including system load, cost and/or other QoS attributes. The system load can be considered by a benefit function ([15]). Definition 1 shows the utility function definition. Users can set the number of QoS values to be considered as well as their weights according to their requirements. In our study each user has m QoS attribute constraints in their QoS requirements: $\mathbb{Q}_c = [Q^1, .., Q^m]$ $(1 \leq m \leq n)$.

Definition 1 (Utility Function). *Suppose there are α QoS values to be maximized and β QoS values to be minimized. The utility function for candidate k in a service class is defined as:*

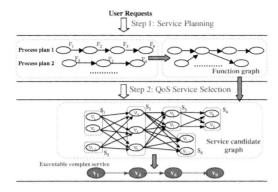

Fig. 1. QoS Web service composition model

$$\mathcal{F}(k) = \sum_{i=1}^{\alpha} w_i * \left(\frac{q_{ai}(k) - \mu_{ai}}{\sigma_{ai}}\right) + \sum_{j=1}^{\beta} w_j * \left(1 - \frac{q_{bj}(k) - \mu_{bj}}{\sigma_{bj}}\right)$$

where w is the weight for each QoS parameter set by a user ($0 < w_i, w_j < 1$, $\sum_{i=1}^{\alpha} w_i + \sum_{j=1}^{\beta} w_j = 1$, $\alpha + \beta = m$). μ and σ are the average value & the standard deviation of the QoS attribute for all candidates in the service class.

In our study, the QoS Web service composition is conducted in two steps: *service planning* and *service selection,* as shown in Figure 1. For each user request, the Composition Manager in the QoS broker first matches the request with one or more process plan(s). Each of them is an abstract process that defines a flow of component functions ($\mathcal{F}$, each can be accomplished by a service class) as well as their relationships. All potential process plans together constitute a function graph. The Selection Manager then maps the function graph into a service candidate graph and constructs an executable complex service. The mapping from a user request to process plans (*step 1*) only considers the functional requirements of the user request and does not handle the QoS requirement. It performs the parametric consistency checking of service classes in order to integrate them with each other. This problem has been addressed by several research work such as [13, 6]. The mapping from a function graph to an executable complex service (*step 2*) is decided by the distributed performance of services and a user's QoS requirements. Step 2 is the focus of this paper.

The QoS attributes of the complex service are decided by the QoS attributes of its component services as well as their integration relationships, such as sequential, parallel, conditional or loop. In this paper, we only consider the sequential composition model in which the QoS attribute and the utility of the complex service is the sum of its component services' QoS attributes and utilities at the selected service level. If a QoS attribute is the product of its component QoS, such as reliability and availability, we can apply a logarithm operation to convert it into a summation relationship. For QoS attribute with convex/concave characteristic, it may be processed by a filter operation and is not considered in this paper. Other composition models, such as parallel, conditional or loop, may be reduced or converted to the sequential model.

4   Service Selection Algorithms

In this section, we present the service selection algorithms used by the QoS broker for service composition with two or more QoS constraints. There are two models to solve the problem: *the combinatorial model* and *the graph model*.

4.1   The Combinatorial Algorithm

The *Multi-choice, Multi-dimension 0-1 Knapsack Problem (MMKP)* [12] is defined as follows: Suppose there are K groups, each has l_i ($1 \leq i \leq K$) items, where each item has a profit p_{ij} and requires resource $r_{ij} = (r_{ij1}, ..r_{ijm})$. The total amount of available resources in the knapsack are $R = (R_1, .., R_m)$. The objective of MMKP is to select exactly one item from each group to be included in the knapsack within the resource constraint while maximizing the total profit.

For a complex service that contains N service classes $(S_1, S_2, ..., S_N)$ in a process plan and with m QoS requirements, the service selection problem can be mapped to an MMKP as follows: (1) each service class can be viewed as a group in MMKP; (2) every candidate in a service class represents an item in a group; (3) the QoS attributes of each candidate are equivalent to the resources needed by the item; (4) the utility a candidate produces is mapped to the profit of the item; (5) a user's QoS requirements are considered as the available resources of the knapsack. The objective of service selection is to select one candidate from each service class to construct a complex service that meets a user's QoS requirements yet maximize the total utility. The problem is formulated as:

$$Max \quad \sum_{i=1}^{N} \sum_{j \in S_i} \mathcal{F}_{ij} x_{ij}$$

$$Subject\ to \quad \sum_{i=1}^{N} \sum_{j \in S_i} q_{ij}^{\alpha} x_{ij} \leq Q^{\alpha} \ (\alpha = 1, .., m) \tag{1}$$

$$\sum x_{ij} = 1$$

$$x_{ij} \in \{0, 1\} \quad i = 1, ..., N, \ j \in S_i$$

The MMKP problem is NP-hard [12]. [7] proposes a branch and bound algorithm (BBLP) to find the optimal solution for MMKP. The branch and bound method uses a search tree to find a solution. A node in the search-tree represents a solution state where some classes are fixed (an item has been chosen in these classes) and some others are free (no item has been selected). A node that has free classes may be expanded to generate new nodes. BBLP has a very high complexity and is not suitable for large size problems. The detailed description about the BBLP algorithm can be found in [7].

A heuristic algorithm (HEU) for MMKP has been presented in [8]. The idea of the algorithm is to find a feasible solution at first, then iteratively improve the solution by replacing items with a low utility with items with higher utilities in each group while keeping the solution feasible. If no such item can be found, it tries to replace items with a higher utility in a group (which makes the solution infeasible) followed by replacing items in other groups with a lower utility and less resource requirements to keep the solution feasible. This method of upgrades followed by downgrades may increase the total utility of the solution.

We modify HEU by always selecting a feasible solution (if one exists) at first without considering those infeasible ones. (In HEU, an infeasible solution may be picked at first and iterations are needed to make it feasible.) The modification can shorten the algorithm execution time. The modified algorithm WE_HEU is presented in Algorithm 1. The algorithm is used to select services for one process plan. If a user request can be matched with more than one process plans, we need to apply the algorithm to every plan and produce several executable complex services. Among them, the one with the highest utility is the final solution.

Algorithm 1. WS_HEU

Step 1: Select item ρ_i from each group i ($i = 1, 2, .., N$), such that $\rho_i = min_j\{max_\alpha\{\frac{q_{ij}^\alpha}{Q^\alpha}\}\}$; if $\forall \alpha$, $\sum_{i=1}^{N} q_{i\rho_i}^\alpha \le Q^\alpha$, use it as the initial feasible solution and proceed to *step 2* ; If no feasible solution exists, stop;

Step 2: Iteratively upgrade the current solution with another solution;
(a) For each item in the solution, find an item with a higher utility from the same group under resource constraint with the highest $\triangle a_{ij} = (q_{i\rho_i} - q_{ij}) \times \mathbb{C}/ \mid \mathbb{C} \mid$, where $q = [q^1, .., q^m]$, $\mathbb{C} = \sum_{i=1}^{N} q_{i\rho_i}$. $\mathbb{C}$ is the current resource usage;
(b) If no such item is found in group i, then select the item under resource constraint that maximizes the value gain per unit of extra aggregate resource: $\triangle p_{ij} = (\mathcal{F}_{i\rho_i} - \mathcal{F}_{ij})/ \triangle a_{ij}$;
(c) If no feasible upgrade is possible, go to *Step 3*;

Step 3: Upgrade the solution by using one upgrade followed by downgrades;

Step 3.1: Find a higher-utility item in any group with the highest value of $\triangle p_{ij}' = (\mathcal{F}_{i\rho_i} - \mathcal{F}_{ij})/ \triangle t_{ij}'$ and $\triangle t_{ij}' = (q_{i\rho_i} - q_{ij})/(\mathbb{Q} - \mathbb{C})$. $\mathbb{Q}_c = [Q^1, .., Q^m]$ indicates user's QoS requirements;
Step 3.2: Find a lower-utility item in any group with the highest value of $\triangle p_{ij}'' = (\mathcal{F}_{i\rho_i} - \mathcal{F}_{ij})/ \triangle t_{ij}''$ and $\triangle t_{ij}'' = (q_{i\rho_i} - q_{ij})/(\mathbb{C} - \mathbb{Q}_c)$ while after downgrade, the total utility is still higher than achieved in *Step 2*;
Step 3.3: If an item ρ_i' is found in *Step 3.2* and ρ_i' satisfies the resource constraint, use ρ_i' to replace ρ and go back to *Step 2*. If ρ_i' is found in *Step 3.2* but violates the resource constraint, go back to *Step 3.2* for another downgrade. If no item can be found in *Step 3.2*, the algorithm stops.

To include the network performance factor in the model, we could add the network QoS attribute (such as transmission delay) to the sender service. That is, if service $a \in S_i \rightarrow b \in S_j$ ($b = 1, 2, ...l$), the corresponding network QoS attribute can be set to $q = \frac{1}{l} \sum_{b=1}^{l} q^\alpha(a, b)$ ($\alpha = 1, ..m$), and $q_a^\alpha = q_a^\alpha + q^\alpha$. The utility of every candidate in a service class can be computed according to Definition 1 after the network attributes are included.

4.2 The Graph Algorithm

Algorithms designed for the graph model can process more than one process plans at a time to find the best solution, although they have a higher complexity than the combinatorial algorithms. We first generate a candidate graph as follows: (1) Each candidate item in the service class is represented by a node in the graph, with a benefit value and several QoS attributes; (2) If service s_i is connected to service s_j, all service levels in s_i are connected to all service levels in s_j; (3) Set the network QoS attributes of every links; (4) Add a virtual source node v_s and sink node v_d. v_s is connected to all nodes without incoming link and v_d is connected to all nodes without outgoing links. The QoS attributes of these links are set to zero; (5) Add QoS attributes of the node to its incoming link and compute the utility of every link according to Def. 1.

After these steps, we have a Directed Acyclic Graph (DAG), in which every edge has a set of QoS attributes and a utility value. A service candidate graph is shown in Figure 2. The selection problem is to find a path that produces the highest utility from source v_s to sink v_d subject to the multiple constraints $\mathbb{Q}_c = [Q^1, .., Q^m]$. This is the well-known multi-constraint optimal path problem in the graph theory. Based on the CSP algorithm designed for one QoS constraint [15], we propose the MCSP algorithm to solve the MCOP problem. Same as CSP, during the execution of MCSP, each node needs to keep several paths from the source to it.

MCSP is shown in Algorithms 2 and 3. One potential problem for MCSP is that, for every intermediate node, the number of paths a node needs to keep may be huge if none of them dominates each other. That may cause the algorithm to run very slow. In order to speed up the algorithm and reduce the space needed, we modify the MCSP algorithm by keeping only K paths on each node. This

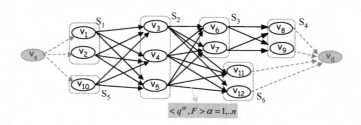

Fig. 2. Service Candidate Graph

Algorithm 2. MCSP

MCSP $(G = (V, E), v_s, v_d, \mathbb{Q}_c)$
// every node ν keeps $\mathcal{L}(\nu)$paths $p(\mu, q, \mathcal{F})$ from source to it that satisfy constraints requirements

1 Topologically sort nodes in G;
2 **for** each node μ, in topological order
3   **for** each $\nu \in adj[\mu]$
4   **if** (μ==s) **then**
5   q^α:=$q^\alpha(\mu, \nu)$ $\forall \alpha = 1, 2, ..., m$
6          $\mathcal{F}$:= $\mathcal{F}(\mu, \nu)$
7   MCSP_RELAX(μ,ν,q,$\mathcal{F}$)
8   **else** for each $p \in \mathcal{L}(\mu)$
9   q^α=$q^\alpha(p)$+$q^\alpha(\mu, \nu)$ $\forall \alpha = 1, 2, ..., m$
10         $\mathcal{F}$:= $\mathcal{F}(p) + \mathcal{F}(\mu, \nu)$
11   MCSP_RELAX(μ,ν,q,$\mathcal{F}$)

12 $p^* \leftarrow \exists p^* \in \mathcal{L}(v_d), \forall p \in \mathcal{L}(v_d), \mathcal{F}(p^*) \geq \mathcal{F}(p)$

Algorithm 3. MCSP_RELAX

MCSP_RELAX $(\mu, \nu, q, \mathcal{F})$

1   **if** ($\exists \alpha, q^\alpha > Q^\alpha$) **then return**;
2   **for** each $p \in \mathcal{L}(\nu)$
3   **if** $\mathcal{F}(p) > \mathcal{F}$ **and** $\forall \alpha$ $q^\alpha(p) \leq q^\alpha$**then return**
4   **if** $\mathcal{F}(p) < \mathcal{F}$ **and** $\forall \alpha$ $q^\alpha \leq q^\alpha(p)$ **then**
5   remove p from $\mathcal{L}(\nu)$
6   **Add** $(\mu, q, \mathcal{F})$ to $\mathcal{L}(\nu)$

---

heuristic algorithm is called MCSP-K. The K-path selection criteria are based on the nonlinear cost function concept that is used to combine the multiple constraints into one [9]. The cost function for any path p can be defined as:

$$g_\lambda(p) \triangleq (\frac{q^1(p)}{Q^1})^\lambda + (\frac{q^2(p)}{Q^2})^\lambda + ... + (\frac{q^m(p)}{Q^m})^\lambda$$

where $\lambda \geq 1$. $q^i(p)$ is the aggregated i^{th} QoS attribute for path p . As $\lambda \to \infty$, $g^*(p) \triangleq \lim_{\lambda \to \infty} g_\lambda(p)$ is equivalent to the cost function

$\xi(p) \triangleq max\{(\frac{q^1(p)}{Q^1}), (\frac{q^2(p)}{Q^2}), ..., (\frac{q^m(p)}{Q^m})\}$. The paths with K minimum g_λ/ξ values will be kept at each intermediate node. This ensures that MCSP-K will never prune out a feasible path if there exists one.

Compared to MCSP, the only difference of MCSP-K lies on the relax function, in which it needs to check the number of paths it has currently and remove the path with the maximum g_λ/ξ if the maximum number K is reached. The relax function for MCSP-K is shown in Algorithm 4. MCSP-K drastically reduces the space cost and speeds up the MCSP algorithm while keeps the result close to the optimal. The simulation results and comparison of the two algorithms are shown in the next section.

Algorithm 4. MCSP-K RELAX

MCSP-K_RELAX (μ, ν, q, $\mathcal{F}$, λ)

1   **if** ($\exists \alpha$, $q^\alpha > Q^\alpha$) **then return;**
2   **for** each $p \in \mathcal{L}(\nu)$
3   **if** $\mathcal{F}(p) > \mathcal{F}$ **and** $\forall \alpha$ $q^\alpha(p) \leq q^\alpha$**then return**
4   **if** $\mathcal{F}(p) < \mathcal{F}$ **and** $\forall \alpha$ $q^\alpha \leq q^\alpha(p)$ **then**
5   remove p from $\mathcal{L}(\nu)$
6   **Add** $(\mu, q, \mathcal{F})$ to $\mathcal{L}(\nu)$
7   **if** size($\mathcal{L}(\nu)$) $> K$ **then**
8   **if** $\lambda == \infty$ **then**
9   remove $p' \in \mathcal{L}(\nu)$, $\forall p \in \mathcal{L}(\nu)$, $\xi(p') \geq \xi(p)$
10   **else**
11   remove $p' \in \mathcal{L}(\nu)$, $\forall p \in \mathcal{L}(\nu)$, $g_\lambda(p') \geq g_\lambda(p)$

5   Performance Study

For systems with only one process plan connected in a sequential flow model, which contains N service classes and each class has l candidates, the worst-case time complexity of BBLP using the simplex method [11] is an exponential function 2^{Nl}. Using WS_HEU, suppose the number of QoS requirements is m, the worst case time complexity is $O(N^2(l-1)^2 m)$ [8]. The worst case time complexity for MCSP is $O(Nl^2 + l^{2N-1}) = O(l^{2N-1})$ and the maximum space needed in v_d to keep all feasible paths is $O(l^N)$. For MCSP-K, the maximum time complexity is $O(Nl^2 + Kl^{N-1}) = O(Kl^{N-1})$ and the maximum space needed in v_d is $O(lK)$. Although the worst case complexity of MCSP and MCSP-K is not a polynomial function, they perform very well in practice. In this section, we study their performance by simulations.

5.1   Evaluation Methodology

We have compared the performance of BBLP, WS_HEU, MCSP and MCSP-K algorithms by extensive simulations. First, we use the degree-based Internet topology generator Inet 3.0 [14] to generate a power-law random graph topology with 4000 nodes to represent the Internet topology. Then we randomly select 25 ~2500 (depends on different test cases) nodes as the service candidate nodes and 2 other nodes as source and sink. In our study, we assume an equal-degree random graph topology for the service candidate graph. For simplicity, we only consider one process plan with the sequential composition model. The number of service class and candidates in each service class involved in the process plan range from 5 to 50.

For our evaluation we also need to generate the service and network QoS attributes and utility. Suppose all QoS attributes have the summation properties. Five QoS attributes are considered for each service/link, each is associated with a randomly generated values: $q^k(\mu,\nu)$ ($k = 1, 2, 3, 4, 5$) with a uniform distribution between [1,100]. We also generate the utility $\mathcal{F}(\mu, \nu)$ of each link as a random value with a uniform distribution between [1,200]. For QoS attributes of each service candidate, a base value is first generated with a uniform distribution between [1,100]. Then an impact factor (ε) is multiplied to each service. We consider two different situations with different network impact factors: (1) large: network QoS value is comparable to services and varies; (2) small: network QoS value is less than $\frac{1}{10}$ of services. The ε is set to 2 and 200 for the two cases respectively. The utility of each service is also generated as random value with a uniform distribution between [1, 200].

For the combinatorial model, we compute the average value of QoS attributes and utility for all outgoing links of a service and add to that service. For services in the first class, it also needs to add the values of link from the source to it. For the graph model, we add the QoS attributes and the utility of the service candidate to every incoming link of it. The number of user's QoS requirements ranges from 2 to 5.

Our study includes two parts: (1) *Optimal and heuristic algorithms comparison*; (2) *The comparison of combinatorial and graph models*. The metrics we measure for Part 1 include *run time, approximation ratio* (heuristic utility vs. the optimal value), *memory usage* (for the graph approach). The metric we use for Part 2 is the *provisioning success rate, running time and utility*. We compare two heuristic algorithms: WS_HEU and MCSP-K. A composed service provisioning is said to be successful if the generated result satisfies a user's QoS requirements. From the description of MCSP-K, we know its success rate is always 1 since it never prunes out the optimal path in all intermediate steps. But for MMKP, since the network QoS attributes are only estimated, the generated results may not meet a user's requirements.

In our study, for each test case (representing different numbers of service classes and service candidates combinations), we randomly generate 10 instances and run 10 times for each instance. We then use the average value of the 100 rounds as the result for comparison.

5.2   Result Analysis

For performance evaluation about the MCSP-K and MCSP algorithms, 25 test cases are used in the simulation (Table 1). The cases are divided into 5 groups; each group has the same number of candidates. For each group, we test different numbers of service classes (from 10 to 50). There are two parameters: λ is used to compute the non-linear cost for MCSP-K and k is the number of paths each intermediate node keeps. We conducted tests on $\lambda = 5, 10, 15, 20, 25, 30, \infty$ and $k = 5, 10, 15, 20$. We find that $\lambda = \infty$ always gets a better performance (in terms of utility) than other values. So here we only report the results for $\lambda = \infty$ under different k values.

Figures 3 and 4 show the running time and memory usage comparison of MCSP-K and MCSP under 2 and 5 QoS constraints, respectively. For both k values, MCSP-K can achieve a near optimal performance (producing utility $> 90\%$ of MCSP). For the cases of 2 QoS constraints, MCSP-K is not attractive since not much space can be saved and the running time is even longer than MCSP in some cases ($k = 10, 15, 20$). The extra time is used to compute the

Table 1. Test Cases

Test Case	1	2	3	4	5	6	7	8	9	10	11	12	13	14	15	16	17	18	19	20	21	22	23	24	25
Test Group	1	1	1	1	1	2	2	2	2	2	3	3	3	3	3	4	4	4	4	4	5	5	5	5	5
No. Candidates	10	10	10	10	10	20	20	20	20	20	30	30	30	30	30	40	40	40	40	40	50	50	50	50	50
No. Service Class	10	20	30	40	50	10	20	30	40	50	10	20	30	40	50	10	20	30	40	50	10	20	30	40	50

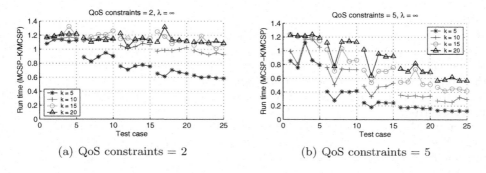

(a) QoS constraints = 2   (b) QoS constraints = 5

Fig. 3. Running time comparison (MCSP-K/MCSP)

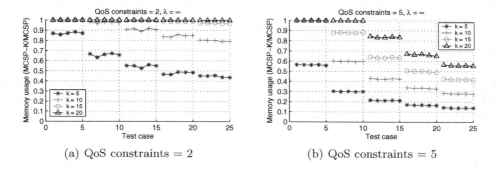

(a) QoS constraints = 2   (b) QoS constraints = 5

Fig. 4. Memory usage comparison (MCSP-K/MCSP)

non-linear cost and decide the paths to be pruned out. As the numbers of service classes and candidates in each class increase, MCSP-K outperforms MCSP. The advantage of MCSP-K is more obvious in the cases of 5 constraints. Both running time and space needed are significantly lower while the performance remains nearly optimal ($> 95\%$ for $k = 10, 15, 20$). So if the process plan contains a large number of service classes or there are many candidates in each service class, using the heuristic algorithm MCSP-K can get a close to optimal solution quickly and avoid the memory growth problem. $\lambda = \infty$ and $k = 10$ or 15 are the best setting for MCSP-K.

Figure 5 shows the running time and utility comparison between BBLP and WS_HEU algorithms when the number of QoS constraints is from 2 to 5, respectively. The number of service classes ranges from 5 to 50 and the number of

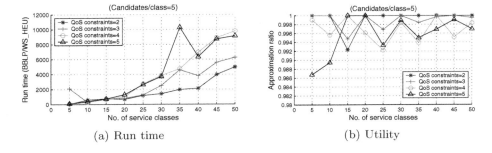

(a) Run time

(b) Utility

Fig. 5. WS_HEU vs. BBLP

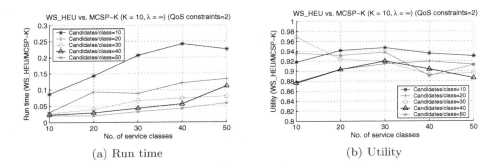

(a) Run time

(b) Utility

Fig. 6. WS_HEU vs. MCSP-K ($K = 10, \lambda = \infty$)

candidates in each service class is 5. We can see that the performance of WS_HEU is near optimal ($> 98.5\%$) while the running time is dramatically reduced.

The heuristic algorithms in both models perform very well. To see which one should be used for service composition, we test the provisioning success rate for WS_HEU under 2 and 5 constraints. (The provisioning success rate for MCSP-K is 1). When the network factor is comparable to the service, the success rate of WS_HEU is very low (0.32 for 2 constraints and 0.04 for 5 constraints). If the network impact factor is small, the success rate is high (0.96 in both cases). The reason for the low success rate lies on that MMKP does a combinatorial selection without the flow concept. Figure 6 shows the run time and utility comparison of WS_HEU and MCSP-K with $k = 10$ and $\lambda = \infty$ in the situation that the network impact factor is small. It shows that WS_HEU outperforms MCSP-K. So the combinatorial approach should be used in the situation when the network impact is small. It can also be used in the situation where the network condition for all services is uniform, such as all are on the same LAN.

From our experiments, we can see that different algorithms should be used under different system conditions. Table 2 presents a comparison of the four algorithms presented in this paper and suggests when they should be used.

Table 2. Comparison of Algorithms

	BBLP	WS_HEU	MCSP	MCSP-K
Running Time	*very slow*	*fast*	*slow*	*fast*
Memory Usage	*low*	*low*	*high*	*low*
Optimality	*optimal*	*near-optimal*	*optimal*	*near-optimal*
Network Cost	*inaccurate*	*inaccurate*	*accurate*	*accurate*
Algorithm Usage	*very small size problem, small or uniform network factor*	*large size problem, small or uniform network factor*	*small size problem, network factor is large*	*large size problem, network factor is large*

6   Conclusions

In this paper, we study the problem of complex service composition with multiple QoS constraints. Two problem models are proposed: the combinatorial model, by defining the problem as an MMKP, and the graph model, by defining the problem as an MCOP. The utility function may be defined by an extended set of system parameters, including static server information (service level), client QoS requirement (QoS constraint), dynamic server capacity (service benefit), and network factor. We have presented various algorithms, both optimal and heuristic, to compose and select services under multiple QoS constraints as well as to achieve the maximum utility. We have also compared the pros & cons between the two models and suggested their usage context. We believe the proposed models and algorithms provide a useful engineering solution to the end-to-end QoS problem for building distributed complex services.

References

1. Aggarwal, R., et al.: Constraint driven Web service composition in METEOR-S. Proc. of IEEE Conf on Service Computing (SCC'04), Shanghai, China, Sep. 2004
2. BPMI.org.: Business Process Modeling Language (BPML), Version 1.0, http://www.bpmi.org/bpml.esp, November, 2002
3. Casati, F., Ilnicki, S., Jin, L., Krishnamoorthy, V. and Shan, M.: Adaptive and dynamic service composition in eflow. Technical Report, HPL-200039, Software Tech Lab, March 2000
4. Curbera, F., Goland, Y., Klein, J., Leymann, F., Roller, D., Thatte, S. and Weerawarana, S.: Business Process Execution Language for Web services, Version 1.1. http://www-106.ibm.com/developerworks/webservices/library/ws-bpel, May 2003
5. Dan, A. et al. : Web services on demand: WSLA-driven automated management, IBM Systems Journal, Vol. 43, No. 1, 2004, pp. 136-158
6. Fu, X., Shi, W., Akkerman, A. and Karamcheti, V.: CANS: Composable, Adaptive Network Services Infrastructure. Proceeding of 3rd USENIX symposium on Internet Technologies and Systems, March 2001
7. Khan, S.: Quality Adaptation in a Multisession Multimedia System: Model, Algorithms and Architecture, Ph.D. Dissertation, Department of ECE, University of Victoria, Canada, May 1998

8. Khan, S., Li, K.F., Manning, E.G. and Akbar, M.: Solving the knapsack problem for adaptive multimedia systems, Studia Informatica Universalis, Volume 2, Number 1, September 2002, pp. 157-178
9. Korkmaz, T., Krunz, M.: Multi-Constrained Optimal Path Selection. Proceeding of 20th Joint Conf. IEEE Computer & Communications (INFOCOM 2001), 2001, pp. 834-843
10. Ludwig, H., Keller, A., Dan, A., King, R.P. and Franck, R.: Web Service Level Agreement (WSLA) Language Specification, Jan. 2003, http://www.research.ibm.com/wsla/WSLASpecV1-20030128.pdf
11. Maros, Istvn: Computational Techniques of the Simplex Method, Springer Publisher, December 2002
12. Martello, S. and Toth, P.: Algorithms for Knapsack Problems. Annals of Discrete Mathematics, 31:70-79, April 1987
13. Ponnekanti, S.R. and Fox, A.: Sword: A developer toolkit for Web service composition. In 11th World Wide Web Conference, Honolulu, Hawaii, May 2002
14. Winick, J. and Jamin, S.: Inet 3.0: Internet Topology Generator. Tech Report UM-CSE-TR-456-02 (http://irl.eecs.umich.edu/jamin/), University of Michigan, 2002
15. Yu, T. and Lin, K.J.: Service Selection Algorithms for Web Services with End-to-end QoS Constraints., Journal of Information Systems and E-Business Management, Volumn 3, Number 2, July 2005
16. Yu, T. and Lin, K.J.: A Broker-based Framework for QoS-Aware Web Service Composition, Proceeding of IEEE International Conference on e-Technology, e-Commerce and e-Service (EEE-05), Hong Kong, China, March 2005
17. Zeng, L., Benatallah, B., Dumas, M., Kalagnanam, J. and Sheng, Q.Z.: Quality Driven Web Service Composition. Proceeding of 12th International World Wide Web Conference (WWW), 2003

On Service Discovery Process Types

Peer Hasselmeyer

C&C Research Laboratories, NEC Europe Ltd.,
53757 Sankt Augustin, Germany
hasselmeyer@ccrl-nece.de

Abstract. With the growing adoption of service-oriented computing, locating services becomes increasingly commonplace. Accordingly, a large number of systems for service discovery have been developed. Although all these systems perform the same function, they do it in lots of different ways. Finding commonalities of and differences between these systems can be hard due to the lack of criteria to compare and classify various discovery schemes.

This paper identifies the processes of registration and look-up as a distinguishing feature of the various discovery systems. It describes the possible types of processes, shows how they are distributed across the lifecycles of the involved entities and classifies existing service discovery systems according to these criteria. Some hints are given on how the process-based view can help guide the selection of a particular discovery style for a problem at hand.

1 Introduction

The use of service-oriented computing and service-oriented architectures becomes increasingly prevalent. The main principle of service-oriented architectures is the loose coupling between service providers and service users. Service providers can be internal to an organization as well as third parties external to the service user's organization. In any case, the service user needs to know the service's location and communication protocol before he can access it. Accordingly, all service-oriented architectures offer some facility for locating services. Although the functionality of these facilities is always the same (i.e. finding an access point to a desired service), its realizations vary significantly among the available architectures. The systems have different methods for describing services, they offer different query possibilities, they use different transport protocols, and they have different registration and query interfaces. The multitude of these features can make comparing different architectures hard. Hidden below these features are the processes for service registration and look-up. These processes are usually not mentioned explicitly, although they make comparing and classifying different architectures possible.

This paper analyzes the processes used for registration and look-up. It is discovered that both processes have a static and a dynamic form. These forms are distinguished by how the processes are spread across the lifecycles of the

B. Benatallah, F. Casati, and P. Traverso (Eds.): ICSOC 2005, LNCS 3826, pp. 144–156, 2005.

components performing registration or look-up. It is described how the different processes affect certain aspects of systems using service discovery, e.g. application development. Existing discovery systems are classified according to their types of processes. In addition, it is shown how a process-based view can guide the selection of a discovery architecture.

The paper starts in section 2 with definitions of the terms used throughout the paper. It continues in section 3 with a detailed description of the various types of processes commonly found in service discovery systems. Section 4 describes a number of systems providing a discovery facility and classifies them according to the process types. Some advice on selecting a particular service discovery system using the proposed process-based view is given in section 5. Related work is discussed in section 6 and some conclusions are presented in section 7.

2   Definitions

There are many different understandings of the terms involved in service-oriented architectures. For example, the term "service" means different things to different people. It is therefore necessary to first define the terms used throughout this paper to avoid ambiguity.

Service. A service is a component that provides a certain set of functions to other entities over a communications network. *Service instance* is a synonym for service.

Service Type. A service type names the functionality of a service. Services are of a certain service type if they provide at least the set of functions referred to by this type. The actual description of these functions is called *service type description*. It is assumed that this is a syntactic (interface) description.

Service Description. Description of non-functional service attributes. Service descriptions can be used in registrations as well as in queries. In registrations, they provide information about actual service properties, while in queries, they state desired service properties.

Service Metadata. The service metadata includes all the information a service is registered with. It consists of the service type, the service description, and the service's endpoint.

Service Provider. An entity that operates one or more services.

Client. An entity acting in the role of a service consumer in a specific service interaction. A client can be a "real" client, i.e., it only consumes services, or a service that happens to be in the client role in this particular interaction but provides services in other interactions.

Service-Oriented Architecture. A service-oriented architecture (SOA) is based on services as the main entities. Services provide certain functions to other entities. These entities can be pure clients or services themselves. Services and their functions are discovered using a service registry.

Service Discovery. The process of finding services and their endpoints. This includes registration and look-up.

Endpoint. A communication port at which a service can be contacted. Services might offer multiple endpoints.

Service Registry (often just called *registry*). A service that provides references to other services. It accepts requests for registration from services (or other entities that act on behalf of a service) and relays registration information on demand to clients.

Registration. Registries keep records of available services. The resources that such a record consumes at a registry are called a registration. Also, the process of having registries store information about a service is called registration.

Look-up. The process of mapping queries to service endpoints. Clients looking for certain services send queries to service registries. The queries contain some description of what kind of service clients are looking for. Registries return a set of available services matching the query. Services are represented by their endpoints.

3   Discovery Processes

Service discovery consists of two main processes: the registration process and the look-up process. Registration is used by services or their operators to announce service availability. Look-up is used by clients to find the endpoints of needed services.

Different service discovery architectures employ different processes for registration and look-up. These will be described in the following sections. The method for distinguishing them involves looking at how the individual steps in the process are allocated to the stages in the lifecycles of the entities executing the process. The registration process is executed by services, the relevant lifecycles therefore are the ones of the services. The look-up process is executed by clients, the relevant lifecycles therefore are the ones of the clients. As both services and clients are software components, they follow a software lifecycle. The stages of that lifecycle that are relevant to the registration and look-up processes are the development, the deployment, the operation, and the undeployment phases.

3.1   Registration Process

The basic lifecycle of a registration is rather simple. The registry creates a registration when a service is registered. From that point on, the registry includes the registered data in responses to matching queries. The registration is deleted when a service is removed from a registry.

As registrations belong to registries, their lifecycles can be observed at registries. The process for performing registration is executed by services (or their providers), though. For the registration process, only the lifecycle of the associated service is relevant. This is the lifecycle considered here. Two different types of service registration processes can be identified: a static and a dynamic type. Figure 1 presents an overview of these two types. Interactions with the registry are shown as rounded rectangles while supplied information is shown as bubbles.

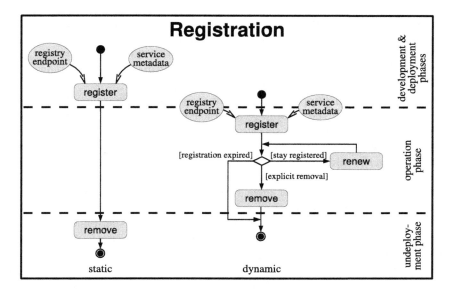

Fig. 1. Registration Process Types

Static Registration Process Type. In systems using static registrations, services are registered once and stay registered for an extended period of time. Registration and removal are usually initiated by human staff members of the service's provider. Registrations are rarely updated. Different parts of the service's metadata are supplied at different stages of the service's lifecycle. The service type is usually encoded in the implementation, i.e., it is supplied during the development phase. The service endpoint is only known at deployment time and is therefore supplied in the deployment phase. Some default values for the service description and the service registry's endpoint can be supplied in the development phase, but they will likely be modified during the deployment phase.

The actual registration of a service following a static process type happens when it is initially deployed. The registration is removed when the service is discontinued. Between registration and removal no communication is going on between the service (or its provider) and the registry. The exception to this rule is a possible maintenance phase in which the service's metadata is changed. Obviously, the new metadata needs to be supplied to the registry which involves communication between the service (provider) and the registry. A consequence of the absence of communication is that static registrations do not contain any current information, e.g. about the availability of services.

Dynamic Registration Process Type. Systems supporting a dynamic registration process type usually employ automated methods for service registration. Services or their supporting middleware initiate service registration upon startup. Human intervention is not needed. Registries use soft-state (lease-based) registrations [3]. Such registrations are valid for only a limited amount of time, most commonly minutes to hours. To stay registered, services must periodically extend the lifetime of their registrations. Upon expiration, registrations are automatically removed from the registry. The system is therefore automatically cleaned from stale registrations and can be considered self-managing. The manual removal of services is nevertheless possible as well.

Service metadata is again supplied at different stages in the lifecycle. Service type information is handled the same way as in the static case – it is supplied during the development phase. The service description can be supplied in the development, the deployment, and, contrary to the static case, in the operation phase. Depending on the middleware used, the service endpoint is either supplied at deployment time or run-time. With technologies like CORBA (Common Object Request Broker Architecture) or Java RMI (Remote Method Invocation), the endpoint will be supplied at run-time as it can change across restarts. Using web service technologies, the endpoint may be supplied during the deployment phase as it rarely changes. The registry location can, as in the static case, be supplied during the deployment phase. Alternatively, as the actual registration happens during the operation phase, supplying the registry location can be postponed to that phase. One popular solution for this is to use a multicast scheme to discover the registry location at run-time.

3.2   Look-Up Process

Just as service registrations can be static or dynamic, so can be service look-up process types. The two different types are shown in figure 2. Although the figure

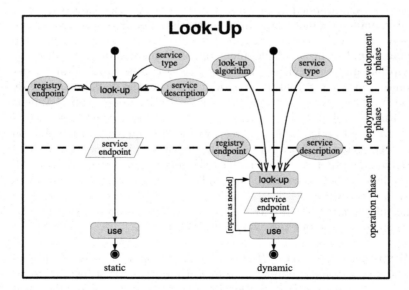

Fig. 2. Look-up Processes

shows look-up as a single step, it might actually consist of multiple steps, e.g. if some iterative method to slowly narrow down the selection is used. The look-up method is independent of the use of a static or a dynamic look-up process type.

Static Look-Up Process Type. In a static environment it is common practice to look up services during the application development phase and put their locations in the code. Alternatively, a configuration file can be used and the look-up process can be moved to the deployment phase. In this case, only the service type is supplied during the development stage. The service description (i.e. the query) as well as the registry's endpoint only need to be known during the deployment phase. In both cases, the registry is not accessed at application run-time.

Dynamic Look-Up Process Type. In a dynamic system, services are assumed to be volatile and those available during the development or deployment phases might not exist during the operation phase. Applications in dynamic environments therefore usually perform look-up at run-time to find currently available services and their endpoints. Information supplied during the development phase are the service type and the look-up algorithm. This algorithm is rather simple in "traditional" discovery systems, but is an important part of the discovery process in content addressable networks [8].

The registry endpoint and the service description can be supplied during the deployment or the operation phase. During deployment, this information goes into some configuration file. If the endpoint is supplied at run-time, it can be retrieved via some multicast scheme or calculated with the help of the look-up algorithm. The service description might be affected by user input and might therefore only be available at run-time.

The choice of a static or dynamic look-up process type is not directly related to the choice of a particular registration process type. A dynamic look-up style can be used in conjunction with a static registry. A static look-up style is ill-suited for a dynamic registry, though, as service information is expected to change during the lifetime of the service client. It is therefore common to bundle static look-up with static registration and dynamic look-up with dynamic registration.

3.3   Foreknowledge

To perform service registration or look-up, the endpoint of the registry needs to be known. This information is called "foreknowledge" in [10]. Such information is needed by all entities using the service registry, i.e. services as well as clients. It is important to note that the information does not need to be available explicitly. In content addressable networks the location of the registry can be derived from registration metadata and look-up queries at run-time. The foreknowledge in this case is embedded in the queries or the service metadata and the algorithm mapping that information to the registry location. Another important observation is the fact that the foreknowledge does not need to exist in all phases of the registration and look-up lifecycles. The knowledge needed and the lifecycle phase in which it is supplied are shown in Figures 1 and 2 in the form of bubbles. The foreknowledge needed does not depend on whether a process' type is static or dynamic. Only the lifecycle phase in which it is used varies with the process type.

In a system using static registrations information about the registry is only needed at development or deployment time. It is therefore sufficient that the human developer or deployer has access to the registry's endpoint information. As that data is not needed at run-time, it is not kept anywhere in a running client.

In a dynamic system, information on the registry's endpoint must be available at run-time. The required information can be supplied in different ways. It could for example be read from some configuration file. A multicast scheme can be employed when a local registry is used thereby reducing configuration effort to a minimum.

3.4   Process Type Implications

The adoption of a particular type of process influences the functionality of registries, the development of entities using discovery, and the performance of a service-oriented system as a whole.

Functionality. The functionality of a registry depends on the registration style. In the dynamic case, it must support soft-state registrations and the associated functionality which is not needed in the static case. Furthermore, lifetime extensions happen quite frequently and those changes to the registration database need to be accommodated. In systems using a static registration process type, registrations have to be made persistent as they occur only once. For systems using a dynamic registration process type it is okay to forget all the registrations every once in a while as services will eventually re-register.

Implementation. Entities that are using service discovery, i.e., services performing registration and clients using look-up, are implemented in different ways depending on the type of the registration and look-up processes. When using static registrations, services do not need to care about the actual registration as this is supposed to be done by human operators before the service's operation phase. In systems using dynamic registrations, services must register at run-time and need to take care of their registrations. This job can be delegated to the infrastructure, though. In that case, services do not need to care about registrations and their renewal. In fact, they do not even need to be aware of what kind of registration process is used.

The situation is a bit different for look-ups. There is a difference in the program logic depending on when look-up is performed. If a static look-up process type is adopted, the client code does not need to contact the registry at run-time. With a dynamic look-up process type, though, some communication with the registry has to occur at run-time. The program code therefore needs to be different depending on the look-up type. It is nevertheless possible to always use code that assumes a dynamic look-up style and let the infrastructure map this to a static environment.

Performance. The registration and look-up process types also affect the performance of systems using service discovery. Obviously, a static system has a better run-time performance as no communication between services or clients and the registry has to occur during the operation phase. Depending on what kind of discovery technique is used, the run-time penalty of dynamic look-up can be significant. On the other hand, using dynamic registration and look-up improves a system's failure resilience. If look-ups follow a static process type, the disappearance of an endpoint to a particular service renders all clients unusable. A dynamic look-up process type allows this failure to be masked by being able to switch over to other instances/endpoints of services.

4   Classifying Discovery Systems

This section briefly describes a number of well-known service discovery systems. The main part of each description deals with registration and look-up properties. Each system is classified according to its use of static or dynamic registration and look-up process types. The results of the analysis are shown in Figure 3.

4.1   UDDI

The Universal Description, Discovery and Integration (UDDI) specification [7] is the most well-known service discovery standard for the web services world. It defines a centralized registry service, the interface to access it, and a data model to describe services. The UDDI registry is modeled after the telephone book. It lists companies ("white pages") and the services that they provide ("yellow pages"). Sticking to the telephone book analogy, data in UDDI registries is stored

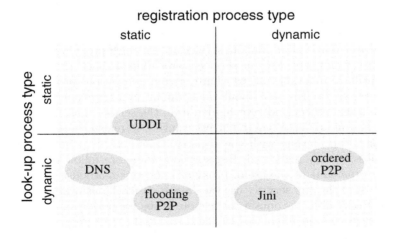

Fig. 3. Classification of Popular Service Discovery Systems

once and stays in them until it is actively removed. UDDI registries obviously employ a static registration lifecycle and therefore follow a static registration process type.

Look-up in UDDI registries usually follows a static process type as well. The structure of the data in the directory makes drill-down operations a convenient way of finding a needed service. A common approach to finding services in UDDI registries is looking at the list of companies, finding a few that are trusted and presumably offer the needed service, have a look at their service offers, and then choose one of them. As trust is a complicated concept for machines, the described process is always done by human beings. Usually, the developer of a service client is looking for an appropriate service, not the deployer. The reason for this is the lack of standardized interfaces that would make exchange of services a simple configuration option. Currently, more often than not, the program code needs to be modified to accommodate a different service provider.

Although dynamically exchanging a service provider in a web-service-based world is currently not widely practiced, performing look-up at run-time is still a sensible option. In this case, it is not used to make the choice of a service provider configurable or dynamic, it is used to automate locating the current endpoint of a well-known service of a well-known provider. A service client would perform a look-up with a predefined query that returns the current endpoint of the needed service. With this scheme, a provider can change the location of his services without explicitly telling his clients. Dynamic look-up can increase the looseness of the coupling between service provider and service client.

Because UDDI-based systems can work with both static and dynamic look-up, the system appears in both sections with a tendency towards the static side.

4.2   Jini

Jini [9] is a Java-based infrastructure for handling service discovery. Registries can be statically configured, or found at run-time via a multicast-based protocol. Registrations contain service descriptions and, instead of the endpoint of a service, a Java object that enables remote service access. Such proxy objects are stored at the registry and copied to the service user's address space at run-time. There, they adapt local function calls to whatever communications protocol the associated service uses. Information about the endpoint of a service is therefore stored inside the proxy object and kept hidden from the service user.

Registrations in Jini are lease-based. Clients wanting to register a service negotiate the registration lifetime with the registry. Leases need to be renewed in time for services to stay registered. Registrations therefore follow a strictly dynamic process type. Due to the use of proxy objects, this method is the only viable option. Most of the Jini services use the Java RMI mechanisms for remote procedure calls. Proxy objects contain the remote stubs for performing invocations. These in turn contain references to the associated server object. As the server object might change with every restart of the server, previously handed out references become invalid. Registration data therefore needs to be updated at the registry. With an automated update system (as used with dynamic registrations), this is no problem. Performing updates by hand is rather tedious, though. A static model is therefore not an optimal solution.

Look-ups also follow a dynamic process type, basically for the same reason why registrations are dynamic. Remote object references may change frequently. Embedding fixed, static references in client code is no option. In addition to that, Jini transfers around proxy objects. These consist of data (e.g. object references) and code. Just as the data changes, the code might change as well. As the code is supplied by the service provider, it is impractical to statically embed that code in service clients.

4.3   DNS

The Domain Name System (DNS) [6] is the most commonly used method for resolving human-readable internet host names. The DNS system translates those names to machine-understandable Internet Protocol (IP) addresses. DNS can store mappings for different types of services, e.g. for mail relays. It can therefore be considered a service discovery system.

The assumption for the DNS is that internet host names and the corresponding addresses do not change frequently. As a result, registrations follow a static process type. New internet host and domain names are stored at designated name servers. The mapping stays at the name server until it is removed.

DNS look-ups follow a dynamic process type. To find a host, clients send a query to the DNS sub-system on the local host. Queries that cannot be answered locally are passed on to DNS servers one level up in the hierarchy. The path followed by a query is statically configured by the administrators of the involved DNS servers. The location information of the registry (the next DNS server) is therefore configured for a host, not an individual client.

4.4   Peer-to-Peer Systems

Peer-to-peer (P2P) systems are dynamic networks of entities that cooperate to provide certain services to participants. At present, P2P system are aimed mostly at locating content, usually media files, but the same concepts can be used to locate arbitrary services. As the set of participants in a P2P system is dynamic, the set of offered services (or content) is dynamic as well. Searching (i.e. look-up) in P2P systems therefore always follows a dynamic process type.

Regarding registrations, two different kinds of peer-to-peer systems can be distinguished. Most of the P2P systems popular today employ a flooding search approach. They send queries to all (or at least a large subset of) the service providers. Service providers also act as registries. Content files are registered locally and they are usually registered implicitly by putting them in specific places on the local file system. They are unregistered by removing the files from that location. It is therefore a registration process of the static type.

As flooding is not a scalable query mechanism, a second type of P2P systems uses a controlled search approach. Systems of this type designate responsibility for a subset of the whole search space to certain nodes in the system. A responsible node can be found at a predictable location by applying a well-known algorithm to the service's metadata. An example of such a system is described in [2]. In such systems, all nodes act as registries, but each service is registered with just a (small) subset of them. Registrations are constrained in the temporal domain and therefore need to be renewed. This is necessary because not only the set of service providers (and with it, the set of services) changes, but so does the set of registries and therefore the set of registries responsible for a specific service. Registrations therefore follow a dynamic process type.

5 Architecture Selection

Besides offering a method for classification, a process-based viewpoint can also guide the selection of a particular discovery architecture for a given problem. For selecting a discovery system, a large number of different criteria exist, including description capabilities, performance, scalability, supported platforms, protocols used, etc. Most of these are of a low-level, technical nature. The process-based viewpoint proposed here is on a higher level of abstraction, working more on the architectural level than the implementation level.

The guidelines given here are not necessarily the most important ones. Depending on the circumstances in which a discovery system is to be used, different criteria have different priorities. Nevertheless, we think that looking at discovery process types gives a hint on what kind of discovery system is suitable to a given problem. As it works on a comparatively high level of abstraction, it might actually be the first criterion to consider.

When thinking of discovery, the processes for registration and look-up are not a natural starting point. And indeed, they are not the first thing to look at, as they only exist in conjunction with the entities that enact them, i.e., the services and clients.

Therefore, to select a discovery architecture, one should first analyze the services that are to be found by discovery. If these services are rather volatile, their registrations are as well. Dynamic process types for registration and look-up are therefore appropriate. A matching service discovery system should be chosen.

If the set of services is small and the services' metadata is static, a system using static registrations is sufficient. Whether to use a static or dynamic look-up process type in this case is a delicate trade-off. Static look-ups require some manual configuration effort when services migrate. Dynamic look-ups need some additional infrastructure that usually causes some initial set-up costs. The decision therefore depends on the estimate of how frequently service registrations change and thereby cause additional configuration costs.

It is important to note that even if individual services are rather static, but there is a large set of services, the set as a whole becomes volatile, because some changes in the set of services and their metadata always occur. Such a system would benefit from at least a dynamic look-up style. Making registrations dynamic can be a good idea as well, because static registrations become stale eventually and their removal or update is often forgotten [5].

6   Related Work

There is a host of literature that compares various discovery systems. Most of this literature, e.g. [1, 4], compares systems primarily aimed at ubiquitous computing, especially SLP, UPnP, Bluetooth, and Jini. Among the criteria used for distinction are the network protocol used for communication, the type of service description, and the functionality of the systems. None of these comparisons deal with higher level abstractions or give guidance on where to use which architecture.

To the knowledge of the author, only one paper [10] compares service discovery systems on a more abstract level. Vanthournout et al. introduce a taxonomy of discovery systems distinguishing them by design aspects. They analyze discovery systems with respect to their structure, their foreknowledge, their registration behavior, their query routing, the supported resources, and resource naming. Although these represent a large set of criteria, the registration and look-up processes are neither mentioned nor evaluated. As described here, those processes influence the architecture of service discovery systems as well as the design of applications. In fact, some of the above mentioned design aspects are influenced by the processes. Namely, these are the foreknowledge, the registration behavior, and the supported resources.

7   Conclusion

In this paper, we have identified the registration and look-up processes as distinguishing aspects of service discovery systems. Registration as well as look-up can be either static or dynamic. A particular choice for either the registration or the look-up process type does not influence the choice of the other process type. The only caveat is that a static look-up process type does not match a dynamic registration scheme.

We showed that individual registration and look-up process steps are distributed differently across component lifecycle phases depending on the type of process used. We classified a number of well-known discovery architectures according to the process-based view and showed that for each viable combination of processes an examplar exists. We also described how the choice of a particular process type influences the functionality of the registry, the implementation of the entities, the performance of the system as a whole, and how foreknowledge is spread across the lifecycle phases.

We hope that the presented work makes developers adopting service-oriented architectures aware of the discovery processes and their interaction with component lifecycles. We think that a classification according to process types facilitates the selection of a particular style of discovery and therefore the selection of a particular discovery architecture.

Acknowledgements

This work has been supported by the NextGRID project and has been partly funded by the European Commission's IST activity of the 6th Framework Programme under contract number 511563. This paper expresses the opinions of the author and not necessarily those of the European Commission. The European Commission is not liable for any use that may be made of the information contained in this paper.

References

1. Christian Bettstetter and Cristoph Renner. A Comparison of Service Discovery Protocols and Implementation of the Service Location Protocol. In: Proceedings EUNICE Open European Summer School, Twente, Netherlands, September 2000.
2. Jun Gao and Peter Steenkiste. Design and Evaluation of a Distributed Scalable Content Discovery System. Journal on Selected Areas in Communications, 22(1):54–66, January 2004.
3. Cary G. Gray and David R. Cheriton. Leases: An Efficient Fault-Tolerant Mechanism for Distributed File Cache Consistency. In: Proceedings of the 12th ACM Symposium on Operating System Principles, pages 202–210, December 1989.
4. Sumi Helal. Standards for Service Discovery and Delivery. IEEE Pervasive Computing, 1(3):95–100, July 2002.
5. Mike Clark. UDDI – The Weather Report, November 2001. http://www.webservicesarchitect.com/content/articles/clark04.asp
6. Paul V. Mockapetris. Domain Names - Concepts and Facilities, November 1987. Internet RFC 1034.
7. OASIS Open. UDDI Version 3.0.2, October 2004. http://www.oasis-open.org/committees/uddi-spec/doc/spec/v3/uddi-v3.0.2-20041019.htm.
8. Sylvia Ratnasamy, Paul Francis, Mark Handley, Richard Karp, and Scott Schenker. A Scalable Content-Addressable Network. In: Proceedings of the 2001 Conference on Applications, Technologies, Architectures, and Protocols for Computer Communications (SIGCOMM 2001), pages 161–172, August 2001.
9. Sun Microsystems Inc. Jini Architecture Specification – Version 2.0, June 2003. http://www.sun.com/software/jini/specs/jini2_0.pdf.
10. Koen Vanthournout, Geert Deconinck, and Ronnie Belmans. A Taxonomy for Resource Discovery. Personal and Ubiquitous Computing Journal, 9(2):81–89, February 2005.

SPiDeR: P2P-Based Web Service Discovery*

Ozgur D. Sahin, Cagdas E. Gerede, Divyakant Agrawal,
Amr El Abbadi, Oscar Ibarra, and Jianwen Su

Department of Computer Science,
University of California at Santa Barbara, Santa Barbara, CA 93106
{odsahin, gerede, agrawal, amr, ibarra, su}@cs.ucsb.edu

Abstract. In this paper, we describe SPiDeR, a peer-to-peer (P2P) based framework that supports a variety of Web service discovery operations. SPiDeR organizes the service providers into a structured P2P overlay and allows them to advertise and lookup services in a completely decentralized and dynamic manner. It supports three different kinds of search operations: For advertising and locating services, service providers can use keywords extracted from service descriptions (*keyword-based search*), categories from a global ontology (*ontology-based search*), and/or paths from the service automaton (*behavior-based search*). The users can also rate the quality of the services they use. The ratings are accumulated within the system so that users can query for the quality ratings of the discovered services. Finally, we present the performance of SPiDeR in terms of routing using a simulator.

1 Introduction

The adoption and evolution of the Web services technology continue to happen in many different domains from business environments to scientific applications. This technology promises to enable dynamic integration and interaction of heterogeneous software artifacts, and thereby, to facilitate fast and efficient cooperation among the entities in cooperative environments. Lately, there has been a lot of attention drawn to this promising technology from both industry and academia and it has been supported with various emerging standards and proposals such as SOAP[1], WSDL[2], BPEL[3], and OWL-S[4]; accompanying technologies such as IBM's Web Sphere, Microsoft's .NET, and Sun's J2EE; and several research efforts (see recent conferences such as [5, 6, 7, 8]).

Web services are "software applications identified by a URI, whose interfaces and bindings are capable of being defined, described, and discovered as XML artifacts. A Web service supports direct interactions with other software agents using XML-based messages exchanged via Internet-based protocols"[9]. The main research challenges services oriented computing poses include automated composition, discovery, invocation, monitoring, validation and verification[10]. Service discovery, in particular, refers to the problem of how to search for and locate

---

* This research was supported in parts by NSF grants CNF 04-23336 and IIS 02-23022.

B. Benatallah, F. Casati, and P. Traverso (Eds.): ICSOC 2005, LNCS 3826, pp. 157–169, 2005.

services, the descriptions of which are usually considered lying in well-defined service repositories.

Recently, a substantial progress has been done in this area thanks to several research and industrial efforts including UDDI registries [11, 12], similarity search [13], the query languages and indexing efforts [14, 15, 16], peer-to-peer (P2P) discovery techniques [17, 18, 19, 20, 21], semantic web approaches and ontological matching [22, 23]. These solutions, however, are typically limited for 2 reasons:

1. They are usually **centralized** where there is a single central server (e.g., UDDI registry) that keeps track of all available services. Centralized approach has well-known limitations. It is not scalable since the server has to keep information about all services and answer all queries. It is not fault tolerant because the server is a single point of failure and if the server goes down, the whole service discovery mechanism becomes unusable.
2. They usually offer limited search capabilities. There are different techniques to increase the accuracy of service discovery including functional matching (what a service does), behavioral matching (how a service performs), semantic matching (the underlying semantics of a service) and ontological matching (how a service relates to other services). Each of these provides a different metric to measure the relevance among different services and therefore, each one is important. Many existing approaches, on the other hand, concentrate on a single one or a small subset of these techniques.

In this paper, we address above issues by introducing SPiDeR, a P2P based Web service discovery framework that supports a rich set of search operations. A subset of the participating service providers (those that have good resources) are dynamically assigned as super peers and organized into a structured P2P system. Due to its P2P based design, SPiDeR distributes the tasks of indexing available services and resolving service lookups among the participants, thus providing decentralization, scalability, dynamicity, and fault tolerance. It supports 3 different types of search operations based on keywords, global service ontology, and service behavior. It also has a reputation system component for assessing the quality of the services based on the experiences of other services. The ratings given to the services are stored in the system so that users can lookup for service quality ratings when deciding which of the discovered services to use.

The rest of the paper is organized as follows. The related work is surveyed in Section 2. Section 3 introduces SPiDeR, a P2P based distributed Web service discovery framework. Section 4 describes how the different types of discovery operations (keyword-based search, ontology-based search, and behavior-based search) are supported in the framework. The quality rating scheme that enables the ranking of discovered Web services is also explained in that section. In Section 5, dynamic peer operations are discussed in detail. Those include installing and refreshing service advertisements, performing composite lookups, and indexing at the super peers. Additionally, an evaluation of SPiDeR in terms of routing performance using a simulator is presented in Section 5.4. Finally, the last section concludes the paper and outlines the future work.

2   Related Work

P2P Systems: P2P systems are a popular paradigm for exchanging data in a decentralized manner. They distribute the data and load among the peers and thus appear as a good alternative to the centralized systems. Early P2P systems, such as Napster [24] and Gnutella [25], are mainly used for file sharing. These systems are referred to as *unstructured P2P systems* [26] since the overlay network is constructed in a random manner and the data can be anywhere in the system. As a result, search and routing in these systems tend to be inefficient. *Structured P2P systems*, on the other hand, impose a certain structure on the overlay network and control the placement of data. These systems provide desirable properties such as scalability, fault tolerance, and dynamic peer insertion and departure. For example, *Distributed Hash Tables (DHTs)* [27, 28, 29, 30] partition a logical space among the peers and assign each object to a peer dynamically by hashing the object's key onto the logical space. DHTs offer efficient routing and exact key lookups, which are logarithmic or sublinear in the number of peers.

Web Service Discovery: There are several proposals to increase the accuracy and efficiency of service discovery mechanisms. [13] introduces Woogle, a similarity search technique based on clustering the services according to the information gathered from their WSDL documents. It is a centralized approach and do not allow behavioral search. In [17], the authors propose a behavioral search mechanism on a P2P architecture where the service behaviors are represented as finite state automata and the services are indexed in the P2P system with keys extracted from their service automata. It only provides behavior-based search mechanism, but not the others.

SPiDeR shares similarities with [14, 15, 16]. In [14], services are represented as finite state machines which are then transformed into a form that can be indexed for efficient matching. [15] proposes an integrated directory system and a query language. The matching and ranking of the services are done via matching and ranking functions which can be customized by the users. In [16], the services are represented as message-based guarded finite state machines and behavioral signatures are used for discovering relevant services. The behavioral signatures are represented using temporal logic statements. All three approaches mentioned above consider a centralized index structure, whereas in our approach, the index is distributed over a structured P2P system.

SPiDeR also has architectural similarities with [18, 19, 20, 21]. [18] uses DAML-S (previous version of OWL-S) for service representation and uses Gnutella P2P protocol for service discovery. [19] proposes a federation of service registries in a decentralized fashion where federations represent service groups of similar interests. Similarly, [20] and [21] consider a P2P infrastructure. While [20] uses ontologies for publishing and querying purposes, [21] describes each Web service with a set of keywords and then map the corresponding index to a DHT using Space Filling Curves. SPiDeR differs from these proposals as it can also consider the functionality and process behavior of services during discovery and supports quality rating lookups.

In terms of use of ontologies and semantic matching, we also would like to mention [22] and [23]. In [22], the authors integrate semantics and ontological matching via domain-independent and domain-specific ontologies, and propose an indexing method, namely attribute hashing. In [23], a federated registry architecture is proposed where ontologies are to provide a domain-based classification of the registries.

3   SPiDeR Overview

SPiDeR allows distributed Web service discovery over a P2P system and supports a variety of different lookup operations (those operations will be discussed in Section 4). It organizes the participants into a super-peer based structured P2P overlay and allows them to advertise their own services as well as search for other available services.[1] Chord [28] is used as the underlying P2P overlay due to its simplicity and robustness [31], though any other DHT could have been used instead. In this section we briefly introduce the Chord system and then describe the super-peer based architecture of SPiDeR.

3.1   Chord

Chord [28] is a P2P system that implements a DHT. It uses an m-bit identifier ring, $[0, 2^m - 1]$, for routing and locating objects. Both the objects and the peers in the system are assigned m-bit keys through a uniform hash function and mapped to the identifier ring. An object is stored at the peer following it on the ring, i.e., its *successor*. Figure 1 depicts a 4-bit Chord system with 5 peers. It shows the peers that are responsible for a set of keys with different IDs. For example, key 15 is assigned to its successor P_0, which is the first peer after ID 15 on the Chord ring in clockwise direction.

Routing and Lookup: Each peer maintains a finger table for efficient routing. The finger table of a peer contains the IP addresses and Chord identifiers of $O(logN)$ other peers, i.e., its neighbors, that are at exponentially increasing distances from the peer on the identifier ring, where N is the number of peers in the system. The finger table for peer $P3$ is shown in Figure 1. Peers periodically exchange *refresh* messages with their neighbors to keep their finger tables up to date. Chord is designed for very efficient exact-key lookups. A lookup request is delivered to its destination via $O(logN)$ hops. At each hop, the request is forwarded to a peer from the finger table whose identifier most immediately precedes the destination point. In Figure 1, peer $P3$'s request for key 15 is routed through $P13$ to 15's successor $P0$, by following the finger pointers.

Peer Join and Departure: Chord is a dynamic system where peers constantly join and leave the system. When a new peer wants to join, it is assigned an identifier and it sends a join request toward this identifier through an existing

---

[1]   In the rest of the paper, the terms *participants* and *peers* will be used interchangeably.

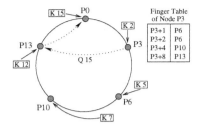

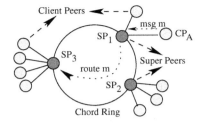

Fig. 1. 4-bit Chord System   **Fig. 2.** Architecture of SPiDeR

peer. Thus the new peer locates its successor, from which it obtains the keys it is responsible for. The affected finger tables are then updated accordingly. Similarly, upon departure of a peer, its keys are assigned to its successor and the affected finger tables are updated.

3.2 SPiDeR Architecture

Chord supports efficient exact key lookups. However dynamic peer join and departure might be costly due to finger table updates and key transfers. Additionally, Chord does not consider the heterogeneity of the peers and treats each peer equally. Thus SPiDeR uses a super peer based overlay built on top of Chord. Instead of inserting all participants into the Chord ring, only a subset of the participants are assigned as *super peers* and join the Chord ring. The super peers are selected among the peers that have good resources such as high availability, high computing capacity, etc. In this architecture, the super peers do all the indexing and query routing. The remaining peers are called the *client peers* and they use the system by connecting to a super peer. Each client peer forwards its requests to its super peer, which processes the requests on its behalf.

The super peer overlay can be maintained dynamically without any central control [32]. Each new peer joins the system as a client peer (except the initial peer starting the system). Whenever a new super peer is required (e.g., an existing super peer leaves or gets overloaded), a super peer assigns one of its client peers with good resources as a new super peer. The super peer based architecture of SPiDeR provides the following advantages:

- Peer capabilities vary widely in terms of computing/storage resources, bandwidth and availability/reliability. Peers with lots of resources will be designated as super peers and will do all the message routing and indexing. Client peers, on the other hand, just ask queries and answer service requests.
- With less peers on the Chord ring, both the routing cost and join/leave overhead are less. Client peers can join (leave) the system by simply connecting to (disconnecting from) their super peers. Thus the system is more resilient to high churn (frequent peer joins and departures).

Figure 2 depicts the architecture of SPiDeR. Note that the central UDDI registry is replaced with the Chord ring in SPiDeR. Any peer in Figure 2 (super or client) can be offering services, which are indexed within Chord by super peers. Similarly, the lookup requests are resolved in a decentralized manner by routing them to the corresponding super peer.

4   Distributed Discovery

SPiDeR organizes service providers into a structured P2P overlay that efficiently supports exact key lookups. In this section we will discuss how this overlay is used to support different types of discovery operations.

4.1   Web Service Description

Web services are software artifacts that consist of a set of operations. There are several competing and complementary languages to describe Web services such as WSDL[2], BPEL[3], OWL-S[4], WSDL-S[33], SWSL[34], and WSML[35]. Among these, WSDL defines the service interface by specifying the following:

- **Service Information:** Contains the address, name and the textual description of the service.
- **Operation Information:** Contains the name and the description of each operation.
- **Input/Output Information:** Defines the names and the types of the operation parameters.

The interface of a service describes how to access and invoke a service. WSDL-S extends WSDL by supporting inline semantic annotation. The service behavior (choreography), on the other hand, defines how to interact with the service, i.e., the possible interaction sequences the service can go through during a communication with other parties. BPEL, OWL-S, SWSL, and WSML are some examples of complimentary languages to capture service behavior.

4.2   Keyword-Based Search

The first discovery method supported by SPiDeR is keyword search. In this method, each service is advertised in the system with a set of keywords. Interested parties can then locate the services they are looking for by querying the system with keywords. When keyword-based search is used, all services that are advertised for the specified keyword will be returned.

Extracting Keywords: The keywords associated with a service can be extracted from its description, e.g., its WSDL document. Popular information retrieval tools such as Smart [36] can be used to automatically extract the tokens from the description file. These tools can also be configured to remove stop words and do stemming. The tokens that appear in *name* and *description* fields can then be used as keywords. For more accuracy during keyword extraction from

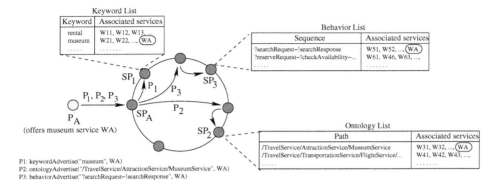

Fig. 3. Advertising Services

tokens, a thesaurus can be used or common naming conventions can be considered. A detailed discussion of extracting keywords from service description files can be found in [22].

Advertising Services: Once the keywords for advertising a service are determined, the peer offering the service sends a *keywordAdvertise* message into the system for each keyword. This message contains the keyword and the necessary information to contact the service (i.e., the address of the service). The keyword string is used as the key, so that the super peer processing the message hashes the keyword to determine its location on the Chord ring. The message is then routed and the corresponding super peer stores the service in its keyword list. For example, in Figure 3, peer P_A advertises its service W_A for keyword *museum* by sending `keywordAdvertise('museum',`W_A`)` message `P1` to its super peer SP_A. The message is then routed to SP_1, which is responsible for the key *"museum"*. SP_1 stores the association $(museum, WA)$ in its keyword list.

Locating Services: When the system is queried for a keyword, the message is routed to the corresponding super peer P_S by hashing the keyword. P_S then searches its keyword list and returns all matching services to the querying peer.

4.3 Ontology-Based Search

Another important search operation is category search, where the user wants to find all services within a certain category.

Common Ontology: SPiDeR assumes that there is a common domain ontology that is known by all peers in the system. This can be achieved by having each new peer download the ontology from the peer it contacts during join. This ontology identifies all possible categories for which the services can be advertised in the system. Figure 4 shows an example domain ontology for a system composed of travel related services.

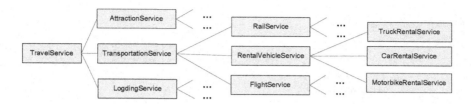

Fig. 4. Example Domain Ontology

Advertising Services: Service providers can advertise their services for each related category from the domain ontology. For each selected category, an *ontologyAdvertise* message is sent to the system. In this case, the path from the root to the corresponding node in the domain ontology is used as the key to determine the message destination. The message is routed to the super peer responsible for the path string. That peer then stores the corresponding information in its ontology list (see advertise message P2 in Figure 3 for an example).

Locating Services: When ontology-based search is used, the path string is hashed and the corresponding super peer returns all matching services from its ontology list to the querying peer.

4.4   Behavior-Based Search

Considering Web services as simple method invocations might not be sufficient in some cases. Web services can interact with other services, send and receive messages, and perform a set of activities. Such service behaviors can be defined by means of, for instance, process flow languages like BPEL. When this information is available, it can be used to improve the accuracy of service discovery by allowing users to specify the desired service behavior. For instance, Figure 5 illustrates a travel service. The automaton describes the message exchanges between the service and a user. If we examine the service behavior, we can see that the service allows its users to cancel their reservations and purchases until it finalizes the transaction. Some users may look for such specific behaviors. A behavior-based analysis can facilitate the system to differentiate among services based on their behaviors and perform the service discovery more accurately.

Advertising Services: For a given finite state automaton representing the service behavior of a Web service (such a finite automaton can be automatically extracted from the service's BPEL document[37]), we extract all the accepting paths from the automaton. An accepting path starts from the initial state of the automaton and ends in an accepting state without any loops (semantically the path implies a sequence of activities successfully performed by the service). Each accepting path is then advertised in the system using the path as a key. The entire service automaton of the service is included in the advertise message and stored in the behavior-list. For the service automaton given in Figure 5, two of the accepting paths are $<$ *?searchRequest - !searchResponse* $>$ and $<$ *?reserveRequest - !checkAvailability - !notAvailable* $>$. The advertise message P3 in Figure 3 shows

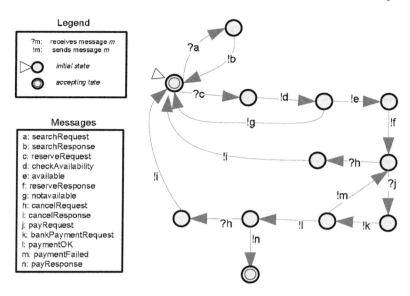

Fig. 5. Example Service Automaton

how service WA is advertised for the first accepting path above. A detailed discussion of the behavior-based search can be found in [17].

Locating Services: Users can ask behavior-based lookup queries for accepting paths they are looking for. In this case, the super peer that is responsible for that path will search through its behavior-list to find the service automata that matches with the query path and return them.

Overview

SPiDeR allows peers to search for Web services in 3 different ways: keyword-based, ontology-based, and behavior-based. All three of these techniques leverage the basic exact key lookup functionality provided by the super-peer overlay, but they incorporate different semantic meanings and thus enable SPiDeR to provide a richer set of querying capabilities. For example, a user P_x looking for services related to museums might not be able to find a relevant service S_m using keyword search just because the service is not advertised for the keyword(s) provided by P_x. However, if S_m is advertised based on ontology, P_x can locate it by issuing an ontology-based search on */TravelService/AttractionService/MuseumService*. Similarly, consider a user P_y looking for flight booking services with express delivery option. If keyword-based or ontology-based search is used, P_y will have to investigate the set of returned services to determine the ones that have express delivery option. Instead, P_y can use behavior-based search so that only the services with express delivery option are returned.

4.5   Ranking Services

In addition to the above search methods, SPiDeR provides a rating discovery mechanism. After using a Web service, a user can rate the quality of the service. The user (P_U) sends a message containing its own address, the address of the service being rated (WS), and the corresponding score (a real value between 0 and 1, where 1 is the highest score). The message is then routed in the system by hashing the address of the service being rated. The corresponding super peer stores all ratings given to WS in its rating list.

The rating of a Web service then can be retrieved by querying for its address. This query will return the average of all the scores the service had been given. The quality ratings are useful for selecting the service to use once a list of matching services are obtained.

5   Peer Operations in SPiDeR

In this section, we provide a more detailed discussion of some peer operations such as advertising services, composite lookups, and indexing services. We also show the routing performance of SPiDeR.

5.1   Advertising Services

After joining the system, each peer P periodically advertises the services it provides. For advertising a service, P_n sends the necessary information to its super peer (if it is not a super peer). This message specifies the address of the service, advertisement type(keyword-based, ontology-based or behavior-based), and the additional information (keyword, ontology path, service automaton). The super peer then routes the corresponding message within the Chord so that the responsible super peer stores the index information.

Peers periodically refresh their service advertisements to avoid stale index entries (super peers remove the index entries that are not refreshed) and to recover lost index information (if a super peer leaves without transferring its index information to another super peer).

5.2   Composite Lookups

Peers can use any of the supported search methods to locate the services they are looking for. The query message contains the address of the querying peer, query type (keyword/ontology/behavior/rating), and the corresponding arguments (keyword/ontology path/request automaton/service address, respectively). The super peer responsible for the argument receives the message and searches through the corresponding index. It then returns the list of matching services to the querying peer. SPiDeR can also be used for composite lookups such as searching for multiple keywords or for services with a keyword within a category. In this case, the user can retrieve the result of each elementary lookup and locally compute the intersection.

5.3   Indexing at Super Peers

In SPiDeR, super peers index the information about Web services they are assigned through Chord hashing. Each super peer keeps 4 different lists for supporting the corresponding discovery operations: keyword list, ontology list, behavior list, and rating list. SPiDeR is flexible in the sense that each super peer can individually choose the indexing methods it uses. For example, a peer might choose to keep each list as a sequential file, which might not be very efficient. More efficient index lookups can be achieved by using more efficient indexing schemes. For keyword, ontology, and rating lists, hashtable-like indexing methods are desirable since these lists only require exact key lookups. For behavior list, the matching regular expressions should be identified, so an RE-tree (Regular Expression tree) [38] might be suitable.

5.4   Routing Cost

We measured the performance of SPiDeR in terms of routing using a simulator implemented in Java. To measure the routing cost, we measured the average number of peers visited for routing a message in the super peer ring for different number of peers. For each message, the initiating peer is selected uniformly at random from the existing super peers and the message destination is set to a random Chord identifier. Figure 6 shows the results, where each data point is the average over 1000 runs. The routing cost is low and also increases gracefully with increasing number of peers. For example, routing a message takes 3.7 overlay hops on the average in a 50 peer system, whereas it takes 5.4 hops when the peer number increases to 500. Note that the peer numbers shown on the graph are the number of super peers and do not include the client peers. The actual number

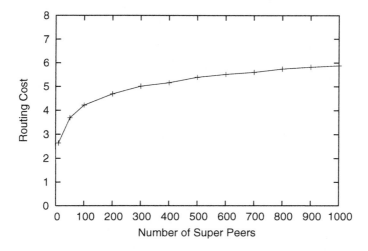

Fig. 6. Routing Performance of SPiDeR

of peers in the system can be much more than the number shown in the graph. Thus we conclude that SPiDeR is both scalable and efficient in terms of routing. Compared to a centralized service discovery system, SPiDeR is more robust and scalable, and supports a richer set of discovery operations at the expense of a little routing overhead.

6   Conclusion

With the proliferation of Web services technology and the increase in the number of Web services, the service discovery problem gets more challenging. There are different dimensions like functionality, behavior and semantics each describing a service from a different perspective. In this paper, we proposed a structured P2P framework which unifies these perspectives by means of providing different search methods in a distributed environment without a central component. We believe our results will contribute to the efforts towards comprehensive service discovery systems. As future work, we plan to look into other possible perspectives that users may be interested in and improve our system with the addition of new search methods.

References

1. Simple Object Access Protocol (SOAP) 1.2: http://www.w3.org/TR/SOAP/ (2003)
2. Web Services Description Language (WSDL) 2.0: http://www.w3.org/tr/ (2001)
3. Business Process Execution Language (BPEL) 2.0: http://www.oasis-open.org/committees/download.php/10347/wsbpel-specification-draft-120204.htm (2004)
4. OWL-S 1.1: http://www.daml.org/services/owl-s/1.1/ (2004)
5. Aiello, M., Aoyama, M., Curbera, F., Papazoglou, M., eds.: Proceedings of the International Conference of Service Oriented Computing (ICSOC'04), November 15-19, 2004, New York City, NY, USA,. In Aiello, M., Aoyama, M., Curbera, F., Papazoglou, M., eds.: ICSOC, ACM Press (2004)
6. Proceedings of the IEEE International Conference on Web Services (ICWS), San Diego, California, USA. (2004)
7. Proceedings of the IEEE International Conference on Services Computing (SCC), Shanghai, China. (2004)
8. Ellis, A., Hagino, T., eds.: Proceedings of the 14th international conference on World Wide Web, Chiba, Japan, May 10-14, 2005. In Ellis, A., Hagino, T., eds.: WWW, ACM (2005)
9. Web Services Architecture Requirements: http://www.w3.org/tr/wsa-reqs (2004)
10. Alonso, G., Casati, F., Kuno, H., Machiraju, V.: Web Services: Concepts, Architectures and Applications. Springer (2004)
11. Binding Point: http://www.bindingpoint.com/ (2005)
12. Web Service List: http://www.webservicelist.com/ (2005)
13. Dong, X., Halevy, A., Madhavan, J., Nemes, E., Zhang, J.: Similarity search for web services. In: VLDB. (2004)
14. Mahleko, B., Wombacher, A., Frankhauser, P.: A grammar-based index for matching business processes. In: ICWS. (2005)

15. Constantinescu, I., Binder, W., Faltings, B.: Flexible and efficient matchmaking and ranking in service directories. In: ICWS. (2005)
16. Shen, Z., Su, J.: Web service discovery based on behavior signatures. In: Proceedings of International Conference on Services Computing. (2005)
17. Emekci, F., Sahin, O.D., Agrawal, D., El Abbadi, A.: A peer-to-peer framework for web service discovery with ranking. In: ICWS. (2004) 192–199
18. Paolucci, M., Sycara, K., Nishimura, T., Srinivasan, N.: Using daml-s for p2p discovery. In: ICWS. (2003) 203–207
19. Papazoglou, M.P., Kramer, B., Yang, J.: Leveraging web-services and peer-to-peer networks. In: CAISE. (2003) 485–501
20. Schlosser, M., Sintek, M., Decker, S., Nejdl, W.: A scalable and ontology-based p2p infrastructure for semantic web services. In: P2P. (2002) 104–111
21. Schmidt, C., Parashar, M.: A peer-to-peer approach to web service discovery. In: WWW. (2004) 211–229
22. Syeda-Mahmood, T., Shah, G., Akkiraju, R., Ivan, A., Goodwin, R.: Searching service repositories by combining semantic and ontological matching. In: ICWS. (2005)
23. Verma, K., Sivashanmugam, K., Sheth, A., Patil, A., Oundhakar, S., Miller, J.: Meteor-s wsdi: A scalable p2p infrastructure of registries for semantic publication and discovery of web services. Inf. Tech. and Management **6** (2005) 17–39
24. Napster: (http://www.napster.com/)
25. Gnutella: (http://www.gnutella.com/)
26. Lv, Q., Ratnasamy, S., Shenker, S.: Can heterogeneity make gnutella scalable? In: IPTPS. (2002) 94–103
27. Ratnasamy, S., Francis, P., Handley, M., Karp, R., Schenker, S.: A scalable content-addressable network. In: SIGCOMM. (2001) 161–172
28. Stoica, I., Morris, R., Karger, D., Kaashoek, M.F., Balakrishnan, H.: Chord: A scalable peer-to-peer lookup service for internet applications. In: SIGCOMM. (2001) 149–160
29. Rowstron, A., Druschel, P.: Pastry: Scalable, distributed object location and routing for large-scale peer-to-peer systems. In: Middleware. (2001)
30. Zhao, Y.B., Kubiatowicz, J., Joseph, A.: Tapestry: An infrastructure for fault-tolerant wide-area location and routing. Technical Report UCB/CSD-01-1141, University of California at Berkeley (2001)
31. Gummadi, P.K., Gummadi, R., Gribble, S.D., Ratnasamy, S., Shenker, S., Stoica, I.: The impact of dht routing geometry on resilience and proximity. In: SIGCOMM. (2003) 381–394
32. Yang, B., Garcia-Molina, H.: Designing a super-peer network. In: ICDE. (2003) 49–60
33. Web Service Semantics - WSDL-S: http://www.w3.org/2005/04/fsws/submissions/17/wsdl-s.htm (2005)
34. Semantic Web Services Language - SWSL: http://www.daml.org/services/swsl/ (2005)
35. Web Service Modeling Language - WSML: http://www.wsmo.org/wsml/ (2005)
36. Buckley, C.: Implementation of the SMART information retrieval system. Technical Report 85-686, Cornell University (1985)
37. Fu, X., Bultan, T., Su, J.: Wsat: A tool for formal analysis of web services. In: International Conference on Computer Aided Verification. (2004)
38. Chan, C.Y., Garofalakis, M.N., Rastogi, R.: Re-tree: An efficient index structure for regular expressions. In: VLDB. (2002) 263–274

An Approach to Temporal-Aware Procurement of Web Services *

Octavio Martín-Díaz, Antonio Ruiz-Cortés,
Amador Durán, and Carlos Müller

Dpto. Lenguajes y Sistemas Informáticos,
ETS. Ingeniería Informática - Universidad de Sevilla,
41012 Sevilla (Spain - España)
{octavio, aruiz}@tdg.lsi.us.es
{amador, cmuller}@lsi.us.es

Abstract. In the context of web service procurement (WSP), temporal–awareness refers to managing service demands and offers which are subject to validity periods, i.e. their evaluation depends not only on quality of service (QoS) values but also on time. For example, the QoS of some web services can be considered critical in working hours (9:00 to 17:00 from Monday to Friday) and irrelevant at any other moment. Until now, the expressiveness of such temporal–aware specifications has been quite limited. As far as we know, most proposals have considered validity periods to be composed of a single temporal interval. Other proposals, which could allow more expressive time–dependent specifications, have not performed a detailed study about all the underlying complexities of such approach, in spite of the fact that dealing with complex expressions on temporality is not a trivial task at all. As a matter of fact, it requires a special design of the so–called *procurement tasks* (consistency and conformance checking, and optimal selection). In this paper, we present a constraint–based approach to temporal–aware WSP. Using constraints allows a great deal of expressiveness, so that not only demands and offers can be assigned validity periods but also their conditions can be assigned (possibly multiple) validity temporal subintervals. Apart from revising the semantics of procurement tasks, which we previously presented in the first edition of the ICSOC conferences, we also introduce the notion of the *covering set of a demand*, a topic which is closely related to temporality.

Keywords: services, procurement, quality, temporality, constraint programming.

1 Introduction

Web service procurement (WSP)—including automated search and selection—of the best web services according to their offered quality of service (QoS) is an activity which is gaining importance in the development of enterprise–level systems with a service–oriented architecture (SOA) [18, 24].

---

* This work has been funded by the Spanish Government under grant TIC2003-02737-C02-01, AGILWEB project.

B. Benatallah, F. Casati, and P. Traverso (Eds.): ICSOC 2005, LNCS 3826, pp. 170–184, 2005.

Web services, as a particular case of *software packages*, must be selected according to user requirements [3,4]. On the one hand, these user requirements, to which we refer to as *demands*, are usually specified using boolean expressions, i.e. conditions on attributes describing the desired QoS of a service, for example[1] $MTTF \geq 100$. On the other hand, web service providers usually guarantee the QoS of the service they provide, i.e. their *offers*, for example $100 \leq MTTF \leq 120$.

Procurement is the process of finding the best offer for a given demand [18]. Its typical scenario is: (1) a provider advertises its offers in a repository, (2) a customer asks its matchmaker for an offer to meet its demands, and (3) the matchmaker searches for matching offers, returning a result which may be an optimal offer according to a given customer criterion, or a failure message if no matching offer is found [21].

Temporality is an important aspect of WSP. If a demand or offer is subject to a validity period, it is said to be *temporal–aware*. As an example, in order to specify a (part of a) demand as *"the MTTF of the web service at working hours (9:00 to 17:00, Monday to Friday) should be (at least) of 99%, otherwise 90%"*, we would require to define multiple, periodical validity periods associated to concrete conditions of the demand. Other temporal aspects to be taken into consideration are the granularity of time points, periods and durations, and the different time zones in which demands and offers (D&O) can be available.

Not only it is necessary to extend the current models in WSP in order to improve their expressivess regarding temporality, but it is also needed to re–think the so–called procurement tasks, i.e. consistency and conformance checkings, and optimal selection, because of the non-trivial, intrinsic semantics of temporal expressions. For example, in a non-temporal-aware context we define the notion of *pessimistic conformance* so that an offer is conformant to a demand iff all the quality values guaranteed by the offer satisfy the conditions imposed by the demand. Let imagine a dummy demand and offer which were constituted by only a validity period, with no conditions regarding any quality attribute. If the validity period of the offer were included in the validity period of the demand, then such offer could be considered as conformant. But this is not the case, because the offer does not cover the validity period of the demand, so the offer is not conformant. In general, if temporality is taken into account, the notions of consistency, conformance, and optimal selection must be revised.

Until now—to the best of our knowledge— proposals allow a demand or an offer to have a validity period composed of only a single temporal interval. Only a few of them allows more complex temporal expressions, but most of them have not provided a detailed study about the underlying complexities of operations due to temporal semantics.

In this paper, we present an approach to temporal–aware WSP which is based on constraint programming (CP). It is based on notions introduced in our previous non–temporal–aware, constraint–based approach to WSP [15,18]. Using CP for WSP entails some advantages. First, D&O can be stated declaratively, endowing the symmetric model with a very powerful expressiveness so that D&O can be specified with the same expressiveness. Thus, offers are not limited to single parameter–value pairs. Moreover,

---

[1] MTTF stands for *mean time to failure*.

```
// Service Demand for IVideoServer

using Reliability, Hosting;          guarantees {
product  IVideoServer;                 D4: HOST = SPAIN;
                                     }
valid zone GMT +1 {
  global { during 01/JUN/2005..31/AGO/2005; }
  WORKING { from 9..17 on MON..FRI; }
  HOME { global except WORKING; }      assessment {
  SEASON { during 15/JUL/2005..15/ AGO/2005;   MTTF { importance = VERY_HIGH, {
  }                                        WORKING { (0,0), (80,0), (100,0.5), (120,1) }
}                                      };
                                           HOME { (0,0), (60,0), (90,0.5), (120,1) }; }
requires {                             }
  D1: MTTF ≥ 100 and MTTR ≤ 10 on WORKING;   MTTR { importance = LOW, {
  D2: MTTF ≥ 90 and MTTR ≤ 15 on HOME;     global { (0,1), (5,1), (10,0.5), (15,0) }; }
  D3: COST ≤ 10 on SEASON;             }
}                                    }
```

Fig. 1. An example of temporal-aware demand written in QRL

it is not necessary to write specific procedures for procurement tasks because they are implemented by checking properties of D&O by means of a constraint solver.

Figure 1 shows an illustrative example of a temporal-aware demand. It is written in QRL (*Quality Requirements Language*), which is a language specifically devised for that purpose by one of the authors of this work as part of his PhD thesis [17]. This example is intended to be self–explanatory, in order to give an overview of the expressiveness of our approach. First, the demand establishes the Central Europe time zone (UTC/GMT+1). Then, it defines the global validity period (VP) together with other validity periods. The *working hours* VP is composed of some periodical temporal intervals, whereas the *home hours* VP is computed from the global VP and the previous one. Another valididy period is *season* which is non-periodical.

Note the validity periods can be assigned to conditions of the demand, so that the conditions on the same quality attributes are different at *working hours* or *home hours*. The *season* VP indicates the dates between which the cost of using the service should not be greater than 10 €. The demand's host is always in Spain at any time of the global VP.

Note also the assessment criteria include utility functions which depends upon time. These functions are defined in a piecewise–like way. Each point is associated to the corresponding utility value (between 0 and 1), so that two consecutive points form a segment of the function. Utility functions are weighted by their grades of importance.

We also introduce the notion of *covering*. Since it is possible that none of the available offers were conformant to a given demand because they did not cover it, one could think of selecting several offers which are grouped together, in order to *build* a conformant offer which covers the validity period of the demand.

The rest of the paper is structured as follows. First, Section 2 introduces the theoretical basis for interpreting the temporal-aware procurement tasks by means of CSP, so that Section 3 presents our proposal to model them. Next, Section 4 provides a review of the state–of–the–art. Finaly, Section 5 concludes the paper and presents the future work.

2   Constraint Programming in a Nutshell

Constraint programming (CP) is the study of computational models and systems based on contraints. CP is becoming a very interesting alternative to the modeling of optimization problems because of its potential to solve hard, real–life problems, and its declarative nature. A problem expressed as a set of constraints is formalized as a *contraint satisfaction (optimization) problem* (CSP) [5, 7, 8].

2.1   Basic Definitions

In this section, we introduce CP as the underlying formalism of our approach for expressing D&O. The core of our proposal was a set of definitions used to rigorously define the so–called procurement tasks.

Definition 1 (CSP). *A CSP is a three–tuple of the form* (V, D, C) *where* $V \neq \emptyset$ *is a finite set of variables,* $D \neq \emptyset$ *is a finite set of domains (one for each variable) and* C *is a set of constraints defined on* V.

For instance, for the following CSP $(\{x, y\}, \{[0..2], [0..2]\}, \{x+y < 4, x-y \geq 1\})$, the assignment $\sigma = \{x \mapsto 2, y \mapsto 0\}$ is one of its solutions.

Definition 2 (Solution Space). *Let* ψ *be a CSP of the form* (V, D, C), *its solution space, denoted as* $\mathrm{sol}(\psi)$, *is composed of all its possible solutions.*

$$\mathrm{sol}(\psi) = \{\, \sigma \in V \to D \mid \sigma(C) \,\}$$

where $\sigma(C)$ *holds iff each assignment in* σ *satisfies every constraint in* C.

In the previous example the solution space is $\{\{x \mapsto 1, y \mapsto 0\}, \{x \mapsto 2, y \mapsto 0\}, \{x \mapsto 2, y \mapsto 1\}\}$.

Definition 3 (Satisfiability). *Let* ψ *be a CSP of the form* (V, D, C), ψ *is said to be satisfiable, denoted as* $\mathrm{sat}(\psi)$, *iff its solution space is not empty.*

$$\mathrm{sat}(\psi) \Leftrightarrow \mathrm{sol}(\psi) \neq \emptyset$$

Definition 4 (Minimum Space and Value). *Let* ψ *be a CSP of the form* (V, D, C), *its minimum space with regard to an objective function* O, *denoted as* $\min_S(\psi, O)$, *is composed of all the solutions of* ψ *that minimize* O. *Its minimum value with regard to* O, *denoted as* $\min_V(\psi, O)$, *is the value the objective function takes on* $\min_S(\psi, O)$.

$$\min_S(\psi, O) = \{\, \sigma \in \mathrm{sol}(\psi) \mid \forall \sigma' \in \mathrm{sol}(\psi) \cdot O(\sigma) \leq O(\sigma') \,\}$$
$$\min_V(\psi, O) = m \Leftrightarrow \forall \sigma \in \min_S(\psi, O) \cdot O(\sigma) = m$$

For instance, consider the CSP in the previous example and an objective function defined as $O(x, y) = x^2 y$. In this case, $\min_S(\psi, O) = \{\{x \mapsto 1, y \mapsto 0\}, \{x \mapsto 2, y \mapsto 0\}\}$. The minimum value is 0.

2.2 Filters and Projections

In general, the solution space of a CSP can be restricted by means of intersecting a second CSP.

Filters. A filter is a kind of selection, which allows to obtain a CSP whose solution space has been restricted to those solutions containing a (possibly partial) assignment over the variables.

Definition 5 (Filtering). *Let* ψ *be a CSP of the form* (V, D, C), *and* $\sigma_\pi = \{v_1 \mapsto d_1, \dots, v_k \mapsto d_k\}$ *an assignment defined over the k variables in* $\pi \subseteq V$, *the filtering of* ψ *on* σ_π, *denoted as* $\psi_{v_1 \mapsto d_1, \dots, v_k \mapsto d_k}$, *is another CSP defined on V and D whose constraint set* C' *is C wherein as many equality constraints as assignments in* σ_π *have been added.*

$$C' = C \cup \bigcup_{i=1}^{k} \{v_i = d_i\}$$

In the previous example, the filtering over $\sigma_\pi = \{y \mapsto 0\}$ results in a CSP whose solution space is $\{\{x \mapsto 1, y \mapsto 0\}, \{x \mapsto 2, y \mapsto 0\}\}$.

Projections. A projection is another kind of selection, which allows to obtain those values which take a set of variables whenever the CSP is satisfiable.

Definition 6 (Projection). *Let* ψ *be a CSP of the form* (V, D, C), *and* π *a set of variables such that* $\pi \subseteq V$, *the projection of* ψ *over* π, *denoted as* $\psi_{\Downarrow\pi}$, *is another CSP defined on* π *and* D_π *whose solution space is composed of values of variables in* π *which are part of any solution in* $\mathrm{sol}(\psi)$.

$$\mathrm{sol}(\psi_{\Downarrow\pi}) = \{\, \sigma_\pi \in \pi \rightarrow D_\pi \mid \exists\, \sigma \in \mathrm{sol}(\psi) \cdot \sigma_\pi \subseteq \sigma \,\}$$

where $D_\pi \subseteq D$ *is the set of domains of variables in* π.

In the previous example, the projection of the solution space over $\pi = \{x\}$ results in $\{\{x \mapsto 1\}, \{x \mapsto 2\}\}$.

3 Temporal-Aware Procurement Using Constraint Programming

In [15, 18], we described how CP can help automating the procurement tasks, i.e. the checking for consistency and conformance, and selection of optimal offers. The key to automating the procurement tasks is to map D&O onto CSPs. In order to do so, each attribute must be mapped onto a variable with its corresponding domain, and each condition must be mapped onto a constraint.

In this section, we review these notions in order to make them temporal-aware. We assume a linear, discrete time-structure based on natural numbers. Time elements are point times and temporal intervals. A temporal interval is given by two time points representing their extremes.

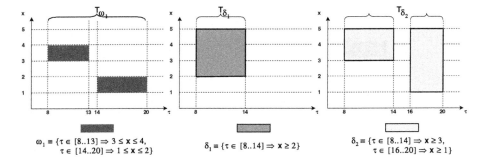

$\omega_1 \equiv \{\tau \in [8..13] \Rightarrow 3 \leq x \leq 4,$
$\tau \in [14..20] \Rightarrow 1 \leq x \leq 2\}$

$\delta_1 \equiv \{\tau \in [8..14] \Rightarrow x \geq 2\}$

$\delta_2 \equiv \{\tau \in [8..14] \Rightarrow x \geq 3,$
$\tau \in [16..20] \Rightarrow x \geq 1\}$

Fig. 2. Solution spaces of temporal-aware offers and demands

3.1 Demands and Offers

Demands assert the conditions the provider shall meet, whereas offers assert the conditions a provider guarantees[2]. Regarding temporality, all D&O are considered as (by default) temporal-aware, i.e. they all have a *validity period* and their inner conditions can (optionally) establish time-dependent demand requirements or offer guarantees. If a D&O does not have an explicit validity period, it will be supposed to have an infinite temporal interval.

Let δ denote a demand, and ω denote an offer. Their corresponding CSP are denoted as ψ_δ and ψ_ω, respectively. Let α denote a demand or offer. Any demand or offer α has an (implicit) temporal variable, denoted as τ, so that its domain D_τ corresponds to the validity period. Inner conditions of D&O are based on QoS attributes and (eventually) the temporal variable, so that distinct temporal subintervals can be assigned to them, provided these subintervals are included in the validity period.

T_α stands for a CSP of the form $(\tau, D_\tau, true)$ whose its solution space corresponds to the validity period of α. Note $\tau' \in T_\alpha$ is a shorthand for an assignment at time τ' which belongs to the validity period.

For instance, the following tuples denote an offer ω_1 and two demands δ_1 and δ_2:

$$\omega_1 = (\{x, \tau\}, \{[0..5], [8..20]\}, \{\tau \in [8..13] \Rightarrow 3 \leq x \leq 4, \tau \in [14..20] \Rightarrow 1 \leq x \leq 2\})$$
$$\delta_1 = (\{x, \tau\}, \{[0..5], [8..14]\}, \{\tau \in [8..14] \Rightarrow x \geq 2\})$$
$$\delta_2 = (\{x, \tau\}, \{[0..5], [8..14] \cup [16..20]\}, \{\tau \in [8..14] \Rightarrow x \geq 3, \tau \in [16..20] \Rightarrow x \geq 1\})$$

Their solution spaces are shown graphically in Figure 2. The offer ω_1 has the temporal interval $[8..20]$ as validity period, representing the office hours of a day. Each guarantee of this offer is assigned a temporal subinterval which is included in the validity period, covering the overall temporal interval. The first guarantee of ω_1 is valid at times in $[8..13]$. The second guarantee of ω_1 is valid at times in $[14..20]$.

Note the "$\Rightarrow$" operator is the logic implication with its usual meaning.

---

[2] For the sake of simplicity, we are assuming a one-way matchmaking, i.e. demands only require something from offers, and offers only guarantee something to demands, but not viceversa. The interested reader is referred to [18] wherein a two-way matchmaking is presented.

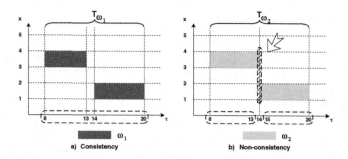

Fig. 3. Temporal-aware consistency

The first demand δ_1 has a unique requirement whose temporal subinterval is regarded to the overrall validity period [8..14]. This demand is not defined at any other time of a day.

The second demand δ_2 has a validity period composed of two subintervals [8..14] and [16..20] so that each requirement is assigned to every subinterval.

3.2 Consistency

Checking a demand or offer for consistency allows to unveil whether they have internal contradictions or not along the times whenever it is defined. If temporality is taken into account, consistency must also involve a checking of their validity periods. Moreover, since their requirements or guarantees can be also assigned one or more temporal intervals, they should be included in the validity period in order to be considered as consistent.

Note that it is also possible different demand requirements or offer guarantees have to be fulfilled at the same time. Checking the consistency of conditions and validity periods separately is not enough, but once validity periods have been checked, the consistency of conjunction of all demands requirements or offer guarantees at any time of the validity period has to be checked, as well.

Definition 7 (Consistency). *A demand or offer α is said to be consistent iff the projection over time of its corresponding CSP ψ_α equals its non-empty validity period.*

$$consistent(\alpha) \Leftrightarrow sol(\psi_{\alpha \Downarrow \tau}) = sol(T_\alpha)$$

For instance, consider the offer ω_1 in the previous example, and another offer ω_2 defined on the same attributes and domains but with the following conditions:

$$\{\tau \in [8..14] \Rightarrow 3 \leq x \leq 5, \tau \in [14..20] \Rightarrow 1 \leq x \leq 3\}$$

Both of them are shown in Figure 3. Note that the offer ω_1 is consistent (see Figure 3.a) because there are no contradictory conditions at any time in the validity period. However, the offer ω_2 is not consistent (see Figure 3.b) because at time $\tau = 14$ (marked with an arrow) there exist two contradictory conditions, so that the solution space of their conjuction at such a time is empty, and that point time is not included in the projection. Therefore, since the projection does not equal the validity period, the offer ω_2 is not consistent.

3.3 Conformance

Checking if an offer conforms to a demand allows to know whether the values guaranteed by a party (the offer from a provider) meet the values required by the other party (the demand of a client) whenever the demand is defined. A non-temporal-aware offer ω and a non-temporal-aware demand δ is said to be pessimistic-conformant iff the solution space of ψ_ω is a subset of the solution space of ψ_δ. In terms of CP, this can be expressed by means of Marriott and Stuckey expression [14]:

$$conformant(\omega, \delta) \Leftrightarrow \neg sat(\psi_\omega \wedge \neg \psi_\delta)$$

If temporality is taken into account, this checking must be carried out at any time of the validity period of the demand. In Section 1, we have introduced the need of revising the conformance notion, so that if an offer and a demand were defined exclusively by their validity periods, then they would be considered as conformant iff the validity period of the offer covered the validity period of the demand.

Definition 8 (Conformance). *An offer ω and a demand δ are said to be conformant iff the validity period of ω covers the validity period of δ, and the projection over time of the CSP representing those solutions of ω which are not a solution of δ is disjoint to the validity period of δ.*

$$conformant(\omega, \delta) \Leftrightarrow sol(T_\delta) \subseteq sol(T_\omega)$$
$$\wedge \; sol(\{\psi_\omega \wedge \neg \psi_\delta\}_{\Downarrow \tau}) \cap sol(T_\delta) = \emptyset$$

For instance, consider the offer ω_1 and the demand δ_1 in the previous example, together with the demands δ_3 and δ_4 whose definitions are:

$$\delta_3 = (\{x, \tau\}, \{[0..5], [8..20]\}, \{\tau \in [8..13] \Rightarrow x \geq 3, \tau \in [14..20] \Rightarrow x \geq 1\})$$
$$\delta_4 = (\{x, \tau\}, \{[0..5], [7..20]\}, \{\tau \in [7..13] \Rightarrow x \geq 3, \tau \in [14..20] \Rightarrow x \geq 1\})$$

Their conformance relationships are shown in Figure 4. Note that the offer ω_1 is not conformant to the demand δ_1 (see Figure 4.a) because at $\tau = 14$ (marked with an arrow) the solution space of the offer is not a subset of solution space of the demand. Note this situation is detected by the above formula, because the time $\tau = 14$ belongs to the projection over time of those solutions of ω_1 which are not included in the solution space of the demand δ_1, and it is also included in its validity period T_{δ_1}. The offer ω_1 is conformant to the demand δ_3 (see Figure 4.b) because it is conformant at any time of its validity period, covering it completely as well. Finally, the offer ω_1 is not conformant to the demand δ_4 (see Figure 4.c) because it does not cover its validity period since it does not supply anything at $\tau = 7$ (marked with an arrow). The striped zones in Figure 4 represent the solution spaces of the negated CSP corresponding to the demands.

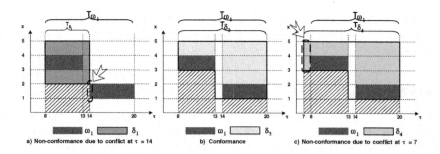

Fig. 4. Temporal-aware conformance

3.4   Finding the Optimal Offers

The final goal of matchmaking is, given a demand, finding a conformant offer that is optimal from the customer's point of view. This task is interpreted as a contraint satisfaction *optimization* problem (CSOP), which requires a preference order defined on the offer set. It is usual to establish such an order by means of a weighted composition of utility functions, whose general form is as follows:

$$\mathcal{U}(a_1, \ldots, a_n) = \sum_{i=1}^{n} k_i U_i(a_i) \quad k_i \in [0,1] \quad \sum_{i=1}^{n} k_i = 1$$

where each a_i denotes a quality attribute, each k_i its associated weight, and each U_i its associated utility function ranging over $[0,1]$ and describing how important the values of attribute are for the client.

Definition 9 (Set of Optimal Offers). *Let Ω_δ be a set of conformant offers to the demand δ, and $\mathcal{U}$ the assessment criteria given by an utility function, the set of optimal offers, denoted as $\Omega_{\delta,\mathcal{U}}^*$, is constituted of those offers in Ω_δ which maximize $\mathcal{U}$.*

$$\Omega_{\delta,\mathcal{U}}^* = \{\omega \in \Omega_\delta \mid \forall \omega' \in \Omega_\delta \cdot \mathcal{U}(\omega) \geq \mathcal{U}(\omega')\}$$

where $\mathcal{U}(\omega)$ stands for the utility of the offer ω given $\mathcal{U}$.

In a non-temporal-aware context, the utility of an offer corresponds to the worst case, that is to say, the utility of those values which minimize the utility function:

$$\mathcal{U}(\omega) = \min_V(\psi_\omega, \mathcal{U})$$

If temporality is taken into account, utility functions can be dependent upon time, so that quality attributes can have different utility values at distinct temporal intervals. The utility of an offer is the average utility during the validity period of δ:

$$\mathcal{U}(\omega) = \frac{1}{|sol(T_\delta)|} \sum_{\tau' \in T_\delta} \min_V(\psi_{\omega, \tau \mapsto \tau'}, \mathcal{U})$$

where $\psi_{\omega, \tau \mapsto \tau'}$ stands for the CSP which corresponds to ω filtered at time $\tau = \tau'$.

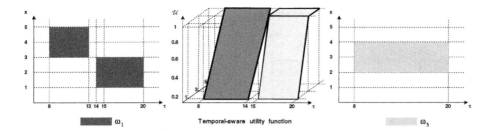

Fig. 5. Optimal selection with temporal-aware utility functions and offers

For instance, consider the offer ω_1 in the previous example, and another offer ω_3 defined on the same attributes and domains but with the following condition $\{\tau \in [8..20] \Rightarrow 2 \leq x \leq 3\}$. Assume these offers are conformant to a demand δ whose validity period is $[8..20]$, so that the assessment criteria is given by the utility function $\mathcal{U}$ in Figure 5. Note it gives different utility values for intervals $\tau \in [8..14]$ and $\tau \in [15..20]$. The set of optimal offers is $\Omega^*_{\delta,\mathcal{U}} = \{\omega_3\}$, according to their utility values:

$$\mathcal{U}(\omega_1) = \tfrac{1}{13}\{\tfrac{3}{5} \times 6 + \tfrac{1}{5} \times 1 + \tfrac{1}{3} \times 6\} = 0.45$$
$$\mathcal{U}(\omega_3) = \tfrac{1}{13}\{\tfrac{2}{5} \times 7 + \tfrac{2}{3} \times 6\} = 0.52$$

The utility of ω_1 is computed in this way. Note that the number of time points which belongs to T_δ is 13. If $\tau \in [8..13]$ (six time points) then $x = 3$ is given an utility of $3/5$, if $\tau = 14$ (one time point) then $x = 1$ is given an utility of $1/5$, and if $\tau \in [15..20]$ (another six time points) then $x = 1$ is given an utility of $1/3$. The utility of ω_3 is computed in a similar way.

3.5   Finding the Optimal Covering

Since it is possible that none of the available offers were conformant to a given demand because they did not cover it, one could think of selecting several offers so that all together are conformant to the demand, covering all the validity period. The covering problem is to find such a set of offers, optimizing according to assessment criteria from demand and other (optional) criteria, in order to adopt different strategies such as, for example, to minimize the number of offers.

Definition 10 (Covering). *Let δ be a demand and Ω a set of available offers*[3]. *Ω is said to be a covering set of δ iff there exists (at least) a conformant offer in Ω at any time of the validity period of the demand.*

$$isCoveringSet(\Omega, \delta) \Leftrightarrow \forall \tau' \in T_\delta, \exists \omega \in \Omega \cdot conformant(\omega_{\tau \mapsto \tau'}, \delta_{\tau \mapsto \tau'})$$

where $\omega_{\tau \mapsto \tau'}$ and $\delta_{\tau \mapsto \tau'}$ stand for the offer ω and the demand δ at time $\tau = \tau'$, respectively.

---

[3] An offer is available iff it provides the functionality required by a demand.

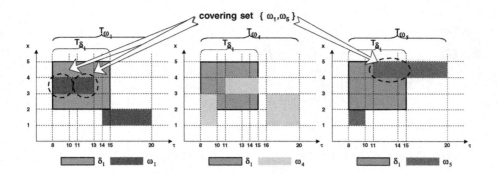

Fig. 6. Covering and temporal-awareness

For instance, consider the demand δ_1 whose valid period is $T_{\delta_1} = [8..15]$ and the assessment criteria given by the utility function $\mathcal{U}$, and the offer ω_1 in the previous example, together with the following offers ω_4 y ω_5 which are also defined on the same attributes and domains as ω_1, but with the following constraints:

$$C_{\omega_4} = \{\tau \in [8..10] \Rightarrow 1 \leq x \leq 3, \tau \in [11..15] \Rightarrow 3 \leq x \leq 4, \tau \in [16..20] \Rightarrow 1 \leq x \leq 3\}$$
$$C_{\omega_5} = \{\tau \in [8..10] \Rightarrow 1 \leq x \leq 2, \tau \in [11..20] \Rightarrow 4 \leq x \leq 5\}$$

The demand and offers are shown in Figure 6. None of them is conformant to the given demand, but if it were possible to join two (or more) of them, then one would be able to build a conformant offer, i.e. the so-called covering set of a demand.

Figure 6 shows the covering set of δ_1 which is constituted by the offers $\{\omega_1, \omega_5\}$ (marked with the arrows). It is a covering set because at any time of T_{δ_1} there exist (at least) a conformant offer:

$$\tau \in [8..10] \rightarrow \omega_1; \tau \in [11..13] \rightarrow \omega_1, \omega_5; \tau \in [14..15] \rightarrow \omega_5$$

The sets of offers $\{\omega_1, \omega_4\}$ and $\{\omega_1, \omega_4, \omega_5\}$ also conform a covering set of the demand. However, the set of offers $\{\omega_4, \omega_5\}$ is not a covering set, because at time $\tau \in [8..10]$ there is no offer conformant to the demand.

Among all the covering sets which can be conformed from a set of offers, one should be able to select the best one. Therefore, we need to compute their utility according to assessment criteria attached to a demand.

Let Ω be a covering set of the demand δ_1, and $\mathcal{U}$ the utility function of δ_1, the utility of a covering set is given by the aggregation of maximum utilities at any time in the validity period of δ_1:

$$\mathcal{U}(\Omega) = \frac{1}{|sol(T_\delta)|} \sum_{\tau' \in T_\delta} \max_{\omega \, \in \, \Omega_{\delta, \tau \mapsto \tau'}} \{\min_V(\psi_{\omega, \tau \mapsto \tau'}, \mathcal{U})\}$$

where $\Omega_{\delta, \tau \mapsto \tau'}$ is the subset of offers in Ω which are conformant to δ at time $\tau = \tau'$:

$$\Omega_{\delta, \tau \mapsto \tau'} = \{w \in \Omega \mid conformant(\omega_{\tau \mapsto \tau'}, \delta_{\tau \mapsto \tau'})\}$$

For instance, consider the set of offers $\Omega = \{\omega_1, \omega_4, \omega_5\}$ available to the demand δ_1, whose assessment criteria is $\mathcal{U}$, in the previous example, the utility values of the covering sets of δ_1 are:

$$\mathcal{U}(\{\omega_1, \omega_4\}) = \tfrac{1}{7}\{\tfrac{3}{5} \times 3 + \tfrac{3}{5} \times 3 + \tfrac{3}{5} \times 1 + \tfrac{3}{3} \times 1\} = 0.74$$
$$\mathcal{U}(\{\omega_1, \omega_5\}) = \tfrac{1}{7}\{\tfrac{3}{5} \times 3 + \tfrac{4}{5} \times 3 + \tfrac{4}{5} \times 1 + 1 \times 1\} = 0.86$$
$$\mathcal{U}(\{\omega_1, \omega_4, \omega_5\}) = \tfrac{1}{7}\{\tfrac{3}{5} \times 3 + \tfrac{4}{5} \times 3 + \tfrac{4}{5} \times 1 + 1 \times 1\} = 0.86$$

The utility of the covering $\{\omega_1, \omega_5\}$ is computed in this way. Note that the number of time points which belongs to T_δ is 7. If $\tau \in [8..10]$ (three time points) then the offer ω_1 has the conformant value $x = 3$ which is given an utility of $3/5$, if $\tau \in [11..13]$ (three time points) then both offers are conformant, but the best one is ω_5 because it offers a conformant value $x = 4$ which is given an utility of $4/5$ whereas ω_1 has a conformant value $x = 3$ which is given a worse utility of $3/5$, if $\tau = 14$ (one time point) then the offer ω_5 has the conformant value $x = 4$ which is given an utility of $4/5$, and if $\tau = 15$ (another one time point) then the offer ω_5 has the conformant value $x = 4$ which is given an utility of 1. The utility of the remaining coverings is computed in a similar way.

Definition 11 (Set of Optimal Coverings). *Let δ be a demand, $\mathcal{U}$ an utility function as assessment criteria, and Ω_δ^+ the set of all coverings given a set of available offers. The set of optimal coverings, denoted as $\Omega_{\delta,\mathcal{U}}^+$, is constituted of those covering sets which maximize the utility function $\mathcal{U}$.*

$$\Omega_{\delta,\mathcal{U}}^+ = \{\Omega \in \Omega_\delta^+ \mid \forall \Omega' \in \Omega_\delta^+ \cdot \mathcal{U}(\Omega) \geq \mathcal{U}(\Omega')\}$$

Given the offers and demand in the previous example, the set of optimal coverings is $\{\{\omega_1, \omega_5\}, \{\omega_1, \omega_4, \omega_5\}\}$.

Note that these covering sets have the same utility, although the latter seems to be redundant because values from ω_5 override those from ω_4. We can establish a preference order by means of any secondary assessment criteria, for example, by minimizing the number of offers. In this case, the optimal subset regarding $min_{|\Omega|}$ of $\{\{\omega_1, \omega_5\}, \{\omega_1, \omega_4, \omega_5\}\}$ is $\{\{\omega_1, \omega_5\}\}$.

4   Related Work

Figure 7 shows a brief comparison among related proposals, showing their characteristics on temporality at a first sight. Because of the limited extension of this paper, this section is devoted solely to temporal–aware proposals. A broader outline, which also includes the non–temporal–aware proposals, is available in [15, 18].

Note that our point of view is different from the perspective of service workflows, which is interested in the problem of finding an optimal execution plan of services in the context of a workflow [24]. We are interested in the procurement of web services whose demands and offers are temporal–aware. Of course, the workflow issue is very related to our problem, and they can be studied as a whole.

	Non-Periodical VP Entire Demand/Offer	Periodical VP Inner Conditions	Non-Periodical VP Inner Conditions	Multiple Intervals	Covering	Temporal Reasoning /Solving with Decidable Satisfiability
UDDIe	V					
WS-QoS	V					
WSOL		V				
WSLA			V	V		
WSML	V	V		V		
OWL-TIME	V	V	V	V		~
QRL	V	V	V	V	V	V

Fig. 7. A comparison among temporal–aware proposals

4.1 Proposals Based on Ad-Hoc Formalisms

These proposals do not have any formalism for temporal specifications, such as the *UDDI Extension* [20] and the *WS-QoS* ontology [22]. In general, they only allow to define an unique validity period for an entire demand or offer.

Fortunately, other proposals do allow to assign a validity period to every condition of a demand or an offer, such as the *IBM WSLA Web Services Level Agreement* language [6, 11] and the *WSOL Web Service Offerings Language* [23]. The *HP WSML Web Services Level Agreement Management* language [19] allows to specify both a single validity period for the entire agreement and also a periodic temporal interval to every condition. Both WSLA and WSML languages allow validity periods to be composed of multiple sub-intervals in distinct, limited ways as well.

4.2 Proposals Based on Semantic Web

These proposals are based on formalisms of the semantic web, having a much greater deal of expressiveness. The *OWL+TIME Ontology* [9, 10] is a very expressive language which is used by semantic-web-based approaches of WSP, such as the *Web Ontology Language - Services (OWL-S)* [2, 13, 16].

However, having a greater deal of expressiveness leads to several computation problems of the *Description Logics* (DL) reasoners able to reason about such temporal specifications. As a matter of fact, in logics there exist a tradeoff between expressiveness and the computability of reasoning procedures [12], so the more expressive temporal DL languages are known to be undecidable, that is to say, there is no algorithm for computing the satisfiability of a DL specification. Most of temporal DL reasoners overcome this problem by making the language less expressive, or treating the time as a concrete domain in order to use hybrid reasoners so that temporal specifications are processed by external solvers, such as the CSP solvers. In general, both (1) the reasoning on less expressive temporal DL specifications, or (2) solving a CSP, are known to be NP-complete [1].

5   Conclusions and Future Work

In this paper, we have presented an approach to add temporal–awareness to WSP by using CP, which endows our proposal with a declarative way to specify demands and offers so that the procurement tasks can be carried out by means of constraint satisfaction problems. We have introduced the notion of covering of a demand. We have also shown the need to review the semantics of procurement tasks if temporality is taken into account, and proposed a rigorous definition for them.

Our approach allows to specify a global validity period for a demand or an offer, and other validity periods which can be periodical or not, or composed of multiple intervals. These validity periods can be assigned to different conditions of the demand or the offer. Utility functions can be temporal–aware too, so that different utility values for a quality attribute can be defined at distinct time periods. The expressiveness of our approach is similar to semantic web–based proposals, though their major drawback is the undecidable nature of more complex temporal DL languages.

For future work, we are currently finishing the development of a proof–of–concept implementation, by adapting the prototype introduced in [18] so that it becomes temporal–aware. At operational level, consistency, conformance, and optimality have not to be computed at every time point of validity periods, just as they were defined in theory. A pre–processing step is needed in order to get the concrete time intervals of interest, then such tasks can be carried out on such time intervals.

Experiments need to be carried out in order to characterize the complexity of temporal–aware procurement tasks. As a result, it is expected to know what kind of temporal expressions to avoid because of their impact on the exponential behavior of CSP solving.

References

1. A. Artale and E. Franconi. A Survey of Temporal Extensions of Description Logics. *Annals of Mathematics and Artificial Intelligence*, 30(1-4):171–210, 2000.
2. The OWL Services Coalition. OWL-S: Semantic Markup for Web Services. Technical report, DARPA, 2004. http://www.daml.org.
3. A. Finkelstein and G. Spanoudakis. Software Package Requirements and Procurement. In *Proc. of the 8th Int'l IEEE Workshop on Software Specification and Design (IWSSD'96)*. IEEE Press, 1996.
4. X. Franch and J.P. Carvallo. Using Quality Models in Software Package Selection. *IEEE Software*, 20(1):34–41, 2003.
5. E.C. Freuder and M. Wallace. Science and substance: A challenge to software engineers. *Constraints IEEE Intelligent Systems*, 2000.
6. P. Grefen, H. Ludwig, and S. Angelov. A Three-Level Framework for Process and Data Management of Complex E-services. *International Journal of Cooperative Information Systems*, 12(1):455–485, December 2003.
7. P. Hentenryck. Constraint and Integer Programming in OPL. *Informs Journal on Computing*, 14(4):345–372, 2002.
8. P. Hentenryck and V. Saraswat. Strategic directions in constraint programming. *ACM Computing Surveys*, 28(4), December 1996.

9. J. Hobbs and J. Pustejovsky. Annotating and Reasoning about Time and Events. In *Proc. of the AAAI Spring Symposium on Logical Formalization of Commonsense Reasoning*, Stanford, CA, March 2003.

10. J. Hobbs and J. Pustejovsky. An Ontology of Time for the Semantic Web. *ACM Transactions on Asian Language Processing, Special Issue on Temporal Information Processing*, 3(1):66–85, March 2004.

11. Y. Hoffner, S. Field, P. Grefen, and H. Ludwig. Contract-driven Creation and Operation of Virtual Enterprises. *Computer Networks*, (37):111–136, 2001.

12. H.J. Levesque and R.J. Brachman. Expressiveness and Tractability in Knowledge Representation and Reasoning. *Computational Intelligence*, 3(2):78–93, May 1987.

13. L. Li and I. Horrocks. A Software Framework for Mathmaking based on Semantic Web Technology. In *Proc. of the 12th ACM Intl. Conference on World Wide Web (WWW'03)*, pages 331–339, 2003.

14. K. Marriottt and P.J. Stuckey. *Programming with Constraints: An Introduction*. The MIT Press, 1998.

15. O. Martín-Díaz, A. Ruiz-Cortés, A. Durán, D. Benavides, and M. Toro. Automating the Procurement of Web Services. In *1st Int.l Conf. on Service-Oriented Computing*, volume 2910 of *LNCS*, pages 91–103, Trento, Italy, 2003. Springer Verlag.

16. F. Pang and J. Hobbs. Time in OWL-S. In *Proc. of the AAAI Spring Symposium on Semantic Web Services*, pages 29–36, Stanford, CA, 2004.

17. A. Ruiz-Cortés. *A Semiqualitative Approach for the Automatic Management of Quality Requirements (in Spanish)*. PhD thesis, University of Seville, 2002.

18. A. Ruiz-Cortés, O. Martín-Díaz, A. Durán, and M. Toro. Improving the Automatic Procurement of Web Services using Constraint Programming. *Int. Journal on Cooperative Information Systems*, 14(4):439–467, December 2005.

19. A. Sahai, V. Machiraju, M. Sayal, L.J. Jin, and F. Casati. Automated SLA Monitoring for Web Services. Research Report HPL-2002-191, HP Laboratories, 2002.

20. A. ShaikhAli, O. Rana, R. Al-Ali, and D. Walker. UDDIe: An Extended Registry for Web Services. In *Proc. of the IEEE Int'l Workshop on Service Oriented Computing: Models, Architectures and Applications at SAINT Conference*. IEEE Press, January 2003.

21. K. Sycara, M. Klusch, S. Widoff, and J. Lu. Dynamic Service Matchmaking among Agents in Open Information Environments. *SIGMOD Record*, 28(1):47–53, 1999.

22. M. Tian, A. Gramm, T. Naumowicz, H. Ritter, and J. Schiller. A Concept for QoS Integration in Web Services. In *Proc. of the IEEE Int'l Web Services Quality Workshop (at WISE'03)*, pages 149–155, 2003.

23. V. Tosic, K. Patel, and B. Pagurek. Reusability Constructs in the Web Service Offering Language (WSOL). Research Report SCE-03-21, The Department of System and Computer Engineering, Carleton University, Ottawa, Canada, 2003.

24. L. Zeng, B. Benatallah, A.H.H. Ngu, M. Dumas, J. Kalagnanam, and H. Chang. QoS-Aware Middleware for Web Services Composition. *IEEE Transactions on Software Engineering*, 30(5):311–327, May 2004.

Approaching Web Service Coordination and Composition by Means of Petri Nets. The Case of the Nets-within-Nets Paradigm*

P. Álvarez, J.A. Bañares, and J. Ezpeleta

Department of Computer Science and Systems Engineering,
Instituto de Investigación en Ingeniería de Aragón (I3A),
University of Zaragoza. María de Luna 3, E-50015 Zaragoza (Spain)
{alvaper, banares, ezpeleta}@unizar.es

Abstract. Web service coordination and composition have become a central topic for the development of Internet-based distributed computing. A wide variety of different standards have been defined to deal with the composition of Web services (usually represented as workflows) and the execution of coordination protocols. On the other hand, some relevant research proposals have already pointed to the use of the same formalism for both aspects, being Petri nets one of the adopted formalisms. In this work we present a case study showing how the adoption of the *Nets-within-Nets* paradigm helps in the modelling of complex coordination protocols and workflows. We first propose a Petri net model for a Web service peer able to run any workflow and to dynamically interpret the coordination required protocols. The execution of these protocols allows the peer to integrate functionalities offered by external peers. The *Linda* communication model has been used to support the integration among peers.

Keywords: Service Composition and Coordination, Formal Methods for Service-Oriented Architectures, Petri nets, Nets-within-Nets paradigm.

1 Introduction

In service-oriented computing, Web services are the basic building blocks to create new applications. Many efforts have been devoted to define some standards to access Web services. As pointed in [1], some research should be done on how to weave those services together and subsequently expose the resulting artifacts as new Web services, namely, service coordination and composition (choreography and orchestration terms are also used alternatively to refer to them). The cornerstone of this style of building Web-based applications is a communication

---

* This work has been partially supported by the Spanish Ministry of Education and Science through the project TIC2003-09365-C02-01 from the National Plan for Scientific Research, Development and Technology Innovation.

B. Benatallah, F. Casati, and P. Traverso (Eds.): ICSOC 2005, LNCS 3826, pp. 185–197, 2005.

middleware able to glue Web services using new interaction models, more complex than the provided by the client/server model (asynchronous, event-based communication, etc.).

Service composition is an aspect related to the implementation of a Web service whose internal logic involves the invocation of operations offered by other Web services. From this definition, it is obvious that composition requires interactions between different Web services: a Web service may require specific dialogs (sequences of interchanged messages) in order to respond to a service requested by another participant. A *conversation* is a dialog among two or more Web services participating in these complex interactions, whereas a *coordination protocol* describes a set of accepted conversations (the external observable behavior of involved Web services) [1].

Most coordination and composition standard initiatives have been launched with industry-wide support. For Web service coordination, behavioral descriptions (i. e., the set of protocols and their conversations) of Web services can be defined using high-level declarative languages, such as WCSI [2], WS-CDL [3] and OWL-S [4]. On the other hand, many composition tools are available in the marketplace, most of them offering some type of modelling mechanism based on the BPEL4WS specification [5]. In any case, despite all the efforts invested in the standardization of coordination and composition languages and tools, an important problem is the lack of a clear methodology to develop complex Web services. Another interesting question refers to the fact that both, composition and coordination, have quite similar aspects, which lead us to the question of why not to use the same tool/formalism to work with them.

Different solutions can be adopted to deal with this last point, being Petri nets a quite natural approach. Petri nets [6] are a well-known formalism in the world of concurrent systems, which easily fits into Web service environments to deal with composition and coordination aspects (see for instance [7, 8, 9, 10]). The Petri net family of formalisms are of interest for the Web service community because they provide a clear and precise formal semantics, an intuitive graphical notation and many techniques and tools for their analysis, simulation and execution [7]. However, Petri nets are not the unique formalism that can be used for that purposes: in [11, 12] alternative solutions can be found using automata-based specifications of the peers' behaviors, using queues as intermediate message stores; and, in [13] is investigated the use of process-calculus techniques for providing distributed protocols in a mobile agent-based environment.

In this paper we propose a formal model based on Petri nets to represent a Web service peer able to run workflows representing composed services, to dynamically interpret the coordination protocols required by them during the execution and to communicate with other external peers via an abstraction of a communication middleware. The use of Petri nets as the same formalism to represent together conversations and workflows and the adoption of the *Nets-within-Nets paradigm* allow a natural integration of the coordination and composition models, making their interactions easier. The model imposes a methodology for avoiding the confusion between workflows and conversations, and provides a coordination space based on the *Linda* paradigm [14] to model the asynchronous communications among peers. The choice of *Linda* is motivated because its communication primitives are particulary well-suited for Web service environments allowing an uncoupled communication and requiring a minimum prior knowledge between the cooperating peers.

Our approach is similar to the one in [15]. Moldt et al. follow a more agent-centric view to cope with adaptability for workflows in the Web service field. They use *Nets-within-Nets* to deal with different aspects related with Web services, such as the deployment of Web services into physical hosts, the service container, and the internal and external service flows. Our proposal provides a more concrete model based on a *Linda*-like communication model. This simpler and narrower point of view allows us to provide a more detailed representation of peers, recovering the explicit separation between protocols (workflows) and conversations of agent models presented in [16].

The paper is organized as follows. Section 2 presents a brief introduction to the *Linda* communication model and the *Nets-within-Nets* paradigm. These formalisms constitute the framework for modelling Web service composition and coordination. Section 3 introduces our view of a Web service peer able to execute complex workflows involving complex conversations, which is then applied to the development of a concrete example from [17]. Finally, Section 4 contains some concluding remarks and future work directions.

2   Underlying Technologies: *Linda* and *Nets-Within-Nets*

Let us briefly introduce *Linda* and *Nets-within-Nets* as the underlying technologies used in the approach we are proposing.

2.1   *Linda* as the Communication Model

Linda is a coordination model based on generative communication. If two or more processes need to communicate, they cooperate exchanging messages through a shared memory. In *Linda*, messages are represented as *tuples*, while the common tuple repository is called a *tuple space* [14]. Informally speaking, a tuple is a list of untyped atomic values, as (`"a string"`, `18`), for instance. A few simple operations have been defined to insert (withdraw) tuples into (from) the tuple space: `out` places a tuple into the tuple space; `rd` returns a copy of a tuple from the space that matches with a template tuple (a template is a query tuple composed of values and wildcards, like (`"a string"`, `???`); the matching is free for the wildcard and literal for the constant values); finally, `in` works like `rd`, except that the matched tuple is removed from the space. If no matching tuples are into the space, the `rd` and `in` operations block the calling process until a convenient tuple appears (until a matching occurs). In this paper, the *Linda* operations have been renamed according to the point of view of the external processes: `write` (out), `read` (rd) and `take` (in).

The use of *Linda* in distributed and open environments is promising because it allows for an uncoupled cooperation in space and time and a flexible modelling of interactions among processes without adapting or announcing themselves. However, due to the fact that processes distributed over Internet communicate exchanging XML-encoded data, and the reading operations can involve long waits if no matching tuple is available in the space, *Linda* must be extended for improving its data representation capabilities and the set of associated operations. In this sense, the definition of tuple has been broadened to be able to represent data according to the XML encoding-format by means of attribute/value pairs, and new non-blocking reading operations inspired by an event-based communication style have been added to coordinate Web services [18].

2.2   The *Nets-within-Nets* Paradigm

Assuming the reader knows about Petri nets, let us now briefly introduce the class of Reference nets [19], which is a subclass of the *Nets-within-Nets* family of Petri nets [20]. *Nets-within-Nets* are an extension of the Colored Petri net formalism [21]. They fall into the set of object oriented approaches. In classical Petri nets, the net structure is static, and tokens move inside the net. *Nets-within-Nets* have a static part (the environment, also called *system net*) and a dynamic part, composed of instances of *object nets* that move inside the system net. These instances can be created in a dynamic way. Each object net can have its own internal dynamic behavior and can also interact with the system net by means of *interactions*. The system net can also move (*transport*) object nets by its own.

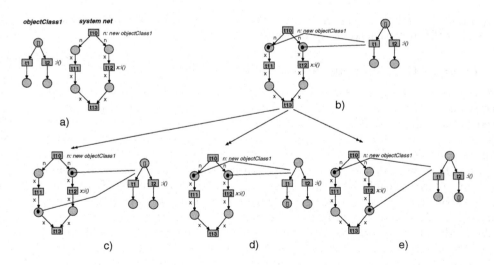

Fig. 1. a) A reference *Net-within-Net* example with the *system net* and an *object net*. b) The previous systems once transition **t10** has been fired. c) Evolution from the state in Figure-b) when **t11** fires (*transport*). d) Evolution from the state in Figure-b) when **t1** fires (*autonomous object event*). e) Evolution from the state in Figure-b) when the synchronized firing of **t12** and **t2** occurs (*interaction*).

Reference nets are a special subclass of *Nets-within-Nets* in which tokens in the system net, instead of object nets, are references to object nets, so that it is possible for different tokens to refer to the same object net. Figure 1-a) depicts a system net and an object net class. Firing transition **t10** creates two references to a new instance of **objectClass1**, moving the system to the state in Figure 1-b). In *Nets-within-Nets* three different types of transition firings are possible. The first one corresponds to the case in which an object instance executes an *object autonomous action*: in the state in Figure 1-b), transition **t1** of the object net is enabled, and can fire independently of the system net, leading to the state in Figure 1-d). The second one corresponds to the initiative of the system net: in the state in Figure 1-b), transition **t11** of the system net is enabled, and can fire moving the reference from the input place of transition **t11** to its output place, leading to the state in Figure 1-c) (notice that nothing has changed in the internal state of the object net). This is the reason why these firings are called *transports*. The last case corresponds to the synchronized firing of a transition of the system net with a transition of an object: in the state in Figure 1-b), transitions **t12** and **t2** can synchronize their firings (this is indicated by the common part in their inscriptions, **:i()**), whose firing will give the state in Figure 1-e). This way of firing is called an *interaction*. It is important to remark that the mentioned inscriptions may optionally consist of a common-separated list of parameters (e.g., **:i(x,y,z)**), which are used to communicate values between the synchronized nets.

Reference nets have a powerful tool called **Renew** [22] that allows to execute reference nets. It is developed in Java, and allows an easy integration of reference nets and Java code associated to transitions (it is possible to access Java code from the net, but also to access the net from Java code). This makes Renew to become a very interesting and useful tool to work on Web services environments.

3   *Nets-within-Nets* for Web Services Composition and Coordination

In this section we describe the architectural design of the approach we propose. In order to introduce the way we propose to integrate Web service composition and coordination, an example from the literature is developed.

3.1   The System Components

Figure 2 depicts the Petri net model we propose for a Web service peer. Basically, a Web service peer has the following elements. First, it contains a *work-space*. This is a kind of process space where the services in which the peer is involved are being executed. These can be either simple ("atomic" services) or composite services. Composite services are described by means of workflows where a component is a service provided by either an external peer or the peer itself. On the other hand, the interactions between the peer and other peers usually require the execution of (simple or complex) interaction protocols (choreographies) whose

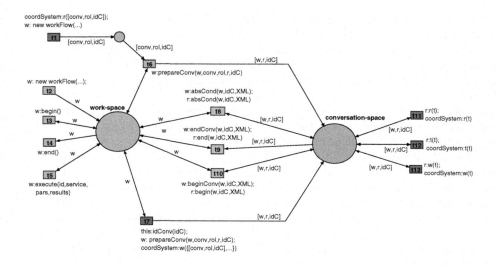

Fig. 2. The general architecture of a Web service peer

possible executions correspond to possible conversations. Conversations may involve two or more peers and, in each conversation, each peer has to execute a given part (the peer must play a given "role"). The set of roles that a peer is playing at a given moment stay in the *conversation-space*.

Adopting the *Nets-within-Nets* paradigm, Figure 2 corresponds to the "system net". Place *work-space* corresponds to the work space as described in the precedent paragraph, while place *conversation-space* contains the active roles in which the peer is involved in. Tokens inside these places will be Petri nets (*object nets* in *Nets-within-Nets* terminology) corresponding to workflows and roles in execution, respectively. Let us first take a closer look at the system net. Notice that transitions t1 and t2 both contain the `new workFlow(...)` action; these transitions are the way of starting the execution of new workflows. The main difference is that t2 corresponds to the case of a new workflow generated by the initiative of the peer itself, while transition t1 corresponds to the case of a workflow started in response to the requirement of a service initiated by another peer

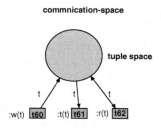

Fig. 3. A *Linda* coordination system

(accepting to participate in a conversation demanded by another peer requires to be able to execute a given role of a conversation).

A workflow whose execution has started can execute a set of different actions, corresponding to transitions around the work-space place:

- The workflow must execute a **begin** action (transition t3) as a first step after creation and, once terminated, it must execute an **end** action (transition t4).
- The workflow may require the execution of inner services, this is the task of transition t5. For that, a call to a local service or application is generated with a set of input and output arguments. For instance, once a set of data has been received, some local processing can be necessary before continuing an active conversation.
- Transitions t6 and t7 are the ones that generate new conversations, which are inserted into the conversation space. There are two different situations in which insertion of new conversations can occur (in fact, new roles corresponding to either a new conversation or an existing one): 1) the workflow requires the new conversation and starts it (transition t7); this means that a new conversation correlator **idC** is generated, a role (or set of roles) is assumed by the initiating workflow and a set of peers are demanded putting the corresponding service demands on the coordination system; 2) the workflow decides to meet the requirements of another peer to participate in an started conversation, in which a required role is assumed (transition t6).
- Once a given in-execution workflow starts the execution of a role of a conversation, some interactions are needed between the workflow and the conversation (these typically involve the necessity of passing information between the workflow and the role in order to be able to execute the conversation). They must synchronize the conversation begin and end points (transitions t10 and t9, respectively). On the other hand, the execution of a role of a given conversation by a peer sometimes requires the invocation of proper services, whose results may also be needed to continue the conversation (for instance, to do some calculations, to take some decisions, etc.). This approach is similar, but more flexible, to *abstract properties* (WSCI notation [2]) or *variables* (WS-CDL notation [3]) used by declarative XML-based coordination languages for the evaluation of conditions against the internal implementation of the service. This is the task of transition t8.

Obviously, Web services must interact, usually in an asynchronous way. This means that some mechanism must be provided allowing Web services to interact. Its asynchronous nature made interesting to adopt the *Linda* coordination system [14]. In fact, independently of its implementation, a *Linda* system will be considered along all the paper. Figure 3 is a model of a *Linda* coordination space. The three transitions t60,t61,t62 correspond to the **write**, **take** and **read** *Linda* operations, respectively, while place *tuple space* holds the tuples inserted into the *Linda* space. The peer will execute the communication operations by firing transitions t11,t12,t13, which will synchronize with t62,t61,t60, respectively.

Workflows and conversations have some common elements, which pushed us to model both using the same formalism. Among other common elements, the following can be considered: a) there may have some partial ordering to be imposed (on the way services are composed and also on the way messages are exchanged); b) the same way as some services can be satisfied in parallel, a peer, inside a given conversation, can dialog with a set of involved peers (even if the different dialogs would be executed in an interleaved way). This leads to the use of Petri nets for both types of elements. Since these elements must live and evolve inside a peer, to model them by means of object nets in the *Nets-within-Nets* paradigm is a quite natural approach. Let us introduce in the next subsection an example and to explain how it can be viewed from our perspective.

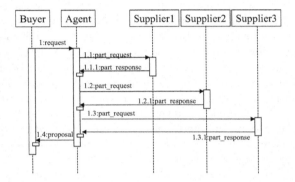

Fig. 4. The case study sequence considered in [17]

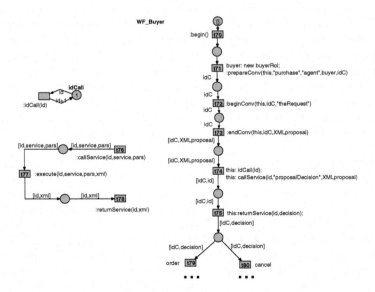

Fig. 5. The (partial) workflow of the buyer peer

3.2   An Example

Let us use the same case study in [17] to show how Petri nets can be used for composition and coordination, and how the *Nets-within-Nets* paradigm allows a natural integration with the previously defined architecture. The case corresponds to a PC manufacturer which needs to build a set of PC machines with different configurations, and using a list of available component suppliers. In the process, a buyer uses a purchasing agent to fulfill the inventory requests. The purchasing agent communicates with a set of suppliers, each of them offering specific components needed to build the PC machines. Once a complete configuration can be build (using components of one or multiple suppliers), a proposal is constructed and sent to the buyer, which can either place the parts order or cancel the request. Figure 4 shows a possible view of the process just described.

Figure 5 is a Petri net model of the workflow a buyer executes (by now, do not pay attention to the left small Petri nets in the figure: they are just technical elements to get a unique local identifier for local service calls, the upper one, and to implement the local service calls, the bottom one). Firing transition t2 in Figure 2 generates a new instance of this workflow, which is inserted into the work-space place. The synchronized firing of transitions t3 and t70 makes the execution of the workflow to start. The synchronized firing of transitions t7 and t71 makes a lot of work. First, a net instance of the role "buyer" (left part of

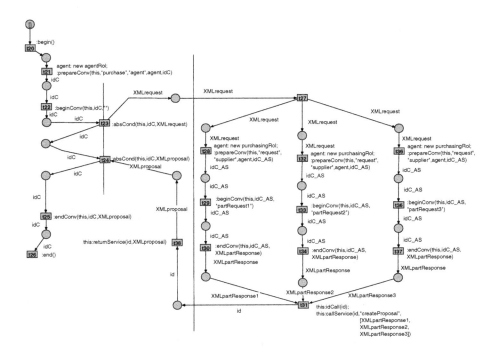

Fig. 6. The workflow of the agent peer

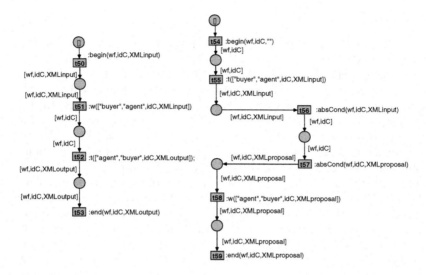

Fig. 7. A PN model of the buyer-agent interaction protocol (the "purchase" protocol). The left part corresponds to the "buyer" role, while the right one to the "agent" role.

Figure 7) of the coordination protocol "purchase" is created (the buyer: new buyerRol is executed); then the coordination protocol is prepared (a new correlator, idC, is generated and associated to the pair (workflow,coordination protocol)). The generated instance of the buyer role in the coordination protocol is then inserted into the conversation space. Finally, a request of the form ["purchase","agent",idC] is sent to the coordination system, which means that a peer playing the "agent" role of a coordination protocol of type "purchase" is looked for. Firing transition t72 starts the execution of the buyer role of the coordination protocol.

On the other side, Figure 6 is a Petri net model of the workflow an agent must execute as the answer to the request just commented. Notice that firing transition t21 prepares an instance of the agentRol; the conversation between the buyer and the agent takes place while both roles are executing. Figure 7 is the communication protocol where transitions t51,t52, t55 and t58 execute asynchronous communication operations on the *Linda*-like asynchronous communication system.

Let us now concentrate on the agent workflow to remark some important elements. Once the instance of the agent role net has been created, the synchronized firing of transitions t10, t22 and t54 is possible, which means that the agent part of the "purchase" conversation can start. When possible, the synchronized firing of t9, t25 and t59 will terminate that conversation. But previously, a lot of things must occur. The synchronized firing of t8, t23 and t56 allows the agent role part of the "purchase" coordination protocol to pass to the associated workflow, in form of an XML string/file, for instance, the description of the request. With this information, that workflow initiates, in parallel, a set of **request** coordination protocols with the three suppliers (transition **t27**). Once the offers from the suppliers arrive (firing transition **t31**), the local service *createProposal* is called, using the set of offers as parameter. By firing transition **t24**, the workflow of the agent peer communicates the proposal elaborated from the set of offers to its role (**"agent"** role) of the current conversation. The mentioned proposal is sent to the buyer by firing transition **t58**. The conversation between the buyer and the agent is then terminated, as well as the agent workflow (synchronized firing of transitions **t9**, **t25** and **t59**).

4   Conclusions

Most of the XML-based languages for modelling coordination protocols and workflows are declarative and cannot, by itself, be executed. Moreover, different languages are used as appropriate. In this work, Petri nets and the *Nets-within-Nets* paradigm are used as the same formalism to deal with complex coordination protocols and workflows. Its intuitive graphical notation, its formal semantics and the possibility of doing some properties analysis offer interesting advantages.

We have proposed a Petri net model for a Web service peer able to execute workflows and dynamically interpret the required coordination protocols. This proposal allows the development of complex Web based systems by the description of the workflows and protocols of the involved services, and subsequently, their distributed execution over a set of physical hosts. The cooperation among these distributed peers has been done by a *Linda*-like communication model, which is orthogonal to the formalism in which it is embedded. The decision of using a more concrete communication model, and a more concrete and delimited view of a Web services architecture which, as a counterpart, looses generality with respect to the proposal in [15], distinguishes our proposal from the approach followed by Moldt et al.

At present, we have also implemented *Linda* as a Petri net of the class of the *Nets-within-Nets*, so that we are able, using the Renew tool, to execute Web service peers and *Linda*-like coordination primitives on distributed physical hosts. We will study, in further work, the incorporation of some new functionalities to use Renew as a well-adapted tool for the modelling and prototyping of Web Services. It should include some important aspects as the automatic translation OWL-S into Petri nets, as pointed in [16], the addition of some horizontal coordination protocols, and the inclusion of transaction processing or time related aspects, as timeouts, for instance.

References

1. Alonso, G., Casati, F., Kuno, H., Machiraju, V.: Web Services. Concepts, Architectures and Applications. Springer Verlag (2004)
2. A. Arkin et al.: Web Service Choreography Interface (WSCI). Technical report, World Wide Web Consortium (W3C) (2002)

3. N. Kavantzas et al.: Web Service Choreography Description Language (WS-CDL). Technical report, World Wide Web Consortium (W3C) (2004)
4. D. Martin et al.: Bringing Semantics to Web Services: The OWL-S Approach. Number 3387 in Lecture Notes in Computer Science. In: First International Workshop, SWSWPC 2004. Revised Selected Papers. Springer Verlag (2004) 26–42
5. T. Andrews et al.: Business Process Execution Language for Web Services (BPEL4WS). Technical report, BEA Systems & IBM & Microsoft & SAP AG & Siebel Systems (2003)
6. Murata, T.: Petri nets: Properties, analysis and applications. In: Proceedings of IEEE. Volume 77. (1989) 541–580
7. Aalst, W., Hee, K.: Workflow Management: Models, Methods, and Systems. MIT Press, Cambridge, MA, USA (2004)
8. M. Mecella, F.P. Presicce, B.P.: Modeling E-Service Orchestration Through Petri Nets. Number 2444 in Lecture Notes in Computer Science. In: Proceedings of the 3rd VLDB International Workshop on Technologies for e-Services (VLDB-TES 2002). Springer Verlag (2002) 38–47
9. Hamadi, R., Benatallah, B.: A Petri net-based model for Web service composition. In: CRPITS'17: Proceedings of the Fourteenth Australasian database conference on Database technologies 2003, Darlinghurst, Australia, Australia, Australian Computer Society, Inc. (2003) 191–200
10. Yi, X., Kochut, K.J.: Process Composition of Web Services with Complex Conversation Protocols: a Colored Petri Nets Based Approach. In: Proceedings of the Design, Analysis, and Simulation of Distributed Systems Symposium (DASD'04), Advanced Simulation Technology Conference 2004. (2004) 141–148
11. Hull, R., Benedikt, M., Christophides, V., Su, J.: E-services: a look behind the curtain. In: PODS '03: Proceedings of the twenty-second ACM SIGMOD-SIGACT-SIGART symposium on Principles of database systems, New York, NY, USA, ACM Press (2003) 1–14
12. Fu, X., Bultan, T., Su, J.: Analysis of interacting BPEL Web services. In: WWW '04: Proceedings of the 13th international conference on World Wide Web, New York, NY, USA, ACM Press (2004) 621–630
13. Fournet, C., Gonthier, G., Lévy, J.J., Maranget, L., Rémy, D.: A calculus of mobile agent. In: Proc. of CONCUR'96. Volume 1119 of Lecture Notes in Computer Science. Springer-Verlag, Berlin (1996) 406–42
14. Carriero, N., Gelernter, D.: Linda in context. Communications of the ACM **32** (1989) 444–458
15. Moldt, D., Offermann, S., Ortmann, J.: Proposal for Petri Net Based Web Service Application Modeling. Number 3140 in Lecture Notes in Computer Science. In: Web Engineering: 4th International Conference, ICWE 2004. Springer Verlag (2004) 93–97
16. Moldt, D., Ortmann, J.: A Conceptual and Practical Framework for Web-based Processes. Unpublished manuscript (2004)
17. Peltz, C.: Web Service Orchestration and Choreography. A look at WSCI and BPEL4WS. Web Services Journal (2003) 1–5
18. Álvarez, P., Bañares, J.A., Muro-Medrano, P.: An Architectural Pattern to Extend the Interaction Model between Web-Services: The Location-Based Service Context. Number 2910 in Lecture Notes in Computer Science. In: First International Conference on Service Oriented Computing –ICSOC 2003. Springer Verlag (2003) 271–286
19. Kummer, O.: Introduction to Petri Nets and Reference Nets. Sozionik Aktuell (**1**)

20. Valk, R.: Petri nets as token objects - an introduction to elementary object nets. Lecture Notes in Computer Science: 19th Int. Conf. on Application and Theory of Petri Nets, ICATPN'98, Lisbon, Portugal, June 1998 **1420** (1998) 1–25
21. Jensen, K.: Colored Petri nets: A high level language for system design and analysis. In Rozenberg, G., ed.: Advances in Petri Nets 1990. Volume 483 of Lecture Notes in Computer Science. Springer Verlag, Berlin (1991) 342–416
22. Kummer, O., Wienberg, F.: Renew - the reference net workshop. In: Tool Demonstrations, 21st International Conference on Application and Theory of Petri Nets, Computer Science Department, Aarhus University, Aarhus, Denmark (2000) 87–89

Modeling and Analyzing Context-Aware Composition of Services

Enzo Colombo[1], John Mylopoulos[2], and Paola Spoletini[1]

[1] Politecnico di Milano, Dipartimento di Elettronica e Informazione,
Via Ponzio 34/5, 20133, Milano, Italy
{colombo, spoleti}@elet.polimi.it
[2] Dept. of Computer Science, University of Toronto,
40 St. George Street, Toronto, Canada M5S 2H4
jm@cs.toronto.edu

Abstract. Service-oriented modeling and analysis is a promising approach to manage *context-aware* cooperation among organizations belonging to the same value chain. Following this approach, a value chain is modeled as a composition of services provided by different partners and coordinated in a way that their interactions can be reorganized according to changes in the environment. However, so far, most of the research work in this area has been focused on the design of architectures handling service discovery, compatibility and orchestration. Little attention has been given to the specification and verification of context-aware composition of services during the requirement engineering process. The goal of this paper is to fill this gap through a methodological approach based on the strict coupling between a social and a process model. The methodology is discussed through a simple example.

1   Introduction

Industrial districts consist of a number of enterprises, often small-to-medium (SME), that are physically close. These enterprises often collaborate through short-term projects to deliver products and services. In such a setting, enterprises strive to exploit flexible forms of collaboration with their business partners as a means to extend the boundaries of their planning activities, increase performance through cooperation and reduce TCO (Total Cost of Ownership). Industrial districts often include alliances, temporary or permanent, between two or more legal entities that exist for the purpose of furthering business or social objectives without causing the participants to lose their autonomy. In general, this cooperative environment is characterized by organizations that own heterogeneous information systems, with their own processes, procedures, data schemes, internal roles and responsibilities.

As a consequence, industrial districts represent an ideal environment for the implementation of a cooperative environment that supports the automation of inter-organizational business processes through the *logical composition* of distributed services representing public views on organizations' private workflows.

B. Benatallah, F. Casati, and P. Traverso (Eds.): ICSOC 2005, LNCS 3826, pp. 198–213, 2005.

In this context, ebXML is an example of a stable architectural solution that provides a specification language and an architecture shifting the logic of composition from information to service exchange [14].

However, ebXML does not support inter-organizational business processes that are context-aware in the sense that they are run-time customizable, i.e., they can readily adapt their structure according to feedbacks from the environment. For example, a previous agreement cannot be re-negotiated during the execution of a collaborative activity and a partner cannot be automatically replaced when cooperative goals are not fulfilled. In order to overcome these limitations, researchers and practitioners have focused much effort on implementing service-oriented architectures supporting context-aware collaborations among organizations [17, 10]. In such settings, an inter-organizational process is implemented through a composition of services supplied over multiple channels by different actors. In particular, a composition of services describes the relationships among cooperating organizations according to a global, neutral perspective, in terms of valid *control* and *coordination* mechanisms. Moreover, a service composition is usually public, since it specifies the common rules defining a valid interaction among distributed business processes.

Unfortunately, the fruits of this research on context-aware applications does not have counterparts in methods, models and tools supporting the requirements engineering process. Indeed, according to [3], the conceptual modeling and analysis of context-aware composition of services is in its early stage even if this is the phase where the most and costliest errors are introduced to a design.

The goal of this work is to present a methodological framework that supports the conceptual modeling and formal analysis of requirements for context-aware service compositions through a social and a complementary process perspective. The paper also explores how modelers can analyze different process alternatives complying with the same social specification. Finally, our approach supports the formal verification of critical properties of a service composition (e.g., termination, structural soundness and achievement of shared goals). This work represents therefore a first step toward the design of service compositions aligned with different requirements policies.

In the remainder of the paper, we first motivate this work in terms of the state of the art. Then in Section 3, we define a set of different requirements policies adopted from the autonomic computing literature [9, 13] that modelers can adopt during the requirements analysis and process specification. Section 4 discusses the requirements analysis process supporting the implementation of a composition of services. Finally, Section 5 discusses an example highlighting how our model formalizes service compositions with respect to different requirements.

2   Related Work

Most of the current work on context-aware composition of services is focused on service orchestration, discovery and semi-automatic management of compositions. For example, a theoretical model supporting service orchestration through colored Petri nets is proposed in [12]. In particular, this work proposes a novel formal approach to the distribution of control responsibilities among different actors.

Moreover, formal models of service compositions supporting e-service discovery and composition are discussed in [1, 18]. The work of Bultan et al. is mainly focused on providing a model of compositions for detailed design. Under this framework, individual services communicate through asynchronous messages and each service maintains a queue for incoming messages. Moreover, a global *watcher* keeps track of messages as they occur. However, this work pays little attention to the problem of specifying and analyzing service compositions, even though this is a key factor to improve collaboration among organizations. Notice that these modeling techniques are particularly important within industrial districts where the final output of a composition must comply with strategic goals shared among different organizations. Moreover, the violation of goals requires compensation actions aimed at leading the composition to a consistent state.

A promising starting point for a methodology supporting the specification of context-aware composition of services is the adoption of a social model. Indeed, this model facilitates goal refinement, the discovery of goal interactions, and the identification of services that can contribute to their achievement. Moreover, social models are consistent with coordination theory that constitutes the conceptual background for modeling service compositions [11]. Requirements specification through social models is discussed within the Tropos project, where the i^* model for early and late requirements analysis is discussed and formally defined. The i^* framework supports the modeling of social relationships among actors and has been widely experimented within the context of Multi-Agent System (MAS) development [3]. However, social specifications alone are inadequate for modeling control and coordination mechanisms. In particular, they lack a formal semantics to represent the standard and exceptional control flow for the actions constituting a service composition. Accordingly, i^* needs to be supplemented in order to be adopted in our particular application domain.

3   Policies for Context-Aware Service Composition

In the following, we define a core set of policies that modelers should evaluate during the requirements engineering process associated with the specification and verification of context-aware composition of services. This core set involves a level of self error detection, i.e. *controllability*, that defines the strategies to identify anomalous situations within a composition, and two levels of self-management, *flexibility* and *adaptability*. Flexibility (also, self-repair) concerns the management of problems repaired through the specification of ad-hoc compensation flows, while adaptability (also, self-configuration) addresses cooperation scenario changes when the same problem occurs over time. It should be noted that self-repair and self-composition are generally acknowledged as key features of autonomic systems [13].

Flexibility. Flexibility is referred to as the run-time management of service self-repair intended to bring a composition in a consistent state at the lowest cost and it is formalized according to three dimensions of analysis: *automation level*, *compensation classes* and *sparsity*.

Automation level is concerned with the degree of human intervention in conducting self-repair. We recognize three levels of intervention: automatic, manual and semi-automatic. If the system can self-repair by itself in the presence of anomalous events, the automation level is automatic, while if it only provides monitoring capabilities the automation level is manual. Finally, if a system does require some input to perform a compensation action, the automation level is semi-automatic.

Compensation actions are distinguished into five classes that, as discussed in [16], represent an exhaustive set of tasks that organizations may implement to return a composition to a consistent state.

- *Delay class* calls for simply waiting a predefined time interval hoping that the anomalous event is resolved; for example, missing information received after waiting beyond the due date.
- *Informative class* calls for actions that communicate a particular anomalous state of affair; for example a violation is notified to a business partner.
- *Re-negotiatiation class* involves either relaxation or tightening of goals and constraints a result of process failures.
- *Re-execution class* involves the re-execution of one or multiple services, possibly starting the execution of the whole process.
- *Re-transact class* involves the re-execution of the entire composition with other potential business partners. This kind of actions always involves the failure of the current composition and, possibly, the replacement of one or more process partners.

Sparsity formalizes where compensation actions take place with respect to where the violation of goals occurs [2]. When the compensation is executed by the business actor that detects the violation, the compensation is called centralized. On the other hand, when the action is executed elsewhere it is called delegated. A delegated compensation can be based on either a centralized or a delegated decision. When the actor raising the anomalous event specifies the compensation that its business partner should perform, the decision is centralized, otherwise it is delegated. Moreover, a delegated compensation can be deterministic or not depending on the knowledge of the identity of the business partners involved in the composition. A typical example of non-determinism is the delegation of a compensation action to any actor that plays a given role within the system. Finally, a compensation is participative if it is performed by more than one actor. For example, re-negotiation is intrinsically participative since it requires to establish a new agreement between two or more counterparts.

Controllability. During a service composition, anomalous events are detected and communicated by control activities whose aim is to evaluate the fulfillment of goals. Controllability concerns the level of visibility on the private business process that implements a service, or the localization of control activities. Notice that, in our environment, control activities typically monitor quality of service goals (for example, service lead-time, productivity and use of resources).

Controllability is defined through two dimensions of analysis: service view and control policy. In service compositions such as the purchase of commodities by an occasional buyer, control is typically targeted to the end of the service with no intermediate checks during service execution. This view can be seen as black box since control is only possible when service outputs are delivered. Conversely, when control is possible on different activities during service execution, the service provides a public view on the private production process (i.e., grey-box).

Moreover, three control policies can be implemented when a service composition takes place. If control activities are performed where operating activities are executed, control is said to be centralized. On the other hand, control is delegated when control activities are performed elsewhere. Finally, if control activities are performed where operating activities are executed and repeated elsewhere, the control policy is redundant.

Let us consider a scenario that involves a service supplier and an occasional buyer. The former always monitors service lead-time since it have to guarantee an high quality of service (a violation of this commitment reduces the reputation of the buyer). The latter monitors the same attribute since it does not trust the supplier completely. This short-term relationship represent a simple case of redundancy since control is repeated by the buyer. However, we note that these two control activities could return different results if compared each other since service lead-time measured by the supplier could not consider network delays. As a consequence, redundant does not mean superfluous.

Adaptability is concerned with modifications of the standard and exceptional behavior of a composited process depending on the environment within which the composition is deployed. The environment is modeled through (i) the set of organizations involved within a composition (i.e., stakeholders) and through (ii) their goals over time.

In particular, adaptability is required when stakeholders' goals are repetitively violated over time. According to the stakeholder dimension, a designer may want to model different compositions as a function of the actors participating in the cooperative process. For example, when a business-to-consumer relationship is deployed, a provider could require payment before service delivery. On the contrary, for business-to-business interactions, payment could be required after delivery. We note that the specification of this adaptive behavior requires the formalization of two roles, i.e., corporate and retail. A stakeholder could be also modeled through either the channel or the device used during a service composition and, as a consequence, the behavior of a composition may vary accordingly. For example, a device could be a desktop, a laptop or a mobile phone. A channel could be a Virtual Private Network (VPN), Internet, a Wireless LAN or the GSM network. For each channel a designer may want to consider the bandwidth and the level of security of the channel (e.g., low, medium, high). Therefore, a composition may vary depending on channel since organizations may decide that strategic information provided by a given service can be shared on a VPN (high-security, high-bandwidth) but not when the same service is required over the Internet. Moreover, a composition with an information service provided for a laptop (e.g., querying a warehouse to check the availability of a product) can be simpler if compared with a composition modeled for a desktop.

As discussed before, adaptation is especially desired when stakeholders' goals are repetitively violated over time. In this context, modelers should identify different alternatives to adapt the composition in order to reduce the violation of their goals. In our framework, we identify a main composition and a set of alternatives corresponding to other configurations when a goal/softgoal is repetitively violated. As a consequence, a composition shifts from an alternative to another depending on nature and number of violations. We note that violations can be either interleaved or not depending on the policy that we adopt for counting anomalous events. If the counter is reset every time a desired behavior is reached, the policy is not interleaved, otherwise it is.

4   Domain Requirements Analysis of Services Composition

Figure 1 shows the methodological steps through which modelers can perform the requirements modeling and analysis for a service composition. These steps comply with coordination theory that provides a theoretical foundation [11]. In particular, the methodology consists of a social analysis, a process analysis and a verification phase. In the following we present each step. We note that a social representation of a composition could generate different scenarios with different business rules and, as a consequence, different process models. These alternatives are evaluated studying the impact of different specification policies (see Sect. 3) on strategic goals. The evaluation process is performed adopting the labeling notation proposed in the NFR framework. Labels are defined as follows: satisfied ($\checkmark$), weakly satisfied ($\mathcal{W}^+$), undecided ($\mathcal{U}$), weakly denied ($\mathcal{W}^-$), denied ($\times$), conflict ($\rightsquigarrow$) [5].

4.1   Social Analysis

The social specification of a service composition is organized in the following steps:

- *Step 1.1.* Identification of market players and dependencies; this step determines the organizations involved in the composition and their business relationships;
- *Step 1.2.* Refinement of business relationships, i.e., the actual pruning of intentional elements according to control and coordination policies.

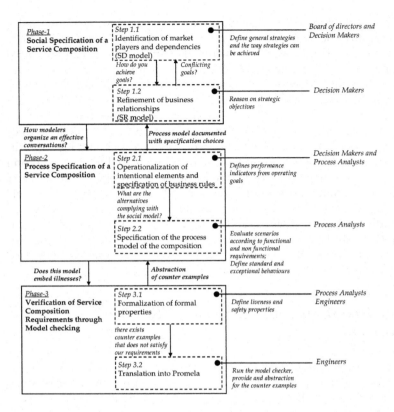

Fig. 1. Methodological steps supporting the analysis and specification of a composition of services

Our social analysis concerns a description of service composition that formalizes the strategy and the rationale of organizations interacting within a cooperative environment (i.e., *who, why* and *what*). In particular, directors and decision makers receive feasibility analysis and define the general goals that the composition should satisfy and the strategies through which these can be achieved. Then, general strategies are refined into more operating goals and the corresponding services fulfilling these goals are identified. The output of this step is an *i** social model of service composition and its level of detail is at the discretion of modelers.

In particular, our *i** specification embeds intentional elements such as softgoals, goals, service (i.e., a task in the traditional *i** notation) and information resources [3, 6]. Goals represent requirements to be fulfilled (○= goal); softgoals are similar to goals but their fulfillment is not clearly defined (⬡= softgoal). A service is a structured sequence of decisions and actions aimed at producing an added value transformation of inputs into outputs (○= service) and, finally, information resources represent inputs/outputs to services (□= resource).

Intentional elements are related to each other through Strategic Relationships (SR) and Strategic Dependencies (SD). The SD model concerns with the specification of social dependencies among organizations. In particular, an SD model is a graph where each node represents an organization and each link between two actors describes a dependency in terms of intentional entities. A dependency formalizes an agreement between two organizations, i.e. a depender and a dependee (depender − D − int. entity − D − dependee). The type of dependency defines the nature of the agreement. In particular, a goal (or softgoal) dependency represents the delegation of responsibility over the fulfillment of a goal (or softgoal) from a depender to a dependee. A service dependency represents the delegation of responsibility over the execution of a service from a depender to a dependee. With respect to goal (or softgoal), a service dependency is stronger since the depender also specifies how the service needed to fulfill a goal (or a softgoal) must be implemented. Finally, a resource dependency represents the need for an input that must be provided to a depender by a dependee. On the other hand, the SR model supports the refinement process of stakeholder goals through decomposition (—|−), contribution (→) and means-end (−▷) links. Directors and decision makers (see Figure 1) define their high-level goals and strategies and then, following a refinement process, elicit the set of services (and the corresponding resources) that should be performed to achieve their goals (and softgoals).

4.2   Process Analysis

The process specification of a service composition is organized according to the following steps:

- *Step 2.1.* Operationalization of intentional elements and specification of business rules managing either goals fulfillment or violation.
- *Step 2.2.* Specification of the process model of composition complying with both *(i)* the social model and *(ii)* the core set of policies that could be adopted when modeling context-aware compositions (see Sect. 3).

Our process analysis describes the control and coordination mechanisms of a service composition. In particular, decision makers receive a social model from the previous step and, together with process analysts, define the business rules modeling the standard and exceptional behavior of a service composition. Our approach to the transformation of a social model into business rules has been discussed in [6]. Moreover, business rules are specified according to ECA (event, condition, action) rules complying with the following semantics [4]:

Events are only of two types $End(sv), Begin(sv)$ where sv is a service, with the natural meaning of beginning and end of the service passed as argument.

Let S be a set of symbols representing actors, RO a set of symbols representing roles played by actors in S, G a set of symbols representing strategic goals, R a set of symbols representing information resources, X_t a set of discrete clocks and CH and DV sets of symbols representing respectively channels and devices used to supply a service in the conversation. A *condition* is a predicate p, that can be categorized in the following classes:

1. If p has the form $Achieved(g)$, $g \in G$, it is a *goal condition*.
2. If p has one of the forms $Fulfilled(a)$ or $Done(a)$, $a \in A$, p is called *compensation condition*.
3. If p has one of the forms $Actor(s)$, $Role(s, ro)$, $Device(dv)$, $Channel(ch)$, p is called *user condition*. $Actor(s)$ is satisfied when the current actor is $s \in S$; $Role(s, ro)$ is satisfied when the actor $s \in S$ plays the role expressed by $ro \in RO$; $Device(dv)$ is satisfied when the current device is $dv \in DV$ and $Channel(ch)$ is satisfied when the current channel is $ch \in CH$.
4. If p is a conjunction of predicates of the form $[\rho \bullet c]_t$, where $\bullet \in \{\leq, \geq, =, <, >\}$, $\rho \in X_t$ is a discrete clock, $c \in \mathbb{N}$ is a constant and the subscript t indicates a time measurement unit, it is a *temporal condition*.
5. If p has the form *(i)* $[\rho \bullet c]_t$, where $\bullet \in \{\leq, \geq, =, <, >\}$, ρ is a variable, c is a constant and the square brackets with the index t denote that ρ and c are of the same measurement unit t or *(ii)* $Received(x, s, r) \wedge x \in X$, where $r \in R$, $s \in S$ and X is a set of temporal conditions, p is a *resource condition*.

Actions can be composed by means of logical (i.e., $\neg$, $\vee$, $\wedge$) and *Sequence* operators. When actions are composed with $\vee$, the action to be enacted is selected non-deterministically. The *Sequence* operator involves the execution of a finite number of compensation actions in a sequence. However, compensation stops at the first successful compensation action in the sequence. Moreover, compensation actions are grouped into classes (see Sect. 3), i.e. *delay* (e.g., wait for, delay, ...), *informative* (e.g., notify, urge,...), *re-execute* (e.g., re-execute, skip,...), *re-negotiate* (e.g., relax, tighten,...) and *re-transact* (e.g. delegate execution,...).

For example, $Wait\_for([t_0, t_1], r)$ requires to wait for a resource within t_0 and t_1 time units, $Re\_execute([t_0, t_1], sv)$ requires the re-execution of a service sv, $Urge([t_0, t_1], sv, r)$ urges to the service sv the delivery of a resource r and $Relax$ $([t_0, t_1], sv, [\rho \bullet c]_m)$ requires to service sv the relaxation of the constraint $[\rho \bullet c]_m$.

Finally, business rules are then mapped into a process model, i.e. a particular instance of statechart [7] where transitions are labeled by the set of business rules defined so far and where states labels are defined as follows [4].

A state label l_q is a 5-uple $l_q = <sv, \{s_1, \ldots, s_n\} / \{ro_1, \ldots, ro_n\}, x, ch, dv>$, with $sv \in SV$, $s_i \in S$ $\forall i \in [1 \ldots n]$, $ro_j \in RO$ $\forall j \in [1 \ldots n]$, $x \in X$, $ch \in CH$, $dv \in DV$. The initial state q_0 has no label. Final state labels are modeled as $< [commit, abort, pending]$, null, null, null, null$>$.

We note that the symbol ξ in the action part of an ECA rule means that no action is performed during the transition from a state to another.

4.3   Verification Phase

The verification phase is organized as follows:

- *Step 3.1.* Formalization of safety and liveness properties [15] related to our process model.
- *Step 3.2.* Translation of the process model into the Promela language of the SPIN model checker [8].

This final step verifies that the process model is correct, or otherwise provides a counter example that points to specification inconsistencies.

Properties are generally defined by process analysts on the basis of requirements and then specified as LTL logic formulas by engineers. Hence, the process description of a composition of services C is accepted *iff* it satisfies a set of LTL formulas. Formally, let φ the conjunction of all LTL formulas, the process model is accepted *iff* $C| = \varphi$.

Our properties can be classified as follows:

- **Structural properties**, modeling the functional characteristics of a composition of services. Critical structural properties include the verification that a composite system is deadlock-free (i.e., absence of invalid end-states), that it does not embed infinite cycles and that each service belonging to the process is invoked (i.e., total functional coverage). More in general, structural properties model each functional expectation from a run of a composition of services involving a particular sequence of invocations, the ownership of each service and the device/channel used to deliver a service.
- **Temporal properties**, modeling time constraints of a composition. In particular, temporal requirements state that a service belonging to the composition can not be invoked in a time less then or equal to t. Moreover, we can also require that a service is not invoked before t.
- **Quality of Service (QoS) properties**, modeling the quality requirements of a composition. Critical QoS properties formalize strategic business goals whose fulfillment depends from the satisfaction of Service Level Agreement (SLA) parameters such as productivity, yield, price and throughput.

Accordingly, LTL formulas can formalize the following critical scenarios:

- a scenario involving a single property. For instance, we may require that the process lead-time is always constrained below a given threshold (i.e., $\Box(lead - time < threshold)$);
- a scenario involving dependencies among properties belonging to the same class. For instance, we may require that when a particular quality requirement is not fulfilled, the overall price of the composition must be below a predefined threshold (i.e., $\Box[(throughput \le .5) -> \diamond(price < InitialPrice)])$;
- a scenario involving dependencies among properties belonging to different classes. In particular, assertions relating either temporal and QoS properties with structural properties are useful to validate scenarios involving the behavior expected from a composite system as a consequence of exceptions. For instance, we may require that the violation of a quality requirement always lead to a negotiation of the initial agreement and viceversa (i.e., $\Box[(throughput \le .5) \Leftrightarrow \diamond\mathbf{Done}(negotiation)])$.

Notice that verification is possible since we generate non-deterministically all the possible values of temporal and QoS variables. These values are obtained by discretizing the domain of each variable into a finite number of significant values. In this way, we keep finite the number of alternatives. For sake of the simplicity, the reader can assume that each state of the model is mapped into a Promela process and that transitions among states are represented through the exchange of messages between Promela processes. Under such sattings, the non-deterministic generation of a temporal and QoS variable associated with a service is implemented within its corresponding Promela process. An in-depth discussion of the performances of our model checking technique has been provided in [4].

5   Example

This section illustrates how the social and process models proposed in Sect. 4 support the specification of a service composition according to different degrees of flexibility, controllability and adaptability. Hence, our goal in this section is threefold. First, we provide an intuitive use of our specification models through a simple example. Second, we discuss how a single social specification can be mapped into multiple alternative process models. Finally, we show how model checking supports the identification of inconsistent behaviors in the process specification thus guiding modelers in their work.

Let us suppose that, within an industrial district, a buyer company buys laptop components on the market and supplies assembled laptops to a selected network of retailers. Moreover, this buyer company decides to control components before assembly since it aims at minimizing laptop malfunctions (i.e., errors). In order to reduce total costs, the buyer also aims at minimizing the interaction with the supplier. On the other hand, potential sellers within the district does not provide any visibility on their production process. The production process is thus private. However, during component delivery, they provide component technical features required by the buyer to make quality control. We note that this example precisely defines our requirements for controllability (i.e., control delegation, black-box control). We note that control is considered delegated since it is not implemented by the seller locally.

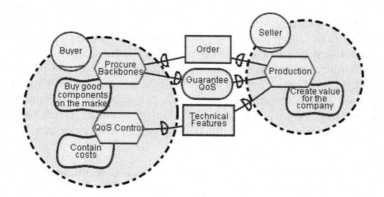

Fig. 2. Social model involving a buyer company and its laptop components supplier

Table 1. Contribution of different alternatives on strategic goals (NFR Analysis)

Policy		Result	
Flexibility	*Controllability*	*Subgoals*	*Goal*
1 ×	black-box control ✓ delegated control ✓	minimize interactions $\mathcal{W}^+$	Contain Cost $\mathcal{W}^+$
		minimize errors $\mathcal{W}^-$	
2 centralized decision ✓	black-box control ✓ delegated control ✓	minimize interactions ×	Contain Cost $\mathcal{W}^+$
		minimize errors ✓	
3 delegated decision ✓	black-box control ✓ delegated control ✓	minimize interactions $\mathcal{U}$	Contain Cost ✓
		minimize errors ✓	

However, there are several possible choices with respect to flexibility that need to be explored and compared during the design process. The social model associated with this cooperating scenario is shown in Figure 2.

At this stage, the buyer may want to evaluate the impact of different policies (see Sect. 3) on its high-level *Contain Costs* softgoal under the hypothesis that this goal is decomposed into *Minimize Errors* and *Minimize Interactions*. Table 1 studies the impact of controllability and flexibility on these softgoals through the NFR framework. In particular, flexibility impacts negatively on the *Minimize Interaction* softgoal but, on the contrary, it contributes positively to *Minimize Error*.

First of all, let us consider the simplest specification scenario, i.e. flexibility is not satisfied. This means that violations of the *Guarantee QoS* goal are not managed. The analysis of the NFR three shows that this configuration weakly satisfies the *Contain Cost* softgoal. In particular, the *Minimize Interaction* softgoal is weakly satisfied and the *Minimize Error* softgoal is weakly denied. If the buyer is happy with the adoption of a strategy resulting in a weak satisfaction of its high-level softgoal, the process model formalizing our cooperating scenario is shown in Figure 3(a). This specification presents a black-box delegated control where compensation is not implemented since when the QoS goal is violated the composition automatically aborts.

The second alternative (see Table 1) is intended to specify a cooperating scenario where the buyer wants to be sure that the compensation action raised by violations of the *Guarantee QoS* goal brings the composition in a consistent state. Accordingly, the buyer requires the implementation of a centralized decision, but this requirement denies the *Minimize Interactions* softgoal. On the other hand, the implementation of a centralized decision guarantees the satisfaction of *Minimize Errors*. The final result is weak satisfaction of *Contain Costs*, as with the first alternative. This means that the fulfillment of the *Minimize Errors* softgoal balances the structural complexity derived by more interactions.

Figure 3(b) shows the process model associated with our second alternative. With respect to the previous specification, from the perspective of controllability, our scenario is unchanged since control is black-box and delegated. However, the specification is a little bit more complex since compensation classes are introduced together with sparsity. Figure 3(b) enriches the scenario described in Figure 3(a) by allowing the re-execution of the production service when the QoS goal is violated. Moreover, since re-execution is allowed exactly once, if the QoS

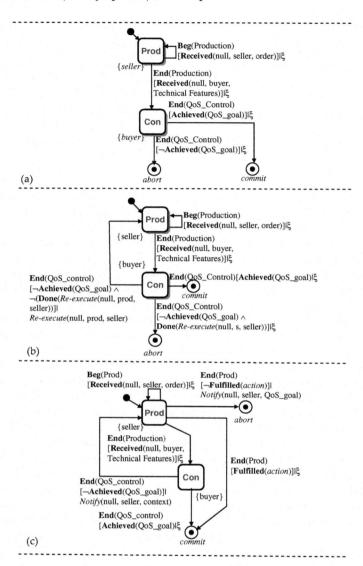

Fig. 3. Poor flexibility (a), centralized decision (b), delegated decision (c)

goal is still violated the composition aborts. Re-execution is performed according to the following guard condition: $\neg Achieved(QoS\_goal) \wedge \neg(Done(Re-execute(null, s, seller))$.

In summary, from the perspective of *flexibility*, this scenario is automatic, uses re-execute compensation class and compensation is delegated with a centralized decision. The compensation is delegated since it is executed by an actor different from the one raising the exception, i.e. the seller. Moreover, decision is centralized since the compensation action is decided by the actor raising the exception (i.e., the buyer).

Finally, the third alternative in Table 1 studies the impact of flexibility on high-level softgoals in case of delegated decision. According to this scenario, the impact of flexibility on the *Minimize Interaction* softgoal improves from *break* to *hurt* [5]. As a consequence, the *Minimize Interaction* softgoal is not *denied* but *undecided*. Moreover, the *Minimize Errors* softgoal is still satisfied meaning that the *Contain Costs* softgoal is satisfied as well. Hence, with respect to previous two alternatives, this current alternative seems to capture a better compromise.

Figure 3(c) shows the process model associated with this third alternative. In this case, a notification is provided to the seller that will perform a corresponding compensation action. If the compensation fails the composition is aborted, otherwise committed. Since the service view is black-box, the buyer is not aware of the rules followed to compensate the violation. The buyer is only aware of the behavior of the composition, independently of whether the compensation fails or not.

Once the better policy has been identified, our last step is requirements verification. Indeed, checking that the behavior of the compensation is consistent with our requirements is a critical activity of our modeling process. Under this scenario, we have two main vital requirements for our composition of services.

- An instance of the composition always terminates: $\Box\Diamond(commit \vee abort)$.
- The composition commits either if the QoS goal is fulfilled or if its violation is successfully compensated:
  $\exists q_n \in F[l_n = \langle commit,\ null,\ null,\ null,\ null \rangle \rightarrow$
  $(\exists a : Action,\ qs : QoSGoal(Achieved(qs) \vee Fulfilled(a)))].$

The analysis of the process model through model checking shows that *Prod* is an invalid end state [8]. In particular, the generated counter-example shows that the composition does not terminates into either commit or abort since our specification does not model what happens when the *order* information resource is not received. Hence, our model is enriched with a transition from *Prod* to *abort* labeled as following:
$Beg(Production)[\neg Received(null,\ seller,\ order)]\|\xi.$

Moreover, a successive analysis shows the same problem for the *Con* state. However, in this case *Production* has been already executed and modelers want to avoid, if possible, an abort of the composition. As a consequence the process model is completed as follows:

- A self-loop on the *Prod* state is added to urge the provisioning of *Technical Resources* This transition is labeled as follows:
  $End(Production)[\neg Received(null,\ seller,\ TechnicalFeatures)]\|$
  $Urge([1, 3],\ buyer,\ TechnicalFeatures).$
- A *pending* state modeling that control is given to a human operator is added to the composition to handle a failure of the *Urge* compensation action. The transition from *Prod* to pending is labeled as follows:
  $End(Production)[\neg Fulfilled(Urge([1, 3],\ buyer,\ TechnicalFeatures)]\|\xi.$

This new version of the original process model fully satisfies the two critical requirements formalized for our composition of services.

6   Conclusion and Future Work

This paper has presented a methodological framework that supports the modeling and formal analysis of service compositions extending the i^* social model adopted in Tropos [3] with a complementary process perspective. Moreover, this work has discussed a set of policies that designers should consider when shifting the attention from a social representation of the cooperative environment to one of the possible process scenarios. In summary, our proposal represents the first step toward the implementation of autonomic inter-organizational business processes, i.e., business processes that can self-repair, self-configure and self-tune on the basis of feedbacks from the environment [13]. Specifically, we envision an environment where several service compositions exist, but one is selected for execution. If there are problems with this execution, the system can self-repair or self-reconfigure by shifting to an alternative composition to improve its performance with respect to the fulfillment of stakeholder goals. Mechanisms for changing the composition on the basis of different types of feedback have not been studied yet in our work.

Future research direction will include the development of a theory of robustness for service compositions. In particular, we will study techniques to ensure that a composition behaves in a reasonable way even when part of the goals are inconsistent, implausible or unrealizable with the resources available.

References

1. T. Bultan, X. Fu, R. Hull, and J. Su. Composition specification: a new approach to design and analysis of e-service composition. In *Proceeding of the International Conference on the World Wide Web (WWW'03)*, ACM press, pages 403–410, 2003.
2. F. Casati and G. Pozzi. Modeling exceptional behaviours in commercial workflow management systems. In *Proceeding of the CoopIS/DOA/ODBASE 1999*, LNCS, pages 127–138, 1999.
3. J. Castro, M. Kolp, and J. Mylopoulos. Towards requirement-driven information systems engineering: the tropos project. *Information Systems*, 27:365–389, 2002.
4. A. Cherubini, E. Colombo, C. Francalanci, and P. Spoletini. A formal approach supporting the specification and verification of business conversation requirements. In *Proceeding of the IADIS International Conference on Applied Computing*, 2005.
5. L. Chung, B. A. Nixon, E. Yu, and J. Mylopoulos. *Non-Functional Requirements in Software Engineering Series*, volume 5. Kluwer Internationale Series in Software Engineering, 2000.
6. E. Colombo, C. Francalanci, and B. Pernici. Modeling cooperation in virtual districts: a methodology for e-service design. *International Journal of Cooperating Information Systems, Special Issue on Service Oriented Modeling*, 13(4):337–369, 2004.
7. D. Harel and A. Naamad. The statemate semantics of statecharts. *ACM Trans. on Soft. Eng. and Method.*, 5(4):293–333, 1996.

8. G.J. Holtzmann. *The SPIN Model Checker*. Addison-Wesley, 2004.
9. J. Kephard, M. Parashar, V. Sunderam, and R. Das, editors. *Proceedings of the International Conference on Autonomic Computing*, 2004.
10. Mais project. http://black.elet.polimi.it/mais/index.php.
11. T.W. Malone and K. Crowston. The interdisciplinary study of coordination. *ACM Comp. Surveys*, 26(1):87–119, 1994.
12. M. Mecella, F. Parisi-Presicce, and B. Pernici. Modeling e -service orchestration through petri nets. In *Proceedings of the 3nd VLDB International Workshop on Technologies for e-Services*, pages 38–47, 2002.
13. R. Murch. *Autonomic Computing*. Prentice Hall, 2004.
14. ebxml project. www.ebXML.org.
15. A. Pnueli. A temporal logic of concurrent programs. *Theoretical Computer Science*, 13:45–60, 1981.
16. W. R. Scott. *Organizations: Rational, Natural and Open Systems*. Prentice Hall, 1992.
17. Vispo project. www.casaccia.enea.it/vispo.
18. A. Wombacher and B. Mahlenko. Finding trading partners to establish ad-hoc business processes. In *Proceeding of the CoopIS/DOA/ODBASE 2002*, LNCS, pages 339–355, 2002.

Towards Semi-automated Workflow-Based Aggregation of Web Services

Antonio Brogi and Razvan Popescu

Computer Science Department, University of Pisa, Italy

Abstract. Service aggregation is one of the main issues in the emerging area of service-oriented computing. The aim of this paper is to contribute to the long-term objective of lifting service aggregation from manual hand-crafting to a semi-automated engineered process. We present a methodology which, given a set of service contracts, tries to construct an aggregation of such services. Service contracts include a description of the service behaviour (expressed by a YAWL workflow), as well as an (ontology-annotated) signature. The core aggregation process basically performs a control-flow and an (ontology-aware) data-flow analysis of a set of YAWL workflows to build the contract of an aggregated service.

1 Introduction

Service-oriented computing [18] is emerging as a new promising computing paradigm that centres on the notion of *service* as the fundamental element for developing software applications. In this scenario, two prominent issues involved in the development of next generation distributed software applications can be roughly synthesised as: (1) discovering available services that can be exploited to build a needed application, and (2) suitably aggregating such services to achieve the desired result. A typical example [16] of the need of aggregating services is a client wishing to make all the arrangements necessary for a trip (flights, hotel, rent-a-car, and so on). Such a client query may not be satisfied by a single service, while it could be satisfied by composing several services. Complex Web service interactions however require more than SOAP, WSDL and UDDI can offer [7], and semi-automatic aggregation frameworks based on such standards are not available yet.

The aim of this paper is to contribute to the long-term objective of lifting service aggregation from manual hand-crafting to a semi-automated engineered process. We present a methodology which, given a set of service contracts, tries to construct an aggregation of such services. Service contracts include a description of the service behaviour (expressed by a YAWL [23] workflow), as well as an (ontology-annotated) signature. The core aggregation process basically performs a control-flow and an (ontology-aware) data-flow analysis of a set of YAWL workflows to build the contract of an aggregated service. Technically, these analyses are defined by first expanding the services' workflows with dummy YAWL flow constructs, and by exploiting ontology-matching mechanisms to perform

B. Benatallah, F. Casati, and P. Traverso (Eds.): ICSOC 2005, LNCS 3826, pp. 214–227, 2005.

a semantics-aware data-flow analysis. It is worth noting that the aggregation process is parametric with respect to the type of semantic annotations and the matching mechanism. Namely different ontology-matching mechanisms can be plugged-in (e.g., [4, 5, 17]), including the "void" one for syntactic matching (matching=identity) in absence of ontological information. The result of the aggregation process is a YAWL workflow which describes the interplay among all the services considered, namely all the control-flow and data-flow relationships among them.

In this paper we will try to focus on the aggregation process, and directly consider the problem of how to aggregate a given set of service contracts. We will not describe here how service contracts can be generated from service implementations. (A thorough analysis of how to transform BPEL [3] specifications into workflows can be found in [26].) We will not describe either how the initial set of services is chosen. We may assume that it has been selected by some matchmaking algorithm in response to some client query. For instance, the composition-oriented matchmaking algorithm in [4] returns a candidate set of services which may collectively satisfy a client query. It is worth observing that the aggregation process is completely separated from the process of selecting the initial set of services. For instance, the latter can be also performed by a user browsing a (semantics-enabled) UDDI registry and selecting some services.

It is worth noting that the proposed aggregation process can accept both black-box and glass-box queries to drive the aggregation. Black-box queries simply specify the sets of inputs and outputs that the aggregated service should request and offer respectively. Glass-box queries specify instead a process behaviour (i.e., a workflow and not just inputs/outputs) and can be used to check whether it can be aggregated together with a given set of services.

The description of the proposed aggregation process can by synthesised in three main steps: (1) perform control-flow and data-flow analysis on the input services to determine their aggregation, (2) generate the contract of the aggregated service, (3) deploy the aggregated service. We will concentrate on steps (1) and (2) in this paper, and it is worth stressing the importance of separating the phase of contract generation from the deployment of the aggregated service, thus allowing multiple deployments of the latter.

2 Aggregation Framework

2.1 Service Contracts

We consider services that are described by *contracts* [13], and we argue that contracts should in general include different types of information: (a) **Ontology-annotated signatures**, (b) **Behaviour**, and (c) **Extra-functional properties**. Following [16], we argue that WSDL signatures should be enriched with ontological information (e.g., expressed with OWL [10] or WSDL-S [15]) to describe the semantics of services, necessary to automatise the process of overcoming signature mismatches as well as service discovery and composition. Still, the information provided by ontology-annotated signatures is necessary but *not* sufficient to ensure a correct inter-operation of services. Following [13], we argue that contracts should also expose a (possibly partial) description of the interaction protocols of services. Indeed, such information is necessary to ensure a correct inter-operation of services, e.g., to verify absence of locks. We argue that YAWL [23] (see below) is a good candidate to express service behaviour as it has a well-defined formal semantics and it supports a number of workflow patterns. Finally, we argue that service contracts should expose, besides annotated signatures and behaviour, also so-called extra-functional properties, such as performance, reliability, or security. (We will not however consider these properties in this work, and leave their inclusion into the aggregation framework as future work.)

We intend to build an aggregation framework capable of translating the behaviour of a service described using existing process/workflow modelling languages (e.g., BPEL, OWL-S [16], etc.) into equivalent descriptions expressed through an abstract language with a well-defined formal semantics, and vice-versa. An immediate advantage of using such an abstract language is the possibility of developing formal analyses and transformations, independently of the different languages used by providers to describe the behaviour of their services. We consider that YAWL [23] is a promising candidate to be used as an abstract workflow language for describing service behaviour. YAWL is a new proposal of a workflow/business processing system, which supports a concise and powerful workflow language and handles complex data, transformations and Web service integration. YAWL defines twenty most used workflow patterns gathered by a thorough analysis of a number of languages supported by workflow management systems. These workflow patterns are divided in six groups (basic control-flow, advanced branching and synchronisation, structural, multiple instances, state-based, and cancellation).[1] YAWL extends Petri Nets by introducing some workflow patterns (for multiple instances, complex synchronisations, and cancellation) that are not easy to express using (high-level) Petri Nets. Being built on Petri Nets, YAWL is an easy to understand and to use formalism. With respect to process algebras, YAWL features an intuitive (graphical) representation of services through workflow patterns. Furthermore, as illustrated in [22], it is likely that a simple workflow which is troublesome to model for instance in π-calculus may be instead straightforwardly modelled with YAWL. A thorough comparison of workflow modelling with Petri Nets vs. π-calculus may be found in [22]. With respect to the other workflow languages (mainly proposed by industry), YAWL relies on a well-defined formal semantics. Moreover, not being a commercial language, YAWL supporting tools (editor, engine) are freely available.

2.2   Aggregation Phases

As mentioned in the Introduction, a prerequisite of our framework is the set of services to be aggregated which may be obtained either by manual selection or as

---

[1] Space limitations do not allow us to illustrate these patterns. A thorough description of them may be found in [24].

output of a service discovery framework. It is worth noting that our aggregation approach copes both with black-box and glass-box queries. On the one hand, a black-box query specified only in terms of offered inputs and requested outputs is transformed into an equivalent service which is then added to the registry of matched services. On the other hand, one may submit services as glass-box queries. By doing so one may also check whether the corresponding service can be aggregated with a given set of services.

The semi-automated aggregation framework we propose can be synthesised by the following phases:

0. **Service Translation.** This preliminary phase deals with translating real-world descriptions (e.g., BPEL + semantics, or OWL-S, etc.) of the services to be aggregated into equivalent service contracts using YAWL as an abstract workflow language for expressing behaviour, and OWL for example for expressing the semantic information. One may note that such a translation may be done off-line and hence it is not a burden for the aggregation process. (A thorough analysis of how to transform BPEL specifications into workflow patterns can be found in [26].)

1. **Core Aggregation.** During this phase YAWL processes are expanded with explicit data- and control-flow (dummy) constructs, also called Input/Output Control/Data enabler processes (or ICs/IDs/OCs/ODs for short). We then express the initial control-flow connections in terms of the newly added ICs and OCs. Next, we use data-flow dependencies (i.e., operation and message mapping among the involved parties) provided by an ontology-aware matching algorithm (e.g., [4, 5, 17]) to derive a data-flow mapping. We express such mapping by suitably linking IDs and ODs.

2. **Contract Generation.** Firstly, we perform a basic check to see whether the aggregated service does not have processes with unsatisfied inputs. Should this be the case, we adequately eliminate unlinked ODs and other redundant dummies introduced by the previous phase, and we cancel redundant control-flow constructs. The ontology-annotated signature and behaviour we obtain form the service contract of the aggregated service. The generated contract can be further analysed (e.g., lock analysis) and optimised.

3. **Service Deployment.** Finally, the aggregated service can be deployed as a real-world Web service (i.e., described using OWL-S, or BPEL + semantics, etc.). Clients will hence see the aggregation as another Web service that can now be discovered and further aggregated with other services. This operation is the inverse of the operation done during the Service Translation phase.

As already mentioned in the Introduction, we will describe phases (1) and (2) in the following, after introducing some definitions.

2.3   Definitions

We shall use the term "service" to denote the YAWL notion of "workflow specification", "process" to denote a YAWL "task" as well as "start" and "end" to denote YAWL "input condition" and "output condition", respectively.

We consider a set or registry of service contracts to be aggregated, where each contract corresponds to an original service implementation (e.g., described with BPEL and OWL for semantics, etc.). A contract S consists of an ontology-annotated signature (i.e., semantic information, Sem for short) and of a behaviour description (Beh).[2]

Sem specifies the set of processes ($Procs$) as well as the name ($Sname$) and the type ($Stype$) of the service. Indeed we argue that services, processes as well as parameters (i.e., messages) should be annotated with ontological information describing their types. Such information can be used by discovery frameworks to better match services. For example, considering ontologies for services, processes and parameters, we may have for example a "stock_quote" service type, a "flight_reservation" process type, or a "notebook_computer" parameter type, and so on. $Procs$ consists of the m processes of S together with $start$ and end, which are two special dummy processes used to mark the entry end exit points, respectively, of S. A process P contains the sets of input (I) and output (O) parameters, its name ($Pname$) and type ($Ptype$). Similarly to services and processes, a parameter exposes its name ($Iname$) and type ($Itype$). Note that the matching concerns types — rather than names — of parameters, processes or services[3]. Name matching should be employed in absence of ontology-annotations. The $start$ and end dummy processes are defined similarly to the other processes P yet they do not have IOs and ontological values associated. They are named "$DummyStart$ of P" and "$DummyEnd$ of P", respectively.

Beh contains information about both the control-flow constructs used by processes in $Procs$ (PC), as well as information about the control-flow dependencies among such processes (PD). PC associates one join and one split construct to each process P. A join or split control construct may be one of the following: AND, OR, XOR, or EMPTY. Intuitively, the join specifies "how many" processes before P are to be terminated in order to execute P, while the split construct specifies "how many" processes following P are to be executed. The EMPTY join (split) is used when at $most$ one process execution precedes (follows, respectively) the execution of P. PD defines the control-flow of S by means of a set of process pairs. A pair $< P, Q >$ specifies that P must be executed before process Q (i.e., Q may begin its execution provided P has finished its execution).

Consider the following example which will be used as a basis for presenting the applicability of our methodology, and for enhancing the description of the proposed approach. A youngster passionate about winter sports and computer science, decides to publish on her homepage a Web service providing information on the conditions of her favourite slope. Basically, she wishes that other winter

---

[2] When necessary, indexes shall be used for disambiguation.

[3] Roughly, service matching may restrict the set of services to be considered, while process matching may help refining further the selection (e.g., matching a "computer_selling" process of an "e_shop" service) to possibly aggregate sub-services rather than whole services. Finally, parameter matching can provide the data-flow information necessary to achieve the aggregation.

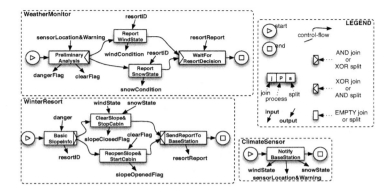

Fig. 1. Example registry with three services to be aggregated

sports enthusiasts like her may access her page in order to see whether the slope is practicable and the cabin is working.

One may assume that she locates the ontologically-enriched WR^4 service (see Figure 1[5]) from a (semantically anotated) UDDI registry. Next, she feeds this service as a black-box query to a discovery framework (e.g., [9] or [5]). This may lead to selecting the other two services in Figure 1.

It is important to note that the example is not supposed to present a software masterpiece as we would like to underline the fact that different services written by different persons with different programming styles and backgrounds may present (aggregation) issues. It is likely that the selected services do not match perfectly, or that the ensemble is not optimal, and so on. Redundancies (e.g., redundant outputs) may occur as well. The three services are as follows:

CS basically gathers data from sensors located on top of the mountain. Upon invocation, it executes process NBS which outputs the sensor's location and the warning level for the slope it is monitoring sLW, as well as the snow's condition sS (e.g., indication of avalanche danger) and the wind's condition wS (e.g., strong wind leads to stopping the cabin). We may assume that CS runs periodically (e.g., every hour).

WM (or $BaseStation$) centralises data gathered from various CSs. It firstly performs a preliminary analysis (e.g., reasoning based on a history record over the past X years) through the execution of PA. On the one hand it specifies whether there is an avalanche danger by enabling dF or, on the other hand whether the slope is safe (e.g., it may be (re)opened). In the latter case cF is enabled. The AND split of PA indicates that *both RWS and RSS* are to be executed after it. RWS makes its own prediction on the wind state based on the rID input. Similarly, RSS sets the snow state based on its prediction. The AND join construct of WRD states that WRD may be executed provided *both RWS*

---

[4] Due to space limitations, we shall use abbreviations throughout the paper (e.g., WR instead of $WinterResort$).

[5] In addition to the representation of YAWL tasks (i.e., processes) we graphically describe their parameters as well.

and RSS finished execution. WRD is in charge of waiting for a report from a WR service (i.e., the decision of the latter on whether to close or to (re)open the slope).

WR is a service that manages access to a slope and cabin. From a workflow point of view, WR behaves differently from WM in the way that it uses a XOR split in the BSI process and a XOR join in the $SRBS$ process. The former indicates that *either $CSSC$ or $RSSC$* will be activated for execution, while the latter indicates that $SRBS$ will be invoked after each execution of *either $CSSC$ or $RSSC$*. BSI inputs the danger flag produced by the WM and it decides either to clear the slope and stop the cabin (by executing the $CSSC$ process), or to (re)open the slope and (re)start the cabin (by executing the $RSSC$ process). Finally, $SRBS$ sends a report to the WM service with its decision.

2.4   Core Aggregation

During this phase, all processes (except *start* and *end* ones) are expanded with explicit control- and data-flow dummies. Then, a control-flow analysis expresses the initial flow dependencies in terms of the newly added dummies. Last but not least, a data-flow analysis coordinates processes of (possibly) different services by taking into account a given data-flow mapping. The three steps are detailed hereafter.

PROCESS EXPANSION

Let us consider the empty (aggregated) service A. For each process P of each service S, we generate the following five dummy processes:

- P^* corresponding to process P "stripped off" its join and split control constructs, and augmented with AND join and split constructs,
- an Input Control enabler IC_P which inherits the initial join of P,
- an Output Control enabler OC_P which inherits the initial split of P,
- an Input Data enabler ID_P which is in charge of gathering all inputs needed for the execution of P (if P has at least one input), as well as
- an Output Data enabler OD_P which "offers" all outputs of P to other processes (if P has at least one output).

With the exception of P^*, all such processes lack IOs and ontological values. Their purpose is to explicitly separate the control- and data-flow logic of P. From a control-flow point of view, IC_P and ID_P are linked as inputs of P^* while OC_P and OD_P are linked as outputs. All added dummies as well as the corresponding dependencies have to be added to Beh_A.

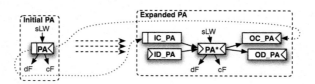

Fig. 2. Expansion of PA

Figure 2 describes the process expansion step applied to process PA of service WM. As one may note, PA^* employs AND join and split constructs as, on the one hand, both IC_PA and ID_PA have to finish execution before executing PA^* and, on the other hand, both OC_PA and OD_PA are to be executed after PA^* terminates. From a data-flow point of view, the AND join of ID_PA indicates that all inputs of PA must be available in order to execute PA. Dually, the AND split of OD_PA specifies that after PA finishes its execution, all its outputs will be available to all processes requesting at least one of them as input.

Once all processes have been expanded, two more processes are introduced. They are IC_A and OC_A corresponding to the input and the output control enabler dummies of A. IC_A has an AND split in order to activate ICs of all services to be aggregated. Dually, OC_A has an AND join in order to wait for OCs of all services to finish execution. Links from $start\_A$ to IC_A as well as from OC_A to end_A are added to Beh_A.

CONTROL-FLOW ANALYSIS

During this step, control-flow dependencies of each service S are specified in terms of the newly added ICs and OCs, as well as IC_A and OC_A, and then added to Beh_A. The result of applying this step on the WM service may be seen in Figure 3.[6]

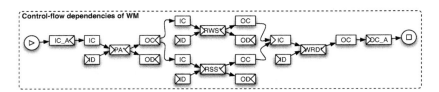

Fig. 3. Control-flow analysis for WM

For example, the initial link between PA and RWS has been translated to a link between OC_PA and IC_RWS. Moreover, one should note that $start\_WM$ and end_WM are now connected to IC_A and OC_A respectively. That is, IC_A enables (from the control-flow point of view) IC_PA for execution. Dually, OC_WRD is connected to OC_A and hence (from the control-flow point of view) its execution is to be interpreted as the termination of WM.

DATA-FLOW ANALYSIS

In order to derive data-flow information linking processes of (possibly) different services, one has to match requested inputs with offered outputs. Our flexible methodology allows for an ontology-based matching algorithm (e.g., [17,5]) to be plugged-in. "An input i of process P matches an output o of process Q if and only if $Itype_i$ is in an *exact* or *subsumes* relation with $Otype_o$". Dually, "an output o of process Q matches an input i of process P if and only if $Otype_o$ is in an *exact* or *plug-in* relation with $Itype_i$". One should note that the notion of

---

[6] All enabler dummies shall be abbreviated in figures from now onwards (e.g., IC instead of IC_PA, and so on).

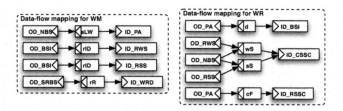

Fig. 4. Data-flow analysis for our example

"match" used in this paper is in line with the one defined in [17, 16]. We shall call such a match a *data-flow dependency* and a set of them as *data-flow mapping*.

From a data-flow point of view, a process P must have all its inputs available in order to be executable. In this paper we assume that such data-flow dependencies are provided by the matching framework. A maximal such mapping can be obtained by employing a one-to-one matching between all process parameters of the services to be aggregated. One should note that the user should be allowed to modify, cancel or add dependencies in the mapping. A data-flow mapping can be expressed in terms of IDs and ODs as follows. If input x of process P matches output(s) y of process(es) Q then we generate the following:

1. A dummy process P_x[7] with no IOs or ontological value. However, it is important to note that such a dummy employs a XOR join and an EMPTY split. This is due to the fact that values for x may be obtained from different ys, yet only one is needed. Furthermore, a link from P_x to ID_P is added to Beh_A.
2. A link from OD_Q to P_x which is added to Beh_A for every matched y.

Figure 4 illustrates the data-flow mapping for our example. Due to space issues, P_x dummy names will be abbreviated to x in figures from now onwards. One should note that the CS service is not depicted as its only process (NBS) does not have inputs.

2.5   Contract Generation

During this phase, the algorithm employs an input-driven basic check and then it cleans the aggregated service A of redundant constructs.

Basic Validation

We firstly assume that all services are "well defined" in the sense that each initial process P has at least one incoming link (with the exception of "*start*") and at least one outgoing link (with the exception of "*end*"). This means that each IC has at least one incoming link, and that each OC has at least one outgoing link. At this point one may encounter two situations:

- All processes P have their inputs satisfied. In other words, every input x of P has been matched with at least one output y of a process Q. This

---

[7] For simplicity we assume here that all P_x are unique.

translates to the fact that the P_x dummy process has at least one incoming link. Should this be the case, we say that the aggregation is successful — in the way that there are no unsatisfied data- (and control-) flow constraints.

– At least one process P is missing some inputs. In other words there exists an input x of P which has not been matched to any output(s) y of process(es) Q. This translates to the fact that the P_x dummy process has no incoming links. Should this be the case, we say that the aggregation has not succeeded — in the way that there is at least one unsatisfied data-flow constraint. The (additional) missing inputs must be provided by other services, hence either a refined query can be launched or the needed services can be manually added to the set of services to be aggregated.

We chose to consider as valid such a "closed" workflow (i.e., without unsatisfied inputs) in order to enforce a necessary yet not sufficient condition for the execution of (all) processes. Given a valid service contract, one may use analysis tools in order to verify (dead-)lock freedom for example. As YAWL is built upon Petri Nets (PN), analysis tools for the latter can be exploited to check properties of PN translations of the former. For example WofYAWL [25] is an analysis tool for YAWL workflows. WofYAWL maps an input YAWL workflow into a PN with inhibitor arcs, and then analyses semi-positive transitions in the short-circuited net. If the net is bound, it performs a relaxed soundness check in the regular net. Finally the results are mapped back into a YAWL workflow, possibly annotating the output with warnings (e.g., in the case of unbounded nets). Figure 5 describes the aggregation contract we have obtained so far for our example.[8] One should note that all ICs (e.g., IC_PA and so on) have at least one incoming link, as well as, all OCs (e.g., OC_PA and so on) have at least one outgoing link. Moreover, all process with the exception of OD_CSSC and OD_RSSC have at least one incoming and one outgoing link. We can say that the aggregation is successful as there are no unsatisfied data- (or control-) flow constraints.

ELIMINATING REDUNDANCIES

As one may have noted, not all dummy constructs introduced during the **Core Aggregation** phase are necessary. Given the aggregated service is valid, we can (repeatedly) eliminate redundant items, that is, dummies and join/split constructs. One obtains at the end of this step the final service contract of A. We hereafter describe three elimination criteria.

Dummy Absorption. Assume a dummy (i.e., control or data process enabler, or process added during the data-flow analysis) iD connected as input of another process P such that the pair $< join_{iD}, join_P >$ is one of the following – $\{< EMPTY, EMPTY >, < EMPTY, \alpha >, < \alpha, \alpha >\}$ –, where $\alpha \in \{AND, XOR, OR\}$. Then, we "absorb" iD into P which remains unchanged. If $< join_{iD}, join_P >$ is $< \alpha, EMPTY >$ then we absorb iD into P with the observation that P inherits the join of iD (i.e., $join_P := join_{iD}$). The scenario is dual

---

[8] Due to its verbosity we chose not to represent dummies introduced during the DATA-FLOW step – with the exception of wS and sS. Moreover, the full graphical form of the workflow (i.e., including process parameters and so on) has been omitted.

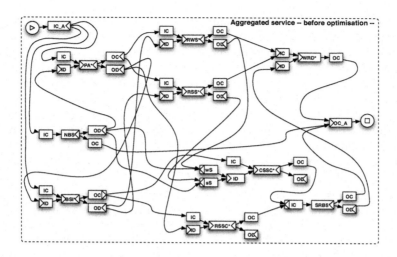

Fig. 5. Service contract A (before eliminating redundancies)

for absorbing output dummies. Absorbing means eliminating iD and updating Beh_A correspondingly.

Dummy Elimination. An OD_P employing an EMPTY split construct and that does *not* have at least one outgoing link to other join of an ID_Q can be eliminated together with its corresponding link (from P to OD_P) from Beh_A. One should note that the initial AND split of OD_P should be cancelled first by the following criteria.

Join/Split Elimination. A $join_P \neq$ EMPTY has to be set to EMPTY provided P has *only one* incoming link. The dual (i.e., the "reset" of $split_P$ given P has *at most one* outgoing link) is resolved in similar way.

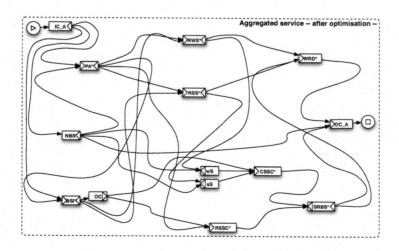

Fig. 6. Final service contract A

Let us come back to our example. Figure 4 indicates that all dummies introduced during the data-flow analysis are redundant, except for wS (input of $CSSC$) and sS (input of $RSSC$). The redundant joins are cancelled first and then the respective redundant processes are absorbed into IDs and ODs. Moreover, the elimination criteria allow us to cancel almost all dummies introduced during PROCESS EXPANSION with the exception of OD_CSSC, OD_RSSC, and OC_BSI. The former two are tackled by the dummy elimination criterion. The final version of A is given in Figure 6.

3   Concluding Remarks

The aim of this paper is to contribute to the long-term objective of lifting service aggregation from manual handcrafting to a semi-automated engineered process. We have presented the kernel of a semi-automated workflow based aggregation framework of Web services. It consists of a methodology which, given a set of service contracts, tries to construct an aggregation of such services.

We have synthesised three main phases of the proposed aggregation process: (1) *Core Aggregation* – perform control- and data-flow analysis on the input services to determine their aggregation, (2) *Contract Generation* – generate the contract of the aggregated service, (3) *Service Deployment* – deploy an implementation of the aggregated service. While we concentrated on steps (1) and (2) in this paper, it is worth stressing the importance of separating the phase of contract generation from the deployment of the aggregated service, which allows multiple deployments of the latter.

The main features of our approach are: (a) It can be used to aggregate services written with different description languages (e.g., BPEL + semantics, OWL-S), (b) It is (semi-)automatic – both with respect to service translation and co-ordination (core aggregation and contract generation), (c) It allows a seamless integration with service discovery systems (third-party matchmaking frameworks can be straightforwardly plugged in), (d) It supports both black- and glass-box queries (i.e., behaviour-less and behavioural queries), (e) It features compositional aggregation (e.g., the aggregation of A, B, and C can be computed by first aggregating A and B and then aggregating the obtained service with C), and finally (f) It supports multiple deployments of the aggregated service.

Regrettably, space limitations do not allow a thorough discussion of related work (e.g., manual [3, 28], semiautomatic [9, 12] or fully automatic approaches [2, 11, 19, 20, 21, 27]). Surveys on Web service composition can be found in [1, 6, 8, 14]. In manual Web service composition the requester acts as the service composer as well. She has to browse the registry, find the desired service operations and model their interactions into a flow structure. Fully automatic composition of services is very difficult to achieve as the requester has to specify all input requirements of registered service operations that make the composite service. Furthermore, processing the request is a very time consuming process. A significant number of fully automatic approaches employ planning techniques. A downside of planning is that both the goal and the status are difficult to represent. Another issue is that all services involved in the composition have to be known a priori. It is however worth observing that, while some of the previously mentioned features ((a) – (f)) are considered in some existing approaches, our approach is the first — at the best of our knowledge — that provides all of them in a single framework.

A key ingredient of our framework is the notion of service contract, which includes a description of the service's behaviour (expressed by a YAWL [23] workflow), as well as an (ontology-annotated) signature. Contracts are the basis for linking services through data-flow dependencies as well as for overcoming signature and behaviour mismatches. They also pave the way for aggregrating services written in different languages and for multiple deployments of the aggregated service.

Further investigation will be devoted to extend the core aggregation process in order to ensure stronger formal properties of computed aggregations, and to account for the adaptation of signature and behavioural mismatches in contracts. Future work will also be devoted to the development of the semi-automated derivation of contracts from real service implementations (considering first BPEL and OWL-S, and exploiting the techniques described in [26]), and of the service deployment phase (again considering BPEL and OWL-S first).

References

1. W. Aalst, M. Dumas, and A. Hofstede. Web service composition languages: Old wine in new bottles? In *Proceedings of Euromicro '03*, pages 298–307. IEEE Computer Society, 2003.
2. D. Berardi, G. D. Giacomo, M. Lenzerini, M. Mecella, and D. Calvanese. Synthesis of underspecified composite e-services based on automated reasoning. In *ICSOC '04: Proceedings of the 2nd international conference on Service oriented computing*, pages 105–114, New York, NY, USA, 2004. ACM Press.
3. BPEL4WS Coalition. Business Process Execution Language for Web Services (BPEL4WS), 2002. http://www-106.ibm.com/developerworks/webservices/library/ws-bpel/.
4. A. Brogi, S. Corfini, and R. Popescu. Flexible Matchmaking of Web Services Using DAML-S Ontologies. In P. Traverso and S. Weerawarana, editors, *Proceedings of Second International Conference on Service Oriented Computing (ICSOC04 - short papers), IBM Research Report. NY, USA*, pages 30–45, November 15-18 2004.
5. A. Brogi, S. Corfini, and R. Popescu. Composition-oriented Service Discovery. In F. Gschwind, U. Assmann, and O. Nierstrasz, editors, *Proceedings of Software Composition '05, LNCS, vol. 3628*, pages 15–30, 2005.
6. Y. Charif and N. Sabouret. An Overview of Semantic Web Services Composition Approaches. To appear in Proceedings of the International Workshop on Context for Web Services 2005, Elsevier.
7. H.-P. Company. Web Services Concepts – a technical overview. http://www.hpmiddleware.com/downloads/pdf/web_services_tech_overview.pdf. Technical report, 2001.
8. J. Koehler and B. Srivastava. Web Service Composition: Current Solutions and Open Problems. ICAPS Workshop on Planning for Web Services, pp. 28-35, 2003.
9. Q. Liang, L. N. Chakarapani, S. Y. W. Su, R. N. Chikkamagalur, and H. Lam. A Semi-Automatic Approach to Composite Web Services Discovery, Description and Invocation. *International Journal of Web Services Research*, 1(4):64–89, 2004.

10. D. McGuiness and F. van Harmelen (Eds). OWL Web Ontology Language Overview. Web guide, February 2004. http://www.w3.org/TR/owl-features.
11. S. McIlraith and C. T. Son. Adapting Golog for composition of semantic Web services. Proceeding of 8th Conference on Knowledge Representation and Reasoning (KR'02), 2002.
12. B. Medjahed, A. Bouguettaya, and A. K. Elmagarmid. Composing Web services on the Semantic Web. *The VLDB Journal*, 12(4):333–351, 2003.
13. L. Meredith and S. Bjorg. Contracts and types. *CACM*, 46(10), 2003.
14. N. Milanovic and M. Malek. Current Solutions for Web Service Composition. *IEEE Internet Computing Online*, 8(6):51–59, Dec. 2004.
15. J. Miller, K. Verma, P. Rajasekaran, A. Sheth, R. Aggarwal, and K. Sivashanmugam. WSDL-S: Adding Semantics to WSDL - White Paper. http://lsdis.cs.uga.edu/library/download/wsdl-s.pdf.
16. OWL-S Coalition. OWL-S 1.1 release. http://www.daml.org/services/owl-s/1.1/.
17. M. Paolucci, T. Kawamura, T. Payne, and K. Sycara. Semantic Matchmaking of Web Services Capabilities. In I. Horrocks and J. Hendler, editors, *First International Semantic Web Conference on The Semantic Web, LNCS 2342*, pages 333–347. Springer-Verlag, 2002.
18. M. P. Papazoglou and D. Georgakopoulos. Service-Oriented Computing. *Commun. ACM*, 46(10):24–28, 2003.
19. R. Ponnekanti and A. Fox. SWORD: A developer toolkit for building composite Web services. Computer Science Department, StanfordUniversity, 2002. http://www2002.orgCDROM/alternate/786/.
20. S. Thakkar, A. C. Knoblock, and L. Ambite. A view integration approach to dynamic composition of Web services. Proceedings of the ICAPS '03 Workshop on Planning for Web Services, Italy, 2003.
21. P. Traverso and M. Pistore. Automated Composition of Semantic Web Services into Executable Processes. In *International Semantic Web Conference*, pages 380–394, 2004.
22. W. M. P. van der Aalst. Pi calculus versus Petri nets: Let us eat humble pie rather than further inflate the Pi hype, 2004. Available from http://tmitwww.tm.tue.nl/staff/wvdaalst/pi-hype.pdf.
23. W. M. P. van der Aalst and A. H. M. ter Hofstede. YAWL: Yet Another Workflow Language. Technical report, Queensland Univ. of Technology, FIT-TR-2003-04, 2003.
24. W. M. P. van der Aalst, A. H. M. ter Hofstede, B. Kiepuszewski, and A. P. Barros. Workflow Patterns. *Distrib. Parallel Databases*, 14(1):5–51, 2003.
25. E. Verbeek. WofYAWL Version 0.3. Technical report available online at http://home.tm.tue.nl/hverbeek/wofyawl03.pdf.
26. P. Wohed, W. M. P. van der Aalst, M. Dumas, and A. H. M. ter Hofstede. Analysis of Web Services Composition Languages: The Case of BPEL4WS. In I.-Y. Song, S. W. Liddle, T. W. Ling, and P. Scheuermann, editors, *Proceedings of the 22nd International Conference on Conceptual Modeling*, volume 2813 of *Lecture Notes in Computer Science*, pages 200–215. Springer, 2003.
27. D. Wu, E. Sirin, J. Hendler, D. Nau, and B. Parsia. Automatic Web services composition using SHOP2. Proceedings of the ICAPS '03 Workshop on Planning for Web Services (P4WS '03), 2003.
28. J. Yang and M. P. Papazoglou. Service components for managing the life-cycle of service compositions. *Information Systems*, 29(2):97–125, 2004.

Choreography and Orchestration: A Synergic Approach for System Design*

Nadia Busi, Roberto Gorrieri, Claudio Guidi,
Roberto Lucchi, and Gianluigi Zavattaro

Department of Computer Science, University of Bologna, Italy
{busi, gorrieri, cguidi, lucchi, zavattar}@cs.unibo.it

Abstract. Choreography and orchestration languages deal with business processes design and specification. Referring to Web Services technology, the most credited proposals are WS-CDL about choreography and WS-BPEL about orchestration. A closer look to such a kind of languages highlights two distinct approaches for system representation and management. Choreography describes the system in a top view manner whereas orchestration focuses on single peers description. In this paper we define a notion of conformance between choreography and orchestration which allows to state when an orchestrated system is conformant to a given choreography. Choreography and orchestration are formalized by using two process algebras and conformance takes the form of a bisimulation-like relation.

1 Introduction

In the design and deployment of service oriented applications two different and opposite features should be taken into account. On the one hand, it is important to program single peers services, which could be involved in different systems at different times, preserving their composionality, and on the other hand, it is fundamental to guarantee overall systems functionalities. Orchestration and choreography deal with such a kind of issues where the former focuses on single peers description whereas the latter describes a system in a top view manner.

In this paper we present a notion of conformance between two simple formal languages we have developed for representing choreography and orchestration. They are inspired by Web Services technical specifications as WS-CDL [W3C] and WS-BPEL [OAS]. Here we intend to give a mathematical *liaison* between the two different approaches of choreography and orchestration in order to give a powerful mechanism for designing systems where peers behaviours and systems functionalities are developed together in a complementary fashion.

The choreography language has been presented in our previous works [BGG+] [GGL05] whereas the orchestration one is introduced in this work. They are based both on basic Web Services interaction mechanisms, the so called *operations*, defined in WSDL specifications. Briefly, we remind that an operation contains

---

* Research partially funded by EU Integrated Project Sensoria, contract n. 016004.

B. Benatallah, F. Casati, and P. Traverso (Eds.): ICSOC 2005, LNCS 3826, pp. 228–240, 2005.

the definition of an incoming message for a service and, when used, the definition of the response one.

The orchestration language takes inspiration from WS-BPEL. More precisely we have been inspired by the abstract non-executable fragment of WS-BPEL used to specify the observable behaviour of services abstracting away from internal details. Abstract WS-BPEL exploits opaque variables (i.e. variables without a specified content) to indicate which state variables could influence a choice taken from a service, without specifying the internal decision procedure of the service. In our language, all variables are opaque; this permits us to focus on interaction mechanisms and data flow abstracting away from variable values.

The choreography language is named CL_P and is used to describe the behaviour of a system by defining the involved roles and their interactions whereas the orchestration language is called OL and it allows to program communicating behaviours of the single peers which can be composed for obtaining an orchestrated system. We define the semantics of such languages by using two different labelled transition systems and we present a notion of conformance based on a bisimulation between them with some similarities with branching bisimulation [vGW96]. In particular, we define a so called *joining function* in order to associate the orchestrators of the orchestrated system to the roles of the choreography and we construct the definition of conformance on a bisimulation which exploits such a function in order to compare the labels of the two different labelled transition systems.

In section 2 we present the choreography language whereas in section 3 we present the orchestration one. Then in section 4 we present the joining function and we give the notion of conformance. Furthermore, in section 5, an example is reported and in section 6 conclusions are presented.

2   A Formal Model for Choreography

In this section we introduce the formal model for representing choreography which is based on a declarative part and on a conversational one. The former deals with roles, operations and variables whereas the latter deals with a language for describing the conversations (interactions composition) among the roles.

Declarative Part. Here we explain the declarative part of our choreography formal model which is based on the concept of *role*. A role represents the behaviour that a participant has to exhibit in order to fulfill the activity defined by the choreography. Each role can store variables and exhibit operations.

As far as variables are concerned, we associate to each role a set of variables which represent the information managed by the role and which will be used in the interactions between roles. In this model we abstract away from the values and we consider variables as names which are exploited for representing the data flow among the roles.

As far as operations are concerned, each role is equipped with a set of operations it has to exhibit which essentially represent the access points that will be used by the other roles to interact with the owner one. Operations can have one of the following interaction modalities: *One-Way* or *Request-Response*. Indeed, in WSDL specifications, the most significant types of operations are the *One-Way*, where only the incoming message is defined, and the *Request-Response*, where both the incoming message and the response one are defined.

Let us now introduce the formalization of *roles*, *variables* and *operations*.

Let Var be the set of variables ranged over by x, y, z, k. We denote with $\widetilde{x}$ tuples of variables, for instance, we may have $\widetilde{x} = \langle x_1, x_2, ..., x_n \rangle$.

Let $OpName$ be the set of operation names, ranged over by o, and $OpType = \{ow, rr\}$ be the set of operation types where ow denotes a One-Way operation whereas rr denotes the Request-Response one. An operation is described by its operation name and operation type. Namely, let Op be the set of operations defined as follows where each operation is univocally identified by its name.

$$Op = \{(o, t) \mid o \in OpName,\ t \in OpType\}$$

A role is described by a role name, the set of operations it exhibits and by a set of variables. Namely, let $RName$ be the set of the role names, ranged over by ρ. The set *Role*, containing all the possible roles, is defined as follows:

$$Role = \{(\rho, \omega, V) \mid \rho \in RName,\ \omega \subseteq Op, V \subseteq Var\}$$

Conversational Part. The conversations among the roles are defined by using the following grammar:

$$C_P ::= \mathbf{0} \mid \mu \mid C_P; C_P \mid C_P | C_P \mid C_P + C_P$$
$$\mu ::= (\rho_A, \rho_B, o, \widetilde{x}, \widetilde{y}, dir)$$

In the following we use CL_P, ranged over by Con, to denote the set of conversations of such a language. C_P denotes a conversation which can be the null one ($\mathbf{0}$), the interaction μ, the sequential composition ($C_P; C_P$), the parallel composition ($C_P \mid C_P$) or the choice one ($C_P + C_P$). ($\rho_A, \rho_B, o, \widetilde{x}, \widetilde{y}, dir$) means that an interaction from role ρ_A to role ρ_B is performed. In particular, o is the name of the operation $(o, t) \in Op$ on which the message exchange is performed. Variables $\widetilde{x}$ and $\widetilde{y}$ are those used by the sender and the receiver, respectively. They represent that after the interaction the information stored in $\widetilde{x}$ are assigned to the variables $\widetilde{y}$. Finally, $dir \in \{\uparrow, \downarrow\}$ indicates whether the interaction is a request ($\uparrow$) or a response ($\downarrow$) one. Choreography well-formedness rules can be found in [BGG⁺].

Semantics of CL_P. The semantics of CL_P is defined in terms of a labelled transition system [Kel76] which describes the evolution of a conversation. Let Act_C be a set of parameterized actions ($\rho_A, \rho_B, o, \widetilde{x}, \widetilde{y}, dir$) ranged over by μ. $C_P \xrightarrow{\mu} C'_P$ means that the conversation C_P evolves in one step in a configuration C'_P performing the action μ. We define $\rightarrow \subseteq \mathtt{CL}_P \times Act_C \times \mathtt{CL}_P$ as the least relation which satisfies the axioms and rules of Table 1 and closed w.r.t. $\equiv$, where $\equiv$ is the least congruence relation satisfying the axioms at the end of Table 1. The structural congruence $\equiv$, which equates the conversations whose

Table 1. Semantics of CL_P conversations

(SEQUENCE)
$$\frac{C_P \xrightarrow{\mu} C'_P}{C_P; D_P \xrightarrow{\mu} C'_P; D_P}$$

(INTERACTION)
$$\mu \xrightarrow{\mu} \mathbf{0}, \ \mu = (\rho_A, \rho_B, o, \widetilde{x}, \widetilde{y}, dir)$$

(PARALLEL)
$$\frac{C_P \xrightarrow{\mu} C'_P}{C_P \mid D_P \xrightarrow{\mu} C'_P \mid D_P}$$

(CHOICE)
$$\frac{C_P \xrightarrow{\mu} C'_P}{C_P + D_P \xrightarrow{\mu} C'_P}$$

(STRUCT)
$$\frac{C'_P \equiv C_P, C_P \xrightarrow{\mu} D_P, D_P \equiv D'_P}{C'_P \xrightarrow{\mu} D'_P}$$

(STRUCTURAL CONGRUENCE)
$$\mathbf{0}; C_P \equiv C_P \qquad C_P \mid \mathbf{0} \equiv C_P \qquad C_P + \mathbf{0} = C_P$$
$$C_P + D_P \equiv D_P + C_P \qquad C_P \mid D_P \equiv D_P \mid C_P$$
$$(C_P + D_P) + E_P \equiv C_P + (D_P + E_P) \qquad (C_P \mid D_P) \mid E_P \equiv C_P \mid (D_P \mid E_P)$$

behavior cannot be distinguished, expresses that $(C_P, +)$ and $(C_P, \mid)$ are abelian monoids where $\mathbf{0}$ is the null element. Furthermore, the rule $\mathbf{0}; C_P \equiv C_P$ means that when a conversation completes then the other one which follows in sequence can be performed.

The description of axioms and rules follows. The axiom INTERACTION describes that an interaction μ, which is a request or a response one depending on the value of dir, is performed. When a request is performed ($dir = \uparrow$) the information contained in the variables $\widetilde{x}$ within the sender role ρ_A are passed to the variables $\widetilde{y}$ within the receiver role ρ_B exploiting the operation o of the role ρ_B. When a response is performed ($dir = \downarrow$) the information contained in the variables $\widetilde{y}$ within the request receiver role ρ_B are passed to the variables $\widetilde{x}$ within the request sender role ρ_A exploiting the operation o of the role ρ_B. Response must be performed always after a request interaction from ρ_A to ρ_B. The rules SEQUENCE, PARALLEL, CHOICE and STRUCT are standard.

Now we are ready to define a choreography. A choreography, denoted by C, is defined by a pair (Con, Σ) where $Con \in CL_P$ and $\Sigma \subseteq Role$ with Σ finite.

3   A Formal Model for Orchestration

In this section we introduce a formal language for orchestration called OL. An orchestrator can be seen as a process, associated to an identifier, that can exchange information, represented by variables, with other processes. Our model takes inspiration from the abstract non-executable fragment of WS-BPEL and abstracts away from variables values focusing on data-flow. Let Var be the set of variables used for choreography ranged over by x, y, z, k and ID be the set of possible identifiers ranged over by id. We denote with $\widetilde{x}$ tuples of variables. The language syntax follows:

$$P ::= \mathbf{0} \mid o \mid \bar{o} \mid o(\widetilde{x}) \mid \bar{o}(\widetilde{y}) \mid o(\widetilde{x}, \widetilde{y}, P) \mid \bar{o}(\widetilde{x}, \widetilde{y}) \mid P; P \mid P + P \mid P \mid P$$
$$E ::= [P]_{id} \mid E \parallel E$$

An orchestrated system E is a pool of named processes. An orchestrator $[P]_{id}$ is a process P identified by id. Informally the idea is that orchestrators are executed on different locations, thus they can be composed by using only the parallel operator ($\|$). Processes can be composed in parallel ($|$), sequence (;) and alternative composition ($+$). **0** represents the null process. Communication mechanisms model Web Services One-Way and Request-Response operations. In particular, we have three kinds of primitives for synchronization, one for the internal synchronization and two for the external one. The former simply consists of a channel o that different threads of the process running in parallel, can use to coordinate their activities. In this case no message is exchanged; this is because the orchestrator variables are shared by any processes running on that orchestrator. The primitives for external synchronization, that is between different orchestrators, are the following ones: $o(\tilde{x})$ and $\bar{o}(\tilde{y})$ represent the input and the output of a single message whereas the primitives $o(\tilde{x}, \tilde{z}, P)$ and $\bar{o}(\tilde{y}, \tilde{k})$ represent coupled messages exchanges. In particular we have that $o(\tilde{x})$ represents a One-Way operation whose name is o where the received information are stored in the tuple of variable $\tilde{x}$ of the receiver. $\bar{o}(\tilde{y})$ represents a One-Way invocation whose name is o and the sent information are stored in the tuple $\tilde{y}$ of the sender. $o(\tilde{x}, \tilde{z}, P)$ represents a Request-Response operation whose name is o. In this case the process receives a message and stores the received information in $\tilde{x}$ then it executes the process P and, at the end, sends the information contained in $\tilde{z}$ as a response message to the invoker. Finally, $\bar{o}(\tilde{y}, \tilde{k})$ represents the invocation of a Request-Response operation whose name is o. The process sends the information contained in $\tilde{y}$ as a request message and stores the information of the response message in $\tilde{k}$.

Semantics of OL. The semantics of OL is defined in terms of a labelled transition systems which describes the evolution of an orchestrated system. We define $\rightarrow$ as the least relation which satisfies the axioms and rules of Table 2. Let $Act_{OL} = \left\{ \bar{o}, o, \bar{o}(\tilde{y}), o(\tilde{x}), \bar{o}(\tilde{y}, \tilde{k})(n), o(\tilde{x}, \tilde{z})(n), \bar{o}_n(\tilde{y}), o_n(\tilde{x}), \sigma, \tau \right\}$, ranged over by γ, be the set of actions. σ is a parameterized action of the form $(id, id', o, \tilde{x}, \tilde{y}, dir)$ where id, id' are orchestrators ids, o is an operation name, $\tilde{x}, \tilde{y}$ are tuples of variables and $dir \in \{\uparrow, \downarrow\}$.

Table 2 is divided into two parts describing the rules and structural congruence for processes and orchestrated systems respectively. IN, OUT, ONE-WAYOUT, ONE-WAY-IN, REQ-OUT, REQ-IN, RESP-OUT, RESP-IN are axioms where it is important to note the behaviour of the REQ-IN one. It stands that after the reception of a request on a Request-Response operation the process P must be executed before sending the response. Rule INT-SYNC deals with internal synchronization whereas PAR-IN and CHOICE ones deal with internal parallel and choice respectively. SEQ describes the behaviour of sequentially composed processes. CONGRP deals with internal structural congruence denoted by $\equiv_P$.

Rule ONE-WAYSYNC deals with the synchronization on a One-Way operation between two orchestrators whereas the rules REQ-SYNC and RESP-SYNC deal with that on a Request-Response one. Rule REQ-SYNC exploits a fresh label n which is generated in order to univocally link the response synchronization

Table 2. OL operational semantics

(Rules over P)

(In)
$$o \xrightarrow{o} \mathbf{0}$$

(Out)
$$\bar{o} \xrightarrow{\bar{o}} \mathbf{0}$$

(One-WayOut)
$$\bar{o}(\tilde{y}) \xrightarrow{\bar{o}(\tilde{y})} \mathbf{0}$$

(One-WayIn)
$$o(\tilde{x}) \xrightarrow{o(\tilde{x})} \mathbf{0}$$

(Req-Out)
$$\bar{o}(\tilde{x}, \tilde{y}) \xrightarrow{\bar{o}(\tilde{x}, \tilde{y})(n)} o_n(\tilde{y})$$

(Req-In)
$$o(\tilde{x}, \tilde{y}, P) \xrightarrow{o(\tilde{x}, \tilde{y})(n)} P; \bar{o}_n(\tilde{y})$$

(Resp-Out)
$$\bar{o}_n(\tilde{y}) \xrightarrow{\bar{o}_n(\tilde{y})} \mathbf{0}$$

(Resp-In)
$$o_n(\tilde{x}) \xrightarrow{o_n(\tilde{x})} \mathbf{0}$$

(Int-Sync)
$$\frac{P \xrightarrow{o} P' , \ Q \xrightarrow{\bar{o}} Q'}{P \mid Q \xrightarrow{\tau} P' \mid Q'}$$

(Par-Int)
$$\frac{P \xrightarrow{\gamma} P'}{P \mid Q \xrightarrow{\gamma} P' \mid Q}$$

(Seq)
$$\frac{P \xrightarrow{\gamma} P'}{P; Q \xrightarrow{\gamma} P'; Q}$$

(Choice)
$$\frac{P \xrightarrow{\gamma} P'}{P + Q \xrightarrow{\gamma} P'}$$

(CongrP)
$$\frac{P \equiv_P P' , \ Q' \equiv_P Q , \ P' \xrightarrow{\gamma} Q'}{P \xrightarrow{\gamma} Q}$$

(Structural Congruenge over P)

$$P + \mathbf{0} \equiv_P P \qquad P \mid \mathbf{0} \equiv_P P \qquad \mathbf{0}; P \equiv_P P \qquad (P + Q) \equiv_P (Q + P)$$
$$(P \mid Q) \equiv_P (Q \mid P) \qquad (P + Q) + R \equiv_P P + (Q + R) \qquad (P \mid Q) \mid R \equiv_P P \mid (Q \mid R)$$

(Rules over E)

(One-WaySync)
$$\frac{[P]_{id} \xrightarrow{\bar{o}(\tilde{x})} [P']_{id} , \ [Q]_{id'} \xrightarrow{o(\tilde{y})} [Q']_{id'} , \sigma = (id, id', o, \tilde{x}, \tilde{y}, \uparrow)}{[P]_{id} \parallel [Q]_{id'} \xrightarrow{\sigma} [P']_{id} \parallel [Q']_{id'}}$$

(Req-Sync)
$$\frac{[P]_{id} \xrightarrow{\bar{o}(\tilde{z}, \tilde{k})(n)} [P']_{id} , \ [Q]_{id'} \xrightarrow{o(\tilde{x}, \tilde{y})(n)} [Q']_{id'} , n \ fresh, \sigma = (id, id', o, \tilde{z}, \tilde{x}, \uparrow)}{[P]_{id} \parallel [Q]_{id'} \xrightarrow{\sigma} [P']_{id} \parallel [Q']_{id'}}$$

(Resp-Sync)
$$\frac{[P]_{id} \xrightarrow{o_n(\tilde{k})} [P']_{id} , \ [Q]_{id'} \xrightarrow{\bar{o}_n(\tilde{y})} [Q']_{id'} , \sigma = (id, id', o, \tilde{k}, \tilde{y}, \downarrow)}{[P]_{id} \parallel [Q]_{id'} \xrightarrow{\sigma} [P']_{id} \parallel [Q']_{id'}}$$

(Par-Ext)
$$\frac{E_1 \xrightarrow{\gamma} E_1'}{E_1 \parallel E_2 \xrightarrow{\gamma} E_1' \parallel E_2}$$

(CongrE)
$$\frac{E_1 \equiv E_1' , \ E_2' \equiv E_2 , \ E_1' \xrightarrow{\gamma} E_2'}{E_1 \xrightarrow{\gamma} E_2}$$

(Int-Ext)
$$\frac{P \xrightarrow{\gamma} P'}{[P]_{id} \xrightarrow{\gamma} [P']_{id}}$$

(Structural Congruence over E)

$$\frac{P \equiv_P Q}{[P]_{id} \equiv [Q]_{id}} \qquad E_1 \parallel E_2 \equiv E_2 \parallel E_1 \qquad E_1 \parallel (E_2 \parallel E_3) \equiv (E_1 \parallel E_2) \parallel E_3$$

defined in rule REQ-RESP. Considering the axiom REQ-OUT and REQ-IN indeed, the Request-Response primitives will be transformed into two ONE-WAY (invocation and reception) identified by the label n which is unique and univocally determined during the synchronization. It is worth noting that all the synchronizations which are performed between different orchestrators are labelled with an action σ. This fact will be fundamental for the definition of the conformance notion presented in the next section. PAR-EXT deals with external parallel composition and CONGRE is for external structural congruence denoted by $\equiv$. INT-EXT expresses the fact that an orchestrator behaves accordingly with its internal processes.

4   Conformance Between Choreography and Orchestration

Our proposal defines a conformance notion based on a bisimulation-like relation between the labelled transition system of choreography and the labelled transition system of the orchestrated system where orchestrators are associated to roles. Such a kind of machinery allows us to test if all the interactions performed by the orchestrated system are coherent with the conversations expressed in the choreography. Furthermore, it guarantees, by exploiting the fact that the name of the variables must be the same, that the data flow of the orchestrated system is conformant with that expressed by choreography conversations. In particular, let C be a choreography where Con represents the conversation rules and let E be an orchestrated system. We define a *joining function*, named Ψ, for associating the orchestrators of E to the roles of C and we test the conformance, up to Ψ, of E and C by using a bisimulation-like relation where the σ labels of the former are compared with the μ ones of the latter.

Definition 1 (joining function). *A joining function is an element of the set* $\{\Psi \mid \Psi : ID \to RName \cup \{\bot\}\}$ *containing functions which associate to each orchestrator identifier id a choreography role ρ or the $\bot$ value.*

Given a joining function Ψ and an action $\sigma = (id, id', o, \tilde{x}, \tilde{y}, dir)$ of a given orchestrated system where id and id' are orchestrator identifiers, o is an operation, $\tilde{x}$ and $\tilde{y}$ are tuples of variables and $dir \in \{\uparrow, \downarrow\}$, we denote with $\Psi[\sigma] = (\Psi(id), \Psi(id'), o, \tilde{x}, \tilde{y}, dir)$ the renaming of the orchestrator identifiers with the joined roles.

Now we introduce the conformance notion, namely *conformability bisimulation*, between an OL system and a CL_P one. It is based on a relation which resembles branching bisimulation and it tests that, given a joining function Ψ, all the conversations σ produced by the OL system are equal to the μ produced by the CL_P one excluding τ actions.

Definition 2 (Conformability bisimulation). *Let Ψ be a joining function. A relation $\mathcal{R}_\Psi \subseteq (CL_P \times OL)$ is a conformability bisimulation if $(C, E) \in \mathcal{R}_\Psi$ implies that for all $\mu \in Act_C$ and for all $\sigma \in Act_{OL}$:*

1. $C \xrightarrow{\mu} C' \Rightarrow E \xrightarrow{\tau}^* E' \wedge E' \xrightarrow{\sigma} E'' \wedge (C', E'') \in \mathcal{R}_\Psi \wedge \Psi[\sigma] = \mu$
2. $E \xrightarrow{\tau} E' \Rightarrow (C, E') \in \mathcal{R}_\Psi$
3. $E \xrightarrow{\sigma} E' \Rightarrow C \xrightarrow{\mu} C' \wedge (C', E') \in \mathcal{R}_\Psi \wedge \Psi[\sigma] = \mu$

We write $C \triangleright_\Psi E$ if there exists a conformability bisimulation $\mathcal{R}_\Psi$ such that $(C, E) \in \mathcal{R}_\Psi$.

Such a kind of notion is not enough for defining conformance because it is possible that there exist synchronizations between orchestrators on operations which are not considered in choreography. Furthermore, there could be orchestrators which are not joined with the roles of the choreography (this case corresponds to those identifiers that Ψ maps in $\perp$) and which are used for coordinating the others. To the end of conformance, only the interactions which are performed on the operations within the choreography roles and which involve only orchestrators joined with roles must be considered relevant (i.e. observable). The following definition defines the notion of conformance between a choreography and an OL system exploiting a hiding operator which makes observable those interactions which contain operations included in the choreography and orchestrators joined with roles.

Definition 3 (Conformance Notion). *Given a choreography $C = (Con, \Sigma)$, an orchestrated system $E \in OL$ and a joining function Ψ such that $Im(\Psi) = \Sigma_\rho \cup \{\perp\}^1$ where Σ_ρ is the set of role names contained in Σ, let ω_C be the set of the operations involved within the choreography C, let ω_o be the set of operations exhibited by the processes of E and let $E_{OP} = \omega_o \backslash \omega_C$ be the set of operations exhibited by E and which do not appear within the roles of C. Let $E_\perp$ be the set of orchestrator identifiers id of E for which $\Psi(id) = \perp$. We say that E is conformant to C if the following condition holds:*

$$C \triangleright_\Psi E/E_{OP}//E_\perp$$

where $/E_{OP}$ is a hiding operator which hides (replaces with τ moves) all the transitions which contain operations contained in E_{OP} and $//E_\perp$ is a hiding operator which hides all the transitions which contain orchestrators not joined with any role.

5 Example

Here we reason about the meaning of conformance by using an example. Let us now consider a business scenario where a customer invokes a store service in order to buy a good and where, depending on the customer's credit card type, the store service will invoke the respective payment service. In order to define the choreography let us consider four roles: ρ_C which represents the customer behaviour, ρ_S which represents the store service, ρ_V which represents the VISA

---

[1] $Im(\Psi) = \{\Psi(id) \mid id \in ID\}$.

payment service and ρ_{AE} which represents the American Express payment service. For each role we define the following operations:

$$\omega_C = \{(\text{RECEIPT}, ow)\}, \quad \omega_S = \{(\text{BUY}, rr)\},$$
$$\omega_V = \{(\text{PAY-VISA}, rr)\}, \quad \omega_{AE} = \{(\text{PAY-AE}, rr)\}.$$

Referring to the role definitions described in Section 2 the role ρ_C exhibits a One-Way operation named RECEIPT whereas the other roles exhibit a Request-Response operations (respectively BUY, PAY-VISA, PAY-AE).

Let $type_C$ and $type_S$ be the variables which hold the credit card type of role ρ_C and ρ_S respectively, let $\tilde{d}_C$, $\tilde{d}_S$, $\tilde{d}_V$ and $\tilde{d}_{AE}$ be the tuples of variables representing the customer data respectively owned by each role and let ack_C, ack_S, ack_V and ack_{AE} be the variables used for modelling the response information into the Request-Response operations. We denote with $\circ$ (e.g. $\tilde{d}_C \circ type_C$) the concatenation of tuples. We define the variable sets of each role in the following way:

$$V_C = \left\{ type_C, \tilde{d}_C, ack_C \right\}, \; V_S = \left\{ type_S, \tilde{d}_S, ack_S \right\},$$
$$V_V = \left\{ \tilde{d}_V, ack_V \right\}, \; V_{AE} = \left\{ \tilde{d}_{AE}, ack_{AE} \right\}$$

Let Σ be the set of roles defined in the following way:

$$\Sigma = \{(\rho_C, \omega_C, V_C), (\rho_S, \omega_S, V_S), (\rho_V, \omega_V, V_V), (\rho_{AE}, \omega_{AE}, V_{AE})\}.$$

Let Con be the following conversation:

$Con ::= CustBuyReq;$
  $(VisaPay; CustBuyResp ; VisaReceipt$
  $+$
  $AEPay; CustBuyResp ; AEReceipt)$
$CustBuyReq ::= (\rho_C, \rho_S, \text{BUY}, \tilde{d}_C \circ type_C, \tilde{d}_S \circ type_S, \uparrow)$
$CustBuyResp ::= (\rho_C, \rho_S, \text{BUY}, ack_C, ack_S, \downarrow)$
$VisaPay ::=$
  $(\rho_S, \rho_V, \text{PAY-VISA}, \tilde{d}_S, \tilde{d}_V, \uparrow); (\rho_S, \rho_V, \text{PAY-VISA}, ack_S, ack_V, \downarrow)$
$VisaReceipt ::= (\rho_V, \rho_C, \text{RECEIPT}, \tilde{d}_V, \tilde{d}_C, \uparrow)$
$AEPay ::=$
  $(\rho_S, \rho_{AE}, \text{PAY-AE}, \tilde{d}_S, \tilde{d}_{AE}, \uparrow); (\rho_S, \rho_{AE}, \text{PAY-AE}, ack_S, ack_{AE}, \downarrow)$
$AEReceipt ::= (\rho_{AE}, \rho_C, \text{RECEIPT}, \tilde{d}_{AE}, \tilde{d}_C, \uparrow)$

In Fig. 1 are graphically represented the interactions among the roles set by Con without showing the order they are performed. The circles are the roles with their own variables depicted inside, the bold segments are the operations and the arrows are the interactions. $CustBuyReq$ is the request interaction from the customer to the store service for purchasing a good. Depending on the information held by the variable $type_S$ the Visa payment interaction $VisaPay$ or the American Express one $AEPay$, will be enabled. After the payment is performed the store service can send the response to the customer ($CustBuyResp$).

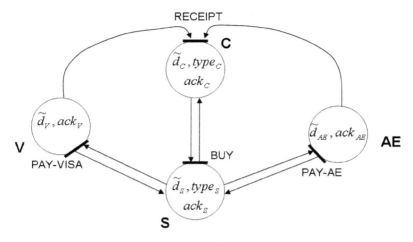

Fig. 1. Interactions among the roles

At the end the receipt from the credit card agency can be sent to the customer (*VisaReceipt* or *AEReceipt*). We consider the choreography $C = (Con, \Sigma)$.

In the following we present two possible orchestrated systems where the former is not conformant with the choreography C and the latter satisfies the notion given in the previous section.

1. We consider an orchestrated system E_1 with four orchestrators: C, S, V and AE whose definition follows:

$$E_1 ::= C \parallel S \parallel V \parallel AE$$
$$C ::= [\overline{\text{BUY}}(\tilde{d}_C \circ type_C, ack_C) \mid \text{RECEIPT}(\tilde{d}_C)]_C$$
$$S ::= [\text{BUY}(\tilde{d}_S \circ type_S, ack_S, Payment)]_S$$
$$\quad Payment ::= (\overline{\text{PAY-VISA}}(\tilde{d}_S, ack_S) + \overline{\text{PAY-AE}}(\tilde{d}_S, ack_S))$$
$$V ::= [\text{PAY-VISA}(\tilde{d}_V, ack_V); \overline{\text{RECEIPT}}(\tilde{d}_V)]_V$$
$$AE ::= [\text{PAY-AE}(\tilde{d}_{AE}, ack_{AE}); \overline{\text{RECEIPT}}(\tilde{d}_{AE})]_{AE}$$

We consider a joining function Ψ where C, S, V and AE embody roles ρ_C, ρ_S, ρ_V and ρ_{AE}, that is:

$$\Psi(C) = \rho_C, \Psi(S) = \rho_S, \Psi(V) = \rho_V, \Psi(AE) = \rho_{AE},$$
$$\Psi(id) = \bot \; for \; id \notin \{C, S, V, AE\} \,.$$

Analysing system E_1 is possible to note that it is not conformant with the choreography C because of the RECEIPT operation. Indeed, there exist some paths where the interaction on the RECEIPT operation is performed before the response interaction on the BUY operation. Such a kind of behaviour is in contrast with that of choreography C where the receipt interaction must be performed after the response interaction on the BUY operation. For this reason the conformance notion is not satisfied. **2.** We consider a system E_2 where there is an additional orchestrator whose identifier is B which is not joined with any role of the choreography and which is a bank service. The store service invokes the bank service when it has performed the credit card request (PAY-VISA or PAY-AE) for charging its transactions. The bank service will invoke the respective credit card service for charging the purchase order of the customer whose behaviour is the same of previous case E_1 as well as for the *Payment* process. At the end the credit card service will send the receipt to the customer.

$$E_2 ::= C \parallel S \parallel V \parallel AE \parallel B$$
$$S ::= [\mathrm{BUY}(\tilde{d}_S \circ types_S, ack_S, Payment); \overline{\mathrm{CHARGE}}(\tilde{d}_S)]_S$$
$$V ::= [(\mathrm{PAY\text{-}VISA}(\tilde{d}_V, ack_V); \mathrm{CH\text{-}VISA}(\tilde{d}_V); \overline{\mathrm{RECEIPT}}(\tilde{d}_V)]_V$$
$$AE ::= [\mathrm{PAY\text{-}AE}(\tilde{d}_{AE}, ack_{AE}); \mathrm{CH\text{-}AE}(\tilde{d}_{AE}); \overline{\mathrm{RECEIPT}}(\tilde{d}_{AE})]_{AE}$$
$$B ::= [\mathrm{CHARGE}(\tilde{d}_B); (\overline{\mathrm{CH\text{-}VISA}}(\tilde{d}_B) + \overline{\mathrm{CH\text{-}AE}}(\tilde{d}_B))]_B$$

We consider the same joining function Ψ of the example above. E_2 is conformant to the choreography C. Indeed, differently from E_1, the receipt interaction always follows the response on the BUY operation. This condition is guaranteed by the fact that the receipt interactions from the two credit card orchestrators are blocked by the CH-VISA and the CH-AE operations which are performed after the CHARGE operation in B. Indeed, the CHARGE operation in S is invoked after the response on the BUY operation.

It is important to note that the operations CHARGE, CH-VISA and CH-AE are not described in the choreography C. Considering the conformance notion given at Section 4 all the interactions which involve such a kind of operations are hidden in τ actions by using the operator $/E_{2OP}$ where $E_{2OP} = \{\mathrm{CHARGE, CH\text{-}VISA, CH\text{-}AE}\}$. In the same way, all the interactions which involve the orchestrator B must be hidden by using the operator $/E_{2\perp}$ where $E_{2\perp} = \{B\}$. Thus we can write that: $C \rhd_\Psi E_2/E_{2OP}/E_{2\perp}$.

6 Conclusions

In this work we have formalized a notion of conformance between choreography and orchestration. To this end we have exploited previous work where the choreography language CL_P were defined, and we have introduced here a language for orchestration equipped with a formal semantics. Choreography abstracts away from some aspects (e.g., coordination activities that should be performed by roles to preserve the conversation rules) while orchestrated systems can be seen as a further development step of systems described by choreography which must take into account also coordination activities between roles. We consider that the usage of a bisimulation-like technique, of the hiding operators and of the joining function between orchestrator identifiers and roles permits to capture such a relationship.

The notion of conformance between the choreography and the orchestration languages we introduce in this paper provides a methodology to approach both the system design and the development phase which allows us to verify whether the implementation, that is the orchestrated system, behaves accordingly with the conversation rules of the choreography. As future work we intend on one hand to extend the two languages by introducing the notion of variables state and, on the other hand, to investigate how to capture the conformance between choreographies and more structured solutions at the level of orchestrated systems. Variables states can be used to express behaviours depending on the values stored in the variables and, on the orchestration side, to be closer to executable languages and in particular with the executable fragment of WS-BPEL. As for the conformance we intend to refine the notion in order to perform conformance tests also in cases where, for instance, more orchestration processes embody a certain role, or viceversa.

While there are several works which separately deal with services orchestration or choreography that we list below, to the best of our knowledge the only related work is [BBM+05] where, by means of automaton, defines a conformance notion which allows us to test whether interoperability is guaranteed. Such a notion is limited to systems involving only two peers.

Papers [BMM05, BHF04, LZ05, ML04] investigate mechanisms for supporting long running transactions in orchestration languages and security issues have been investigated in [BFG04]. Another aspect related with orchestration is the correlation sets mechanism (used, e.g., by WS-BPEL) which provides a mean for correlating some interactions between services; such a mechanism have been formalized in an orchestration language in [Vir04]. Besides our work on choreography we have mentioned in the paper, here we cite [BCPV04] where the Web Service Choreography Interface (WSCI) language is modeled.

References

[BBM+05]   M. Baldoni, C. Badoglio, A. Martelli, V. Patti, and C. Schifanella. Verifying the conformance of web services to global interaction protocols: a first step. In *Proc. of Web Services and Formal Methods Workshop (WS-FM'05)*, volume 3670 of *LNCS*, pages 257–271. Springer-Verlag, 2005.

[BCPV04]   A. Brogi, C. Canal, E. Pimentel, and A. Vallecillo. Formalizing web services choreographies. In M. Bravetti and G. Zavattaro, editors, *Proc. of 1st International Workshop on Web Services and Formal Methods (WS-FM 2004)*, volume 105 of *ENTCS*. Elsevier, 2004.

[BFG04]   K. Bhargavan, C. Fournet, and A.D. Gordon. A semantics for web services authentication. In *Proceedings of the 31st ACM SIGPLAN-SIGACT Symposium on Principles of Programming Languages (POPL)*, pages 198–209. ACM, 2004.

[BGG+]   N. Busi, R. Gorrieri, C. Guidi, R. Lucchi, and G. Zavattaro. Towards a formal framework for Choreography. In *Proc. of 3rd International Workshop on Distributed and Mobile Collaboration (DMC 2005)*. IEEE Computer Society Press. To appear. [http://www.cs.unibo.it/%7Elucchi/papers/dmc.pdf].

[BHF04]   Michael Butler, C. A. R. Hoare, and Carla Ferreira. A trace semantics for long-running transactions. In *25 Years Communicating Sequential Processes*, pages 133–150, 2004.

[BMM05]   R. Bruni, H. Melgratti, and U. Montanari. Theoretical foundations for compensations in flow composition languages. In *POPL '05: Proceedings of the 32nd ACM SIGPLAN-SIGACT symposium on Principles of programming languages*, pages 209–220, New York, NY, USA, 2005. ACM Press.

[GGL05]   R. Gorrieri, C. Guidi, and R. Lucchi. Reasoning on the interaction patterns in choreography. In *Proc. of Web Services and Formal Methods Workshop (WS-FM'05)*, volume 3670 of *LNCS*, pages 333–348. Springer-Verlag, 2005.

[Kel76]   Robert M. Keller. Formal verification of parallel programs. *Commun. ACM*, 19(7):371–384, 1976.

[LZ05]   C. Laneve and G. Zavattaro. Foundations of Web Transactions. In *Proc. of International Conference on Foundations of Software Science and Computation Structures (FOSSACS'05)*, volume 3441 of *LNCS*, pages 282–298, 2005.

[ML04]   M. Mazzara and R. Lucchi. A Framework for Generic Error Handling in Business Processes. In M. Bravetti and G. Zavattaro, editors, *Proc. of 1st International Workshop on Web Services and Formal Methods (WS-FM 2004)*, volume 105 of *ENTCS*. Elsevier, 2004.

[OAS]   OASIS. *Web Services Business Process Execution Language Version 2.0, Working Draft.* [http://www.oasis-open.org/committees/download. php/10347/wsbpel-specification-draft-120204.htm].

[vGW96]   Rob J. van Gabbeek and W. Peter Weijland. Branching time and abstraction in bisimulation semantics. *J. ACM*, 43(3):555–600, 1996.

[Vir04]   M. Viroli. Towards a Formal Foundation to Orchestration Languages. In M. Bravetti and G. Zavattaro, editors, *Proc. of 1st International Workshop on Web Services and Formal Methods (WS-FM 2004)*, volume 105 of *ENTCS*. Elsevier, 2004.

[W3C]   W3C. *Web Services Choreography Description Language Version 1.0. Working draft 17 December 2004.* [http://www.w3.org/TR/2004/WD-ws-cdl-10-20041217/].

PerfSONAR: A Service Oriented Architecture
for Multi-domain Network Monitoring

Andreas Hanemann[1], Jeff W. Boote[2], Eric L. Boyd[2], Jérôme Durand[3],
Loukik Kudarimoti[4], Roman Łapacz[5], D. Martin Swany[6],
Szymon Trocha[5], and Jason Zurawski[6]

[1] German Research Network (DFN), c/o Leibniz Supercomputing Center,
Barer Str. 21, D-80333 Munich, Germany
hanemann@lrz.de
[2] Internet2, 1000 Oakbrook Drive, Suite 300, Ann Arbor, MI 48104, USA
{boote,eboyd}@internet2.edu
[3] GIP Renater, 151 Boulevard de l' Hôpital, 75013 Paris, France
Jerome.durand@renater.fr
[4] DANTE, 126-130 Hills Road, Cambridge CB2 1PG, United Kingdom
loukik.kudarimoti@dante.org.uk
[5] Poznan Supercomputing and Networking Center, Noskowskiego 12/14,
61-704 Poznan, Poland
{romradz,szymon.trocha}@man.poznan.pl
[6] Department of Computer and Information Sciences, University of Delaware,
Newark, DE 19716, USA
swany@cis.udel.edu, zurawski@eecis.udel.edu

Abstract. In the area of network monitoring a lot of tools are already available
to measure a variety of metrics. However, these tools are often limited to a single
administrative domain so that no established methodology for the monitoring of
network connections spanning over multiple domains currently exists. In addition, these tools only monitor the network from a technical point of view without
providing meaningful network performance indicators for different user groups.
These indicators should be derived from the measured basic metrics.

In this paper a Service Oriented Architecture is presented which is able to perform multi-domain measurements without being limited to specific kinds of metrics. A Service Oriented Architecture has been chosen as it allows for increased
flexibility and scalability in comparison to traditional software engineering techniques. The resulting measurement framework will be applied for measurements
in the European Research Network (GÉANT) and connected National Research
and Education Networks in Europe as well as in the United States.

1 Introduction

The administrators of a network domain can currently make use of a lot of available
tools to monitor a variety of metrics. However, the situation gets much more complicated if information about the performance of a connection involving different administrative domains is requested. Besides of examples like transnational videoconferences

B. Benatallah, F. Casati, and P. Traverso (Eds.): ICSOC 2005, LNCS 3826, pp. 241–254, 2005.
© Springer-Verlag Berlin Heidelberg 2005

the monitoring of multi-domain connections is especially interesting for Grid projects which are currently being deployed across Europe and elsewhere.

The subproject *Joint Research Activity 1* of the GN2 project [4] aims at providing a framework for performing multi-domain measurements in the European Research Network (GÉANT) and the connected National Research and Education Networks (NRENs). It is carried out in close cooperation with Internet2's End-to-End piPEs [6] initiative and will result in a common system called *PerfSONAR* (Performance focused Service Oriented Network monitoring ARchitecture). The name reflects the choice of a Service Oriented Architecture for the system implementation.

A survey performed in the requirement phase of the project showed the diversity of measurements that are currently applied in different networks together with the demand for a common framework. The survey has also been useful to derive a list of metrics being of common interest. These metrics can be retrieved by active and passive measurement methodologies as well as by requesting SNMP variables. Metrics of primary interest for the users include round-trip time and one-way delay as well as its variation (aka jitter), round-trip and one-way packet loss ratio, bandwidth utilization, IP available bandwidth, and interface errors/drops. For each metric a differentiation can be made between IPv4 and IPv6, unicast and multicast, different classes of service as well as between different time-scales ranging from short-term for performance debugging to long-term for trend observation. The metric definition in the project is done in accordance with current recommendations (such as those from IETF IPPM (IP Performance Metrics) and IPFIX (IP Flow Information Export)). Currently, most public networks provide information about the core network topology, link bandwidth, and current utilization data (sometimes with some limitations), while information about other metrics is hardly provided.

The rest of the paper is organized as follows. In Section 2 requirements from different user groups concerning the networking monitoring functionality are motivated. Related Work is examined in Section 3 which includes the examination of previous projects and different software architectures interesting for the framework implementation. Our Service Oriented Architecture is presented in Section 4, while the current status of its prototypical implementation is subject to Section 5. Conclusion and future work can be found in the last section.

2   Requirements

The multi-domain monitoring framework that is addressed in the project should be able to fulfill the requirements of different user groups.

NOC/PERT: For the Network Operation Center (NOC) or people from the Performance Emergency Response Team (PERT) the framework shall provide a multi-domain perspective on the networks and juxtapose a variety of metrics. This is needed to link several information sources in order to allow for a better understanding of performance degradations in the network.

Network Managers: The framework should also allow for different kinds of policies with regard to user groups and metrics. An example policy could be that the access to interface packet drops is only allowed for NOC and PERT staff. Therefore, it should be easy for the network managers to apply their network policies for information filtering to the framework.

Projects: A dedicated view is required for projects spanning over multiple administrative domains to show to each partner the performance of the underlying backbone network. This information complements the end-to-end view of the projects gathered by their own systems (e.g. DataGrid WP7 software [5]) to gain a better understanding of the network behavior and its impact for application tuning. Furthermore, special kinds of metrics have to be offered for the project links, e.g. an aggregated metric showing the performance of the connections to important partners.

End Users: For end users the framework shall provide a view of the backbone networks which allows to easily track whether a problem is located in the backbone or is supposed to be present in the user's local area network. This is a major improvement in comparison to the current situation (see Figure 1). Today, a user who experiencies a network performance problem is often able to get information about the local area network, but it is hardly possible to get timely information about the performance of the national research backbone and of Geant. The use of simple test tools like ping

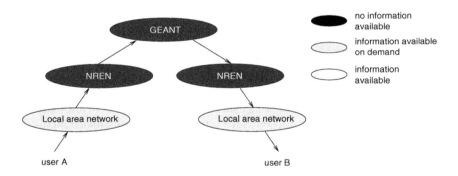

Fig. 1. Network transparency today

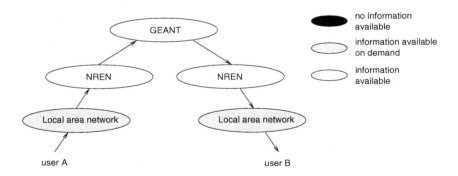

Fig. 2. Network transparency after PerfSONAR deployment

and traceroute cannot be regarded as satisfactory. The aim in the project is to provide an edge-to-edge view of the research backbones facilitating the easy identification of problems in the networks for the user (see Figure 2).

3   Related Work

This section deals with monitoring projects related to the purpose of JRA1. In addition, the different possibilities for the realization of the PerfSONAR framework using the Service Oriented Architecture paradigm are evaluated.

3.1   Monitoring Projects

One of the issues of the EU-funded INTERMON [10] project was inter-domain QoS monitoring. The modeling in the project is based on abstractions for traffic, topology, and QoS parameter patterns. This allows to run simulations for network configuration planning. To fulfill these goals, the project has based its entire design on a huge centralized and complex database for topology, flow, and test information, collecting all network data in a single location. However, such model is not acceptable in a multi-domain environment. It is not conceivable that an entity supersedes the others and has a complete control of other networks. Also, while INTERMON centralizes the collection of pre-defined measurements, JRA1 provides an architecture where any entity can, based on authentication and authorization rules, schedule new types of measurements and run tests over the multi-domain network. JRA1 has a more focused goal and has real production constraints from NOCs, requesting data for day-to-day operation of the networks. There are also many constraints for allowing distributed policies among the different networks, for exchange of monitoring data and access to on-demand test tools.

The MonALISA project [13] has also provided a framework for distributed monitoring. It consists of distributed servers which handle the metric monitoring for each configured host at their site and for WAN links to other MonALISA sites. JRA1 shares the idea of servers acting as a dynamic service system and providing the functionality to be discovered and used by any other services or clients that require such information. Even though MonALISA has similar concepts to our approach, JRA1 details its application to multi-domain environments with mechanisms for measurements spanning independently managed domains, especially with respect to metrics concatenation and aggregation. The MonALISA system relies on JINI (see Section 3.2) for its discovery service.

The PlanetLab [15] initiative is also related to our work. It is a huge distributed platform over currently 568 nodes, located in 271 different sites. It enables people being members of the consortium to access the platform (or a part of it) to run networking experiments. Most of the projects which run over the PlanetLab infrastructure deal with network monitoring and management in general. Those tests aim at properly designing services at a large scale. The architecture is similar to PerfSONAR - resources are made available through designed architecture services. In PlanetLab a node manager (i.e. access interface for each node) has been proposed which just allocates local resources based on a policy enforced by the infrastructure service. Even though analogies between the components defined in the two projects can be identified, the PlanetLab infrastructure service is centralized and relies on a single database. Similar to INTER-MON it can therefore not be applied as is to a multi-domain environment.

The Enabling Grids for E-SciencE (EGEE) project, which has been launched in April 2004 and is funded by the European Commission, continues the work of the DataGrid project [5]. The project aims at network service deployment for the Grid community. This includes the development of network interfaces and the use of network services like performance measurements and advance reservations. The task of its subactivity JRA4 [7] is to retrieve network measurements from a set of domains by using Web Services. The measurement services being accessed can be divided into end-to-end measurements (host-to-host) and backbone measurements using dedicated monitoring equipment.

EGEE JRA4 has in total designed and developed three prototypes which communicate with both kinds of measurement services. The third protoype communicates with PerfSONAR instances located in different domains to retrieve backbone measurements for capacity, bandwidth utilization, and available bandwidth. It decides on the correct service end point to contact by using a discovery functionality which is currently statically configured. The transportation layer of EGEE being implemented as a Web Service translates between different versions of the GGF NMWG schema [14].

3.2   Implementation Options

In JRA1 it has been decided to realize the network monitoring framework by adopting the Service Oriented Architecture (SOA) paradigm. This new paradigm in software engineering proposes to use independent pieces of software (called "services") which can be orchestrated to collaborate in order to reach a common goal.

A SOA has several advantages in comparison to traditional software architectures. A large task can be split into independent services which helps to avoid monolithic software blocks being difficult to maintain. At runtime, the services can be dynamically added/dropped which results in an increased flexibility and robustness. Furthermore, different implementations of a SOA design do not have to realize all services if only a part of the functionality is needed.

The most common technology for the realization of a SOA are Web Services. From the evolving Web Service standards WS-Notification is of particular interest for the project and is going to be adapted in multiple scenarios. It deals with the communication between services using publish/subscribe mechanisms and therein supports two data flow models: Direct notifications (WS-BaseNotification) from service to client, where the service itself maintains a list of interested clients, and brokered notifications (WS-BrokeredNotification), where a client can act as a broker and can have several clients of his own. The specification contains standardization of message exchanges and XML schema specifications.

In JRA1 several options have been considered for the implementation of the framework using a SOA. Besides of Web Services are also other possibilities as described in the following.

JINI. One possibility to implement a distributed Service Oriented Architecture is to apply JINI [11] which is provided by Sun Microsystems under an open source licence.

It is a set of Java APIs and runtime conventions that facilitate the building and deploying of distributed systems. JINI itself is fully implemented in Java and uses its integral mechanisms such as remote method invocation (RMI).

Applications using JINI are treated as a set of cooperating distributed services. There is one specialized service called Lookup Service where other services can register and client applications can fetch information about required services.

The default communication between services is done in RMI offering remote procedure calls, but also any other protocol offering message passing is allowed (one can choose UDP or TCP on transport level and any protocol on application level). The discovery of the Lookup Service depends on the existence of multicast in the network. Without multicast the address(es) of Lookup Service(s) need to be well-known.

Even though some mechanisms like the lookup procedure are interesting for the project, it has been decided not to use JINI because of its tight Java coupling and limitations like the necessity to use multicast.

JXTA. Sun Microsystems also promotes the open source peer-to-peer software architecture JXTA [12] which can be regarded as complementary to JINI. The basic entities defined by JXTA are peers which can interact by using defined protocols. These protocols deal with peer discovery, peer information exchange, peer-to-peer routing, and the establishing of communication channels (called pipes).

A variety of different types of low-level message transport protocols, such as HTTP, TCP/IP, and TLS (Transport Layer Security) can be used in the current reference implementation of JXTA. One of the JXTA protocols enables the communication between peers connected to different low-level network types.

There is a reference implementation of the architecture in Java, but other implementations in C, Ruby, Phyton, or Perl are also available. Like in other P2P architectures peers can be added/dropped at any time. To allow for a service provisioning change using other resources, no physical network addresses are used, but a JXTA addressing scheme is applied.

JXTA is supposed to be suitable for peer-to-peer applications, even though only few information about successful JXTA-related projects can be found best to our knowledge. The measurement framework in JRA1 cannot be classified as a true peer-to-peer scenario as we have different classes of service in our framework (see Section 4). Therefore, JXTA would have to be combined with JINI or Web Services.

Apache Axis. For the implementation of Web Services Apache Axis [1] which is a popular Simple Object Access Protocol (SOAP, [18]) implementation has been examined. Axis is mainly a Java platform for creating and deploying Web Services. A C/C++ version of Axis is available as well. The Axis package also provides an application called SOAPMonitor to view and debug SOAP communications received and replied to by deployed Web Services. A web-based interface for viewing and managing services is also part of the package. Application servers such as Tomcat [19] are required to use the Java version of Apache Axis. The C/C++ version needs a Web Server (such as Apache) and uses Xerces C++ [20] to parse SOAP. The examination of Axis in the project has focused on the Java version.

Deploying services can be done in many ways with all of them requiring the use of Web Service Deployment Descriptors (WSDD). It can work with or without server side stubs and can also create service descriptions in Web Service Description Language (WSDL) at run time. It is also possible to have clients without stubs thus making it easier to have dynamic invocations.

In the Axis case, a client connects to the web (application) server and feeds a SOAP message, which conforms to the service WSDL definition. Axis converts the SOAP message to proper method calls of the classes that implement the service (business logic). Axis is therefore called a *SOAP proxy*. A Document Type/Literal Style of Web Service, which uses an XML document as input in the request, can be deployed by using Axis. Information required by the service to handle and satisfy the request (including the operation name) are "derived" from this XML Document.

The use of SOAP, WSDLs and the possibility to use Document Type/Literal Style of Web Services makes it easy to deploy services without worrying about how the clients are built (using Java/C++/Perl/Python/etc.). The clients only need to build acceptable XML documents (conformant to a defined schema) and use the standard SOAP protocol in order to make use of the service. The operating system or the platform used on the client side bears no importance or effect on the entire process. Consequently, the use of Web Services (and hence Axis, which provides an "easy-to-use" Web Service (SOAP) implementation) has an edge over its competitors.

Globus Toolkit. The Globus Toolkit 4.0 [9] has evolved from a Web Services-based reimplementation of a software suite from the Grid community. It is based on Axis, but has build several modules on top of it which can be used independently. Its modules include implementations of the Grid Resource Allocation Manager (WS-GRAM), Replica Location Service, Monitoring and Discovery Service (MDS), etc.

It intends to implement a stable reference implementation of the Web Services Resource Framework (WSRF, refactoring of the Open Grid Services Infrastructure specification, OGSI) in Java, C, and Python. The management of stateful resources provided by WSRF is interesting, as stateful resources like links are encountered in the JRA1 context.

The Globus Toolkit is much more difficult to deploy than Axis. Even though some modules are application agnostic so that they are supposed to be suitable for network monitoring, it needs to be examined whether it makes sense to incorporate some Globus Toolkit modules in the framework or to implement some more lightweight functionalities for the JRA1 purpose on top of Axis directly. A sophisticated module of Globus is the implementation of the Grid Security Infrastructure which is hard to deploy due to the needed certificates which have to be provided and managed.

Summary. In the project it has been chosen to implement the monitoring framework by using Web Services. Web Services provide a lot of flexibility in the client programming as these only have to be conformant to an XML description, i.e. there are no dependencies from operating systems or programming languages. The communication can happen via the easy-to-use SOAP. Our examination of Apache Axis showed that it is a mature open source tool for implementation. Some modules of the Globus Toolkit could be adopted in later stages of the project.

4   Multi-domain Monitoring Framework and Service Oriented Architecture

The monitoring framework which is designed by JRA1 as well as JRA1's PerfSONAR system being applied for the middle layer of the framework are outlined in this section.

4.1   Monitoring Framework

The general monitoring framework which is explained in detail in the following is depicted in Fig. 3.

The Measurement Points are the lowest layer in the system and are responsible for measuring and storing network characteristics as well as for providing basic network information. The measurements can be carried out by active or passive monitoring techniques. The Measurement Point Layer of a domain consists of different monitoring components or agents deployed within the domain. A monitoring agent provides information on a specific metric (e.g., one-way delay, jitter, loss, available bandwidth) by accessing the corresponding Measurement Points. Each network domain can, in principle, deploy Measurement Points of its choice.

The Service Layer is the middle layer of the system and consists of administrative domains. It allows for the exchange of measurement data and management information between domains. In each domain, a set of entities (services) is responsible for the domain control. Each of them is in charge of a specific functionality, like authentication and authorization, discovery of the other entities providing specific functionalities, resource management, or measurement of network traffic parameters. The interaction of the entities inside a domain as well as the access to the Measurement Point Layer or other domains may not be visible to the end user. Some of the entities contain an interface which can be accessed by the User Interface Layer.

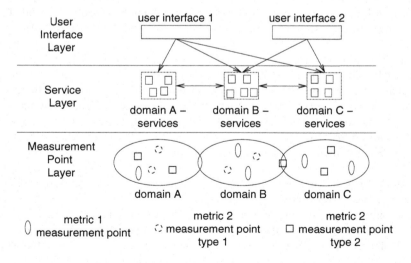

Fig. 3. JRA1 architecture proposal

The User Interface Layer consists of visualization tools (user interfaces) which adapt the presentation of performance data to be appropriate for the needs of specific user groups. In addition, they may allow users to perform tests using the lower layers of the framework. From the user interface perspective, the Service Layer provides an additional level of abstraction to hide the differences between Measurement Points deployed in the different domains.

The design aim is to provide the main functionalities in the Service Layer as independent entities to allow for an increased flexibility of the system: existing elements may be easily replaced or new ones inserted. Even if the number of entities is large each one can be identified and invoked using discovery functionalities.

4.2   Service Oriented Architecture

There are three general categories of performance measurement data, i.e., active and passive measurement results as well as network state variables (SNMP variables) that can be thought of as data producers and are provided by the Measurement Point Layer. From the user or network administrator point of view, analysis tools, threshold alarms, and visualization graphs can be thought of as data consumers which are contained in the User Interface Layer. Between data producers and data consumers is a pipeline of aggregators, correlators, filters, and buffers, which can be regarded as data transformers and data archives. Data producers, consumers, transformers, and archives are all resources that need to be discovered and (possibly) protected from over-consumption using authentication and authorization.

A services-based measurement framework implements each of these roles as an independent service: Lookup (LS), Authentication (AS), Measurement Archive (MAS), Transformation (TS), and Resource Protector (RPS). These services form the Service Layer. The Measurement Point Layer is also regarded as it contains Measurement Point Services (MPS).

Users of any service, whether they are end user applications or other services, are specified as clients. Providers of any service are denoted as servers. Therefore, many services can be both client and server, depending upon the context. To achieve this, all data providers implement a publisher interface and all data consumers implement a subscriber interface. When a data flow is requested, the consumer provides a handle to a subscription interface if it wants a push interaction. If it does not provide a subscription handle, the data producer creates a publisher interface that the consumer can poll.

The service interactions are depicted in Fig. 4 and are referenced at the end of the description of each service. In [2] use case examples for the application of the framework can be found.

Measurement Point Service (MPS). The Measurement Point service creates and publishes measurement data by initiating active measurements or querying passive measurement devices [3]. A common interface to these capabilities is required for ease of integration into the monitoring system as a whole. MPSs use a measurement setup protocol to allow the user to request measurements to be made for a specified set of parameters and then publish the results of these measurements to one or more sub-

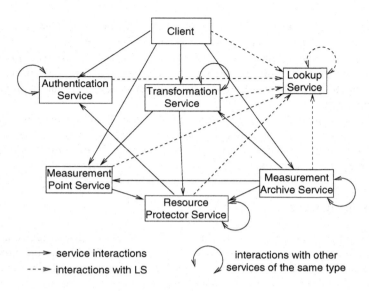

Fig. 4. Interactions of Services

scriber interfaces. Legacy capabilities (e.g., existing active measurement tools, Netflow, SNMP) can be wrapped within an MPS.

When acting as a server, the MPS accepts measurement requests and uses a push method for data publishing. In this case the client has to provide in advance one or more subscriber handles to send the results directly to it. It is also possible to send data indirectly via a TS (see below). When acting as a client, the MPS registers its own presence with an LS and publishes measurement data to subscribers. The MPS may send resource availability and authorization requests to the Resource protector service.

Lookup Service (LS). Services register their existence and capabilities, subject to locally-determined policies and limits, with a Lookup Service. The registration is performed using a join protocol. A service may register for a limited period of time or leave without disrupting the interaction of other services. Clients discover needed services by querying an LS using the lookup protocol. The first LS is found by one of several approaches, including multicast, well-known servers, or internal configuration. Once an LS is found, additional LSs are identified by querying the first one. LSs register themselves with other LSs and are organized using peer-to-peer distribution techniques.

The lookup protocol of the service network defines the kinds of queries a client can make when looking for a resource. The LS is not a simple name-based directory service. Queries about the services are based upon attributes such as service type, required authentication attributes, and service capabilities, as well as more complex constructs, such as network location or community affiliations. It is expected that the information in the LS will be much more expansive than a typical UDDI directory, although this could be one way to implement the LS information store. It is likely a more generic store will be put in place to allow for more targeted service specific information to be registered. This could be implemented using a direct XML database with XQuery capabilities.

When the service acts as a server the LS accepts requests for service-related information, registration and deregistration requests (including advertisements from other LSs announcing their existence), and keep-alive requests. When acting as a client, the LS registers its own presence to other LSs. The service can also work in peer-to-peer networks where an LS shares directory information with other LSs.

Measurement Archive Service (MAS). The Measurement Archive service stores measurement data in database(s) optimized for the corresponding data type and publishes measurement data produced by MPSs and/or TSs. In addition to providing a historical record for analysis, the MAS serves to reduce queries to the MPS by effectively offloading the publication to multiple clients. MAS makes use of a set of protocols: storage setup protocol which is used to setup the MAS to accept and store measurement data from a publisher, e.g. MPS and measurement data retrieval protocol to get measurement data from MAS by the client.

In case the MAS is perceived as a server, it accepts and stores setup requests as well as publication requests. The publication request includes a subscription handle and the results are sent directly to the client (or indirectly via a TS). As a client, the MAS registers its own presence with an LS, subscribes to an MPS, other MAS, or TS, and publishes measurement data to subscribers. The MAS may send resource availability and authorization requests to the RPS.

Authentication Service (AS). The Authentication service provides the authentication functionality for the framework as well as an attribute authority. The AS supports clients with multiple identities, including individual identities that represent different roles at different times. Role-based authentication using attribute assertion style authorization protects the privacy of the user [17]. This typically means a handle is created to provide additional information about the attributes of that user and that resources can use that handle to make queries about the user subject to the privacy policy. Communities of multiple administrative domains that accept each other's authentication can be formed by federating ASs. Federation details are held solely in the AS and are hidden from other services within a given administrative domain. In other words, the *trust* relationship within a domain is between the domain's services and the local AS domain, while the *trust* relationship between any two federated domains is managed by the ASs.

When acting as a server, the AS accepts authentication requests and attribute requests via its interfaces. As a client, it registers its own presence with an LS and may query other ASs for attributes of a federated identity.

Transformation Service (TS). The Transformation service performs a function (e.g., aggregation, correlation, filtering, or translation) upon measurement data. The TS subscribes to one or more servers and publishes to one or more clients, making it a key component of a data pipeline within the measurement framework. For example, a TS might compress datasets from more recent, high-resolution data to less recent, low-resolution data and publish that data to an MAS. A TS also might read from multiple data publishers to create a specific correlation. A very simplistic data analysis example would be a threshold detection operation that then pushed data out for the purposes of triggering a Network Operations Center alarm. For the Alarm Notification Service (a type of TS) the WS-Notification standard is going to be applied for distributing alarms.

When considering the TS as a server, it accepts publication requests. If the request includes a subscription handle, the results are sent directly. If no subscription handle is included, the TS returns a publisher handle to the client which is then responsible for initiating dataflow. When TS acts as a client, it registers its own presence with an LS, subscribes to one or more MPs, MAs, or TSs, and publishes measurement data to subscribers. The TS may send resource availability and authorization requests to the RPS.

Topology Service (ToS). The Topology service is a specific example of a TS used to make topological information about the network available to the framework. It collects topological information from a variety of sources (i.e. multiple MPSs) and uses algorithms to derive the network topology. The ToS also reflects multiple network layers. That is, the topology can be described on the domain level through network elements, but also by wavelengths representing the physical level. Understanding the network topology is necessary for the measurement system to optimize its operation. For example, the LS relies on the ToS to determine MPS that are "closest to" interesting network locations (e.g. routers). Thus, in the same way that a host may ask for an MPS instance that has a particular set of properties, a service component can also request information about node proximity. Additionally, the Topology service may be used for overviews/maps that illustrate the network with relevant measurement data.

Resource Protector Service (RPS). The Resource Protector service is used to arbitrate the consumption of limited resources, such as network bandwidth. This service is distinct from the individual MPSs to allow the consumption of resources that are common across multiple types of MPSs to be tracked in a single place. (For example, a one-way latency test would be adversely effected by a throughput test going over the same network interface.) The RPS also has a scheduling component to deal with the consumption of time-dependent resources. When measurement activities are involved, resources may be related to the measurement infrastructure or real network resources. The RPS can allocate portions of a resource based upon configuration rules and can schedule the time-dependent resources. Services that consume resources contact the associated RPSs to allocate them. Because RPSs reduce scheduling flexibility, RPSs should only be deployed to protect limited resources. In other words, some MPSs do not have to contact an RPS at all.

Authenticated requests provide a way of making attribute assertion queries back to the authenticating entity. A handle is included within the Authentication Token that is sent with the request. This makes it possible for the RPS to determine whether a particular resource requestor has the right to access a given resource without being completely aware of the identity of the requestor.

If the RPS acts as a server, it accepts authorization and resource availability requests. If it acts as a client, the RPS registers its presence with an LS. The RPS may request authorization and resource availability for other resources from other RPSs. The RPS may request additional attribute information about an authenticated identity from an AS.

5   Prototypical Implementation

This work is based upon lessons learned from many European and international initiatives and deployed measurement frameworks, including DANTE's perfmonit project [4] and Internet2's piPEs project [6]. The work is also carried out with respect to efforts of the GGF Network Measurement Working Group [14] to develop schemas for interoperable measurement frameworks.

A prototypical implementation is currently carried out to realize the model as Web Services aiming at the retrieval of link utilization data from several networks. The focus of this implementation is to validate the framework design and the service interactions.

Simplified versions of the services are applied to reduce the complexity of the architecture at the first stage. The number of services and their complexity will increase over time by adding additional modules, features, and measurement types. The initial service is the Lookup Service which is needed to locate other services (in this case MAS and MPS). The crucial portion of the prototype system is the MAS, which is initially a wrapper around Round Robin Databases (RRD) [16] and provides link utilization statistics. in the beginning, several MASs have been deployed in multiple domains, making use of different RRD collections already performed in these networks and providing a picture of a few research networks' utilization both from Europe (e.g. GÉANT) and North America (e.g. ESnet [8]). As mentioned before, the prototypical implementation is already used by EGEE [7] to retrieve link utilization data for enabling its own Grid network monitoring.

Two other phases are targeted in the prototype. The first extension will be to add auto-registration capabilities to the LS, so that any service coming into live could register its capabilities and will automatically be known by the LS. It is also intended to add new measurement capabilities like packet loss and interface errors to the MAS. It is considered to replace user scripts with intuitive graphical interface for test setup, data retrieval and presentation.

6   Conclusion and Future Work

In this paper a motivation has been given for the necessity of a multi-domain network monitoring framework. Due to the deficits of existing frameworks with respect to flexibility and the disregard of organizational boundaries such a framework is subject to the JRA1 project. The examination of different implementation options has resulted in choosing a Web Services approach using Apache Axis and maybe some modules of the Globus Toolkit.

While the project primarily aims to provide a monitoring framework for the involved research networks, the open source tool development will also make it feasible to apply the framework to other multi-domain network monitoring scenarios.

Acknowledgments

The authors wish to thank Nicolas Simar (DANTE) and Thanassis Liakopoulos (GR-NET) for the collaboration in the project and their valuable comments on previous versions of the paper.

References

1. Apache Axis. http://ws.apache.org/axis.
2. J. Boote, E. Boyd, J. Durand, A. Hanemann, L. Kudarimoti, R. Lapacz, N. Simar, and S. Trocha. Towards multi-domain monitoring for the european research networks. In *Proceedings of the Tenera Networking Conference 2005 (TNC 2005)*, Poznan, Poland, June 2005. TERENA.
3. T. Chen and L. Hu. Internet performance monitoring. *Proceedings of the IEEE*, 90(9):1592–1603, September 2002.
4. DANTE homepage including information about GÉANT, performit and GN2 projects. http://www.dante.net/.
5. Wp7 - network services, DataGrid project. http://ccwp7.in2p3.fr.
6. E2Epi performance evaluation system (piPEs), Internet2, End-to-End Performance Initiative. http://e2epi.internet2.edu/.
7. Joint Research Activity 4, Enabling Grids for E-SciencE (EGEE) project. http://egee-jra4.web.cern.ch/EGEE-JRA4/.
8. Energy Sciences Network. http://www.es.net.
9. Globus toolkit, version 4.0. http://www.globus.org/.
10. INTERMON project. http://www.intermon.org/.
11. JINI network technology, Sun Microsystems. http://www.sun.com/software/jini and http://www.jini.org.
12. JXTA, Sun Microsystems. http://jxta.org/.
13. MONitoring Agents using a Large Integrated Services Architecture (MonALISA), California Institute of Technology. http://monalisa.caltech.edu/.
14. Network measurements working group (NMWG), Global Grid Forum. http://www-didc.lbl.gov/NMWG.
15. PlanetLab project. http://www.planet-lab.org/.
16. Round robin database tool homepage. http://people.ee.ethz.ch/ oetiker/webtools/rrdtool/.
17. Specification of the general architecture, protocolas, and message formats of the shibboleth mechanism. http://shibboleth.internet2.edu/docs/draft-mace-shibboleth-arch-protocols-06.pdf.
18. Simple Object Access Protocol, World Wide Web consortium. http://www.w3.org/-2000/xp/Group.
19. Apache Tomcat, Apache Jakarta project. http://jakarta.apache.org/tomcat/.
20. Xerces xml parser, c++ version, Apache project. http://xml.apache.org/xerces-c/.

DySOA: Making Service Systems Self-adaptive

Johanneke Siljee, Ivor Bosloper, Jos Nijhuis, and Dieter Hammer

Department of Computing Science, University of Groningen,
P.O. Box 800, 9700 AV Groningen, The Netherlands
{b.i.j.siljee, i.e.bosloper, j.a.g.nijhuis,
d.k.hammer}@rug.nl

Abstract. Service-centric systems exist in a very dynamic environment. This requires these systems to adapt at runtime in order to keep fulfilling their QoS. In order to create self-adaptive service systems, developers should not only design the service architecture, but also need to design the self-adaptability aspects in a structured way. A key aspect in creating these self-adaptive service systems is modeling runtime variability properties. In this paper, we propose DySOA (Dynamic Service-Oriented Architecture), an architecture that extends service-centric applications to make them self-adaptive. DySOA allows developers to explicitly model elements that deal with QoS evaluation and variable composition configurations. Having the DySOA elements explicit enables separation of concerns, making them adaptable at runtime and reusable in next versions. We demonstrate the use of DySOA with an example.

1 Introduction

Building systems from services has been emerging as a software paradigm [1], [2]. Service-centric systems consist of multiple services, possibly from different service providers, working together to perform some functionality. A service implemented by combining the functionality provided by other services is a *composite service* [3], and the way a composite service is structured and behaves is the *service composition.*

Service-centric computing provides new techniques that allow for greater runtime flexibility. Services are located, bound, and executed at runtime using standard protocols such as UDDI, WSDL, and SOAP [4]. Because services are loosely-coupled and have an explicit interface, it is relatively easy to integrate third-party services, and to substitute one service for another at runtime.

Although the techniques for runtime adapting service systems are available, it currently happens seldom. The reason is that no standards exist for *self-adaptation*, the process where the service system autonomously makes decisions on when and what to change and autonomously enacts the changes. Because technologies for self-adaptation still miss, the burden for adaptation would fall on service users or service providers. But users just want to use the service system, without being bothered with collecting and composing the right services to make up the system. And service providers might provide service systems that have thousands of users, making manual adaptation an impossible task. This results in service-centric systems that, once bound, will always call the same services.

B. Benatallah, F. Casati, and P. Traverso (Eds.): ICSOC 2005, LNCS 3826, pp. 255–268, 2005.

Having such "static" service systems would not provide any problems, if nothing changes during the period that a user makes use of the service system. Unfortunately, this is not the case. Almost every service system exists in a very dynamic environment that makes it nearly impossible to keep delivering the quality of service (QoS) that the user pays for. The QoS that the service system has to deliver is often formalized in a Service Level Agreement (SLA), and not fulfilling these QoS requirements may result in penalties, e.g. the provider has to pay a fine or will loose customers. Examples of the dynamics that service systems are confronted with are:

- *Unreliable third-party services*: third-party services are not controlled by the service system provider and can fail unexpectedly.
- *User changes*: a service composition may serve multiple users, with each a different SLA and thus different QoS requirements. These QoS requirements can change when the user's context changes, for example because the user moves or starts using the same service on a different device. An example is a changing security requirement, caused by a user leaving the office building and going out on the street. Data transfer should then be better encrypted and limited to non-secure documents.
- *Network irregularities*: available network bandwidth and throughput rates between distributed services vary over time, potentially causing services to be unreachable.

The dynamic context of service systems requires them to adapt to context changes in order to keep fulfilling the QoS requirements. Service systems should be self-adaptive, because, as explained earlier, manual adaptations by users or service providers are not a feasible solution. In order for service systems to be self-adaptive, they must be able to self-detect when and what to change and make this change autonomously. This ability requires, among other things, runtime evaluating if the current QoS fulfills the QoS requirements, and knowing the runtime variability options. In this paper, we focus on modeling the possible configurations (i.e. the variability) in self-adaptive service systems.

1.1 Design of Self-adaptive Systems

A software architecture provides a global perspective on the software system in question. Architecture-based design of large-scale software systems provides major benefits [5]. Designing the architecture for a software system shifts the focus away from implementation issues towards a more abstract level. This enables designers to get a better understanding of the big picture, to reason about and analyze behavior, and to communicate about the system with others.

Part of a service architecture is the service composition, which can be described with languages like BPEL and UML. Many other Web Service standards are used to describe other aspects of the system. Each standard allows developers to specify a certain part of self-adaptive service systems, but no approach exists for developers to design variability options of these systems. This void results in ad-hoc solutions at the implementation level, which hinders the development, reuse and evolution of systems.

In this paper we present DySOA, a Dynamic Service-Oriented Architecture. DySOA extends service applications to make them self-adaptive in order to guarantee the QoS, despite the dynamic context of service systems. DySOA structures the elements that deal with self-adaptation and variability, making them easier for developers to model and reason about. DySOA provides explicit components that deal with QoS evaluation and composition variability. Having all major self-adaptation elements first-class makes it easier to develop them, to runtime update them, and to reuse them for other systems.

The remainder of this paper is structured as follows. We describe the DySOA architecture in section 2. We show the use of DySOA with an example in Section 3. Section 4 covers related work and Section 5 concludes the paper.

2 DySOA

DySOA stands for Dynamic Service-Oriented Architecture, and is an architectural extension for service-based application systems. DySOA provides a framework for monitoring the application system, evaluating acquired monitoring data against the QoS requirements, and adapting the application at runtime.

The purpose of DySOA is to assist the service application system in maintaining its QoS. At design time, an application developer designs a system that is targeted to fulfill the requirements. However, some of the QoS requirements are only known at runtime (e.g. negotiated in an SLA), and service systems live in dynamic environments, of which the properties cannot always be foreseen at design time. In order to keep delivering the QoS requirements, the application system should be able to self-adapt when necessary.

Many different aspects need to be taken into consideration for the development of a self-adaptive system. It is very difficult to address all concerns in one model, and this one model would be hard to evolve. The complexity can be reduced by splitting the process from monitoring to reconfiguration into several steps. The different concerns are then addressed in different components and models within each step. Having explicit, separate models for the different aspects allows better communication between different stakeholders (e.g. service providers or service users) and independent evolution of the aspects. Furthermore, in order to evolve at runtime, the specific models have to be available at runtime. In the next sections we describe the architectural model of DySOA and the relation with service-based applications.

2.1 The DySOA Adaptation Process

Figure 1 shows the activity diagram of the DySOA runtime adaptation process. First, monitors collect data about the application context. From the collected monitoring data the QoS is determined. Some QoS attributes are directly measurable (e.g. response time), but the values of many QoS attributes cannot be directly monitored and need to be inferred from other context information. The determined QoS is compared with the QoS requirements. If the result of this evaluation indicates the QoS is good enough, then monitoring continues. If the QoS is not good enough, a new configuration is chosen that will satisfy the QoS requirements. Finally, the changes are enacted in the application. Possible changes are substituting a bound service for an alternative service or changing the structure and the flow of the service composition.

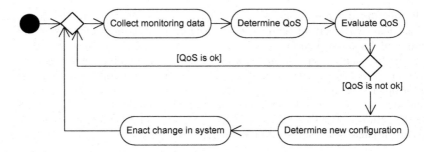

Fig. 1. Activity diagram of the DySOA monitoring and adaptation process

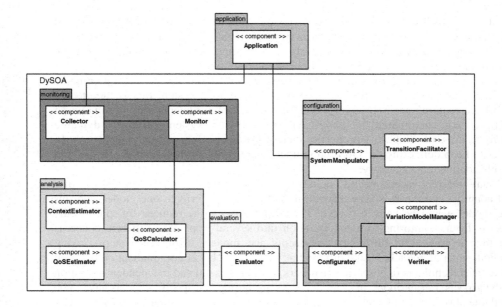

Fig. 2. Overview of the DySOA component architecture

2.2 Overview of the DySOA Architecture

Figure 2 shows an overview of the DySOA architecture. It consists of four component packages: the Monitoring component, the Analysis component, the Evaluation component, and the Configuration component. The Application component does not belong to the DySOA architecture, but refers to the service-based application system that DySOA monitors and configures. Next we describe the functionality of each component and its subcomponents.

2.2.1 Monitoring
The Monitoring component deals with acquiring information about the running application and its environment. The *Collectors* gather the data necessary to

determine the current application QoS. A Collector can, for example, intercept and inspect service messages, or monitor a system resource. The kind of data collected depends on the application domain and the QoS requirements itself, but it typically involves data about individual services in the application (e.g. response times, failure rates, exceptions), the execution environment (e.g. network bandwidth, processor load), and the context of the application users (e.g. user GPS coordinates).

Collectors are runtime created, deployed and removed by the Monitor, which does not interfere or deal with monitoring data itself, but manages the Collectors based on a list of collectors needed per QoS attribute. Upon application reconfiguration the Monitor re-evaluates the list and removes or deploys Collectors where necessary. The Collectors provide the monitoring data to the QoSCalculator.

2.2.2 Analysis

The QoSCalculator uses monitoring data to determine the current QoS of the running application. The determination may be executed in two steps; this depends on whether QoS attribute information can be monitored directly. We distinguish three cases:

1) The QoS can be directly monitored, and the QoSCalculator just sends the monitoring data on to the *Evaluator*. For instance, response time is directly measurable.

2) The monitoring data contains information on the application or user context, and has to be combined with e.g. information on the current application configuration to determine the current QoS. In this case the QoSCalculator sends the monitoring data to the *QoSEstimator* for QoS determination. The result is provided to the Evaluator.

3) Again, the monitoring data only contains information on the application or user context, but of such a low level that first a better understanding of the context is necessary before the QoSEstimator can be used. In this case the QoSCalculator transforms the monitoring data with the *ContextEstimator*. The returned context information is used by the QoSEstimator to determine the QoS sent to the Evaluator. For example, the GPS-coordinates of the user location first need to be translated to country and corresponding language.

The ContextEstimator determines the context by analyzing the monitoring data. A context model is used to associate monitoring data with context situations. A context model can be based on a table or ontology (e.g. OWL [6]), and may be designed by experiments. In the example of the GPS-coordinates, the context model associates them with a language.

The QoSEstimator determines the QoS of the application, based on the context information or the monitoring data. For example, to determine the availability of the entire application system, the down-times of the individual services making up the application are monitored. Because the overall availability depends on the workflow between several services (e.g. parallel or in series), to determine the overall availability the monitoring data is combined with a representation of the dynamic structure of the application.

The QoSEstimator may use a composition model, containing the current configuration of the application and QoS metrics, to calculate the QoS from the monitoring data. Another option is a number of formulas to calculate the QoS. Distinguishing between ContextEstimator and QoSEstimator allows both to be adapted separately: the former when the context interpretation has to be changed and the latter when the translation to QoS has to be changed.

2.2.3 Evaluation

The *Evaluator* determines if the current QoS satisfies the application QoS requirements. For this purpose, it uses the QoS information provided by the QoSCalculator, and uses a model containing the QoS requirements. The Evaluator compares the QoS information to the QoS requirements; if the current QoS does not satisfy, a reconfiguration is needed. The Evaluator sends this evaluation, including a description of how well each QoS requirement is fulfilled and (expected) reasons of failure, to the *Configurator*.

2.2.4 Reconfiguration

The Configurator is responsible for determining new application configurations. Configuring the application is only possible if the configuration options are known. Furthermore, the system should be able to determine if a configuration is valid. Also, the Configurator should be able to enact a new configuration in the application system. Having these features, Dysoa can reconfigure the service system.

Configuration Variability

In DySOA, designers can model the runtime variability of the self-adaptive service system in a variation point view; a view that can be used as a supplement to other design views. Variation points have been recognized as elements that facilitate systematic documentation and traceability of variability, assessment, and evolution [7]. Thus, variation points are perfectly suited as central elements in managing variability, which holds for runtime variability as well. The variation model behind this view is available at runtime, and is used by the Configurator. Our variation point view is largely based on the one presented in [8]. In this paper, we have altered some aspects to tailor the variation point view to self-adaptive software.

Variation Model

A variation point is uniquely identified by its *name*, and contains a *description* of the variability it provides. This description can be informal or formal, as long as the software developers can describe and understand the rationale behind each variation point. A variation point identifies a location where variation occurs, and is therefore associated with one or more *variants*. The variants of a variation point are, for example, several services that provide the same functionality but with different QoS characteristics, or several *composition fragments*: sets of services organized in different process flows (e.g. BPEL activities).

An intrinsic variation point constraint restricts the variant selection of one variation point. An extrinsic variation point constraint restricts the selection of two or more variants from different variation points. The selection of variant *a* for variation point vp1 might, for instance, demand the selection of variant *b* of variation point vp2, or it might prohibit the selection variant *c* of variation point vp3.

Part of the specification of a variant is the *realization*, which can be described as a recipe with instructions for realizing the binding of the variant dynamically. The current bindings of a variation point are its currently bound variants.

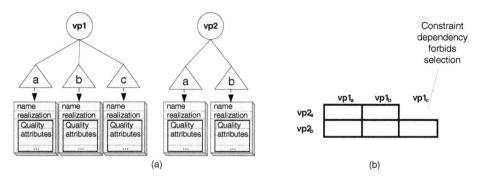

(a)   (b)

Fig. 3. (a) Two variation points. (b) The VariationModel containing the set of possible configurations of the associated variants. The VariationModel does not contain configuration (*vp2a, vp1c*) because an extrinsic constraint forbids its selection.

Furthermore, service systems often have *open variation points*: variants can be added to or removed from an existing variation point while the system is running. For service compositions this means that at runtime newly discovered services can be added to the composition.

The *VariationModel* of a set of variation points *vps* is the set of possible configurations of the variants belonging to *vps*, together with the (possibly estimated) QoS attribute values of the variants. A DySOA VariationModel only represents configurations possible at runtime. Furthermore, if an intrinsic or extrinsic constraint forbids a certain configuration, then that configuration is not part of the VariationModel. For example, Figure 3 (a) shows two variation points: vp1 and vp2. vp1 has three variants, $vp1_a$, $vp1_b$, and $vp1_c$, and vp2 has two variants, $vp2_a$ and $vp2_b$. An extrinsic constraint forbids the selection of both $vp1_c$ and $vp2_a$. Each variant has an explicit realization and quality attributes. Figure 3 (b) shows the corresponding VariationModel. Five possible configurations exist, as the selection of ($vp2_a$,$vp1_c$) is forbidden by the extrinsic constraint.

The VariationModel is not static; new services can be automatically discovered at runtime or inserted by the user or provider of the service system. Additionally, the QoS characteristics of a variant are not static and should be updatable as well. New QoS values can be determined by monitoring, or a service provider can publish a new QoS specification of its services. The *VariationModelManager* manages all the runtime variability options of the application. The VariationModelManager is responsible for keeping the available variability options up-to-date, e.g. by using service discovery techniques to update the available services (e.g. UDDI).

Configuration Verification
The *Verifier* checks the correctness of new configurations proposed by the Configurator. Examples of checks include variability constraints and deadlock detection.

Configuration Realization
When a new configuration has been verified, the *SystemManipulator* deploys the new configuration in the running system, e.g. by deploying a new orchestration in the BPEL engine of the application system or by reconfiguring a service proxy. The

SystemManipulator makes sure that application state and transactions are managed safely by using the *TransitionFacilitator*. This component can for instance make sure that no transactions are running during configuration, by postponing the start of new transactions. A different approach is to interrupt transactions, send the appropriate exceptions, and execute rollback- or compensation-actions. The state of the running business process (e.g. contained in variables) is copied to the new application state if necessary.

Configuration Selection

Now we are able to deploy new application configurations safely, the Configurator should be able to choose a new configuration, based on the results of the Evaluator. There are several strategies to deal with evaluation results. The Configurator could *optimize*, by always looking for a better configuration, handle *pro-actively*: switching the configuration when danger for QoS failure appears, or *recover*: only choose a new configuration if the QoS fails. Also, the timing for dealing with insufficient QoS is variable; instead of immediate action, it might be allowable to wait for a while to see if the QoS failure is not temporary. Additionally, choosing a new configuration can be based on a formal trade-off of quality attributes (e.g. linear programming), a random choice (in case no quality characteristics of variants are available in the VariationModel) or anything in between. For instance, if time is no issue, the Configurator can test many different configurations before making a decision.

These aspects are specified in the Strategy, a data structure that explicitly represents how to act on the Evaluation results. The Configurator bases the decision process on the currently chosen Strategy.

To summarize: the Configurator uses information from the Evaluator, the Strategy, and the VariationModel to determine a new configuration, and uses the Verifier to verify the correctness of the new configuration.

3   Example

In this section we show how to use DySOA to make a service application self-adaptive. The service application is a video-on-demand service, consisting of third-party services. In order to provide the user with the best QoS for his video stream, the service application needs to be self-adaptive.

The Streaming Video Service (SVS) offers different kinds of streaming video: movies and television series. Users contact the SVS on the internet and select a movie or series episode to watch. For the actual delivery of the video, the SVS uses services from video content suppliers. Each content supplier offers a certain set of streaming video, in several resolutions, and with specific quality characteristics. The SVS discovers the available video suppliers at runtime using a registry.

The SVS automatically binds to a video supplier service that provides the required video content. For the actual streaming, the SVS invokes a proxy service that handles the network connection between the video supplier and the user. The proxy buffers the video stream, in order to protect against short discontinuities and to provide the capability to rebind to another supplier without the user noticing. See Figure 4 for an overview of the streaming video system. Below we show how the components and data structures of the DySOA architecture are instantiated.

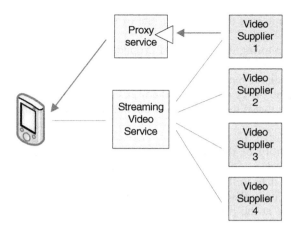

Fig. 4. Service composition of the SVS application

Qos Requirements

Because of space limitations, we do not specify DySOA for all QoS requirements that can trigger adaptations, like performance or cost. Here, we concentrate on two requirements:

- Req 1: continuous availability of the video stream. The video should not stop unless the user explicitly turns it off.
- Req 2: best possible video quality for the user. This is related to the user's display resolution, bandwidth and available streams from video suppliers.

Figure 5 shows the requirements representation.

Monitoring

The quality attributes referred to in the requirements cannot be directly measured. In order to be able to evaluate whether the system fulfills these two requirements, DySOA inserts the following collectors:

```
<wsp:Policy>
 <wsp:All>
  <qos:Policy
     serviceName="VideoProxy">
  <qos:QoS name="Availability">
   <qos:Value>
    <qos:Min>0.95</qos:Min>
    <qos:Pref>1</qos:Pref>
   </qos:Value>
  </qos:QoS>
```
```
<qos:QoS name="VideoQuality">
 <qos:Value>
  <qos:Min>0.8</qos:Min>
  <qos:Pref>1</qos:Pre>
 </qos:Value>
</qos:QoS>
</qos:Policy>
</wsp:All>
</wsp:Policy>
```

Fig. 5. The QoS Requirements

1. A collector monitoring the output bit rate of the proxy video stream sent to the user.
2. A collector monitoring the number of dropped packets on the proxy-to-user connection. From time to time, the collector sends a small burst of packets to estimate the available bandwidth.
3. A collector at the proxy monitoring the user video resolution. The streaming protocol defines that if the video is resized, the collector is notified.

Analysis

Req 1 specifies availability of the video stream at the user playback device. The measured proxy bit rate does not directly define this video stream availability; we need to relate measured data to the video stream availability at the playback device. For this example, the ContextEstimator uses a context model based on the simple heuristic that the bit rate at the playback device is equal to the bit rate at the proxy output. The advantage of having this rule explicit is that it is possible to adapt this heuristic when it turns out to be incorrect.

The ContextEstimator returns the bit rate to the QoSCalculator. The latter sends this information, together with the estimated bandwidth and resolution, to the QoSEstimator, which calculates the availability and video quality.

The QoSEstimator is implemented by several functions that relate the data coming from the QoSCalculator with the QoS requirements on availability and video quality. The availability is specified in terms of the Mean Time To Failure (MTTF) and the Mean Time To Repair (MTTR) of the video stream at the user, see Table 1. The MTTF is determined from the bit rate as follows:

Let B be the bit rate at the playback device. A failure F_i refers to the event that the bit rate drops to 0, where $F_i(B)$ refers to failures in B. $R_i(F_i)$ is the repair time after F_i. If n is the number of failures during time t, then:

$$MTTF = \frac{t}{\sum_{i=1}^{n} F_i(B)} \qquad\qquad MTTR = \frac{R_i(F_i)}{\sum_{i=1}^{n} F_i(B)}$$

The video quality is determined from the bit rate B, the available bandwidth A and the horizontal resolution of the offered stream ($R_{offered}$) and of the playback device R_{user}, see Table 1.

Table 1. Table with the functions for estimating the QoS attributes

QoS Attribute	Function
Availability	$\dfrac{MTTF}{MTTF + MTTR}$
VideoQuality	$1 - \dfrac{\left| R_{offered} - R_{user} \right|}{R_{user}} - \dfrac{\left| B - A \right|}{A}$

The data flow in the Analysis is as follows; the QoSCalculator sends the collector monitoring data to the ContextEstimator, which returns context information on the playback device's bit rate. The QoSCalculator sends the context information and monitoring data to the QoSEstimator. After the QoSEstimator has determined the current QoS for availability and video quality, the QoS values are sent back to the QoSCalculator, who provides it to the Evaluator.

Evaluation

The Evaluator compares the determined QoS values from the QoSCalculator with the QoS requirements. In our example, the Evaluator checks if the current Availability value is higher than 0.95, and if the current VideoQuality is higher than 0.8. The results of this evaluation specify how each QoS requirement performs, and this is sent to the Configurator. In this example we do not include possible causes for the failure in the message.

Configuration

The VariationModel contains two variation points; a *sup* variation point for choosing between movie suppliers, and a *res* variation point for choosing the video resolution (see Figure 6). The VariationModelManager initially creates the list of variants for *sup* by discovering available services that fulfill the functional requirements (i.e. provide the selected movie). Each variant has a realization that specifies how to invoke the variant. A *supplier* variant is realized by binding to the video supplier, and a *resolution* variant is realized by passing the right parameters during binding.

These variation points cannot be configured independently, as not every supplier provides all resolutions. Choosing a supplier can therefore rule out the choice for a certain resolution. The VariationModel also models these dependencies.

When a QoS requirement is violated, a new configuration is chosen. In this case the Strategy is a recovery strategy that acts immediately if the required QoS is not met. The Configurator asks the VariationModelManager to look up alternative variants, and to update the VariationModel with the observed QoS properties of the

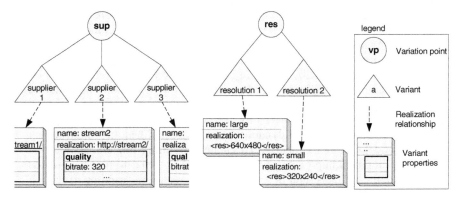

Fig. 6. The SVS VariationModel; the *sup* variation point has discovered video suppliers as variants. The *resolution* variation point has two variants.

failing variant. The Strategy is configured to select the variants that best match the QoS requirements. The selected variants are bound as described by their realizations, and the SystemManipulator is implemented by calling a management method on the proxy to switch the variant.

In this example we have shown how DySOA is instantiated for a simple example. Because all data structures and components that deal with the self-adaptation of DySOA are explicit in the architecture, it is relatively easy to runtime adapt these elements, and to reuse the design for new service applications.

4   Related Work

Most methods for developing runtime self-adaptive systems concentrate on a specific application domain or only on the implementation mechanisms for runtime change. This related work discussion is limited to the more general development approaches at the architectural level.

Some research focuses on a specific part of a dynamic architecture. Yang [9] for example proposes a modeling method for a dynamically extendable adaptation kernel that monitors whether changes should be made. The "adaptation rules" are composed of a condition, which determines when to change, and an action, which specifies how and what to change. The Lasagne framework [10] models runtime variability with "extension identifiers" and provides composition policies attached to a component to change its (messaging) behavior. Tsai [11] presents a framework and tool to specify constraints and audit these constraints at runtime. Service providers register their services at the framework, which tests the service to verify the constraints. Services that pass the tests are available to incorporate in service compositions. Tsai's approach enables quality assurance beforehand, but limits the amount of services that can be used by requiring testing every service before it is published, as not all services and all quality constraints can be tested.

Architecture description languages (ADLs) are used to formally describe a software architecture [12], and several ADLs support dynamism with specific first-class language elements. Dynamic Wright [13] allows defining a variation model by having explicit definitions of variable components. A "configuror" enacts changes and contains a rule block that specifies when to exchange certain components for other components. Weaves [14] provides explicit elements called "instruments" to collect context information. "Observers" are modeled to evaluate this information. "Actors" support enacting change by translating high-level to low-level changes.

Software construction methodologies go beyond modeling and additionally define how to implement dynamic software. Bapty [15] presents an overall design approach called Model Integrated Computing (MIC) for the development of a domain-specific dynamic system. The models of a dynamic system are defined in "multi-aspect domain-specific modeling environments". To create a resulting implementation, the MIC defines a development approach for "system synthesis tools" to turn the created models into executable artifacts, and describes how to create the "runtime execution environment".

The architecture of a dynamic system can systematically be evaluated. Brusilovsky [16] presents a layered evaluation framework for dynamic systems, designed to determine what parts of the architecture should be adapted if the dynamic behavior does not resemble the required dynamic behavior. The framework separates the responsibilities in the architecture of a dynamic system in two layers. The "adaptation decisions" layer focuses on the architecture for reconfiguration, and the "interaction assessment" layer describes the part of the architecture that monitors environment data and transforms it into information.

5 Conclusion

Designing self-adaptive service systems is a major undertaking and requires software engineering modeling methods and tools. The dynamic context of service systems requires them to adapt to context changes in order to keep fulfilling the QoS requirements. Current standards and techniques for service system engineering typically provide an implementation-level solution for a single aspect of the dynamic behavior. DySOA combines, at the architecture level, the necessary components and data structures for the entire process. This allows separation of concerns and enables developers to manage the complexity of the self-adaptive behavior.

The DySOA architecture can be used to develop service systems that autonomously and dynamically adapt to a changing context and changing user requirements. We demonstrated how the runtime variability is modeled in the architecture for a self-adaptive service application example. Currently we are working on the implementation of DySOA.

Acknowledgements

This research has been sponsored by SeCSE (Service-Centric System Engineering) under contract no. IST-511680.

References

1. Microsoft, Service-Oriented Architecture: Implementation Challenges, http://msdn.microsoft.com/library/en-us/dnmaj/html/aj2soaimpc.asp (2004)
2. Schmelzer R., "Service-Oriented Process Foundation Report", ZTR-WS108, ZapThink (2003)
3. Alonso G., Casati F., Kuno H., Machiraju V., Web Services - Concepts, Architectures and Applications, Springer Verlag (2004)
4. Tsai W. T., Song W., Paul R., Cao Z., Huang H., "Services-Oriented Dynamic Reconfiguration Framework for Dependable Distributed Computing", *COMPSAC 2004*, Hong Kong (2004) 554-559
5. Shaw M., Garlan D., Software Architecture: Perspectives on an Emerging Discipline, Prentice Hall, Upper Saddle River, New Jersey (1996)
6. W3C Recommendation, OWL Web Ontology Language Overview, Recommendation, http://www.w3.org/TR/REC-owl-ref-20040210 (2004)
7. Bosch J., Design & Use of Software Architectures - Adopting and Evolving a Product Line Approach, Addison-Wesley, Boston (2000)

8. Sinnema M., Deelstra S., Nijhuis J., Bosch J., "COVAMOF: A Framework for Modeling Variability in Software Product Families", *The Third Software Product Line Conference (SPLC 2004)*, Boston, USA (2004)

9. Yang Z., Cheng B., Stirewalt K., Sadjadis M., Sowell J., Mckinley P., "An Aspect-Oriented Approach to Dynamic Adaptation", *Proceedings of the Workshop on Self-Healing Systems (WOSS'02)*, ACM SIGSOFT, Charleston, SC (2002)

10. Truyen E., Vanhaute B., Nørregaard Jørgensen B., Joosen W., Verbaeten P., "Dynamic and selective combination of extensions in component-based applications", IEEE, Toronto, Ontario, Canada (2001) 223-242

11. Tsai W. T., Song W., Paul R., Cao Z., Huang H., "Services-Oriented Dynamic Reconfiguration Framework for Dependable Distributed Computing", Hong Kong (2004) 554-559

12. Allen R., Douence D., Garlan D., "Specifying and analyzing Dynamic Software Architecture", Springer-Verlag (1998) 21-37

13. Magee J., Kramer J., "Dynamic Structure in Software Architectures", *Fourth Symposium on the Foundation of Software Engineering (FSE 4)*, ACM SIGSOFT (1996) 24-27

14. Gorlick M. M., Razouk R. R., "Using Weaves for Software Construction and Analysis", *13th International Conference on Software Engineering (ICSE 13)* (1991) 23-34

15. Bapty T., Scoot J., Neema S., Sjtipanovits S., "Uniform Execution Environment for Dynamic Reconfiguration", *IEEE Conference and Workshop on Computer-Based Systems*, Nashville, Tenessee (1999)

16. Brusilovsky P., Karagiannidis C., Sampson D., "The benefits of layered evaluation of adaptive applications and services", *Workshop on Empirical Evaluation of Adaptive Systems*, Sonthofen, Germany (2001)

Towards Dynamic Monitoring of WS-BPEL Processes

Luciano Baresi and Sam Guinea

Dipartimento di Elettronica e Informazione - Politecnico di Milano,
Piazza L. da Vinci 32, I-20133 Milano, Italy
{baresi, guinea}@elet.polimi.it

Abstract. The intrinsic flexibility and dynamism of service-centric applications preclude their pre-release validation and demand for suitable probes to monitor their behavior at run-time. Probes must be suitably activated and deactivated according to the context in which the application is executed, but also according to the confidence we get on its quality. The paper supports the idea that significant data may come from very different sources and probes must be able to accommodate all of them.

The paper presents: (1) an approach to specify monitoring directives, called monitoring rules, and weave them dynamically into the process they belong to; (2) a proxy-based solution to support the dynamic selection and execution of monitoring rules at run-time; (3) a user-oriented language to integrate data acquisition and analysis into monitoring rules.

1 Introduction

The flexibility and dynamism of *service-centric* applications impose a shift in the validation process. Conventional applications are thoroughly validated before deployment, and testing is the usual means to discover failures before release. In contrast, service-centric applications can heavily change at run-time: for example, they can bind to different services according to the context in which are executed or providers can modify the internals of their services. New versions of selected services, new services supplied by different providers, and different execution contexts might hamper the correctness and quality levels of these applications. Testing activities cannot foresee all these changes, and they cannot be as powerful as with other applications: we need to shift validation to run-time, and introduce the idea of *continuous monitoring*.

Runtime monitors [6] are the "standard" solution for assessing the quality of running applications. Suitable probes can control functional correctness, and also the satisfaction of QoS parameters, but web services introduce some peculiar aspects. Functional correctness can be easily monitored by analyzing the data exchanged among services, but service-centric applications also require that the many QoS aspects be monitored with data that can be collected at different abstraction levels. We can analyze the SOAP messages exchanged between client and provider, trace the events generated during execution, and collect data from external metering tools. All these options must be accommodated in a general framework that lets designers choose the values of interest and the way they want to collect them.

B. Benatallah, F. Casati, and P. Traverso (Eds.): ICSOC 2005, LNCS 3826, pp. 269–282, 2005.

Current technology for executing (composed) services, like the WS-BPEL engines available in these days, does not support monitoring. It only allows designers to inter-twine the business logic with special-purpose controls at application level, thus hamper-ing the separation between the definition of the application (i.e., the WS-BPEL process) and the way it can be monitored. Designers must be free to change monitors without af-fecting the application, and the actual degree of control must be set at run-time. In fact, since monitoring impacts performance, the user must be able to change the amount of monitoring while the application executes to adjust the ratio between control and performance.

In this context, the paper presents an approach towards the *dynamic* monitoring of WS-BPEL processes. It proposes external *monitoring rules* as means to dynamically control the execution of WS-BPEL processes. This separation allows different sets of rules to be associated with the same process. Monitoring rules abstract Web services into suitable UML classes, and use this abstraction to specify constraints on execution. Assertions are specified in WS-CoL (Web Service Constraint Language), a special-purpose assertion specification language that borrows its roots from JML (Java Model-ing Language [11]), and extends it with constructs to gather data from external sources (i.e., to interact with external data collectors).

Besides constraining the execution, monitoring rules provide parameters to govern the degree of run-time checking. After weaving selected rules into the process at de-ployment time, the user can set the amount of monitoring at run-time by means of these parameters (see Sections 3 and 4). The weaving introduces a proxy service, called *moni-toring manager*, which is responsible for understanding whether a monitoring rule must be evaluated, interacting with the external services, and calling known data analyzers (monitors) to evaluate specified constraints. This solution can be seen as a feasibility study (proof of concept) before embedding the manager in a WS-BPEL engine and letting monitoring rules become part of the execution framework.

The approach is demonstrated on a simple example taken from [8]. Even if the pro-posal is suitable for checking both functional and non-functional constraints, here we only address QoS related monitoring rules since functional aspects were already studied in [7].

This paper is the natural continuation of the work already presented in [7], and its novel aspects are: (1) the idea of monitoring rules, (2) WS-CoL to specify constraints on execution, (3) the capability of setting the degree of monitoring at run-time, and (4) the proxy-based solution to enact the monitoring rules.

The rest of the paper is organized as follows. Section 2 introduces the monitoring approach, while Section 3 describes monitoring rules and Section 4 introduces the mon-itoring manager. Section 5 surveys similar proposals and Section 6 concludes the paper.

2   Monitoring Approach

The ideas behind the monitoring approach presented in this paper come from assertion languages, like Anna (Annotated Ada [4]) and JML (Java Modeling Language [11]), which let the user set constraints on program execution by means of suitable comments added to the source code. Similarly, we propose monitoring rules to annotate WS-BPEL processes and constrain their executions both in terms of functional correctness and satisfiability of the QoS agreements set between the client, which runs the WS-BPEL specification, and the providers, which supply the services invoked by the WS-BPEL process.

Monitoring rules are blended with the WS-BPEL process at deployment-time. The explicit and external definition of monitoring rules allows us to keep a good separation between business and control logics, where the former is the WS-BPEL process that implements the business process, and the latter is the set of monitoring rules defined to probe and control the execution. These rules also comprise meta-level parameters that allow for run-time tailoring of the degree of monitoring activities. This separation of concerns lets designers produce WS-BPEL specifications that only address the problem they have to solve, without intertwining the solution and the way it has to be checked. Different monitoring rules (and/or monitoring parameters) can be associated with the same WS-BPEL process, thus allowing the designer to tailor the degree of control to the specific execution context without any need for reworking the business process. Moreover, a good separation of concerns allows for a neater management of monitoring rules, and it is an effective way to find the right balance between monitoring and performance.

Besides separation of concerns, the approach was conceived with the goal of reusing existing technology to ease the acceptability of the approach and foster the adoption of monitoring techniques.

All these reasons led to the monitoring approach summarized in Figure 1. It starts as soon as a WS-BPEL process exists (or the designer starts working on it):

– Monitoring rules are always conceived either in parallel with the business process or just after designing it. These rules are associated with specific elements (for example, invocations of external services) of the business process, and are stored in monitoring definition files.
– When the designer selects the rules to use with a specific execution, $BPEL^2$ instruments the original WS-BPEL specification to make it call the monitoring manager.

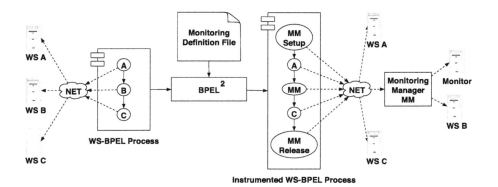

Fig. 1. Our Monitoring Approach

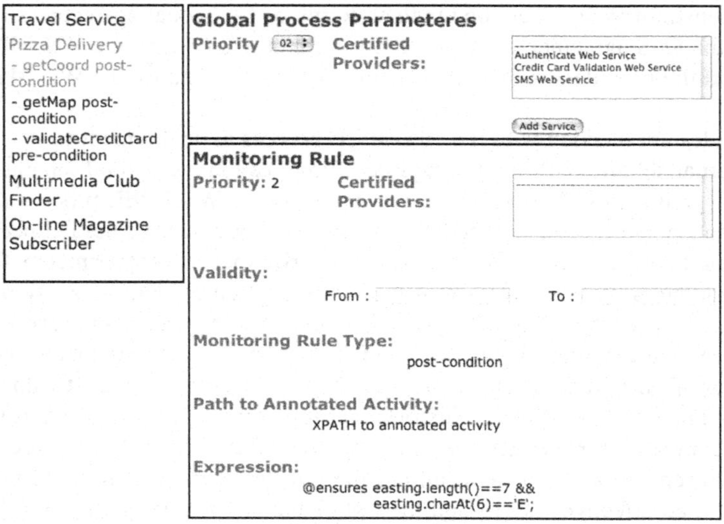

Travel Service	**Global Process Parameteres**		
Pizza Delivery	**Priority** `02 ⬍` **Certified**		
- getCoord post-condition	**Providers:**	Authenticate Web Service	
- getMap post-condition		Credit Card Validation Web Service	
- validateCreditCard pre-condition		SMS Web Service	
		(Add Service)	
Multimedia Club Finder	**Monitoring Rule**		
On-line Magazine Subscriber	**Priority:** 2 **Certified**		
	Providers:		
	Validity:		
	From :	To :	
	Monitoring Rule Type:		
	post-condition		
	Path to Annotated Activity:		
	XPATH to annotated activity		
	Expression:		
	@ensures easting.length()==7 &&		
	easting.charAt(6)=='E';		

Fig. 2. The monitoring manager's interface

- When the instrumented WS-BPEL process starts its execution, it calls the monitoring manager whenever a monitoring rule has to be considered. The actual invocation of the monitor, that is, the actual analysis of execution/QoS data depends on the current status of the manager. For example, if a rule has priority lower than the current one, the manager skips its execution and calls the actual service directly.
- The designer has a special-purpose user interface (see Figure 2) to interact with the monitoring manager and change its status. This happens when the designer wants to change the impact of monitoring at run-time without re-deploying the whole process.
- If some constraints are not met, that is, if some monitoring rules are not satisfied, the monitoring manager is in charge of letting the WS-BPEL process know. It could also activate *recovery actions* specified in the monitoring rules, but this topic is not part of this paper, and recovery actions are still work in progress.

2.1   Weaving

Code weaving is performed by the BPEL[2] pre-processor. Its job is to parse the monitoring rules associated with a particular process and to add specific WS-BPEL activities to the process in order to achieve dynamic monitoring . If the rule embeds a post-condition to the invocation of an external web service, BPEL[2] substitutes the WS-BPEL invoke activity with a call to the monitoring manager (Figure 3), preceded by WS-BPEL assign activities that prepare the data that have to be sent to the monitoring manager, and followed by a switch activity which checks the monitoring manager's response. The monitoring manager is then responsible for invoking the web service that is being monitored and for checking its post-condition with the help of an external data analyzer.

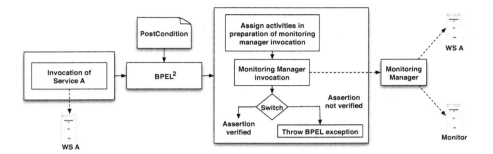

Fig. 3. The effects of weaving

Depending on the response it receives from the monitoring manager, the process flow can either continue or stop (see Figure 3). Pre-conditions are treated the same way, except that the monitoring manager first checks the pre-condition, and only if it is verified correctly does it then proceed to invoke the web service being monitored.

If the rule represents an invariant on a scope, $BPEL^2$ translates it as a post-condition associated with each of the WS-BPEL activities defined in the scope. If the rule is a punctual assertion then a single call to the monitoring manager is added, together with the corresponding WS-BPEL assign and switch activities.

$BPEL^2$ always adds to the WS-BPEL process an initial call to the monitoring manager to send the initial configuration such as the monitoring rules and information about the services it will have to collaborate with (see MM Setup in Figure 1). $BPEL^2$ also adds a "release" call to the monitoring manger to communicate it has finished executing the business logic (see MM Release in Figure 1). This permits the monitoring manager to discard any configurations it will not be needing anymore. Every call to the monitor manager (which is not a setup or a release call) is also signed with a unique incremental identifier. This is used for matching the manager call to the specific rules and the data stored in the monitoring manager during setup.

This solution does not require any particular tool to run and monitor WS-BPEL processes. Once the weaving of rules has been performed, the resulting process continues to be a standard WS-BPEL process which simply calls an external proxy service to selectively apply specified monitoring rules.

3   Monitoring Rules

Monitoring rules reflect the "personal" monitoring needs that single users of WS-BPEL processes may have. Every time a WS-BPEL process is run, different monitoring activities should be enacted, depending on "who" has invoked the process. This requires the ability to define and associate monitoring activities to a single WS-BPEL process instantiation, or execution. These definitions are conceived by producing a monitoring definition file.

The monitoring definition file follows the structure illustrated in Figure 4. The information it provides is organized into three main categories: *General Information, Initial*

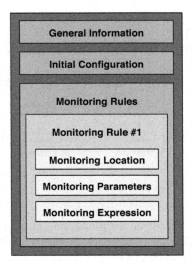

Fig. 4. Monitoring Definition

Configuration, and *Monitoring Rules*. The first part provides generic data regarding the WS-BPEL process to which the monitoring rules will be attached. The second part contains values that are associated with the process execution as a whole and can impact the amount of monitoring activities that will be performed at run-time. This concept will be further analyzed in Section 4. The third part, the monitoring rules, represent the core of the monitoring definition. They are organized in *Monitoring Location*, *Monitoring Parameters*, and *Monitoring Expressions*.

The first element indicates the exact location in the WS-BPEL process in which the monitoring rule must be evaluated. The second element contains a set of monitoring parameters, meta level information that define the context of the monitoring rule itself. These parameters influence the actual evaluation of the rule, and can even impede its run-time checking. Since we envisage the existence of multiple external monitors, the type of monitor that should be used for the given rule is an important parameter. Besides this, we currently consider three parameters (but many others could easily be added in the future[1]). The three parameters considered so far are:

Priority. It is a number between one and five indicating the level of importance that is associated with the rule. A priority level of one indicates a very low priority level, while a priority level of 5 indicates a very high priority level. The idea is that a process can run at various levels of priority. Given a process priority, any monitoring rule with a priority level inferior to this threshold would not be considered at run-time. This makes it possible to execute the same business logic with different degrees of monitoring.

---

[1] The context could be more complex and address the physical location in which the process is executed, or interact with the device on which the process executes through interfaces such as WMI (Windows Management Instrumentation).

Validity. The user defining the monitoring rules can decide to associate a time-frame with a monitoring rule. Every time a process execution occurs within this time-frame, the monitoring rule is checked; while, should it occur outside the time-frame, it would be ignored. This can be useful when a service invocation must be initially monitored for a certain amount of time before deciding that it can be trusted.

Certified Providers. It is a list of providers that gives us a way of indicating that the monitoring activity does not have to be executed if the actual service is supplied by one of the providers in the list. This is because we envisage monitoring playing a key role in systems living in highly dynamic environments, and for this reason we imagine that a specific service with which to do business could be chosen dynamically. We are never entirely sure of "who" will really be providing that service at run-time. In fact, even when a service has been chosen statically, it can still need to be substituted at run-time in the wake of erroneous situations.

The third and last element, the monitoring expression, states the constraint that has to be evaluated.

The monitoring definition file is mainly a container for the definition of the monitoring rules that are to be executed at run-time and of the conditions at which they can be ignored. Obviously, this leads to the need of specific languages for identifying the locations and for defining the expressions embedded in the rules.

3.1   Locations

In our approach we want to monitor pre- and post-conditions associated with the invocations of external web services, invariants that can be attached to WS-BPEL scopes, and punctual assertions indicating a property that must hold at a precise point of execution. While defining locations, we specify two things: the kind of condition we want to monitor, and in which point of the process definition we want to monitor it. For the first part, we use a keyword indicating whether the monitoring rule specifies a *pre-condition*, a *post-condition*, an *invariant*, or an *assertion*. For the second part, we use an XPATH query capable of pointing out where the rule has to be checked in the process, independently of the fact that the run-time checking could later be dynamically switched off. In the first two cases (pre- and post-conditions) the XPATH query indicates the WS-BPEL invoke activity to which we associate the rule, in the case of an invariant it indicates the WS-BPEL scope to which we associate it, and in the case of an assertion it indicates any point of the WS-BPEL process (in this case we indicate the WS-BPEL activity prior to which the assertion must hold). Regarding pre- and post-conditions, we are only interested in attaching monitoring rules to WS-BPEL activities that can in some way modify the contents of the process' internal variables. We are not interested in attaching monitoring rules to activities that are used by WS-BPEL to define the process topology. Therefore, we assume that pre- and post-conditions can be attached to WS-BPEL invoke activities, post-conditions to receive activities, and pre-conditions to reply activities. We also assume that post-conditions can be associated with *onMessage* branches in WS-BPEL pick activities. The reason for this is that although pick activities contribute to the process topology, they also help define the internal state of the process, and therefore should be monitored.

For example, recalling the *Futuristic Pizza Delivery* example presented in [8], if we want to define a post-condition on the invocation of the operation named `getMap` published by the `MapWS` web service and linked to the WS-BPEL process through partnerlink `MapServicePartnerLink`, we would define the location as[2]:

```
type = "post-condition"
path = "//:invoke[@partnerLink="lns:MapServicePartnerLink" and
                  @operation="getMap"]"
```

3.2 Expressions

For monitoring expressions, we propose to reason on an abstraction of the WSDL definitions of the services the WS-BPEL process does business with. Depending on the degree of dynamism, these could be the actual services used by the application, or abstract descriptions of the services the process would like to bind to (dynamic binding is not treated in this paper). To do this we use a tool based on Apache AXIS WSDL2Java [2]. The tool permits us to reason on stereotyped class diagrams that represent the classes that are automatically extracted from a WSDL service description. In the tool, a web service becomes a ≪service≫ class that provides one public method for each service operation and no public attributes. Similarly, for each message type defined in the WSDL a ≪dataType≫ class is introduced, containing only public attributes and no methods. Figure 5 shows a `MapWS` ≪service≫ class that provides a single method called `getImage`. The exposed method takes a `GetImageRequest` ≪dataType≫ as input and produces a `GetImageResponse` ≪dataType≫ as output. This way we can state our pre- and post-conditions by referring to these classes. If we want to express an invariant, we can only express conditions on variables visible within the WS-BPEL scope to which the invariant is attached. Since internal WS-BPEL variables are structured as simple or complex XSD types, the automatic translation to stereotyped class diagrams can still be achieved. The same holds for expressions that are punctual assertions. The only difference lies in the visibility of the variables the expression can refer to.

Expressions are defined using WS-CoL, inspired by the light-weight version of JML (Java Modeling Language [11]). WS-CoL further simplifies it and introduces a set of instructions for specifying how we can retrieve data that are external to the process. This may be the case in which the monitoring rule defines a relationship that must hold between data existing within the process in execution and data that can be obtained by interacting with external data collectors.

WS-CoL does not make use of keywords \old and \result[3]. The first is not useful because services are black-boxes that take input messages and produce output messages. Therefore, it is never necessary to refer to the value a certain "variable" possessed prior to the invocation of the operation. The second keyword is useless because we can refer to returned messages with their names.

---

[2] This is what the system produces but the user defines locations by pointing to the specific WS-BPEL elements directly in the graphical editor, and by choosing the annotation type.

[3] Lack of space does not allow us to thoroughly introduce the language, but JML uses \old to refer to old values in post-conditions, and \result to identify the value returned by a method.

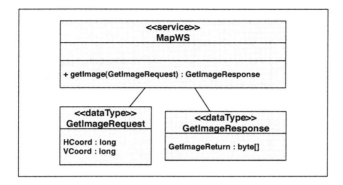

Fig. 5. The MapWS Web Service

WS-CoL adds a set of keywords that represent ways of obtaining data from external data collectors. A different extension is introduced for each of the standard XSD types that can be returned by external data collectors: \returnInt, \returnBoolean, \returnString, etc. Therefore, while defining a monitoring expression, we can use these extensions. All follow the same design pattern. They take as input all the information necessary for interacting with the external data collector, such as the URL location of its WSDL description, the name of the operation to be called upon it, the parameters to be passed to the data collector service, etc (see Section 4).

For example, if we want to specify a post-condition for the getImage operation in Figure 5 and state that the returned map must have a resolution less than "80x60" pixels we would define the expression as:

```
@ensures \returnInt(wsdlLoc, getResolution,
'image', GetImageResponse.GetImageReturn,
HResolution) <= 80 &&
\returnInt(wsdlLoc, getResolution, 'image',
GetImageResponse.GetImageReturn, VResolution) <= 60;
```

In this example, a getResolution operation is invoked on a service that publishes its interface at the URL wsdlLoc. The array of bytes GetImageReturn (see Figure 5) is passed as an input value and mapped onto the image message part defined at wsdlLoc. HResolution and VResolution, on the other hand, are the message parts defined in the output message at wsdlLoc that should be returned as integers. These returned values are compared with the desired resolution (80 pixels for the horizontal dimension and 60 pixels for the vertical dimension).

4 Monitoring Manager

The *Monitoring Manager* is the key component of our proxy-based solution for dynamic monitoring. This section illustrates its architecture and how it can be used by a WS-BPEL process that requires monitoring. We also analyze how its structure impacts the transformation produced by the BPEL^2 pre-processor.

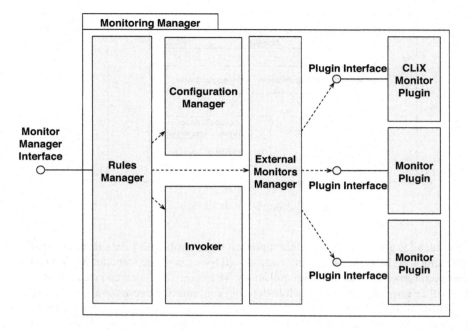

Fig. 6. The Monitoring Manager

The manager, whose architecture is shown in Figure 6, is capable of interpreting monitoring rules, of keeping trace of the configuration with which a user wants to run a process, of interacting with external data collectors to obtain additional data for monitoring purposes, and of invoking external monitor services.

We illustrate its use in the case of monitoring of pre- and post-conditions; its usage for the other cases is similar. To evaluate pre-conditions, the manager is used in substitution to the services which have rules associated with them. In fact, it is called *instead* of the service to be monitored. When called, it decides if the rule is to be evaluated by looking at its associated monitoring parameters and if it is, it proceeds to evaluate it. If the condition is verified correctly, it then invokes the original web service being monitored. Post-conditions are evaluated in the same way.

The manager is constructed to keep a configuration table for each process execution. These configurations are managed by the *Configuration Manager*. In particular, the manager needs to know: the initial overall process configuration (contained in the monitoring definition file), the monitoring rules, and all the information necessary for interacting with external services (the service being monitored, the external data collectors, and the external monitor service). Most of these data can be sent to the manager at the beginning of the process by invoking the setup method published by the manager (see Figure 1). In particular, everything except the input/output values that will be exchanged at run-time can be sent at the beginning of the process, before starting to perform the real business logic. This solution is preferable, with respect to sending all the data every time the process needs to interact with the manager, since an initial slowdown is certainly better than slowing down all the intermediate steps. All the in-

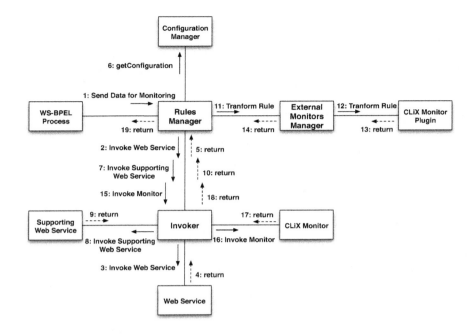

Fig. 7. The Monitoring Manager

formation sent during the setup phase is stored in the *Configuration Manager* and is associated with a process execution through the unique identifier produced by the WS-BPEL engine. Similarly, at the end of a process execution the manager is warned to free itself of the burden of keeping the corresponding configuration table.

The manager also supplies a graphical interface to the user. It permits the run-time consultation and modification of the values contained in the configuration table. For example, it is possible to modify the priority level at which a process is being run or to add a new provider to the list of certified providers that are associated with a given monitoring rule.

Figure 7 shows the step by step interaction of the components that cooperate to execute the service presented in Section 3 and to check its post-condition[4]. Initially, the BPEL process sends the data that will be necessary to the manager (Step 1). Since no pre-condition needs to be checked, the *Rules Manager* asks the *Invoker* to go on and invoke the external web service (in our case service MapWS) (Steps 2 and 3). When the *RulesManager* receives the results of the service invocation (Steps 4 and 5), it interacts with the *Configuration Manager* to retrieve the monitoring rule (i.e. the post-condition) that has to be checked (Step 6). By examining the monitoring parameters attached to the rule, the *Rules Manager* dynamically decides if the rule is to be checked or not. For example, if we consider the expression presented in Section 3, we could imagine the

---

[4] More complete running examples are available at : http://www.elet.polimi.it/upload/guinea.

associated priority parameter to be 4. If the process is then run with a priority value
of 3, the rule would be checked since its priority parameter is higher than the value
associated with the process.

Then, *Rules Manager* decides whether additional data are required from external
data collectors. If this is the case, it calls the *Invoker* to obtain them (Step 7). This
component is built around Apache WSIF (Web Service Invocation Framework [3]) and
is capable of invoking a web service without previously creating client-side stubs but
by dynamically interacting with the service through its WSDL description. The *Invoker*
can be used to invoke any service provided it knows: the URL of the WSDL of the
service to be invoked, the name of the operation that is to be invoked on that service,
a list of keys that help map the operation's input values onto the operation's message
parts as defined in the WSDL description, a list of input values for the operation to
be invoked, and a list of keys for indicating the parameters (as indicated in the output
message parts contained in the WSDL description) we want to receive as output. The
Invoker can also be called when an expression uses a WS-CoL to obtain additional
monitoring data from external data collectors. In this case, the list of output keys is
reduced to a single key that corresponds to a part of the output message as described in
the WSDL description of the service (see the expression given in Section 3.1).

Once all the data necessary have been obtained (Steps 8, 9, and 10), the *RulesManager* begins its interaction with the *External Monitors Manager* (Step 11). This component is responsible for managing the different kinds of external monitors that the
manager is capable of working with. In particular, it manages the set of plugins that
contain the logic necessary for converting the WS-CoL syntax used for defining the
monitoring expressions into the proprietary syntax used by each external monitor. The
monitor plugin also prepares the data that must be sent to the monitor by formatting
them in a way that the monitor is capable of interpreting (Step 12). In this paper, we
use a monitor built around XlinkIt [1]. For this monitor the WS-CoL expressions
must be re-written as CLiX rules and the data expressed as XML fragments. When the
External Monitors Manager has finished adapting the monitoring data and the monitoring rules (Steps 13 and 14), the *Invoker* is called once again for invoking the external
monitor (Step 15). If the monitor responds with an error, meaning the condition is not
satisfied, the *Rules Manager* communicates it to the WS-BPEL process by returning a
standard fault message, as published in the WSDL description of the manager. If the
monitor's response is that the condition is satisfied, the manager can then proceed to
return the original service response to the *WS-BPEL Process* (Step 19).

5   Related Work

The research initiatives undertaken in the field of web service monitoring share the
common goal of discovering erroneous situations during the execution of services. They
differ, although, in a number of ways: degree of invasiveness, abstraction level at which
they work, reactiveness or pro-activeness.

For example, Spanoudakis and Mahbub [9] developed a framework for monitoring requirements of WS-BPEL-based service compositions. Their approach uses eventcalculus for specifying the requirements that must be monitored. Requirements can be behavioral properties of the coordination process or assumptions about the atomic or joint behavior of deployed services. The first can be extracted automatically from the WS-BPEL specification of the process, while the latter must be specified by the user. Events are then observed at run-time. They are stored in a database and the run-time checking is done by an algorithm based on integrity constraint checking in temporal deductive databases. Like our approach, it supports reactive monitoring since erroneous situations can be found only after they occur, but it is less intrusive since it proceeds in parallel with the execution of the business process. This leads to a lesser impact on performance but also to a lesser responsiveness in discovering run-time erroneous situations. The approach also proposes a lower abstraction level, placing therefore a heavier burden on the designer.

Lazovik et al. [10] proposes another approach based on operational assertions and actor assertions. The first can be used to express properties that must be true in one state before passing to the next, to express an invariant property that must hold throughout all the execution states, and to express properties on the evolution of process variables. The second can be used to express a client request regarding the entire business process, all the providers playing a certain role in the process execution, or a specific provider. The system then plans a process, executes it, and monitors these assertions. This approach shares with ours the fact of being assertion-based. Once the assertions are inserted, it is completely automatic in its setup and monitoring. It lacks although the possibility of dynamically modifying the degree of monitoring. It also lacks adoptability since it is based on proprietary solutions.

Our approach must also be compared with the proposals that integrate Aspect Oriented programming and WS-BPEL. An example can be found in the work by Finkelstein et al. [5]. It exploits the semantic analyzers present in their development toolkit (called SmartTools) to implement a WS-BPEL engine as an interpreter. Abstract syntax trees are built for each process and are then traversed by the semantic analyzer that implements the visitor design pattern. These methods facilitate aspect oriented adaptation. The approach concentrates more on weaving at the engine level and less at the process level, which is where our approach works.

6   Conclusions and Future Work

The paper has presented an approach to support the *dynamic monitoring* of WS-BPEL processes. It is an evolution and refinement of the ideas already presented in [7]. The proxy-based solution is dictated by the wish of using available technology, instead of inventing new non standard executors, but this proposal can also be seen as a feasibility study to better understand the different pieces of the approach, and evaluate the possibility of embedding them in an existing WS-BPEL engine.

Our future work will concentrate on further studying the possibility of embedding the *monitoring manager* into a WS-BPEL engine, on experimenting with new *data collectors* and *data analyzers*, on extending the language to support other types of monitoring (e.g., the capability of predicating on histories instead of concentrating on punctual values), and on providing real-world results of the performance "overhead" that can be introduced by our approach.

References

1. XlinkIt: A Consistency Checking and Smart Link Generation Service. *ACM Transactions on Software Engineering and Methodology*, pages 151–185, May 2002.
2. AXIS. Apache AXIS Web Services Project, 2005. http://ws.apache.org/axis/.
3. Web Service Invocation Framework. Apache WSIF Project, 2005. http://ws.apache.org/wsif/.
4. D.C. Luckham. Programming with Specifications: An Introduction to Anna, A Language for Specifying Ada Programs. *Texts and Monographs in Computer Science*, Oct 1990.
5. C. Courbis and A. Finkelstein. Towards Aspect Weaving Application. *In Proceedings of the 25th International Conference on Software Engineering*, 2005.
6. N. Delgado, A.Q. Gates and S. Roach. A Taxonomy and Catalog of Runtime Software-Fault Monitoring Tools . *IEEE Transactions on software Engineering*, pages 859-872, December, 2004.
7. L. Baresi, C. Ghezzi and S. Guinea. Smart Monitors for Composed Services. *In Proceedings of the 2nd International Conference on Service Oriented Computing*, 2004.
8. L. Baresi, C. Ghezzi and S. Guinea. Towards Self-healing Service Compositions. *In Proceedings of the First Conference on the PRInciples of Software Engineering*, 2004.
9. K. Mahbub and G. Spanoudakis. A Framework for Requirements Monitoring of Service Based Systems. *In Proceedings of the 2nd International Conference on Service Oriented Computing*, 2004.
10. A. Lazovik, M. Aiello and M. Papazoglou. Associating Assertions with Business Processes and Monitoring their Execution. *In Proceedings of the 2nd International Conference on Service Oriented Computing*, 2004.
11. Gary T. Leavens, Albert L. Baker, and Clyde Ruby. Preliminary Design of JML: A Behavioral Interface Specification Language for Java. *Department of Computer Science, Iowa State University, TR 98-06-rev27*, April, 2005.

Template-Based Automated Service Provisioning – Supporting the Agreement-Driven Service Life-Cycle

Heiko Ludwig[2], Henner Gimpel[1], Asit Dan[2], and Bob Kearney[2]

[1] Universität Fridericiana zu Karlsruhe (TH), Englerstrasse 14,
76131 Karlsruhe, Germany
gimpel@iw.uni-karlsruhe.de
[2] IBM T.J. Watson Research Center, 19, Skyline Drive,
Hawthorne, NY, 10025, USA
{hludwig, asit, firefly}@us.ibm.com

Abstract. Service Level Agreements (SLAs) are a vital instrument in service-oriented architectures to reserve service capacity at a defined service quality level. Provisioning systems enable service managers to automatically configure resources such as servers, storage, and routers based on a configuration specification. Hence, agreement provisioning is a vital step in managing the life-cycle of agreement-driven services. Deriving detailed resource quantities from arbitrary SLA specifications is a difficult task and requires detailed models of algorithmic behavior of service implementations and capacity of a – potentially heterogeneous – resource environment, which are typically not available today. However, if we look at, e.g., data centers today, system administrators often know the quality-of-service properties of known system configurations and modifications thereof and can write the corresponding provisioning specifications. This paper proposes an approach that leverages the knowledge of existing data center configurations, defines templates of provisioning specifications, and rules on how to fill these templates based on a SLA specification. The approach is agnostic to the specific SLA language and provisioning specification format used, if based on XML.

1 Introduction

Agreements, particularly Service Level Agreements (SLAs), play an important role in the binding process of service-oriented architectures. They are used for the reservation of service capacity at defined service levels for a specific customer. Agreements enable a service provider to learn about future demand in advance – as stated in the agreements – and provision the required resources for the agreed service capacity.

The use of agreements to reserve and bind to services is relevant for various types of services. Agreements are used for reserving capacity of software-as-a-service, e.g., Customer Relationship Management services, for scheduling Grid jobs, and also for resource-level services within a complex system such as storage capacity, network bandwidth, computing nodes, and memory. Furthermore, the mechanism of binding to services by agreement is applied within an organization and across organizational boundaries – with changing security requirements, though.

B. Benatallah, F. Casati, and P. Traverso (Eds.): ICSOC 2005, LNCS 3826, pp. 283–295, 2005.

Traditionally, SLAs have been used primarily between organizations in a, mostly, paper-based process. SLA creation was then followed by a phase of service provisioning that could take once more a significant amount of time, depending on the degree of automation of the design of the resource infrastructure that provisions the service and of the provisioning process.

Recently, however, a number of efforts were undertaken to streamline the creation and monitoring of SLAs for service-oriented architectures by representing SLA contents in a machine-readable format and using electronic (Web services) interactions to negotiate and sign them. WSOL [15] and WSLA [12] are research approaches proposing agreement representations. SNAP is a proposal for an agreement negotiation protocol [4]. WS-Agreement [1] is a specification of the Global Grid Forum that standardizes a top-level agreement structure, a simple negotiation protocol and a compliance monitoring interface. Standardized representations of agreements and negotiation processes enable dynamic service acquisition processes for capacity-aware service clients. However, to be effective in practice, they also demand automation of the provisioning process of service providers, which is the subject of this paper.

Provisioning is the act of deploying, installing and configuring a service [9]. It is an important aspect of management of data centers and networks. Provisioning typically involves the following steps:

1. Identifying the target system state that delivers the service as intended; this involves the derivation of the system's topology, the configuration of firewalls, application servers, database servers and the like, as well as the quantification of those resources, i.e. how many servers of each type.
2. Deriving a process that transitions the system from its current state to the target state, often referred to as change management [10];
3. Executing the process consistently, usually driven by a workflow or script system accessing instrumentation on those resources.

The term provisioning is applied to both, low-level provisioning of servers or other raw resources, i.e. installing and configuring operating systems, as well as to high-level application provisioning, installing, updating and configuring applications on resources that underwent low-level provisioning earlier. Given the complexity of the steps of the provisioning process listed above, particularly steps 1 and 2, a generic solution for automating the end-to-end service provisioning process is a daunting task. While some approaches address partial aspects such as deriving a service topology [6] and deriving and optimizing a provisioning workflow [9], no generic, derivative provisioning solution is available as of now.

The approach presented here tackles exactly this problem, i.e. the automation of end-to-end service-provisioning based on agreement terms. More precisely, we propose a template mechanism that automatically handles service requests: it derives resource types and quantities necessary to guarantee quality requirements, it determines the resource configuration and assembly, and acquires resources from heterogeneous resource managers.

To make provisioning work in practice, service providers capture the experience of their system administrators in provisioning process templates and rules of thumb for capacity planning, an approach that is often pragmatic. The approach proposed in this paper leverages this pragmatic approach for agreement-driven provisioning. It provides a formal representation for templates of an executable provisioning process and an executable way of defining how to fill in these templates based on content of a formal agreement, which we call the *Agreement Implementation Plan Template (IP Template)*. These templates are predefined parametric examples of how to provision services of a given basic structure. Thus, the presented mechanism does not go against the administrators' rules of thumb or best practices on a general basis, but embraces them in providing an automatically executable process, and thus more appropriate if time is a crucial factor. The approach enables dynamic acquisition of service capacity in a service-oriented environment in a pragmatic way.

To this end, the remainder of the paper is structured as follows: Section 2 establishes relevant terminology by defining a model of provisioning in the service livecycle. Section 3 outlines the problem definition in more details, presents a sample scenario where the proposed mechanism is applicable, and points out the major requirements. Section 4 presents the proposed template structure along with the processing of agreement offers to derive resource requirements and trigger provisioning. Finally, Section 5 reviews related work and concludes.

2   Provisioning in the Agreement-Driven Service Life-Cycle

The life-cycle of any electronic service goes through at least four broad stages:

1. a high level service modeling stage for mapping a business problem to a service description,
2. a design and implementation stage where the service technology, usually the application code is developed in support of the above service description,
3. a resource mapping and deployment stage, where a specific set of resources, its topology and quantity, is defined on which the service is deployed, and
4. a runtime monitoring and management stage for managing resources delivering the service.

Supporting performance-related quality of service as part of an agreement requires additional activities throughout these four life-cycle stages. At the modeling stage, in addition to the service definition, associated qualities of service are defined. The service implementation must be implemented in a way that it can be deployed on a variable set of resources. The resource mapping and deployment stage, the service provisioning as defined here, must be able to derive the set of resources required to achieve a given performance level and at runtime, the instrumentation of the service must allow us to assess QoS compliance and adjust resource allocations.

2.1   Provisioning in an Agreement-Driven Service-Oriented Architecture

This life-cycle is managed in the context of an *agreement-driven service-oriented architecture (ADSOA)*. In this ADSOA, the agreement-related interaction between service provider and customer precedes, and is orthogonal to, the service interaction taking place between service and service client [1]. In an implementation architecture, the *Service Delivery* layer, which exists in any service-oriented architecture, is driven by the *Agreement Management* layer through Agreement Delivery Management as outlined in Figure 1.

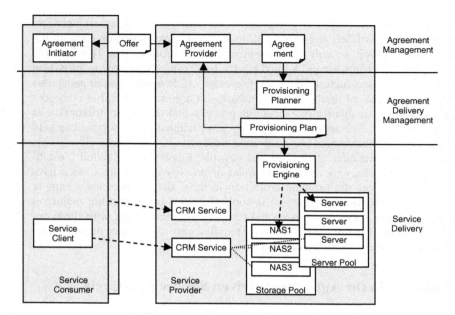

Fig. 1. Provisioning in an Agreement-Driven Service Architecture

The *Service Delivery* layer addresses the implementation of a service on a set of re-sources. In Figure 1, a CRM service is implemented by resources from two pools, storage and servers (dotted lines). It can be accessed by one or more clients. Re-sources are configured for a particular service using a provisioning engine, which executes provisioning plans, acquiring resources from resource pools and executing provisioning workflows. Resources can be shared between services or be exclusive. The Service Delivery layer per se is independent of agreements and is present in any non-trivial SOA implementation architecture.

The *Agreement Management* layer manages the portfolio of agreements and enters new agreements by exchanging offers. It also exposes the current state of the agree-ment, according to the WS-Agreement model.

The *Agreement Delivery Management* layer relates the Service Delivery and Agree-ment Management. Offers and Agreements are input to a Provisioning Planner, which creates a Provisioning Plan, comprising the set of resources required and the provision-ing workflow. This Provisioning Plan can be used by the Agreement Management layer to assess an agreement offer or it can be passed on to the Provisioning Engine of the Service Delivery layer. Mapping the state of the Service Delivery layer to the state of compliance of an agreement is also part of this layer but not the focus of this paper [11].

2.2 Use of Templates

In an ADSOA, service capabilities can be published by an agreement provider as *agreement templates*, potentially in addition to and complementing other forms such as policy-annotated UDDI entries. WS-Agreement defines a template format that con-tains a partially completed agreement, a definition of named locations where an agreement initiator can fill in agreement content, i.e. the "fields", and constraints that limit what can be filled in [1]. In the context of a CRM Web service, for example, a field could be the value for the response time of an operation and a constraint could limit the choice to one, two or five seconds. The use of agreement templates, particularly their constraint mechanism, enables service providers to advertise services only at performance levels whose resource implications they have experience with and understand. A service can be advertised using multiple agreement templates.

To capture the provisioning expertise of system administrators, these agreement templates can be associated with *agreement implementation plan templates*. An agreement implementation plan template contains a partially filled provisioning plan, corresponding to the agreement template approach, and a definition how to fill these fields depending on content of agreements. The details of this approach are described in Section 4. Agreement implementation plan templates can be changed independently of agreement templates but must be adapted if agreement templates change. Hence, the joint use of agreement templates and agreement implementation plan templates enables a service designer to anticipate the decision-making of the first three stages of the service life-cycle and automate the execution of provisioning planning for particular agreements in the life-cycle.

3   Problem Definition

The use of agreements in managing service interactions, and hence, agreement-based provisioning is required in all scenarios where service configurations need to be customized based on client requirements. As mentioned earlier, the use of customer-specific SLAs is equally applicable for configuring a business service between enterprises or for managing interactions across resource managers in a complex distributed environment, e.g., having a storage manager, workload manager, cluster manager, etc. The complexity of an agreement driven provisioning process in different scenarios depends on the service and the complexity of customization. For example, in an agreement-based job submission, where the agreement specifies a preference of resources over which the job is to be run, the Provisioning Planner simply invokes the scheduling system with the information on resource preferences. In this case, the agreement implementation plan template specifies the end-point of the scheduling system and how to extract resource preference information to be passed to the scheduling system. Similarly, incremental provisioning for setting up a shared application/web service with a client specific service level objective on average response time simply requires passing the service level objective information to the workload manager managing this service. Again, the associated agreement implementation plan template consists of the end-point of the workload manager and how to extract service level objective information.

3.1   Use Case

A more complex example of agreement-based provisioning may involve multiple steps of deriving information to be passed to one or more provisioning services and/or multiple methods to be invoked. Consider, setting up a CRM software-as-a-service hosted by an application service provider. Also, assume the agreement includes many details such as how to upload client data, application isolation, firewall and other security requirements, performance and availability requirements, requirement on storage size and data back up, network connectivity requirements, details of metering and billing, etc. Clearly, provisioning such a service requires interaction with many components and deriving resource configuration parameters to be used.

3.2 Requirements

The previous discussion leads to a set of requirements to be addressed by an agreement-driven provisioning approach:

- The approach must not be specific for a single service or a class of services, like, for example, a CRM application service. It should generically enable SLAs for a *wide range of services*, from resources to business services.
- The approach must deal with a *variety of provisioning engines*, including schedulers.
- *Agnosticism to the specific SLA language* is desirable as there is no unique way to specify SLAs and this reduces re-implementation and adaptation.
- The approach must provide means for *capturing externalized know-how* of system administrators.
- The overall provisioning process should be *automatically executable*, the main motivation for automatic provisioning.
- The approach has to provide functionality for *deriving resource types and quantities* for a given SLA.
- Furthermore, there has to be a detailed plan of the necessary *resource configuration and assembly* for provisioning these resources.
- Allowing for the *acquisition of resources* from a resource pool is an integral step in provisioning.
- Finally, the mechanism has to be *adaptive to the resource load and availability*, as the system state is non-constant.
- Finally, it might be favorable if the system is able to simultaneously cope with *heterogeneous resource pools* like, for example, different data centers; at its best, this works *across organizational boundaries*.

Manually provisioning an infrastructure that delivers a service as defined in a SLA fulfills all functional requirements outlined above but the automation. However, automation opens up the potential of speeding up the provisioning process. To forestall its properties one can say that it satisfies all above requirements. One more point about the agnosticism to the SLA language is noteworthy: the examples presented in this paper assume SLAs specified according to the WS-Agreement specification and the template itself is exemplified via XML. However, the general components and processes are as well applicable to other languages by adapting the location pointers used in the implementation plan template.

4 Template-Based Agreement Provisioning Framework

Addressing the detailed requirements defined in the previous section, this section introduces the template-based agreement provisioning framework, specifically addressing provisioning planning of the agreement delivery layer of the ADSOA. This framework comprises two elements, a representation for Agreement Implementation Plan Templates and a Definition of the Provisioning Planning process based on these templates.

4.1 Agreement Implementation Plan Templates

The framework aims at determining the resources required to provision a given SLA which might, for example, be specified as a WS-Agreement for the above-mentioned CRM application service. To this end, the framework's core element is the *agreement implementation plan template* (IP template for short). The IP template contains a description how to create a complete provisioning plan from a given agreement offer. To this end, an IP template comprises four sections:

1. *Agreement parameter identifiers,*
2. *Partial provisioning plan,*
3. *Instance completion description,*
4. *Provisioning engine invocation section.*

The components of an IP template are sketched in Figure 2 and discussed in more detail in the following.

Agreement Parameter Identifiers. The purpose of the agreement parameter identifiers section is to relate the IP template to agreements to which it can be applied. When designing the IP template one has to relate it to a class of potential agreements that follow a similar structure, potentially being created according to an agreement template, as, for example, the WS-Agreement specification draft suggests. However, this is an example and the IP template itself and the process that uses it are agnostic to the semantics of agreements, if based on XML. The section contains an arbitrary number of agreement parameter identifiers – each of which having a unique name and a location pointer. The location pointer points to exactly one location in an agreement, referred to as agreement part. Agreement parts can be any clearly identified substructure of an agreement. The pointer concept is sketched in Figure 2.

In the CRM application service example agreement parts might be performance requirements like response time and throughput, the pricing scheme, and the firewall configuration. If the agreement is specified in an XML data structure, the XPath format can be employed to represent location pointers; the author of such an XPath expression has to make sure that it resolves to one and only one single location in an agreement document. A corresponding agreement parameter identifier using XPath is exemplified below:

```
...
<AgreementParameterIdentifiers>
  <ParameterIdentifier name="AverageResponseTime">
    <LocationPointer>
      //wsag:GuaranteeTerm[@wsag:Name='resTime']/*Value
    </LocationPointer>
  </ParameterIdentifier>
  ...
</AgreementParameterIdentifieres>
...
```

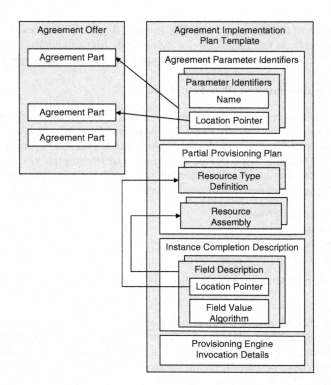

Fig. 2. Pointer structure in agreement implementation plan templates

Partial Provisioning Plan. The partial provisioning plan has a format that is interpreted by a provisioning engine. The plan has open or modifiable fields that will be filled in with values as described in the instance completion description. Most provisioning systems today have their proprietary format but some standards are under development such as CDDLM [2] or IUDD [16]. The presented approach only relies on an XML representation.

We present a simple proprietary example language that we use for provisioning prototypes; in a productive environment, CDDLM or IUDD can easily be used, as the overall mechanism is agnostic to the specific XML language employed. The description comprises the definition of resource types and one or more definitions of resource assembly which are alternatives and among which can be chosen depending on resource availability and cost considerations. Different alternatives might for example be whether to employ a mainframe or a cluster for the CRM application service example. The definition of resource types contains the information to uniquely identify the type of resources to a resource pool, e.g., the cluster management system of a data center, to query the resources availability. The following XML listing exemplifies the definition:

```
...
<PartialProvisioningPlan>
  <ResourceTypeDefinitions>
    <ResourceType name="P-Series">
      <HostType description="pSeries550">
        <HostArchitecture>
          <CPUCount>4</CPUCount>
        </HostArchitecture>
        ...
      </HostType>
    </ResourceType>
    ...
  </ResourceTypeDefinition>
  ...
</PartialProvisioningPlan>
...
```

The definition of resource assembly comprises resource quantity definitions, indicating how many resources for which type are needed for this assembly. Furthermore, the assembly contains a definition how and in which order the resources will be configured and provisioned. This definition might be written in a script language such as Unix shell script or Perl, or in a workflow language such as BPEL4WS.

Instance Completion Description. The instance completion description section of the IP template defines what parts will be filled in and substituted in the partial provisioning plan. For this, the instance completion description comprises a set of field descriptions, each of which explains how to create a value for a specific part of the partial provisioning plan. Such a field description is made up of a location pointer and an algorithm for deducing the field value. The location pointer is analogous to the above-mentioned location pointer. The algorithm is represented in a format that can be automatically interpreted – any such format is possible; the PMAC Expression Language [8], for example, is a suitable representation, as the following code illustrates:

```
...
<InstanceCompletitionDescription>
  <FieldDescription>
    <LocationPointer>
      //ProvisioningProcessDescription/*NumberOfServers
    </LocationPointer>
    <FieldValueAlgorithmDescription>
      <exp:Plus>
        <exp:FloatConstant>
          <Value>02.000</Value>
        </exp:FloatConstant>
        <exp:Divide>
          <exp:FloatConstant>
            <Value>01.000</Value>
          </exp:FloatConstant>
          <exp:Variable name="AverageResponseTime"/>
```

```
      </exp:Divide>
     </exp:Plus>
    </FieldValueAlgorithmDescription>
   </FieldDescription>
   ...
  </InstanceCompletitionDescription>
  ...
```

In this example the number of servers to be provisioned increases the shorter the average response time is chosen. The desired response time is extracted from the agreement, i.e. the SLA, via the parameter identifier, as shown in the example above. The deduced number of servers is filled in the partial provisioning plan. Besides the sketched expression language, a field value algorithm can contain a call to an external algorithms, functions, and programs performing more complex estimations for the resource requirements.

Provisioning Engine Invocation. The fourth section of the IP template gives details on the provisioning engine to use. This enables environments with multiple provisioning engines by defining the endpoint reference to which a complete provisioning plan instance is sent. An example in the simplest case is:

```
  ...
  <ProvisioningEngineInvocationDetails>
    <wsa:EndpointReference>
      http://manamgement.ibm.com:8080/provisioning
    </wsa:EndpointReference>
  </ProvisioningEngineInvocationDetails>
  ...
```

4.2 Provisioning Process

The outlined template mechanism (1) identifies the parts of a SLA which are relevant for supplying resources, (2) derives quantities for different resource types, determines and outlines alternative resource assemblies that might be used, and (3) compiles a provisioning plan detailing the required resources, their configuration, and their provisioning. The processing of such an IP template is implemented by the Provisioning Planner; the provisioning itself is carried out be the Provisioning Engine.

Provisioning Planner: Upon receiving an agreement, the Provisioning Planner analyzes it and checks its syntactic correctness. Subsequently, a set of implementation plan templates associated with the agreement offer is retrieved from a template repository and is subsequently used to devise a provisioning plan.

The first applicable template is chosen and processed up to a provisioning plan. The provisioning engine then executes this provisioning plan – it acquires and configures the respective resources and reports the result of this provisioning process back to the agreement provisioning planner. In case of failure, the agreement provisioning planner can devise an alternative provisioning plan from the next IP template retrieved from the repository.

Processing a single IP template involves the following:

1. Verify for each location pointer of each parameter identifier if it points to one and only one location in the received agreement.
2. Retrieve values from the agreement as specified by the parameter identifiers and store them indexed by their respective names.
3. Write a copy of the provisioning process description.
4. For all field descriptions in the instance completion description:
   a. Execute the field value algorithm.
   b. Insert the value returned in the provisioning plan instance at the location given by the field description's location pointer.

With completion of these steps – possibly for several IP templates if there might be failures – the algorithm yields a complete and executable instance of the provisioning plan. Hence, there is no need for the Provisioning Planner to understand the semantics of the provisioning plan as the semantics, e.g., a system administrator's knowledge on how many servers are to utilize to meet a given response time goal, is captured in the IP template itself.

Provisioning Engine. The Provisioning Engine interprets the output of the Provisioning Planner. Although our approach can work with different engines, we illustrate the workings of the provisioning engine along a simple prototypical implementation.

When one of the IP templates results in a complete provisioning plan, the provisioning planner retrieves endpoint reference of the provisioning engine to be used from the provisioning engine invocation details in the IP template. It sends the completed provisioning plan to this provisioning engine which proceeds with the following steps:

1. Select the first resource assembly within the provisioning plan.
2. Check whether the resources can be acquired from the resource pool in the quantity indicated by the resource quantity definition of the respective resource assembly.
   If not, this step is repeated with the next resource assembly, if any. If there is no resource assembly left, a failure notice is returned the provisioning planner and the process is terminated here.
3. Acquire resources in the desired quantity, as step 2 assured that they are available.
4. Execute the assembly provisioning plan to configure the assembly.

If step four completes, the provisioning is complete and the service can be used. The provisioning engine reports the successful resource acquisition back to the provisioning planner which in turn informs the service client that presented the service offer in the first place. The service management then starts the service by making it available to the service client.

Heterogeneous Resource Pools. Up to now, the nature of resource pools and the specific acquisition mechanism was not addressed. The template-based approach is applicable to different resource pools: it can equally be applied for provisioning of resources within a single host, within one data center, across different data centers run by the same organization, and to inter-organizational resource acquisition. The crucial factor is that the provisioning engine has to be able to communicate with the resources or resource providers respectively. The easiest way is direct access to the scheduler; a more sophisticated acquisition – which might be applied across organizational boundaries and maybe even within a single data center – might be market-based. The provisioning engine could, for example, negotiate with several resource providers as outlined by Czajkowski et al. [4] and Gimpel et al. [7] or it could acquire the resources on a structured marketplace as presented by Buyya et al. [3] and Schnizler et al. [14]. With this, a service provider might become a service broker and distributor, potentially operating without putting forth own resources.

5 Summary and Conclusion

In this paper, we proposed a template-based agreement-driven service provisioning process to facilitate automated service provisioning and by that enable an agreement-driven service-oriented architecture providing dynamic service capacity acquisition. In the template-based agreement provisioning framework introduced in this paper, an agreement implementation plan template is associated with an agreement template. It defines a partially filled provisioning plan with a description how to fill the variable, incomplete elements with input from an agreement. A processor for agreement implementation plans is also defined, implementing a template-based provisioning planner. The provisioning planner has been implemented using Java and tested with a set of agreement templates defined using the WS-Agreement standard.

Provisioning planning is very complex and hard to solve with derivative approaches in the general case. However, the proposed approach based on an agreement implementation plan templates associated with agreement templates can capture the experience of system administrators and, hence, solve the provisioning planning problem pragmatically for service delivery environments in which the relationship of typical customer performance requirements and resource capacity is well understood. The proposed approach is also agnostic to the specific agreement language and the language of the provisioning plan, as both can vary depending on the application domain.

In future work, we will investigate how this template-based approach can be combined with derivative approaches for specific application, leveraging the strength of different approaches.

References

1. Andrieux, A., Czajkowski, K., Dan, A., Keahey, K., Ludwig, H., Pruyne, J., Rofrano, J., Tuecke, S., Xu, M.: Web Services Agreement Specification. Version 1.1, GGF GRAAP working Group Draft 18, May 14, 2004.
2. Bell, D., Kojo, T., Goldsack, P., Loughran, S., Milojicic, D., Schaefer, S., Tatemura, J., Toft, P.: *Configuration Description, Deployment, and Lifecycle Management (CDDLM) Foundation Document.* January 2003, http://forge.gridforum.org/projects/cddlm-wg.
3. Buyya, R., Abramson, D., Giddy, J., Stockinger, H.: Economic models for resource management and scheduling in grid computing. *The Journal of Concurrency and Computation: Practice and Experience*, 14(13-15), pp. 1507–1542, 2002.

4. Czajkowski, K., Foster, I., Kesselman, C., Sander, V., Tuecke, S.: SNAP: A Protocol for Negotiation of Service Level Agreements and Coordinated Resource Management in Distributed Systems. *Job Scheduling Strategies for Parallel Processing: 8th International Workshop (JSSPP 2002)*. Edinburgh, 2002.

5. Dan, A., Dumitrescu, C., Ripeanu, M.: Connecting client objectives with resource capabilities: an essential component for grid service management infrastructures. *Service-Oriented Computing - ICSOC 2004, Second International Conference*, New York, NY, USA, Proceedings, pp. 57-64, ACM 2004.

6. Eilam, T., Kalantar, M., Konstantinou, A., Pacifici, G.: Reducing the Complexity of Application Deployment in Large Data Centers. Proceedings of the *9th International IFIP/IEEE Symposium on Integrated Management (IM 2005)*, IEEE Press, 2005.

7. Gimpel, H., Ludwig, H., Dan, A., Kearney, B.: PANDA: Specifying Policies for Automated Negotiations of Service Contracts. *Service Oriented Computing – Proceedings of ICSOC 03*, Springer LNCS 2910, pp. 287-302, 2003

8. IBM Corporation: PMAC Expression Language Users Guide. Alphaworks PMAC distribution, www.alphaworks.ibm.com, 2005.

9. Keller, A., Badonnel, R.: Automating the Provisioning of Application Services with the BPEL4WS Workflow Language. *Proceedings of DSOM 2004*, Davis, CA, USA, 2004.

10. Keller, A.: Automating the Change Management Process with Electronic Contracts. Proceedings of the *First IEEE International Workshop on Service oriented Solutions for Cooperative Organizations (SoS4CO '05)*, IEEE Computer Society Press, 2005.

11. Ludwig, H., Dan, A., Kearney, R.: Cremona: an architecture and library for creation and monitoring of WS-Agreements. *Service-Oriented Computing - ICSOC 2004, Second International Conference*, New York, NY, USA, Proceedings, pp. 65-74, ACM 2004.

12. Ludwig, H., Keller, A., Dan, A., King, R.: A Service Level Agreement Language for Dynamic Electronic Services. *Proceedings of WECWIS 2002*, Newport Beach, 2002.

13. Ludwig, H.: A Conceptual Framework for Electronic Contract Automation. *IBM Research Report*, RC 22608. New York, 2002.

14. Schnizler, B., Neumann, D., Weinhardt, C.: Resource Allocation in Computational Grids – A Market Engineering Approach, Proceeding of the WeB 2004, Washington, 2004

15. Tosic, V., Pagurek, B., Patel, K.: WSOL - A Language for the Formal Specification of Classes of Service for Web Services. *Proceedings of ICWS 2003*, pp. 375-381, CSREA Press 2003.

16. Vitaletti, M., Draper, C., George, R., McCarthy, J., Poolman, D., Miller, T., Middlekauff, A., Montero-Luque, C.: *Installable Unit Deployment Descriptor Specification Version 1.0*. W3C Member Submission, 12 July 2004. http://www.w3.org/Submission/2004/SUBM-InstallableUnit-DD-20040712/

Proactive Management of Service Instance Pools for Meeting Service Level Agreements

Kavitha Ranganathan and Asit Dan

IBM T J Watson Research Center,
19 Skyline Drive, Hawthorne, NY, 10025, USA
{kavithar, asit}@us.ibm.com

Abstract. Existing Grid schedulers focus on allocating resources to jobs as per the resource requirements expressed by end-users. This demands detailed knowledge of application behavior for different resource configurations on the part of end-users. Additionally, this model incurs significant delay in terms of the provisioning overhead for each request. In contrast, for interactive workloads, services are commonly pre-configured by an application server according to long-term steady-state requirements. In this paper, we propose a framework for bridging the gap between these two extremes. We target application services beyond simple interactive workloads, such as a parallel numeric application. In our approach, end users are shielded from lower-level resource configuration details and deal only with service metrics like average response time, expressed as SLAs. These SLAs are then translated into concrete resource allocation decisions. Since demand for a service fluctuates over time, static pre-configurations may not maximize utility of the common pool of resources. Our approach involves dynamic re-provisioning to achieve maximum utility, while accounting for overheads incurred during re-provisioning. We find that it is not always beneficial to re-provision resources according to perceived benefits and propose a model for calculating the optimal amount of re-provisioning for a particular scenario.

1 Introduction

Existing Grid [1,3,4] scheduling technologies – as described in commercial products [5,12], prototypes [15,7,8], requirement specifications [13,14] and papers [11, 16,17, 9] – have primarily focused on allocation of resources to incoming jobs as per the resource requirements expressed directly by end users. An experienced end-user of an application, say a scientist submitting a numerically intensive application, is quite knowledgeable of the application execution behavior over different resource configurations. Thus the scientist is able to manually translate the requirements on timeliness and data size into a set of requested resources over which the application is to be run. Current resource provider capabilities do not permit a client to use high level objectives such as a deadline or desired throughput. Note that a service could be an invocation of an interactive workload or a longer running numeric intensive application. As pointed out in [2], to bridge the gap between a high level client request and the resource provider capabilities to make available any requested resources, an intermediate layer

B. Benatallah, F. Casati, and P. Traverso (Eds.): ICSOC 2005, LNCS 3826, pp. 296–309, 2005.

must translate high level objectives to detailed resource requirements based on application execution profiles.

To illustrate a long running parallel application service, consider a financial application for portfolio risk evaluation consisting of two phases as described in [2]. The first phase invokes a service that solves a large system of linear equations, and is implemented as a parallel, tightly-coupled, compute and network intensive computation. The result of this phase along with new input is used to compute the risk profiles of a set of trades in the second phase. The computation of this phase is organized as a master-worker interaction: each worker node independently computes the risk profile for a set of trades, and the master assembles the information received from workers into the final result. The overall computation must be completed by a fixed deadline (say 7:00 AM of each trading day). The client application breaks down the overall objective, by setting service level goals (such as completion time or number of trade risk computation per second) for each phase of the portfolio computation.

Setting up a service instance with the required resource configuration involves acquiring the required set of resources, starting up a (parallel) application on these nodes, and finally after execution, shutting down the application and releasing allocated nodes. To avoid delay and overheads associated with provisioning resources on a per-request basis, an application service instance can be reused for serving another user request with similar requirements; as is done when managing interactive workloads. Note that an available pre-configured application instance may not always match the resource requirements of a new user request. Hence, the new user request may have to wait until a matching application instance is available. If no such instance has been pre-configured or existing instances are insufficient, a new instance could be created on-demand. The resources for the new instance may be obtained by destroying one or more less frequently used pre-configured instances. Once an application instance is acquired by an end-user, it is either used to run a single (long running) request, or is used to invoke a series of short operations by the end-user. The end-user therefore, expresses an SLA that not only translates to resource configuration requirements of an instance, but also defines service level objectives like the wait time to acquire a matching service instance.

In this paper, we propose a layered framework for managing application level SLA objectives for all types of services (not just interactive workloads), including invocation of parallel applications. The framework addresses the translation of end-user SLA requirements into concrete resource requirements to be used for configuring a service instance based on a prior application execution profile. It also addresses (1) scheduling user requests to matching available pre-configured service instances, (2) pro-active management of a pool of pre-configured service instances for meeting SLA objectives on waiting time, (3) allocation and de-allocation of physical resources to service instances, and (4) provisioning and de-provisioning of service instances.

We then explore key issues and strategies in pro-active management of service instance pools, taking into account SLA objectives. We incorporate the provisioning overhead - often ignored in steady state analysis – as well as gauge the effect of different user request arrival patterns. We find that it is not always beneficial to re-provision resources according to perceived benefits. In fact, in certain cases the re-provisioning overheads make it detrimental to adapt service pools according to user request arrival patterns. We hence propose a model for calculating the optimal amount of re-provisioning for a particular scenario. Preliminary simulation results also show that we are able to effectively manage service instance pools, based on user defined SLAs. Additional experimental results are described in [18].

The rest of this paper is organized as follows. Section 2 proposes a layered framework for managing application level end-user SLA and scheduling user service requests. Section 3 provides details on dynamic management of service pools, including SLAs and workloads used, algorithm tested, and a model for calculating the optimal level of re-provisioning. Section 4 contains the experimental setup, parameters and simulation results. We conclude in Section 5.

2   Overview of the Architecture for Service Instance Scheduling and Management

We now detail the proposed layered architecture for managing application level SLAs using pre-configured service instances (See Figure 1). Before invoking a service, a client application establishes a SLA with the service provider, that expresses not only the capabilities of the service instance to be assigned, but also timeliness in receiving a service instance. The SLA for service capabilities can be expressed either as a deadline or as the number of transactions per unit time supported by such an instance.

The primary components of this architecture and their interactions are detailed below.

Application Service Level Manager (ASLM): A service client interacts with the ASLM for establishing a new SLA, and subsequently monitors the status of the SLA. Our prototype supports the WS-Agreement protocol [10] for the above interactions, which additionally includes customizing predefined agreement templates to create a new SLA.

In addition to establishing the SLA, the ASLM translates higher level SLA objectives into detailed resource requirements to be used for configuring a service instance in support of this SLA. To estimate required resource configurations, the ASLM maintains an application execution profile consisting of multiple observed performance points for various resource configurations. The focus of this paper is not on this translation method, and hence, details of how to obtain the execution profile, bounding the number of observations to be obtained for defining execution profile, etc. are not discussed here. We mention in passing that the execution profile captures only the effects of changes in key resource attributes, such as the number of nodes, processor MIPS, and memory size per node.

Service Instance Request Scheduler (SIRC): Once an SLA is established, a service client requests a service instance that is configured according to the SLA. Depending on the type of a service, this request may be explicit or implicit. If the service instance is to be used for a single invocation (e.g., a long running application), the request for a service instance can be combined with the service invocation request, i.e., assignment of service instance is implicit. Alternatively, a client may request a binding to an explicit service instance, and perform multiple service invocation on this instance (as in the second phase of the financial application example, discussed in Section 1).

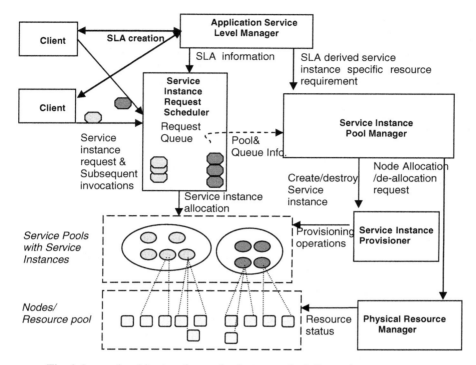

Fig. 1. Layered architecture for service Instance scheduling and management

The SIRC assigns a matching service instance to an incoming service instance request, if such an instance is available. Otherwise, it queues the incoming request, and prioritizes requests in the queue to meet SLA waiting time objectives. The service instance pool manager monitors the queuing delay, and possible SLA violations, and pro-actively signals provisioning of new service instances.

Service Instance Pool Manager (SIPM): The SIPM makes dynamic decisions on the number of services instances to be maintained for each service type. Multiple SLAs may specify the same set of service objectives, referred to as a service type. The decision is based on the business values associated with SLA objectives, required resource configuration for each service instance derived by ASLM and the current state of objectives. Following this decision, the SIPM creates and/or destroys service instances of different service types by invoking the two components discussed next, the Physical Resource Manager and the Service Instance Provisioner. The focus of the current paper is on the strategy of managing service instance pool, and we will provide more details in Sections 3 and 4.

Physical Resource Manager (PRM): The PRM manages allocation of nodes to service instances, and is invoked by the SIPM to allocate nodes for a new service instance to be created or to release nodes when a service instance is destroyed. Upon destruction of a service instance, the nodes are made available for reallocation.

Service Instance Provisioner (SIP): Actions involved in provisioning a service instance depends on the type of the service, as well as differences across services sharing the same resource pool. For a relatively simple scenario, this involves merely starting up an application on one or more nodes. For a parallel application this may involve synchronization with the master node. In a more complex scenario, where different applications require different execution environments (e.g., J2EE version), a completely new software stack needs to be loaded for reassigning a node to another application. In all scenarios, once a service instance is created, the SIRC is notified of this new instance.

3   Service Instance Pool Management

We now discuss issues involved with the dynamic management of service pools. The characteristics of the service request streams (henceforth referred to as the workload) and SLAs used play a key role in the implementation and effectiveness of dynamic service instance pool management. We then propose an algorithm that is used by the SIPM to manage these service instance pools. Other key issues explored are the overheads involved in re-provisioning service instances i.e. moving nodes across service pools – and the extent of adaptability for the SIPM.

3.1   Request Workloads, SLAs and Key Issues

Workload Characteristics: If requests for each particular service-type arrive at a steady rate (say according to a uniform or Poisson distribution) then it is relatively easier to decide the number of service instances to be instantiated per service, to meet the SLA goals. Many systems today assume steady-state parameters to calculate resource allocation. However, in many cases, the workload may change over time, either gradually or suddenly (for example, there might be a sudden spike in demand for one particular service) warranting the increase in the number of instances of certain service types. A successful adaptation technique should be able to detect the changes in the workload and re-provision instances accordingly.

We look at both cases in our experiments: (1) a steady-state scenario where requests for different services may arrive at different rates but follow Poisson distributions and (2) when the workload varies over time.

Higher Level SLA Objectives: The Service Level Agreements between the provider and client could take a number of forms [10]. In this paper we assume business values associated with objectives are defined as explicit utility functions, where a client specifies how much utility is gained (or in other words, how much she is willing to pay) for a certain response time for acquiring the service instance. The same utility function also applies to the scenario of how much penalty should be assessed for deviations from the specified goal.

Key Issues in Dynamic Adaptation: Often, there might be inherent costs associated with re-provisioning a node. At one extreme, the overheads might be negligible if switching from one service to another just involves linking different libraries. On the other extreme, it may involve, draining the node of current jobs and software, I/O operations to load the software for the new service and extensive re-configuration. Thus the "dead time" defined as the time when the node is unavailable for any service, could be substantial in many cases of re-provisioning. Moreover, re-provisioning might require I/O or other operations which access bottleneck resources like the network or shared disk access. Thus, the time to re-provision 'k' nodes may not be the same as the time to re-provision one node. Depending on how costly the re-provisioning step is, and the relative increase in utility it may actually be disadvantageous to re-provision more than a certain number of nodes at a time. Our proposed model for estimating these costs is described later.

3.2 Algorithm for Incremental Adaptation

We now describe the algorithm employed by the SIPM to make decisions regarding the number of service instances to maintain for each service pool. Since the SIPM has access to the different utility functions for each service type, it can make re-provisioning decisions with the aim of maximizing utility (henceforth called revenue) across all resources it controls. We assume that we know how long a particular service instance will be used by a client (This can be derived either by employing predictive techniques or by requiring that the user submit an estimate of the usage time).

We first establish some terms that will be used in the algorithm. As explained earlier, the revenue acquired by a service is a function of the response time (as defined in the SLA). Hence the revenue gained for time interval t0-t1 is captured in the following expression:

*Revenue(t0-t1) = Number of requests fulfilled in t0-t1 * utility_function(average response time for fulfilling requests in t0-t1)*

Thus, given a request queue for a particular service type, the number of service instances (i.e. the size of the service instance pool) and the estimated run-time for each request in the queue; the predicted average response-time to obtain a service instance, can easily be calculated. This can then be used to derive the predicted revenue.

Predicted Revenue = function of (Size of Service Instance Pool, Run time estimates of Requests in Queue).

Thus, if a Service Instance was added to a pool that already had s Service Instances, the advantage of adding that new Instance (the 'Incremental Revenue' gained) could be calculated as follows :

Incremental Revenue = (Predicted Revenue with $s+1$ instances) – (Predicted Revenue with s instances).

The algorithm for incremental adaptation is then a simple calculation to maximize revenue, as the following pseudo code describes :

At each time period (the periodicity factor is discussed in the next section):

1) Each service instance pool donates at-least 'k' nodes to a common virtual pool. If a certain service instance pool does not contain enough resources to contribute 'k' nodes to the common pool, it does not contribute nodes in that iteration, but is however considered a candidate to receive nodes. Note that nodes are not de-provisioned at this stage (The size of 'k' is discussed shortly).

2) Now the SIPM calculates how best the nodes in the common pool could be re-distributed across service instance pools. Assume here that each service instance requires one node. Variations are discussed below.

> *For each node (n) in the common pool :*
> > *For each Service Instance Pool (p):*
> > > *Calculate 'Incremental Revenue' gained if node n is added to Service Instance Pool p*
> > > *Assign node n to Service Instance Pool with maximum 'Incremental Revenue'*
> > > *Update size of that Service Instance Pool*
> > *Record new assignments*

Note that if each service type requires more nodes than one, then instead of one node, groups of nodes of the required size, are considered at each iteration.

3) Re-provision nodes according to the new assignment that was calculated. (Note that actual re-provisioning only happens in Step 3).

The incremental adaptation algorithm, reassigns nodes to where they might be most useful, but at the same time, ensures that this re-assignment is gradual. Temporary variations in the request workload may cause a small number of service instances to be re-provisioned. Massive re-structuring can only occur if there is a sustained change in external parameters like SLAs or service demand.

3.3   Model for Estimating Optimal Amount of Simultaneous Re-provisioning

A key factor for dynamic adaptation is that while a node is being re-provisioned, it is unavailable for providing any service. These so called "dead times" could be significant. Moreover, as discussed earlier, concurrently re-provisioning multiple nodes could lead to larger dead-times than when only one node is re-provisioned. Hence this cost has to be factored in when deciding the adaptation algorithm parameter of how many nodes to consider for re-provisioning in each iteration of the algorithm. The following model aims to estimate this parameter, by calculating the loss in revenue caused by the dead times and the gain in revenue, resulting from running a different service on the nodes.

Assume there are two service types, $s1$ and $s2$, which currently generate revenue $r1\_old$ and $r2\_old$ per time interval t. There are n service nodes in the system and they are initially partitioned into the two service types ($x1$ nodes provide service $s1$, and $x2$ provide service $s2$). Suppose we now want to re-provision k nodes from serving $s1$ to serving $s2$ and the new revenues that will be generated by each are $r1\_new$ and $r2\_new$ per time interval. (To recall, the revenue generated is a function of the average response time, which will change when the number of instances per service type changes).

Now the cost of moving k nodes from service type $s1$ to service type $s2$, is at the very least the revenue lost by not serving $s1$, for the duration of the dead time of those k nodes. Assume that if it takes T seconds to re-provision one node, it will take $T + delta * (k-1)$ to re-provision k nodes, where $delta$ is the simultaneous re-provisioning cost factor. Hence the dead time for one node = T where as the dead time for k nodes is $kT + k(k-1)*delta$. Thus the revenue lost if k nodes are re-provisioned = $(kT + k(k-1) * delta) * r1\_old$.

The benefit gained by the re-provisioning can be quantified as the increase in revenue, that is Revenue(old) – Revenue(new). We assume here, that there is enough demand to use up all nodes. Suppose, the time-interval for periodically adapting is *Ta*. The revenue made by the nodes for the non-adaptive case: Revenue(old) = *(r1_old * s1 + r2_old * s2) * Ta*. The Revenue made in the adaptive case: Revenue(new) can be split into 2 stages T1 and T2 where Ta = T1 + T2. T1 is the time for the re-provisioning to occur [which was earlier calculated as = *T + delta * (k-1)*] and T2 is the time when the re-provisioning has already succeeded.

During T1, there are *x1-k* nodes serving *s1*, *x2* nodes serving *s2* and *k* nodes unavailable.

Therefore, Revenue(T1) = ((x1-k) * r1_new + x2 * r2_old) * T1
Similarly, Revenue (T2) = ((x1-k) * r1_new + (x2 + k) * r2_new) * T2

Hence, the increase in revenue for a particular *k* can be calculated as *Revenue(T1) + Revenue(T2) – Revenue(old)* . The optimal value for *k* can be derived by calculating the maxima of this resulting function. Figure 3 plots the revenue gain for some sample values of *x1*, *x2*, *utility curves* and *delta*. It is clear from the figure that for a given *delta*, there is a certain range for *k*, when it is most beneficial to re-provision those many nodes simultaneously. Re-provisioning more nodes than this value leads to a steady decline in revenue and even to losses.

Frequency of Adaptation: Closely related to the overheads of re-provisioning is the frequency with which adaptation occurs. In our architecture the SIPM periodically recalculates if nodes need to be re-provisioned. If this frequency is too high, then minor fluctuations from the steady state may cause unnecessary re-provisioning; if too low, then the adaptive machinery may be too slow to react to genuine surges.

We tackle this issue by using an incremental adaptation process. At each time-period (which is relatively short) only a certain number of nodes are considered for re-provisioning. If the surge that triggered the re-provisioning was small or short-lived, this adaptation is corrected in the next time interval. If however the surge is a genuine one, and has lasted beyond a couple of time-periods, subsequent adaptations further create the necessary services.

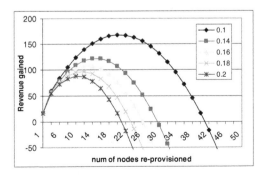

Fig. 2. Revenue gained for different values of Delta. Total nodes = 100, r1 old and r1 new = 2, r2 old and r2 new = 4, T =1 and Ta = 10.

This incremental adaptation has a twofold advantage: (1) temporary aberrations to the steady-state workload don't falsely trigger a huge amount of costly re-provisioning (2) by re-provisioning smaller batches of nodes at a time (around the optimal value of k as explained earlier), we decrease the dead times of nodes and hence maintain higher revenues.

4 Experiments and Results

To test the effectiveness of our dynamic adaptation algorithm, we simulate a cluster of nodes providing different services. Our in-house simulation program generates various service requests, and allocates and executes them on the services running on the cluster. We then use the prototype we have built for incremental-adaptation; the SIPM, to manage the service instances provided on this simulated cluster. We measure both the net revenue gained by adaptation and improvement in performance in terms of response time.

4.1 Experimental Setup

In the start of each experiment, all the nodes in the cluster are equally pre-divided into two logical service instance pools. There is a fixed utility function associated with each service type, and we assume here that both service types run on the same number of nodes. Client requests for a service are generated according to a Poisson distribution. Each service instance pool has an associated queue of requests waiting to acquire a service instance from that pool, and incoming requests are added to this queue as the simulation progresses. Requests are allocated to service instances by the Service Instance Request Scheduler, using a FIFO (First In First Out) algorithm.

The Service Instance Pool Manager (SIPM) kicks in periodically to re-provision service instances if needed. The input to the SIPM consists of the size of each service instance pool, the size of request queues for each service instance pool and the respective utility functions. The SIPM then calculates the desired size of each service instance pool, so as to maximize revenue. The Service Instance Provisioner then re-provisions nodes, so as to meet the new assignment. Note that nodes do not physically belong to certain pools, but form logical pools on the basis of the type of service instance they belong to.

The experimental parameters used are provided in Table 1.

Table 1. Parameters used in simulations

Experimental Parameter	Value
Total number of nodes in cluster	100 - 200
Number of requests per service type	varies by experiment ; 250-1000
Job run time	60 seconds
Nodes per service instance	5
Periodical adaptation	Varies; typically 200 seconds
Time to re-provision one node	Varies; 5 – 100 seconds
Delta : factor that determines overhead of re-provisioning n nodes simultaneously	Varies; 0.5 - 20

4.2 Simulation Results

We first want to compare our incremental-adaptation approach against the case were no adaptation takes place, to ascertain whether dynamic adaptation does result in higher revenues for the provider. We then go on to study parameters like workload variations and cost of re-provisioning, that might impact the algorithm. The results are an average of three runs, where the varying factor in each run was the generated workload. We did not find significant variations between runs.

Effectiveness of Incremental Adaptation
We first consider the case of two services types, S1 and S2, each offering 10 service instances each. We test two cases (1) where both services have the same utility function but different request arrival rates and (2) where they have the same request arrival rate but different utilities.

(A) Heterogeneous Request Arrival Rates: We specify the same utility function for both services but different request arrival rates. Maximum revenue is gained if requests for a service instance do not incur any delay. If the response time goes beyond 40 seconds, then there is a penalty associated with that request. The request arrival rates for the two services differ by a factor of two. Requests for S1 arrive twice as often as requests for S1 (Poisson inter-arrival time for S1 = 5, S2= 10).

Table 2. Performance comparison of static provisioning and SIPM's dynamic re-provisioning for heterogeneous request arrival rates

	Avg. Response Time (secs)		Revenue ($)	
	Static	SIPM	Static	SIMP
S1	578	31	-2662	44
S2	02	14	95	63
Total	na	na	-2567	107

Table 2 contains the average response time (the time it takes to allot a particular service instance to a request) and net revenue gained when the above utility function is used, for both the static case when no adaptation takes place, and the dynamic case where the SIPM re-provisions service instances to increase revenue gained. As seen, in the static case, the average response time for S1 in very high, leading to a large penalty imposed on the provider. When the SIPM is used, the response times for S1 are effectively brought down to 91 seconds whereas the response time for S2 goes up slightly, resulting in positive revenues. Note that the revenue numbers are entirely dependant on the utility function used to interpret the gains, but the average response times are independent of whatever utility function is used.

These results can be explained as follows: since there are many more outstanding requests for S1 than S2, the SIPM successfully detects this, re-provisions nodes serving S2 to serve S1 and decreases wait-times for S1 requests.

(B) Heterogeneous Utility Functions: For this experiment, requests for both services arrive at the same rate, but the services have different utility functions as shown in Figure 3(left). S2 is a relatively more critical application than S1 and hence the client offers higher revenues if the ideal response time is met for S2. Thereafter, the utility curve for S2 decreases more rapidly than for S1. If the response time for S2 is greater than 100 seconds, the provider incurs a penalty. We model the same request arrival rate for both services: a Poisson arrival rate with inter-arrival time of 6 seconds.

Table 3 provides the results of this experiment for both the static and SIPM cases. As the results show, the SIPM is able to effectively increase net revenue earned, as compared to the static node distribution case. Figure 3(right) shows the number of service instances as the simulation progresses, for one particular run. Initially, the SIMP re-provisions some nodes to serve S2, since the revenue gained from S2 is higher. As the simulation progresses, the request queue for S1 grower longer (as lesser nodes now serve S1), effectively making it more lucrative to switch some nodes back to S1. The SIPM also detects small bursts in traffic and adapts slightly, bringing down the average response time considerably.

Effect of Workload Variations
To test how the SIPM reacts to a sudden increase in requests for one service type, we generated a workload where after a short while, requests for S2 start arriving more frequently. Requests for S1 have a constant inter-arrival time of 6 throughout the workload, where as after 500 seconds, S2 requests start arriving much faster (with an inter-arrival time of 2 seconds). S2 jobs cease arriving at time 1150.

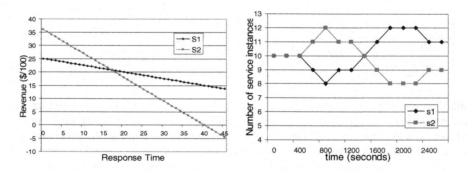

Fig. 3. (left) Utility functions used for re-provisioning and (right) number of service instances as simulation progresses

Table 3. Performance comparison of static provisioning and SIPM's dynamic re-provisioning for heterogeneous utility functions

	Avg. Response Time (secs)		Revenue ($)	
	Static	SIPM	Static	SIMP
S1	178	66	-98	41
S2	165	39	-56	18
Total	na	na	-154	59

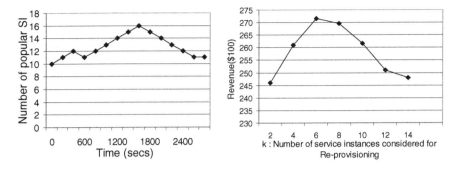

Fig. 4. (left) Number of service instances as simulation progresses for an unstable workload (right) Revenue generated as the amount of simultaneous re-provisioning increases

Figure 4(left) shows the number of service instances for S2 as the simulation progresses (the remainder of a total of 20 instances are S1 instances). As can be seen, the SIPM is quickly able to detect the surge in S2 requests (at time 600) and increases service instances of S2. However, once most S2 requests are met, nodes are switched to S1 instances (starting at time 1600), to better respond to S1 requests.

Effect of Cost of Re-provisioning
While we have ascertained that the SIPM is able to re-provision nodes according to workload fluctuations and utility definitions, we want to study the effect of the overheads of re-provisioning.

The next experiment quantifies the effect of simultaneously re-provisioning instances, the k factor, as explained in Section 3.3. Each service type in this experiment starts off with 20 instances each, and k instances (that is k/2 from each service instance pool) are periodically considered by the SIPM for re-provisioning. One service type is defined as having consistently higher returns than another, prompting the SIMP to re-provision as many nodes as permitted by the value of k. Figure 4(right) plots the revenue gained as the number of instances being simultaneously re-provisioned (k) is increased.

As can be seen from the figure, there is a distinct advantage in increasing k to a certain point. The adaptation process succeeds in generating higher revenues. But beyond the threshold value ($k = 6$ in this case) it is less advantageous to re-provision more nodes simultaneously. This is because, as explained in our model in Section 3.3, the loss in revenue caused by the dead-times over-weigh whatever increase in revenue the new service type generates. It should be noted here that the value of delta determines the cost of simultaneous re-provisioning. In future work, we plan to run experiments on a real test-bed to obtain realistic ranges for delta.

5   Conclusions and Future Work

Existing scheduling solutions require end-users to express exact resource requirements for each request in the form of a job submission. We have proposed a framework where end-users need not be aware of specific resource configurations needed to realize their service level objectives. Our framework translates high-level end-user service level objectives like desired response-time to specific resource scheduling and provisioning actions based on application execution profiles. Since configuring a new service instance, especially for parallel applications, can incur both delay and over-head, the proposed framework furthermore, reuses existing pre-configured service instances in serving a new user. An end-user first establishes a SLA, and receives a service instance configured to meet SLA objectives, which is then used for subsequent invocations. To avoid a long delay in acquiring a service instance, SLAs also specify response time objectives in acquiring a new instance.

Additionally, our framework also enables dynamically re-provisioning nodes to meet SLAs provided by users. To this end, we put forth an incremental adaptation algorithm for dynamically re-provisioning services and an analytical model for estimating the optimal amount of re-provisioning. Initial simulation results to evaluate our prototype show that not only is it successful in adapting service instance pools, for maximizing utility, but also that the optimal amount of adaptation depends on the cost of provisioning.

In future work, we plan to run more experiments on test-beds using real workloads to better quantify the overheads of simultaneously re-provisioning nodes.

Acknowledgements. The authors would like to acknowledge the contributions of and thank Cait Crawford, Liana Fong, Kevin Gildea, Alan King, H. Shaikh, and Annette Rossi on the broader formulation of reusable parallel application service instances.

References

1. I. Foster, C. Kesselman, J. Nick, and S. Tuecke, "The Physiology of the Grid: An Open Grid Services Architecture for Distributed Systems Integration," Globus Project 2002.
2. A. Dan, C. Dumitrescu, and M. Ripeanu, "Connecting Client Objectives with Resource Capabilities: An Essential Component for Grid Service Management Infrastructures", 2nd International Conference on Service Oriented Computing (ICSOC), November 2004, New York, NY.
3. A. S. Grimshaw and W. A. Wulf, "The Legion Vision of a Worldwide Virtual Computer," Communications of the ACM, vol. 40, pp. 39-45, 1997.
4. I. Foster, "The Grid: A New Infrastructure for 21st Century Science," Physics Today, vol. 55, pp. 42-47, 2002.
5. I.B.M Corporation. IBM LoadLeveler: User's guide. Technical report, IBM, September 1993.
6. H. Ludwig, A. Keller, A. Dan, and R. King, "A Service Level Agreement Language for Dynamic Electronic Services," presented at 4th IEEE International Workshop on Advanced Issues of E-Commerce and Web-based Information Systems (WECWIS'02), Newport Beach, California, USA, 2002.
7. R. Raman, M. Livny, and M. Solomon, "Matchmaking: Distributed Resource Management for High Throughput Computing", Proceedings of the Seventh IEEE International Symposium on High Performance Distributed Computing, July 28-31, 1998, Chicago, IL
8. The Globus Resource Allocation and Management http://www.unix.globus.org/toolkit/docs/3.2/gram/ws
9. C Liu, L Yang, I Foster, D Angulo, "Design and Evaluation of a Resource Selection Framework for Grid Applications", HPDC, Edinburgh, July 2002.

10. A. Andrieux, C. Czajkowski, A. Dan, K. Keahey, H.Ludwig, J. Pruyne, J. Rofrano, S. Tuecke, M. Xu., Web Services Agreement Specification (WS-Agreement). Version 1.1, Draft 20, June 6th 2004.

11. D.Feitelson, L Rudolph and U Schwiegelshohn, Proceedings of the Job Scheduling Strategies for Parallel Processing, 10th International Workshop, JSSPP 2004, New York, NY, USA, June 13, 2004.

12. C Smith, "Open Source Metascheduling for Virtual Organizations with the Community Scheduler Framework (CSF) , White Paper, Platform Computing Inc.

13. The JSDL Specification https://forge.gridforum.org/projects/jsdl-wg/document/draft-ggf-jsdl-spec/en/21

14. The Globus Resource Specification Language RSL v1.0: http://www-fp.globus.org/gram/rsl%5Fspec1.html

15. The NorduGrid Project. http://www.nordugrid.org

16. J. Gehring and A. Reinefeld. MARS - a framework for minimizing the job execution time computing environment. Technical report, Paderborn Center for Parallel Computing, Jan 1995.

17. G. Allen, D. Angulo, I. Foster, G. Lanfermann, and C. Liu. "The Cactus Worm: Experiments with dynamic resource discovery and allocation in a Grid environment", International Journal of High Performance Computing Applications, 15(4),Jan 2001.

18. K. Ranganathan and A. Dan, "Proactive management of Service Instance Pools for meeting Service Level Agreements", Technical Report, I.B.M - RC23723, September 2005.

Adaptive Component Management Service in ScudWare Middleware for Smart Vehicle Space

Qing Wu and Zhaohui Wu

College of Computer Science, Zhejiang University,
Hangzhou, Zhejiang, China, 310027
{wwwsin, wzh}@cs.zju.edu.cn

Abstract. Due to the complexities of increasing prevalence of ubiquitous computing, it poses a large number of challenges for middleware and component technologies. We believe that service-oriented component adaptation provides a principled means to achieve the flexibility and scalability required. The focus of this paper regards an adaptive component management service in the ScudWare middleware architecture for smart vehicle space. The contribution of our work is twofold. First, an adaptive component management service framework, including a resource abstract framework, is put forward to implement adaptive mechanism. Second, a component hook proxy is proposed in detail for adaptation. In addition, this service is validated by a series of experimental results.

1 Introduction

In recent years, many kinds of smart devices come into our life such as PDAs, mobile phones, and smart cameras. The physical world and information space integrate seamlessly and naturally. The computation is becoming embedded and ubiquitous [1], which provides more facilities for people. This computing environment demands plenty of computation resources for functional requests and performance requirements. However, the computation resources in environments are limited in terms of CPU computation capabilities, network bandwidth, memory size, and device power, etc. As a result, sometimes it cannot provide enough resources to execute applications successfully. In addition, changes of the heterogeneous contexts including people, devices, and environments are ubiquitous and pervasive. Therefore, it results in many problems in software middleware design and development. We consider "adaptation" is the key issue for software systems and applications to meet the different computing environments and the diverse run-time context. On the other hand, component-based and service-oriented software (CBSOS) architecture provides a novel infrastructure and a development platform for ubiquitous computing. Components are abundant, heterogeneous, autonomic, and multiple categories. Because ubiquitous computing aims at building a human-centric ideal world, all entities should communicate and cooperate with each other transparently and spontaneously. The CBSOS system provides a flexible and adaptive computing framework. Taking into account the influence of dynamic changes on computation adequately, we use the service-oriented, context-aware, and component-based methods for adaptation.

B. Benatallah, F. Casati, and P. Traverso (Eds.): ICSOC 2005, LNCS 3826, pp. 310–323, 2005.

Vehicles play an important role in our daily life. People require more safety, comfort, and facilities in vehicles. We select a vehicle space[2] as a representative scene to study ubiquitous computing. Cho Li Wang[3] has proposed five types of software adaptation, consisting of data adaptation, network level adaptation, energy adaptation, migration adaptation, and functionality adaptation. Our current work focuses at the design-time and run-time adaptation including the computation resource, logic behavior semantic, and run-time context adaptation. We emphasize on adaptive component management at design-time and run-time in the ScudWare[4] middleware for smart vehicle space. An experiment prototype called "mobile music system" is built to demonstrate the feasibility and reliability of our methods and techniques. The paper brings forward the ScudWare middleware platform and an adaptive component management service framework. In addition, we have made experiments to test the performance of this service.

The rest of the paper is organized as follows. Section 2 describes the ScudWare middleware platform including smart vehicle space, CCM (CORBA Component Model) [5] specification overview, and the ScudWare middleware architecture. Then an adaptive component management service framework is proposed in Section 3. Specially, a resources abstract framework and the functions of this service are presented particularly. Section 4 gives a run-time component hook proxy mechanism. In Section 5, we give experiments study and evaluate the efficiency and performance of the service. Next, some related work is stated in Section 6. Finally, we draw a conclusion in Section 7.

2   ScudWare Middleware Platform

To implement smart vehicle space naturally and adaptively, we have built the ScudWare middleware platform conformed to the CCM (CORBA Component Model) specification. We use the ACE (Adaptive Communication Environment) [6] and the TAO (The ACE ORB) [7]. TAO is a real-time ORB (Object Request Broker) developed by Washington University. According to the application domain of smart vehicle space, we reduce the TAO selectively and add some adaptive services such as adaptive resource management service, context service, and notification service. ScudCCM, a part of ScudWare, is responsible for adaptive component management comprising component package, assembly, deployment, and allocation at design-time, and run-time component monitoring. As following, we introduce smart vehicle space, CCM specification and ScudWare architecture briefly.

2.1   Smart Vehicle Space

In recent years, a lot of developers have applied embedded, AI, and biology authentication technologies to vehicles. The drive capability, dependability, comfort, and convenience of the vehicle are improved greatly. When people go into smart vehicle space, they find many intelligent devices and equipments around

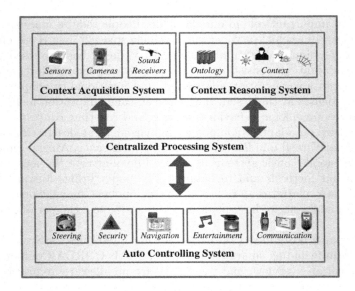

Fig. 1. Smart Vehicle Space

them. They communicate with these tools naturally and friendly. It forms a harmonious vehicle space where people, devices, and environments co-operate with each other adaptively.

Figure 1 describes the structure of smart vehicle space, which has four parts and is defined as $SVS=(CA,\ CR,\ AC,\ CP)$. CA is a context acquisition system. $CA = ((\Delta State(pe, de, en), (sen, cam, sou))$ aims at sensing status changes of people, devices, and environments in the vehicle, including sensors, cameras, and sound receivers. CR is a context repository reasoning system. $CR=(context, ontology, domain, inference)$ uses the correlative contexts and application domain ontology to make the manipulating strategy for adaptation. AC is an auto controlling system. $AC=(ste,\ com,\ ent,\ nav,\ sec)$ consists of steering, communication, entertainment, navigation, and security subsystem. CP is a centralized processing system. Particularly, CP is the kernel of smart vehicle space, which controls above third parts co-operating effectively.

2.2   CCM Specification Overview

CORBA (Common Object Request Broker Architecture) is one of software middlewares, which provides language and operating system independences. CCM is an extension to CORBA distributed object model. CCM prescribes component designing, programming, packaging, deploying and executing stages.

CCM specification defines component attributes and ports. Attributes are properties employed to configure component behavior. Specially stated, component ports are very important, which are connecting points between components. There are four kinds of ports: facets, receptacles, event sources, and event sinks.

Facets are distinct named interfaces provided by component for client interaction. Receptacles are connection points that describe the component's ability to use a reference supplied by others. Event sources are connection points that emit events of a specified type to one or more interested event consumers, or to an event channel. Event sinks are connection points into which events of a specified type may be pushed.

In addition, CCM specification defines component home, which is a meta-type that acts as a manager for component instances of a specified component type. Component home interfaces provide operations to manage component lifecycle. CIF (Component Implementation Framework) is defined as a programming model for constructing component implementations. CIDL (Component Implementation Definition Language), a declarative language, describes component implementations of homes. The CIF uses CIDL descriptions to generate programming skeletons that automate many of the basic behaviors of components, including navigation, identity inquiries, activation, state management, and lifecycle management. The component container defines run-time environments for a component instance. Component implementations may be packaged and deployed. A CORBA component package maintains one or more implementations of a component. One component can be installed on a computer or grouped together with other components to form an assembly.

2.3 ScudWare Middleware Architecture

As Figure 2 shows, ScudWare architecture consists of five parts defined as $SCUDW = (SOSEK, ACE, ETAO, SCUDCCM, SVA)$. $SOSEK$ denotes SMART OSEK [8], an operating system of vehicle conformed to OSEK [9] specification developed by us. ACE denotes the adaptive communication environment, providing high-performance and real-time communications. ACE uses inter-process communication, event demultiplexing, explicit dynamic linking, and concurrency. In addition, ACE automates system configuration and reconfiguration by dynamically linking services into applications at run-time and executing these services in one or more processes or threads. $ETAO$ extends ACE ORB and is designed using the best software practices and patterns on ACE in order to automate the delivery of high-performance and real-time QoS to distributed applications. $ETAO$ includes a set of services such as the persistence service and transaction service. In addition, we have developed an adaptive resource management service, a context service and a notification service. Specially, the context service is based on semantic information [10]. $SCUDCCM$ is conformed to CCM specification and consists of adaptive component package, assembly, deployment, and allocation at design-time. Besides, it comprises component migration, replacement, updating, and variation at run-time. In addition, the top layer is SVA that denotes semantic virtual agent [11]. SVA aims at dealing with application tasks. Each sva presents one service composition comprising a number of meta objects. During the co-operations of SVA, the SIP(Semantic Interface Protocol) [11] set is used including sva discovery, join, lease, and self-updating protocols. Due to the limited space, we don't detail SVA in this paper.

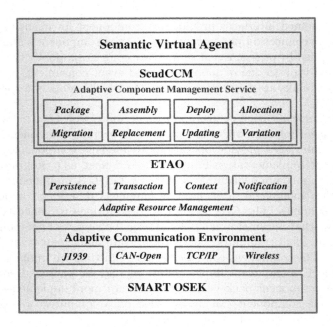

Fig. 2. ScudWare Architecture

3   Adaptive Component Management Service Framework

In this section, we describe the architecture of the adaptive component management service in a structural method. Because the component management is
resource-constrained, we firstly give a resource abstract framework, and then we
details this service.

3.1   Resource Abstract Framework

As Geoff Coulson [12] said, the goal of the resource abstract model is to support
component adaptation. In refining this goal, two additional requirements have
been identified. First, the framework must be extensible to capture diverse types
of resources at different levels of abstraction, including CPU processing resources
(e.g., threads, virtual processors), memory resources (e.g., ram, disk storage),
communication resources (e.g., network bandwidth, transport connections), OS
resources (e.g., Windows, Linux, Unix) and component container resource (e.g.,
CCM, EJB, .Net). Second, the framework must provide maximum control to
applications according to resource adaptation.

A resource is a run-time entity that offers a service for which one needs to
express a measure of quality of service. In ubiquitous computing environments,
various smart devices provide amount of resources on deferent level. On the other
hand, a large number of components are distributed on these devices, consuming
computation resources when executing tasks. Due to the joinment and departure

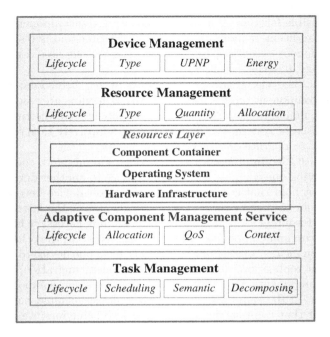

Fig. 3. Resource Abstract Framework

of the smart devices and components are dynamic, it forms a relationship between the producer and consumer based on computation resources. For instance, when a new smart device d goes into a system s, the components in s can use the resources provided by d. In addition, when a new component c enters a system s, it will be decided that how to allocate c automatically and adaptively. Specially, component c can migrate from the one device to another device.

The resource abstract framework $RAF = (DM, RM, CM, TM, PS)$ shows in Figure 3. DM is a smart device manager that monitors the device lifetime, type, and energy. In addition, it provides a mechanism for devices to UPNP (Universal Plug and Play). RM is a resource manager, administering resource lifecycle, type, quantity, and allocation. CM is an adaptive component management service, which is responsible for component lifecycle, allocation, QoS, and context management. To emphasize CM, we will give a detailed description in Section 3.2. TM is a task manager. When an application comes, TM will decompose it into several tasks based on semantic information. TM monitors tasks lifetime and schedules them in an adaptive way. Besides, PS is a set of management policy sets for these four parts, which can be well defined and reconfigured dynamically.

3.2 Adaptive Component Management Service

In terms of the resource abstract framework, we have developed an adaptive component management service. According to the different run-time contexts, this service is responsible for allocating and re-allocating the components in an appropriate way. In addition, it monitors component lifetime and is responsible for the QoS of component execution. Importantly, this service uses a run-time component hook proxy, described in Section 4.

In one component lifecycle, there are two kinds of key behaviors: component migration and component replication. These two behaviors are essential for adaptive component management. Because the components are distributed in such dynamic and discrete system, this service should adaptively take measures about when and how to migrate or replicate components.

Components are installed in different smart devices. On on hand, component migration means moving one component from one device to another device. The former device will not hold that component, and the latter device becomes the new resource carrier for that component. Emphatically stated, the latter device should have suitable resources for that component, including necessary hardware resources, OS resources, and component container resources. On the other hand, component replication means copying one component from one device to another device. In component replication, different from component migration, the former still has that component. As a result, there are two same components in two different devices. In the same way, two different devices should have same suitable resources for that component. To illustrate two behaviors, we give the cases shown in Figure 4. At first, component c_1 is distributed in smart device d_1, and d_1 also has other components such as c_2 and c_3. Assume that c_2 is exe-

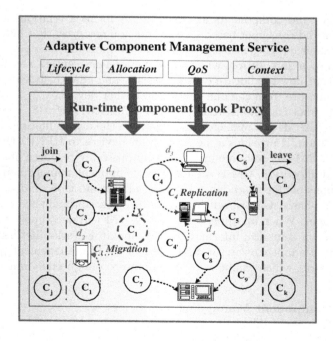

Fig. 4. Adaptive Component Management Service

cuting and occupies more hardware resources of d_1, it induces that c_1 cannot be executed for hardware resources limited when one invocation comes. Under this condition, component management service will decide to migrate c_1 to another device d_2. Next, in one appropriate time, the component migration of c_1 will take place. Following that, c_1 will execute on d_2 successfully. Here is another case of component replication. At beginning, c_4 is distributed in smart device d_3. Different form the former case, the number of invocations of c_4 is very large. For load balance, the component manger will decide to copy c_4 to another device. Assume that d_4 is satisfied with resource demands of c_4 and is not busy at that time, c_4', the backup of c_4, will be distributed in d_4 to decrease the invocations of c_4 in d_3.

4 Run-Time Component Hook Proxy Mechanism

In the framework of adaptive component management service, we introduce a proxy mechanism called run-time component hook proxy that plays an important role in component management. This section firstly presents a component interdependence graph, and then proposes an architecture of this hook proxy.

4.1 Component Interdependence Graph

During component management, the relationships among components are very important. In order to describe the interdependent relationships among components, we introduce a component interdependence graph composed of component nodes and link paths.

For each component, we associate a node. In addition, the link paths are labelled with a weight. We define the component interdependence graph $A_{ig} = (CN, LP, W)$. (1) $CN = \{cn_i\}_{i=1..n}$ denotes a set of component nodes. (2) $LP = \{l_{i,j}\}_{i=1..n, j=1..m}$ denotes a set of component links, describing the dependent targets. $l_{i,j}$ is the link between the nodes cn_i and cn_j. (3) $W = \{w_{i,j}\}_{i=1..n, j=1..m}$ denotes a set of interdependent weight. $w_{i,j}$ is a non-negative real number, which labels $l_{i,j}$. In addition, $w_{i,j}$ reflects the importance of the interdependence between the associated components. These weights used, for instance, to detect which links becomes too heavy or if the systems rely too much on some components. In terms of this weight, we can decide which component should be allocated preferentially. Extremely, this graph changes according to the different contexts. Therefore, this interdependence is not static. It can be modified when a new component is added, or one component disappears. Moreover, based on the different application domain contexts and the run-time environments, the interdependent relationships will change.

For example, Figure 5 shows a case of the component interdependence graph. The dependence weight of component c_2 on component c_5 is 0.8, and component c_5 on component c_2 is 0.6. We call component c_2 and c_5 are mutual and direct component interdependent. Besides, we can also calculate indirect component dependent weight by decomposing each direct dependent relationship. In this case, we can conclude the indirect dependence weight of component c_1 on

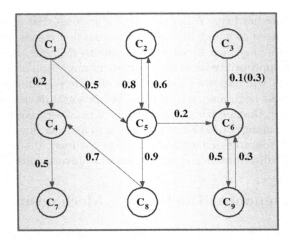

Fig. 5. A case of Component Interdependence Graph

component c_7 is a sum of weight of component c_1 on component c_4, and weight of component c_4 on component c_7. As a result, the weight is 0.7. In addition, we can also see dependence weight of component c_3 on component c_6 is 0.1 in one context, while this weight changes to 0.3 in another context. Therefore we should consider the effect of context variety on component interdependence in component allocation design.

4.2   Run-Time Component Hook Proxy Architecture

In the large and complex ubiquitous computing environments, the multiple resources are restricted. Software components are distributed, and connected with each other. They compute and communicate frequently under different conditions. As a result, they are interdependent. However, some relationships are casually and others are perpetual, which means the components do not always depend on special components for co-operations. Therefore, we use the component interdependence graph to describe run-time component self-adaptation. In executing time, the dynamic interdependence graph is generated automatically by the components hook proxy that is responsible for acquiring information to analyze and update interdependence graph to manage the components lifetime. Under the changes of the contexts, the components hook proxy uses the different strategies. Here gives a simple example. For a mobile music program, there are four components: c_1, c_2, c_3, c_4. c_1 is responsible for acquiring music information. c_2 is responsible for playing music with stereo tune. c_3 is responsible for playing music with mono tune. c_4 is responsible for outputting the music. At first, the network bandwidth is enough, the component hook proxy selects c_1, c_2, c_4 to deal with this task, and forms a component interdependence graph. However, when the component hook proxy finds the network bandwidth is scarcity, and cannot to transmit stereo track successfully, it will stop the actions of c_2,

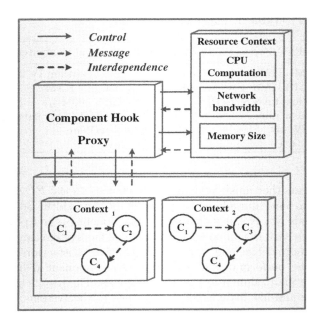

Fig. 6. A case of Component Hook Proxy

and then choose c_3 to work. As a result, the component interdependence graph changes. Figure 6 shows this case.

5   Experiment Study and Evaluation

We have made some preliminary experiments using the adaptive component management service to build the mobile music system of smart vehicle space. A large number of components are distributed on the various platforms to acquire, play, transmit, and output the music information. These components interact with the request and reply process. If one component sends the request for some music information, the component management service will select one appropriate component to work and reply to the demander. Since the context of the application is very dynamic, the strategy of component allocation should be done automatically and dynamically. Our experiments are tested on the following platforms, as shown in Table 1. The iPAQ is connected to the PC via the wireless LAN using 802.11b protocol. The middleware platform uses the ScudWare.

Mobile music system runs on some PDAs and PCs. Many components are distributed on the PDAs and PCs randomly. The functions of these components consist of acquiring the music source information, transmitting the music, and playing the music. To illustrate this, we give a case. First, the playing component c_1 on the PDA_1 is playing the music with stereo tune. When the component hook proxy finds the network bandwidth is not enough, it will stop the component c_1.

Table 1. Experiment Test Bed

	HP iPAQ Pocket PC H5500	Personal Computer
CPU	400 MHz Intel, XScal-PXA255	Intel Pentium IV 2.4G
Memory	128 MB RAM + 48 MB Flash ROM	256 MB RAM
Network	Wireless LAN 802.11b	LAN 100MB/s
OS	Familiar Linux v0.8.0-rc1	RedHat Linux 9.0 (2.4.20)
Middleware	ScudWare	ScudWare
Dev-Language	g++, QT	g++

Then the proxy finds another music playing component c_2 on the PDA_2, which plays music with mono tune and adapts to low network bandwidth. Because the current playing frame is No. 168, it will start the component c_2, and play music from the No. 168 frame with the mono tune. In this way, the system can continue successfully without more delays and provide comparative satisfaction for users.

In order to test the performance of the adaptive component management service, we have made many simulations and evaluations. The results show that our method is flexible and has little negative influence to the systems.

Due to adaptive component migration and replication, it must induce the execution performance cost through component manager monitoring. As a result, we focus on the performance test for measuring the cost. Because components in ubiquitous computing environments form a large, complex and rich world, the number of components in the tests is a key issue. In our tests, we choose the component number n in this way: the first value is 50, the last is 500, and the

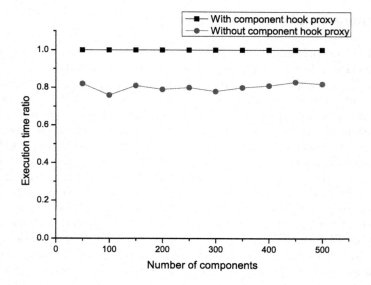

Fig. 7. Performance Cost

step is 50. We have done the experiments 10 times, and each time we use $n/25$ PCs and $n/50$ iPAQs. As shown in Figure 7, the average execution time for each n is given about two kinds: one is a mobile music system without the component hook proxy monitoring, and the other is with it. As a whole, the difference is small and the execution time is acceptable.

6   Related Work

Service-oriented adaptive middleware plays an important role in software engineering. It has the large potential for enhancing the system's flexibility and reliability to a very wide range of factors. Many efforts are put in this research area. For instance, Philip K. Mckinley has made a lot of research on adaptive software. He considers the compositional adaptation enables software to modify its structure and behavior dynamically in response to changes in its execution environment. He also gives a review of current technology comparing how, when, and where re-composition occurs [13]. In addition, he describes Petrimorph [14], a system that supports compositional adaptation of both functional and non-functional concerns by explicitly addressing collateral change. Kurt Wallnau and Judith Stafford [15] discuss and illustrate the fundamental affinity between software architecture and component technology. They mainly outline criteria for the component integration. Jiri Adamek and Frantisek Plasil [16] discuss the problem of defining a composition operator in behavior protocols in a way, which would reflect false communication of the software components being composed. Besides, we have proposed a semantic and adaptive middleware for data management in smart vehicle space [2]. In component adaptation, we should consider both the task decomposing completely at design-time and the executing effectively and reliably at run-time [17]. However, many researches consider incompletely, ignoring some aspects. Additionally, it needs an integrated computation model to describe adaptive component management. The goal of our research is to overcome this deficiency. Smita Bakshi and Daniel D. Gajski [18] present a cost-optimized algorithm for selecting components and pipelining a data flow graph, given a multiple implementation library. This method focuses on performance analysis, which is short of the run-time adaptive mechanism. Belaramani and Cho Li Wang [3] propose a dynamic component composition approach for achieving functionality adaptation and demonstrate its feasibility via the facet model. However, they do not integrate the design-time adaptation to form a synthetical computation model. Shige Wang and Kang G. Shin [19] give a new method for component allocation using an informed branch-and-bound and forward checking mechanism subject to a combination of resource constraints. Nevertheless, their method is static, and focuses on design-time instead of runtime adaptation.

7   Conclusions and Future Work

Now, adaptive component management is playing a more important role in ubiquitous computing environments, which is a significant research issue. In this paper, we firstly analyze the problem area caused by dynamic characters of ubiquitous computing, and give a short introduction of the software adaptation. Next, we mainly present an adaptive component management service, which is integrated into the ScudWare middleware. In addition, we have made a large number of experiments to test the performance cost of this service.

Our future work is to improve the adaptive component management service including some algorithm analysis. In addition, we will take other methods to realize more component management flexibility and reliability both at design-time and run-time.

Acknowledgments

This research was supported by 863 National High Technology Program under Grant No. 2003AA1Z2080, 2003AA1Z2140 and 2002AA1Z2308.

References

1. Weiser M: The Computer for the 21st Century. Scientific American, pp.94-100 (1991)
2. Qing Wu, Zhaohui Wu, Bin Wu, and Zhou Jiang: Semantic and Adaptive Middleware for Data management in Smart Vehicle Space. In proceedings of the 5th Advances in Web-Age Information Management, LNCS 3129, pp. 107-116 (2004)
3. Nalini Moti Belaramani, Cho-Li Wang, and Francis C.M. Lau: Dynamic Component Composition for Functionality Adaptation in Pervasive Environments. In proceedings of the Ninth IEEE Workshop on Future Trends of Distributed Computing Systems, (2003)
4. Zhaohui Wu, Qing Wu, Jie Sun, Zhigang Gao, Bin Wu, and Mingde Zhao: Scud-Ware: A Context-aware and Lightweight Middleware for Smart Vehicle Space. In proceedings of the 1st International Conference on Embedded Software and System, LNCS 3605, pp. 266-273 (2004)
5. http://www.omg.org/technology/documents/formal/components.htm (2005)
6. http://www.cs.wustl.edu/ schmidt/ACE.html (2005)
7. http://www.cs.wustl.edu/ schmidt/TAO.html (2005)
8. Mingde Zhao, Zhaohui Wu, Guoqing Yang, Lei Wang, and Wei Chen: SmartOSEK: A Dependable Platform for Automobile Electronics. In proceedings of the first International Conference on Embedded Software and System, LNCS 3605, pp. 437-442 (2004)
9. OSEK/VDX: OSEK/VDX Operating System Specification Version 2.2.2. http://www.osek-vdx.org (2005)
10. Qing Wu and Zhaohui Wu: Integrating Semantic Context Service into Adaptive Middleware for Ubiquitous Computing. In "Advances in Computer Science and Engineering Series", Imperial College Press, London, UK, to appeare (2005)
11. Qing Wu and Zhaohui Wu: Semantic and Virtual Agents in Adaptive Middleware Architecture for Smart Vehicle Space. In proceedings of the 4th International Central and Eastern European Conference on Multi-Agent Systems, LNAI 3690, pp. 543-546 (2005)
12. Hector A. Duran-Limon, Gordon S. Blair, Geoff Coulson: Adaptive Resource Management in Middleware : A Survey. IEEE Distributed System 5(7), (2004)

13. Philip K. McKinley, Seyed Masoud Sadjadi, Eric P. Kasten, Betty H.C. Cheng: Comosing Adaptive Software. IEEE Computer Society, pp. 56-64 (2004)
14. E.P. Kasten, P.K.McKinley: Perimorph: Run-time Composition and State Management for Adaptive Systems. In proceedings of the 4th International Workshop on Distributed Auto-adaptive and Reconfigurable Systems, pp. 332-337 (2004)
15. Kurt Wallnau, Judith Stafford, Scott Hissam, Mark Klein: On the Relationship of Software Architecture to Software Component Technology. In proceedings of the 6th International Workshop on Component-Oriented Programming (2001)
16. Jiri Adamek, Frantisek Plasil: Component Composition Errors and Update Atomicity : Static Analysis. Journal of Software Maintenance and Evolution: Research and Practice (2005)
17. Qing Wu and Zhaohui Wu: Adaptive Component Allocation in ScudWare Middleware for Ubiquitous Computing. In proceedings of the 2005 IFIP International Conference on Embedded And Ubiquitous Computing, LNCS, to appeare (2005)
18. Smita Bakshi, Daniel D.Gajski:A component Selection Algorithm for High-Performance Pipelines. In proceedings of the conference on European design automation, ACM, pp. 400-405 (1994)
19. Shige Wang, Jeffrey R. Merrick, Kang G. Shin: Component Allocation with Multiple Resource Constraints for Large Embedded Real-time Software Design. In proceedings of the 10th IEEE Real-Time and Embedded Technology and Applications Symposium (2004)

Semantic Caching for Web Services[*]

Stefan Seltzsam[1], Roland Holzhauser[2], and Alfons Kemper[1]

[1] TU München, D-85747 Garching, Germany
⟨first name⟩.⟨last name⟩@in.tum.de
[2] Universität Passau, D-94030 Passau, Germany
holzhaus@fmi.uni-passau.de

Abstract. We present a semantic caching scheme suitable for caching responses from Web services on the SOAP protocol level. Existing semantic caching schemes for database systems or Web sources cannot be applied directly because there is no semantic knowledge available about the requests to and responses from Web services. Web services are typically described using WSDL (Web Service Description Language) documents. For semantic caching we developed an XML-based declarative language to annotate WSDL documents with information about the caching-relevant semantics of requests and responses. Using this information, our semantic cache answers requests based on the responses of similar previously executed requests. Performance experiments—based on the scenarios of TPC-W and TPC-W Version 2—conducted using our prototype implementation demonstrate the effectiveness of the proposed semantic caching scheme.

1 Introduction

Service-oriented architectures (SOAs) based on Web services are emerging as the dominant application on the Internet. Mission critical services like business-to-business (B2B) or business-to-consumer (B2C) services often require more performance, scalability, and availability than a single server can provide. Server side caching, e.g., [1, 2], and some kind of cluster architecture alleviate some of these problems. A major drawback remains: all clients must still access the Web service directly over the Internet, which is possibly resulting in high latency, high bandwidth consumption, and high server load.

There are many Web services characterized by read-mostly interactions, e.g., B2C and B2B services offering query-like interfaces to access product catalogues. Such services are also used in standard benchmarks like TPC-W [3] and TPC-W Version 2 [4]. Another important category of Web services includes information services like stock quote services, news services, weather services, etc., which typically offer read-only access. There are Web services with different access patterns but since the Web service categories described above are very common and important, this paper focuses on them.

---

[*] This research is supported by the Advanced Infrastructure Program (AIP) group of SAP and the German National Research Foundation under contract DFG Ke 401/7-2.

B. Benatallah, F. Casati, and P. Traverso (Eds.): ICSOC 2005, LNCS 3826, pp. 324–340, 2005.

Our generic approach to achieving higher performance and scalability is called *Semantic SOAP Protocol Level Cache* (SSPLC). The performance increase is based on semantic caching of responses from Web services in request/response message exchange patterns on the SOAP [5] protocol level. Clients are not directly accessing the origin service anymore; instead they are accessing instances of SSPLC. As long as requests can be answered based on cached data, the origin server hosting the Web service is not involved anymore. Therefore, the load at the origin server is reduced, bandwidth consumption is diminished, and latency is reduced. The advantage of a semantic cache is that it reuses the responses to prior requests to answer similar requests, not only the exact same requests. Thus, if request R_1 retrieves all books written by "Rowling" and afterwards a request R_2 retrieves all books written by "Joanne Rowling", a semantic cache reuses the response to R_1 to answer the more selective request R_2.

Our proposed cache can be used like traditional HTTP proxies, i.e., SSPLC instances need not be hosted by service providers themselves, but can easily be run by, e.g., companies and universities, just like HTTP proxies nowadays. However, SSPLC can also be used as reverse-proxy cache or edge server cache. with the additional advantage that server-driven cache consistency techniques are applicable.

Our approach relies on service provider cooperation. All instructions to control the SSPLC are embedded by the provider of a service in SOAP result documents and in the WSDL [6] description of a service. The SOAP results are augmented with information about cache consistency. This is the only modification to a Web service required for the use of SSPLC. The effort necessary to generate these annotations depends on the consistency strategy and the complexity of the application logic and is subject to further investigations. Simple annotations, e.g., TTL values, can be inserted by the SOAP-engine in a post-processing step without modifications of the Web service. More complex annotations demand some coding effort. Additionally, the WSDL document of the service is annotated with information about the caching-relevant semantics of a service. This is done manually using an XML-based declarative language because automatic reasoning about the semantics normally results in a very conservative caching behavior. Writing these annotations is considered to be quite easy for the developers of a Web service as they already have the required knowledge. Altogether, we assume that the additional effort for the provider to make a Web service cachable is clearly outweigh by its benefits.

The remainder of the paper is organized as follows: In Section 2 we present background information and introduce an example Web service used as running example. Several basic design decisions are described in Section 3. A detailed description of SSPLC, the embedded control instructions of service providers, and some sophisticated features of the SSPLC are presented in Section 4. Experimental results follow in Section 5. Section 6 surveys related work and Section 7 presents our conclusions.

2   Background Knowledge and Running Example

2.1   Fundamentals of Semantic Caching

Semantic caching is a client-side caching technique introduced in the mid 90s for DBMSs to exploit the semantic locality of queries [7, 8]. A semantic cache is managed as a collection of *semantic regions* which group together semantically related objects. Regions are composed of *region descriptor* and *region content*. The descriptor basically contains a predicate (like 'author = "Joanne Rowling" ') describing the region content. The content stores the objects related to a region descriptor. Access history is maintained and cache replacement is performed at the granularity of semantic regions.

Every query sent to a semantic cache is split into two disjoint parts: a *probe query* and a *remainder query*. The probe query extracts the relevant portion of the result already available in the cache while the remainder query is sent to the origin server to fetch the missing, i.e., not cached, part of the result. If the remainder query is empty, the cache does not interact with the origin server. In the context of DBMSs or Web sources, all participating components have been full-fledged DBMSs. Since Web services normally have a more constrained query interface, semantic caching must be adapted to these limitations (see Section 4).

2.2   Running Example

Amazon offers a SOAP-based Web service interface which is very similar to their broadly known HTTP interface. Since Amazon is in fact a "real-world implementation" of the TPC-W benchmark, we use parts of their interface for our example and the TPC-W benchmark scenario as basis for performance experiments conducted using our prototype implementation. Our example service is called *Book Store Light* and is a slim version of Amazon. The relevant operation of this service is a search for books written by certain authors (*author search*). The XML documents used by Amazon are too large to be presented entirely in this paper. We shortened and simplified them to a reasonable degree and removed all namespaces and types from the presented documents for better readability and a more concise presentation.

2.3   The Communication Protocol SOAP

SOAP [5] is an XML-based communication protocol for distributed applications. The root element of a SOAP message is an `Envelope` element containing an optional `Header` element for SOAP extensions and a `Body` element for the payload. SOAP is designed to exchange messages containing structured and typed data and can be used on top of several different transfer protocols like HTTP, SMTP, and FTP. The usage of SOAP over HTTP is the default in the current landscape of Web services. Figure 3 shows an example SOAP response corresponding to the request shown in Figure 1.

2.4   The Description Language WSDL

WSDL (*Web Service Description Language*) [6] is an XML-based language to describe the technical specifications of a Web service, in particular the operations offered by a Web service, the syntax of the input and output documents, and the communication protocol to use for communication with the service. The exact structure of a WSDL document is complex and out of the scope of this paper, but we will give a brief overview of the WSDL standard. At first, a service in WSDL is described on an abstract level and afterwards bound to a specific protocol, network address (normally a URL), and message format. On the abstract level *port types* are defined. A port type is a set of operations (like author search). Every operation has a number of input and output messages associated defining the order and type of the messages sent to/received from the operation. The messages themselves are assembled from several typed *parts*. The types are defined using XML Schema.

On the non-abstract level, port types are bound to concrete communication protocols and concrete formats of the messages using so-called *bindings*. At last, a service in WSDL is defined as a set of *ports*, i.e., bindings with associated network addresses (normally URLs).

Since SSPLC is currently mainly based on annotations at the abstract level we will focus on this level. Figure 4 shows a fragment of a WSDL document defining the port type of the Book Store Light service (`BookStoreLightPort`) having one operation (`AuthorSearchRequest`). This operation expects an `AuthorSearchRequest` message as input and produces an `AuthorSearchResponse` message as an output document. These messages are defined just above the `portType` element. Messages are composed of several `part` elements. As shown in the figure, the request message has one part of type `AuthorRequest` and the response message has one part of type `ProductInfo`. These types are defined using XML Schema in another fragment of the WSDL document, shown in Figure 2. An element of type `AuthorRequest` has the elements `author` and `levelOfDetail`, both of type `string`, in its content. In our example, `levelOfDetail` can be "heavy" or "lite" and influences the level of detail of the result. Figure 1 shows an example SOAP message requesting the most important information about books written by "Joanne Rowling".

An element of type `ProductInfo` contains the two subelements `TotalResults` and `DetailsArray`. The former is of type `int`, whereas `DetailsArray` is, in short, an array of `Details` elements. `Details` is another type defined inside the WSDL document, having the three subelements `Asin`, `Title`, and `Authors`. The first two subelements are of type `string`, the last one is of type `AuthorArray` which is an array of `strings` representing the authors of the book. For our example, we assume that `Asin` is only present in a result if `levelOfDetail` was "heavy".

```
<Envelope encodingStyle="http://...">
 <Body>
  <AuthorSearchRequest>
   <AuthorSearchRequest>
    <author>Joanne Rowling</author>
    <levelOfDetail>lite</levelOfDetail>
   </AuthorSearchRequest>
  </AuthorSearchRequest>
 </Body>
</Envelope>
```

Fig. 1. Example SOAP Request

```
<types><schema>
 <complexType name="AuthorRequest"><all>
  <element name="author" type="string" />
  <element name="levelOfDetail"
           type="string" />
 </all></complexType>
 <complexType name="ProductInfo"><all>
  <element name="TotalResults" type="int" />
  <element name="DetailsArray"
           type="DetailsArray" />
 </all></complexType>
 <complexType name="DetailsArray">
  <complexContent>
   <restriction base="Array">
    <attribute ref="arrayType"
               arrayType="Details[]" />
   </restriction>
  </complexContent></complexType>
 <complexType name="Details"><all>
  <element name="Asin" type="string" />
  <element name="Title" type="string" />
  <element name="Authors"
           type="AuthorArray" />
 </all></complexType>
 <complexType name="AuthorArray">
  <complexContent>
   <restriction base="Array">
    <attribute ref="arrayType"
               arrayType="string[]" />
   </restriction>
  </complexContent></complexType>
</schema></types>
```

Fig. 2. Type Definitions

```
<Envelope encodingStyle="http://...">
 <Body>
  <AuthorSearchRequestResponse>
   <return>
    <TotalResults>200</TotalResults>
    <DetailsArray arrayType="Details[200]">
     <Details>
      <Title>
       Harry Potter and the Sorcerer's Stone
      </Title>
      <Authors arrayType="string[2]">
       <Author>Joanne K. Rowling</Author>
       <Author>Mary GrandPré</Author>
      </Authors>
     </Details>
     <!-- 199 more Details elements -->
    </DetailsArray>
   </return>
  </AuthorSearchRequestResponse>
 </Body>
</Envelope>
```

Fig. 3. Example SOAP Response

```
<message name="AuthorSearchRequest">
 <part name="AuthorSearchRequest"
       type="AuthorRequest" />
</message>
<message name="AuthorSearchResponse">
 <part name="return" type="ProductInfo" />
</message>
<portType name="BookStoreLightPort">
 <operation name="AuthorSearchRequest">
  <input message="AuthorSearchRequest" />
  <output message="AuthorSearchResponse" />
 </operation>
</portType>
```

Fig. 4. Messages and Port Types

```
<CacheControlHeader>
 <CacheConsistency>
  <TTL>P0Y0M0DT12H00M00S</TTL>
 </CacheConsistency>
</CacheControlHeader>
```

Fig. 5. Cache Consistency Information

```
<binding name="BSLBinding" type="BookStoreLightPort">
 <binding style="rpc" transport="http://schemas.xmlsoap.org/soap/http" />
 <operation name="AuthorSearchRequest">
  <operation soapAction="BookStoreLight" />
  <!-- ...mappings of input and output message... -->
  <OperationCacheControl>
   <fragmentationXPath>
    /Envelope/Body/AuthorSearchRequestResponse/return/DetailsArray/Details
   </fragmentationXPath>
   <reassemblingXQuery> <![CDATA[
    let $details := ##RESULT_FRAGMENTS##
    return
    <Envelope encodingStyle="http://schemas.xmlsoap.org/soap/encoding/">
     <Body>
      <AuthorSearchRequestResponse>
       <return type="ProductInfo">
        <TotalResults type="int">##COUNT_RESULT_FRAGMENTS##</TotalResults>
        <DetailsArray arrayType="Details[##COUNT_RESULT_FRAGMENTS##]" type="Array">
         {$details}
        </DetailsArray>
       </return>
      </AuthorSearchRequestResponse>
     </Body>
    </Envelope> ]]>
   </reassemblingXQuery>
  </OperationCacheControl>
 </operation>
</binding>
```

Fig. 6. Annotation of the AuthorSearchRequest Operation

3   Basics of the Web Service Cache

We will now discuss our design decisions on several basic caching aspects. These concerns are not the main focus of our work so we used existing solutions as far as possible and adapted existing work where necessary.

3.1   Replacement Policy

Since cache memory is a limited resource, the cache may have to discard some regions to free memory for new regions. After experimenting with some different replacement strategies, we decided to use our own modified version of the 2Q strategy [9], which is a low overhead approximation to LRU-2. Empirically, standard 2Q is a smart choice because of good replacement decisions and low CPU overhead, but this algorithm is designed to handle objects of uniform size. As semantic regions can be of different size, we had to modify the standard 2Q strategy by introducing a simple but efficient *cost-to-size ratio*. More details on our modifications of 2Q can be found in the extended version of this paper [10].

3.2   Distribution Control/Cache Consistency

SSPLC gives providers exclusive control over distribution and cache consistency using a SOAP header extension. Since cache consistency mechanisms are not the focus of this work, we assume service-specific TTL in the following discussion. If a provider allows caching, it must explicitly state some cache consistency information. For example, the `CacheControlHeader` element shown in Figure 5 allows caching and states that the response is *fresh* for at least the given duration (12 hours). After this duration, the cached version of the response must be removed from the cache.

3.3   Physical Storage of Semantic Regions

Using a cache requires a large amount of memory to be able to serve lots of clients based on a reasonably large number of semantic regions. Since disks are considerably larger and cheaper than main memory, it is obviously a good idea to use them for the storage of semantic regions. Since it is orthogonal to the issues discussed in this paper whether the cache is based on main memory, disk, or both, we assume for the rest of the paper that the cache is only based on main memory. Our prototype system is main memory-based as well.

4   Semantic Caching in SSPLC

Basically, semantic caching in SSPLC is done by annotating WSDL documents with information about the caching-relevant semantics of services using the language presented in the next section. This information is used for mapping SOAP requests to predicates, for fragmenting responses, and for reassembling responses. Thus, adapted semantic caching algorithms can be applied.

4.1 WSDL Annotations

Our language is designed both to cover common capabilities of existing Web service interfaces and to preserve efficient solvability of the *query containment problem*, which is intrinsic to semantic caching. The annotation of WSDL documents is done using XML Schema annotation elements and WSDL extensibility elements. Thus, compatibility to the original WSDL document is preserved, because applications which cannot handle the annotations ignore them.

Fragmentation and Reassembling. Since Web services deliver monolithic XML documents rather than tuple-oriented responses, SSPLC needs some information about how to fragment such documents to obtain fine-granular response units comparable to tuples in database caching. These units are called *fragments*. We use an XPath-expression to specify the fragmentation. Additionally, SSPLC needs further instructions regarding the generation of a complete response document based on fragments of prior requests. This information is specified using the XQuery language. Both the XPath-expression and the XQuery, are provided using an additional element (`OperationCacheControl`) inside the `binding` element of the WSDL document of a service because it depends on the actual coding of the messages.

Figure 6 gives an example for our Book Store Light. The marked region depicts the annotated information for the SSPLC while the rest of the document constitutes a standard SOAP binding. Referring to our book store example, we are interested in the individual books, i.e., `Details` elements, contained in a response document of our example service. The XPath-expression inside the `fragmentationXPath` element in Figure 6 fragments a response document accordingly. The XQuery to reassemble a response is shown in the figure inside the `reassemblingXQuery` element. The macros `##COUNT_RESULT_FRAGMENTS##` and `##RESULT_FRAGMENTS##` are expanded by the SSPLC before evaluating the XQuery and represent exactly the fragments (respectively their number) which should be reassembled to a complete response document. Since an introduction to XQuery lies outside the scope of this paper, we will not explain the XQuery shown in the figure. It should be obvious that the result of the XQuery is a SOAP response like the one shown in Figure 3.

Predicate Mapping. We need predicates to describe the fragments stored in a region. Thus, we need some information about the semantics of requests. Moreover, we want to be able to filter semantic regions, e.g., if we are looking for all books written by "Joanne Rowling" in a region storing all books written by "Rowling". Therefore, we need to know how to access the individual "attributes" (elements) of a tuple (fragment). This information is annotated to the type definitions of requests in WSDL documents.

We will explain the annotations using our Book Store Light example. The original type definition of `AuthorRequest`, which is the request type of our service, is shown in Figure 2. Currently, we assume that if there are several parameters defined in a request, i.e., `levelOfDetail` and `author`, they are combined by an

```
<complexType name="AuthorRequest"><all>
  <element name="author" type="string">
    <annotation><appinfo>
      <CacheControl context="AuthorSearchRequest"
                    bindingContext="BSLBinding">
        <StringParameter>
          <required>true</required>
          <fragmentXPath>
          Authors/Author/text()
          </fragmentXPath>
          <implicitOperator>contains_wwo</implicitOperator>
          <caseSensitive>false</caseSensitive>
          <operators>
            <and> </and><and>,</and>
          </operators>
        </StringParameter>
      </CacheControl>
    </appinfo></annotation></element>
  <element name="levelOfDetail" type="string">
    <annotation><appinfo>
      <CacheControl context="AuthorSearchRequest"
                    bindingContext="BSLBinding">
        <StringParameter>
          <required>true</required>
          <implicitOperator>equals</implicitOperator>
          <caseSensitive>true</caseSensitive>
        </StringParameter>
      </CacheControl>
    </appinfo></annotation></element>
</all></complexType>
```

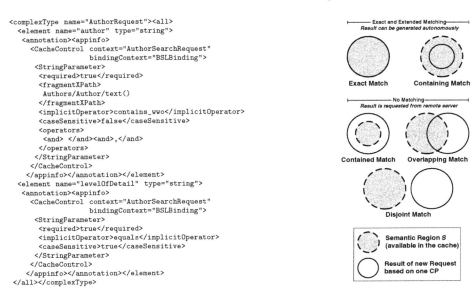

Fig. 7. Annotated WSDL Type Definition   **Fig. 8.** Match Types

AND operator. Thus, the request shown in Figure 1 means that we are looking for all books written by "Joanne Rowling" and we are only interested in the most important facts of the books. Additionally, we assume that if there are several elements inside an array, the elements are logically ANDed together, too. This is also true for responses (see the `Author` elements inside the `Authors` element shown in Figure 3). The annotated version of the `AuthorRequest` type is shown in Figure 7.

We annotate every parameter of the request using one or more `CacheControl` elements. It is necessary to specify some context information because a parameter can be used for several operations having different semantics. Also, if another binding is used, the coding of the parameter might be different, requiring some modifications inside the `CacheControl` element. Thus, the context information given by the attributes of `CacheControl` defines when to use the information inside the `CacheControl` element. A `StringParameter` element defines that the parameter is of type string. The content of this element gives more detailed information about how to handle this string parameter. We also defined elements for other parameter types, e.g., an `IntegerParameter` element. Each of these elements contains further information (e.g., operators) depending on the parameter type.

Looking at the example in Figure 7, we observe that the author parameter is mandatory (`required` element). If a parameter is optional, a default value of the parameter that is used in case of absence of the parameter in a request must be specified using a `default` element (not available in the example document). The `fragmentXPath` element specifies how to extract the information from result fragments that correspond to this parameter (compare Figure 3). For example, if we ask for books written by an author, the `fragmentXPath` can be used to find the authors in the result fragments. If, as in our example, an XPath is specified, the cache can inspect the fragments to look up the actual author(s) of a book. This information can be used to filter all fragments contained in a semantic region. If there is no XPath specified, the cache is not able to do such filtering because it is constrained to the information obtained from the request.

The element `implicitOperator` defines the operator of the parameter. Currently, we support the following operators (for appropriate parameter types): $>$, $\geq$, $<$, $\leq$, $=$ (or *equals*), *contains*, *contains_wwo*, *starts_with*, and *ends_with*. In our example, the operator is *contains_wwo* which is a contains operator that looks for "whole word only" occurrences of the given pattern in a string, i.e., "Joanne Rowling" does not contain_wwo "Rowl", but contains_wwo "Rowling". The comparison of strings is case insensitive as defined by the `caseSensitive` element.

Additionally, we support the logical operators AND and OR to support complex predicates. We also support parentheses for precedence control. Currently, we are not supporting the $\neg$ operator (logical NOT operator) because there are virtually no Web services offering this operator and we are interested in keeping the query containment problem efficiently solvable. The `operators` element in Figure 7 defines two AND operators for the author parameter: a space character and a comma.

The second parameter is `levelOfDetail`. This is also a mandatory string parameter. The implicit operator is a case sensitive "equals". There is no `fragmentXPath` defined because in the response document of our Web service no explicit information about whether it is a "heavy" or a "lite" result is contained. As this information is stored as part of the region predicate, this information is not lost.

Using these annotations SSPLC can figure out the semantics of a request and is able to extract relevant elements from fragments. Also, it is able to generate a predicate from a request. The request shown in Figure 1 is mapped to the following predicate:

$$\begin{aligned}
&\text{author \ contains\_wwo\_case\_insensitive \ "Joanne"} \land \\
&\text{author \ contains\_wwo\_case\_insensitive \ "Rowling"} \land \\
&\text{levelOfDetail \ equals\_case\_sensitive \ "lite"}
\end{aligned}$$

4.2   Matching and Control Flow

Using our annotations we are now able to understand the caching-relevant semantics of requests and responses. We will now describe how this information is used for caching. First of all, a SOAP request R is mapped to a predicate P as described above. Although the Book Store Light does not offer a logical OR operator for the author parameter, we will use the following predicate P (operator names are shortened) for demonstration purposes throughout this section:

(author contains "Rowling" ∨ author contains "GrandPré") ∧
levelOfDetail = "lite"

After the mapping, P is transformed into *disjunctive normal form* (DNF)
and split into *conjunctive predicates* (CPs), i.e., predicates only containing
simple predicates connected by logical AND operators. If there is no logical OR
in a request, P is processed as is. The transformation of our example predicate
P results in:

CP_1: author contains "Rowling" ∧ levelOfDetail = "lite"
CP_2: author contains "GrandPré" ∧ levelOfDetail = "lite"

All CPs are processed in parallel. First, match types of a CP with all semantic
regions are determined, i.e., the correlation between every semantic region S and
the result of CP is determined. There are five different match types as shown in
Figure 8. The best match type for a CP and a semantic region S is, of course,
the exact match. The next best match type is a containing match because we
only have to filter S by eliminating all fragments fulfilling the region predicate
but not CP to get the fragments for the response. The other three match types
require server interaction because we do not have all fragments cached to answer the request. Since most Web services do not have adequate interfaces to
be able to process complicated remainder requests, we handle all three match
types as disjoint match. Thus, we are sending a request generated from the CP
to the Web service even though there already might be some relevant fragments
available in the cache. Even if a Web service can process complicated remainder requests, processing of such complex requests is likely to be costly. As one
of the goals of SSPLC is to reduce processing demands of the central servers,
usage of complex remainder requests could be counterproductive. The response
of the Web service is fragmented and afterwards stored in the cache. If there
are already regions in the cache that are a subset of the response (i.e., in the
case of a contained match), these semantic regions are replaced with the new
(larger) semantic region. In all other cases, the fragmented response is inserted
as a new semantic region using CP as the region predicate. After all CPs have
been processed, SSPLC calculates the result of P as the union of the results
of all CPs. By default, duplicates are eliminated, i.e., SSPLC implements the
very common set semantics. Alternatively, SSPLC calculates the result without
duplicate elimination. This behavior is controlled by an optional **distinct** element inside the **OperationCacheControl** element (not shown in the example
document). Fragments are considered equal if their contents are equal or if keys
are defined, their keys are equal. Keys can be defined via a **key** element inside
the **OperationCacheControl** element using the standard XML Schema syntax
for keys. Usage of keys considerably speeds up duplicate elimination. We do not
further investigate keys in the scope of this paper. The result of P is (conceptually) written to an XML document D. After that, the **reassemblingXQuery**
is evaluated with the macro **##RESULT_FRAGMENTS##** expanded to D and the
macro **##COUNT_RESULT_FRAGMENTS##** expanded to $|D|$. Finally, the response is
sent back to the client.

4.3   Sorting and Generalization

Since the order of elements can be important in XML documents, SSPLC is aware of it. XML documents are inherently ordered by the sequence of the elements (*document order*). As long as the document order generated by a Web service offers no real added value (e.g., lexicographical order by title), it does not matter in which order the fragments emerge in the response. Also, as long as we are using fragments of only one semantic region (filtered or not), order is abided and we can generate correctly ordered results as in the Book Store Light example.

If a Web service orders fragments using some information available in the response, there are two possibilities to establish the same order even if we are merging fragments of several semantic regions to generate the response. First, if the order is fixed, i.e., always the same, the `reassemblingXQuery` can be modified to do the sorting using the *order by* clause of XQuery. Second, if the order depends on a request parameter, we can annotate this parameter using a `SortParameter` element. This element contains a mapping from the service's sorting facilities to order by clauses of XQuery. For example, if a Web service has a parameter `sort` and the value "+title" means "sort by title", a mapping to XQuery could look like "order by $fragment/Title". The appropriate order by clause is inserted into `reassemblingXQuery` before evaluation. The value of a sorting parameter is stored in the region descriptor because it is relevant for determining the match types.

Another enhancement of our semantic caching scheme is the usage of generalization for better decisions on the query containment/predicate subsumption problem. Our SSPLC supports two different types of generalization. First, tree-structured containment relations for values of parameters can be defined. For example, if there is a parameter defining whether we are interested in paperback, hardcover, or both, we are able to annotate this parameter to point out that "hardcover $\subseteq$ both" and "paperback $\subseteq$ both". This information is used during match type computation and for filtering of semantic regions. The second type of generalization can be seen in our example. There is a parameter `levelOfDetail` that influences the level of detail of the response. Since "heavy" fragments simply contain some extra elements, it is possible to define an XQuery filter to transform "heavy fragments" to "lite fragments" by removing the surplus elements like the `Asin` elements in our example. This information is also used during match type computation and region filtering.

5   Performance Evaluation

We implemented a prototype of SSPLC for the service platform ServiceGlobe [11] using Java and conducted several performance experiments based on the scenarios of TPC-W [3] and TPC-W Version 2 [4].

5.1   Benchmark Scenario 1 (TPC-W)

The first scenario is related to the online bookstore scenario of the TPC Web commerce benchmark (TPC-W). Because TPC-W does not aim at SOAP Web services and semantic caching, but instead at traditional Web servers and back-end servers, major modifications to TPC-W (system architecture as well as data generation) are necessary to adjust the benchmark to the context of our SSPLC in a reasonable way. Thus, we decided to model our benchmark scenario on the SOAP interface of Amazon, just as the scenario of TPC-W is modeled on the HTTP interface of Amazon. We chose to use Amazon's author search request for our benchmarks because this search functionality is also addressed in TPC-W.

Experimental Setup. Due to space restrictions, we only present a survey of the experimental setup of benchmark scenario 1. A detailed description can be found in the extended version of this paper [10].

To show the effectiveness of our semantic cache, we implemented a simulation service rather than using Amazon directly because Amazon delivers its results page-wise (i.e., 10 books per SOAP response), which is an unusual behavior for Web services. The requests and responses of our simulation service are identical to those of the Amazon service despite the fact that our service delivers all results to a request in one response. For that purpose, we materialized some of the data of Amazon to be able to work with real data. Since our simulation service delivers these materialized results extremely fast, we are delaying results to simulate processing time of a Web service. We conducted some experiments to assure that SSPLC is able to deliver its results as fast or faster on average than the origin Web service. Since these results depend heavily on the performance of the origin server and of the machine running SSPLC, we do not present quantitative results.

Our benchmark scenario is based on several top-300 bestseller lists (top selling science books, top selling sports books, ...) of Amazon. We used these different bestseller lists to generate different traces as described below and we always present the average of all performance experiments conducted using these different traces. If an author's book is present on the bestseller list, people will be interested in other books published by the same author, too. Thus, an author search request is more likely for authors whose books are ranked high on the best-seller list. Since studies [12] have found that the request characteristics of many Internet applications are adequately modeled through a Zipf-like distribution, we use such a distribution (with parameter theta (θ) set to 0.75) on the top-300 bestseller lists to select books. Using the names of the authors of a book, we generate a request for our simulation service. We randomly choose which names (surnames, first names) are used for the request. Every request contains at least one surname of an author. This is done to challenge semantic caching. We generated traces of 2000 requests each for the performance experiments. Additionally, we conducted some experiments using traces of 10000 requests showing similar results.

Some of the requests produce very large response documents containing up to 32000 fragments. Since the size of such documents is about 40 MB, it is very likely that Web services do not generate such large responses. Rather, they generate a fault response informing the caller that there are too many results and that the request has to be refined. Thus, our simulation service sends fault

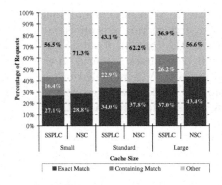 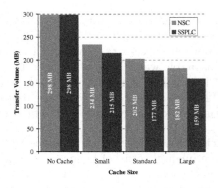

Fig. 9. Match Distribution (Left) and Transfer Volume (Right) Varying Cache Size

messages for results containing more than 2000 fragments. SSPLC caches these fault messages because they are marked cachable in the SOAP header.

We conducted several performance experiments varying different parameters and we present the results in this section. For the experiments in this section, the TTL of responses was set to 30 minutes, if not explicitly stated differently. The maximum size for responses to be cached was set to about 1000 fragments (1.2 MB). Larger responses were fetched from the remote Web service and forwarded to the client without caching. We conducted the experiments using three different cache sizes: small (10% of the data volume of the unique-trace[3]), standard (20%), and large (30%). The cache was warmed up by running every trace twice and measuring the second one, although there are only minor differences between the two runs.

Experimental Results. Due to space restrictions, we only present the core results of benchmark scenario 1. Detailed experimental results are presented in the extended version of this paper [10].

The main goal of the SSPLC is to improve scalability of Web services. Figure 9 shows[4] that already the smallest semantic cache is able to answer 43.5% (exact matches + containing matches) of all requests using data stored in the cache, reducing processing demands on the central servers significantly. A traditional (non-semantic) cache (NSC) achieves much smaller hit rates (28.8%). The bigger the caches are, the better the hit rates become even though the increase rate is not linear with the cache size increment. This is due to the fact that already the standard cache size is large enough to cache most of the hot spot responses. The only advantage of a larger cache is that it is able to additionally store some of the less frequently requested responses. SSPLC benefits more from a larger cache than NSC because SSPLC can exploit the semantics of the requests.

---

[3] The term *unique-trace* refers to a trace where all duplicates are removed.

[4] Please note that the sum of exact matches, containing matches, and other matches is not always exactly 100% due to rounding errors.

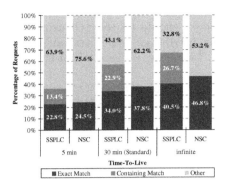

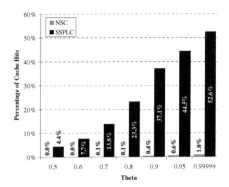

Fig. 10. Match Distribution Varying TTL   **Fig. 11.** Cache Hits Varying Theta

Figure 9 demonstrates the reduction of bandwidth consumption. Running the trace without cache results in the transfer of 298 MB across the network. The smallest semantic cache reduces the transfer volume by approximately 28%, the standard semantic cache by approximately 41%. The large semantic cache reduces the transfer volume even more, but the difference is not linear with the cache size increment due again to the reasons above. The increased hit rate of SSPLC does not 1:1 translate into equally large bandwidth savings in this scenario. For example, the hit rate of SSPLC is about 19% higher compared to NSC using the standard cache size. This hit rate increment translates into about 14% bandwidth savings. The correlation between hit rate increment and bandwidth savings depends on the size of the cached semantic regions and the traces. Nevertheless, the transfer volume of NSC is on average more than 12% larger than that of SSPLC.

Figure 10 shows results for varying time-to-live periods. Of course, the longer the TTL period is, the more effective the caches are. Depending on the TTL, SSPLC performs about 43% to 50% better than NSC.

5.2 Benchmark Scenario 2 (TPC-W 2)

The Transaction Processing Performance Council published a first draft of TPC-W Version 2 (TPC-W 2) for public review. This new version of TPC-W is aiming at Web services. Thus, we decided to conduct some additional performance experiments based on TPC-W 2. Due to incomplete specifications and time constraints, we did not implement the full benchmark. Rather, we chose the "product detail Web service interaction" of TPC-W 2 to conduct our experiments. The data was generated conforming to the rules of TPC-W Version 2, i.e., 100000 books were generated and stored in the DBMS. We configured our remote business emulator (RBE) to run 8 emulated businesses (EB) concurrently. The TTL was set to 5 minutes[5] and a total of 3000 requests were sent to the SSPLC. The cache was able to store about 2500 books. Every request asked

---

[5] Every benchmark run lasted for about 20 minutes.

for detailed information about a randomly chosen number (1 to 10) of books. According to the TPC-W 2 specifications, the books should be selected using a given non-uniform random distribution, but this distribution generates values which are distributed too uniformly for any cache. Therefore, we used a Zipf-like distribution to select the books.

If a client requests product details for, e.g., book 2 and book 8, SSPLC translates the request to the predicate "book $= 2 \vee$ book $= 8$". Thus, SSPLC splits up the request into two CPs, as described above, and generates a request for every single book if not available in the cache. For this reason, there are only exact matches and disjoint matches in this scenario. If not all books of a request are available in the cache, the SSPLC rates the request as exact match and disjoint match according to the ratio of books available in the cache to books not available in the cache. For example, if a client requests details about eight books and six books are available in the cache, the request is rated as 0.75 exact match and 0.25 disjoint match.

Figure 11 shows the exact matches for the benchmark varying theta of the Zipf-like distribution. A non-semantic cache (NSC) is virtually useless in this scenario because the cache hits are less than 1%, even if $\theta = 0.99999$. This is because NSC can only answer requests from the cache if two requests are exactly the same, i.e., the number of product details requested must be the same, the books must be the same, and the order of the books must be the same. SSPLC works very well for sufficient large θ, even though the cache size is small (about 5% of the data volume available at the origin server) and the TTL is short. For a realistic θ, i.e., greater or equal to 0.8, the SSPLC is able to answer more than 23% of the requests.

6   Related Work

Caching in the context of Web services has been addressed, e.g., by the usage scenarios S032 and S037 of the World Wide Web Consortium [13]. The proposed approaches are either described very abstractly, or are limited to a more or less straightforward store-and-resend of SOAP responses. Our approach differs in that it takes advantage of the fact that query-style requests can be cached more efficiently using semantic caching. Thus, this paper proposes an alternative solution which is more flexible and powerful.

A solution for a similar but simpler problem in the area of Web sources and respectively Web databases, was presented by [8]. They focus on wrapper[6] level caching. Therefore, they are able to take advantage of the semantics of the declarative query language SQL, i.e., they automatically deduce region predicates from SQL queries. In the area of Web services, no such standardized declarative language exists. Due to our declarative language for the annotation of WSDL documents with information about caching-relevant semantics, we are able to apply semantic caching to Web services in, e.g., B2B and B2C scenarios. Additionally, we investigate sorting and generalization issues. Thus, our solution

---

[6] Wrappers are used to extract data from Web sources.

is more comprehensive and more flexible. The basic techniques of both SSPLC and [8] are based on prior work on semantic caching, e.g., [7].

A different usage of caching for Web services is presented in [14]. They use caching techniques for reliable access to Web services from, e.g., PDAs or similar unreliably connected mobile devices. The authors use one representative service to demonstrate the benefits of a Web service cache and expose a number of issues in caching Web services. They do not present a generic solution, but they do conclude that extensions to WSDL are needed to support cache managers. We think that the language presented in this paper constitutes a good base for such extensions.

7   Conclusions and Future Work

We presented the semantic cache SSPLC that is suitable for caching responses from Web services on the SOAP protocol level. We introduced an XML-based declarative language to annotate WSDL documents with information about the semantics of services. We demonstrated the validity of our proposed caching scheme by performing a set of experiments.

We plan to investigate some ideas on how SSPLC can be further improved. The declarative language can be extended to integrate additional semantic knowledge like *fragment inclusion dependencies* [8] to transform as many overlapping or contained matches as possible into exact or containing matches. Furthermore, we intend to improve our caching scheme by taking advantage of richer interfaces of services.

References

1. Yagoub, K., Florescu, D., Issarny, V., Valduriez, P.: Caching Strategies for Data-Intensive Web Sites. In: Proceedings of the International Conference on Very Large Data Bases (VLDB), Cairo, Egypt (2000) 188–199
2. Larson, P., Goldstein, J., Zhou, J.: MTCache: Transparent Mid-Tier Database Caching in SQL Server. In: Proceedings of ICDE, Boston, MA, USA (2004) 177–189
3. Transaction Processing Performance Council: TPC Benchmark W Version 1.8 (2002) http://www.tpc.org/tpcw/spec/tpcw_V1.8.pdf.
4. Transaction Processing Performance Council: TPC Benchmark W Version 2.0r (2003) http://www.tpc.org/tpcw/spec/TPCWV2.pdf.
5. Box, D., et al.: Simple Object Access Protocol (SOAP) 1.1. http://www.w3.org/TR/SOAP11 (2000)
6. Christensen, E., et al.: Web Services Description Language (WSDL) 1.1. http://www.w3.org/TR/2001/NOTE-wsdl-20010315 (2001)
7. Dar, S., Franklin, M.J., Jónsson, B.T., Srivastava, D., Tan, M.: Semantic Data Caching and Replacement. In: Proceedings of VLDB, Mumbai (Bombay), India (1996) 330–341
8. Lee, D., Chu, W.W.: Towards Intelligent Semantic Caching for Web Sources. Journal of Intelligent Information Systems (JIIS) **17** (2001) 23–45

9. Johnson, T., Shasha, D.: 2Q: A Low Overhead High Performance Buffer Management Replacement Algorithm. In: Proceedings of VLDB, Santiago de Chile, Chile (1994) 439–450
10. Seltzsam, S., Holzhauser, R., Kemper, A.: Semantic Caching for Web Services – Extended Version. http://www-db.in.tum.de/research/publications/techreports/SemCachingExtended.pdf (2005)
11. Keidl, M., Seltzsam, S., Kemper, A.: Reliable Web Service Execution and Deployment in Dynamic Environments. In: Proceedings of the International Workshop on Technologies for E-Services (TES). Volume 2819 of Lecture Notes in Computer Science (LNCS)., Berlin, Germany (2003) 104–118
12. Adamic, L., Huberman, B.: Zipf's Law and the Internet. Glottometrics **3** (2002) 143–150
13. He, H., Haas, H., Orchard, D.: Web Services Architecture Usage Scenarios. http://www.w3.org/TR/ws-arch-scenarios (2004)
14. Terry, D.B., Ramasubramanian, V.: Caching XML Web Services for Mobility. ACM Queue **1** (2003) 70–78

ODEGSG Framework, Knowledge-Based Annotation and Design of Grid Services

Carole Goble[1], Asunción Gómez-Pérez[2], Rafael González-Cabero[2], and María S. Pérez-Hernández[3]

[1] Department of Computer Science, University of Manchester,
Oxford Road, Manchester M13 9PL, UK
[2] Ontology Engineering Group, Universidad Politécnica de Madrid,
Campus de Montegancedo s/n, 28660 Boadilla del Monte, Madrid, Spain
[3] DATSI, Facultad de Informática, Campus de Montegancedo s/n,
Universidad Politécnica de Madrid, 28660 Boadilla del Monte, Madrid, Spain
{asun, rgonza, mperez}@fi.upm.es

Abstract. The convergence of the Semantic Web and Grid technologies has resulted in the Semantic Grid. The great effort devoted in by the Semantic Web community to achieve the semantic markup of Web services (what we call Semantic Web Services) has yielded many markup technologies and initiatives, from which the Semantic Grid technology should benefit as, in recent years, it has become Web service-oriented. Keeping this fact in mind, our first premise in this work is to reuse the ODESWS Framework for the Knowledge-based markup of Grid services. Initially ODESWS was developed to enable users to annotate, design, discover and compose Semantic Web Services at the Knowledge Level. But at present, if we want to reuse it for annotating Grid services, we should carry out a detailed study of the characteristics of Web services and Grid services and thus, we will learn where they differ and why. Only when this analysis is performed should we know how to extend our theoretical framework for describing Grid services. Finally, we present the ODESGS Framework, which is the result of having applied the extensions identified to the aforementioned Semantic Web Services description framework.

1 Introduction

The Semantic Grid is the result of the convergence of the Semantic Web and the Grid technologies. Its definition of is created by modifying the Semantic Web definition given in [1]. The Semantic Grid is defined thus as an extension of the current Grid, in which information and services are given well-defined meaning for better enabling computers and people to work in cooperation. The requirements and research challenges of the Semantic Grid are identified in an unimpeachable manner in [2] and updated in [3], of which the most related to the knowledge-based markup are a) process descriptions that allow the (semi)automatic composition of services; b) annotation of all the contents in the system (resources, services, provenance data, etc.), which allows automatic discovery and must be done by means of an agreed interpretation (i.e. ontologies); c) context-aware decision support, or the context of the

B. Benatallah, F. Casati, and P. Traverso (Eds.): ICSOC 2005, LNCS 3826, pp. 341 – 352, 2005.

Grid environment that must be annotated ; and d) the communities that users should be able to form, maintain and disband (this community term correspond with the Grid idea of Virtual Organization (VO) to be analyzed later) .

In addition to these requirements, the Semantic Grid should also be service-oriented, as the Grid is since the emergence of OGSA (Open Grid Service Architecture) [4]. Grid resources are wrapped with services and exposed via a WSDL file (i.e. a set of operations written in a standard XML language). OGSA redefines the concept of VO, a key element for Grid computing. They were considered a group of organizations and/or individuals that share resources in a controlled fashion [5]. Now VOs are considered to be the set of services that these organizations and/or individuals operate on and share [4] (plus some security policies). This idea of service-oriented VO, mixed with agent-oriented and dynamic view, is also described in [3]; in that paper, VOs are considered dynamic agents marketplaces. All these ideas of service orientation have became even more relevant since the appearance of GT4[1] and WSRF [6] which make Grid environments compliant with the most widely accepted Web services standards and technologies (WSDL, SOAP, etc.).

The Semantic Grid may reuse all the emerging technologies related to Semantic Web Services (i.e. IRS [7], OWL-S [8], ODESWS [9], WSMO [10], WSDL-S [11], etc.). These technologies and initiatives should not be considered as off-the-shelf technologies for the Semantic Grid because of the different nature of a Web service and a Grid service, and therefore between a Semantic Web Service (SWS) and a Semantic Grid Service (SGS).

In this paper we present the ODESGS Framework, an ongoing work carried out in the Ontogrid Project[2] (FP6-511513), which is the adaptation of the ODESWS Framework developed in the context of the EU project Esperonto[3] (IST-2001-34372); which was developed for annotating and creating complex SWSs, working at the Knowledge Level [12] thus enabling their discovery and (semi)automatic composition. As we have mentioned, we will start this paper enumerating the differences between SWS and SGS. Then, we will present the ODESGS Framework, which contains all the extensions that we have identified as necessary. This description of the ODESGS Framework comprises an enumeration of its design elements and a detailed description of a stack of ontologies used to describe SGSs. This stack will be called the ODESGS Ontology.

2 From SWSs to SGSs: Minding the Gap

As we have stated, one of the main points for the convergence of the Semantic Web and the Semantic Grid may lie in their service-oriented view. Before reusing the SWSs technology in the Grid, we should analyze the different nature of a Grid service (GS) and a Web service (WS). This analysis will help to clarify the terminology used.

A Web Service is an interface that describes a collection of operations that are network-accessible through standardized Web protocols whose features are described using a standard XML-based language [13][14]. Although there are other ways of

---

[1] http://www.globus.org/toolkit/
[2] http://www.ontogrid.net
[3] http://www.esperonto.net/

defining a WS, in this paper we adopt the aforementioned definition because it is the one that best captures the interface nature of what a WS is (and where its benefits come from). Other definitions consider WSs as modules or components, but these definitions break the low coupling principle that motivated the creation of WSs. In short, "It's not the components, it's the interfaces" [15].

SWSs, in the context of the Semantic Web, are the markup of WSs that will make them computer-interpretable, use-apparent and agent-ready [16]. This definition raises a simple but important question. Should SWSs be constrained with all the characteristics and limitations that the WS definition imposes (i.e. stateless interfaces, XML compliant, etc.)? Depending on our answer to this question we will distinguish between Semantic (Web Services) or (Semantic Web) Services. More precisely:

- A *Semantic (Web Service)* (S(WS)) retains all the characteristics of a WS, adding just semantic annotations to its domain, its inputs and outputs, and describing its functional properties (precondition, postconditions, etc.). However, It says nothing about the internal structure of the service, its state, etc. (as it remains   being an interface). It is just a WSDL file plus some semantics (a clear example of this is WSDL-S [11]). S(WS)s have the great advantage of being upgraded easily from current technology to a semantically enhanced one.

- A *(Semantic Web) Service* ((SW)S) it is not constrained by the nature of a WS, as it can be a WS, an agent or anything that provides a service-oriented functionality for the Semantic Web. The description of a (SW)S goes far beyond the idea of an interface since we may find internal reasoning process descriptions, explicit lifecycle, state handling, and many other elements. Therefore, they can be considered a superset of S(WS)s.

Current SWSs initiatives are closer to the idea of (SW)Ss, because most of them describe, at least, the internal structure of complex SWSs (thus, they fall outside the semantic description of a simple net-work accessible interface).

Once we have briefly defined WSs and SWSs, let us see what GSs are. As we stated in the introduction, the service-oriented view of the Grid appeared in OGSA [4], where a service is defined as a network-enabled entity that provides some capability. GSs serve to achieve the virtualization (i.e. encapsulation independent of the implementation of physical resources such computational resources, storage resources, networks, programs, data-bases, etc.) of the shared resources.

Thus, by analogy with the aforementioned definition of SWS [16], a SGS is the markup of a GS that makes it computer-interpretable, user-apparent and agent-ready. Note that due to the more generic definition of what a GS is, we are less constrained in the markup of a GS than in the markup of a WS (remember the S(WS) and (SW)S differentiation that we stated above). A GS is not defined as an interface at all, which makes a big difference. However, and for the sake of completeness, we will also introduce a differentiation between Semantic (Grid Services) and (Semantic Grid) Services. Note that this differentiation is made by considering other terms than the S(SW)/(SW)S one.

Thus, we propose the following definitions:

- A *Semantic (Grid Service)* is just a "conventional" GS annotated to achieve its design, discovery, invocation and composition in a (semi)automatic way. In other words, a knowledge-aware GS.

- A *(Semantic Grid) Service* is a grid compliant knowledge service, a GS situated in the Knowledge Layer [3] that provides any kind of information, which is understood as knowledge that can be applied to achieve a goal, to solve a problem or to enact a decision. Possible examples could be a service that provides ontologies, a SGSs discovery service, a reasoner, etc.

From these definitions and after analyzing the nature of WSs SWSs, GSs and SGSs we have identified the following key features of a SGS not described by a SWS:

- *VO.* This is the first and, perhaps, the most important concept to remember. Despite trendy words like services and virtualization, Grid is about sharing resources under a certain set of rules. We should provide a formal and explicit description of a) the institution that is created by the sum of these services; b) the rules that govern the interaction between the entities involved; and c) the entities themselves (i.e. providers, consumers, and all the other roles that may coexist in a VO). The concept of VO does not exist in the SWSs field; SWSs are considered as isolated elements.

- *Non-functional Properties.* Non-functional properties are especially important in Grid environments. This is because a) discovery and composition is usually performed manually and depend on them; and b) many issues such as trust, quality of service and workload distribution are dependant on non-functional properties, and have much more importance in the Grid environment than in the Web environment. SWSs focus mainly on functional properties currently. Both types of information (functional and non-functional) should be handled (and therefore annotated).

- *Provenance.* Provenance information gives the origin and metadata information of a concrete enactment of a GS. With this information we are able to interpret the enactment results. Provenance seems to be very important in Grid environments, since Grid applications often deal with experiments where knowing which data and services are used to generate the results is very important.

- *Complex Interactions.* Interactions for SWSs tend to composed by the pair invoker/invoked-service (a refurbished XML version of the classic client/server interaction). In a Grid environment we should permit more complex interactions, i.e., defining more complex message exchanges and defining the different roles of the participants. These interactions plus the context of the enactment of the services can also be seen as service contracts [3].

- *Resources.* Although GSs hide resources, they should be also annotated and considered first-class citizens in a SGS description. Additionally, the handling of resources plus the nature of Grid environments clarify the definition of the real world, which is defined as the set of Grid resources that a SGS handles. In SWSs descriptions, the concept of the real world and the concept of the domain model (the abstract and formal representation of the world) are often confusing and confused.

- *Transient GS Instances.* This is one of the trickiest differences between SWSs and SGSs. The discovery, creation, and invocation of transient SGSs instances are a must. The possibility of specifying a concrete instance of a SWS, or even an scheduled invocation of one of its operations is not contemplated by current SWSs orchestrations and descriptions. SWSs work at a "class of services" level while SGSs should allow working at an "instance of service" level instead.

3 The ODESGS Framework

ODESGS Framework is a theoretical framework for annotating, discovering and composing SGSs in a (semi)automatic way. Its main assumptions are: the use of Problem-Solving Methods (PSMs) and ontologies for describing GSs in a formal and explicit way; thus the design and implementation phases of a SGS are clearly separated; VOs will be defined as the sum of SGSs plus some additional information about the hierarchy of roles of each SGS inside the VO; and some security and provenance related issues.

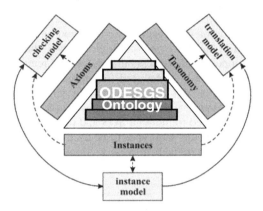

Fig. 1. ODESGS Framework design elements

This framework (see Figure 1) should provide a) service and stateful resource ontologies, rich enough to express the semantics required for service discovery and composition in a Grid environment; b) a set of rules to check whether the proposed design (for complex SGSs and VOs) is correct; and c) a way to translate from this design into a concrete implementation once the SGS has been designed. According to all these requirements, the following elements have been identified:

- **ODESGS Ontology.** To describe the features of VOs, SGSs, Grid resources, etc. a set of ontologies will be used. Ontologies are useful to represent their features in a formal and explicit way, which we will use in order to reason about them. This set of ontologies will be described in detail later.
- **Instance Model.** To design SGSs or VOs means to instantiate each of the ontologies of the stack and its relations. Each instance constitutes a model that specifies a SGS and VO.
- **Checking Model.** Once the instance model has been created, it is necessary to guarantee that such model does not present inconsistencies. Design rules will be needed to check this, particularly when ontology instances have been created automatically (as in the case of (semi) automatic composition). A set of design rules will be used to check both the SGSs annotated and designed by the user, and the different VOs created by aggregating these SGSs.
- **Translation Model.** Although SGSs and VOs are modelled in a high level of abstraction, they must be specified in different representational languages to enable

programs and external agents to access their capabilities. Therefore, once the instance that describes the SGS is created and checked, it should be automatically translated into any of the existing SGS or Grid service representational language.

4   ODESGS Ontology

Our aim is to come up with a service and data ontology, rich enough to express the semantics required for VOs formalization and SGSs discovery and composition. This means that VOs and service features should be explicitly and formally described. For this task, the use of ontologies seems to be the most appropriate solution. We propose a stack of ontologies that will complement each other in annotating all the features of a SGS. The stack is composed of the following ontologies a) one that describes VOs; b) another that describes the upper-level concepts that define the features of a SGS; c) a third ontology that describes the PSM to be used for representing both the internal structure and functional features of a SGS and the domain in which the service will be used (and, consequently, the domain of the VO); d) an ontology that defines the knowledge representation entities used to model a SGS and the domain ontology; and, finally, e) an ontology that describes the data types to be used in the domain ontology. Each of these ontologies is explained in the following sections.

4.1   SGS Ontology

The SGS ontology presumes that a SGS is decomposed in a set of operations. Each of these operations will be related to its corresponding Choreography, Model and Profile. Let us see each of these elements in detail and how they are related to elements of the PSM Description Ontology (which appears in Figure 2 and is fully explained below):

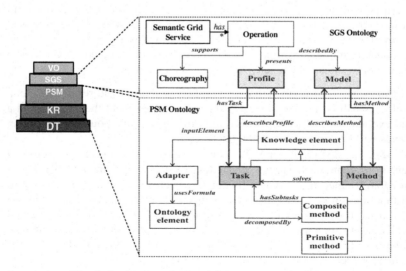

Fig. 2. Stack of ontologies main concepts and relations

- **Profile.** The profile stores both functional and non-functional properties of the SGS operation. We have identified a set of useful non-functional properties such as authors, description, accuracy, quality of service, performance, robustness, trust, etc. For describing the functional properties, the profile concept establishes relationships (*hasTask*) with the Task concept of the PSM ontology.

- **Model.** The Model concept defines a relationship (*hasMethod*) with the concept Method of the PSM Ontology. This means that a service operation will be described by a method, which solves or decomposes the task associated with the profile of the service operation. Moreover, the consistency in the relationships among the concepts of Task, Method, and SGS Operation are guaranteed; if a SGS operation is functionally described by a task, and executed by a method, there must be a relationship between this task and this method, being this method one of the set of methods that can solve this task.

- **Choreography.** The choreography of the operation describes the interaction that should be made to invoke its addressed operation in a formal way. Choreography describes both the messages inter-changed and the roles of those sending and receiving those messages. We will use those formalisms to those presented in [17] to formalize Web services choreographies and their concept of module replaceability, but we will extend it in some ways: a) we will use π-calculus [18] instead of CSS [19] (due to the changing and dynamic nature of the Grid); b) we will add semantic annotation to the messages exchanged, using the domain ontologies; and c) we will map the different actors appearing in the choreography with the roles that we have defined in the VO Roles Model (we will define them later).

4.2 PSM Ontology

Our approach for describing SGSs is based on the Problem-Solving Method paradigm. To decouple the functional features of a service from its internal specification, we propose to apply PSMs [20][21] when modelling SGSs (following the same approach that we did for describing SWSs in ODESWS [9]. A PSM is defined as a domain-independent and knowledge-level specification of the problem solving behaviour that can be used to solve a class of problems [21]. Our ontology for the description of PSM is based on the Unified Problem-solving Method Language (UPML) [23]. The UPML language was developed in the context of the IBROW project [23] with the aim of enabling the (semi) automatic reuse and composition of PSMs distributed throughout the Web. This objective seems to be similar to that of composing services; thus, it can be considered that the IBROW project highlights the close relation between PSMs and SWSs [24] (and SGSs by analogy since OGSA apparition).

- **Task.** It describes an abstract operation of independent domain to be solved, specifying the input/output parameters and the task competence; This task competence is composed of 1) preconditions and postconditions, which are logical expressions about the abstract representation of the domain (how this domain should be before and after the execution of the operation, respectively); and 2) assumptions and effects, which are logical expressions about the state of the real world (how the world should be for this operation to be applicable and how will be after the execution of the operation, respectively), being the real world the set of available Grid resources. Note that this task description is independent of the method used for solving the task and that the PSM paradigm distinguishes between what we want to solve and how we are going to solve it.

- **Method.** It details the abstract reasoning process which is domain independent to achieve a task, describing both the decomposition of the general tasks into sub-tasks and the coordination of those sub-tasks to reach the required result. Note that we based our PSMs descriptions on UPML, and it does not define nor impose a language for describing the reasoning processes carried out by the methods. We propose to add a minimal set of programming primitives to describe the operational description of a composite method, a combination of which allows us to derive several basic workflow-like patterns [25]. The formalism that we will use beneath this workflow representation will be Kripke Structures and their translation to temporal logic (see [26] for a complete reference).
- **Adapter.** It specifies mappings among the knowledge components of a PSM, adapting a task to a method and refining tasks and methods to generate more specific components [27]. Therefore, adapters are used to achieve the reusability, since they bridge the gap between all the elements of a PSM.
- **Domain Model.** Domain Model introduces domain knowledge, and by means of adapters it is attached to the methods and tasks in order to represent a concrete description of an operation in a concrete domain (task and methods are domain independent, as defined before).

4.3 VO Ontology

VOs were originally defined in [5] as a set individuals/institutions defined by a set of resource sharing rules (these sharing rules specify what is shared, who is allowed to share, and the conditions under which sharing occurs). When OGSA appeared, VOs became defined by the services that they operate on and share and this was due to the wrapping of resources by means of Grid services. So, our VOs descriptions will initially be a set of SGSs descriptions. But there are still open issues that an additional formalism should solve. One of these challenges appearing in [28] is to make automatic decisions about which services could be in a VO and what should be their roles these services should have in the VO. We will try to solve this challenge by formalizing what VOs are. One advantage of formalizing VOs is the possibility of discovering VOs; we may think of several VOs and a user wanting to know which VO fits his/her expectations better. We will decompose a VO in:

- **Metadata Properties.** Additional non-functional information about the VO (security and trust information, geographical issues, date of creation, involved "real world" institutions, etc.).
- **Roles Model.** We will define the roles of SGSs in the VO by means of role taxonomies and a set of restrictions for each role.
  - Each VO will have a set of role taxonomies linked by subsumption relationships. This tree-shaped structure (or structures) contains the possible roles of the services (or external agents) that may interact or belong to the VO.
  - A set of different restrictions for belonging to a role will be defined for each of them. These restrictions will cover different aspects of what SGSs are in our definition. We will distinguish between: *non-functional restrictions*, which

constraint SGSs non-functional properties; *competence restrictions*, i.e., functional properties that a role membership imposes; *choreography restrictions*, (a role may impose certain message interchange compliance to the SGS just by defining an abstract choreography and a type of relationship (bisimulation, strong bisimulation, weak simulation, etc.) that the choreography of the service should have (see [18] for a definition of them); and *method restrictions* (we may impose certain restrictions to the orchestration/dataflow of a complex SGS).

With all these roles and restrictions, we may be able to a) know if a SGS can be added to a certain VO; b) know, in case that a service may belong to a certain VO, which of the different roles the SGS may play inside the VO; and c) use these roles to annotate the actors that appear in each SGS choreography, relating thus the interaction of a concrete service with the other SGSs that compose the VO.

- *Provenance Model.* We will initially follow the ideas formulated in [my]Grid Project[4] (for a detailed explanation we remit the reader to [29]). Provenance information provides the origin as well as and metadata information of a concrete enactment of a Grid service so as to be able to interpret the results.

4.4   KR Ontology and DT Ontology

The Knowledge Representation (KR) Ontology describes the primitives of the KR model, which contains descriptions about the knowledge and data used by the SGS. We have selected the WebODE knowledge model [30] as KR ontology. The KR Ontology is constructed on top of an ontology that describes the types of the concepts and attributes. This ontology will be based on the XML Schema Datatypes (XSD).

5   A Simple Example

Due to the lack of space we have chosen a very simple example to illustrate how a SGS description is defined, and how it is seamlessly included in the context of a semantically enhanced VO.

Let us suppose that we have a Grid portal that offers some functionality in some given domain. Before accessing any of the services that belong to the portal, the client (user, service, agent, whatever) should provide its identification and some kind of key that guarantees its identity. Note that we suppose that this must be done always before the invocation of any operation of the offered services in the portal.

Needless to say, the first step is the creation of all the ontologies that will be used for the definition of all the elements and models of the VO and all the SGSs that may fit in it. We suppose that in these ontologies, at least, concepts such us *Key, Credential, Identification* are defined, as top level concepts. We also assume that they are also refined, in order to achieve finer grained descriptions of these concepts.

Our very simple VO will comprise the set of GSs that are invoked from outside the portal to obtain some functionality, and some services that are used for authenticating and finding the privileges of the invokers. Therefore, we will define a very simple Roles Model, in which we define two roles, *Authentication Services* and

---

[4] http://www.mygrid.org.uk/

Offered Services. How are we going to characterize each of them? We may define them by setting restrictions on their operations and in their choreographies. An *Authentication Service* will be defined as a service that should have at least an *authenticate* operation, and this operation should receive, in its invocation process, first an instance of the *Identification* concept and then an instance of the *Key* concept, giving as a result a *Credential* instance. An *Offered Service* in our VO could be any service that works in its domain. We just impose that the first action performed by each of its operations Choreography is to invoke the *authenticate* operation of an *Authentication Service* belonging to the VO.

Once we have defined this simple VO (we left out the Provenance Model and all the Metadata information for the sake of simplicity), we are going to show how to describe two SGSs that belong to the VO. We already know, thanks to the aforementioned Role Model constraints, that an *Authentication Service* should have at least one *authenticate* operation. In this example we will show how to describe this *authenticate* operation of two services. One of them is a simple service called *SimpleSignIn,* which *authenticate* operation receives a user name and its password (both as a string of characters). The other is *SequreSignIn (*a complex SGS that invokes other SGSs), whose *authenticate* operation receives more complete identification information, and an X.509 digital certificate as its key.

In both services operations, the inputs are instances of concepts subsumed by the concepts *Identification* and *Key* and the output in both cases is a credential, so both operations can be described using the same abstract high level task, that we will call *Authenticate,* even thought their methods may be completely different.

Once we have defined the *Authenticate* task, we have described what the *authenticate* operation does. But how does the *Authenticate* task achieve its results? We define that by means of methods. We build two methods, an atomic method called *SimpleAuthenticationProcess*, and a complex method called *ComplexAuthentication Process*. Atomic method means that it does not decompose the task into subtasks, as the complex method does. Because of that, the complex method should define a) what are the subtasks in which *ComplexAuthenticationProcess* decompose the *Authenticate* task; b) how they interchange data between them, i.e. the dataflow; and c) how they are orchestrated, i.e. the controlflow. Figure 3 shows how the *ComplexAuthenticationProcess* is defined, by means of a dataflow diagram and a workflow.

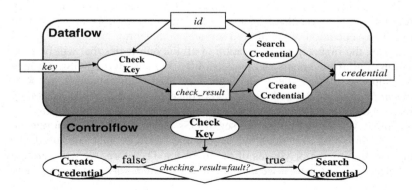

Fig. 3. Dataflow and Controlflow of the *ComplexAuthenticationProcess* method

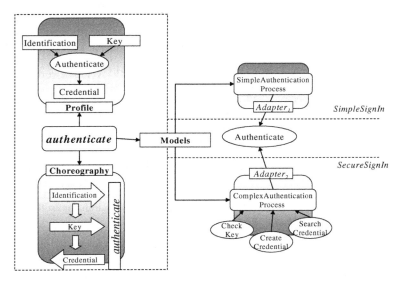

Fig. 4. The different elements that describe the *authenticate* operation

These methods will be glued to the *Authenticate* task by means of adapters. Adapters will also be used to glue the tasks and methods to the domain knowledge.

To sum up, the semantic description of the model of the *authenticate* operation of the *SimpleSignIn* GS will be the *Authenticate* task, the *SimpleAuthenticationProcess* method and all the assumptions and mappings that *Adapter₁* may contain. The semantic description of the model of the *SequreSignIn authenticate* operation will be also the *Authenticate* task, the *ComplexAuthenticationProcess* method and all the assumptions and mappings that *Adapter₂* may state.

Figure 4 shows a simplified summary of how both *autenthicate* operations are described, defining their Choreography, Profile (that we have supposed to be equal) and respective Models.

Acknowledgements

This work has been partially financed by the Ontogrid Project (FP6-511513) and by a grant provided by the Comunidad Autónoma de Madrid (Autonomous Community of Madrid).

References

1. Hendler, J. 2001. Agents and the Semantic Web. IEEE Intelligent Systems, 16(2):30–37.
2. De Roure D., Jennings N. R., and Shadbolt N. R.,(2001) Research Agenda for the Semantic Grid: A Future e-Science Infrastructure, NeSC, Edinburgh, UK UKeS-2002-02.
3. De Roure, D., Jennings, N. R. and Shadbolt, N. R. (2005) The Semantic Grid: Past, Present and Future. Procedings of the IEEE.
4. Foster I., C. Kesselman, J. N., and Tuecke S., (2002) Grid Services for Distributed System Integration Computer, vol. 35.

5. Foster I., Kesselman C., and Tuecke S. (2001) The anatomy of the Grid: Enabling scalable virtual organi-zations. Lecture Notes in Computer Science 2150
6. Czajkowski K., Ferguson D.F., Foster I., Frey J., Graham S., Sedukhin I., Snelling D., Tuecke S., Vam-benepe W., (2003) The WS-Resource Framework
7. Motta, E., Domingue, J., Cabral, L., Gaspari, M.:(2003) IRS-II: A Framework and Infrastructure for Semantic Web Services. ISWC 2003. LNCS Vol. 2870. Springer-Verlag
8. OWL Services Coalition (2004), OWL-S 1.1 Release: Semantic Markup for Web Services", Available: http://www.daml.org/services/owl-s/1.0/owl-s.pdf
9. Gómez-Pérez, A., González-Cabero, R., and Lama, M. (2004), A Framework for Design and Composing Semantic Web Services", IEEE Intelligent Systems, vol. 16, pp. 24–32
10. WSMO Working Group, (2004) http://www.wsmo.org/2004/d2/v1.0/
11. Akkiraju, R., Farrell, J. Miller J. Nagarajan M.(2005) WSDL-S Technical NoteVersion 1.0 Web Service Semantics
12. Newell, A.(1982) The knowledge level Artificial Intelligence., vol. 18, pp. 87--127.
13. Kreger, H. (2001) Web Services Conceptual Architec-ture. http://www.ibm.com/software/solutions/webservices/pdf/WSCA.pdf
14. Curbera, F.; Nagy, W.A.; and Weerawana, S. (2001). Web Service: Why and How?. In Proceedings of the OOPSLA-2001 Workshop on Object-Oriented Ser-vices. Tampa, Florida.
15. Kayne D. (2003) Loosely Coupled, The Missing Pieces of Web Services Rds Associates Inc
16. McIlraith, S.; Son, T.C. and Zeng, H. (2001) Semantic Web Services. IEEE Intelligent Systems, 16(2):46–53.
17. Brogi A.,Canal C.,Pimentel E.,and Vallecillo A..(2004) Formalizing WS choreographies. In Proc. of First International Workshop on Web Services and Formal Methods
18. Milner R., (1999) Communicating and Mobile Systems: the Pi-Calculus Cambridge University Press ISBN: 0521658691
19. Milner, R., Communication and Concurrency (1989) Prentice Hall. ISBN: 0131149849
20. Benjamins, V.R., and Fensel, D. eds. (1998). Special Issue on Problem-Solving Methods. International Journal of Human-Computer Studies, 49(4): 305–313.
21. Motta, E. (1999), Reusable Components for Knowledge Modelling, IOS Press
22. Fensel D., Motta E., van Harmelen F., Benjamins V.R., Crubezy M., Decker S., Gaspari M., Groenboom R., Grosso W., Musen M., Plaza E., Schreiber G., Studer R., and Wielinga B. (2003), The Unified Problem-Solving Method Development Language UPML. Knowledge and Information Systems (KAIS): An International Journal
23. Benjamins, V.R.; Wielinga, B.; Wielemaker, J.; and Fensel, D. (1999). Brokering Problem-Solving Knowledge at the Internet. In Proc. (EKAW-99): Springer-Verlag.
24. Benjamins, V.R. (2003), Web Services Solve Problems, and Problem-Solving Methods Provide Services. IEEE Intelligent Systems, 18(1):76–77.
25. van der Aalst, W.P.; ter Hofstede, A.H.; Kiepuszewski, B.; and Barros, A.P.. Workflow patterns. Distrib-uted and Parallel Databases, 14(2):5–51.
26. Clarke E. M., Grumberg O., Peled D.A., (2000), Model Checking The MIT Press ISBN: 0262032708
27. Fensel, D. (1997), The Tower-of-Adapter Method for Developing and Reusing Problem-Solving Methods. In Proc. of the 7th Knowledge, Modeling and Management Workshop, 97–112: Springer-Verlag.
28. Foster I., Jennings N. R., and Kesselman C (2004) Brain meets brawn: Why grid and agents need each other. In Proc. 3rd Int. Conf. on Autonomous Agents and Multi-Agent Systems, New York, USA
29. Zhao J., Stevens R., Wroe C., Green-wood M. and Goble C. (2004) The Origin and History of in silico Experiments In Proc. of the UK e-Science All Hands Meeting.
30. Arpírez J.C., Corcho O., Fernández-López M., and Gómez-Pérez A (2003).: WebODE in a nutshell. AI Magazine.

Implicit Service Calls
in ActiveXML Through OWL-S

Salima Benbernou, Xiaojun He, and Mohand-Said Hacid

LIRIS,University Claude Bernard Lyon 1,
43 bld du 11 Novembre 1918, 69622 Villeurbanne-France
{sbenbern, x-he04, mshacid}@bat710.univ-lyon1.fr

Abstract. In this paper, we present a framework for implicit service calls in data centric Peer to Peer Active XML language. Active XML is a language devoted to the management of distributed data by embedding Web service calls into XML document. The aim of implicit calls is to allow dynamic data sources discovey through dynamic services discovery and composition. Implicit service calls are based on the use of ontologies for describing the domain and functionality of services to call and an Active XML engine for calls evaluation. The evaluation process deals mainly with dynamic service composition. It consists in matching OWL-S descriptions contained in a query with service descriptions in a peer-to-peer network. Such a network is structured in such a way that peers with similar functionalities are grouped together and each peer makes itself acquainted with matching relationships between its inputs/outputs and those of other peers.

1 Introduction

Web services can be viewed as a programming paradigm that extracts and integrates data from heterogeneous information systems by providing interface standards [7]. They can be described, published, located, invoked, and can even operate with other services to form a new, composed service over a network. When they are used to manage data on the Web, services bring new features : (1) the discovery of Web services based on their functionality leads to the discovery of data sources that contains expected data (i.e., retrieval of dynamic data sources) ; (2) the dynamic composition of Web service allows to retrieve dynamic data; (3) the invocation of web services on demand allows retrieval of dynamic data.

Our work deals with the integration of the two first tasks into Active XML framework which is a language for Web-scale data integration by embedding calls to Web services into XML document [1]. Active XML allows retrieval of dynamic data by including features in XML documents to indicate the location of the service to be called, and to control three elements: the timing of the service invocation , the lifespan of data and the extensional and intensional data exchange. A service call which explicitly makes reference to a service location is called explicit call.

B. Benatallah, F. Casati, and P. Traverso (Eds.): ICSOC 2005, LNCS 3826, pp. 353–365, 2005.
© Springer-Verlag Berlin Heidelberg 2005

In order to enable dynamic data source discovery and dynamic data retrieval (i.e., when an update on data source occurs) by means of dynamic service composition in Active XML, we introduce implicit service calls. By resorting to ontologies, we provide a way to specify service domain and service functionality with Active XML documents.

The rest of the paper is organized as follows: Section 2 presents our motivation through examples. Section 3 briefly describes Active XML. Section 4 presents our framework for incorporating implicit service calls within Active XML documents. Section 5 describes an Active XML architecture with implicit calls. We conclude in Section 6.

2 Motivating Examples

1. **Dynamic data sources discovery.** Let us consider a scenario where we want to make an inventory of books stored in city libraries. We assume that each library has an Active XML peer with a service offering its own book inventory. The implementation and the outputs of the services can be different.

   Now we want to make an inventory of the books stored in all the local libraries of the "GuangZhou" city. By means of explicit service calls, we have to be aware of locations of all relevant services and then invoke an explicit service call. Figure 1 shows an explicit call for book inventory. A drawback with this method is that it is not resilient to changes. If Web services locations change, then we have to manually encode the changes (by modifying service calls).

   With implicit service calls, it is sufficient to be aware of the service domain (*service category*) of the data that we can offer (inputs of service) and of the data that we expect to be returned (outputs of service). In our example, the required service belongs to the *Book* domain, it has no data offered but a list of books is expected as output. Figure 2 shows an implicit call. When it is decided to activate this implicit service call drawn up by using these descriptions, the evaluation of the required service location is launched and terminates after a period of time. Then the user can decide which discovered services he would like to invoke later. Finally, the chosen services are invoked. As a result, we obtain the book inventories of the cities in spite of the dynamism of the data sources. The other motivation of implicit service calls is that we can invoke the relevant service without any knowledge regarding its location.

2. **Dynamic data retrieval.** We want to build up a personal Portuguese-Chinese dictionary. With explicit service call, we need to be aware of the Portuguese-Chinese dictionary service location and invoke the service. In the case a Portuguese-Chinese service does not exist, while two other dictionary services – Portuguese-English and English-Chinese– exist and are locatable, we will not expect an answer to the explicit call. However, with an implicit service call by composing services through input and output descriptions, the call will return an answer.

```
<?xml version="1.0" encoding="UTF-8" ?>
- <Inventory>
    Inventory of the books of city libraries
  - <city name="GuangZhou">
      <sc>zhongshan.com/getBooks()</sc>
      <sc>GuangZhou.com/Books()</sc>
    </city>
</Inventory>
```

```
<?xml version="1.0" encoding="UTF-8" ?>
- <Inventory>
    Inventory of the books of city libraries
  - <city name="GuangZhou">
    - <sc serviceCat="hierachicalProfile.owl#book">
        <output param_data_type="Concepts.owl#booklist" />
      </sc>
    </city>
</Inventory>
```

Fig. 1. Explicit call   **Fig. 2.** Implicit call

Instead of describing how to obtain the data, an implicit service call describes the domain, the inputs and outputs of a required service based on ontologies (here we use OWL-S). In our example, the required services in the *translator* domain have a Portuguese word as input and a Chinese word as output. The evaluation process of the implicit call is launched in the same way as in the previous example.

3   Background

Active XML is a declarative language for distributed information management and an infrastructure to support the language in a peer-to-peer framework. It has two fundamental components: Active XML documents and Active XML service [1, 13, 12].

ActiveXml document. Active XML documents are based on the simple idea of embedding calls to Web services within XML documents. An XML syntax is defined to denote service calls and the elements conforming to this syntax are allowed to appear anywhere in an Active XML document. The presence of these elements makes the document intensional, since these calls represent some data that are not given explicitly, but intensionally, by providing means to acquire the corresponding data when necessary. Active XML documents may also be seen as dynamic since the same service called at different times may give different answers if, for example, the external data source changed. So an active XML document is capable of reflecting world changes, which means that it has different semantics at different times. Figure 3 is an example of an Active XML document that represents databases of books. This document contains some extensional information such as records of the publishers and one record of a book *The Economics of Technology and Content for Digital TV*, and at the same time some intensional information: a service call to get the books published by the *publisher* described by Xpath.

Service call elements in ActiveXML. The Service Call *(sc)* element is defined in the special namespace mentioned above and has a set of attributes and children XML elements defining:

– The Web service to call which is defined by serviceURL, serviceNameSpace, methodName, and useWSDLDefinition.

```
<?xml version="1.0" encoding="UTF-8" ?>
- <Inventory axml:docName="Inventory" xmlns:axml="http://www-
  rocq.inria.fr/verso/AXML">
    <publisher>Addison-Wesley</publisher>
    <publisher>Morgan Kaufmann Publishers</publisher>
  - <books>
    - <book year="1999">
        <title>The Economics of Technology and Content for Digital TV</title>
      - <editor>
          <last>Gerbarg</last>
          <first>Darcy</first>
          <affiliation>CITI</affiliation>
        </editor>
        <publisher>Kluwer Academic Publishers</publisher>
        <price>129.95</price>
      </book>
    - <axml:sc frequency="every 3600000" methodName="GetBooksByPublisher"
      mode="replace" serviceNameSpace="GetBooksByPublisher"
      serviceURL="http://lirispbu.univ-
      lyon1.fr:8080/axml/servlet/AxisServlet">
      - <axml:params>
        - <axml:param name="publisher">
            <axml:xpath>../../publisher/text()</axml:xpath>
          </axml:param>
        </axml:params>
      </axml:sc>
    </books>
  </Inventory>
```

Fig. 3. Active XML document: Inventory of books

- The attributes that provide information on how and when to invoke the service call
- the attributes that influence the behaviors imposed on the results,
- parameters that are accepted by the web service.
- frequency states when the Web service should be instantiated and the validity of the returned results.

Frequency attribute has two modes: (1) *immediate* mode, means that service calls have to be activated as soon as they expire (2) *Lazy* mode, means that a service call will be activated only when its result is useful to the evaluation of a query or when the instantiation of a service Call parameter, defined through an XPath expression is necessary. The presence of lazy calls may cause dependencies among call activations.

According to the expression of parameters, we distinguish two kinds of service calls:(1) *a concrete*service call is one whose parameters do not include XPath expressions (2) *a non-concrete* service call is one whose parameters do include at least one XPath expression.

Service Call Evaluation. The notion of *task* is introduced to track the evaluation of each particular service call. Since the service call is concrete or non concrete, tasks can be concrete or non-concrete. There are two types of evaluation for each invoked mode: (1) service call with immediate mode, where the evaluation is done first by selecting the service calls and processing the selected service call; (2) Service call with lazy mode, where the evaluation is performed by first evaluating the dependencies between calls through a dependency graph i.e. before instantiating XPath parameters, it is necessary to know which call is affected by some updates in a node, and selecting the service that can be activated according to the attribute frequency and dependency graph, and finally processing the selected service call by the algorithm for the non-concrete task.

4   Implicit Calls in ActiveXML Documents

As we have seen previously, the service call defined in Active XML is *explicit* since the service to call is indicated explicitly in the element *axml:sc* by a set of attributes that specify *"the service to call"*. It requires a user to be aware of its exact location. However, we expect to call a relevant service by its description (service query), i.e. implicit service call, instead of its identification (location). In order to realize an implicit service call, we have to know how to integrate the automated service discovery and composition [9] [6] in Active XML. At first glance, we describe how to add the semantic description in the service call and then how to obtain the query based on these descriptions that are used for the

```
<?xml version="1.0" encoding="UTF-8"?>
<Inventory axml:docName="Inventory"
 xmlns:axml="http://www-rocq.inria.fr/verso/AXML">
  <publisher>Addison-Wesley</publisher>
  <publisher>Morgan Kaufmann Publishers</publisher>
  <books>
    <book year="1999">
      <title>The Economics of Technology and Content for Digital TV</title>
      <editor>
        <last>Gerbarg</last><first>Darcy</first>
        <affiliation>CITI</affiliation>
      </editor>
      <publisher>Kluwer Academic Publishers</publisher>
      <price>129.95</price>
    </book>
    <axml:sc serviceCat=
    "http://lirispbu.univ-lyon1.fr/services/hierarchicalProfile.owl#Book"
    frequency="every 3600000" mode="replace" >
        <axml:params>
          <axml:param name="publisher"
           param_type=
           "http://www.daml.org/services/owl-s/1.1/Process.owl#Input"
           param_data_type=
           "http://lirispbu.univ-lyon1.fr/services/Concepts.owl#publisher">
             <axml:xpath> ../../publisher/text()</axml:xpath>
          </axml:param>
          <axml:param name="booklist"
           param_type=
           "http://www.daml.org/services/owl-s/1.1/Process.owl#Output"
           param_data_type=
           "http://lirispbu.univ-lyon1.fr/services/Concepts.owl#booklist">
             <axml:value />
          </axml:param>
        </axml:params>
    </axml:sc>
  </books>
</Inventory>
```

Fig. 4. Active XML document with implicit service call

service discovery and composition. Then, we describe how to answer a query by peer-to-peer composition in a network. Finally, we present how to evaluate implicit service calls.

4.1 Implicit Calls and OWL-S Queries

Figure 4 shows the syntax of an implicit service call which is different from the explicit service call in two respects.

1. The implicit service call does not specify the attributes (*serviceURL*, *serviceNameSpace*, *methodName*, *signature*, and *useWSDLDefinition*) that identify the service to be called, but a new attribute *serviceCat* allows to specify the domain of a service. In our example, the domain of the query is `http://lirispbu.univ-lyon1.fr/services/hierarchicalProfil.owl#Book;`

2. It adds two attributes *param_type* and *param_data_type* to the *param* element. *Param_type* specifies the type (Inputs, Outputs) of a parameter.

   Param_data_type describes the class the values of the parameter through a concept belong to. In our example, we want to call a service that provides a list of books based on the publisher's name. The implicit service call is defined as having two parameters:

   (1) *publisher* being the input of the service whose value is of type `http://lirispbu.univ-lyon1.fr/services/Concepts.owl#publisher;`

   (2) *booklist* being the output of the service whose value is of type `http://lirispbu.univ-lyon1.fr/services/Concepts.owl#booklist.`

4.2 Data Model for Implicit Service Calls

An implicit service call can be represented by a tuple $< p, f, x_1, ..., x_n >$,

- p : the peer that contains the expected service. It has to be evaluated by Active XML. Initially, it has NULL as default value since we do not know which service will be invoked.
- f : the domain of the expected service.
- $x_1, ..., x_n$: the inputs and outputs annotated by concepts of the expected service.

Based on the description of the implicit call, a query represented as an OWL-S profile description [3, 4] is generated for the service discovery and composition. The benefit of this representation is that the service discovery can be accomplished by performing matching between service profiles.

4.3 Peer-to-Peer Composition for Query Answering

Once the query is formalized with OWL-S profile, the discovery and composition tasks can take place.

1. **The choice of the peer-to-peer composition**
   There are two computing types for service discovery and composition: centralized computing [10, 14, 4, 11] and distributed computing [8, 5, 2].

   In the former case, a centralized registry exists; every Web service coming on line advertises its existence and eventually its functionalities and thereafter, every service requester has to contact the registry to discover a particular service or to compose services and gather information about them. Whereas such a structure is effective since it guarantees the discovery of services it has registered, it suffers from problems such as performance bottlenecks, single points of failure, and timely synchronization between the providers and registries (i.e. by updating the changes of service availability and capabilities) [8].

   Alternatively, distributed computing allows the registry to be converted from its centralized nature to a distributed one. In the current Active XML context, each peer in the network provides the other peers with its own data as Web services using XQuery queries raised over the Active XML documents in their repository. Hence, changes are frequent and numerous in the service availability and functionalities in an Active XML peer. Furthermore, we envision that the number of implicit service calls is enormous. As we have seen previously, centralized computing is not suitable for such a situation, while the distributed computing can resolve the availability, reliability and scalability problems in this environment.

2. **A composition network**
   In order to reduce the complexity of the peer-to-peer composition, we suggest to compute it in a network, structured into two dimensions based on the one proposed in [2]. In this network, each peer can provide some web services dealing with particular domains. The peers that provide services for the same domain are grouped together. Each peer is a member of at least one domain. Each domain has both *a master peer* and *a backup peer*. The master peer in each domain maintains two lists: (1) the list of master and backup peers of other domains and (2) the list of all peers within the master peer domain together with the services they provide as well as the input and output parameters they accept and generate respectively. The backup peers have a replica of these lists. Furthermore, each peer maintains its master, backup peer and the predecessor-successor lists for its respective services. A predecessor of a service means the outputs match the inputs of this service, while a successor of a service has the inputs matching the outputs of this service. So, discovery of peers that can participate in the composition through these predecessor-successor relationships, starts from the peer(s) providing the query's outputs, up to those accepting the inputs (provided by the query) required for the composition.

3. ***SearchService*:The peer-to-peer composition structure**
   A peer-to-peer composition service component in ActiveXML system, namely *searchService*, should be defined in order to achieve the service discovery and composition task for implicit service call in the network described previously. Its structure is based on WSPDS [5]. WSPDS (Web services

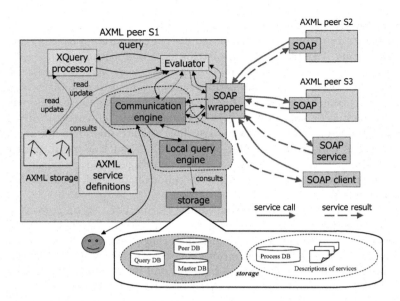

Fig. 5. Architecture for Active XML with implicit service calls

peer-to-peer discovery service) is a distributed discovery service implemented as a cooperative service.

SearchService is composed by two engines: the communication engine and the local query engine. Figure 5 depicts the proposed structure for *search-Service*:

(a) **The communication engine:** It provides the interfaces to the Active XML *evaluator*, to the user and to the other peers. It is responsible for the following tasks:

- Receiving service queries from *evaluator*, answering the queries by local query (through the local query engine) and global query (via the other peers) based on the query phase, merging the different answers in order to allow the user to choose the services (particular or composite) to be invoked, and finally delivering to the *evaluator* the list of locations of chosen services;

- Receiving queries from the other peers in the peer-to-peer network, resolving the queries by local query engine, and sending the response to the caller as well as forwarding to the candidate peers the query whose lifetime is not yet over ($TTL > 0$). The parameter TTL (Time To Live) is used to restrict the dissemination of a query in the network and to control the depth of the composition. For example, we can suppose the value for TTL to be 7, and then the query can be propagated in the network with only a depth of 7.

(b) **The local query engine:** It answers the query received by the communication engine to the local peer. It contains three modules: *ServiceCat*, the *Outputs* and the *Inputs* which are respectively responsible of the service domain, outputs matching , and inputs matching between the OWL-S profile description of the query and those of existing services.

4. **Composition algorithm used by *searchService*** The Algorithm 1 describes the process of discovery and composition in *searchService*. When a peer's *searchService* receives the query from its *evaluator*, it forwards the

---

Algorithm 1 sketch-Composition Algorithm – *searchService*

Require: LQD – Location of Query in OWL-S profile Description
   QP – Query Phase: $toMaster, choiceMaster, choicePeer, choiceComponent$
   TTL – Time To Live
Ensure: $SLLD$ – Service (composite or simple) Location List with matching Degree
 if Query comes from the evaluator, i.e. QP = toMaster **then**
  Transmit this query with choiceMaster phase to its master and communicate the result($SLLD$) returned with the user
 else
  if QP = choiceMaster **then**
   Transmit this query with choicePeer phase to the masters whose services are in the same domain of the query
   Fusion the results($SLLD$) received and range the services in the results($SLLD$) based on their matching degrees
  else
   if QP = choicePeer **then**
    if $\exists query \in QueryDB$ is similar to this query **then**
     Return the results of the similar query as the responds
    else
     Transmit the query with choiceComponent phase to the member peers that provides the services whose outputs match those of the query
     Calculate the matching degree for each composition returned and add the composition returned in $SLLD$
     Save the query with the results($SLLD$) obtained in its Data bases of query
    end if
   else
    Reduce the TTL of the query
    if the inputs of candidate service match those of the query **then**
     Generate a composition that contains the service matched with its matching degree and add it to the local composition list $SLLD$
    else
     if $\exists predecessors$ for the candidate service and the TTL $<> 0$ **then**
      Transmit this query to its predecessors
      Add the candidate service to the compositions in the list $SLLD$ returned by its predecessors
     end if
    end if
    Fusion the local composition list with those returned by their predecessors
   end if
  end if
 end if

---

query to the master in its domain, communicates its master's response with the user and returns the list of compositions selected by a user to the *evaluator*. The master of the initiator peer determines the candidate domains for the query and then relays the request to the master peers of these domains. It orders the compositions by the matching degree and returns the result to the initiator, when the master peers return the result. To respond to the query, the masters then consult their proper *Query DB* to find whether some of the existing queries match this query. If such queries exist, an answer is sent. Otherwise, they search in their *Peer DB* to determine which services in their domain provide all the expected outputs of the query and transmit the query to the hosts of these candidate services. When these host peers return the list of compositions, the master peers compute the matching degree for each composition based on the output matching degree, the input matching degree and the number of its components. Then the master peers update their own *Query DB* and return the list of compositions. To answer the query, the host determines whether the service requires inputs that can be provided by the query inputs. If they match, the host adds the service to the list of compositions. Otherwise, it relays this query to the peer providing the predecessor of this service and waits for an answer from its predecessor peer.

4.4   Evaluation of Implicit Service Calls

We have seen that in the case where an Active XML document contains the service call in a lazy mode, the service call evaluation consists in three steps: (1) evaluating a dependency graph for each non-concrete service call; (2) selecting the service call that can be executed based on the *frequency* attribute and the dependency graphs; and (3) processing the selected service.

However, for the implicit call, the evaluation of the service location is necessary. Then the , in the evaluation process, the third step deals with the evaluation of the evaluation of the service location and processing of the selected service.

Algorithm 2 describes the processing of an *implicit non-concrete* task t. A local process *queryGenerator* that takes the parameters annotated as inputs will produce a query based on OWL-S profile description and will return the address of the query. A local service *searchService* takes as parameters, the location of the OWL-S query, the query phase (QP), the TTL and the service name as inputs to achieve this task. Then, it returns the locations of services fulfilling the query. When the evaluation of the service location is completed, the XPath parameters that are not annotated as "output" of the service call are evaluated. Once the evaluation is done, each p_i has the value of an Active XML forest f_i. Then the implicit non-concrete service call is unrolled into explicit concrete calls. Each service candidate has to be called and takes as parameters each element in the cartesian product of the forest f. The processing of t will end when all these concrete tasks complete their execution. Similarly, the processing of a concrete call can be adapted to accomplish the processing of implicit concrete calls.

Algorithm 2 peer P, implicit non-concrete task $t(d, P_f, f, p_1, p_2, ..., p_n)$

---

if $P_f = NULL$ then
  $LQD \longleftarrow queryGenerator(P_f, f, p_1, p_2, ..., p_n)$ – Location of OWL-S Query Description
  $QP \longleftarrow toMaster$ – Query Phase
  $TTL \longleftarrow 7$
  $servieN \longleftarrow NULL$ – service Name
  $SLL \longleftarrow$ call local service $searchService(LQD, PQ, TTL, serviceN)$. – Services' Location List
else
  $SLL \longleftarrow (P_f, f)$
end if
evaluate the XPath parameters $p_1, p_2, ..., p_m$ – the parameters annotated as *input*.
for all $p_i \in (p_1, p_2, ..., p_m)$ do
  let f_i be the value obtained for x_i (an AXML forest)
end for
for all $(P_{f'_1}, f'_1), ..., (P_{f'_t}, f'_t) \in LSL$ do
  for all $x = x_1, x_2, ..., x_m \in f_1 \times f_2 \times ... \times f_m$ do
    create $t_x(t.root, P_{f'_1}, f'_1, (t.root, P_{f'_2}, f'_2, (...(P_{f'_t}, f'_t, x_1, x_2, ..., x_m)...)))$
    insert t_x in W
  end for
end for
suspend until all t_x finish

---

5   Architecture

In this section, we propose a new architecture for Active XML in order to take into account the implicit service call. Figure 5 depicts the internal architecture of Active XML with implicit service call. We add two new modules to the original structure:

1. ***searchService.*** It contains two components: the communication engine and the local query engine. It is in charge the reception of the query from the *evaluator.*
2. The ***storage.*** It maintains the components describing its own peer. Each peer in the network contains two components in the storage:
   (a) *Description of services*, is a registry of OWL-S descriptions of the services provided by the peer. These service descriptions will be compared to the service query by the local query engine.
   (b) *Process DB* is a database maintaining the predecessor-successor relations dealing with the services provided by the peer. The directed graph with input/output compatibility provided by *Process DB* can reduce the computing complexity of the composition.
   The master peers and backup peers contain three additional components in the storage:
   (a) *Peer DB* contains the peers providing the services of the community presented by the master.

(b) *Master DB* contains the master peers and backup peers of the other domains. This database is necessary for the query propagation between different domains.

(c) *Query DB* maintains the query, together with its solution.

6 Conclusion

In this paper, we have presented the benefits of embedding implicit service calls in Active XML and its realization by the discovery and composition of services. The introduction of implicit service calls in Active XML leads to dynamic data sources discovery by which we can obtain the expected data without knowledge on the data location. To enable implicit service calls, we integrate some techniques in the Active XML framework: (1) OWL-S is used to draw up the query based on the annotation in the implicit service call, (2) A peer-to-peer composition service is defined to be used in a structured network.

References

1. Omar Benjelloun. *Active XML: A data centric perspective on Web services.* PhD thesis, Paris XI university, 2004.
2. Boanerges Aleman-Meza Budak Arpinar, Ruoyan Zhang and Angela Maduko. Ontology-driven web services composition platform. *e-Commerce Technology, 2004. CEC 2004. Proceedings. IEEE International Conference*, July 2004.
3. The OWL Services Coalition. Owl-s: Semantic markup for web services. *http://www.w3.org/Submission/OWL-S/*, November 2004.
4. James Hendler Evren Sirin and Bijian Parsia. Semi-automatic composition of web services using semantic descriptions. *In Web Services: Modeling, Architecture and Infrastructure workshop in ICEIS 2003, Angers, France*, April 2003.
5. Ching-Chien Chen Farnoush Banaei-Kashani and Cyrus Shahabi. Wspds: Web services peer-to-peer discovery service. *International Symposium on Web Services and Applications(ISWS'04), Nevada*, June 2004.
6. Anupriya Ankolekar Katia Sycara, Massimo Paolucci and Naveen Srinivasan. Automated discovery, interaction and composition of semantic web services. *Journal of Web Semantics*, 1(1), September 2003.
7. Stuart Madnick Mark Hansen and Michael Siege. Data integration using web services. *MIT Sloan Working Paper*, May 2002.
8. Takuya Nishimura Massimo Paolucci, Katia Sycara and Naveen Srinivasan. Using daml-s for p2p discovery. *Proceedings of the International Conference on Web Services*, 2003.
9. Terry R. Payne Massimo Paolucci, Takahiro Kawamura and Katia P. Sycara. Semantic matching of web services capabilities. *in Proceedings of the First International Semantic Web Conference*, 2002.
10. Marie desJardins Mithun Sheshagiri and Tim Finin. A planner for composing services described in daml-s. *AAMAS Workshop on Web Services and Agent-Based Engineering*, 2003.
11. Christophe Rey Mohand-Sad Hacid, Alain Leger and Farouk Toumani. Dynamic discovery of e-service. *the proceedings of the 18th French conference on advanced databases. Paris*, 2002.

12. Omar Benjelloun Serge Abiteboul and Tova Milo. The active xml project: an overview. *ftp://ftp.inria.fr/INRIA/Projects/gemo/gemo/GemoReport-331.pdf*, 2004.
13. Omar Benjelloun Serge Abiteboul and Tova Milo. Positive active xml. *In Proc. of ACM PODS*, 2004.
14. Evren Sirin, Bijan Parsia, and James Hendler. Composition-driven filtering and selection of semantic web services. *In AAAI Spring Symposium on Semantic Web Services*, 2004.

Semantic Tuplespace

Liangzhao Zeng[1], Hui Lei[1], and Badrish Chandramouli[2]

[1] IBM T.J. Watson Research Center, Yorktown Heights, NY 10598
{lzeng, hlei}@us.ibm.com
[2] Duke University, Durham, North Carolina 27708-0129
badrish@cs.duke.edu

Abstract. The tuplespace system is a popular cooperative communication paradigm in service-oriented computing. Tuple matching in existing tuplespace systems is either type-based or object-based. It requires that both tuple writers and readers adhere to the same approach of information organization (i.e., same terminologies or class hierarchy). Further, it examines the value of the tuple contents only. As such, these tuplespace systems are inadequate for supporting communication among services in heterogeneous and dynamic environments, because services are forced to adopt the same approach to organizing the information exchanged. In order to overcome these limitations and constraints, we propose a semantic tuplespace system. Our system uses ontologies to understand the semantics of tuple contents, and correlates tuples using relational operators as part of tuple matching. Therefore, by engineering ontologies, our system allows different services to exchange information in their native formats. We argue that a semantic tuplespace system like ours enables flexible and on-demand communication among services.

1 Introduction

The tuplespace paradigm is a simple, easy to use, and efficient approach for supporting cooperative communication among distributed services. Typically, a tuplespace system contains three roles: (i) tuple writers, who write tuples into sharespace, (ii) tuple readers, who read/take tuples that they are interested in, by specifying templates, and (iii) the tuplespace server, who is responsible for managing the sharespace and routing the tuples from writers to readers. The earliest tuplespace systems were *type-based*. A tuple in Linda [4] is a series of typed fields. For example, a tuple can be $t('Sports Car', 400,000)$. Tuple matching is based on a template that consists of a series of typed fields or type definitions. For instance, a template can be $\varphi(\langle 'Sports Car' \rangle, \langle ?float \rangle)$, where typed field (e.g., $\langle 'Sports Car' \rangle$) requires value identical matching (e.g., string that is the same as $'Sports Car'$); while the type definition (e.g., $\langle ?float \rangle$) only concerns the type matching (e.g., any float value). Obviously, such systems have limitations on specifying filtering criteria: either exact value or type matching. For above example, any tuples with type float in the second field can satisfy the template's requirement on second field, regardless of the value of the field.

Consequently, as an improvement to type-based solutions, *object-based* tuplespace systems have been proposed [10]. Instead of exact type matching, these systems

B. Benatallah, F. Casati, and P. Traverso (Eds.): ICSOC 2005, LNCS 3826, pp. 366–381, 2005.

enable *object compatibility* based type matching. Further, these systems allow tuple readers to specify queries on fields, which provides the flexibility of choosing filtering criteria along multiple dimensions. For example, the template in the vehicle dealer example may be refined as $\varphi'(\langle \texttt{SportsCar}\rangle, \langle \texttt{CarInsurance},$ $\texttt{CarInsurance.premium} < 2000\rangle)$. This template indicates that those tuples that first field's type is $\texttt{SportsCar}$ or descendent of $\texttt{SportsCar}$ (e.g., $\texttt{USSportsCar}$, if $\texttt{USSportsCar}$ is a descendent class of $\texttt{SportsCar}$ in the implementation of the class hierarchy) and the second field's type is $\texttt{CarInsurance}$ or descendent of $\texttt{CarInsurance}$ and the $\texttt{premium}$ is less than 2000, will be delivered to the reader.

Considering the adaptability and flexibility requirements from services that operate in dynamic environments, we argue that both type-based and object-based tuplespace systems are not sufficient in two aspects:

- Value-based matching. Currently, in object-based tuplespace systems, the type matching is based on object compatibility, wherein the relationship among the objects is deduced from the implementation of the class hierarchy. Without semantic support to understand the meaning of the field, the matching algorithm assumes that both tuple writers and readers share the same implementation of class hierarchy. Such an assumption is hard to enforce when the relationship of tuple writers and readers is dynamically formed.
- One-to-one matching. Presumably, services read multiple tuples in a transaction as no single tuple can provide all the necessary fields, when they interact with a collection of partner services. However, in current tuplespace systems, correlation of interrelated tuples is not supported, which requires custom implementation by application programmers. The implementation of tuple correlation is often a challenging and involving task. Further, it requires that the application programmers be aware of all the tuples that are provided by partner services in advance at development time. Such a requirement is impractical when a service has a dynamic collection of partners.

In this paper, we introduce a semantic tuplespace system. Our system enables semantic tuple matching, wherein semantic knowledge is maintained in ontologies. This releases the constraints in object-based tuplespace systems that writers, readers and the server must share the same implementation of class hierarchy. Unlike traditional tuplespace systems, tuple correlation in our system is performed by the tuplespace server, which is transparent to tuple readers. Therefore, services in dynamic environments become easier to develop and maintain as tuple semantic transformation and correlation can be provided as part of the tuplespace system. In a nutshell, the salient features and contributions of our system are:

1. Efficient semantic tuple matching. A naive approach to enabling semantic tuple matching is term generation, in which more generic fields (i.e., objects) are generated based on ontologies. For example, from an object of $\texttt{sportsCar}$, the system can generate a more generic object about $\texttt{car}$. Such an approach is clearly very inefficient, since it generates unnecessary redundant tuples. In our framework, instead of adopting term generation approach, the system enables semantic tuple routing by rewriting templates, wherein no redundant tuples need to be generated.

2. Semantic-based, correlation matching. With ontology support, it is possible for the system to conduct tuple correlation based on tuple content semantics using relational operators. For example, two tuples in a sharespace can be correlated to one by the join operator and then delivered to tuple readers. We extend tuple matching in traditional tuplespace systems with two kinds of correlation matchings, namely those based on common fields across tuples and those based on attribute dependence. Correlation matching can automatically search available tuples which can only provide partial information required by a read/take template, and correlate them to one tuple that contains all the fields required by the template.

The remainder of this paper is organized as follows: Section 2 introduces some important concepts and presents the overview of the semantic tuplespace system. Section 3 and 4 discuss two main features of the proposed system. Section 5 illustrates some aspects of the implementation. Finally, Section 6 discusses some related work and Section 7 provides concluding remarks.

2   Preliminaries

In this section, we first introduce some important concepts in ontology, and then present the proposed system architecture of the semantic tuplespace system. Finally, we outline the tuple matching algorithm.

2.1   Ontology

In our system, we adopt an object-oriented approach to the definition of ontology, in which the type is defined in terms of *classes*[1] and an instance of a class is considered as an *object*. In the subsection, we present a formal description of class and object. It should be noted that this ontology formulation can be easily implemented using OWL [11] framework. We will present details on how to use ontology to perform semantic matching and correlation matching in following sections.

Definition 1 (*Class*). A class C is defined as the tuple $C = \langle N, S, P, R, F \rangle$, where

- N is the name of the class;
- S is a set of synonyms for the name of class, $S = \{s_1, s_2, ..., s_n\}$;
- P is a set of properties, $P = \{p_1, p_2, ..., p_n\}$. For $p_i \in P$, p_i is a 2-tuple in form of $\langle T, N_p \rangle$, where T is a basic type such as integer, or a class in an ontology, N_p is the property name.
- R is a set of parent classes, $R = \{C_1, C_2, ..., C_k\}$;
- F is a set of dependence functions for the properties, $F = \{f_1, f_2, ..., f_l\}$. Each function is in form of $f_j(p_1', p_2', ..., p_m')$ and associated with a predicate c, where the output of f_j is a property p_i of class C and p_i' is property from a class other than C and the predicate c is used to correlate p_i'.   □

---

[1] Some notations used in this paper are summarized in Table 1.

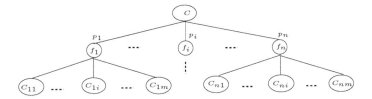

Fig. 1. A Dependence Tree of the Class C

In the definition of class, the *name, synonyms,* and *properties* present the connotation of a class; while *parent classes* and *dependence functions* specify relationships among the classes, i.e., present the denotation of a class. In particular, dependence functions provide information for searching candidate tuples for correlation. A class may have parent classes for which it inherits attributes. For example, class `sportsCar`'s parent class is `Car`, so the class `sportsCar` inherits all the attributes in class `Car`.

Other than inheritance relationships, different classes may have value dependence on their properties. In our framework, dependence functions are used to indicate the value dependence among the different classes' properties. For example, we have three classes `ShippingDuration`, `Arrival` and `Departure`. In `ShippingDuration`, the attribute `duration` has a dependence function `minus(Arrival.timeStamp, Departure.timeStamp)`, where the predicate is `ShippingDuration.shippingID = Arrival.shippingID = Departure.shippingID`.

Based on dependence functions, a dependence tree can be constructed for each class. Assuming that the class C has a set of dependence functions F, a *dependence tree* can be generated as in Figure 1. There are three kinds of nodes in a dependence tree, namely *class node, operator node* and *dependant class node*. It should be noted that the depended class node may also have its own dependence tree (e.g., C_{11}). A class C's *complete dependence set* (denoted as $\mathbb{D}_C$) is defined as a collection of depended classes that can be used to calculate the value of the property. For example, the set $\{C_{11}, C_{12}, ..., C_{1m}\}$ is a complete dependence set of the class C's property p_1.

Once a class is defined, instances of the class can be created as objects (See 2). In the definition, the *ID* is the universal identifier for an object, while V gives values of attributes in the object.

Definition 2 (*Object*). An object o is a 3-tuple$\langle ID, N_c, V \rangle$, o is an instance of a class C, where

- ID is the id of the object;
- N_c is the class name of C;
- $V = \{v_1, v_2, ..., v_n\}$, are values according to the attributes of the class C. For $v_i \in V$, v_i is a 2-tuple in form of $\langle N_p, V_p \rangle$, where N_p is the property name, V_p is the property value. □

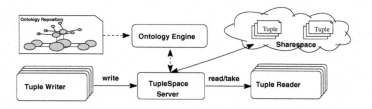

Fig. 2. Semantic Tuplespace System Architecture

Table 1. Notations

Notation	Definition
C	a class
$\mathbb{C}$	a set of classes
p_i	a class property
f_i	a dependency function
$\mathbb{D}_C$	a complete dependence set for class C
o	an object
$t(o_1, o_2, ..., o_n)$	a tuple
$\mathbb{C}_t$	the set consists of all t's field classes
$\mathbb{T}$	a set of tuples
$\mathbb{C}_{\mathbb{T}}$	the set consists of all field classes of tuples in $\mathbb{T}$
$\varphi(t_1, t_2, ..., t_n)$	a read/take template
$\mathbb{C}_\varphi$	the set consists of all the field classes required by template φ
q_i	a query predicate
$t_i = \langle C_i, q_i \rangle$	a formal field in template

2.2 System Architecture

Our semantic tuplespace system (see Figure 2) consists of an *ontology repository*, an *ontology engine*, *tuple writers*, *tuple readers*, *sharespace* and a *tuplespace server*. A tuple in the semantic tuplespace system is denoted as $t(o_1, o_2, ..., o_n)$, where each field in a tuple is an object o_i[2] and the class is C_i. An example of a tuple can be t_s(sportsCarA, carInsuranceB, carFinanceC), which contains three objects.

As in the traditional tuplespace system, the basic operations in semantic tuplespace include *write*, *read* and *take*. For tuple providers, the write operation is used to save tuples into the sharespace. For tuple consumers, the operations can be either read or take. The difference between read and take is that after a take the tuple is removed from the sharespace, while read leaves the tuple object in sharespace.

When performing a read/take operation, a template $\varphi(t_1, t_2, ..., t_n)$ that defines tuple matching conditions is specified . For each t_i in φ, it can be either *formal* or *non-formal* field. A formal field is specified as a pair $\langle C_i, q_i \rangle$, where the C_i specifies the class of the field and the q_i is a query predicate (a boolean expression of attributes in class C_i). A non-formal field is specified as $\langle o_i \rangle$ that indicates expecting an identical

---

[2] In the rest of the paper, we use term *object* and *field* interchangeably.

Table 2. Examples

Entity	Example
template	$\varphi_s(\langle$ Car, Car.price.amount< 5000 $\rangle$,
	$\langle$ carInsuranceB $\rangle$, $\langle$ CarFinance, null $\rangle$)
candidate tuple	$t($ sportsCarA, carInsuranceB, carFinanceC $)$
tuple set	$\mathbb{T}_k=\{t_1, t_2\}$, where
	$t_1($ sportsCarA, sportsCarInsuranceB $)$,
	$t_2($ sportsCarA, carFinanceC $)$
generated template for t_1	$\varphi_1(\langle$ SportsCar, SportsCar.price.amount<5000 $\rangle$,
	$\langle$ carInsuranceB $\rangle$)
generated template for t_2	$\varphi_2(\langle$ SportsCar, SportsCar.price.amount<5000 $\rangle$,
	$\langle$ CarFinance, null $\rangle$)
tuple set	$\mathbb{T}_f=\{t_1, t_2, t_3, t_4\}$, where
	$t_1($ sportsCarA, licenceB $)$, $t_2($ licenceB, carOwnerC $)$,
	$t_3($ carOwnerC, carInsuranceD $)$, $t_4($ sportsCarA, carFinanceE $)$

object as o_i is contained in matched tuples. There are two options in read/take operation: *all* or *any*. Option all returns all the matched tuples, while option any only returns one of the matched tuples. In the rest of the paper, for sake of presentation, we only discuss option all; however, in our design, we support both options.

An example of template can be φ_s (see Table 2). In this example, the first field required by the template is an object of class Car, where the associated query predicate is Car.price.amount<5000. The second field is non-formal: object carInsuranceB, indicating that the tuples need to provide identical information as specified in the object. Actually, the non-formal field $\langle o_i \rangle$ can be converted to a formal field as $\langle C', \bigwedge_{j=0}^n (C'.p_j = o_i.p_j) \rangle$, where object o_i's class is C' that has n properties p_j. As such, in the rest of this paper, we only discuss the case of formal field.

2.3   Tuple Matching in Semantic Tuplespace System

By introducing ontologies into tuplespace system, other than *exact matching*, we extend the tuple matching algorithm with two extra steps: *semantic matching* and *correlation matching*. Therefore, three steps are involved in our matching algorithm:-

- **Step 1. Exact Matching.** The first step is to find exact matches, which returns tuples that have exactly the same field classes as the template;
- **Step 2. Semantic Matching.** The system searches tuples that have field classes which are semantically compatible with the template and delivers tuples if the tuples' contents can satisfy the filtering conditions;
- **Step 3. Correlation Matching.** The system searches a set of tuples and correlates them to one tuple, in order to match all required fields of the template.

It is worth noting that the type-based tuplespace system only performs step 1. The object-based tuplespace systems perform another step of matching that is based on object compatibility, which is different from semantic matching in step 2. In object-based tuplespace system, the object compatibility is deduced from the implementation of class hierarchy. In our semantic tuplespace systems, the relationships among the objects are declaratively defined by ontologies. As such, the steps 2 and 3 are unique to our semantic tuplespace system. In this paper, we assume that both readers and writers use the same ontology for a domain. If a tuple writer and a tuple reader use different ontologies for a domain, then a common ontology can be created for both writer and reader. Detailed discussion on creating a common ontology is outside the scope of the paper. Therefore, by engineering ontologies, our system allows different services to exchange information using their native information format to construct tuples. The cost of engineering ontologies is much less than that of developing object adaptors for object-based tuplespace systmes as ontologies are declaratively defined. Further, ontologies are reusable. Details of semantic and correlation matching are presented in the following sections.

3   Semantic Matching

As an extension of object-based tuplespace system, semantic matching is used to determine whether a tuple in the sharespace satisfies a tuple retrieval request (read/take). The difference between object-based matching and semantic matching comes from the adopted approaches that determine the relation among the objects. As discussed earlier, object-based matching tuple matching is based on object compatibility, where the subclass relation is deduced from the implementation of class hierarchy. This requires all the tuplespace users to adopt the same implementation of class hierarchy. In our semantic matching, we adopt the notion of *semantic compatibility* (see 3), wherein the semantic knowledge of synonyms and subclasses can be declaratively defined in ontologies.

Definition 3 (*Semantic Compatibility*)**.** Class C_i is semantically compatible with class C_j, denoted as $C_i \overset{s}{=} C_j$, if in the ontology, either (i) C_i is the same as C_j (same name or synonym in an ontology) , or (ii) C_i is a superclass of C_j.   □

By adopting the definition of semantic compatibility, we say a class C semantically belongs to a class set $\mathbb{C}$ (denoted as $C \in_s \mathbb{C}$) if $\exists C_i \in \mathbb{C}, C \overset{s}{=} C_i$. Using the notion of semantic compatibility, we define a *candidate tuple* (see 4) as a tuple that contains all the fields that are semantically compatible with the fields required by a read/take operation. In the definition, each of the fields of the tuple needs to be semantically compatible with the corresponding field of the template. For example (see Table 2), with regard to the template φ_s, the tuple t can provide all the fields required in φ_s since the first field sportsCarA "is a" Car (semantic compatibility) and the rest two fields are exactly matched. Therefore, t is a candidate tuple for φ_s.

Definition 4 (*Candidate Tuple*)**.** t is a tuple in tuplespace where $\mathbb{C}_t$ is the set that contains all the field classes in t; φ is the template for read or take operation, where the feild class set is $\mathbb{C}_\varphi$. t is a ***candidate tuple*** for φ iff: $\forall C_i \in \mathbb{C}_\varphi, C_i \in_s \mathbb{C}_t$.   □

It should be noted that a candidate tuple may not be able to satisfy the filtering condition given in templates. Further examination of the contents of the tuple is required, in order to determinate whether the tuple should be delivered to tuple readers.

In our system, when inspecting the contents of tuples, in most cases, the tuplespace server needs to rewrite fields in the template, except when all the field classes in the candidate tuple are exactly the same as those of the template, i.e., $\mathbb{C}_t = \mathbb{C}_\varphi$. Therefore, each $\langle C_i, q_i \rangle$ in φ, assuming the class type of candidate tuple is C' for the corresponding field, should be rewritten as $\langle C', q_i' \rangle$, where q_i' is transformed from q_i by replacing property references of class type C with C'.

4 Correlation Matching

As a further extension of object-based tuple matching, our system also enables correlating multiple tuples for a template. In the following subsections, we first present how to search a collection of tuples that are correlatable and are able to provide all compatible fields for read/take operation. This is followed by details on composing results from a collection of tuples.

4.1 Searching Correlatable Tuple Set for Read/Take Operation

In our framework, multiple tuples in the sharespace can be correlated to one that can provide all the necessary fields required by a template, wherein the correlation can be done by the join operator. Correlation can be either based on common fields and/or attribute dependence functions. In this subsection, we discuss the case of field-based correlation first, and then illustrate the case of attribute dependence function correlation.

Field-Based Correlation. Obviously, multiple tuples can be correlated using the join operator to one if they contain same field. For example, two tuples t_1 and t_2 in $\mathbb{T}_k$ (see Table 2) can be correlated using the join operator as they both have field sportsCarA. Therefore, when the tuplespace server performs the correlation matching, in order to compose tuples that can provide all the fields that are required by the template, it first searches a *key-based correlation tuple set*, i.e., a set of tuples that are correlatable by a key field that is specified by the template and can provide all the fields required by the template. The formal definition of key-based correlation tuple set is as follows.

Definition 5 (*Key-based Correlation Tuple Set* S_{kc}). $\mathbb{T}$ ($\mathbb{T} = \{t_1, t_2, ..., t_n\}$) is a set of tuples in tuplespace, $\mathbb{C}_{t_i}$ is the set that consists of all the field classes in tuple t_i and $\mathbb{C}_\mathbb{T}$ ($\mathbb{C}_\mathbb{T} = \cup_{i=1}^n \mathbb{C}_{t_i}$) is aggregation of all the field classes in $\mathbb{T}$; φ is the template for read/take operation, C_k is the key field's class type and $\mathbb{C}_\varphi$ is the set that consists of all the field classes of φ. $\mathbb{T}$ is a *Key-based Correlation Tuple Set* of φ iff:

1. $\forall C \in \mathbb{C}_\varphi, C \in_s \mathbb{C}_\mathbb{T}$;
2. $\forall \mathbb{C}_{t_i}, \exists C_k' \in \mathbb{C}_{t_i}, C_k \stackrel{s}{=} C_k'$, and $o_1^k = o_2^k = ... = o_n^k$, where o_i^k is the field with class C_k' in t_i;
3. $\forall \mathbb{C}_{t_i}, \exists C, C \in (\mathbb{C}_{t_i} - (\cup_{j=1}^{i-1} \mathbb{C}_{t_j} \bigcup \cup_{j=i+1}^n \mathbb{C}_{t_j}))$ and $C \in_s \mathbb{C}_\varphi$. $\square$

In this definition, three conditions need to be satisfied when considering a set of tuples as a correlation tuple set for a read/take template: (i) Condition (1) indicates for each field class required by the template, there is at least one tuple that contains a compatible field class, which is a necessary condition of the definition. (ii) Condition (2) implies all the field classes are correlatable by the key field. (iii) Condition (3) evinces any tuples in the set contributes at least one unique field. It should be noted that condition (2) and (3) are the sufficient conditions for the definition. Using above example, the aggregation of t_1 and t_2 provides all the required fields in template, which satisfy condition (1), and they can be correlated as they share the field `sportsCarA` that is the descendant for the key field `Car` in template φ_s. Also, t_1 (resp. t_2) provides unique field `carInsuranceB` (resp. `carFinanceC`). Therefore, t_1 and t_2 compose a key-based correlation tuple set for the template.

Actually, by releasing the constraint that correlating is based on key field only, our system enables more generic tuple correlation, wherein tuple correlations can be based on any fields. In such a generic correlation, we adopt the notion of `Correlatable Class` (see 6). In this definition, two field classes are correlatable in a set of tuples if either they appear in the same tuple, or when these two classes do not appear in the same tuple and belong to two tuples t_x and t_y respectively, then either (i) t_x and t_y at least have one field that is identical; or (ii) there are a sequence tuples in the set that are correlatable "step by step" and aiming for correlating t_x and t_y in the end. Actually, if we consider t_x and t_y are `entities` in ER model, then these tuples between t_x and t_y in the sequence are `relationships`: in order to joint two entities without common attributes, a collection of relationships $[t_{x+1}, t_{x+2}, ... t_{y-1}]$ are required. For example, class `SportsCar` and `CarInsurance` are correlatable in $\mathbb{T}_f$ (see Table 2), as class `SportsCar` and `CarInsurance` appear in t_1 and t_3 respectively; and t_2 is considered as a relationship to bridge `SportsCar` and `CarInsurance`.

Definition 6 (*Correlatable Class*). *Class C_i, C_j are correlatable in tuple set $\mathbb{T}$ ($\mathbb{T} = \{t_1, t_2, ..., t_n\}$), iff either*

- *C_i and C_j appear in same tuple (i.e., $\exists t_x \in \mathbb{T}$, both C_i and $C_j \in \mathbb{C}_{t_x}$); or*
- *C_i and C_j do not appear in same tuple (i.e., $\nexists t \in \mathbb{T}$, where C_i and $C_j \in \mathbb{C}_t$), then $\exists t_x, t_y \in \mathbb{T}$, $x \neq y$, $C_i \in \mathbb{C}_{t_x}$, $C_j \in \mathbb{C}_{t_y}$, and either:*
  - *$\exists o_x$ from t_x and $\exists o_y$ from t_y, $o_x = o_y$; or*
  - *there is a correlation tuples sequence $[t_x, t_{x+1}, t_{x+2}, ... t_{y-1}, t_y]$ in $\mathbb{T}$, and for any t_i, t_{i+1} in the sequence, $\exists o_i$ from t_i and $\exists o_{i+1}$ from t_{i+1}, so that $o_i = o_{i+1}$.* □

Definition 7 (*Field-based Correlation Tuple Set S_{fc}*). $\mathbb{T}$ ($\mathbb{T} = \{t_1, t_2, ..., t_n\}$) is a set of tuples in tuplespace, $\mathbb{C}_{t_i}$ is the set that consists of all the field classes in tuple t_i and $\mathbb{C}_{\mathbb{T}}$ ($\mathbb{C}_{\mathbb{T}} = \cup_{i=1}^n \mathbb{C}_{t_i}$) is aggregation of all the field classes in $\mathbb{T}$; φ is the template for read/take operation, and $\mathbb{C}_\varphi$ is the set that consists of all the field classes of φ. $\mathbb{T}$ is a *Field-based Correlation Tuple Set* of φ iff:

1. $\forall C \in \mathbb{C}_\varphi, C \in_s \mathbb{C}_{\mathbb{T}}$;
2. for $\forall C_i', C_j' \in \mathbb{C}_\varphi, i \neq j, \exists C_i, C_j \in \mathbb{C}_{\mathbb{T}}, C_i' \overset{s}{=} C_i, C_j' \overset{s}{=} C_j$, and C_i and C_j are correlatable in $\mathbb{T}$;
3. $\forall t_i \in \mathbb{T}$, at lease one of the following is true:
   - $\exists C \in (\mathbb{C}_{t_i} - (\cup_{j=1}^{i-1} \mathbb{C}_{t_j} \bigcup \cup_{j=i+1}^n \mathbb{C}_{t_j})), C \in_s \mathbb{C}_\varphi$;
   - t_i appears in tuple consequences in condition (2) of this definition. □

Using the notion of correlatable class, we can define the concept of *Field-based Correlation Tuple Set* (see 7). In the definition, there are also three conditions that need to be satisfied when considering a set of tuples as a correlation tuple set for a read/take template: (i)The same as key-based correlation, condition (1) indicates for each field class required by the template. (ii) Different from key-based correlation, instead, Condition (2) implies correlation can be on any fields. (iii) Condition (3) evinces any tuples in the set contributes at least one unique field, either contributes to the required fields by the template, or appearers in tuple sequence for correlation.

Attribute-Dependence Correlation. Other than field-based, multiple tuples can be correlated using dependence functions, in case some required fields can not be provided by any available tuples. Assuming that an absent field's class C_i has a dependence function, the tuplespace server can compute the value for the absent field from the tuples that provide elements in the dependence set. For example, if the class type ShippingDuration is required by the template but not provided by any tuples,

as ShippingDuration's dependence set is {Departure, Arrival}, the system can search tuples that contain Departure or/and Arrival and correlate these tuples and compute the value for ShippingDuration. Again, we first limited the correlation on key field only, wherein *Key-based Attribute-dependence Correlation Tuple Set* can be defined as:

Definition 8 (*Key-based Attribute-dependence Correlation Tuple Set S_{ka}*). $\mathbb{T}$ ($\mathbb{T} = \{t_1, t_2, ..., t_n\}$) is a set of tuples in tuplespace, $\mathbb{C}_{t_i}$ is the set that consists of all the field classes in tuple t_i and $\mathbb{C}_{\mathbb{T}}$ ($\mathbb{C}_{\mathbb{T}} = \cup_{i=1}^{n} \mathbb{C}_{t_i}$) is aggregation of all the field classes in $\mathbb{T}$; φ is the template for read/take operation, the key field's class is C_k and $\mathbb{C}_{\varphi}$ is the set that consists of all the field classes in φ. $\mathbb{T}$ is an **Key-based Attribute-dependence Correlation Tuple Set** of the template φ iff:

1. $\forall C_i \in \mathbb{C}_{\varphi}$, either
   - if $C_i \in_s \mathbb{C}_{\mathbb{T}}$, i.e., $\exists\ C_i' \in \mathbb{C}_{\mathbb{T}}$, $C_i \overset{s}{=} C_i'$; or
   - if $C_i \notin_s \mathbb{C}_{\mathbb{T}}$, then $\mathbb{C}_{\mathbb{T}}$ contains a complete dependence set $\mathbb{D}_{C_i}$ of C_i.
2. $\forall \mathbb{C}_{t_i}$, $\exists C_k' \in \mathbb{C}_{t_i}$, $C_k \overset{s}{=} C_k'$, and $o_1^k = o_2^k = ... = o_n^k$, where o_i^k is the field with class C_k' in t_i;
3. $\forall t_i \in \mathbb{T}$, at lease one of the following is true:
   - $\exists C \in (\mathbb{C}_{t_i} - (\cup_{j=1}^{i-1} \mathbb{C}_{t_j} \bigcup \cup_{j=i+1}^{n} \mathbb{C}_{t_j}))$, $C \in_s \mathbb{C}_{\varphi}$ or $C \in \mathbb{D}_{C_i}$;
   - t_i appears in tuple consequences in condition (2) of this definition.   □

In condition (1) of above definition, unlike field-based correlation tuple set, a field required by the template may not appear in any tuple, however, its properties can be computed using dependence functions (See 2). Like field-based correlation in tuple set, the condition (2) concerns whether tuples can be correlated by the key field. The condition (3) states that each tuple in the set contributes at least one unique attribute. Again, we can release the constraint that correlation is based on key-field only . Therefore, the more generic *Attribute-dependence Correlation Tuple Set* can be defined (see 9). In particular, the condition 2 of the definition indicates that correlation can be done based on any fields.

Definition 9 (*Attribute-dependence Correlation Tuple Set* S_{ac}). $\mathbb{T}$ ($\mathbb{T} = \{t_1, t_2, ..., t_n\}$) *is a set of tuples in tuplespace,* $\mathbb{C}_{t_i}$ *is the set that consists of all the field classes in tuple* t_i *and* $\mathbb{C}_{\mathbb{T}}$ ($\mathbb{C}_{\mathbb{T}} = \cup_{i=1}^{n}\mathbb{C}_{t_i}$) *is aggregation of all the field classes in* $\mathbb{T}$; φ *is the template for read/take operation;* $\mathbb{C}_{\varphi}$ *is the set that consists of all the field classes in* φ. $\mathbb{T}$ *is an **Attribute-dependence Correlation Tuple Set** of the template* φ *iff:*

1. $\forall C_i \in \mathbb{C}_{\varphi}$, *either*
   - *if* $C_i \in_s \mathbb{C}_{\mathbb{T}}$, *i.e.,* $\exists C_i' \in \mathbb{C}_{\mathbb{T}}$, $C_i \overset{s}{=} C_i'$; *or*
   - *if* $C_i \notin_s \mathbb{C}_{\mathbb{T}}$, *then* $\mathbb{C}_{\mathbb{T}}$ *contains a complete dependence set* $\mathbb{D}_{C_i}$ *of* C_i.
2. *Assuming* $\mathbb{C}'$ *is the class set for all the* C_i' *in condition 1 of this definition, also assuming* $\mathbb{D} = \bigcup \mathbb{D}_{C_i}$ *for all* $C_i \notin_s \mathbb{C}_{\mathbb{T}}$, *and* $\mathbb{C} = \mathbb{C}' \bigcup \mathbb{D}$, *then for* $\forall C_i, C_j \in \mathbb{C}$, C_i *and* C_j *are correlatable in* $\mathbb{T}$;
3. $\forall t_i \in \mathbb{T}$, *at lease one of the following is true:*
   - $\exists C \in (\mathbb{C}_{t_i} - (\cup_{j=1}^{i-1}\mathbb{C}_{t_j} \bigcup \cup_{j=i+1}^{n}\mathbb{C}_{t_j}))$, $C \in_s \mathbb{C}_{\varphi}$ *or* $C \in \mathbb{D}_{C_i}$;
   - t_i *appears in tuple consequences in condition (2) of this definition.* □

4.2 Relationship Among Four Kinds of Correlation Tuple Sets

The relationship among the above four kinds of correlation tuples sets is shown in Figure 3. In particular, the relationship can be summarized as:

- $\{S_{kc}\} \subseteq \{S_{fc}\}$
  Proof: Condition (1) in S_{kc} and S_{fc} are same. Further, the tuple set can satisfy condition (2) and (3) of S_{kc} can also satisfy condition (2) and (3) in S_{fc}.
- $\{S_{fc}\} \subseteq \{S_{ac}\}$
  Proof: Condition (1) in S_{fc} is the first situation of condition (1) in S_{ac}. Condition (2) in in S_{fc} is same as Condition (2) in S_{ac} when $\mathbb{D} = \varnothing$, i.e., all the field classes in the template do not have any attribute dependence function. Condition (3) in both S_{fc} and S_{ac} is same.
- $\{S_{kc}\} \subseteq \{S_{ka}\}$
  Proof: Condition (1) in S_{kc} is the first situation of condition (1) in S_{ka}. Condition (2) in in S_{kc} is same as Condition (2) in S_{ka} when $\mathbb{D} = \varnothing$, i.e., all the field classes in the template do not have any attribute dependence function. Condition (3) in S_{kc} is the first situation in condition (3) in S_{ka}.
- $\{S_{ka}\} \subseteq \{S_{ac}\}$
  Proof: Condition (1) and (3) in S_{ka} and S_{ac} are same. Further, the tuple set can satisfy condition (2) of S_{ka} can also satisfy condition (2) in $\{S_{ac}\}$ as $o_1^k = o_2^k = ... = o_n^k$ can guarantee all the required field classes are correlatable in tuple set.

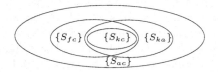

S_{kc}: key-based correlation tuple set
S_{fc}: field-based correlation tuple set
S_{ka}: key-based attribute-dependence correlation tuple set
S_{ac}: attribute-dependence correlation tuple set

Fig. 3. Relationship Among Four Kinds of Correlation Tuple Sets

4.3 Template Generation for Correlation Matching

From the above discussion we know that both types of correlatable tuple sets can only guarantee that the fields required for the template can be provided or computed. However, further inspection of the contents of tuples is required, in order to determine whether the filtering conditions given in templates can be satisfied. In our solution, this is realized by generating a template for each tuple in the set and then using the generated templates to inspect the contents of each tuple individually.

Assuming there are n tuples t_i in the correlation set $\mathbb{T}$ ($t_i \in \mathbb{T}$), We distinguish two types of fields in $\mathbb{T}$: *unique* and *non-unique* fields: unique fields are the fields that are required by the template φ and only appear in one tuple in the tuple set ($\mathbb{C}_{\mathbb{T}}^u$ denotes the collection of all the unique fields), while non-unique fields appear in more than one tuple in the set. From the definition of correlation tuple set, $\forall C \in \mathbb{C}_{\mathbb{T}}^u$, $\exists C' \in \mathbb{C}_\varphi$, C' either is the same as C or super class of C. Therefore, for each $\langle C', q' \rangle$ in a template, in the case of $C' = C$, then in the template φ_i for tuple t_i, $\langle C', q' \rangle$ is used without any changes; while in the case of C' is super class of C, $\langle C', q' \rangle$ need to be transformed to $\langle C, q \rangle$, where query predicate q is transformed from q' by replacing referenced property of C' with property in C.

For example, considering the tuple set $\mathbb{T}_k$ for the template φ_s, two temples φ_1 and φ_2 are generated respectively (see Table 2). In particular, the query predicate SportsCar.price.amount<5000 in φ_1 is transformed from Car.price.amount<5000 in φ, where Car is replaced by SportsCar.

Once a template φ_i is generated for each t_i in $\mathbb{T}$, the tuplespace server needs to test the query predicates for fields in each template and correlate tuples. In the case of field-based correlation tuple set, when inspecting the tuple using the generated template, the false result of query predicate on any tuple in the set will result in discarding the whole tuple set from further correlation processing. After testing all templates, if the tuple set is not discarded, the tuple set is correlated to one tuple. Again, we differentiate two different kinds of fields. For unique field, it can be selected from a tuple. For non-unique field, the tuplespace server prefers a tuple which has same type of field as template required. By selecting each field required by the template, a tuple is created and delivered to the reader.

In the case of attribute-dependence correlation tuple set, another step is required on the correlated tuple: applying the dependence functions to compute the field value and testing the associated query predicate to determinate whether the generated tuple should be delivered to the reader.

5 Implementation Aspects

In this section, we discuss the implementation of the proposed tuplespace server (see Figure 4), which consists of four components: *Write Manager, Runtime Store, Persistent Datastore* and *Read/Take Manager*.

Our tuplespace server supports tuple correlation. This requires the tuplespace server to persist tuples when they are writing into sharespace, for possible correlation operation on them thereafter, as it is unlikely that the main memory can store all the tuples in the sharespace. Further, persistent support also allows tuplespace server restores from

Fig. 4. System Architecture of Tuplespace Server

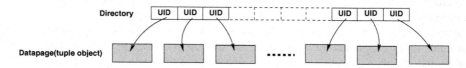

Fig. 5. Hash Index in Runtime Store

runtime failure, which is a key requirement for mission critical applications. There-fore, in our design, the Tuple Writer manages both Runtime Store in main memory and Persistent Datastore in Relational Database. When Tuple Writer receives a write tuple request from users, it saves the tuple object in both the Runtime Store and the Persis-tent Datastore. In case the main memory is full, it needs to remove some tuples from Runtime Store, wherein `First In First Out` update algorithm is adopted. In our design, tuples in the Runtime Store as objects have unique object IDs. As the runtime store is considered as a cache for the tuplespace datastore, we create a *tuple ID-based* hash index, where the unique object ID is used to locate the tuple object. Therefore, when the tuple writer receives a tuple, it saves the tuple with the unique object ID, and then invokes hash functions to update the hash index. When the tuple writer saves a tuple object in runtime store, it also persists the tuple object in tuplespace Datastore. This cache improves the system performance on retrieving tuple contents when tuple UIDs are identified.

The datastore provides persistent storage of tuples. When considering the imple-mentation of datastore, the intuitive choice is adopting object store (i.e., persist tuples as objects). However, it is very costly when inspecting tuples' contents for tuple match-ing: entire tuple objects need to be deserialized in the memory. In fact, in most cases, tuple matching may only concern some attributes of tuples. For the sake of performance and scalability, instead of adopting object store, relation database is used to implement Persistent Datastore. Therefore, when conducting tuple matching, the inspection can only focus on the attributes that are concerted by the templates, without deserialization of entire tuple objects.

When adopting relational approach to persist tuples, mapping between tuple objects and relation tables is required. As user operations on tuples do not explicitly declare the data schema of the tuple (i.e., declaration of tuple schema is not required by the tuplespace system), a tuple can not be stored as a record in a predefined table. In our solution, the tuplespace server separates the data organization of tuple and contents of tuples (see Figure 6), wherein one table `FieldTypes` is used to store the class type information for each field in tuples, while another table `TupleValues` is used to store the contents of tuples. It should be noted that both class type information and the content of the tuples are stored vertically in these tables. In particular, for table

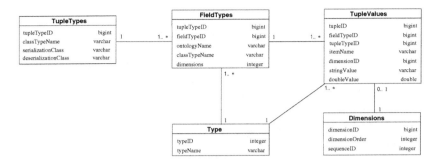

Fig. 6. ER diagram for Persistent Datastore

`FieldTypes`, each field in a tuple occupies a row. For each tuple in tuplespace a unique `tupleTypeID` is assigned for each type of tuple. In table `TupleValues`, each elementary element in a field has a record in the table and `tupleID` is unique for each tuple in tuplespace. Using `tupleID` and `fieldTypeID`, the records in the table can be correlated to individual tuples. Table `Dimensions (D for short)` is used to store the dimension information when there exists any array type of data elements in fields. By specifying `dimensionOrder` and `sequenceID`, the datastore can store any dimension array of data in a tuple. Further, the table `Types` gives type information in tuplespace.

The Read/Take Manager handles tuple read/take requests from users. When it receives read/take requests, it searches for a single tuple that can match the template first. In case there are no single tuple matching the template or users required, the Read/Take Manager searches a correlation tuple set for the temple. In our solution, both semantic and correlation matching is done by generating queries on persistent data store. Details on design of query generation are omitted due to space reasons.

6   Related Work

An effort to provide semantic support in communication paradigm is given in [15], wherein we introduce ontologies into the publish/subscribe systems to understand event contents. This relaxes the constraint in prior content-based pub/sub systems that publishers and subscribers must share the same event schemas. It supports semantic-based, automatic event correlations of multiple event sources for subscriptions, which also overcomes the limitation of relational publish/subscribe systems [8] that requires event consumers to explicitly specify the correlation of event sources. In this paper, we apply the same idea to the tuplespace system, i.e., providing flexibility and adaptability in communication paradigm by leveraging data semantics. Unlike publish/subscribe systems, the tuplespace system does not require the explicit declaration of the data schema when reading and writing tuples, which imposes new challenges when introducing semantic support.

The tuplespace system is a very active area of research and development. Early tuplespace systems [4,7] can be considered as a software implementation of a shared distributed memory. The sharespace appears as a single shared blackboard where tuples can be deposited. Readers are notified when the values of tuples match templates. In this way information can be shared and tuples can be passed among services. As a further development for supporting coordination among services, reactivity was added into tuplespace [3], where local policies could be specified for interactions among the tuple readers and writers. However, in the above systems, expression power of specifying the matching template is very limited for both data type and exactly value matching.

ObjectSpace [12] and T Space [10] added object-orientation to the tuplespace system, wherein a template and a tuple match if the type of the tuple is an instance of the type in the template. The limitation is that object-compatibility assumes both tuple writers and readers adhere to the same implementation of class hierarchy. In our semantic tuplespace system, we externalize the semantic of tuples, wherein ontology is used to understand the content of tuples in matching algorithm. On the other aspect, in order to enhance the tuple retrieval power, PLinda [1] added database functionalities (query predicates, join operator and transaction) into tuplespace systems. In our semantic tuplespace, not only are the database functionalities fully supported, but the join operation is also transparent to tuple readers when correlating multiple tuples for tuple matching.

Triple Space [6,2] provides an asynchronous communication mechanism that supports the four types of autonomy: time, space, reference, and data schema. The data schema is implemented using RDF [13] to understand the communication contents, which is similar to semantic matching in semantic tuplespace system. It should be noted that with the persistent data store, our system also supports these four types autonomy. In additional, our system provides correlation autonomy, i.e., automatic tuple correlation.

An initial effort to provide semantic support for tuplespace matching is given in sTuple [9], which relaxes the constraints in object-based tuplespace that readers and writers must share the same implementation of class hierarchy. However, it only considers one tuple and one template matching. This is similar to the case of semantic matching in our system. Our system proposes a comprehensive schematic tuplespace system. In particular, it supports semantic-based, automatic correlations of multiple tuples for tuple matching, which also overcomes the limitation of PLinda system that requires tuple readers to explicitly specify the correlation of tuples.

Semantic matching is widely adopted to solve the service matching problem in the semantic Web [5,14]. The basic idea of semantic matching is to determine the semantic distance between co-existent terms within shared ontologies, where service queries and descriptions are based on pre-defined schema. However, the semantic matching that enables tuple routing in our tuplespace system is conducted without the user's declaration of data schema when writing and reading tuples.

7   Conclusion

In this paper, we propose a semantic tuplespace system, which is another step forward in the development of current tuplespace systems. We introduce semantics to understand the tuple contents. Our system not only considers single tuple for read/take operation, but also automatically correlates multiple tuples using relational operators based on templates. Unlike object-based tuplespace systems, the tuple correlation in our system is transparent to the tuple reader. We argue that the proposed tuplespace system is essential to enable cooperative service communication in service-oriented computing. Our future work includes optimization of semantic tuple matching and tuple correlation, and a scalability and reliability study of the system.

References

1. B. Anderson and D. Shasha. Persistent Linda: Linda + transactions + query processing, 1991.
2. C. Bussler. A minimal triple space computing architecture. In *2nd WSMO Implementation Workshop, Innsbruck, Austria, June 2005.*
3. G. Cabri, L. Leonardi, and F. Zambonelli. Reactive tuple spaces for mobile agent coordination. *Lecture Notes in Computer Science*, 1477, 1998.
4. N. Carriero and D. Gelernter. Linda in context. *Commun. ACM*, 32(4):444–458, 1989.
5. D. Chakraborty, F. Perich, S. Avancha, and A. Joshi. Dreggie: Semantic service discovery for m-commerce applications, 2001.
6. D. Fensel. Triple-space computing: Semantic web services based on persistent publication of information. In *IFIP Int'l Conf. on Intelligence in Communication Systems 2004*, pages 43–53.
7. Y. S. Gutfreund, J. Nicol, R. Sasnett, and V. Phuah. Wwwinda: An orchestration service for www browsers and accessories. In *WWW Conference '94: Mosaic and the Web*, 1994.
8. Y. Jin and R. Strom. Relational subscription middleware for internet-scale publish-subscribe. In *2nd international workshop on Distributed event-based systems, San Diego, California*, pages 1–8, 2003.
9. D. Khushraj, O. Lassila, and T. Finin. sTuples: Semantic Tuple Spaces. In *First Annual International Conference on Mobile and Ubiquitous Systems: Networking and Services, Boston, Massachussets, USA*, August 22 - 26, 2004.
10. T. J. Lehman, S. W. McLaughry, and P. Wycko. T spaces: The next wave. In *HICSS*, 1999.
11. OWL, 2005. http://www.w3.org/TR/owl-ref/.
12. A. Polze. Using the Object Space: a Distributed Parallel Make. In *The 4th IEEE Workshop on Future Trends of Distributed Computing Systems, Lisbon, September*, 1993.
13. RDF Primer, W3C Recommendation 10 February 2004. http://www.w3.org/TR/rdf-primer/.
14. K. Sycara, S. Wido, M. Klusch, and J. Lu. Larks: Dynamic matchmaking among heterogeneous software agents in cyberspace, 2002.
15. L. Zeng and H. Lei. A semantic publish/subscribe system. In *CEC-EAST '04: Proceedings of the E-Commerce Technology for Dynamic E-Business, IEEE International Conference on (CEC-East'04)*, pages 32–39, Washington, DC, USA, 2004. IEEE Computer Society.

Trust-Based Secure Workflow Path Construction

M. Altunay, D. Brown, G. Byrd, and R. Dean

North Carolina State University, Raleigh, 27695, USA
{maltuna, debrown, gbyrd, ralph_dean}@ncsu.edu

Abstract. Security and trust relationships between services significantly govern their willingness to collaborate and participate in a workflow. Existing workflow tools do not consider such relationships as an integral part of their planning logic: rather, they approach security as a run-time issue. We present a workflow management framework that fully integrates trust and security into the workflow planning logic. It considers not only trust relationships between the workflow requestor and individual services, but also trust relationships among the services themselves. It allows each service owner to define an upper layer of collaboration policies (rules that specify the terms under which participation in a workflow is allowed) and integrates them into the planning logic. Services that are unfit for collaboration due to security violations are replaced at the planning stage. This approach increases the services owners' control over the workflow path, their willingness for collaboration, and avoids run-time security failures.

1 Introduction

Workflow management tools, making use of available services created by the SOC-based communities, play a focal role in dissecting complicated user applications into smaller tasks, assigning each task to a suitable service, and orchestrating the workload among these services. Workflow management, requiring disparate services to collaborate and interact on demand, raises important security and trust issues. At the planning stage, a workflow engine must evaluate the trust relationships among the services as well as the trust relationships between the end user and individual services. The trust relationships among the services may be driven by factors such as industry-specific regulations, existing business partnership agreements, and competition among the services. Moreover, the identities of the workflow requestor and collaborating services, along with the prospective benefits from participation in a workflow, should have an impact on the willingness of a service to join a workflow. Orchestrating services without modeling such complicated trust relationships may result in security violations and reluctance of services for participation.

OGSA [1] and its implementation Globus Toolkit [2] are one of the most significant service-based efforts that provide the necessary middleware to support autonomous inter-organizational sharing of resources and services. Currently, the grid's primary administrative entity, the Virtual Organization (VO) [3], defines a community of users and imposes an "all-or-nothing" style of authentication and authorization. While resource administration is performed locally, in each owner's

B. Benatallah, F. Casati, and P. Traverso (Eds.): ICSOC 2005, LNCS 3826, pp. 382–395, 2005.

domain, the identities and roles of VO members are determined by VO-wide credentials and/or policies, thus making a resource's access control policies conform to the trust model established by the VO. Such uniformity of access eases the problems of resource discovery and selection, and allows the user to form workflows or pipelines of resources to solve complex problems.

The establishment of this community, however, requires infrastructure that can be cumbersome in a more dynamic environment characterized by short-lived collaborations and relationships. The grid-oriented VO requires pre-established trust relationships among the member organization. Service-oriented applications, on the other hand, rely on short-term *ad hoc* collaborations. These collaborating services may not share common goals – rather, they spontaneously collaborate on behalf of a third party, the workflow requestor. Such loose collections of web services may include resources owned by rival companies, be separated by corporate firewalls, otherwise be inhibited from working collaboratively, even on behalf of a third party (the end user) that is authorized for each resource individually. The data, the computations involved, and even the databases and queries used, can all be sensitive and proprietary, due to competitive and regulatory constraints. This style of "co-opetition" is not likely to happen under the VO model – a more dynamic, decentralized collaborative trust model is required.

Based on the characteristics of these new heterogeneous and dynamic environments, we have identified the following list of security requirements for workflow management. Throughout this paper, a *workflow participating entity (WPE)* is any resource (e.g., web service, computational resource, or storage site) that may be chosen to participate in a workflow. An execution path is the specific set of interactions among workflow entities that satisfies the requirements of the workflow. A workflow requestor is the end user on behalf of whom the workflow is executed.

- *Recognition of collaboration requirements among workflow participating entities.* Complex workflows may require a resource owner to interact and collaborate with many other WPEs on behalf of the workflow requestor. Trust models of these WPEs may prevent them from joining a given workflow due to interactions with other participants or the workflow requestor. Ignoring trust relationships between parties during the planning stage may result in security failures (e.g. access denials or firewall failures).

- *A decentralized workflow authorization model.* It is highly likely that WPEs constituting a workflow will have domain-specific security policies and requirements that are confidential [16]. Thus, workflow engines should have decentralized access control models that leave the final access decision to each WPE. Moreover, the workflow engine should not assume any knowledge about the internal security policies of each WPE.

- *Context-based, collaboration-aware access control mechanisms.* Classical identity-based models or the families of role-based (RBAC) [4] and task-based (TBAC) [5] access control models assume that a resource owner has prior knowledge of the user. This assumption is not adequate for today's highly dynamic, market oriented web services paradigm, wherein the services are offered to anyone with the necessary credentials. Proposed access control models based on trust management [6] address this problem. However, trust management-based access control models still need to be incorporated with a high level abstraction that encompasses trust and collaboration policies, as described in Section 2. These policies will allow a resource owner to evaluate incoming access requests based on the context of a workflow and the established trust relationships among the WPEs.

Below, Figure 1 illustrates the workflow path construction throughout the planning stage. The planning engine starts with finding sets of candidate services that are functionally capable of performing the workflow tasks (candidate services are shown in curly brackets in Figure 1). Then each task is mapped to a service, and the workflow path is sent to the execution stage. We propose that the workflow planning engine needs to recognize, identify, and evaluate the complex trust relationships between WPEs during the planning stage. Modeling and evaluating trust relationships during planning stage is requisite if the above requirements are to be met. Thus, the workflow planning engine should (1) identify prospective collaborating parties from a given path, (2) orchestrate the trust evaluations among these parties, and (3) have a robust selection algorithm for building a secure and reliable workflow path from given candidate resources.

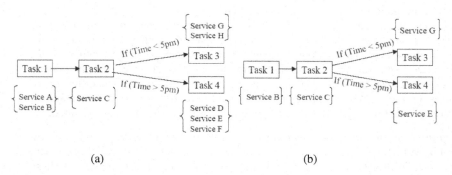

(a)   (b)

Fig. 1. (a) The tentative workflow path at the beginning of planning stage. (b) The workflow path at the end of the planning stage.

To support such environments, we present a workflow management framework (Section 3) that incorporates collaborative trust and security models at the workflow planning stage. Our framework provides an organizational model rather than an architectural specification. The primary component of this framework is a workflow engine that can identify and evaluate complex trust relationships among workflow entities. It provides a decentralized authentication and authorization model, in which each workflow entity is responsible for creating and enforcing its own access control policies. Our framework increases the availability of complex and trusted distributed environments for application communities that are unable or reluctant to create formal virtual organizations. It also provides the tools that support the complex trust relationships that already exist in these domains, allowing new opportunities for collaboration and scientific discovery.

2   New Workflow Paradigm: Collaboration-Based Secure Workflow Path Formation

Conceptually, during the execution of a typical workflow, the data transfer and control flow defined by the workflow engine specifies the neighboring relationships among arbitrary resources. The interactions occurring between WPEs in a workflow path can be examined in two categories: bilateral and indirect.

Any interaction between two WPEs that are immediate neighbors of each other is a *bilateral relationship*, even when the flow of interaction seems to be one-sided. To illustrate this, the simple collaboration scenario shown in Figure 2 seemingly involves a one-sided relationship: Service A presents an input file to Service B and Service B determines if it trusts Service A.   However, there are actually two relationships: (1) Service A determines that it trusts Service B and agrees to share a copy of its result file, and (2) Service B determines that it trusts Service A to access with the specified input file. Both of these actions involve risk: from Service A's perspective, Service B could be a rival company that is not willing to share its results (i.e. application logic); from Service B's perspective, Service A could be a malicious user who sends a Trojan horse.

Indirect interactions occur between WPEs that are not immediate neighbors of each other, such as A and C in Figure 2. The interaction between such WPEs occurs through intermediate services. Based on the level of interaction, a service owner may want to put restrictions on the identities of its non-immediate neighbors. Moreover, the identities of such neighbors may significantly affect the willingness of a WPE to participate in a workflow. There are several reasons why such indirect trust relationships must be carefully evaluated. (1) Confidential documents or the results of a sensitive algorithm are typically passed among several WPEs throughout an execution path; thus even a non-immediate neighbor might have access to confidential data. (2) Industry-specific and government-based regulations [21] place important restrictions on the identity of collaborating partners, even when such collaborations are indirect. In industries such as health care and bioinformatics, every individual organization is held accountable for their direct and indirect collaborators with whom they exchange data. (3) Existing partnership agreements and competition among businesses prevent them from doing business with some certain organizations. Even when such interactions are safe from a security standpoint, the higher-level business logic forbids them.

Current workflow management systems ignore bilateral and indirect interactions, and only apply unilateral security checks, merely checking credentials of the workflow requestor against each WPEs. Two scenarios arise where our proposed framework provides a distinctive advantage over existing workflow planning systems. Presume that the user has authorized access to all WPEs, and has delegated his access rights to them.

In the first scenario, a desired interaction cannot

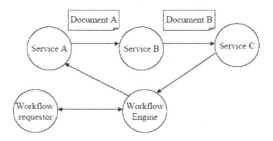

Fig. 2. Collaboration scenario

occur and this is not determined until run-time. For example, Service B needs to access a file from Service A but security policies, perhaps a firewall rule set, deny the interaction. This fault will require a costly run-time re-evaluation of the planning algorithm.

In the second scenario, a desired interaction occurs that, due to higher-level business policies, ought not be allowed. Given the current difficulty in setting up fine-grained, dynamic VO's and the costly nature of security related run-time failures, many installations are overly permissive. For example, Service B's business logic prevents it from interacting with Service A due to its partnership agreement with another business, but since the WPEs are using delegated rights, Service B is unable to recognize its interaction with Service A.

Our framework realizes the evaluation of bilateral and indirect trust relationships, and requires every WPE to express its security requirements through an upper layer of collaboration policies. These policies allow a service owner to explicitly communicate its trust requirements for bilateral and indirect interactions occurring in a workflow. By harnessing such requirements, collaboration policies express the conditions under which a WPE is willing to participate in a workflow and the allowed actions during the workflow execution.

2.1 Collaboration Policies

Collaboration policies define a set of requirements and rules that must be met for participating in a workflow. These policies define trust requirements of neighboring services for collaboration, the propagation of access rights throughout the execution path (delegation policies), and the trust requirements from a workflow requestor. Each collaboration policy is comprised of four attributes: (1) authorization rules for neighboring WPEs, (2) the radius of the partial workflow path that a WPE needs to evaluate in terms of security, (3) the delegation of credentials throughout a workflow, and (4) the trust relationship with the workflow requestor. Separate collaboration policies for upstream and downstream neighbors may be defined.

Authorization rules for neighbor WPEs: The level of interaction between WPEs is determined by the position of services in the execution path. The immediately neighboring services are expected to exchange documents, executables and other arguments directly, whereas non-immediate neighbors interact with each other through intermediate services. A service owner may have different security requirements based on the level of interaction required with each WPE. A collaboration policy must express how all these different requirements combined together and an overall authorization decision is made for a given path.

For example, an immediate neighbor (service B in Figure 2) may be required to have the proper authorization rights to invoke service C, whereas, a non-immediate neighbor (service A in Figure 2) may be applied to a weaker set of authorization rules that covers only a partial set of required authorization attributes such as country location, company information or a reputation value.

At the policy writing time, each service owner must decide (1) the size of the partial workflow path that needs to be examined (i.e. the distance between the service owner and the WPEs that security checks must be applied), and (2) the set of access rules that should be applied to the entities within the partial path. Note that the size of the partial workflow path that should be examined is independent of a specific workflow instance — rather it is dependent on the sensitivity of the resource being offered and the local regulations governing this resource. For example, a service, which is only interested in checking its immediate upstream and downstream neighbors, has a partial workflow path of two nodes. No matter which specific workflow instance this service participates in, it will only examine two WPEs that happen to be at the specified distances from the service owner.

In order to ease writing such policies, we define two security functions, S and A, where S denotes strong authorization requirements and A denotes lighter attribute-based requirements. Both S and A define the access control rules based on the interaction level between entities. We use the distance between WPEs as an indicator of interaction level, which is defined as follows:

Distance (WPE1, WPE2): x, where there are x number of hops between WPE1 and WPE2 for each linear path between them.

S(WPE, obj), where obj denotes the object access is being requested, and WPE denotes the workflow entity requesting access. One way to express a neighbor WPE is by using **direction:distance** pairs. The direction:distance pairs identify the WPE for which this policy rule is applied. Direction could be either upstream (up) or downstream (down). S shows that the requesting WPE must be applied to the same security policies that are applied when the access is requested by this WPE individually (without being part of a workflow).

A(WPE, attr, obj), where obj and WPE are used in the same manner as used in the S function. Attr denotes a list of attribute-based requirements. This list of required attributes for authorization does not constitute the full set of attributes that are required when the access is requested individually. Rather, these attributes are geared towards internal business rules and industrial restrictions such as checking the geographical origin of an organization or the rivalry information.

For example, the below sample policy shows that as long as one of the two upstream neighbors are strongly authorized and they are not a certain rival company, the access for this upstream path is allowed, whereas for the downstream path, only the country information of the immediate neighbor is needed.

CP: {(((S(up:1, obj1) ∧ A(up:2, Organization Name, obj1)) ∨ (S(up:2, obj1) ∧
    A(up:1, Organization Name, obj1))) ∧
    A(down:1, country information, obj2)}

The delegation of credentials throughout the workflow path: During the execution of a workflow, the delegation of credentials from WPEs or workflow requestor may be necessary. Each WPE, before joining a workflow, must express its delegation rules in its collaboration policy. Such rules define (1) if delegated credentials are accepted for authorization, (2) whether the downstream delegation of WPEs' credentials are allowed in case workflow execution requires such an action, and if so the trust requirements from the delegated parties, (3) whether the WPE accepts delegated credentials (delegated from an upstream neighbor) in order to invoke another service or to propagate them to another WPE.

The above rules are necessary for a number of reasons. (1) A WPE or a workflow requestor may be willing to delegate their credentials to a second party in order to complete a job without carefully contemplating the security consequences. The WPE that receives a request with delegated credentials must be able to distinguish such credentials and apply appropriate security policies. Current grid execution environments (Globus Toolkit) do not allow discrimination of delegated credentials from the original ones, due to the usage of proxy credentials that provide single sign-on. Our framework, by allowing a WPE to evaluate its direct and indirect neighbors' credentials, enables a WPE to determine if delegated credentials are used in an execution chain. Armed with such information, a WPE may refuse to allow access to a delegation chain. (2) During workflow execution, WPEs shares their resources on behalf of a workflow requestor. These shared resources may involve a WPE's credentials. Before joining a workflow, each WPE should define their rules for allowing downstream delegation. Once such information is made available to the workflow engine at the planning stage, a more efficient but non-secure path may later be discovered to be suitable, thus increasing the performance of the workflow. (3) A WPE may need to accept delegated credentials from an upstream neighbor either to propagate them along the execution path or to invoke another downstream service. Even though, acceptance of delegated credentials seems relatively safer than delegating one's own credentials, a WPE must carefully analyze the consequences of accepting such credentials.

In order to ease writing collaboration policies, we define three delegation functions:

Du(distance, obj, conditions), where distance shows how many downstream hops the delegated credentials has traveled, obj denotes the object that is being requested, and conditions defines the rules that must be satisfied for accepting access with delegated credentials. Conditions define the authorization requirements in terms of combination of S and A functions. Du communicates under which conditions access to an object with delegated credentials is accepted.

Dd(credential, distance, conditions), where distance shows how many hops of re-delegation is allowed, conditions hold the same meaning as in Du. Credential denotes the credential being delegated downstream. Dd communicates whether this WPE is willing to allow downstream delegation of its credentials.

Dt(credential, distance, transient/final, conditions), where all attributes hold the same meaning as above except transient/final. Transient/final denotes whether the credentials should be passed onto another WPE for the final service invocation or the receiving WPE will perform the downstream service invocation with the delegated credentials. Dt communicates the conditions under which a delegated credential is accepted so that these credentials either be propagated to another WPE or used for a downstream service invocation.

The radius of partial workflow graph for security examination: Based on its collaboration policy, a WPE may require examining a partial graph of the workflow. The radius for such a sub-graph is calculated from the collaboration policy and communicated to the workflow engine. Depending on the policy, the number of neighbors that should be evaluated in the downstream and upstream directions may be different, thus requiring two radii, one calculated for each direction.

The trust relationship with the workflow requestor: In addition to defining the required access rules for its neighboring WPEs', a WPE may also need to define access rules for the workflow requestor. The functions defined previously, S and A, can be used to state such rules with the special keyword **requestor** instead of direction:distance pairs. Note that the distance between a WPE and the workflow requestor is dependent on the specific workflow path instance; however, the collaboration policies must be expressed independent of any specific workflow instances. Therefore, at the policy writing time, the location of the workflow requestor is unknown, and must be signaled by the keyword **requestor** in S and A.

2.2 Collaboration Policy Semantics

A flexible yet expressive collaboration language is needed to express the collaboration policies. XACML allows a resource owner to express access control policies for a resource. Due to its richness and flexibility, we decided to express our collaboration policies in XACML. Collaboration policies, combining existing lower level access control policies with additional constraints, require an extensible language that allows defining new attributes and subject groups easily.

We have also examined several other languages. BPEL4WS is widely accepted as the de-facto flow language for workflow management systems. However, security is not a major concern in the BPEL4WS – rather, BPEL4WS provides a facility to exchange messages between collaborating organizations, and assumes that underlying standards such as WS-SecureConversation and WS-Security would provide the necessary security extension. WS-SecureConversation and WS-Security standards provide "message-level" security on top of the SSL layer by specifying needed security tokens in a SOAP message (Kerberos tickets, X509 credentials, or SAML assertions). However, neither expresses the "business-level" interactions and security/trust requirements among the collaborating partners.

WS-Trust and its allied standards support security token interoperability and traditional bi-partite trust relationship. It does not explicitly model business level trust relationships between entities when they are acting on behalf of a third party.

3   Secure Workflow Management Framework

Typically, workflow planning engines retrieve a list of suitable resources from the discovery service (MDS) [7] [8], and map each task to a resource. During the mapping process, the planning engines evaluate several constraints such as resource availability, current load, wait time, data locations and the cost associated with each resource [18, 19, 20]. For example, The Pegasus [18] planning engine selects resources that are closer to the required data locations. If no resource is particularly close, then a random decision is made. The Nimrod/G [19] planning engine evaluates the computational costs and selects resources within workflow requestor's price range. The GridFlow [20] planning engine focuses on time management. The estimated execution times for each candidate resource is evaluated, and an optimal workflow path is built that can satisfy the time restrictions. Security and trust is of little or no consideration during the mapping process. Rather, classical systems defer authorization and trust evaluation to the execution stage.

The workflow planning logic must evaluate the existing trust relationships, and dynamically build alternative execution paths when a functionally desirable execution

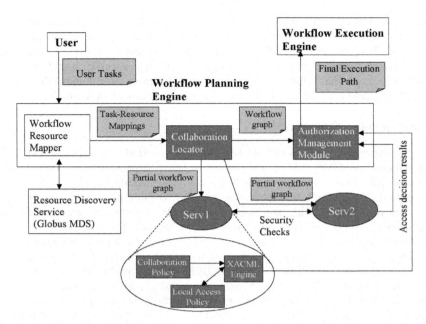

Fig. 3. Secure Workflow Framework, operating with the Globus Toolkit. The dark components indicate the proposed additions to the frameworks. The light gray boxes are the documents exchanged among the components.

path discovered to be infeasible from the security standpoint. To accomplish this, we extend the workflow planning stage with a Collaboration Locator Module (CLM) and the Authorization Management Module (AMM) (see Figure 3).

3.1 Collaboration Locator Module

The Collaboration Locator Module (CLM) is responsible for locating the WPEs that collaborate with each other. Each WPE communicates the required radiuses of partial workflow graphs to CLM. Based on the radius information, the CLM determines the partial graphs that need to be sent to each WPE, and also determines the security checks among the WPEs. Based on these checks, each WPE initiates the security evaluations. (Note that WPE collaboration policies need not be communicated to the CLM.)

The sample scenario shown in Figure 2 is accompanied with the following collaboration policies for each of the WPEs.

CPd(A):{S(down:1, document A); Dd(X.509, 2, Condition1: {S(down:1, credential) for one hop delegation}, Condition2: {(S(down:1,credential) ∧ S(down:2, credential)) for two hops delegation}; radius:2;   S(requestor, service A)},

CPu(B):{S(up:1, service B); Dt(X.509, up:1, final, none); radius:1; S(requestor, service B)}

CPd(B):{S(down:1, document B); none; radius: 1}

CPu(C): {(((S(up:1, service C)) ∨ (S(up:2, service C) ∧ A(up:1, Organization Name (X.509 DN), service C) ∧ Du(2, service C, none))) ; none; radius: 2; S(requestor, service C)}

A's collaboration policy indicates that the strong authorization of an immediate downstream neighbor (expressed by S(down:1, document A)) and the workflow requestor are required (expressed by S(requestor, service A)). Downstream delegation of service A's credentials are allowed under two conditions (expressed by Dd(X.509, 2, Condition1, Condition2)): (1) either the immediate downstream neighbor is strongly authorized and the credentials are delegated for one hop distance (expressed by Condition1: {S(down:1, credential) for one hop delegation}), or (2) two subsequent downstream neighbors are strongly authorized, and the delegation of credentials for distance of two is allowed (Condition2: {(S(down:1,credential) ∧ S(down:2, credential)) for two hops delegation}). Finally, the radius of upstream workflow graph that needs to be evaluated is two (expressed by radius:2). Note that the radius is two due to the conditions for the delegation rule.

B's collaboration policy consists of two parts: upstream and downstream policies. Both policies can be expressed together, however separation eases the job of policy writer. The upstream policy requires the immediate upstream neighbor and the workflow requestor to be strongly authorized ((S(up:1, service B) and S(requestor, service B)). In case of an upstream delegation, B accepts the delegated credentials if it would be the final entity for downstream service invocation (Dt(X.509, up:1, final, none)). B's downstream policy does not allow delegation of B's credentials and indicates that it should strongly authorize its immediate downstream neighbor (S(down:1, document B)).

C's collaboration policy indicates that an upstream path is only authorized if (1) the immediate neighbor is strongly authorized or (2) the non-immediate neighbor at distance 2 must be strongly authorized and should allow downstream delegation of its credentials, and the immediate neighbor must not be a rival company ((S(up:2, service C) ∧ A(up:1, Organization Name (X.509 DN), service C) ∧ Du(2, service C, none))). C requires strong authorization of the workflow requestor (S(requestor, service C)), and does not allow downstream delegation.

Having only received the radius information from the above collaboration policies, CLM decides that following security checks among the WPEs are necessary.

A → C for service C; B → C for service C; C → B for document B; B → A for document A; A → B for service B, and C → A for service A. CLM also prepares partial graphs of the workflow and sends those to each WPE. Finally, CLM passes the list of required security checks to AMM, which orchestrates the communication among WPE and replaces insufficient pairs with matching ones.

3.2 Authorization Management Module

The AMM performs two functionalities: it orchestrates the trust evaluations between WPEs, and based on the access decisions, it finds alternative execution paths.

A key point of AMM is the decentralized authorization framework. Each WPE evaluates the access requests from its candidate neighbors. Based on the results of security checks, each WPE determines whether or not to participate in the workflow and the conditions under which the participation may take place. WPEs send their decisions and conditions on the partial workflow path. AMM examines the WPEs' decisions and checks if the conditions are met. Note that AMM only serves to orchestrate authorization, rather than making the final access control decisions on behalf of resources.

In order to ease the communication between AMM and WPEs, we provide a simple message format.

(WPE, path): {decision, conditions: (required upstream delegation distance, (allowed upstream delegation distance, transient/final), allowed downstream delegation distance)}. Decision denotes if a given partial workflow map is authorized by this WPE. The list of conditions shows if the approval of this partial path is dependent on delegation of credentials. The list, respectively, shows how many hops of upstream delegation is required for authorization (corresponds to Du), how many hops of upstream delegation is accepted along with a transient or final flag (corresponds to Dt), and the number of hops allowed for downstream delegation of this WPE's credentials (corresponds to Dd).

Re-visiting the sample scenario from Figure 2, CLM triggers services A, B and C to start trust evaluations among each other. Assume A is strongly authorized for service C, whereas B is not. However, B's company information indicates that it is not part of a rival organization. Also, B and C are both strongly authorized to A, and finally, A and C are strongly authorized to B. The following messages would be created:

(C, 1): {approved, conditions: (1, 0, 0)}. This message shows that C is willing to authorize this path, but it requires upstream delegation of distance one: neighbor (B) must use the delegated credentials from its immediate upstream neighbor (A) (indicated by 1 in the message). C neither authorizes any downstream delegation nor accepts transient delegation of upstream credentials.

(A, 1): {approved, conditions: (0, 0, 2)}. This message shows that A is only willing to allow downstream delegation of its credentials up to distance of 2.

Note that the authorization of C to A seems like an unnecessary operation for this specific partial graph. However, consider the following scenario: there is a subsequent downstream service, say D, that accepts upstream delegated credentials from distance of two. In the case that C does not have the required credentials for access, the workflow engine would immediately know that this path is still feasible by looking at the message from A indicating that A may delegate its credentials to C (of course given that A is authorized to D). Also note that requirement for authorization of A to D is indicated in D's upstream collaboration policy which would state that credentials delegated up to distance of two are accepted.

(B, 1): {approved, conditions: (0, (1,final), 0)}, which shows that B accepts the upstream delegation of credentials from A to invoke service C (indicated by (1, final)); however it neither allows downstream delegation, nor requires upstream delegation.

Having looked at all the messages, AMM starts checking the conditions on the path. C's conditional approval (shown by (1,0,0)) depends on A's willingness to delegate (which holds true as shown in (0,0,2)) and B's willingness to accept the delegated credentials (which holds true as shown by (0, (1, final), 0)). Therefore, AMM concludes that the required conditions for this path have been achieved and a feasible path is found.

The second important function of AMM is to suggest alternative execution paths in case a chosen path turns out to be infeasible from security standpoint. AMM must select which WPE to replace in a given infeasible path. There could be several WPEs that do not mutually trust each other on a complicated workflow path. Therefore, the algorithms for selecting which WPE to replace become crucial. There are several important issues to consider while replacing an unfit WPE and locating a new one for that task. (1) The number of neighbors of the WPE. A high number of neighbors indicates that replacement is going to cause many re-evaluations of trust relationships. Therefore, it is safer to replace a WPE that has few neighbors. (2) The collaboration policy of a WPE. Replacing a WPE that has a relatively light collaboration policy (i.e. accepts and allows delegation, small radius, does not require strong authorization) with a WPE that has more restrictive requirements may cause more trust re-evaluations. (3) The number of neighbors that do not authorize this specific WPE. In some cases, a WPE may be found to be unfit by only one other WPE, while the rest of the WPEs authorize it. In most cases, it is safer to replace a WPE that is found unfit by the majority. However, a robust selection algorithm must always re-visit issues (1) and (2).

4 Related Work

There are several workflow security frameworks that target the needs of large organizations [9][10][11]. They focus on synchronizing the access to required privileges to execute a task with the progression of a workflow. These approaches require a central workflow authority to have the access rights associated with each workflow subject and transfer these rights to the subjects based on the workflow progress. In a heterogeneous environment, objects and subjects may be web services belonging to different organizations. Therefore, the ownership of such access rights by the central authority becomes impossible, thus making them insufficient for heterogeneous dynamic environments.

Other approaches by Bertino [12], Tan [13], and Hung [14] use authorization constraints to extend RBAC models. A security policy designed by a workflow requestor may express constraints such that the resulting execution path must conform. These efforts approach the authorization problem from the workflow requestor's perspective, and allow her/him to express trust requirements sought from a candidate resource to perform a job. However, this approach does not touch upon the other side of the authorization problem: the authorization of workflow requestor to the candidate resources and the trust relationships among the resources.

Kang [15], Koshutanski [16], and WAS framework [17] recognize the inter-organizational, heterogeneous nature of new-generation workflows. Kang requires each participating organization to map its entire role structure to the role domain of the workflow. The WAS framework focuses on deciding the required rights in order to run a task through different domains, and on providing restricted delegation by using source-code analysis of tasks. Both approaches require a central authority, with access to the internal policies of each WPE, that can assign each task with a pool of privileges and roles. The main drawback of this model is that it does not allow building dynamic workflows, where the workflow engine assumes no knowledge about the internal security policies of a participating organization.

Koshutanski's framework focuses on providing authorization mechanisms between a workflow requestor and WPEs. Instead of revealing access policies, each organization sends a mobile process to the end user. Upon executing the mobile processes on the user side, an access control decision is made. The reliance on mobile processes introduces other security issues, such as how the end user can verify the code, and how the code should identify the credentials required to make the authorization decision. Moreover, this framework does not consider the trust relationships among WPEs.

5 Conclusion

Construction of heterogeneous and dynamic workflows requires collaboration and interaction among disparate services on demand; necessitating expression and evaluation of trust relationships at the planning stage. Unfortunately, no current workflow tool considers such relationships during the planning stage: rather, they assume homogeneous execution communities where each party shares common long-term goals and implicit trust. Our framework differentiates itself by defining a security architecture for heterogeneous and short-lived collaboration environments. It introduces collaboration policies that express the conditions to enter a workflow and allowed actions during execution, by harnessing existing lower level access control policies and additional workflow-oriented constraints. As a result, workflow entities are assured to abide by their internal security policies, and infeasible execution paths are replaced with suitable service pairs that are willing to collaborate at the planning stage. Our framework, by providing the tools to support complex trust relationships, increases the willingness of services for collaboration where creating formal homogeneous communities are expensive.

References

1. Foster I., Kesselman C., Nick J., Tuecke S.: Open Grid Service Infrastructure WG, Global Grid Forum (2002)
2. Foster I., Kesselman C.: Globus: A Metacomputing Infrastructure Toolkit. Intl J. Supercomputer Applications (1997) 11(2):115-128
3. Foster I., Kesselman C., Tuecke S.: The Anatomy of the Grid: Enabling Scalable Virtual Organizations. Intl. J. Supercomputer Applications (2001) 15(3)
4. Sandhu R.: Role-Based Access Control Models. IEEE Computer (1996) 29(2):34-47
5. Thomas R.K., Sandhu R..: Towards a Task-based Paradigm for Flexible and Adaptable Access Control in Distributed Applications. ACM SIGSAC New Security Paradigms Workshop (1992-93) 138-142
6. Blaze M., Feigenbaum J., Ioannadis J., Keromytis A. D.: The role of trust management in distributed systems security. In Secure Internet Programming: the Security Issues for Mobile and Distributed Objects. Springer-Verlag (1999) 185-210
7. Raman R., Livny M., Solomon M.: Matchmaking: Distributed Resource Management for High Throughput Computing. Seventh IEEE Intl. Symp. on High-Performance Distributed. Computing (HPDC) (1998)

8. Czajkowski K., et al.: Grid Information Services for Distributed Resource Sharing. 10th IEEE Intl. Symp. on High-Performance Distributed Computing (HPDC-10) (2001)

9. Atluri V., Huang W-K.: An Authorization Model for Workflows. Fifth European Symp. on Research in Computer Security (1996) 44-64.

10. Knorr K.: Dynamic access control through Petri net workflows. 16th Conf. on Computer Security Applications (ACSAC'00) (2000) 159-167

11. Huang W-K., Atluri V.: SecureFlow: A Secure Web-enabled Workflow Management System. 4th ACM Workshop on Role-based Access Control (1999)

12. Bertino E., Ferrari E., Atluri V.: The Specification and Enforcement of Authorization Constraints in Workflow Management Systems. ACM Trans. on Information and System Security (1999) 2(1):65-104

13. Tan K., Crampton J., Gunter C. A.: The Consistency of Task-Based Authorization Constraints in Workflow Systems. 17th IEEE Computer Security Foundations Workshop (CSFW'04) (2004) 155-169

14. Hung P.C.K., Karlapalem K.: A secure Workflow Model. Australasian Information Security Workshop Conference (2003) 33-41

15. Kang M.H., Park J. S., Froscher J. N.: Access-Control Mechanisms for Inter Organizational Workflow. Sixth ACM Symp. on Access Control Models and Technologies (2001) 66-74

16. Koshutanski H., Massacci V.: An Access Control Framework for Business Processes for Web Services. ACM Workshop on XML Security (2003) 15-24

17. Kim S-H., Kim J., Hong S-J., Kim S.: Workflow-based Authorization Service in Grid. Fourth Intl. Workshop on Grid Computing (GRID'03) (2003) 94-100

18. Deelman E., Blythe J., Gil Y., Kesselman C., Mehta G., Patil S., Su M-H., Vahi K., Livny M.: Pegasus: Mapping Scientific Workflow onto the Grid. Across Grids Conference (2004) 11-20

19. Buyya R., Abramson D., Giddy J.: Nimrod/G: An Architecture for a Resource Management and Scheduling System in a Global Computational Grid. Fourth Intl. Conference On High Performance Computing in Asia-Pacific Region (HPC ASIA'00) (2000) (1): 283-289

20. Cao J., Jarvis S. A., Saini S., Nudd G. R.: GridFlow: Workflow Management for Grid Computing. Third IEEE/ACM Intl. Symposium on Cluster Computing and the Grid (CCGRID'03) (2003) 198-205

21. Standards for Privacy of Individually Identifiable Health Information (HPR). 45 CFR 164.C. Federal Register (2003) 68(34):8334 – 8381

Reputation-Based Service Level Agreements for Web Services

Radu Jurca and Boi Faltings

Ecole Polytechnique Fédérale de Lausanne (EPFL),
Artificial Intelligence Laboratory, CH-1015 Lausanne, Switzerland
{radu.jurca, boi.faltings}@epfl.ch

Abstract. Most web services need to be contracted through service level agreements that typically specify a certain quality of service (QoS) in return for a certain price.

We propose a new form of service level agreement where the price is determined by the QoS actually delivered. We show that such agreements make it optimal for the service provider to deliver the service at the promised quality. To allow efficient monitoring of the actual QoS, we introduce a reputation mechanism. A scoring rule makes it optimal for the users of a service to correctly report the QoS they observed.

Thus, we obtain a practical scheme for service-level agreements that makes it uninteresting for providers to deviate from their best effort.

1 Introduction

Service oriented computing systems represent an attractive paradigm for the business world of tomorrow. User requests ranging from trip reservations to complex optimization problems, are no longer atomically treated by monolithic organizations, but rather decomposed into smaller components that are separately addressed by different service providers [17]. While the advantages of such a scenario are clear (simplicity, ease of management and customization, fault tolerance and scalability), the fact that services are delivered by independent, self-interested providers poses new challenges.

We assume a scenario where services are contracted through Service Level Agreements (SLAs) that specify a certain quality of service (QoS) in return for a certain price. Independent monitoring of QoS is expensive and technically difficult. Without proper monitoring, selfish service providers can increase their revenues by cheating: they advertise high quality but do not invest the necessary effort to provision the service. Anticipating this behavior, rational clients will not trust the providers, and therefore, will decrease to a minimum the amounts they are willing to pay for the service. Such a market is very inefficient, and will drive away trustworthy providers.

In this paper, we consider scenarios where a group of customers are treated identically by the provider using the same service level agreement. In this case, the SLA can be based on the service provided to them as a group. The first result of this paper is that given correct information about the QoS, such agreements

B. Benatallah, F. Casati, and P. Traverso (Eds.): ICSOC 2005, LNCS 3826, pp. 396–409, 2005.

make it optimal for the service provider to deliver at least the advertised quality to each participant.

This leaves the problem of monitoring this quality of service. As a second main result, we show that independent monitoring can actually be replaced by a reputation system where monitoring is done by the customers themselves. This raises the problems of (a) eliciting honest feedback from clients and (b) preventing collusion. We show how a reputation mechanism can use side-payments (i.e. clients get paid for submitting feedback) to make it rational for all clients to truthfully share their feedback. Moreover, when a reputation mechanism has a small number of "trusted" reports (i.e. feedback that is true with high probability) we prove that rational clients will not collude in order to artificially decrease the reputation of a service provider.

This paper thus describes a practical mechanism that eliminates incentives for selfish service providers to cheat while greatly reducing the QoS monitoring burden on the market. The scheme is safe against strategic lying and bad-mouthing[1] collusion. Section 2 formally describes the setting and the assumptions behind our results, Section 3 describes in detail the service level agreements and their properties while Section 4 addresses the problem of truthful reporting. Section 5 evaluates our mechanism, followed by related work and a conclusion.

2   The Setting

We consider an online market pictured in Fig. 1 where service providers repeatedly offer the same service to the interested clients, in exchange for money. The transactions between service providers and clients are regulated by a Service Level Agreement (SLA) that defines (among others) quality parameters of the delivered service (i.e. the QoS) and the dependence of price on the actual QoS. When there are several QoS parameters, we assume that the SLA can be split into separate agreements for each parameter such that the price is the sum

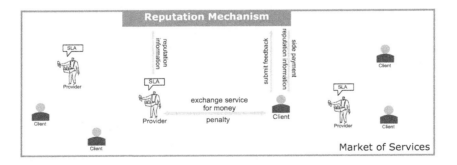

Fig. 1. A market of web services

---

[1] Strategic denigration of a provider's reputation through false negative feedback.

of the prices in the individual SLAs. A precise definition of the SLA for our mechanism is given in Section 3, Definition 1. A practical framework supporting such interactions is described in detail by Dan et al. [3].

We assume there is a large enough group of clients that share the same QoS and SLA during a predefined period of time. Note that a provider can have several customer groups (e.g. silver/gold/platinium customers), as far as all clients in a certain group are treated identically. Therefore, the average satisfaction rate of the customers in a given group, in a given period of time, can be used to estimate the real QoS delivered by the provider. We denote by $\mathcal{Q}$ the set of all possible values for the QoS.

We assume that clients have two degrees of satisfaction: they either perceive *high* quality or *low* quality service. High quality service, for example, is perceived when the answer to the service request is received before a specified deadline. This binary model can be easily extended to finer grained quality levels and multiple quality parameters.

The market has an independent *reputation mechanism* (RM) that collects binary feedback from clients. "1" denotes positive feedback and signals the fact that the client has observed a high quality service. Likewise, "0" denotes negative feedback and signals low quality service. Feedback is collected at the end of each time period, when all transactions are assumed completed. The reputation of a provider is computed by the RM as the percentage of positive reports submitted by the members of a particular customer group, in a given period. Reputation, therefore, equals the average QoS delivered to a given customer group in a given period.

Clients can make involuntary mistakes when submitting feedback. When q percent of the clients perceive high quality, the reputation of the provider equals $q + \eta_r$; the noise η_r is assumed normally distributed around 0 with variance σ_r^2.

We further assume that the RM can (a) pay clients for submitting reports, and (b) obtain a limited number of trusted reports that are true with high probability. Trusted reports can be obtained from specialized agents[2] hired to anonymously test the service delivered by the provider. In Section 4 we show how side payments and trusted reports can be used to elicit honest feedback from rational clients, and prevent collusion.

Service providers differ in their ability and knowledge to provide qualitative services. For example, the time required to successfully answer a service invocation (up to some random noise) depends on the available infrastructure (e.g. hardware, software, network capacity) and on the number of requests accepted by the provider in a given time window.

The infrastructure is assumed fixed and defines the *type* of the provider. Two providers have the same type if they have exactly the same capabilities for providing service. Formally, the set of possible types is denoted by Θ, and members of this set are denoted as θ.

---

[2] Sites like Keynote Systems (www.keynote.com) and Xaffire Inc. (www.xaffire.com) offer such services.

The number of accepted requests, on the other hand, can be strategically decided by the service provider. Given the available infrastructure (i.e. a type), the provider needs to limit the number of accepted requests in order to deliver the required answers before the deadline, with high probability. Providing high QoS requires *effort* (e.g. limiting requests and giving up revenue), and hence, has a cost.

Let $c(\theta, e)$ be the cost incurred by a provider of type θ when exerting effort e in a given period of time. The cost function is private to each provider type, and usually concave (i.e. higher quality demands increasingly more effort). However, our results are independent of the form of the cost function.

The provider's type (e.g. available infrastructure) and effort (e.g. number of accepted requests) determine the actual QoS provided to clients. If we denote by $\mathcal{E}$ the set of possible effort levels, and by $\mathcal{Q}$ the set of possible quality levels, let the function $\phi : \Theta \times \mathcal{E} \rightarrow \mathcal{Q}$ defines the mapping between type, effort and QoS. External factors and noise also influence the QoS. A type θ provider will therefore deliver quality $\phi(\theta, e) + \eta_n$ when exerting effort e. η_n is assumed normally distributed around 0 with variance σ_n^2.

3   Reputation-Based Service Level Agreements

The idea behind the SLA we propose in this paper is to make higher, untruthful, advertisements of QoS unprofitable for service providers. For that, our SLA follows the framework proposed in [3] and specifies a monetary penalty that must be paid by the provider to each client at the end of a given period of time. The penalty is directly proportional to the difference between promised and delivered QoS, such that the total revenue of a provider declaring higher QoS (i.e. the price of the advertised QoS minus the penalty for providing lower QoS) is lower than the price obtained from truthfully declaring the intended QoS in the first place. The novelty of our approach is that we use reputation information to compute the penalties paid by providers.

Definition 1. *A reputation-based Service Level Agreement states the following terms:*

- **per_validity**: *the period of validity. Time is indexed according to a discrete variable t;*
- **cust_group**: *the intended customer group (e.g. silver/gold/platinium customers);*
- **QoS** *(denoted as $\bar{q}_t \in \mathcal{Q}$): the quality of service (e.g. the average probability of delivering high quality service);*
- **price** *(denoted as p_t) : the price of service;*
- **penalty**: *the reputation-based penalty to be paid by the provider to the client for deviating from the terms of the SLA. The penalty $\lambda_t : \mathcal{Q} \times \mathcal{Q} \rightarrow \mathbb{R}^+$ is a function of advertised QoS (i.e. $\bar{q}_t$) and delivered QoS (i.e. the reputation, R_t). $\lambda_t(\bar{q}_t, R_t) = 0$ for all $R_t \geq \bar{q}_t$ and strictly positive otherwise.*

The SLA is defined by the service provider prior to the period of time, t, when the SLA is valid. The provider chooses (a) the advertised QoS (i.e. $\bar{q}_t$), (b) the price charged for service (i.e. p_t), (c) the penalty function (i.e. $\lambda_t(\cdot, \cdot)$), and (d) the exerted effort (i.e. e_t). The first three choices are made public through the SLA (we therefore use the shorthand notation: $sla_t = (\bar{q}_t, p_t, \lambda_t)$) while the forth one is kept private.

As a first result we derive sufficient constraints on the penalty function such that service providers of all types find it optimal to deliver at least the promised QoS. As expected, these constraints are related to the market price of QoS.

Proposition 1. *Let the function $u : \mathcal{Q} \to \mathbb{R}$ define the market price clients pay for a given QoS. When (1) clients truthfully submit feedback, and (2) the penalty function satisfies: $\partial\lambda(q, R)/\partial q \geq 2u'(q)$, for all q and R, the reputation-based SLA makes it rational for all service provider types to deliver at least the advertised QoS.*

Proof. Consider a type θ provider advertising $sla_t = (\bar{q}_t, p_t, \lambda_t)$ in period t. If the provider exerts effort level e_t, his expected revenue is:

$$V_t(e_t, \bar{q}_t) = N_t \cdot (p_t - E[\lambda(\bar{q}_t, R_t)]) - c(e_t, \theta); \qquad (1)$$

where R_t is the reputation of the provider at the end of time period t, N_t is the number of services sold in period t, $c(e_t, \theta)$ is the cost of effort, and the expected penalty is computed with respect to possible values of R_t. V_t does not depend on any past or future decisions of the provider. By individually maximizing the sequence of payoffs, a rational provider also maximizes his life-time revenue.

When the provider exerts effort e_t, the quality of the service equals $\phi(\theta, e_t) + \eta_n$, where η_n is normally distributed around 0 with variance σ_n^2. Clients truthfully report their observations, however, they make mistakes. Assuming that the number of reports is big enough, the value of the reputation $R_t = \phi(\theta, e_t) + \eta_n + \eta_r$ is normally distributed around $\phi(\theta, e_t)$ with the variance $\sigma^2 = \sigma_n^2 + \sigma_r^2$.

Let $(e^*, q^*) = \arg\max_{(e_t, \bar{q}_t)} E[V_t(e_t, \bar{q}_t)]$ be the optimal effort level and advertised QoS. Assuming the provider asks the maximum price for the advertised quality (i.e. $p_t = u(\bar{q}_t)$), the first order condition on q^* becomes:

$$\frac{1}{N_t}\frac{\partial V_t}{\partial \bar{q}_t}(e^*, q^*) = u'(q^*) - E\left[\frac{\partial\lambda}{\partial\bar{q}_t}(q^*, \phi(e^*) + \eta)\right]$$

$$= u'(q^*) - \int_{q<q^*} normpdf(q|\phi(e^*), \sigma)\frac{\partial\lambda}{\partial\bar{q}_t}(q^*, q)dq = 0;$$

where $normpdf(q|\phi(e^*), \sigma)$ is the normal probability distribution function with the mean $\phi(e^*)$ and variance σ^2.

By replacing the condition on λ, we get:

$$\int_{q<q^*} normpdf(q|\phi(e^*), \sigma)dq \leq 0.5 \qquad (2)$$

i.e. the cumulative probability distribution $Pr[q < q^*|\phi(e^*)] \leq 0.5$. For a normal distribution, this is only true if $q^* \leq \phi(e^*)$. In other words, all provider types deliver at least the promised QoS.   □

Clients can check the constraint on the penalty function by analyzing the previous transactions concluded in the market. For every previously negotiated $sla_i = (\bar{q}_i, p_i, \lambda_i)$, clients infer that the market price corresponding to $\bar{q}_i$ must be higher than p_i: i.e. $u(\bar{q}_i) \geq p_i$. Previous interactions thus establish a lower bound on the real market price that can be used to safe-check the validity of the penalty function. Please note that the proof above does not make any assumptions about the market price or the cost function of the providers. Reputation-based SLAs can thus be used for a variety of settings.

All service providers have the incentive to minimize the penalty function specified by the SLA. This happens when the constraint in Proposition 1 is satisfied up to equality. As an immediate consequence, all service providers advertise exactly the intended QoS (Equation 2).

The mechanism assumes that (1) clients submit honest feedback, (2) they are able to submit feedback only after having interacted with the provider, and (3) they submit only one feedback per transaction. The first assumption can be integrated into the broader context of truthful feedback elicitation. The problem can be solved by side-payments (i.e. clients get paid by the reputation mechanism for submitting feedback) and will be addressed in more details in Section 4.

The second and third assumptions can be implemented through cryptographic mechanisms based on a public key infrastructure. As part of the interaction, providers can deliver signed one-time certificates that can later be used by clients to provide feedback. A concrete implementation of such a security mechanism for reputation mechanisms is presented in [7].

4   Truthful Reporting

Reporting honest feedback (as required by the proof of Proposition 1) is not exactly in the best interest of rational clients. By reporting false negative feedback (when she actually experienced a successful service) a client decreases the reputation of the provider, and consequently decreases the overall price (i.e. price minus penalty) she needs to pay for the service. Actually, it is always in the clients' best interest to report negative feedback. Unless this strategic bias can be eliminated, rational clients will consistently downrate providers who will eventually quit the market.

Side-payments (i.e. clients get paid for submitting feedback) can be designed to encourage rational clients to report the truth. This is possible because the observation of a client (i.e. the fact that the service delivered to her had high or low quality) slightly changes the client's belief regarding the experience of future clients. Take a client having experienced a low quality service (e.g. a request failure). The client will infer that the present invocation failure is likely to be caused by a problem affecting the general infrastructure of the provider. Future clients will probably be affected by the failure as well, and therefore, the average QoS experienced by the next clients is slightly lower than expected (prior to observing the failure).

$S(0,0)$	$\dfrac{2(1-\bar{q}_t)(1-2\bar{q}_t+\bar{q}_t^2+\sigma^2)-(\bar{q}_t-\bar{q}_t^2-\sigma^2)^2-(1-2\bar{q}_t+\bar{q}_t^2+\sigma^2)^2}{(1-\bar{q}_t)^2}$
$S(1,0)$	$\dfrac{2(1-\bar{q}_t)(\bar{q}_t-\bar{q}_t^2-\sigma^2)-(\bar{q}_t-\bar{q}_t^2-\sigma^2)^2-(1-2\bar{q}_t+\bar{q}_t^2+\sigma^2)^2}{(1-\bar{q}_t)^2}$
$S(0,1)$	$\dfrac{2\bar{q}_t(\bar{q}_t-\bar{q}_t^2-\sigma^2)-(\bar{q}_t-\bar{q}_t^2-\sigma^2)^2-(\bar{q}_t^2+\sigma^2)^2}{\bar{q}_t^2}$
$S(1,1)$	$\dfrac{2\bar{q}_t(\bar{q}_t^2+\sigma^2)-(\bar{q}_t-\bar{q}_t^2-\sigma^2)^2-(\bar{q}_t^2+\sigma^2)^2}{\bar{q}_t^2}$

Fig. 2. Side-payments for reputation reports, depending on the advertised QoS ($\bar{q}_t$) and noise (σ^2)

Similarly, a high quality service testifies for the well functioning of the provider's infrastructure and encourages more optimistic estimates regarding the QoS observed by future clients. This asymmetry in the beliefs regarding the experience of future clients can be exploited by side-payments that make truthful reporting optimal.

Concretely, we adapt the mechanism described by Miller et al. [13] to our setting. The basic idea behind the mechanism is to use the feedback of a future client (referred to as *rater*) to rate (and compute the payment for) a submitted report. The present report is used to update a probability distribution for the report of the rater. The payment for the report is then computed by comparing the *likelihood* assigned to the rater's rating with the rater's actual rating.

The payment scheme is the following:

- all reports submitted during the same period of time are attributed a unique sequence number, $i \in \{0, \ldots N\}$. N is the total number of collected reports (in a period).
- the feedback r_i is compared against feedback r_{i+1}, and is paid $S(r_{i+1}, r_i)$ defined according to Fig. 2:

The side payments depend on (a) the advertised QoS, and (b) on the variance $\sigma^2 = \sigma_n^2 + \sigma_r^2$ of the observed QoS. The first is specified in the SLA. The second can be approximated by the reputation mechanism from the reputation record of the provider (e.g. the reputation R_i is a noisy approximation of the same intended QoS). The side payments are computed and made public by the reputation mechanism at the beginning of each time period.

To prove that rational clients have the incentive to tell the truth we have to consider their beliefs. Given the SLA ($\bar{q}_t, p_t, \lambda_t$), every client believes that the actual QoS is normally distributed around $\bar{q}_t$ with variance σ_n^2. Having observed a successful service or a failure, the client updates her prior beliefs (described by the pdf[3] $f(q)$) according to Bayes' Law into the posterior pdfs: $f(q|1)$, respectively $f(q|0)$:

$$f(q|1) = \frac{Pr[1|q] \cdot f(q)}{\int_Q Pr[1|q]f(q)dq}; \qquad f(q|0) = \frac{(1-Pr[1|q]) \cdot f(q)}{1 - \int_Q Pr[1|q]f(q)dq};$$

---

[3] Probability distribution funtion.

where $Pr[1|q]$ is the probability of observing 1 given a service with quality q, and $\int_{\mathcal{Q}} Pr[1|q]f(q)dq = \bar{q}_t$ is the overall probability of observing high quality. Consequently, the *likelihood* assigned by the client to the next client's rating is described by:

$$
\begin{aligned}
Pr[r_{i+1} = 1|r_i = 1] &= \int_{\mathcal{Q}} Pr[1|q]f(q|1)dq = \frac{\bar{q}_t^2 + \sigma^2}{\bar{q}_t}; \\
Pr[r_{i+1} = 1|r_i = 0] &= \int_{\mathcal{Q}} Pr[1|q]f(q|0)dq = \frac{\bar{q}_t - \bar{q}_t^2 - \sigma^2}{1 - \bar{q}_t};
\end{aligned}
\tag{3}
$$

It is easy to verify that $Pr[1|1]S(1,1) + Pr[0|1]S(0,1) \geq Pr[1|1]S(1,0) + Pr[0|1]S(0,0)$ and $Pr[1|0]S(1,0) + Pr[0|0]S(0,0) \geq Pr[1|0]S(1,1) + Pr[0|0]S(0,1)$. In other words, when the next client reports the truth, the expected payment of a true report is always greater than the expected payment of a false report. This makes truthful reporting a Nash equilibrium. The side payments can be scaled to be always positive and budget balanced (details in [13]).

Every negative report decreases the price a client has to pay by $\lambda(\bar{q}_t, R_t - 1/N) - \lambda_t(\bar{q}_t, R_t)$. The client cannot benefit from submitting a false negative report if the loss due to lying outweighs the price cut. This can be achieved by multiplying the values in Fig. 2 with the constant[4]:

$$
M = \frac{\lambda_t(\bar{q}_t, R_t - 1/N) - \lambda_t(\bar{q}_t, R_t)}{E(1,1) - E(0,1)}
\tag{4}
$$

where $E(r_i, o_i)$ denotes the expected payment of client i given that she has observed $o_i \in \{0, 1\}$ and reports $r_i \in \{0, 1\}$.

4.1   Enforcing the Truthful Reporting Strategy

The truthful equilibrium defined above is unfortunately not unique. Clients, for example, can always report negative feedback without suffering side payment losses (i.e. always reporting 0 is also a Nash equilibrium strategy). In [8] we suggest the use of *trusted reports* in order to eliminate such *undesired* equilibrium strategies. Trusted reports can be obtained from specialized agents hired to test the service of a provider.

The truthful equilibrium becomes unique when the feedback from clients is rated (as explained in the previous section) only against trusted reports. It is desirable, however, to minimize the number of trusted reports needed in order to enforce the uniqueness of the truthful equilibrium.

We modify the rating scheme from Section 4 such that all client reports are rated against one trusted report, randomly chosen from a small set of available trusted reports. In the extreme case the set could contain only one report; however, the right tradeoff between robustness (against the mistakes of specialized agents) and cost can be achieved by having several trusted reports.

---

[4] Multiplication or addition with a constant does not influence the truthful reporting Nash equilibrium of the side payment mechanism.

In [8] we show that it is not necessary to have trusted reports for every time period. Using the side-payments defined above, we conclude that the truthful reporting equilibrium is very stable. It takes a big proportion (e.g. 20%) of lying agents in order to shift the reporting equilibrium, and make it rational for the other agents to lie as well. As a consequence, trusted reports need only be used in the first periods of time in order to coordinate the clients on the truthful equilibrium. Once the truthful strategy is enforced, the market can do a passive monitoring of the reporting strategy and buy new trusted reports only when a deviation is observed. In this way, the overall number of trusted reports needed by the market becomes insignificant.

4.2 Collusion

Collusion happens when two or more clients conspire to artificially decrease the reputation of a provider, and thus decrease the price they have to pay for the service. The reputation side-payments do not make it interesting for one client to submit negative feedback, however, when several clients form a coalition and adopt a negative reporting strategy, the price-cut is cumulative and every agent benefits from the action of the group.

The use of trusted reports (as described in Section 4.1) also deters collusion. When clients are self-interested and external punishments cannot be inflicted on them, we prove that any feedback-reporting coalition is unstable, and hence, irrational.

Proposition 2. *The reputation-based Service Level Agreements are feedback-reporting collusion proof.*

Proof. The intuition behind this proof is that any coalition of clients (colluding to submit false feedback) is unstable. As member of such a coalition, a rational client finds it more profitable to report the truth rather than stick to the colluding strategy. Clients are free to maximize their revenue, so they will quit the coalition and choose to report truthfully.

Formally, take a subset of clients colluding on a lying strategy, and let the client c, part of the coalition, be expected to lie when submitting feedback. Client c exists, since otherwise all colluding agents report the truth. c can stick to the colluding strategy and lie: she thus benefits from the advantages of collusion, however, expects a loss due to reputation side-payments. On the other hand, c can deviate and report the truth: she thus optimizes her expected payment from the reputation mechanism but the result of collusion is less effective.

The side-payments multiplied by the factor in Equation (4) guarantee that the loss in reputation payment is always greater than the price-cut obtained from one false report. Therefore, it is rational for c to leave the coalition. The same argument can be applied to any colluding client; hence feedback-reporting collusion is not rational.   □

Please note that stronger forms of collusion are still possible. If one client controls multiple online identities (the sybil attack) she can coordinate false reporting in order to decrease the price of service. This type of collusion should be addressed by security and social mechanisms that closely connect online and physical identity.

5   Experimental Evaluation

The use of reputation information greatly reduces the independent monitoring required by markets of web services. In this section we compare the mechanism described in this paper (mechanism A) with an alternative mechanism (mechanism B) where the market only uses trusted reports (i.e. independent monitoring) to compute the penalty to service providers for QoS degradation.

We first investigate the quality of monitoring of the two mechanisms. The precision of the monitored QoS value directly impacts the revenue of service providers. When the monitored QoS value is exactly equal to the delivered QoS, service providers do not have to pay any penalty and thus obtain their maximum payoff. However, practical monitoring schemes always provide noise approximations of the delivered QoS. The noise thus introduced, translates into a non-zero expected penalty that decreases the total utility of service providers. The poorer the approximation offered by the monitoring system, the greater the utility loss of service providers.

The second criterion we employ is the monitoring cost required by the two mechanisms. While general analytical results can be obtained, we believe it is more informative to compare the two mechanisms on a realistic (however simplified) example.

Consider a web service providing closing stock quotes. A reputation-based SLA is advertised every morning and specifies the price of service, the QoS (e.g. the quote is obtained within 5 minutes of the closing time with probability $\bar{q}$) and the penalty function λ. Interested clients request the service, and then wait the answers from the service provider. They experience high quality if the answers is received before the deadline (i.e. 5 minutes after the closing time) or low quality if the answer is late or not received.

The probability of successfully answering the clients' requests depends on the available infrastructure and on the number of accepted requests. For a given provider, Fig. 3 plots the relation (experimentally determined) between the expected QoS (i.e. $\phi(n)$), and the number of accepted requests. The QoS actually provided to the clients is normally distributed around $\phi(n)$ with variance σ_n^2.

We assume that the closing stock quotes represent mission-critical information for the clients present in the market. Late or absent information attracts supplementary planning costs and lost opportunities. Therefore, the market price function, (i.e. $u(q)$) is assumed convex, corresponding to risk-averse clients. When $\bar{q}$ is the advertised QoS, n is the number of accepted requests, $\hat{q}$ is the QoS perceived by the market, and C denotes the fixed costs, the expected revenue of the provider is:

$$V(n, \bar{q}) = E_{\hat{q}} \Big[n \cdot \big(u(\hat{q}) - \lambda(\bar{q}, \hat{q}) \big) - C \Big];$$

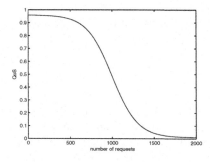

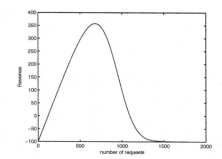

Fig. 3. The QoS as a function of the number of requests accepted by a provider (Experimentally determined)

Fig. 4. The revenue function of the provider depending on the number of accepted requests

By using the mechanism A, the market perceives a QoS equal to: $\hat{q}_A = \phi(n) + \eta_n + \eta_r$ where η_r is the noise introduced by reporting mistakes, normally distributed around 0 with variance σ_r^2. For a price function $u(q) = q^2$, the fixed cost $C = 100$, the standard deviations $\sigma_n = 3\%$, $\sigma_r = 4\%$, and a penalty function $\lambda(\bar{q}, \hat{q}) = 2(p(\bar{q}) - p(\hat{q}))$, Fig. 4 shows the optimal revenue of the provider as a function of n. The optimal value of the payoff function is reached for $n_t = 681$, when $\bar{q} = 0.858 = \phi(681)$, as predicted by Proposition 1. Mechanism B satisfies the same optimality and incentive-compatible properties for the service provider. Different price functions or quality functions generate different optimal parameters, however, they do not modify the qualitative properties of the mechanism: providers deliver at least their declared QoS, and clients have the incentives to report the truth.

The average, per-client, utility loss of a service provider is defined as the expected penalty a provider has to pay as a consequence of an inaccurate approximation of the delivered QoS (as computed by the monitoring mechanisms). When $\hat{q}_A$ and $\hat{q}_b$ are the monitored QoS values provided by the two mechanisms, the utility losses caused by the two mechanisms are:

$$UtilLoss_A = E_{\hat{q}_A}\big[\lambda(\bar{q}, \hat{q}_A)\big]; \qquad UtilLoss_B = E_{\hat{q}_B}\big[\lambda(\bar{q}, \hat{q}_B)\big];$$

computed at the optimal QoS, $\bar{q}$. A higher variance of $\hat{q}$ increases the utility losses of providers. Typically, mechanism B has less information than mechanism A about the delivered QoS and therefore generates higher losses for providers. The difference in the average utility loss per client generated by the two mechanisms is shown in Fig. 5, as a function of the number of trusted reports employed by mechanism B. To reach the same performance, mechanism B needs approximately 75 trusted reports, i.e. 11% of the number of service requests.

The administrative costs of the mechanism A consist of (a) the reputation side-payments and (b) the cost of trusted reports. The cost of mechanism B consists only of trusted reports. The cost of a trusted report is assumed equal

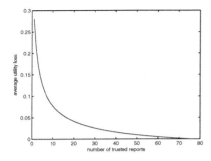

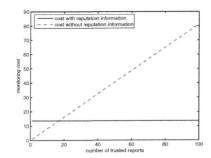

Fig. 5. The difference in client utility loss caused by using only trusted reports

Fig. 6. The monitoring cost of not using reputation information

to $(1 + \delta)$ times the price of service (e.g. the monitoring agent buys the service and receives a commission δ). We take $\delta = 0.1$.

For the same parameter values as above, the reputation side-payments given in Fig. 2 (properly scaled to be positive and multiplied with the correction factor defined by Equation 4) become: $S(1,1) = 2.3\%$, $S(0,1) = 0$, $S(1,0) = 1.6\%$ and $S(0,0) = 1.7\%$ of the price of the perfect service (i.e. $u(1)$). Fig. 6 plots the difference in monitoring costs between the mechanisms A and B for different number of trusted reports employed by mechanism B. For similar performance (i.e. 75 trusted reports) mechanism B has monitoring costs that are 4 times higher.

Please note that the utility loss in Fig. 5 is for every client. When mechanisms A and B have the same monitoring cost (i.e. mechanism B uses approximately 20 trusted reports) a service provider looses on the average approx. 4.5% more utility for every customer as a consequence of not using reputation-based monitoring. This apparently insignificant amount, multiplied by the number of total clients (i.e. 681), generates significant losses for the provider.

6   Related Work

Our work can best be situated at the confluence of two lines of research in service-oriented computing: electronic contract enforcement and reputation-based selection of services.

The legal system is seen as inappropriate for e-commerce disputes [2] and therefore alternative dispute resolution mechanisms have been proposed to avoid the escalation of disputes to the legal stage. Electronic contract enforcement covers both non-discretionary approaches (e.g. preventive security mechanisms) as well as discretionary ones (e.g. different control mechanisms that are applied when contract rules are breached). Concrete progress has been made in the areas of e-contract formal models ([19], [18]), contract performance monitoring([19], [14], [11]), mediation of services through trusted third parties ([15], [16]) and security infrastructures for safe service delivery([6], [5]).

Reputation mechanisms have emerged as efficient tools for service discovery and selection [17]. When electronic contracts cannot be enforced, users can protect themselves against cheating providers by looking at past behavior (i.e. the provider's reputation). Lie et al. [10] present a QoS-based selection model that takes into account the feedback from users as well as other business related criteria. The model is extensible and dynamic. In the same spirit, [9] proposes *verity*, a QoS measure that takes into account both reputation and the terms of the SLA. [12] and [1] propose concrete frameworks for service selection based on provider reputation.

An interesting approach is proposed by Deora et al. in [4]. The authors argue that the expectations of a client greatly influence the submitted feedback, and therefore both should be used when assessing the QoS of a provider.

Our work is novel in three main aspects. First, client feedback becomes a first-class citizen of the interaction model. Reputation has a clear semantics and is used to compute monetary penalties for deviations from the advertised QoS. This makes it possible to rigourously analyze the strategies of rational service providers and give theoretical proofs regarding the properties of the mechanism: e.g. truthful declaration of QoS, low monitoring cost. Second, our model is free from any probabilistic assumptions about the behavior of clients and providers. Clients and providers are assumed to be self interested and free to maximize their revenues. Third, we present a practical mechanism for ensuring truthful feedback from clients that also deters collusion.

7   Conclusion

Without proper monitoring of the delivered QoS, self-interested providers have the incentive to cheat by promising a higher than intended QoS. In this paper we present a new form of SLAs where the final price paid by clients depends on the actual quality delivered by the service provider, as computed by a reputation mechanism. When clients honestly submit feedback, a reputation mechanism is efficient in monitoring the real QoS and makes it rational for all service providers to keep their promises.

As a second contribution we show how a side-payment scheme can be used in a market of web services to elicit honest feedback from rational clients. Moreover, a small number of trusted reports can prevent collusion and enforce truth-telling as a unique strategy. In a previous paper we prove that only few trusted reports are temporarily needed in order to coordinate the clients on the truthful strategy. After this initial phase, the truthful strategy is quite stable (i.e. it takes a large group of agents to change the reporting strategy of the whole community) and the market should only assume a passive, monitoring role. Our mechanism therefore generates significantly lower cost than traditional monitoring mechanisms.

We thus describe a simple, robust mechanism that eliminates incentives for selfish providers to cheat, at a much lower cost. The assumptions behind the mechanism are fairly general, making it a candidate for many practical settings.

References

1. B. Alunkal, I. Veljkovic, G. Laszewski, and K. Amin. Reputation-Based Grid Resource Selection. In *Proceedings of AGridM*, 2003.
2. A. Carblanc. Privacy protection and redress in the online environment: Fostering effective alternative dispute resolution. In *In Proceedings of the 22nd International Conference on Privacy and Personal Data Protection*, Venice, 2000.
3. A. Dan, D. Davis, R. Kearney, A. Keller, R. King, D. Kuebler, H. Ludwig, M. Polan, M. Spreitzer, and A. Youseff. Web services on demand: WSLA-driven automated management. *IBM Systems Journal*, 43(1):136–158, 2004.
4. V. Deora, J. Shao, W. Gray, and J. Fiddian. A Quality of Service Management Framework Based on User Expectations. In *Proceedings of ICSOC*, 2003.
5. R. Handorean and G. Roman. A framework for requirements monitoring of service based systems. In *Proceedings of ICSOC*, 2003.
6. Y.-J. Hu. Trusted Agent-Mediated E-Commerce Transaction Services via Digital Certificate Management. *Electronic Commerce Research*, 3, 2003.
7. R. Jurca and B. Faltings. An Incentive-Compatible Reputation Mechanism. In *Proceedings of the IEEE Conference on E-Commerce*, Newport Beach, CA, USA, 2003.
8. R. Jurca and B. Faltings. Enforcing Truthful Strategies in Incentive Compatible Reputation Mechanisms. In *Proceedings of the Workshop on Internet and Network Economics (WINE)*, Hong Kong, China, 2005.
9. S. Kalepu, S. Krishnaswamy, and S. Loke. Verity; A QoS Metric for Selecting Web Services and Providers. In *Proceedings of WISEW*, 2003.
10. Y. Liu, A. Ngu, and L. Yeng. QoS Computation and Policing in Dynamic Web Service Selection. In *Proceedings of WWW*, 2004.
11. K. Mahbub and G. Spanoudakis. A framework for requirements monitoring of service based systems. In *Proceedings of ICSOC*, 2004.
12. E. M. Maximilien and M. P. Singh. Toward Autonomic Web Services Trust and Selection. In *Proceedings of ICSOC*, 2004.
13. N. Miller, P. Resnick, and R. Zeckhauser. Eliciting Informative Feedback: The Peer-Prediction Method. Forthcoming in Management Science, 2005.
14. Z. Milosevic and G. Dromey. On expressing and monitoring behaviour in contracts. In *Proceedings of EDOC*, Lausanne, Switzerland, 2002.
15. G. Piccinelli, C. Stefanelli, and D. Trastour. Trusted Mediation for E-service Provision in Electronic Marketplaces. *Lecture Notes in Computer Science*, 2232:39, 2001.
16. R. Shuping. A Model for Web Service Discovery with QoS. *ACM SIGecom Exchanges*, 4(1):1–10, 2003.
17. M. P. Singh and M. N. Huhns. *Service-Oriented Computing*. Wiley, 2005.
18. Y.-H. Tan and W. Thoen. A Logical Model of Directed Obligations and Permissions to Support Electronic Contracting. *International Journal of Electronic Commerce*, 3(2), 1999.
19. L. Xu and M. A. Jeusfeld. Pro-active Monitoring of Electronic Contracts. *Lecture Notes in Computer Science*, 2681:584–600, 2003.

Handling Faults in Decentralized Orchestration of Composite Web Services

Girish Chafle, Sunil Chandra, Pankaj Kankar, and Vijay Mann

IBM India Research Laboratory, New Delhi, India
{cgirish, csunil, kpankaj, vijamann}@in.ibm.com

Abstract. Composite web services can be orchestrated in a decentralized manner by breaking down the original service specification into a set of partitions and executing them on a distributed infrastructure. The infrastructure consists of multiple service engines communicating with each other over asynchronous messaging. Decentralized orchestration yields performance benefits by exploiting concurrency and reducing the data on the network. Further, decentralized orchestration may be necessary to orchestrate certain composite web services due to privacy and data flow constraints. However, decentralized orchestration also results in additional complexity due to absence of a centralized global state, and overlapping or different life cycles of the various partitions. This makes handling of faults arising from composite service partitions or from the failure of component web services, a challenging task.

In this paper we propose a mechanism for handling faults in decentralized orchestration of composite web services. The mechanism includes a strategy for placement of fault handlers and compensation handlers, and schemes for fault propagation and fault recovery. The mechanism is designed to maintain the semantics of the original specification while ensuring minimal overheads.

1 Introduction

A composite web service is created by aggregating the functionality of existing web services (which act as its *components*) and can be specified using XML based languages like BPEL4WS [1], WSIPL [9], WSCI [3], *etc.* Typically, a composite service is *orchestrated* by an orchestrator node in a *centralized* manner. The orchestrator node receives the client requests, invokes the component web services and makes the required data transformations as per the service specification. We refer to this mode of execution as **centralized** orchestration. In this mode, all data is transferred between the various components via the orchestrator node instead of being transferred directly from the point of generation to the point of consumption. This leads to unnecessary traffic on the network resulting in poor scalability and performance degradation at high loads. Furthermore, centralized orchestration may not be feasible in scenarios where component web services place constraints on access to the data they provide or on the source from which they can accept data.

B. Benatallah, F. Casati, and P. Traverso (Eds.): ICSOC 2005, LNCS 3826, pp. 410–423, 2005.
© Springer-Verlag Berlin Heidelberg 2005

We have been investigating decentralized orchestration in our prior work [6,7,15,16] in order to overcome the above mentioned limitations imposed by centralized orchestration. In *decentralized* orchestration [15], the composite web service specification is analyzed for data and control dependencies, and broken down into a semantically-equivalent set of partitions known as *topology*. The partitions execute independently without any centralized control and interact with each other directly by transferring data using asynchronous messaging. Our decentralization algorithm [15] reduces the data on the network by sending it directly from its point of generation to point of consumption.

The benefits of decentralization come with the added complexity of the system as decentralization involves partitions which execute independently and interact with each other directly using asynchronous messaging. The global state of the original composite service is now distributed across different partitions. A fault occurring in one partition does not get noticed by other partitions or the client issuing the request. Fault propagation (even in absence of fault recovery) becomes essential so that - a) a fault occurring in one partition does not lead to any other partition waiting indefinitely for an input from the erroneous partition , and b) a client issuing a request is notified about the fault occurring in a partition. Absence of fault propagation in decentralized orchestration will lead to degradation of system performance with increasing load as resources get held up. This is hardly an issue in centralized orchestration as faults are generated locally on the centralized node and the client can be notified easily. Fault recovery, on the other hand, is required in order to correct the effects of partial changes to the state of the system and restore the system to an error free state.

A mechanism for fault handling, has to be designed such that it does not degrade the system performance under normal execution and at the same time be as efficient as possible in case of a fault. However, designing such a mechanism for decentralized orchestration is non trivial because of the following challenges:

- In contrast to centralized orchestration, there is no centralized global state as different partitions execute on different nodes.
- When a composite service specification is partitioned, the fault and compensation handlers have to be placed appropriately amongst the partitions in order to maintain correct semantics of the original service specification. Furthermore, the partitions need to be augmented with additional code to correctly forward and handle faults.
- Composite service languages such as BPEL4WS define "scope" activity to associate fault handlers and compensation handlers with a fault handling and recovery context. However, in decentralized orchestration, a single scope might get partitioned across various partitions and the partitioned scopes might execute at different times and have either overlapping or different lifecycles. No single context exists that can store the data of already completed scopes which is needed to compensate them while recovering from a fault.

In this paper we propose a mechanism for handling faults in decentralized orchestration of composite web services.The mechanism includes a strategy for placement of fault and compensation handlers and schemes for fault propagation and fault recovery. The mechanism is designed to maintain the semantics of the original service specification while ensuring minimal overheads.

2   Background and Related Work

Lot of work has been done in the area of fault handling in distributed systems. Two types of approaches have been proposed for fault recovery - *backward error recovery* and *forward error recovery* [14]. Forward error recovery is based on the use of redundant data that repairs the system by analyzing the detected fault and putting the system into a correct state. In contrast, backward error recovery returns the system to a previous (presumed to be) fault-free state without requiring detailed knowledge of the faults.

Various fault handling models for flat and nested workflow transaction hierarchies have also been proposed in literature [8,18]. BPEL4WS uses a fault handling model that supports nested transactions and allows inner transactions (or sub-transactions) to make their results visible externally (referred to as open nested transactions [18]). In this paper we adhere to the fault handling model used by BPEL4WS and propose mechanisms that help conforming to the BPEL4WS fault handling model during decentralized orchestration of BPEL4WS composite services.

Application partitioning systems (JOrchestra [17], Coign [11], etc) that replace local method calls by remote method calls make use of various forms of forward or backward error recovery scheme as the control for the application remains centralized and there exists a single context in which faults are handled.

Various workflow systems (including systems that employ workflow partitioning) relied heavily on backward error recovery, (although forward error recovery can also be used here) as most of the underlying resources were usually under the control of a single domain. These are specified using proprietary languages and usually do not handle nested scopes [10,13].

Fault recovery becomes a little more complex for composite web services as component web services may be distributed across different autonomous domains. Transactions (which fall under backward error recovery mechanisms), which have been successfully used in providing fault tolerance to distributed systems, are not suited in such cases because of following reasons:

- Management of transactions that span across web services deployed on different domains requires cooperation among the transactional systems of individual domains. These transactional systems may not be compliant with each other.
- Locking resources until the termination of the embedding transaction is in general not appropriate for such web services, still due to their autonomy, and also to the fact that they potentially have a large number of concurrent clients that will not stand extensive delays.

Forward error recovery is extensively used in composite web services in order to handle errors. For instance, BPEL4WS provides support for fault handling to recover from expected as well as unexpected faults, and compensation to "undo" already committed steps by providing user defined fault handler and compensation handler constructs. Apart from the compensation handlers in BPEL4WS, lot of other efforts are also underway for providing transactional support for composite web services (BTP [2], and WS Transaction [4]). Other related work includes Web Service Composition Action (WSCA) [12]. WSCA is an extension of the Coordinated Atomic Action (CA Action) for web services, and is used for handling concurrent exceptions.

Decentralized orchestration of composite web services further complicates fault handling as discussed earlier. In addition to augmenting the existing forward error recovery mechanisms, additional fault propagation and data collection schemes are needed. Not much work has been done in this area.

3   Proposed Fault Handling Mechanism

As discussed in section 2, forward error recovery mechanisms are used for composite web services. The proposed mechanism is also based on the same. It is designed to maintain the semantics of original centralized specification and handles only those faults which are handled either explicitly or implicitly in the original centralized specification. The overall mechanism is based on correct partitioning of the input service specification, such that the fault handlers and compensation handlers are placed appropriately amongst the different partitions, and on augmenting the partitions with additional code that aids in fault propagation, data collection and fault recovery. The fault handling mechanism consists of three runtime phases when a fault occurs. The first phase ensures the propagation of a fault to a partition where its corresponding fault handler resides. The second phase consists of collecting the data, that is needed to initiate fault recovery, from different partitions. The third phase consists of handling the fault in the appropriate fault handler and initiating forward recovery by invoking compensation handlers of already completed inner scope(s). These phases are described in detail in the following subsections with the help of BPEL4WS constructs.

3.1   Placement of Fault Handlers and Compensation Handlers

BPEL4WS specification defines "scope" activities to associate fault handlers and compensation handlers with a fault handling and recovery context . Every BPEL4WS process has an implicit scope of its own. An explicit "scope" activity or an implicit scope can consist of many activities, each of which could itself be a "scope" activity, thereby resulting in *nested scopes*. Since, any activity may generate a fault, the control may flow from any activity to the fault handlers. Further, a fault handler may completely handle the fault or may re-throw it to the outer scope. If a fault handler handles a fault, the execution in the outer scope resumes normally. However, any scope, whose associated fault handler has been invoked, is not considered to be completed normally and compensation is not enabled for it and can not be called on it from an outer scope. Compensation is

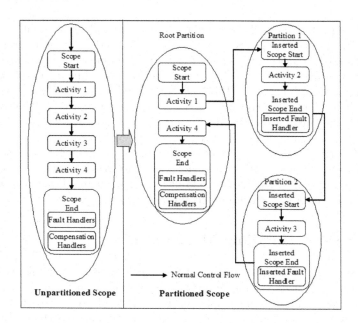

Fig. 1. Partitioning of scope and placement of fault and compensation handlers

enabled only for those scopes that have completed normally and a compensation handler is always invoked from a fault handler or a compensation handler of the outer scope.

In decentralized orchestration, activities inside a scope may get arbitrarily partitioned and thus placement of fault and compensation handlers requires special attention. The overall decentralization algorithm presented in [15] works as follows. In the proposed solution, the decentralization algorithm partitions a scope in such a manner that the start and end of each scope reside in the same partition (which is referred to as the **root** partition of that scope) and the rest of the activities of the scope are placed as per the algorithm described in [15]. We anchor the fault handlers and compensation handlers to the end of scope (refer figure 1). This means that the fault handlers and compensation handlers for a scope always reside in the *root partition* of that scope. Theoretically, the end of each scope can reside on a partition that is the last partition in the control flow of a particular scope. Thus, the start and end can reside on different partitions. The end of the scope partition will then host the fault handlers and compensation handlers according to the scheme given in this paper. However, this will require creation of a logical "scope" that is different from the physical "scope" activity in BPEL4WS. Furthermore, state information will have to be transferred from the start of scope partition to the end of scope partition. To avoid this complexity, the start and end of each scope are placed together. In case of conditional activities like `while` and `switch`, the root partition is the partition that contains the condition itself.

The algorithm given in [15] has been modified to ensure that the fault handlers and the compensation handlers are anchored to the root partition of a scope. We prepare the *Control Flow Graph (CFG)* preserving the fault handlers and compensation handler. A fault handler may have various *Catch* blocks for handling different faults and a *CatchAll* block for handling any fault. A *control flow* edge is added from every activity to the first activity under *CatchAll* since control can flow from any activity to the fault handlers. For all the other fault handlers, a separate control flow edge is added from all those activities which can throw the fault handled by this handler to the first activity of the handler. Similarly, a control flow edge is added from the last activity of the scope to the start activity of the compensation handler because as per BPEL4WS specification, the compensation handler, if invoked, will see a frozen snapshot of all variables, as they were when the scope being compensated was completed. After that we run the *Reaching Definitions* algorithm [5] to generate all the *data flow* edges to discover data dependencies between activities and corresponding activities of the fault and compensation handlers. These data flow edges are used to determine what data needs to be propagated to the root partition during the data collection phase, which is subsequently used during fault handling and recovery.

The data flow edges getting in or out of the fault handlers and compensation handler are marked as fault edges as these are different from the normal data flow edges between activities of the scope. Before we construct the *Control Dependent Graph (CDG)* we cut the sub-trees corresponding to fault handlers and compensation handler from their scopes. After this the *Merge* algorithm (given in [15]) runs on the modified CDG in the normal fashion, ignoring the fault data flow edges. Since, the sub-trees corresponding to fault handlers and compensation handler are absent from the CDG given to *Merge* algorithm, the algorithm will not create partitions for the activities of these handlers. After creating all the partitions, these handlers are added to the their respective scopes during code generation, thereby ensuring that the fault handlers and compensation handlers reside in the root partition.

3.2 Fault Propagation

Since a fault may occur in any partition and the corresponding fault handler resides in the *root partition*, the fault needs to be propagated to the root partition. A partition forwards a fault, that has either occurred within that partition or it has been received from another partition as part of the fault propagation scheme, to one of the following partitions (at the same level in PDG [15]), whichever comes first, in the control flow path

- Root partition of the given scope: All the fault handlers and compensation handlers associated with a scope reside in the root partition of the given scope (shown in figure 1) and all faults occurring within a scope are eventually routed to the root partition (shown in figure 2).
- Next join partition (a partition having more than one incoming links): If there is a join partition (shown in figure 2) in between the given partition

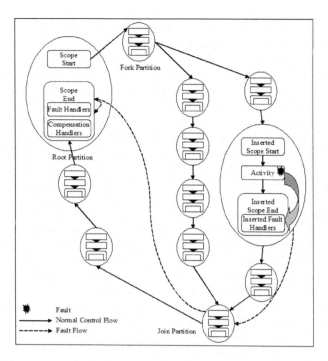

Fig. 2. Fault Propagation Scheme

and the root partition, then the fault is sent to the join partition because a join partition expects input messages from all the incoming links (which execute in parallel legs) and it will continue to wait forever for a message from the leg in which a fault has occurred in one of the partitions. To prevent this condition, the fault is sent to the join partition. The join partition, in turn, upon receiving all the incoming messages (including the fault), forwards the fault to the next partition as per the fault propagation algorithm.

– Next fork partition (a partition having more than one outgoing links): If there is a fork partition (shown in figure 2) in between the given partition and the root partition, then the fault is passed to the fork partition which then forwards the fault on all the outgoing links according to the fault propagation algorithm. A fork partition results in more than one outgoing links and these links may join at some other partition (which becomes a join partition) in the control flow. This join partition will expect an input message from all its incoming links, some of which are the outgoing links of the fork partition. Therefore a fork partition needs to forward a fault on all its outgoing links.

During code generation, all partitions except *root partition* of the process scope, are inserted with additional fault handlers (shown as inserted fault handler in figure 2) that help in fault propagation. These fault handlers are inserted in the outermost scope (which is there implicitly as all partitions consist of a

BPEL4WS `process` activity and a `process` has an implicit scope of its own) of each partition. One handler (a BPEL4WS *Catch* clause) is inserted for each type of fault handled in the original specification. If the original specification does not have a `CatchAll` fault handler, one such handler is inserted to catch other unknown faults which may be generated and need to be propagated to the root of the scope. These fault handlers pack the fault name and fault data associated with the handler and forward it. The fault handlers then wait for a control message to forward data (a snapshot of BPEL4WS variables) required for fault recovery. The `receive` activities in all partitions, to which a fault can be propagated (*i.e.,* root partitions of all scopes, fork partitions and join partitions), are replaced by `pick` activities during code generation. A `pick` activity allows reception of one of n possible incoming messages. Out of these n possible incoming messages, one is an actual input message and the rest $n-1$ incoming messages correspond to the $n-1$ fault messages which a partition can receive due to $n-1$ types of faults handled in that scope in the original specification. In order to receive these n possible messages, a new `operation` is added to the same `port type` (which existed for the actual incoming message) as part of a new `OnMessage` activity inside `pick`, for each of the n possible messages. Upon receiving a fault message, a partition throws a fault (representing the input fault message), which is then caught by the inserted fault handlers in the inserted implicit scope in case of *fork partitions* and *join partitions*, which then propagate the fault according to the fault propagation scheme. In case of a *root partition* the fault is caught and handled by the actual fault handlers associated with the given scope. If a fault handler re-throws a fault, it is automatically caught by the *inserted fault handler* that is associated with the implicit outer scope of the partition in which the inner scope resides. The inserted fault handler is augmented with code to propagate the fault to the root partition of the outer scope using the fault propagation scheme explained above.

3.3   Data Collection

The second phase of the proposed mechanism consists of collecting the data that is required to recover from a fault. All partitions that complete successfully, wait for a control message. If the composite service completes successfully, the *root partition* of the top level scope(*i.e.,* the client facing partition) sends a `NormalComplete` control message along the path traversed by request. All the partitions exit normally on the receipt of this message. In case of a fault, the fault handler of the *root partition* of the scope in which the fault occurred, sends a `DataCollection` control message to its next partition(s) according to the control flow (see figure 3). The message flows along the path traversed by the request till it reaches the partition where the fault occurred. From there, it flows along the path traversed by the fault (as per the fault propagation scheme). Each partition upon receiving the *DataCollection* control message, appends its variables *i.e.,* the data to the payload of the message as a message part. The data that needs to be appended is determined using the modified decentralization algorithm given in section 3.1. The *root partitions* of all the scopes except the top level scope for

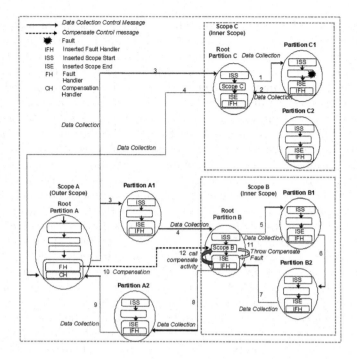

Fig. 3. Flow of control messages in case of a fault

the composite service, now enter a state where they wait for a `Compensation` or `NoCompensation` control message from their outer scope.

In implementation, a set of extra activities are added at the end of each partition. This includes a `pick` to receive either a `DataCollection` or a `NormalComplete` control message from previous partitions, a set of `assign` activities to pack the data to be sent for fault handling and compensation and a set of `invoke(s)` to send the control messages to next partitions in the control flow path. A similar set of activities are also added at the end of the inserted fault handlers (associated with the inserted implicit scope) in all the partitions. The only difference is that instead of a `pick`, a `receive` activity is added as it will never receive a `NormalComplete` control message and can receive only `DataCollection` control message, as a fault has already occurred in that scope.

3.4   Fault Recovery

Once the fault is propagated to the *root partition* of a scope, the corresponding fault handler, if provided, is triggered. If no fault handler is provided, default semantics are provided by the BPEL4WS engine hosting the *root partition*. The data collected during the second phase is used by the root partition for recovering from faults in its scope or faults thrown by its inner scopes. The fault handler associated with the root partition first executes the activities that are specified in the original specification to handle the given fault.

Normally completed scopes may need to be compensated, if a fault occurs in the outer scope or if the outer scope is being compensated. If a fault or compensation handler is provided in the original service specification that consists of explicit `compensate` activities targeted at inner scopes, then these `compensate` activities are replaced with `invoke(s)` that send a `Compensation` control message to the *root partitions* of all such inner scopes. For all other inner scopes (which don't serve as targets for any explicit `compensate` activity), a `NoCompensation` control message is sent to their *root partitions*. If there is no fault handler or compensation handler provided in the original service specification, a `Compensation` message is sent to the *root partitions* of all the inner scopes in the reverse order of their occurrence. This is shown in figure 3, where the outer scope - Scope A, has two inner scopes - Scope B and Scope C, that execute in parallel. Scope B finishes successfully, while a fault occurs in Scope C, which is first propagated to the root partition of Scope C. The root partition of Scope C initiates a data

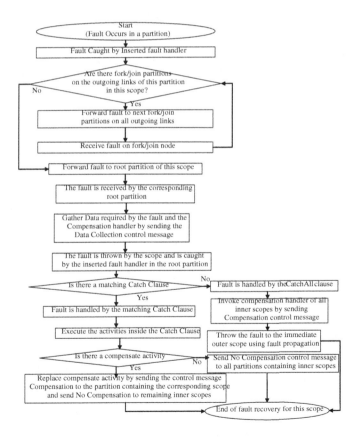

Fig. 4. Flowchart for fault propagation, data collection and fault recovery

collection phase for its scope and then throws the fault to the outer scope - Scope A, as there is no matching fault handler in Scope C. Scope A then initiates the data collection phase for Scope B and Scope C and once the data collection finishes, it compensates Scope B.

The `Compensation` (or the `NoCompensation`) control message is received by the *root partition* of inner scopes (refer figure 3). During decentralization, an additional fault handler is inserted in the top level implicit scope of each root partition, since compensation handler can be invoked only from a fault handler or a compensation handler of the immediately outer scope. When the root partition receives the `Compensation` message, it throws a specific "Compensation" fault which is caught by this inserted fault handler. This fault handler simply invokes the compensation handler of the inner scope by using explicit `compensate` activity as shown in figure 3.

Partitions containing `while` or `switch` blocks require further attention. The `switch` block maintains information about the `case` that was chosen, so that same leg is chosen for data collection and compensation phases. A `while` block can result in a number of iterations each leading to an instance of all the partitions that are part of that block. This raises issues related to the timing of data collection and fault recovery. We are working on augmenting our scheme with all these considerations for `while` loops.

All the code required for the mechanism is automatically generated by the *decentralization tool*, so that developer of the original composite service specification is not burdened with its complexity. The flowchart for the overall fault handling mechanism is shown in figure 4.

4   An Example Scenario

In this section we explain the proposed fault handling mechanism with the help of an example. To highlight all the important aspects of the scheme we created a composite service specification which includes a *switch*, an *inner scope* and few *fork* and *join* points. There are a total of 22 *invoke*s, a *switch* in the outer scope, and an inner scope. The arrangement of various activities in the BPEL4WS code leads to a decentralized topology that helps us in explaining the scheme in its full generality. We exclude the input BPEL4WS specification due to space constraints.

4.1   Fault Propagation

The fault propagation scheme is shown in action for the example scenario in figure 5. Four different requests resulting in four faults originating at different partitions are shown in the figure.

In the first request, fault $F1$ occurs in $P17$, which then forwards it to the next join partition $P13$. Partitions $P18$ (and the inner scope) and $P19$ are skipped and do not get instantiated. The other leg forked at $P12$ proceeds as usual and reaches the join partition $P13$. After receiving the two messages (the fault

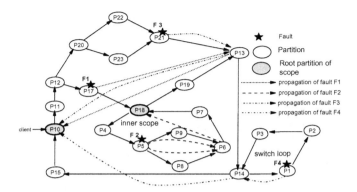

Fig. 5. Fault propagation in an example decentralized topology

message from $P17$ and a normal input message from $P21$), partition $P13$ sends the fault to the end of the scope, $P10$. Remaining partitions after $P13$ in the control flow are skipped and do not get instantiated for this request.

In the second request, fault $F2$ occurs in the inner scope at fork partition $P5$. $P5$ sends two fault messages to the next join partition $P6$, one for each outgoing leg. Partition $P6$ then sends the fault to the *root partition* of the inner scope, $P18$, where it is handled. Partitions $P7$, $P8$, and $P9$ of the inner scope are not instantiated for this particular request.

In the third request, fault $F3$ occurs in partition $P21$ which forwards it to the next join partition $P13$. The other leg forked at $P12$ including the inner scope completes normally. After receiving the two messages,(the fault message from $P21$ and a normal input message from $P19$), partition $P13$ sends the fault to the *root partition* the scope, $P10$. Remaining partitions in the control flow after $P13$ are skipped for this particular request.

In the fourth request, fault $F4$ occurs inside the `switch` block in the outer scope at $P1$, is sent to the root partition of the *switch* block $P14$, and is forwarded to the root partition of the outer scope, $P10$. Partitions $P2$, $P3$, and $P15$ are not instantiated for this particular request. The partitions preceding the switch block in control flow, get completed before the fault occurs and may need to be compensated by the compensation handlers present in the outer scope.

4.2 Data Collection

We demonstrate data collection phase for the second request which results in fault $F2$, occurring inside the inner scope and for the fourth request which results in fault $F4$, occurring inside the `switch` block, as explained above.

For the second request, the fault $F2$ reaches the *root partition* of the inner scope $P18$, which then sends the `DataCollection` control message to first partition ($P4$) in the control flow. The message then travels along the control flow path till partition $P5$ where the fault occurred. After that it follows the fault propagation path. On receiving the message, each partition appends its variables *i.e.,* the data that are required for executing the fault handlers and compensation handlers, to the payload of the message as a message part, and forward the message to the next partition and exit. The collected data finally reaches the root partition, $P18$ which invokes the fault handler for this scope.

For the fourth request, the fault $F4$, reaches the *root partition $P10$* of the outer scope, which then sends the `DataCollection` control message to its first partition ($P11$) in the control flow. The message then travels along the normal control flow covering all partitions which were instantiated (all partitions except $P2$, $P3$, and $P15$) during the course of execution of this particular request. These partitions wait for the data collection message. On receiving the control message, each partition appends its variables *i.e.,* the data that are required for executing the fault handlers and compensation handlers, to the payload of the message as a message part, and forwards the message to the next partition and exits. When the *root partition* of the inner scope, $P18$, gets the `DataCollection` message, it collects the variables that are local to the inner scope as well as those belonging to the outer scope. The variables local to the inner scope are stored at $P18$ and those belonging to the outer scope are appended to the `DataCollection` message, which is then forwarded to partition $P19$. The collected data finally reaches the *root partition* of the outer scope $P10$. All the partitions except the *root partition* of inner scope $P18$ exit after forwarding the data collection message.

4.3   Fault Recovery

The third phase of the scheme consists of execution of the activities inside a fault handler for a given scope in which a fault has occurred and compensating completed inner scopes. It makes use of the data collected during the second phase. For fault $F2$, the root partition of the scope $P18$ executes the fault handlers and the fault is not re–thrown to the outer scope.

For fault $F4$, the completed inner scope (root partition $P18$) needs to be compensated while executing the fault handler associated with the *root partition* of the outer scope - $P10$. The *root partition $P10$* sends a `Compensation` control message to partition $P18$ which executes the compensation handlers for the inner scope using the data collected during the second phase and exits.

5   Conclusions

In this paper we have proposed a mechanism for handling faults in decentralized orchestration of composite web services. We adhere to the fault handling model used by BPEL4WS which employs forward error recovery (through compensation) and supports open nested transactions. The mechanism is designed to maintain the semantics of the original service specification while ensuring minimal overheads. We have implemented the fault propagation part of our scheme in the decentralization tool that we have developed and are currently working on the implementation of the rest of the scheme. We did not touch upon performance or complexity analysis of the proposed mechanism in this paper and plan to investigate it in the near future. The fault management scheme proposed in this paper is centralized as fault handlers and compensation handlers for a scope reside in the root partition. This has been done to keep the scheme simple as the complexities associated with a decentralized fault management scheme might not be worth its benefits. We are going to further explore decentralized fault management in near future.

References

1. Business Process Execution Language for Web Services Version 1.1. http://www.ibm.com/developerworks/library/ws-bpel/.
2. OASIS Business Transaction Protocol, Committee, Specification 1.0. http://www.oasis-open.org/business-transaction.
3. Web Service Choreography Interface (WSCI) 1.0. http://www.w3.org/TR/wsci.
4. Web Services Transaction (WS-Transaction). http://www-106.ibm.com/developerworks/webservices/library/ws-transpec/.
5. A.V. Aho, R. Sethi, and J.D. Ullman. *Compilers: Principles, Techniques and Tools*. Addison-Wesley, 1986.
6. G. Chafle, S. Chandra, V. Mann, and M. G. Nanda. Decentralized Orchestration of Composite Web Services. In *Proceedings of WWW*, 2004.
7. G. Chafle, S. Chandra, V. Mann, and M. G. Nanda. Orchestrating Composite Web Services Under Data Flow Constraints. In *Proceedings of IEEE International Conference on Web Services*, Orlando, USA, July 2005.
8. Q. Chen and U. Dayal. Failure Handling for Transaction Hierarchies. In *Proceedings of International Conference on Data Engineering (ICDE)*, 1997.
9. David W. Cheung, Eric Lo, C. Y. Ng, and Thomas Lee. Web Services Oriented Data Processing and Integration. In *Proceedings of WWW*, 2003.
10. Dickson K.W. Chiu, Qing Li, and Kamalakar Karlapalem. ADOME-WFMS: Towards Cooperative Handling of Workflow Exceptions. *Lecture Notes in Computer Science*, (2677):271–288, 2001. Advances in exception handling techniques.
11. G. Hunt and M. Scott. The Coign Automatic Distributed Partitioning System. In *Proceedings of OSDI*, February 1999.
12. V. Issarny, N. Levy, A. Romanovsky, and F. Tartanoglu. Coordinated Forward Error Recovery for Composite Web Services. In *Proceedings of SRDS*, 2003.
13. Mohan U. Kamath and Krithi Ramamritham. Pragmatic Issues in Coordinated Execution and Failure Handling of Workflow Control Architectures. Computer Science Technical Report 98-28, University of Massachusetts, August 1998.
14. P.A. Lee and T. Anderson. *Fault Tolerance Pinciples and Practice, volume 3 of Dependable Computing and Fault Tolerant Systems*. Springer-Verlag, 1990.
15. M. G. Nanda, S. Chandra, and V. Sarkar. Decentralizing Execution of Composite Web Services. In *Proceedings of OOPSLA*, 2004.
16. M. G. Nanda and N. Karnik. Synchronization Analysis for Decentralizing Composite Web Services. In *Proceedings of SAC*, 2003.
17. E. Tilevich and Y. Smaragdakis. J-Orchestra - Automatic Java Application Partitioning. In *Proceedings of ECOOP 2002*, June 2002.
18. G. Weikum and H. Schek. Concepts and applications of multilevel transactions and open nested transactions. *Transaction Models for Advanced Database Applications*, 1992.

What's in an Agreement?
An Analysis and an Extension of WS-Agreement

Marco Aiello[1], Ganna Frankova[1], and Daniela Malfatti[2]

[1] Dept. of Information and Communication Technologies,
University of Trento, Via Sommarive, 14, 38100 Trento, Italy
{marco.aiello, ganna.frankova}@unitn.it
[2] Corso di Laurea in Informatica
University of Trento, Via Sommarive, 14, 38100 Trento, Italy
daniela.malfatti@studenti.unitn.it

Abstract. Non-functional properties of services and service compositions are of paramount importance for the success of web services. The negotiation of non-functional properties between web service provider and consumer can be agreed a priori by specifying an agreement. WS-Agreement is a recently proposed and emerging protocol for the specification of agreements in the context of web services. Though, WS-Agreement only specifies the XML syntax and the intended meaning of each tag, which naturally leads to posing the question of "What's in an Agreement?" We answer this question by providing a formal definition of an agreement and analyzing the possible evolution of agreements and their terms. From our analysis we identify ways in which to make an agreement more robust and long lived by proposing two extensions to the specification and supporting environment.

1 Introduction

Web Services (WS) are a set of technologies that allow the construction of massively distributed and loosely coupled applications. One of the most thought provoking issues in web services is that of automatically composing individual operations of services in order to build complex added-value services. The research on composition is well under way, but most of the focus is on functional properties of the composition, that is, how does one automatically compose? How does one enrich the services with semantic self-describing information? How does one discover the available services to use for the composition? If, on the one hand, this is crucial, on the other one, it is not enough. Non-functional properties of the composition are also of paramount importance in defining the usability and success of a composed service. Think for instance of desiring a service that performs a biological computation composing the services offered by a number of web service enabled machines. If the user knows that the composition is correct with respect to his goal, he will be satisfied with the answer he receives, but if the answer takes 3 years to be delivered to the user, the correctness is of little use. Therefore, the quality of a composed service is very important when interacting with an asynchronous system built out of independent components.

B. Benatallah, F. Casati, and P. Traverso (Eds.): ICSOC 2005, LNCS 3826, pp. 424–436, 2005.
© Springer-Verlag Berlin Heidelberg 2005

With the term Quality of Service (QoS) we refer to the non-functional properties of an individual service, or a composition of services. The term is widely used in the field of networking. Usually it refers to the properties of availability and performance. In the field of web services, the term has a wider meaning. Any non-functional property which affects the definition and execution of a web service falls into the category of QoS, most notably, accessibility, integrity, reliability, regulatory, and security [15]. Dealing with QoS requires the study of a number of problems. One, the design of quality aware systems. Two, the provision of quality of service information at the level of the individual service. Three, ensuring that a promised quality of service is actually provided during execution. In [2], we addressed the first issue by using the Tropos design methodology, and the second one by resorting to WS-Policy to describe QoS properties. In this paper, we consider the second and third issues; in particular, we show how to provide a framework to negotiate the provision of a service according to a predefined QoS, and how to handle changes during the interactions of web services, and how to prevent the QoS conditions failure.

WS-Agreement is an XML based language and protocol designed for advertising the capabilities of providers and creating agreements based on initial offers, and for monitoring agreement compliance at run-time. The motivations for the design of WS-Agreement stem out of QoS concerns, especially in the context of load balancing heavy loads on a grid of web service enabled hosts [10]. However, the definition of the protocol is totally general and allows for the negotiation of QoS in any web service enabled distributed system. If, on the one hand, the proposal of WS-Agreement is a step forward for obtaining web service based systems with QoS guarantees, on the other hand, the protocol proposal is preliminary. The current specification [3] defines XML syntax for the language and protocol, and it gives a vague textual overview of the intended semantics, without defining a set of formal mathematical rules. Furthermore, a reference architecture is proposed to show how WS-Agreement are to be handled, [13]. Nevertheless, a formal analysis of what an agreement is still missing.

In this paper, we address the question *What's in an Agreement?* In particular, we provide a formal analysis of WS-Agreement by resorting to finite state automata, we provide a set of formal rules that tie together agreement terms and the life-cycle of an agreement. From the analysis, some shortcomings of the protocol become evident. Most notably, there is no checking of how close a term to being violated and, even more, breaking one single term of the agreement results in terminating the whole agreement, while a more graceful degradation is desirable. Therefore, we propose an extension of the protocol for which we provide appropriate semantics, that allows for providing warning before the violation of an agreement and eventually the renegotiation of running agreements by tolerating the break of a term.

Web service QoS issues are gaining attention and have been addressed in a number of recent works. Some approaches are based on the extension of the Web Service Description Language (WSDL) to define not only functional, but also non-functional properties of the service, e.g., [11]. The main idea of the approach is simple: provide syntax to define terms which refer to non-functional properties of operations. The problem with this kind of approach is that the QoS definition is tied to the individual operation, rather than with the service as a whole; furthermore, there is no run-time support. Once a quality is defined, it can not be changed at execution time.

In [18], the authors propose to define WS QoS by using XML schemata that both service consumers and service providers apply to define the agreed QoS parameters. The approach allows for the dynamic selection of WS depending on various QoS requirements. On the negative side, the life-cycle of agreements is not taken into account, and it is not possible to define an expiration for a negotiation. The feasibility of using constraint programming to improve the automation of web services procurement is shown in [16]. A semantic web approach, in which services are searched on the basis of the quality of semantically tagged service attributes is presented in [17]. A predictive QoS model for workflows involving QoS properties is proposed in [6]. In [9], the authors propose a model and architecture to let the consumer rate the qualities of a service. In addition, the industry has proposed a number of standards to address the issue of QoS: IBM Web Service Level Agreement (WSLA) and HP's Web Service Management Language (WSML) are examples of languages used to describe quality metrics of services, [12]. A recent proposal is the specification of a new WS protocol, called Web Services Agreement Specification [3]. In [7], it is presented the Agreement-Based Open Grid Service Management (OGSI-A) model. Its aim is to integrate Grid technologies with Web Service mechanisms and to manage dynamically negotiable applications and services, using WS-Agreement. The WS-Agreement protocol proposal is supported by the definition of a managing architecture: CREMONA–An Architecture and Library for Creation and Monitoring of WS-Agreement [13]. The Web Services Agreement Specification defines the interaction between a service provider and a consumer, and a protocol for creating an agreement using agreement templates. The above approaches show that frameworks for QoS definition and management are essential to the success of the web service technology, but there are a number of shortcomings that still need to be addressed. First, no one has worked out a formal definition of what the semantics of a QoS negotiation should be. Second, the frameworks should be more flexible at execution time because actual qualities of services may change over time during execution.

The remainder of the paper is organized as follows. In Section 2, we present the WS-Agreement protocol defined in [3]. In Section 3, we propose a formal definition of an agreement and of its life-cycle. Section 4 is devoted to the presentation of an extension of WS-Agreement with the goal of improving the duration and tolerance of an agreement in execution. Preliminary experimental results are in Section 5. Concluding remarks are summarized in Section 6.

2   WS-Agreement

In order to be successful, web service providers have to offer and meet guarantees related to the services they develop. Taking into account that a guarantee depends on actual resource usage, the service consumer must request state-dependent guarantees from the service provider. Additionally, the guarantees on service quality must be monitored and service consumers must be notified in case of failure of meeting the guarantees. An agreement between a service consumer and a service provider specifies the associated guarantees. The agreement can be formally specified using the WS-Agreement Specification [3].

A WS-Agreement is an XML-based document containing descriptions of the functional and non-functional properties of a service oriented application. It consists of two main components that are the agreement Context and the agreement Terms. The agreement Context includes the description of the parties involved in the agreement process, and various metadata about the agreement. One of the most relevant components is the duration of the agreement, that is, the time interval during which the agreement is valid.

Functional and non-functional requirements are specified in the Terms section that is divided into Service Description Terms (SDTs) and Guarantee Terms. The first provides information to define the services functionalities that will be delivered under the agreement. An agreement may contain any number of SDTs. An agreement can refer to multiple components of functionalities within one service, and can refer to several services. Guarantee Terms define an assurance on service quality associated with the service described by the Service Description Terms. An agreement may contain zero or more Guarantee Terms.

In [8] a definition for guarantee terms in WS-Agreement is specified and a mechanisms for defining guarantees is provided. An agreement creation process starts when an agreement initiator sends an agreement template to the consumer. The structure of the template is the same as that of an agreement, but an agreement template may also contain a Creation Constraint section, i.e., a section with constraints on possible values of terms for creating an agreement. In [4] enabling of customizations of terms and attributes for the agreement creation is proposed. After the consumer fills in the template, he sends it to the initiator as an offer. The initiator decides to accept or reject the offer depending on the availability of resource, the service cost, and other requirements monitored by the service provider. The reply of the initiator is a confirmation or a rejection.

An agreement life-cycle includes the creation, termination and monitoring of agreement states. Figure 1 shows a representation of the life-cycle. When an agreement is created, it does not imply that it is monitored. It remains in an not_observed state until a service starts its execution. The semantics of the

Fig. 1. The life-cycle of a WS-Agreement

states is as follows: not_observed: the agreement is created and is in execution, but no service involved in the agreement is running; observed: at least one service of the agreement is running; and finished: the agreement has terminated either successfully or not.

3   What's in an Agreement?

The WS-Agreement specification provides XML syntax and a textual explanation of what the various XML tags mean and how they should be interpreted. Thank to the syntax, it is possible to prepare machine readable agreements, but a formal notion of agreement is missing. In this section, we formalize the notion of agreement by defining its main components.

Definition 1 (Term). *A term t is a couple (s, g) with $s \in S$ and $g \in G$, where S is a set of n services and G is a set of m guarantees. $T \subseteq S \times G$ is the set of the terms t.*

In words, a term involves the relationship between a service s and a guarantee g, not simply a specific tag of the agreement structure. If the service s appears in the list of services, which the guarantee g is applied to, it means that the couple (s, g) is a term. The number of terms varies between 0 and $n \cdot m$, where 0 means that there is no association between services and guarantees, and $n \cdot m$ indicates the case where each guarantee is associated with all services.

Definition 2 (Agreement). *An agreement A is a tuple $\langle S, G, T \rangle$, where S is a set of n services, G is a set of m guarantees, and T is the set of the terms t.*

In the following analysis, it is more convenient to consider the agreement as a set of *Terms* rather than a set of related services and guarantees. From the definition of WS-Agreement, we say that an agreement can be in one and only one of three states: not_observed, observed and finished.

Definition 3 (External State). *The external state A_{es} of an agreement A is an element of the set {not_observed, observed or finished}.*

We call the above state external, as it is the observable one. We also define an internal state of an agreement, which captures the state of the individual terms.

Definition 4 (Internal State). *The internal state A_{is} of an agreement A is a sequence of terms' states $ts_1, \ldots, ts_p$ of maximum size $n \cdot m$, where $ts_i = (ss_j, gs_k)$ represents the state of g_k guarantee with respect to the state of the s_j service. Service and guarantee states range over the following sets, respectively:*

- $ss_j \in$ {not_ready, ready, running, finished}, *and*
- $gs_k \in$ {not_determined, fulfilled, violated}.

From the definition of *Term*, we see that services and guarantees are related and we can define the internal state of an agreement, but it is necessary to

	terms are in state	state of the agreement	transitions
(A)	(1)	not_observed	(B)
(B)	(1)(2)	not_observed	(C) (E)
(C)	(1)(2)(3)	observed	(D)(E)(F)(G)
(D)	(1)(2)(3)(5)	observed	(F)(G)
(E)	(1)(2)(4)	observed	(F)(H)
(F)	(1)(2)(3)(4)(5)	observed	(H)
(G)	(5)	finished	
(H)	(1)(2)(3)(4)(5)(6)	finished	

Fig. 2. Transition table for the relation between internal and external states

distinguish between terms that have the same service and terms that have the same guarantee.

Proceeding in our goal of answering the question of what is in an agreement, we define the relationship between the internal and external state of an agreement A. First, we note that not all state combinations make sense. For instance, it has no meaning to say that a guarantee is violated, when a service is in a not_ready state. The only admissible combinations are the following ones.

(1) (not_ready, not_determined)   (2) (ready, not_determined)
(3)   (running, fulfilled)   (4)   (running, violated)
(5)   (finished, fulfilled)   (6)   (finished, violated)

In theory, there are 63 possible combinations of states in which terms can be. That is, $\sum_{i=1}^{6} \binom{6}{i}$ all terms could be in state (1), or in state (2),... or in state (6); there could be terms in states (1) and (2), (1) and (3), and so on. But again, considering the definition of WS-Agreement in [3], one concludes that not all 63 combinations make sense. Furthermore, it is possible to extract the possible evolutions of these aggregated internal states.

When an agreement is created its external state is not_observed, while all services are not_ready and all guarantees are not_determined, i.e., state (1). In the next stage some services will be ready while others will still be not_ready, i.e., there will be terms in state (1) and (2). In this case, the external state is also not_observed. Proceeding in this analysis, one can conclude that there are 8 situations in which terms can be. We summarize these in the table in Figure 2. In the table, we also present the relation between the internal states and the external states, and the set of transitions to go from one set of states to another. The latter transitions are best viewed as an automaton (which is illustrated in [1]).

4   Extension of WS-Agreement

From the semantics and formal analysis presented in Section 3, inspecting the automaton provided, we note that if the agreement arrives into the states (E) or (F) there is a non recoverable failure, and consequently an agreement termination. Even if one single term is violated, the whole agreement is terminated. Furthermore, when an agreement is running there is no consideration on *how* the guarantee terms are fulfilled. Our goal is to provide an extension of WS-Agreement and of its semantics in order to make agreements more long-lived, and robust to individual term violations. In [14] we provide appropriate XML syntax to implement the proposed extension, while an example of using a subset on a concrete case study (DeltaDator Spa, Trento) of the proposed extension can be found in [1].

We propose two extensions to WS-Agreement. The first is used to **(i) anticipate violations**, while the second is devoted to the **(ii) run-time renegotiation**. (i) WS-Agreement considers guarantees of a running service as fulfilled or violated. Nothing is said about how the guarantee is fulfilled. Is the guarantee close or far to being violated? Is there a trend bringing the guarantee close to its violation? We propose to introduce a new state for the agreement in which a warning has been issued due to the fact that one or more guarantees are likely to be violated in the near future. By detecting possible violations, one may intervene by modifying the run-time conditions or might renegotiate the guarantees which are close to being violated. (ii) The WS-Agreement specification does not contemplate the possibility of changing an agreement at run-time. If a guarantee is not fulfilled because of resource overload or faults in assigning availability to consumers, the agreement must terminate. For maintaining the service and related supplied guarantees, it is necessary to create another agreement and negotiate the QoS again. This approach wastes resources and computational time, and increases network traffic. The goal of negotiation terms is to have the chance to modify the agreement applying the negotiation terms rather than respecting the original agreement. Applying the negotiation terms means that the services included in the agreement will be performed according to the new guarantees.

4.1   Life-Cycle and Semantics for the Extended Agreement

To obtain the desired extensions, we expand the set of states in which an agreement and a guarantee term can be and thus update the transition system. More precisely, the definition of an agreement does not change with respect to Definition 2, the difference lies in the fact that the set of terms T is now extended with special *negotiation terms*. These terms are defined as in Definition 1, but have a different role, i.e., they specify new conditions that enable modification of guarantees at run-time.

To account for the new type of terms, we need to extend the definition of external and internal state of an agreement. The external states of an extended agreement are enriched by the `warned` state, `checked` state, the `revisited` state, and the `denied` state. We say that an agreement can be in one of seven states. `not_observed`, `observed` and `finished` have the same meaning as in WS-Agreement, Figure 1. An Agreement is in state `checked` when the monitoring system is checking its services and guarantees. From the `checked` state the agreement can go to five different states: to `finished` if the agreement finishes

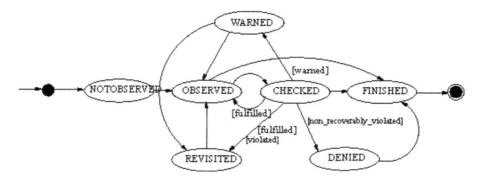

Fig. 3. The life-cylce of the WS-Agreement extension

its life-cycle; to `denied` if the agreement is violated and no *negotiation terms* can be applied, the agreement must terminate; to `warned` if the monitoring system has issued at least one warning for at least one term; back to `observed` if the agreement is fulfilled; to `revisited` if the agreement is fulfilled or violated and a *negotiation term* can be applied.

to `finished` if the agreement finishes its life-cycle;

Definition 5 (Extended External State). *The* extended agreement external state A_{xes} *of an agreement A is an element of the set* {`not_observed`, `observed`, `warned`, `checked`, `revisited`, `denied` *or* `finished`}.

The transitions between states are illustrated by the automaton in Figure 3, which is an extension of the one presented in Figure 1. The automaton represents the new evolution of an agreement where a guarantee can be modified during the processing of a service or a warning can be raised. When a guarantee is violated we have two situations: the first presents a recoverable violation which implies the chance to apply a negotiation term and so the agreement is in a revisited state, the second presents a non recoverable violation which implies that there is no suitable negotiation term for the current violated guarantee and so the agreement must terminate. Otherwise, if a warning is raised, this can be ignored or the agreement can go in a renegotiation state by ending in the revisited state. Also, when a guarantee is fulfilled, it is possible to change the current agreement configuration, applying a negotiation term that changes the QoS.

The internal state definition for the extended agreement is similar to the internal state definition stated before, but a new state for the services is added and two for the guarantees. A new state is `stopped` and is needed to define a state of a service where its associated guarantee is unrecoverable violated and the service must terminate or the guarantee can be revisited. It is an intermediate state. A guarantee can also be `warned` if it is close to being violated in a given time instant. Other state for a guarantee is the `non_recoverable_violated` state in which a guarantee is violated and it has no related negotiation terms for the current violation.

Definition 6 (Extended Internal State). *The* extended internal state A_{xis} *of an agreement A is a sequence of terms' states $ts_1, \ldots, ts_p$ of maximum size $n \cdot m$, where $ts_i = (ss_j, gs_k)$ represents the state of g_k guarantee with respect to the s_j service. Service and guarantee states range over the following sets, respectively:*

- $ss_j \in \{$not_ready, ready, running, stopped, finished$\}$, *and*
- $gs_k \in \{$not_determined, fulfilled, warned, violated, non_recoverably_violated$\}$.

As for Definition 4, one notes that not all the state combinations make sense. The only possible ones are the combinations itemized in Section 3 plus the following four:

(7) (stopped, fulfilled)
(8) (stopped, violated)
(9) (stopped, non_recoverably_violated)
(10) (running, warned)

The state combinations (7), (8) and (9) determine the states when a service is stopped because a guarantee is violated or is being modified. In state (7) a guarantee is fulfilled and we try to improve it applying a positive negotiation term. In (8) and (9) a guarantee is currently violated. In (8) the service is stopped and the guarantee is violated but it is possible to apply a negotiation term and to preserve the agreement again. In (9), instead, the guarantee is irrecoverably violated and the agreement must terminate, there are not any suitable negotiation terms. State (10) represents the fact that a warning has been raised for a running service guarantee.

The relation between internal and external states of an extended agreement is an extension of the one presented in the table in Figure 2, and it is presented in Figure 4. The table respects the original agreement evolution and presents some new transitions.

	terms are in state	state of the agreement	transitions
(A)	(1)	not_observed	(B)
(B)	(1)(2)	not_observed	(C)
(C)	(1)(2)(3)	observed	(D)(E)(F)(G)
(D)	(1)(2)(3)(5)	observed	(F)(G)(I)
(E)	(1)(2)(4)	checked	(F)(H)(I))
(F)	(1)(2)(3)(4)(5)	checked	(H)(I))(J)(K)(L)
(G)	(5)	finished	
(H)	(1)(2)(3)(4)(5)(6)	finished	
(I)	(1)(2)(3)(4)(5)(7)	observed	(D)(E)(F)(G)
(J)	(1)(2)(3)(4)(5)(8)	revisited	(D)
(K)	(1)(2)(3)(4)(5)(9)	denied	(F)(H)
(L)	(1)(2)(3)(5)(7)(10)	warned	(C)(D)(H)(I)(J))

Fig. 4. Extension of the transition table for the relation between internal and external states

4.2 Framework

The proposed extension to WS-Agreement must be handled by an appropriate framework that allows for monitoring and provides run-time renegotiation.

On the one hand, there must be rules specifying when and how to raise a warning for any given guarantee. These rules should be easy to compute to avoid overloading of the monitoring system and be fast to provide warnings. In addition they should provide good performance in detecting as many violations as possible generating the minimum number of false positives. A forecasting method which enjoys this characteristics is the linear least squares method [5]. The method of linear least squares requires a straight line to be fitted to a set of data points such that the sum of the squares of the vertical deviations from the points to the line is minimized. By analyzing such a parameter of the line as a slope ratio, it is possible to predict a change over time.

On the other hand, to allow for renegotiation of guarantee terms at run-time the parties involved in the agreement need to be able to decide whether a renegotation has been agreed upon. Before execution it must be possible to specify negotiation terms. This can be done by using appropriate templates in the spirit of the original work in [13].

5 Preliminary Experimental Results

We have conducted preliminary experimentation to show the feasibility of the warning strategy. We used synthetic data. We generated a sequence of 1100 elements considered as a service guarantee for a single operation over a continuous time interval (for instance the cost of a service which should be below the value 10). The data set and the complete results of the experiments are available at http://www.dit.unitn.it/~frankova/ICSOC05_Exp/. The points were generated by a function that returns a random number greater or equal to 6.00 and less or equal to 14.00, evenly distributed. We split the data set into two subsets. The first part of the data set was used to decide the size of the time window and of the threshold values to be used for prediction. The rest of the data was used for evaluating the system.

To evaluate the method we consider the following performance measures: *Precision* is the ratio of the number of true warnings (i.e., warnings thrown to notify violation points) to the number of total warnings (i.e., true warnings and false warnings). *Recall* is the ratio of the number of warned violations (i.e., violation points for which a warning is issued) to the number of total violation points. Total violation points include warned violations and missed violations.

The following table summarizes the results of the experimentation:

	Warnings		Violations	
	True	*False*	*Warned*	*Missed*
	303	11	156	13
Total	314		169	
Precision	96.50%			
Recall			92.31%	

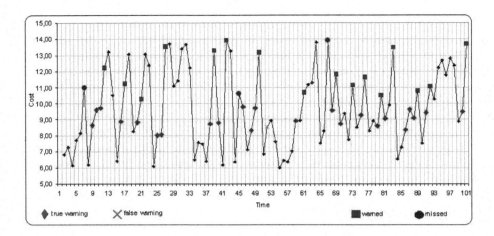

Fig. 5. Experimental results for 100 points

The number of true and false warnings is shown in the first column. The difference in the number of total warnings and violations is due to the fact that more than one warning in the same time window may refer to the same violation. The number of warned and missed violations is reported in the second column of the table. The total sum of warnings and violations is in the "Total" row. The last two rows present the precision and recall of the method.

The results of experimentation on the first 100 points of the data set is shown in Figure 5. In the figure, two types of warnings, true and false, are marked by diamonds and crosses, respectively. A warning is thrown if the cost and tangent of the cost curve are higher then the threshold (8 for cost and 0.1 for the tangent differences). Squares represent warned violation points, while circles indicate missed violation points.

The method shows good performance when the increase in cost is smooth (points 8, 9, and 10), a case that normally takes place during web services execution. If the change in values is abrupt then the method fails to generate warnings, e.g., points 43 (cost is 6.36) and 44 (cost is 10.63). It is difficult to find a violation point if the point is in the very beginning of the process, within or just after the first time window (point 7). The latter cases should be considered exceptional, in fact those occur only 13 times in the whole experiment.

In the experimentation using the method, more than 92% of violation points are warned in advance, and 96.5% of thrown warnings are true warnings. Using bigger time windows does not improve performances, see http://www.dit.unitn.it/~frankova/ICSOC05_Exp/.

6   Concluding Remarks

Describing and invoking an individual functionality of a web service is becoming more and more common practice. One of the next steps is moving from functional properties of basic services to non-functional properties of composed services. The non-functional properties need to be specified by the services, but also to be negotiated among services.

WS-Agreement is a protocol that defines a syntax to specify a number of guarantee terms within an agreement. We looked into the protocol specification with the goal of providing a formalization of the notion of an agreement and proposing a formal representation for the internal and external states in which an agreement can be. From this analysis we discovered that an agreement can be made more long-lived and robust with respect to forecoming violations. We presented the details of the proposed extension in formal terms and provided some preliminary experimentation on synthetic data.

This work prods for more investigation of agreements and of their management. In the next future, we plan to dive into the details of a framework implementing the extended agreement version and then to experiment on real data coming from an actual case study.

Acknowledgments

Marco thanks Asit Dan and Heiko Ludwig for useful discussion on WS-Agreement while visiting IBM TJ Watson.

References

1. M. Aiello, G. Frankova, and D. Malfatti. What's in an agreement? A formal analysis and an extension of WS-Agreement. Technical Report DIT-05-039, DIT, University of Trento, 2005.
2. M. Aiello and P. Giorgini. Applying the Tropos methodology for analysing web services requirements and reasoning about Qualities of Services. *CEPIS Upgrade - The European journal of the informatics professional*, 5(4), 2004.
3. A. Andrieux, K. Czajkowski, A. Dan, K. Keahey, H. Ludwig, J. Pruyne, J. Rofrano, S. Tuecke, and M. Xu. Web Services Agreement Specification (WS-Agreement). Technical report, Grid Resource allocation Agreement Protocol (GRAAP) WG, 2004.
4. A. Andrieux, A. Dan, K. Keahey, H. Ludwig, and J. Rofrano. Negotiability constraints in WS-Agreement. Technical report, Grid Resource Allocation Agreement Protocol (GRAAP) Working Group Meetings, 2004.
5. Rudolf K. Bock. *The data analysis : briefbook.* Springer: Berlin [etc.], 1998.
6. J. Cardoso, A. Sheth, J. Miller, J. Arnold, and K. Kochut. Quality of service for workflows and web service processes. *Journal of Web Semantics*, 2004. To appear.
7. K. Czajkowski, A. Dan, J. Rofrano, S. Tuecke, and M. Xu. Agreement-based Grid Service Management (OGSI-Agreement). Technical report, Global Grid Forum, GRAAP-WG Author Contribution, 2003.
8. A. Dan, K. Keahey, H. Ludwig, and J. Rofrano. Guarantee Terms in WS-Agreement. Technical report, Grid Resource Allocation Agreement Protocol (GRAAP) Working Group Meetings, 2004.
9. V. Deora, J. Shao, W. A. Gray, and N. J. Fiddian. A quality of service management framework based on user expectations. In *Service-Oriented Computing (ICSOC)*, pages 104–114. LNCS 2910, Springer, 2003.

10. I. Foster, C. Kesselman, J. M. Nick, and S. Tuecke. Grid services for distributed system integration. *IEEE Computer*, 35(6), 2002.
11. D. Gouscos, M. Kalikakis, and P. Georgiadis. An approach to modeling web service QoS and provision price. In *1st Web Services Quality Workshop (WQW2003) at WISE*, 2003.
12. H. Ludwig. Web services QoS: External SLAs and internal policies or: How do we deliver what we promise? In *1st Web Services Quality Workshop (WQW2003) at WISE*, 2003.
13. H. Ludwig, A. Dan, and R. Kearney. CREMONA: an architecture and library for creation and monitoring of ws-agreements. In M. Aiello, M. Aoyama, F. Curbera, and M. Papazoglou, editors, *ICSOC*, pages 65–74. ACM, 2004.
14. D. Malfatti. A framework for the monitoring of the QoS by extending WS-Agreement. Master's thesis, Corso di Laurea in Informatica, Università degli Studi di Trento, 2005. In Italian.
15. A. Mani and A. Nagarajan. Understanding quality of service for web services, 2002. http://www-106.ibm.com/developerworks/library/ws-quality.html.
16. O. Martn-Daz, A. Ruiz Corts, A. Durn, D. Benavides, and M. Toro. Automating the procurement of web services. In *Service-Oriented Computing (ICSOC)*, pages 91–103. LNCS 2910, Springer, 2003.
17. M. P. Singh and A. Soydan Bilgin. A DAML-based repository for QoS-aware semantic web service selection. In *IEEE International Conference on Web Services (ICWS 2004)*, 2004.
18. M. Tian, A. Gramm, T. Naumowicz, H. Ritter, and J. Schiller. A concept for QoS integration in web services. In *1st Web Services Quality Workshop (WQW2003) at WISE*, 2003.

SOA in the Real World – Experiences

Manoj Acharya, Abhijit Kulkarni, Rajesh Kuppili, Rohit Mani,
Nitin More, Srinivas Narayanan, Parthiv Patel,
Kenneth W. Schuelke, and Subbu N. Subramanian

Tavant Technologies, 3101 Jay Street, Suite 101, Santa Clara, CA 95054

Abstract. We discuss our experiences in building a real-world, mission-critical enterprise business application on a service-oriented architecture for a leading consumer lending company. The application is composed of a set of services (such as *Credit Report Service, Document Management Service, External Vendor Service, Customer Management Service*, and *Lending Lifecycle Service*) that communicate among themselves mainly through asynchronous messages and some synchronous messages with XML payloads. We motivate the choice of SOA by discussing its tangible benefits in the context of our application. We discuss our experiences at every stage of the software development life cycle that can be uniquely attributed to the service oriented architecture, list several challenges, and provide an insight into how we addressed them in real-life. Some of the hard design and development challenges we faced were related to modeling workflow interactions between services, managing change analysis, and contract specification. In addition, SOA architecture and asynchronous messaging introduces fresh challenges in the area of integration testing (e.g. how do we test a system whose interface points are asynchronous messages) and in testing the robustness of the system (e.g. how do we deal with out of order messages, duplicate messages, message loss?). To address these challenges, we built a tool called *SOA Workbench*. We also discuss the techniques we adopted to address scenario-based validation that go beyond traditional document-centric validation based on XML Schema. Monitoring and error recovery, two key aspects of any mission-critical system, pose special challenges in a distributed SOA-based, asynchronous messaging setting. To address these, we built a tool called *SIMON*. We discuss how SIMON helps error detection and recovery in a production environment. We conclude by listing several opportunities for further work for people in both academia and industry.

1 Introduction

Many mission critical enterprise applications share some common characteristics – they comprise of a variety of functionalities, feature complex interactions among them, should be easy to manage, need to be fault tolerant, and should be isolated in failure. In addition, *constant evolution* required to keep pace with the ever changing business requirements and *distributed ownership of the functionalities* spread across several teams are two other crucial characteristics of such systems. The challenge of building and maintaining such systems is not very different from the challenge of

B. Benatallah, F. Casati, and P. Traverso (Eds.): ICSOC 2005, LNCS 3826, pp. 437–449, 2005.

building a system comprising of complex subsystems (for example a car or a computer) that are products by themselves, have their own product life cycle, and have clearly defined services that are exposed via agreed upon contracts. In this paper, we discuss our experiences in building such an enterprise application for a large consumer lending corporation.

1.1 The Consumer Lending Application

In this section, we briefly introduce the consumer lending application. The application handles the entire lending life cycle that begins with the procurement and management of millions of potential prospective customers (called *leads*). The application has the ability to scrub large amounts of lead data, classify the leads according to various categories, and distribute the leads based on various criteria to the company's sales force. The sales functionalities include ability to make calls to potential customers and keep track of the progress of the conversation and follow-ups via reminders, real-time management visibility to sales force performance, ability to quickly assimilate data critical to the loan offering (such as income, property details, appraisal etc) *real-time* while the sales person is on the phone with the customer, and the ability to order and instantly receive the customer's credit report. The sales functionalities also include the ability to capture the desires of the customer and perform *what-if* scenario analysis to offer the loan product that optimally matches the customer's desire. On successful completion of the sales activities, the system has a set of fulfillment capabilities, also called loan processing capabilities, that involves validating the data obtained from the customer during the sales cycle (such as income verification, appraisal verification, title verification etc). These verifications during the loan processing stage are performed either via supporting paper documentations obtained from the customer such as W2's and income statements or via automated verifications performed through specialized electronic services (such as credit report services or appraisal services) provided by external vendors. The loan processing stage also involves dealing with exceptions that may arise during the verification phase and performing an analysis of their impact on the loan product. Other crucial functionalities in the consumer lending application include (1) a pricing module that given a set of inputs such as the borrower's credit score, income, and property value generates a loan product with the rate, points, and fees information (2) a compliance module that ensures that the loan product does not violate any of the state, federal, and corporation-specific compliance laws (3) a document service that manages storage and retrieval of electronic documents, and (4) a task management service that keeps track of the list of activities (and their statuses) that need to be performed to take the loan application from one stage to the next along its life cycle. Finally, the system has the ability to take a validated and approved loan through a funding process that involves electronic transfer of funds between financial institutions.

1.2 Motivation for SOA

As can be observed, the consumer lending application consists of a set of distinct, related set of functionalities. Not surprisingly, the consumer lending corporation has departments that specialize in these functions. For example, there is a marketing department that owns the lead acquisition and related functions, a sales department that owns the sales functionalities, and a loan processing department that owns the fulfillment functions. Besides taking ownership, these departments also want the ability to evolve their functions and related IT capabilities independent of the others, manage the applications and data, and not be affected by glitches in the other systems. Naturally, the scalability and service level agreement needs of the functions are also different. For example, the marketing functionality is used by a handful of users in the corporate office where as the sales functionality supports thousands of field agents with an expectation of sub-second response time. In addition, there is a need for functionalities to be reused across multiple applications. For example, the document service related functionalities are required by several sales, marketing, and fulfillment applications.

The above set of requirements lend themselves to a natural organization of the software artifacts that comprise of this application as a set of independently deployed components that expose a set of services that can be invoked via predefined messaging protocol – in other words an architecture based on SOA.

Note that the core functional requirements of our lending application can be realized in a traditional, monolithic, non-soa architecture. Indeed, prior to our system, there existed a basic version of the application built on a client-server platform. However, such a tightly-coupled system would not support several critical features such as independent evolution and scaleability of components, isolated deployment and manageability, efficient reusability of common features, and isolated failure.

2 Application Architecture

Figure 1 captures the application architecture of our lending application. Each component (e.g. appraisal service, credit service) is an independently deployable,

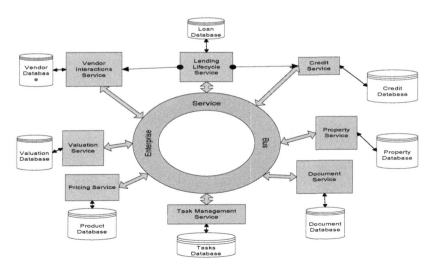

Fig. 1. Application Architecture

maintainable "product" and exposes a set of services related to their specialization that can be invoked by other components that require them in the context of some business workflow. The services can be accessed asynchronously via message interchange on an *Enterprise Service Bus* (ESB) [1] or synchronously via webservice calls.

As illustrated in the figure, the ESB forms the hub of the messaging infrastructure. At a basic level, the ESB provides a reliable messaging infrastructure (we use a commercial ESB product from a third party vendor) that is based on JMS [4]. In addition, it acts as a message router that delivers messages to the appropriate services based on some well-defined routing rules. In order to realize a business transaction, the services communicate among one another via messages that are exchanged on the ESB. In order to standardize the message format and facilitate understanding across teams, we adopted the definition of messages in the form of Business Object Documents (BODs) as defined by The Open Applications Group Integration Specification (OAGIS) [6]. BOD messages are named using a pair consisting of a standardized verb (such as *Get, Show, Process*) and a business relevant noun (such as *loan, credit*).

2.1 Usecase Illustration – Credit Pull

Figure 2 illustrates the realization of a sample business process flow in our architecture. One common usecase in the context of the lending application is the "Credit Pull" workflow – i.e. the functionality that allows a loan sales person to obtain the electronic credit report of a customer in *real-time*. The lending life cycle service initiates the credit pull as a response to a user request on the UI by sending a credit request message to the credit service. The credit service listens to this message, registers its activity with the task management service, and passes the request to the external vendor service which in turn places a request with the credit vendor. The external vendor service obtains the credit report from the right vendor using vendor selection rules (based on established business agreements, service level agreements etc). Once

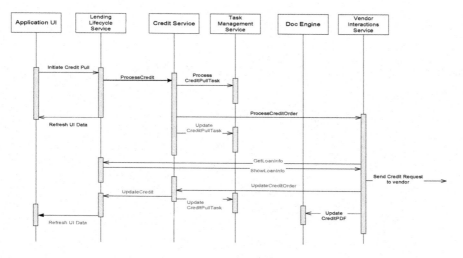

Fig. 2. Credit pull sequence

the vendor responds with the credit report, it is imaged and stored in the document service. The credit report is also sent to the credit service which stores it locally and returns it to the lending life cycle service which performs some local processing and renders the credit report on the UI.

All the service interactions are achieved via asynchronous message interchange on the ESB. Also, the message requests and their names adhere to the OAGIS BOD standards. For example, the lending life cycle service initiates the credit pull request by dropping a *ProcessCredit* message on the ESB.

3   Design Time Challenges

In this section, we motivate the need for new design time tools for SOA applications and describe the *SOA Workbench* tool that addresses these issues. The central elements of the Consumer Lending application described earlier is the notion of "workflows" or "sequences" that is a construction of a higher business services by composing various individual services in interesting ways (e.g., the Credit Pull described in Section 2.1). We need a way to describe such sequences along with their meta-data in a structured way including the details about all its steps, the communication mechanism used for a given step (synchronous via web services or other protocols, or asynchronous via messaging), the structure of the information exchanged (e.g., XML schema info), and several other details specific to the integration between these services. In earlier applications, such information was specified just through design documents. The SOA Workbench is a tool that captures the sequence metadata described above at design time. It then uses this information to do other interesting tasks during the design, test, and production monitoring phases. Additional metadata related to data validation can also be added and is described in the following sections.

3.1   Content Validation

Since the interactions in the sequence are between loosely coupled systems that are usually developed by different teams, it is critical to capture as much information as possible on the validity of the documents exchanged between the services. While some structural and semantic constraints can be expressed in the XML schema, there is a need for validation constraints that cannot be expressed in the schema. For example, the same documents (i.e. same schemas) can be used in different sequences (or even in different steps within a sequence) and the validation constraints may different across these sequences (or across the steps within a sequence). A typical case is that some elements in the schema are mandatory in one sequence but not in another. As discussed in Section 2, we have embraced the OAGIS style of defining documents where key business entities are represented as "nouns" and an XML schema can embed one or more of these nouns within it. Often the same noun is embedded in different schemas that represent different uses of it. For example, we have a Credit noun representing credit information that is used in both ProcessCredit as well ProcessCreditOrder steps in the Credit Pull sequence (Credit noun is also used in several other sequences). The ProcessCredit step mandates some elements within the Credit noun to be present whereas the ProcessCreditOrder mandates a different subset of elements within the Credit noun. The SOA workbench supports such validations by allowing the user to specify mandatory data elements for each step of the sequence. When the communication is asynchronous, our application also uses several custom JMS properties [4] to communicate – the ESB uses the JMS properties to route the message. The SOA workbench tool allows the user to list the JMS properties used in each step and specify whether they are mandatory.

3.2 Advanced Content Validation

XML schemas and the additions described in the previous section about specifying required elements that are sequence-step specific still only validate the message from a structural perspective. The SOA workbench goes further in addressing how one can validate the content of an element (i.e., the *value* of an XML element) as well. In our application, as is typical of many enterprise applications, the data elements in the XML messages are related to or derived from data stored in a database. Services usually consume a message, update the database and generate more messages in response. The content of these generated messages are derived from data in a database. In such scenarios, we need the ability to specify validation checks on the content of the XML messages by validating it against its corresponding data in the database. The tool allows us to specify such validations for each step in the sequence. The XML element to be validated is usually specified via an XPath expression[1]. The tool allows the user to write SQL queries against the database and add a validation that checks if the result of the XPath expression is the same as the result of a SQL query. For example, in the Credit Pull scenario, the Lending Lifecycle Service sends a ProcessCredit document to the Credit Service with borrower's name, social security number (SSN) and address. The Credit Service stores the name and SSN data in its database, but does not have a need to persist the address in its database. It then generates a ProcessCreditOrder document with the borrower name, SSN and address (the address element is just transferred from the ProcessCredit document) and sends it to the External Vendor service. We may want to add a validation constraint that the borrower name and SSN in the Credit Service database is the same as the borrower name and SSN in the ProcessCreditOrder document. SOA workbench allows for specifying such validations.

Notice how the address field was just transferred by the Credit Service from the incoming XML document to the outgoing XML document. In our application, such transient flows of information across XML documents in the sequence are fairly common. It would be useful during testing to validate that the address field in the ProcessCreditOrder document is the same as the address field in the ProcessCredit document. SOA workbench allows to specify whether an XPath expression on a document at a certain step in the sequence has the same value as an XPath expression run on a previous step in that sequence.

---

[1] Ideally, these should be XQueries instead of XPaths as that makes it easier to express more complex validations on the whole document instead of at an element by element basis. This is a simple extension to the current tool and is planned for a future release.

3.3 Reviews, Approval and Impact Analysis

The SOA workbench also allows the interactions to be reviewed and approved by each of the participants in the service. In a loosely coupled system, such review and approval processes are essential to communicate changes and to get all parties to agree to the proposed design.

Another big advantage of laying out the sequences in SOA workbench is its ability to deal with changes. In our applications, we frequently face the need to make changes to the XML schemas for various reasons. Prior to the SOA workbench, it was extremely difficult to manage these changes. A change to a specific element could impact certain sequences and the person making the schema change was not able to easily identify the affected sequences. To address this, the SOA workbench offers a feature by which the person making the schema change can do an impact analysis and identify all the sequences and the specific steps within the sequence where a BOD is used. Furthermore, if a change to a specific element is made, the tool can identify the sequences as well as the exact steps where the changed element is listed as a *mandatory* element. This will help the user to deal with changes in a more controlled manner. In a future version, we plan to add a change request workflow to the tool where a user can propose a change to a schema and all the owners of the services impacted by that change would be required to approve such changes before it is published.

3.4 Comparison with Workflow Tools

It is useful to compare the SOA Workbench to existing Workflow (BPM) tools in the industry. SOA Workbench is similar to BPM tools in that it helps in designing workflows composed of many services and interactions. Workflow systems focus on the ability to change workflows dynamically whereas the SOA workbench primarily deals with the problem of defining sequences across loosely coupled services and managing the *design contracts* (specifications that help answer questions such as what are the required data elements in a XML schema or required JMS properties in each specific interaction, what constitutes a valid document in the context of a specific step in a sequence, how should elements be validated against data in a database etc.), monitoring, and testing of these services. Recently, BPEL[7] has emerged as a potential standard that provides a portable language for coordinating the flow of business process services. BPEL builds on the previous work in the areas of BPM, workflow, and integration technologies. There are a few commercial implementations of BPEL. Weblogic Integration [8] is one such tool that originally focused a lot on integration and workflow capabilities with proprietary ways of defining workflows (called Java Process Definitions) and more recently starting to offer better support for BPEL.

While BPEL and several commercial implementations address the issue of process definition and execution in a distributed SOA environment, they mainly focus on integration and orchestration of services. In particular, they do not address critical aspects associated with design contract definition. The BPEL tools also do not address other design time activities such as reviews and approvals. Furthermore, they also do not deal with the challenges in testing and monitoring as explained in Sections 4 and 5.

Another recent trend is the emergence of tools providing ESB functionality. As explained in Section 2, we use a commercial ESB tool that provides reliable messaging and acts as a message router. Some ESB vendors also provide value added features for service orchestration on top of the basic ESB. Again, in our experience, such features do not focus on specifying design contracts to the level of detail that we have described and also do not sufficiently address the monitoring and testing needs of a SOA application.

We also wish to point out that the work we have done in the areas of design contract specification, testing, and monitoring in the context of SOA are complementary to the current efforts on BPEL and related commercial tools. In fact our work can be easily integrated into the standards or commercial tools as valuable extensions.

4 Challenges in Testing

The main challenges we faced in testing our SOA application were in the areas of checking conformance to contracts specified at design time, automating tests for systems with asynchronous interfaces, testing robustness of applications built based on asynchronous messaging, and testing services in isolation. We now describe the features that we built in the SOA workbench to address each of these challenges.

4.1 Auto-validation During Manually Triggered Tests

In Sections 3.1 and 3.2, we described how a user could add validation criteria to the steps in a sequence at design time. The SOA workbench also provides additional features that enforce these validation rules at *runtime*, which can be leveraged for the testing of the application. The tester would trigger business sequences from the application -- for example, request a Credit Pull for a borrower from the application. This would exercise the entire sequence. All the messages exchanged at each step (including the JMS properties and the payload) are recorded in a Central Logging Database through a tool called SIMON (see Section 5.1). Through the SOA workbench, the tester can then query for the instance of the credit pull sequence that she just triggered (the query can be based on an application specific property such as say the Borrower's Social Security Number) and then "validate" that instance of that sequence. During validation, SOA workbench queries the Central Logging Database for all the messages that are part of that instance of the sequence, and then validates the message at each step against the Content Validation definitions that were specified at design time – i.e., it tests whether the message at each step has all the required elements, and tests the advanced content validations such as checking if the values in the document match the result of the specified queries in the database or if they match the value of an element from a previous step etc. Notice that while this mode of testing automates whether each step in the sequence adhered to its contracts, it still relies on a user to manually start the sequences through the application and to explicitly use the SOA workbench to validate each instance of the sequence. It does not provide a fully automated regression testing mechanism.

4.2 Fully Automated Regression Test Suites

For web-based applications, there are several testing tools that can be used to automate the user interaction to create automated regression tests. Such tools are not common for message-driven applications. To address this, SOA workbench allows a user to create "scenarios" for a sequence each of which represents a test case for that sequence, and then attach sample input messages for the first step in the sequence. An automated test runner just publishes the message to the service that is the message consumer of the first step in the sequence. After the sequence completes, the test runner validates the messages at each step as described in the previous section.

4.3 Proxy ESB Router

The SOA workbench also provides an additional feature by which it can act as a proxy ESB router whereby it routes the messages to the various services instead of letting it happen via the real ESB. This provides the benefit of being able to inspect and validate the messages immediately when the messages go through the proxy ESB as and when the services publish them, instead of waiting for the entire sequence to finish. This feature also eliminates the dependency on other tools (such as SIMON and the Central Logging Database) for SOA workbench to do its testing.

4.4 Robustness Testing – Duplicate, Lost and Out of Order Messages

The proxy ESB feature of the SOA workbench is a key component for executing robustness tests. An application built around messaging has to deal with issues such as lost or timed out messages, duplicate messages, messages arriving out of order or in orders that the application did not normally expect (this can happen because the speed of consumption and processing times of queues can vary dramatically causing events to happen in an order that a programmer didn't imagine in the "normal" flow). While the messaging infrastructure may provide certain guarantees about their quality of service with respect to duplicate and lost messages, some of these issues have to be dealt with by the application in any case. For example, the messaging infrastructure can go down causing messages to not arrive in time, or an application that we cannot control can send a messages twice, or a message may arrive in an order that does not conform to the programmers normal flow of thought. The SOA workbench allows such cases to be simulated in the testing cycle by injecting such behavior (such as losing a message, sending a message twice, or routing messages in different orders) during the routing of messages. Such tests are crucial in creating a robust application that can deal with such situations when they happen in real environments. The proxy ESB makes these tests easy to create which would otherwise be extremely hard to simulate.

4.5 Testing Services in Isolation

Testing a service or groups of services independent of the rest of them is important because (a) not all services may be available at the same time due to different development lifecycles (b) logistical problems can cause services to be unavailable in some environments and (c) it is easier to test a large system by incrementally assembling subsystems and testing them. To facilitate this, the SOA workbench allows the user to attach sample messages for each scenario to the intermediate and last steps in a sequence. When a service is unavailable, the ESB proxy uses these messages as replacements for the real message that would have been produced by the real service. This allows the sequence to be tested even when some services within it are unavailable. A common example in our application is testing the Credit Pull when the External Vendor Service is unavailable (it is difficult to coordinate availability of the External Vendor Service for testing because of external dependencies).

5   Monitoring and Error Recovery

So far we have described the challenges during development and testing phases of building SOA applications. We now describe the challenges that arise when the application is deployed on a production environment. In particular, we discuss the challenges in the areas of monitoring and recovering from error scenarios in a production environment.

5.1 Monitoring

As described earlier, a sequence representing a business process involves interactions with several different services that are deployed independently. A distributed system such as this makes it hard to monitor the application. For example, if the Lending Lifecycle Service initiated a Credit Pull and has not received the credit report back within an estimated time, the problem could have been in any of the several services involved in the sequence. We built a tool called SIMON that makes it easy to monitor the sequences and report on their activity and performance. The architecture of SIMON is illustrated in the figure below.

Each service registers an event when it sends a request to another service and when it processes a request from another service. These events are recorded in a database (called Central Logging Database) on a central server that we call the Central Logging Server. SIMON allows the user to define SLAs (service-level agreements) for the completion time for the various sequences. It then runs a background task periodically (the frequency of which can be configured) that looks at all the sequences that have started and whether they all have completed within the defined SLA time period. If some sequences have gone past the SLA time and are still incomplete, SIMON can identify them as exceptions and raise alerts (such as sending an email to the production support team). The level of alerts can be also configured based on the percentage

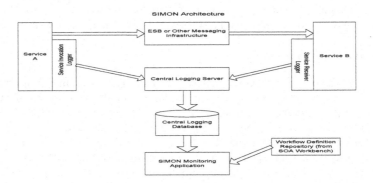

Fig. 3. SIMON Architecture

of occurrence of failures. For example, if less than 1% of the sequences fail, the alert could be a warning, whereas if more than 20% fail, the alert can be made critical. SIMON can also report on the overall performance of the sequences by providing reports such as the average time it took for sequences to complete and also provide response time breakdowns for each step in the sequence. Such reports are very useful to understand the performance of the overall SOA application and to determine the source of bottlenecks within it.

5.2 Error Recovery

Many errors in a production environment can be attributed to (1) services that are down for unexpected reasons, (2) services that didn't produce the correct message as per the contract, or (3) services that didn't consume the message properly due to defects in the code. If a sequence is stuck in the middle because of such problems, we need a way to recover from them. Temporary problems such as intermittent server crashes are usually fixed by using the redelivery features of messaging providers - a message can be delivered a certain number of times if there are failures in processing them. However, some problems such as defects in the code take longer to fix and the design of most messaging systems don't permit messages to be kept in them for a long time. Also, sometimes, we have to fix the message itself to recover from the problem. To deal with these situations, we built a utility that moves messages that have been tried multiple times from the queues into a database. An application allows users to query these messages in the database and move them back to the queue (which will be done once the defects are fixed and the service is redeployed). Also, if the problem is in the content of the message itself, it allows one to transform the message by applying XSL transformations to it before sending it back to the queue. Having these failed messages stored in a database also gives us the flexibility to query for messages related to a specific customer. For example, if a particular customer's credit pull sequence failed and the business wants the business flow for that customer to be completed first, we can query for all the failed messages for that customer and move them back to the queue so that they get processed first.

6 Learnings and Conclusion

SOA architecture offers promise in its ability to integrate loosely coupled systems. However, the principles underlying the design of applications based on SOA are not well established yet. In this section, we discuss the learnings from our experiences with SOA.

A key issue is defining a service at the right level of granularity. Our original architecture started out with defining services around every domain object (noun). For example, in addition to the services discussed earlier, nouns such as *insurance* and *address* were modeled as services in our original architecture. However, we quickly realized that a system based on such fine grained services will have unwanted development, deployment, and performance overhead. What we have learnt is that a service should represent the right abstraction that both IT and business care about. Importantly, it is something that the company wants to *manage independently*. Other factors that defines a service are does it need to be *released separately* from other components, does it provide *services to many different and varying systems*, should its *down time not affect other systems*, does it have *different hardware/scalability requirements*, is there *unique licensing requirements* etc. There is extra cost to managing something as a service and it should be backed by a strong business justification and business ownership.

The area of tools for building SOA applications needs further attention. While the solutions we described in this paper suit most of our needs, there is scope for further improvement. We would like to see more tools that use different approaches to address the challenges in the design, testing and monitoring of SOA applications. We also expect existing workflow and integration tools to start addressing some of these challenges. An interesting area of work is the simplification of the entire development lifecycle by utilizing higher level tools that are fundamentally aware of SOA. As an example, model-driven architectures (MDA [2]) around SOA is an interesting area of study. Another important area of work is the development of systems that intelligently manage schema versioning in SOA.

Adoption of an event driven SOA where back-end services drive events is a difficult challenge for architects and programmers accustomed with the classic UI-driven (e.g. Web) application development. In the web application paradigm, users drive system events by clicking buttons or hyperlinks. The underlying application(s) wait and process individual requests as they arise. Errors are typically handled by raising exceptions that are relayed back to the users, and relying on users to resubmit requests after correcting data and other input problems. In the event driven SOA paradigm, back-end services essentially replace human users. Thus, the back-end systems must be programmed to handle unreliable services, ensure data integrity up-front, resubmit requests, manage transactions etc. This problem is compounded by the fact that services inherently do not have knowledge of the business transaction in which they are a participant. The tools discussed in this paper describe some of means used to mitigate these issues. True defense in depth for the enterprise may require additional audits and batch processing "underneath" the event driven SOA.

Finally, application developers expend valuable time dealing with and designing for failure modes consciously during development (see Section 4.4). Besides the large amount of effort involved, it is difficult to ensure that the developers have thought through the failure scenarios for every use case in the application. It is an imperative to have better programming models and/or more integrated tools that can address these issues in an easier way that removes the burden from the application developers.

Acknowledgements: We would like to acknowledge Fabio Casati for his review of an earlier draft of the paper that has helped improve its quality. We also would like to thank the many members of the Tavant team who helped realize the concepts and features discussed in this paper.

References

[1]   Enterprise Service Bus. David Chappell. O'Reilly 2004.
[2]   MDA Guide Version 1.0.1 Joquin Miller and Jishnu Mukerji. <http://www.omg.org/docs/omg/03-06-01.pdf>, 2003
[3]   Java Business Integration JBI 1.0 http://java.sun.com/integration/1.0/docs/sdk/introduction/introduction.html
[4]   Java Messaging Service Specification version 1.1 http://java.sun.com/products/jms/docs.html

[5]   XML Schemas http://www.w3.org/XML/Schema
[6]   OAGIS Open Applications Group Integration Specification
      http://www.openapplications.org/downloads/oagis/loadform.htm
[7]   BPEL.The BPEL4WS 1.1 Specification.
      http://www-128.ibm.com/developerworks/library/specification/ws-bpel/
[8]   Weblogic Integration http://e-docs.bea.com/wli/docs85/index.html

Appendix -- SOA Workbench Data Model

Figure 4 shows a simplified UML class diagram for the internal object model of the
SOA workbench. The class IntegrationSequence represents the notion of sequences
(such as the Credit Pull) described earlier. Each IntegrationSequence consists of several
steps that is represented by IntegrationSequenceStep. As described in Section 3.1, the
data elements used in an IntegrationSequenceStep and whether they are mandatory for
that step is represented by the class DataElement. Each DataElement is internally represented as an XPath expression on the XML schema used for that IntegrationSequenceStep. The JMS properties associated with a IntegrationSequenceStep is represented by the class JMSProperty. The ValidationDataSource represents the more
complex data validations described in Section 3.2. The class DBValidationDataSource
represents the fact that the data element needs to be validated against the result of some
query which is represented by the class ValidationQuery. The class ConstantValida-
tionDataSource validates the data element against a constant value. The class XPath-
ValidationDataSource validates the data element against the result of another XPath expression on a previous IntegrationSequenceStep within the same IntegrationSequence.
In the interest of space, we have omitted illustrating the classes for other parts of the
SOA workbench such as those related to Reviews and Approvals etc.

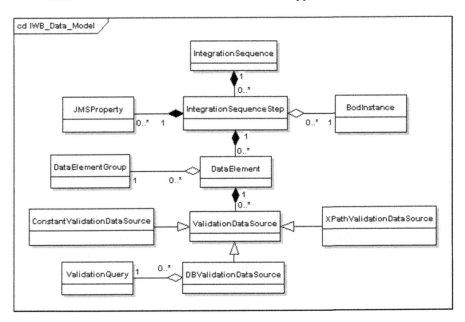

Service-Oriented Design: The Roots

Tiziana Margaria[1], Bernhard Steffen[2], and Manfred Reitenspieß[3]

[1] Service Engineering for Distributed Systems, Universität Göttingen, Germany
margaria@cs.uni-goettingen.de
[2] Chair of Programming Systems, Universität Dortmund, Germany
steffen@cs.uni-dortmund.de
[3] Director Business Development, RTP 4 Continuous Services,
Fujitsu Siemens Computers, Munich, Germany
Manfred.Reitenspiess@fujitsu-siemens.com

Abstract. Service-Oriented Design has driven the development of tele-communication infrastructure and applications, in particular the so-called Intelligent Network (IN) Services, since the early 90s. A service-oriented, feature-based architecture, a corresponding standardization of basic services and applications in real standards, and adequate programming environments enabled flexibilization of services, and dramatically reduced the time to market. Today the current trend toward triple-play services, which blend voice, video, and data on broadband wireline and wireless services builds on this successful experience when reaching for new technological and operational challenges. In this paper, we review our 10 years of experience in service engineering for telecommunication systems from the point of view of Service-Oriented Design then and now.

1 Motivation

Service-Oriented Design has driven the development of telecommunication infrastructure and applications, in particular the so-called Intelligent Network (IN) Services, since the early 90s: IN services are customized telephone services, like e.g., 'Free-Phone', where the receiver of the call can be billed if some conditions are met, 'Virtual Private Network', enabling groups of customers to define their own private net within the public net, or credit card calling', where a number of services can be billed directly on a credit card account. The realization of new IN services was quite complex, error prone, and extremely costly until a service-oriented, feature-based architecture, a corresponding standardization of basic services and applications in real standards, and adequate programming environments came up: they set the market, enabled flexibilization of services, and dramatically reduced the time to market. Today the current trend moves toward triple-play services, which blend voice, video, and data on broadband wireline and wireless services. It builds on this successful experience when reaching for new technological and operational challenges.

In this paper, we review our 10 years of experience in service engineering for telecommunication systems from the point of view of Service-Oriented Design

B. Benatallah, F. Casati, and P. Traverso (Eds.): ICSOC 2005, LNCS 3826, pp. 450–464, 2005.

then and now. In particular, we aim at establishing a link to the notions used by the service-oriented programming (SO) community.

The central observation is that both communities pursue the same goals, a coarse granular approach to programming, where whole programs serve as elementary building blocks. However, they have quite a different view on what a service is and how it is organized. In the terminology of the SO-community, a service is a "nugget" of functionality (essentially a building block) that is directly executable and can be published for use in complex applications. In the telecommunication world, such elementary components are called Service-Independent Building blocks (SIBs), and the notion of service is typically used for the resulting (overall) application. In addition, in the telecommunication world the notion of feature is used to denote substructures of services (applications) that impose additional functionality (like e.g. call forwarding, or blacklisting) on the generic basic telecommunication functionality. In the IN-architecture, the basic functionality was POTS (plain old telephony service), and feature were typically only executable in the context of POTS.

It was always our point of view that some of these distinctions would disappear as soon as one lives in a fully hierarchical context, where services may themselves be regarded as elementary building blocks at a higher level of abstraction. In this scenario, which is supported by METAFrame, our service definition environment, the notion of service capture the corresponding notions of both the SO- and the telecommunication communities. Moreover, the notion of SIB simply characterizes services which cannot be refined, and the notion of feature characterizes subservices that cannot be executed on their own. The remainder of this paper is written from this unifying perspective and it focusses on the impact on formal methods to improve the service development process. This concerns in particular the idea of incremental formalization, which allows users to already exploit very partial knowledge about the service and its environment for verification. In turn, this enables a division of labour, which in particular enables the application expert to directly cooperate in the service definition process.

In the following, Sect. 2 introduces the traditional concept of services in an Intelligent Networks Architecture, Sect. 3 describes the current telecommunication perspective, and Sect. 4 presents a unifying feature-oriented description of services that goes beyond the IN understanding. Finally, Sect. 5 summarizes our conclusions.

2   Services in an Intelligent Networks Architecture

By integrating telecommunication and computer technology, the Intelligent Network concept (see [10] for an overview) helps (network) providers to make new and flexible telecommunication services available for their customers. Particularly complex examples of such services are Universal Personal Telecommunication (UPT), that combines personal mobility with the access to and from telecommunication over a unique number and account, and Virtual Card Calling (VCC), that allows subscribers to make calls from every private or public telephone charging their own VCC account. Widely used IN services are Free-Phone (FPH, the family of 0180- or 800-services), Televoting (VOT, e.g. for selection of Saturday night movies via telephone or for the winner of the European song context), Universal Access Number (UAN, where service subscribers can be reached from anywhere under a unique universal, network-independent directory number), Premium Rate Service (PRM, which enables the service subscriber to supply any information under a unique number and against a usage fee), and Virtual Private Network Service (VPN, which allows subscribers to define a private number plan based on a public telephone exchange).

The underlying *intelligent networks* are composed of several subsystems that together implement the intended functionality. They form complex distributed systems, which require the cooperation of central computers, of databases, of the telephone network, and of a huge number of peripherals under real-time and performance constraints. In particular, the design of new services must take into account requirements imposed by the underlying intelligent network: e.g., system-dependent frame conditions must be obeyed in order to guarantee reliable execution of the new services. Figure 1 shows an abstract functional decomposition of an intelligent network, which comprehends management, control, switch and service creation units. A more detailed description of IN components and their functions can be found in [3,9].

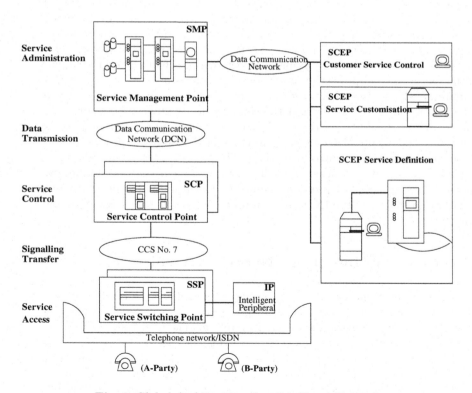

Fig. 1. Global Architecture of an Intelligent Network

- The *Service Management Point* (SMP) serves as the central component for the creation, customization and management of services and service subscribers/users. Based on a database system and on an advanced authorization system, the SMP allows the installation and administration of services and service customers by service subscribers and providers using the associated interfaces (Service Creation Environment, SCE). The SMP also provides interfaces for statistic raw data and for mass data entry.
- The *Service Control Point* (SCP) controls the Service Switching Point according to the control parameters provided by the SMP. The SCP also compiles statistical information of the calling activities and other call-related data and makes them available via the SMP for further processing. Information between SCP and SSP is exchanged via the INAP communication protocol.
- The CCS7 network is used to exchange the signalling information between the SCP and the *Service Switching Point* (SSP). The SSP sets up the call between the calling party and the called party in conjunction with the underlying telephone network (mobile or public exchange). An Intelligent Peripheral (IP) can be attached to the SSP for playing announcements or for other automatic voice services.
- The *Service Creation Environment Point* (SCEP) provides Customer Service Control (CSC), Service Customization (SC) and Service Definition (SD).
  - The *Customer Service Control* component supports the handling of the subscriber-specific service data such as parametrization of a subscribed service, modification and adaptation of service logic and statistics inquiries.
  - The *Service Customization* process serves to define which service functions and features the service subscribers are allowed to use according to their needs.
  - The aim of *Service Definition* is to establish the logic of a service and the parameters which control the processing of the service. The definition of a service begins with the creative process of detailed service specification, in which various aspects such as market requirements, technical performance (load criteria) and serviceability must be taken into account.

The complexity of the new services and the complexity of the distributed environment in which they must correctly function under strict real-time requirements of availability and performance currently make service definition intricate and error prone. In a pure direct programming based approach, the introduction of new complex services like the ones mentioned above used to take several expert years for development and testing.

A model-driven Service Definition approach has supplanted the programming style already in the '90s, supporting a reliable service design and development tailored to the specifica of the intelligent network. This has led to a much shorter time to market (days instead of months), with shortened development and testing phases. It has enabled low-cost development of high-quality services, boosting the differentiation of services to the richness we experience today.

2.1   The METAFrame Environment for Service Definition

The implementation of the Service Design Environment was based on the METAFrame® environment [29]. At that time, the service-oriented terminology was not yet defined, and the IN community defined and standardized own names for the entities they were working with. In the following we stick to that original terminology. The parallel to the modern SO-world is astonishing.

Behaviour-Oriented Development: Application development consists in the behaviour-oriented combination of Service Independent Building Blocks (SIBs) on a *coarse* granular level. SIBs are software components with a particularly simple interface. This kind of interface enables one to view SIBs semantically just as input/output transformations. Additional interaction structures can also be modelled, but are not subject to the formal synthesis and verification methods offered by the METAFrameenvironment. SIBs are here identified on a functional basis, understandable to application experts, and usually encompass a number of 'classical' programming units (be they procedures, classes, modules, or functions). They are organized in application-specific collections. In contrast to (other) component-based approaches, e.g., for object-oriented program development, METAFrame focusses on the dynamic behaviour: (complex) functionalities are graphically stuck together to yield flow graph-like structures called Service Logic Graphs (SLGs) embodying the application behaviour in terms of control. This graph structure is independent of the paradigm of the underlying programming language, which may, e.g., well be an object-oriented language: here the coarse granular SIBs are themselves implemented using all the object oriented features, and only their combination is organized operationally. In particular, we view this flow-graph structure as a control-oriented coordination layer on top of data-oriented communication mechanisms enforced e.g. via RMI, CORBA or (D)COM. Accordingly, the purely graphical combination of SIBs' behaviours happens at a more abstract level, and can be implemented in any of these technologies.

Incremental Formalization: The successive enrichment of the application-specific development environment is two-dimensional. Besides the library of application specific SIBs, which dynamically grows whenever new functionalities are made available, METAFrame supports the dynamic growth of a hierarchically organized library of *constraints*, controlling and governing the adequate use of these SIBs within application programs. This library is intended to grow with the experience gained while using the environment, e.g., detected errors, strengthened policies, and new SIBs may directly impose the addition of constraints. It is the possible *looseness* of these constraints which makes the constraints highly reusable and intuitively understandable. Here we consciously privilege understandability and practicality of the specification mechanisms over their completeness.

Library-Based Consistency Checking: Throughout the behaviour-oriented development process, METAFrame offers access to mechanisms for the verification of

libraries of constraints by means of model checking. The model checker individually checks hundreds of typically very small and application- and purpose-specific
constraints over the flow graph structure. This allows concise and comprehen-
sible diagnostic information in the case of a constraint violation, in particular
as the information is given at the application rather than at the programming
level.

These characteristics are the key towards a well-functioning distribution of
labour, according to the various levels of expertise. The groups that crystallized
were

- **Programming Experts**, responsible for the software infrastructure, the
  runtime-environment for the compiled services, as well as the programming
  of SIBs.
- **Constraint Modelling Experts**, who are experts of the protocols and
  frame conditions of the underlying infrastructure formulate the correctness
  conditions for services to properly run and interact.
- **Application Experts**, who develop concrete applications, by graphically
  combining SIBs into coarse-granular flow graphs. These graphs can be immediately executed by means of an interpreter, in order to validate the intended
  behaviour (rapid prototyping). Model checking guarantees the consistency
  of the constructed graph with respect to the constraint library.
- **End Users** may customize a given (global) service according to their needs
  by parametrization and specialization [6].

The resulting overall lifecycle for application development using METAFrame
is two-dimensional: both the application and the environment can be enriched
during the development process.

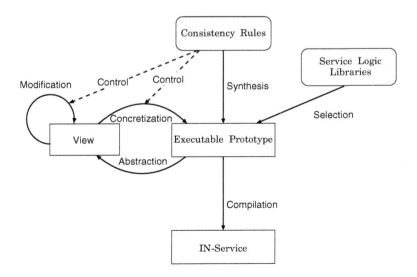

Fig. 2. The Service Creation Process

2.2   Service Definition in Practice

The Service Definition Environment is constructed for the flexible and reliable, aspect-driven creation of telephone services in a 'divide and conquer' fashion [34,4]. As shown in Fig. 2, initial service prototypes are successively modified until each feature satisfies the current requirements. The entire service creation process is supported by thematic views that focus on particular aspects of the service under consideration. Moreover, the service creation is constantly accompanied by on-line *verification*: the validity of the required features and of the executability conditions for intermediate prototypes are checked directly at design time. Design decisions that conflict with the *constraints* and consistency conditions of the intended service are immediately detected via model checking.

The novelty of this SD environment is due the impact of formal verification and abstract views on service creation [33,32]. In fact,

- Formal verification allows designers to check for *global consistency* of each design step with implementation-related or service-dependent frame conditions. Being based on model checking techniques [28], it is *fully automatic* and does not require any particular technical knowledge of the user. This simplifies the service design since sources for typical failures are detected immediately.
- Abstract or thematic *views* concentrate on the required global context and hide unnecessary details. They allow the designer to choose a particular aspect of interest, and to develop and investigate the services under that point of view. This supports a much more focussed service development, which concentrates on the design of the aspect currently under investigation. Of particular interest are error views that concentrate on the essence of a detected error.
- SIBs and reusable services are classified typically according to technical criteria (like their version or specific hardware or software requirements), their origin (where they were developed) and, here most importantly, according to their intent for a given application area. The resulting classification scheme (called *taxonomy*, [32,30,20]) is the basis for the constraint definition in terms of modal formulas.
- Both formal verification and abstract views are fully compatible with the *macro* facility of the environment. This allows developers to define whole sub-services (usually called *features*) as primitive entities, which can be used just as SIBs. Macros may be defined on-line and expanded whenever the internal structure of a macro becomes relevant: this way the SDE supports a truly hierarchical service construction [35].

The design of the taxonomies goes hand in hand with the definition of aspect-specific views, since both are mutually supportive means to an application specific structuring of the design process.

IN services soon reached sizes and complexities which demand for automated support for error detection, diagnosis, and correction. The IN-METAFrame environment encourages the use of the new methods, as they can be introduced *incrementally*: if no formal constraints are defined, the system behaves like standard systems for service creation. However, the more constraints are added, the more reliable are the created services [31].

To allow verification in real time, we use finite-state model checkers [28,23] optimized for dealing with large numbers of constraints. The algorithms verify whether a given model satisfies properties expressed in a modal logic called the modal mu-calculus [18]. In the SD-IN setting:

– the *properties* express correctness or consistency constraints the target IN service is required to respect. They are expressed in a natural language-like macro language, internally based on the temporal logic SLTL (Semantic Linear Time Logic, cf. [30]). This is a linear-time variant of Kozen's mu-calculus [18], which comes together with efficient verification tools;
– the *models* are directly the Service Logic Graphs, where SIB names correspond to atomic propositions, and branching conditions correspond to action names in the SLTL formulas.

Model checking a service, as shown in [35] on a concrete case, may lead to the discovery of paths in the graph that violate some constraints. When the model checker detects such an inconsistency, a plain text explanation of the violated constraint appears in a window. To ease the location and correction of the error, an abstract *error view* is automatically generated, which evidences only the nodes which are relevant to the error detection [5]. Errors can be corrected directly on the error view, and the subsequent view application transmits the modifications to the concrete model. Examples have been already discussed in previous papers [33,32].

3   The Current Telecommunication Perspective

During the last 10 years, smooth but steady transition has taken place from the switch-based IN-Architecture described in the previous section to Computer-Telephony Integrated solutions [12], and more recently to the integrated, open IT-based architectures that are being developed and deployed today as high-availability service solutions [26,24], or as distributed service integration and collaboration platforms [20]. The internet has supplanted the ISDN backbone as basis network, and the picture has reversed: cutting edge telecommunication services are being provided on an IP basic infrastructure.

The transition from the pure telecommunication scenario (which was still dominating the IN architecture) to a holistic service-oriented attitude, that includes also middleware and applications, has been actively pursued in the past years and it starts paying off. An example of this trend are the Open Specifications for Service Availability^{TM}, a collection of specifications spanning from hardware interfaces to the application level, which are available from the SAForum webpage [27]: they are increasingly influencing the way 3G telecommunication services are built. As such, they are a new success story for the feasibility and readiness of adoption of guidelines (a de facto standard) in shaping service

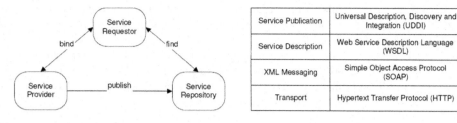

(a) Service Oriented Architecture (SOA)	(b) Web Service Standards Stack

Service Publication	Universal Description, Discovery and Integration (UDDI)
Service Description	Web Service Description Language (WSDL)
XML Messaging	Simple Object Access Protocol (SOAP)
Transport	Hypertext Transfer Protocol (HTTP)

Fig. 3. The Service-Oriented Architecture and the Web Services Standards Stack

interfaces with the aim of granting interoperability also in the software application domain!

The Service Availability Forum itself is a consortium of industry-leading communications and computing companies working together to develop and publish high availability and management software interface specifications. Member companies include e.g. Fujitsu Siemens Computers, IBM, Intel, Motorola, Oracle, Veritas Software, and a large number of smaller companies that offer solution that need to interwork with the platforms of the global players. The goal of the SAForum is to create complete and robust specifications to manage complex, highly-available platforms, with a specific focus on supporting high availability services. The SA Forum then promotes and facilitates specification adoption by the industry.

It is widely perceived by the participating companies that this goal by far exceeds the current aims of the SOA community: the SOA interaction structure establishes a simple, but very generic way of communication shown in Fig.3(a), and there are a number of layers for specific SOA architectures which are object of standardization efforts. SOAP [11] is a standard for XML messaging, the Web Services Description Language [8](WSDL) for service descriptions and UDDI for service repositories are de-facto standards for today's most popular implementation of service orientation: Web services [1]. The Web Services Standards Stack is summarized in Fig.3(b). A Web services implementation aims at allowing loose coupling between business partners. Since all the needed interactions can be automated, it allows also just-in-time queries to find available services.

Still, the standardization in Web services concerns interface programming languages (WSDL), data description languages (XML and derivatives like OWL-S), behaviour composition languages (BPEL4WS) and mechanisms (WSMO [37]), but not services. In other words, it tackles formats - not content, syntax - not semantics. A catalogue of service behaviours that

– service providers in one domain must provide,
– which must satisfy a given standard, but whose implementation might differ, e.g. resorting to different technologies or platforms, and

– which must be capable of interoperation, in the sense that they are guaranteed to be interchangeable,

is not yet in sight. Only such (domain-specific) standardizations will realize the full potential of service orientation in the sense of a major shift of development paradigm.

This is far away from what is customary in the telecommunication world, as described in the previous sections, and far weaker. The concept of concrete sets of *Features* and of *Services* as objects of standardization, which is natural and well accepted in the telecommunication world, is in fact still extraneous to the SOA community. For specific industrial sectors, names for categories and services are slowly becoming established and agreement is building up. Ontology-based approaches are one of the emerging technologies that are being intensively investigated within the semantic web paradigm to handle this. But they are still insufficient since they are island-solutions, not accepted standards. In the IN world, and consequently in the METAFrame environment, this standardized way of thinking was already realized in the '90s.

4   Feature-Oriented Service Description Beyond IN

There are many definitions of features, depending heavily on their context and their use. Although we too learned to know and appreciate the concept and the use of features in the context of Intelligent Networks [14,15,35], our notion of features is meanwhile more general in order to also capture a more general class of services like online, financial, monitoring, reporting, and intelligence services:

Definition 1 (Feature).

1. *A* feature *is a piece of (optional) functionality built on top of a base system.*
2. *It is* monotonic, *in the sense that each feature* extends *the base system by an* increment *of functionality.*
3. *The description of each feature* may *consider or require other features, additionally to the base system.*
4. *It is defined from an* external *point of view, i.e., by the viewpoint of* users *and/or* providers *of services.*
5. *Its granularity is determined by* marketing *or* provisioning *purposes.*

In the IN setting, the base system was a switch that offered POTS (plain old telephone service) functionality, and the features were comparatively small extensions of that behaviour. Instead, today we tend to have a *lean* basis service that deals with session, user, and role-rights management, and a very rich collection of features. Complex internet services with a strongly CSCW-oriented character and online decision support systems like the Online Conference Service described in [17], have been entirely developed this way. This brings a different perspective on the role and purpose of features.

Features were traditionally understood as local modifiers of the basic service: they were individually executed, i.e. a single feature was triggered by some event, executed, and it retuned upon termination to the basic service. This is no longer sufficient: in order to account for complex evolutions of services, we allow in today's SD a *multilevel organization* of features, whereby more specialistic features build upon the availability of other, more basic, functionalities.

In order to keep this structure manageable and the behaviours easily understandable, we restrict us to *monotonic* features, which are guaranteed to add behaviour. Restricting behaviour, which is also done via features in other contexts (e.g. [13]), is done in an orthogonal way in our setting, via constraints at the requirements level.

Additionally, we distinguish between features as implementations and properties of feature behaviours. Both together give the feature-oriented description of services enforced in the ABC.

Definition 2 (Feature-Oriented Description).

1. *A feature-oriented service description of a complex service specifies the behaviours of a base system and a set of optional features.*
2. *The behaviour of each feature and of the basic system are given by means of Service Logic Graphs (SLGs) [15].*
3. *The realization of each SLG bases on a library of reusable components called Service Independent Building-Blocks (SIBs).*
4. *The feature-oriented service description includes also a set of abstract requirements that ensure that the intended purposes are met.*
5. *Interactions between features are regulated explicitly and are usually expressed via constraints.*
6. *Any feature composition is allowed that does not violate any constraint.*

The library of SIBs for IN services was itself standardized [16], thus leading to a well-defined set of capabilities that ensured interoperation between functionalities offered by the different vendors.

In contrast to the proposal by [7], which is still close to the IN point of view, we distinguish the description of the feature's behaviour from that of the legal use of a feature. Restrictions to behaviours are in fact expressed at a different level, i.e. at the requirements level, and they are part of an aspect-oriented description of properties that we want to be able to check automatically, using formal verification methods.

As we successively discovered, the INXpress SDE was already largely organized that way, since it was strongly influenced by more complex IN-services, which themselves were built from a combination of pre-existing individual services. Examples of such leading-edge IN services are the already mentioned UPT and VCC.

– The UPT service examined in [35] combines personal mobility with the access to and from telecommunication over a unique number and account. Using a personal identifier, a service subscriber can access telecommunication services at any terminal and use those services provided by the network which are defined in their own service profile. Personal mobility involves the capability to identify the location of the terminal currently associated with the subscriber. Incoming UPT calls must be routed to the current destination address, and the associated charge may be split between the calling line and the UPT subscriber. Subscribers can use any terminal in the network for outgoing UPT calls, which are charged to their accounts. This requires user identification and authentication on a per-call basis. The use of the optional follow-on feature allows one authentication procedure to continue to be valid for subsequent calls or procedures. The service package can be tailored to the subscriber's requirements selecting from a comprehensive service feature portfolio.

– The VCC service allows subscribers to make calls from every private or public telephone charging their own VCC account. VCC calls are free of charge for the originating telephone line, so that cash or cards are no more needed at public telephones. After dialling the defined access code, VCC subscribers have to identify themselves by entering their virtual card number, used by the VCC service provider to determine the subscriber's account for billing purposes, and a Personal Identification Number (PIN) for personal authorization. If the virtual card number and the PIN are valid and match, the VCC user can dial the desired destination number and will be connected.

5   Conclusions

The INXpress Service Development Environment (SDE), the Siemens solution to Advanced Intelligent Networks that came out of our cooperation in 1995-1996, is a commercial product that shaped the state-of-the-art of IN-service definition in the late '90s. Presented at various international fairs (e.g. CeBIT'97), it was installed at a number of early-adopter customers (e.g. Deutsche Telekom, South Africa's Vodacom, Finnland's RadioLinja), while a number of further key contracts followed, where our SDE was a key factor for the decision of changing to Siemens technology. The success of the IN services since then has clearly demonstrated the validity and adequacy of the service-oriented way of thinking.

The same approach to service definition, composition, and verification has been meanwhile successfully applied in other application domains. With the ABC (Application Building Center) and the jABC (Java ABC)[1] we have meanwhile built internet based distributed decision support systems [19], an integrated test environment for regression test of complex CTI systems [25], a management infrastructure for remote intelligent configuration of pervasive systems [2], as well as many other industrial applications in e-business, supply chain management, and production control systems. In the area of internet-based service orchestration and coordination we have developed since 1997 the Electronic Tool Integration Platform, ETI [30], and its Web services based successor, jETI [21]. jETI is unique in providing (1) lightweight remote component (tool) integration by rregistration, (2) distributed component (tool) libraries, (3) a graphical coordi-

---

[1] The ABC and the jABC are the successors of the METAFrame environment.

nation environment, and (4) a distributed execution environment. Currently its application focus is on tools for program analysis, verification and validation.

The current challenge is to enhance this approach to today's Telecommunication scenarios, e.g. to 3G VoIP solutions, that blend voice, video, and data on broadband wireline and wireless services, and even beyond, reaching to the full range of unified communication and data management scenarios. This should encompasses correctness, interoperability, security, and other aspects which are not yet sufficiently supported by the standards and by the service design and validation environments. In particular, the security issue is new in this dimension to the telecommunication culture, since these concerns have been brought in by the transition to IP-based networks.

Service-level standardization efforts are still going to be the approach of choice in the telecommunication domain. Back then, the IN application consortia of competing vendors like FINNET Group, CSELT/STET, Deutsche Telekom AG, France Tlcom, Swiss Telecom PTT, Telecom Eireann, Telecom Finland Ltd., Telecom Portugal S.A. had joined forces into EURESCOM, and set the (still valid) standard of services and features in that specific domain.

This way of standardizing services and features according to their content is still infant in the area of Web services. Here the accent is still on the application indepedent infrastructure, as in the METEOR-S project [22], with initial catalogues of concrete services being developed (see e.g. the UN/SPSC service taxonomy).

We are convinced that combined approaches, that blend the flexibility of the current SO-scenario with the rigour and semantic standardization culture of the telecommunication community can be the key to the new generation of personalized, secure, and available "triple play" services. Incremental formalization and automatic verification techniques may be again the key to achieving confidence and reliability for services that interact and interoperate on a large distributed scale.

References

1. Alonso, G., Casati, F., Kuno, H., and Machiraju, V. (2004). Web Services - Concepts, Architectures and Applications. Springer Verlag.
2. M. Bajohr, T. Margaria: *MaTRICS: A Management Tool for Remote Intelligent Configuration of (Pervasive) Systems*, Proc. ICPS 2005, IEEE Int. Confer-ence on Pervasive Services, 11-14.July 2005, Santorini, Greece, pp. 457-460, IEEE Computer Society Press, 2005.
3. J. Biala: "*Mobilfunk und Intelligente Netze*," ISBN 3-528-15302-4, Vieweg, Braunschweig (D), 1995.
4. F.-K. Bruhns, V. Kriete, T. Margaria: "*Service Creation Environments: Today and Tomorrow*" tutorial, 4th Int. Conf. on Intelligent Networks (ICIN'96), Nov. 1996, Bordeaux (France).
5. V. Braun, T. Margaria, B. Steffen, H. Yoo: *Automatic Error Location for IN Service Definition*, Proc. AIN'97, 2nd Int. Workshop on Advanced Intelligent Networks, Cesena, 4.-5. Juli 1997, in "Services and Visualization: Towards User-Friendly Design', LNCS 1385, Springer Verlag, März 1998, pp.222-237.

6. V. Braun, T. Margaria, B. Steffen, H. Yoo, T. Rychly: *Safe Service Customization*, Proc. IN'97, IEEE Communication Soc. Workshop on Intelligent Network, Colorado Springs, CO (USA), 4-7 May 1997, IEEE Comm. Soc. Press.
7. J. Bredereke: *On Feature Orientation and Requirements Encapsulation*, in "Objects, Agents, and Features", pp. 26-44, Springer Verlag, LNCS 2975 (2004)
8. Chinnici, R., Gudgin, M., Moreau, J.-J., Schlimmer, J., and Weerawarana, S. (2004). Web Services Description Language (WSDL) version 2.0. http://www.w3.org/TR/wsdl20/.
9. B.E. Christensen, D. Underwood: *"Kommunikationsnetze werden intelligenter,"* Telecom Report 14 (1991), Heft 5, pp. 262-265.
10. J. Garrahan, P. Russo, K. Kitami, R. Kung: *"Intelligent Network Overview,"* IEEE Communications Magazine, March 1993, pp. 30-37.
11. Gudgin, M., Hadley, M., Mendelsohn, N., Moreau, J.-J., and Nielsen, H. F. (2003) SOAP Version 1.2 Part 1: Messaging Framework. http://www.w3.org/TR/soap12-part1/. W3C Recommendation 24 June 2003.
12. A. Hagerer, T. Margaria, O. Niese, B. Steffen, G. Brune, H.-D. Ide: *Efficient Regression Testing of CTI-Systems: Testing a Complex Call-Center Solution*, in *Annual Review of Communication*, Int. Engineering Consortium Chicago (USA), Vol. 55, pp.1033–1039, IEC, 2002.
13. H. Harris, M. Ryan: *Theoretical Foundations of Updating Systems*. ASE 2003, 18th IEEE Int. Conf. on Automated Software Engineering, IEEE-CS Press, 2003.
14. ITU: *General recommendations on telephone switching and signaling intelligent network: Introduction to intelligent network capability set 1*, Recommendation Q.1211, Telecommunication Standardization Sector of ITU, Geneva, Mar. 1993.
15. ITU-T: *Recommendation Q.1203. "Intelligent Network - Global Functional Plane Architecture"*, Oct. 1992.
16. ITU-T: *Recommendation Q.1204. "Distributed Functional Plane for Intelligent Network Capability Set 2: Parts 1-4"*, Sept. 1997.
17. M. Karusseit, T. Margaria: *Feature-based Modelling of a Complex, Online-Reconfigurable Decision Support Service*, WWV'05. 1st Int'l Workshop on Automated Specification and Verification of Web Sites, Valencia, Spain, March 14-15, 2005, – Post Workshop Proc. appear in ENTCS.
18. D. Kozen: *"Results on the Propositional μ-Calculus"*, Theoretical Computer Science, Vol. 27, 1983, pp. 333-354.
19. Tiziana Margaria: *Components, Features, and Agents in the ABC*. In *Objects, Agents, and Features*, Revised and Invited Papers from the International Seminar on Objects, Agents, and Features, Dagstuhl Castle, Germany, February 2003, LNCS 2975, pp. 154-174, Springer Verlag, 2003
20. T. Margaria: Web Services-Based Tool-Integration in the ETI Platform, SoSyM, Int. Journal on Software and System Modelling, Springer Verlag, (available in Online First, DOI: 10.1007/s10270-004-0072-z).
21. T. Margaria, R. Nagel, B. Steffen: Remote Integration and Coordination of Verification Tools in jETI Proc. ECBS 2005, 12th IEEE Int. Conf. on the Engineering of Computer Based Systems, April 2005, Greenbelt (USA), IEEE Computer Soc. Press, pp. 431-436.
22. METEOR-S: see the project site at `lsdis.cs.uga.edu/projects/meteor-s/`
23. M. Müller-Olm, H.Yoo: *MetaGame: An Animation Tool for Model-Checking Games*, Proc. TACAS 2004, LNCS N. 2988, pp. 163-167.
24. J. Neises: *Benefit Evaluation of High-Availability Middleware*, Proc. ISAS 2004, 1st Int. Service Availability Symposium, LNCS N. 3335, pp.73-85, Springer Verlag, 2005.

25. O. Niese, B. Steffen, T. Margaria, A. Hagerer, G. Brune, H.-D. Ide: *Library-Based Design and Con-sistency Checking of System-Level Industrial Test Cases*, Proc. FASE 2001, Int. Conf. on Fundamental Approaches to Software Engineering, Genoa (I), April 2001, LNCS 2029, pp. 233-248, Springer-Verlag.

26. M. Reitenspieß: *High-Availability and Standards - The Way to Go!* Proc. ARCS Workshop 2004 - Organic and Pervasive Computing, Workshops Proceedings, March 26, 2004, Augsburg, Germany. LNI Volume 41, pp. 12-18 - Gesellschaft für Informatik.

27. The Service Availability Forum - http://www.saforum.org .

28. B. Steffen, A. Claßen, M. Klein, J. Knoop. T. Margaria: *"The Fixpoint Analysis Machine"*, (*invited paper*) to CONCUR'95, Pittsburgh (USA), August 1995, LNCS 962, Springer Verlag.

29. B. Steffen, T. Margaria: *METAFrame in Practice: Intelligent Network Service Design*, In *Correct System Design – Issues, Methods and Perspectives*, LNCS 1710, Springer Verlag, 1999, pp. 390-415.

30. B. Steffen, T. Margaria, V. Braun: *The Electronic Tool Integration platform: concepts and design*, [36], pp. 9-30.

31. B. Steffen, T. Margaria, A. Claßen, V. Braun: *"Incremental Formalization: A Key to Industrial Success "*, In "SOFTWARE: Concepts and Tools", Vol. 17, No 2, pp. 78-91, Springer Verlag, July 1996.

32. B. Steffen, T. Margaria, A. Claßen, V. Braun, M. Reitenspieß: *"A Constraint-Oriented Service Creation Environment,"* Proc. PACT'96, Int. Conf on Practical Applications of Constraint Technology, April 1996, London (UK), Ed. by The Practical Application Company, pp. 283-298.

33. B. Steffen, T. Margaria, A. Claßen, V. Braun, M. Reitenspieß: *"An Environment for the Creation of Intelligent Network Services"*, invited contribution to the book "Intelligent Networks: IN/AIN Technologies, Operations, Services, and Applications – A Comprehensive Report" Int. Engineering Consortium, Chicago IL, 1996, pp. 287-300 – also invited to the *Annual Review of Communications*, IEC, 1996, pp. 919-935.

34. B. Steffen, T. Margaria, A. Claßen, V. Braun, M. Reitenspieß, H. Wendler: *Service Creation: Formal Verification and Abstract Views*, Proc. 4th Int. Conf. on Intelligent Networks (ICIN'96), Nov. 1996, Bordeaux (F).

35. B. Steffen, T. Margaria, V. Braun, N. Kalt: *Hierarchical Service Definition*, Annual Review of Communic., Int. Engineering Consortium, Chicago, 1997, pp.847-856.

36. *Special section on the Electronic Tool Integration Platform*, Int. Journal on *Software Tools for Technology Transfer*, Vol. 1, Springer Verlag, November 1997

37. Web Service Modeling Ontology (see www.wsmo.org).

A Service Oriented Architecture for Deploying and Managing Network Services

Victor A.S.M. de Souza and Eleri Cardozo*

Department of Computer Engineering and Industrial Automation,
School of Electrical and Computer Engineering,
State University of Campinas,
13083-970, Campinas, So Paulo, Brazil
{vsouza, eleri}@dca.fee.unicamp.br

Abstract. New generation network services must be deployed and managed according to the customers' specific requirements. In this context, service providers must devise a way to design network services with near zero development time and high degrees of customization and evolution. Customization is necessary to fit the service according to the customers' requirements, while evolution is necessary to adapt the service as soon as these requirements change. In addition, customers are demanding the ability to manage the service in order to keep the usage, configuration, and evolution under their control. This paper presents an approach based on service oriented architecture (SOA) for developing network services able to fulfill the requirements of rapid deployment, customization, and customer-side manageability. The approach considers the network service as a set of interacting elements implemented as Web Services. The service logic is expressed in terms of Web Services orchestration. Two services for the management of connections in optical networks are presented as a case study.

1 Introduction

New network services differ from the present ones in many aspects. Firstly, the development time of the new services must be kept close to zero. In other words, the time between the service design and its effective use must be very short (ideally zero, no more than few hours in special cases). Secondly, the service must take into account the exact customers' requirements (and expectations) such as aspects related to configuration, pricing, and quality. Finally, customers are demanding the ability to manage the main aspects of the service in order to take advantage of their business peculiarities, e.g., traffic patterns and end-user profiles. Of course, price is always an important variable that can be reduced as long as the complexities of service creation, deployment and management decrease.

In this scenario, network providers must devise new ways of designing, deploying and managing network services. We strongly believe that service composition is the key toward this objective. A network service can be created by composing a set of primitive services. This recurrent definition is important in the sense that

---

* The authors would like to thank Ericsson Brazil for its support.

B. Benatallah, F. Casati, and P. Traverso (Eds.): ICSOC 2005, LNCS 3826, pp. 465–477, 2005.

it allows a more complex service be built above a set of already existing services such as back-end, resource management, and network management services. For instance, a Virtual Private Network (VPN) service can be built by composing a connection service, an authentication service, a fault management service, and a resource management service. These composed services are distributed throughout the service provider's enterprise, some of them running on the central office and others running close to the transport network.

Actually, there is a gap between the software entities at the business level and at the network level. Entities at the network level are based on low level signaling protocols such as RSVP-TE (Resource Reservation Protocol - Traffic Engineering) and OIF's UNI (Optical Internetworking Forum's User-to-Network Interface). The access to these protocols are performed via operator's interface, network management protocols (e.g., SNMP - Simple Network Management Protocol), or proprietary application programming interfaces (APIs). The entities at the business level, on the other hand, rely on high level software artifacts such as enterprise components (e.g., Enterprise Java Beans, COM+) and web components (e.g., Java Server Pages, Active Server Pages). Clearly, the gap between the control and management entities at network level and the entities at the business level is a complicating factor when a network service with high level of automation and integration must be designed and deployed in a short period of time.

Service oriented computing (SOC) is an attractive solution to narrow this gap in the sense that it offers a good level of automation, integration, customization, and flexibility in service creation, deployment, and management. This paper proposes a service oriented architecture (SOA) for management and deployment of services in a connection oriented network. The architecture assumes that all the composed services are Web Services and composition is governed by Web Services orchestration and choreography techniques. In this architecture, service creation consists in the edition of an orchestration script while the service deployment consists in the installation of this script in an appropriated software engine. Service management is described via Web Services choreography, an interaction agreement between different organizations or independent processes, in our case service user and service provider. The edition of the orchestration script can be assisted by specialized service creation tools, general purpose text editors or even by software engineering modeling tools.

This paper is organized as follows. Section 2 presents a brief introduction to SOC. Section 3 presents the proposed SOA-based architecture for service creation, deployment, and management focusing on connection oriented networks. Section 4 presents the services developed for assess the proposed architecture. Section 5 discusses some related and recently published works. Finally, Sect. 6 presents some closing remarks.

2   Service Oriented Computing

Service oriented computing is considered by many a step forward in the distributed computing field. Distributed computing, mainly distributed objects and, most recently, components, provide high cohesion, lower coupling, and modularity to the applications. As a consequence, software reuse and evolution are favored, with reduction of development and maintenance costs. Several open standards for distributed computing such as CORBA (Common Object Request Broker Architecture) and CCM (CORBA Component Model) from OMG (Object Management Group), RMI (Remote Method Invocation) and EJB (Enterprise Java Beans) from the Java Community are mature and well accepted. Software platforms supporting these standards are available, both commercially and as open source software.

Unfortunately, these standards and platforms have not been used across enterprises. Security and interoperability issues are the most relevant reasons. Protocols such as IIOP (Internet Inter-ORB Protocol) employed in CORBA and RMI are not "firewall friendly", while the interoperability between different standards has never been completely addressed. Moreover, loose-ends on the standards may result in interoperability problems between platforms implementing the same standard.

It was in this context that SOC emerged, providing a way to interoperate large software entities, independently of software platforms and systems employed by each enterprise. Service oriented computing is defined as "the computing paradigm that utilizes services as fundamental elements for developing applications" [1]. Using orchestration mechanisms we can build a more comprehensive service that can itself be part of a higher level composition [2]. The service workflow is defined in orchestration scripts that is processed by an orchestration engine.

Some relevant characteristics of SOC reported in the literature are summarized below:

- Interoperability - achieved through the use of an independent transport protocol.
- Composability - services can be composed to form another service, providing a flexible, rapid and low cost way of creating new services.
- Reusability - being a modular unit of software, services generally can be reused, reducing the time and effort to build new applications.
- Ubiquity - services can be accessed from anywhere at any time.
- Granularity - services presents higher granularity when compared with objects and components, facilitating the development of complex systems.
- Coupling - loose coupling is achieved in different levels:
  - Just real dependencies among software elements are implemented as long as each service has its own defined interface;
  - Using registering and discovering mechanisms no coupling is made to the service location;
  - Platform and language coupling can be avoided using a platform independent transport protocol;
  - Synchronism due to the request-response invocation style can be attenuated using asynchronous message exchange.

As mentioned in Sect. 1, our objective is to enable a quick and flexible development of new network services in connection oriented networks by addressing interoperability and high coupling issues both inside and outside an administrative network domain. The mentioned SOC characteristics fullfill these requirements. The most relevant consequence of employing SOC in this field is a complete integration of the network and business layers. This integration was proposed more than a decade ago in the scope of TMN (Telecommunication Management Network). However, TMN never achieved such an integration due to the need of gateways (mediation and adaptation functions in TMN) to connect software entities at different layers.

3   The Service Oriented Control and Management Architecture

3.1   Architecture Overview

In SOA every logical entity is seen as a service. Services are built from scratch or from legacy software by adding appropriated wrappers. These existing services can be classified into two levels, the business and the network levels. Services at the business level relate to the enterprise itself (e.g., subscription), while services at the network level relate to the transport network (e.g., routing). As stated before, there is a gap between services located into these two levels in terms of software entities the services are based on. A common approach is to employ a gateway software that converts the high level business decisions to the low level network signaling. This is not a good solution as gateways are always bottlenecks for interoperability, reliability and performance. Moreover, this approach ties too hard the business and network layers, compromising service automatization, customization and evolution.

In order to avoid gateways, we propose to enhance the network elements such as routers and switches with a service interface. In our architecture, every network element offers control and management functions through Web Services. Since the network element already hosts a web server, extending this server toward a Web Service engine is a minor step without significant impact to the equipment final cost. In addition, to allow a smooth integration between the business and network layers, the service interface of the network equipments may eliminate the need of complex network protocols. In our case, the connection establishment protocol (usually RSVP-TE) is replaced by a much simpler orchestration script. In this way we build a single service-based bus of communication, where one central orchestrated service is responsible for receiving client requests and coordinate all calls to the composed services. This architecture is presented in Fig. 1. The orchestrated service exposes a Web Service interface to the service client.

3.2   Service Management

Once installed, the network service provides the client the ability to manage the service, for instance, to alter the topology of a Virtual Private Network.

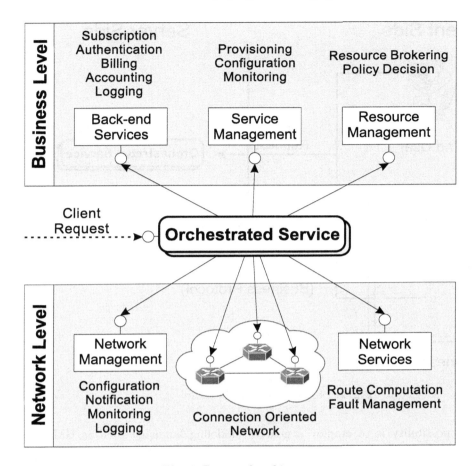

Fig. 1. Proposed architecture

The network service can be accessed via user interfaces (e.g., web interfaces) or via programatic interfaces where the service is accessed by other applications. This allows the composition of end-to-end service over multiple domains, e.g., VPN services, Voice-over-IP (VoIP) services or Virtual LAN (VLAN) services. In this context, it is necessary to precisely and unambiguously describe the collaborations between the client and the service provider. This is exactly what the choreography mechanism proposes [3]. As such, the service interface provided to the client will have their interaction contract described by a choreography script as shown in Fig. 2.

3.3   Service Creation

Service creation is a matter of composing the services with specific functions available at the business and the network levels. The hardest way to create an orchestrated network service is by manually editing an orchestration script.

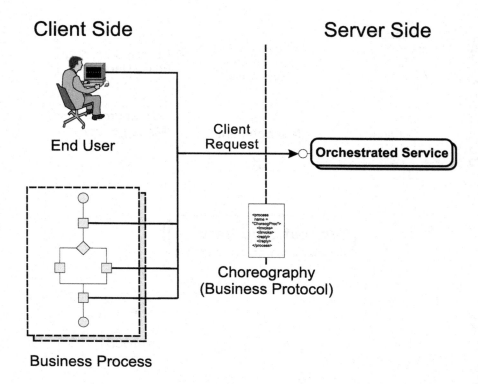

Fig. 2. Proposed client architecture

Another possibility is to employ a general modeling language such as UML (Unified Modeling Language) to specify the interactions among the composed service, using, for instance, an UML activity diagrams [4]. For this, it is necessary to specify a new UML profile in order to represent the particular domain of interest. It is also necessary to use model transformations to translate the UML model to the target orchestration language.

The most convenient way to create services is to use a Service Creation Environment (SCE), a software designed specially to this task [5, 6]. SCEs employ dedicated graphical interfaces with terms, icons, and diagrams known to the network engineer. The output of the SCE is exactly the orchestration script ready to execute in an orchestration engine. In any of the presented possibilities, service composition leads to a reduction in the service development time, a major issue in today's dynamic business environments.

3.4   Service Deployment

Using orchestration, the service deployment consists simply in the installation of the script in the orchestration engine. This can be performed via programatic interfaces (e.g., invoked by the SCE) or manually, via a graphical user interface provided by the orchestration engine.

4 Implementation Description

The architecture proposed in the Sect. 3 is general enough to deploy network services of arbitrary complexity. As a case study, we have developed two optical network services based on the proposed architecture: an Optical Connection Service (OCS) and a Fault Management Service (FMS).

As in any connection oriented network, in optical networks it is necessary to establish a connection before the traffic can be sent over the network. In optical networks, connections are lightpaths that may transverse a number of optical switches. The objective of the Optical Connection Service is to enable network clients to create, manage and destroy lightpaths. The Fault Management Service is aimed at restoring failed connections by setting up protection lightpaths.

Each optical switch in the domain will expose a cross connection service, enabling the composition engine to set up the connections across the domain. As the time required to setup a cross connection inside an optical switch is high (order of ms) it is expected that the Web Service does not introduce a considerable overhead in the connection establishment time.

All other necessary services to provide the connection service could be installed anywhere in the network, even on a third party domain (e.g., the billing service could be provided by a credit card operator).

4.1 Composed Services

We identified the following composed services necessary to implement the Optical Connection Service and the Fault Management Service:

- Optical Switch Service (OSS): a service exposed by the optical switch used to cross connect ports (fibers), wavelengths or wavebands.
- Resource Management Service (RMS): a service responsible for storing data about installed lightpaths, available resources, and Service Level Agreements (SLAs). It also stores protection information associated to a lightpath.
- Routing Service (RS): a service responsible for computing a route inside the optical network, given an ingress node, an egress node, and the available resources on the network. It is also responsible for finding a disjoint route for protection paths. The service must run a Routing and Wavelength Assignment (RWA) algorithm over a topology discovered with the aid of a routing protocol such as Open Shortest Path First - Traffic Engineering (OSPF-TE).
- Authentication Service (AS): a service responsible for authenticating the network users.
- Accounting Service (AcS): a service responsible for keeping track of the resources effectively used by a client for accounting and billing purposes.
- Logging Service (LS): a service responsible for logging errors and any other relevant information.

4.2 Implementation Details

In our system, the OSS, RMS, RS, AS, and LS composed services as previously described were implemented from scratch. In a service provider environment, most of the composed services already exist, although not as Web Services. To expose an existing service as a Web Service, the developer can take advantage of many existing software tools. For instance, some EJB platforms generate Web Service interface for existing enterprise beans (components).

We chose the Business Process Execution Language for Web Services (BPEL) [7], as it is the most mature standard language for orchestration and choreography (through the use of BPEL's *Executable Processes* and *Business Protocols*, respectively). As orchestration engine we chose ActiveBPEL [8] because it is open source and implements all the BPEL 1.1 specification including the full complement of BPEL activities.

Using the compensation mechanism provided by the BPEL language we are able to support rollback in connection establishment. This mechanism defines how individual or composite activities within a process are to be compensated in cases where exceptions occur during service invocations. When an optical switch in the connection path, for any reason, cannot install the cross connection as required, the previous switches that have already set their internal cross connections need to undo the action previously taken. The orchestration engine is in charge of coordinating the compensation actions that must be taken (connection release in this case).

All the topology information about the optical network is stored in a database. We have implemented a web interface where the network administrator can set the physical network topology, including nodes, fibers, wavelengths per fiber, cost of fiber, switching capacity, among other informations. This web interface is shown in Fig. 3. In a real optical network this information could be discovered using a routing algorithm such as OSPF-TE, but this is not relevant for the evaluation of the connection and fault management services.

The RMS is in charge of keeping this database up-to-date. Before any resources can be effectively used the RMS must be notified. This is necessary in order to keep the network state up-to-date. The RS is capable of finding a route inside the network, running a Shortest Path First (SFP) algorithm. It chooses the path with lower cost, where the cost can be any parameter the network administrator defines. After that, it runs a RWA based on the first-fit approach. The RS is also capable of finding a disjoint lightpath for protection purposes. Both RMS and RS were implemented in Java, using Axis Java as SOAP engine and Apache Tomcat as web container.

The AS receives an username and password and verifies if this pair is valid. The LS stores any informations passed to it in a file, with the time that event occurred. In our case we are logging system exceptions and failure informations for statistical purposes. These services are also implemented in Java.

The optical network element was emulated using a modified Linux kernel. This kernel is Multiprotocol Label Switching (MPLS) capable and we used an MPLS label table entry to emulate an optical cross connection. Wavelengths are emulated using MPLS labels. We could use a range of labels to emulate a waveband switching and a whole network interface to emulate a fiber switching. For fiber switching emulation, using a packet filter (as provided by *iptables*) it

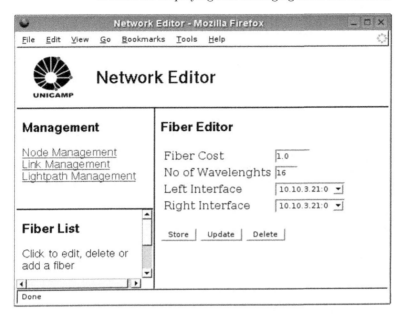

Fig. 3. Web interface of the Network Editor

is possible to redirect a packet arriving at a given network interface to another interface, no matter the packet contents. This is summarized in Fig. 4.

In our emulated scenario the Optical Switch Service must set the MPLS label table at the Linux kernel via system calls. As such, this service must be capable of performing low level actions at the kernel. In a real scenario, this service must run in the optical switch's internal processor (or in an adjunct processor such as a desktop). As a result, the service must be efficient and work with limited resources. Due to these reasons we decided to code this service in C++, as it is an efficient and compact object oriented programming language that still enables low level interactions.

Apache HTTP server and Axis C++ were used to develop this service. We decided to use a document literal wrapped style for all SOAP (Simple Object Access Protocol) bindings, as SOAP encoding is being not recommended for interoperability reasons. SOAP messages using document literal wrapped can be totally validated, as the body part does not contain any type encoding info and the message must be compliant with an agreed XML Schema [9, 10]. Moreover, the method name is present in the SOAP message, what simplifies the dispatching of the message at the server side to the right method implementation. Indications that the industry is abandoning SOAP encoding can be seen from its omission from the WS-I Basic Profile [11].

Using all these composed services the OCS is capable of establishing a connection inside the network. The interaction with the optical switches is accomplished concurrently, i.e., all the switches in the lightpath are cross connected almost at the same time. This can produce a good performance improvement

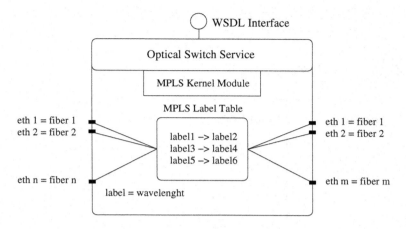

Fig. 4. Emulated optical switch

when compared to signaling protocols where the cross connection are performed sequentially.

When any link failure occurs or is cleared in the network the FMS must be notified. Currently we have implemented the *1:1* and *1:n* protection levels. On a failure the FMS acts on the ingress node, firstly dropping the failed connection and then adding the protection connection. The procedure is analogous when a fault is cleared. The FMS only acts on the ingress node because the rest of the lightpath is already set up.

Finally, all the traffic between the network client and the orchestration engine is transmitted over a secure channel, using Secure Socket Layer (SSL). This aims to protect user's authentication and exchanged data.

4.3   Tests and Evaluation

To test the implemented system we developed a command line client program to interact with the orchestrated service. The language used to code the client software is not relevant, since the SOAP messages exchanged with the service are XML Schema compliant. In our case we used Java language and Axis Java as SOAP engine. The following tests were performed to evaluate the OCS and FMS:

- Lightpath creation;
- Lightpath dropping;
- Fault restoration;
- Clear fault event.

In order to evaluate the performance impact of SOA in network services we focused on response times. As response time we have considered the time between a request message being sent and the response message arrival in client's machine. Further, in these tests we have not emulated the delay to set the cross connection inside the optical elements and, as the cross connections are set concurrently, there was no significant difference when varying the number of nodes in the lightpath. The results of 100 measurements are shown in Table 1.

Table 1. Response time

Test	Response Time (ms)	Standard Deviation (ms)
Lightpath creation	122	13
Lightpath dropping	101	6
Fault restoration	125	5
Clear Fault	136	8

As optical connections generally have long duration the response time for lightpath creation is acceptable. It is important to remember that it includes the time of all processing needed to establish the connection, even those related to the business layer (e.g., logging). Depending on the kind of application, notably phone connections, the restoration response time can be very restrictive. The response time of the FMS for these kind of applications can be considered inadequate if compared to restoration times performed at Layer-2 (such as on Synchronous Optical Networks - SONET). The performance obtained by the FMS is adequate for applications with less stringent recovering requirements such as web browsing and video on demand.

The lightpath dropping and clear fault times are not important issues except in the case where the network is overloaded (all possible lightpaths are installed) and there is need for new connections. Even in these cases, the times obtained are very satisfactory.

The objective of our architecture is to provide quick and flexible development of new network services. With the aid of specialized tools and appropriated languages we consider we achieved our objective. The solutions are simple and robust, and the implementation validates completely the proposed architecture.

5   Related Work

An important related work is being developed under the Canarie [12] User Controlled LightPath (UCLP) Research Program [13], implemented and tested in the Canadian research network CA*Net4. UCLP allows end-users, either people or software applications, to treat network resources as software objects, provisioning and reconfiguring them within a single domain or across multiple, independently managed domains. This research explores new features and enhancements to the current implementation of UCLP through the use of Web Services workflow and orchestration to create "Articulated Private Networks". The main design features of this architecture are [14]:

– All network software, hardware, lightpaths and cross connects are exposed as Web Services;

– Web Services workflow are employed to build a universal control plane across instruments, lightpaths, cross connects, networks and software systems.

Different from UCLP approach, we have not allowed the client interact directly with the network elements inside a domain for security reasons. In our architecture a contractual interface for each administrative domain is exposed in order to provide services for the client, creating a layer over the services offered by the domain. This is more likely to happen, as network providers have serious restrictions in opening their networks for full signaling or management of network elements. Furthermore, using the recurrent service construction provided by SOA we can provide end-to-end services in a very structured way.

The work presented in [15] proposes Web Services as an embedded technology for home appliances. The work argues that this is not an unrealistic assumption as the price and capacity of embedded processors are becoming reasonable for this application. This current work proposes the use of Web Services inside network devices, based on the same arguments.

Similarly to the proposals presented in references [13] and [16] our architecture give the customer the ability to manage a set of service parameters considering customers' specific needs. Moreover, reference [16] gives the customers the ability to build dynamically their application using a service trader. This could improve the level of automation of our architecture and we are now considering a similar approach, but employing UDDI (Universal Description, Discovery and Integration) instead.

6 Closing Remarks

This paper proposes a service oriented architecture for deployment and management of services in connection oriented networks. This architecture brings to the network service provider a higher level of automation, integration and flexibility in the design, deployment, and management of network services. These activities are performed by orchestration scripts executing in standard orchestration engines. Two implementation instances of this architecture in the field of optical networks were developed in order to evaluate the feasibility of the proposed architecture.

One advantage of using composition to build services over an heterogeneous network is the elimination of interoperability bottlenecks. Instead of implementing complex and sometimes poorly standardized protocols, network equipment vendors can implement Web Service interfaces to control and manage their equipments. By publishing this interface, network operators and third party software vendors can control and manage network equipments by incorporating these interfaces into composition scripts. Contrary of network protocols, the Web Service interface need not to be fully standardized (they need only to expose similar functionalities).

As a future work we are considering the incorporation of policies into the orchestrated service in order to adapt the service use and management according to user privileges and profiles.

Finally, we believe that Web Services is a practical way to integrate different network domains. Network operators do not allow network signaling to cross their network boundaries due to stability and security reasons. The offering of inter-domain services via Web Services composition is more feasible and simpler as network providers have full control over the information exchanged in the inter-domain borders.

References

[1] Mike P. Papazoglou and Dimitris Georgakopoulos. Service-oriented computing: Introduction. *Communications of the ACM*, 46(10):24–28, October 2003.

[2] Francisco Curbera, Rania Khalaf, Nirmal Mukhi, Stefan Tai, and Sanjiva Weerawarana. The next step in web services. *Communications of the ACM*, 46(10):29–34, 2003.

[3] World Wide Web Consortium (W3C). *Web Services Choreography Description Language Version 1.0*, December 2004. Working Draft.

[4] Keith Mantell. From UML to BPEL. http://www-128.ibm.com/developerworks/webservices/library/ws-uml2bpel/, September 2003.

[5] ActiveWebflow Professional. http://www.active-endpoints.com/.

[6] Oracle JDeveloper 10g. http://www.oracle.com/.

[7] BEA Systems, International Business Machines Corporation, Microsoft Corporation, SAP AG, Siebel Systems. *Business Process Execution Language for Web Services Version 1.1*, May 2003.

[8] ActiveBPEL. http://www.activebpel.org/.

[9] Russell Butek. Which style of WSDL should I use? http://www-128.ibm.com/developerworks/webservices/library/ws-whichwsdl/index.html, May 2005.

[10] Tim Ewald. The Argument Against SOAP Encoding. http://msdn.microsoft.com/library/default.asp?url=/library/en-us/dnsoap/html/argsoape.asp, October 2002.

[11] Web Services Interoperability Organization. *Basic Profile Version 1.1*, August 2004. http://www.ws-i.org/Profiles/BasicProfile-1.1-2004-08-24.html.

[12] Canarie Inc. http://www.canarie.ca.

[13] Bill St. Arnaud, Andrew Bjerring, Omar cherkaoui, Raouf Boutaba, Martin Potts, and Wade Hong. Web Services Architecture for User Control and Management of Optical Internet Networks. *Proceedings of the IEEE*, 92(9):1490–1500, September 2004.

[14] Bill St. Arnaud. Web Services Workflow for Connecting Research Instruments and Sensors to Networks. http://www.canarie.ca/canet4/uclp/UCLP_Roadmap.doc, December 2004.

[15] Masahide Nakamura, Hiroshi Igaki, Haruaki Tamada, and Ken ichi Matsumoto. Implementing integrated services of networked home appliances using service oriented architecture. In *ICSOC '04: Proceedings of the 2nd international conference on Service oriented computing*, pages 269–278, New York, NY, USA, 2004. ACM Press.

[16] Dirk Thissen. Flexible Service Provision Considering Specific Customer Needs. In *Proceedings of the 10th Euromicro Workshop on Parallel, Distributed and Network-based Processing (EUROMICRO-PDP'02)*, pages 253–260. IEEE, 2002.

Dynamo: Dynamic Monitoring of WS-BPEL Processes

Luciano Baresi and Sam Guinea

Dipartimento di Elettronica e Informazione, Politecnico di Milano,
Piazza L. da Vinci 32, I-20133 Milano, Italy
{baresi, guinea}@elet.polimi.it

Abstract. Dynamo advocates that pre-deployment validation and testing are intrinsically inadequate for tackling the ephemeral and rapidly changing context in which service oriented applications are deployed. Validation must be shifted to run-time and continuous monitoring must be introduced. We propose a simple architecture that, through specific and simple annotations, allows for the automatic creation of instrumented WS-BPEL processes. These processes interact with a special-purpose proxy that enacts the monitoring activities and permits us to dynamically set the level of monitoring through use of a web-based interface.

1 Introduction

Run-time monitoring of functional and non-functional behavior is becoming an important and researched topic in the context of service-based systems. The extreme dynamism in service provisioning (services can change in a great number of ways) makes it difficult to grasp an overall knowledge of the system. This is why testing cannot foresee all the possible variations that may occur during execution, why validation must be shifted towards run-time, and why the idea of *continuous monitoring* must be introduced.

In [2], we propose a proxy-based solution for dynamic monitoring of WS-BPEL processes. Here we demonstrate such solution through its supporting framework called *Dynamo*. Within this work we introduce the idea of *Monitoring Rules*. These define run-time constraints on WS-BPEL process executions and are expressed using a specific language called WSCoL, inspired by the lightweight version of JML [3]. These rules are kept purposely separate from the process definition in order to avoid mixing the business logic with the monitoring logic. This is done because it helps the designer concentrate on solving the business problem without having to contemporarily tackle monitoring, and in order to allow different monitoring directives to be associated with a single process and therefore realize "personalized" monitoring. The monitoring rules are kept external to the WS-BPEL process definition up until deployment time, when they are weaved into the process. The result is an instrumented process which is capable of collaborating with our monitoring proxy (called *monitoring manager*) in order to verify the monitoring rules at run-time.

The monitoring manager is responsible for providing *dynamic monitoring*. We believe it to be of paramount importance to be able to tailor the degree of monitoring after a process has been deployed and, more specifically, at run-time. This is why we associate meta-level parameters to the single monitoring rules. These parameters are

B. Benatallah, F. Casati, and P. Traverso (Eds.): ICSOC 2005, LNCS 3826, pp. 478–483, 2005.

consulted at run-time by the monitoring manager to decide if a monitoring activity is to be performed or ignored. They can also be modified at run-time through a specific graphical interface. Therefore, the real degree of monitoring depends on the values these parameters assume during the execution of the process, which in turn depend on the context of execution (when, where, and by whom the process is performed).

Since data can originate both within the process and outside the process, the monitoring manager is built modularly with respect to the *data collectors* it can use for collecting data at different levels of abstraction, and to the *data analyzers* it can use for verifying the monitoring rules. In this demo we make use of a data analyzer implemented using `xlinkit` [1], and of a dynamic invoker component that can be used as a data collector capable of retrieving data from any source that exposes a web service interface.

2   Context

This demo is based on a slightly modified version of the Pizza Delivery Company example originally proposed in [5].

Suppose that a client wants to eat pizza. With a WAP enabled mobile phone, the client dials the *Pizza Company* and, after suitable identification (`Authenticate Service`), his/her profile (`Profile Service`) determines which kinds of pizza the client likes. The `Pizza Catalog Web Service` then offers the client four kinds of pizza; after selecting the favorite one (Double Cheese), the client provides his/her credit card number (included in the client's profile) which is validated by the `Credit Card Validation Service`. If everything is okay, the client's account is debited and the pizza company's account is credited. Meanwhile, the pizza baker is alerted to the order, because after the selection the pizza appears in his browser, which is integrated with his cooking gear. Using the address contained within the user's profile, the `GPS Service` is called to get the coordinates of the delivery point. These coordinates are then passed onto a `Map Service`, which processes them and sends a map with the exact route to the pizza delivery boy on his PDA. The boy then only needs to deliver the pizza. In the mean time the client is sent an SMS text message on his/her mobile phone to alert about the delivery of the pizza within 20 minutes. This is done using the `SMS Service`.

To demonstrate the actual capabilities of Dynamo, we present two simple examples of monitoring rules and briefly explain their meaning. The first example is a post-condition to the operation `getCoord` published by the `GPS Service`. This operation receives an address as input and returns a UTM (Universal Transverse Mercator) set of coordinates. The set of coordinates comprises a number indicating the zone to which they refer, and two string coordinates called respectively easting and northing. Both are a seven character string made up of six numbers and one character. The final character is either an E or a N, depending if it represents and easting or a northing. The postcondition is that the easting and northing be syntactically correct . The following rule excerpt only checks the easting. Northings are checked in a similar way.

```
Location:
    type = "post-condition"
```

```
   path = "pathToInvokeActivity"
Parameters:
   priority = 2
Expression:
   @ensures easting.length()==7 &&
   easting.charAt(6)=='E';
```

The above states that the easting must be seven characters long and that it must end with a capital 'E'. A priority of 2 is associated with the post-condition. The meaning is that every time the process is executed with a global priority of 2 or less the post-condition is verified. On the other hand, if the global process priority is higher than or equal to 3 then the post-condition is ignored.

The second example is a post-condition to the operation getMap published by the Map Service. This operation takes a UTM set of coordinates and returns a JPEG image of the location. Since the map must be used on the pizza boy's small portable device, the resolution of the map that is returned must not be higher than 80 by 60 pixels. The following rule only presents the horizontal resolution constraint, while the vertical constraint is defined in a similar way.

```
Location:
   type = "post-condition"
   path = "pathToInvokeActivity"
Parameters:
   priority = 4
Expression:
   @ensures \returnInt(wsdlLoc, getResolution, 'image',
   GetImageResponse.GetImageReturn,
   HResolution) <= 80;
```

The above makes use of a special keyword \returnInt which can be called to interact with external collectors which are seen as web services. This makes it possible to write assertions that require information that is not obtainable from the process but that must be searched for elsewhere. In this case an external service is used to calculate the horizontal resolution of the map returned by the service. The operation getResolution is called on the service published at wsdlLoc and the returned HResolution is checked against the desired horizontal resolution of 80 pixels. A priority of 4 is associated with the post-condition.

3   Scenario

Dynamo works as follows[1]:

- The first step is to design the unmonitored version of the process. This can be done using one of the many visual design tools already available on the market. In our

---

[1] In the following, we will use the concept of *priority* as a simplified version of our monitoring parameters.

demo we will use Oracle's BPEL Designer [4] which is available as an Eclipse Plugin.

– The next step is to import the unmonitored WS-BPEL process into Dynamo's Visual Annotation Tool (see Figure 1). By clicking on invoke activities (visualized as boxes), the tool provides information on the partnerlinks established between the process and the external web services. By clicking on the small black dots positioned above and below WS-BPEL invoke activities, it is possible to define either pre- or a post-conditions respectively. After all the monitoring rules have been defined, the tool creates the *monitoring definition file* automatically. The tool also requires that some initial global process parameters be added. They are used at runtime to determine what should be monitored and what not. In the demo, we will start by associating an initial global process priority of 4 to the monitored process. The priorities associated with the example monitoring rules are presented in the previous section.

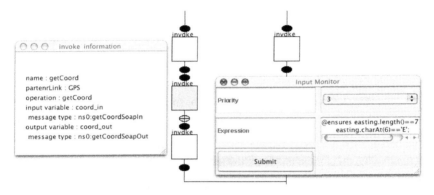

Fig. 1. Annotating the WS-BPEL process

– The third step consists in having Dynamo's BPEL[2] weave the rules contained in the monitoring definition file into the process, thus creating the monitored version of the WS-BPEL process. For each service invocation that has to be monitored (be it a pre- or a post-condition), the instrumented process calls the *Monitoring Manager* instead. This monitoring manager decides wether a monitoring rule has to be checked by confronting its monitoring parameters with the global process parameters. In our simple example, since the global process priority is 4, all monitoring rules with a lower priority are ignored. In this case the post-condition on operation getCoord is ignored and only the operation getMap is checked. In the demo we will show that the process does not terminate correctly because of an error arising somewhere during the execution. However, some of our monitoring activities are not being run due to the global process priority being too high. By changing the global process priority, we can re-activate some monitoring activities that are switched off and discover where the problem lies.

– The global process priority of the process in execution can be changed by re-instrumenting the process or by accessing the monitoring manager at run-time

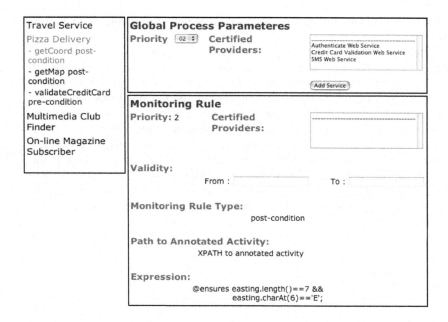

Fig. 2. Monitoring Manager Run-Time Interface

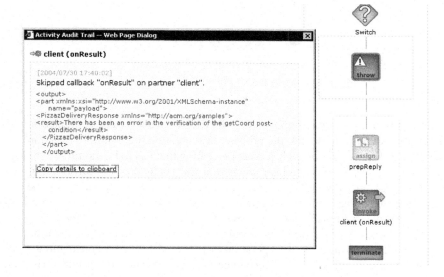

Fig. 3. Error in post-condition at run-time

through a web based interface. In the latter case (see Figure 2), we can choose the process from the list on the left, and set the new global process priority to 2 in order to activate the monitoring of the post-condition on operation `getCoord`.

– Re-running the process, we notice that the process once again does not complete. This time, though, it behaves differently. An error occurs while checking the post-condition on operation `getCoord`. The reason is that the easting returned by the operation is malformed. The process terminates in a more graceful manner and presents us with an error message that explains what is going wrong (see Figure 3).

4   Conclusions

This short demo briefly presents the main capabilities of Dynamo, our toolset for run-time monitoring of WS-BPEL processes. During the demo sessions, the framework will be presented in its entirety by means of the proposed pizza delivery scenario and more monitoring rules. Dynamo is available for download at `http://www.elet.polimi.it/upload/guinea`.

References

1. XlinkIt: A Consistency Checking and Smart Link Generation Service. *ACM Transactions on Software Engineering and Methodology*, pages 151–185, May 2002.
2. L. Baresi, and S. Guinea. Towards Dynamic Monitoring of WS-BPEL Processes. *In Proceedings of the 3rd International Conference on Service Oriented Computing*, 2005.
3. Gary T. Leavens, Albert L. Baker, and Clyde Ruby. Preliminary Design of JML: A Behavioral Interface Specification Language for Java. *Department of Computer Science, Iowa State University, TR 98-06-rev27*, April, 2005.
4. Oracle.   Oracle BPEL Process Manager.   2005.   `http://www.oracle.com/technology/products/ias/bpel/index.html`.
5. IBM T.J. Watson Research Center.   The Futuristic Pizza Company Example.   2004. `http://researchweb.watson.ibm.com`

WofBPEL: A Tool for Automated Analysis of BPEL Processes*

Chun Ouyang[1], Eric Verbeek[2], Wil M.P. van der Aalst[1,2], Stephan Breutel[1], Marlon Dumas[1], and Arthur H.M. ter Hofstede[1]

[1] Faculty of Information Technology, Queensland University of Technology,
GPO Box 2434, Brisbane QLD 4001, Australia
{c.ouyang, sw.breutel, m.dumas, a.terhofstede}@qut.edu.au
[2] Department of Technology Management, Eindhoven University of Technology,
GPO Box 513, NL-5600 MB, The Netherlands
{h.m.w.verbeek, w.m.p.v.d.aalst}@tm.tue.nl

1 Introduction

The Business Process Execution Language for Web Service, known as BPEL4WS, more recently as WS-BPEL (or BPEL for short) [1], is a process definition language geared towards Service-Oriented Computing (SOC) and layered on top of the Web services technology stack. In BPEL, the logic of the interactions between a given service and its environment is described as a composition of communication actions. These communication actions are interrelated by control-flow dependencies expressed through constructs close to those found in workflow definition languages. In particular, BPEL incorporates two sophisticated branching and synchronisation constructs, namely "control links" and "join conditions", which can be found in a class of workflow models known as *synchronising workflows* formalised in terms of Petri nets in [3].

In the field of workflow, it has been shown that Petri nets provide a suitable foundation for performing static verification. Workflow verification engines such as Woflan [7] are able to analyse Petri net-based workflow models for various purposes such as soundness verification. Therefore, by translating BPEL processes to Petri nets and applying existing Petri net analysis techniques, we can perform static analysis on BPEL processes.

To provide tool support for the analysis of BPEL processes, we developed WofBPEL, and a companion tool BPEL2PNML. BPEL2PNML translates BPEL process definitions into Petri nets represented in the Petri Nets Markup Language (PNML). WofBPEL, which is built using Woflan, performs static analysis on the output produced by BPEL2PNML. Currently it supports three types of analysis: detection of unreachable actions, detection of conflicting message-consuming activities, and metadata generation for garbage collection of unconsumable messages, as detailed in Sect. 2.2.

As part of the design of BPEL2PNML, we formally defined a mapping from BPEL to Petri nets. This mapping is described in [5] and compared with other

* Supported by an Australia Research Council (ARC) Discovery Grant (DP0451092).

B. Benatallah, F. Casati, and P. Traverso (Eds.): ICSOC 2005, LNCS 3826, pp. 484–489, 2005.
© Springer-Verlag Berlin Heidelberg 2005

formalisations of BPEL (see [5]). When surveying previous formalisations of BPEL, we found that none of them had led to a publicly available tool that could be used to perform the types of analysis targeted by WofBPEL over the full set of BPEL control-flow constructs. We also found that previous formalisations of BPEL in terms of Petri nets [4, 6] map control links and join conditions to high-level Petri nets, which are usually less suitable for static analysis of control flow properties than plain Petri nets due to complexity issues. Accordingly, we extended the approach previously sketched in [3] to fully capture control links and join conditions in terms of plain Petri nets. This resulted in a detailed and comprehensive mapping that is more detailed and suitable for the types of analysis targeted by WofBPEL than previous proposals.

WofBPEL and BPEL2PNML are available under an open-source license at http://www.bpm.fit.qut.edu.au/projects/babel/tools.

2   Tool Description

2.1   Architecture

Fig. 1 depicts the role of WofBPEL and BPEL2PNML in the analysis of BPEL processes. The BPEL process code may be manually written or generated from a BPEL design tool, e.g. Oracle BPEL Designer. BPEL2PNML takes as input the BPEL code and produces a file conforming to the Petri Net Markup Language (PNML) syntax. This file can be given as input to WofBPEL which, depending on the selected options, applies a number of analysis methods and produces an XML file describing the analysis results. It may also be used as input to general-purpose Petri net analysis tool, e.g. PIPE.[1] In addition, the PNML file obtained as the output from BPEL2PNML also includes layout information, and can thus be used to generate a graphical view of the corresponding Petri nets.

2.2   Automated Analysis

Below we describe the three types of analysis that are currently supported by WofBPEL.

Reachability analysis. Consider the BPEL process definition in Fig. 2 where both the XML code and a graphical representation are provided. During the execution of this process, either A1 or A2 will be skipped because these two activities are placed in different branches of a *switch* activity and in any execution of a *switch* only one branch is taken. Thus, one of the two control links x1 or x2 will carry a negative token. On the other hand, we assume that the join condition attached to activity A3 (denoted by keyword "AND") evaluates to true iff both links x1 and x2 carry positive values. Hence, this join condition will always evaluate to false and activity A3 is always skipped (i.e. it is unreachable).

---

[1] https://sourceforge.net/projects/petri-net

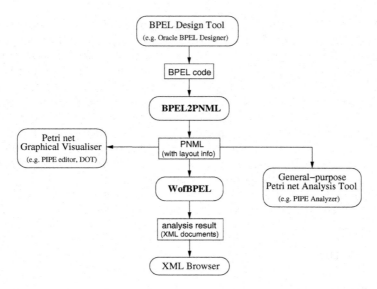

Fig. 1. Analysing BPEL processes using WofBPEL/BPEL2PNML

WofBPEL can detect unreachable activities in a BPEL process such as the one in the previous example. To perform this "unreachability" analysis, Wof-BPEL relies on two different methods, namely *relaxed soundness* and *transition invariants*. The former is complete but more computationally expensive than the latter. Relaxed soundness [2] takes into account all possible runs to get from an initial state (represented by the marking with one token in the designated input place) to the desired final state (represented by the marking with one token in the designated output place). Every transition which is covered by any of these runs is said to be relaxed sound. On the other hand, transitions that are not covered by these runs are called not relaxed sound. If we assume that the goal of the Petri net is to move from the initial state to the desired final state, then transitions that are not relaxed sound clearly indicate an error, because they cannot contribute in any way to achieving this goal.

However, to check for relaxed soundness we need to compute the full state space of the Petri net, which might take considerable time, especially given the fact that our mapping will generate a lot of parallel behaviour (note that even switch and pick activities are mapped onto parallel behaviour, as the unchosen branches need to be skipped). Therefore, computing relaxed soundness might be a problem.

To alleviate this state space problem, we can replace the relaxed soundness by another property known as transition invariants. Basically, a transition invariant is a multiset of transitions that cancel out, that is, when all transitions from the multiset would be executed simultaneously, then the state would not change. It is straightforward to see that any cycle in the state space has to correspond to some transition invariant. However, not all transitions in the state space will be covered by cycles. For this reason, we add an extra transition that removes a

```
<process name="unreachableTask"
  targetNamespace="http://samples.otn.com"
  suppressJoinFailure="yes"
  xmlns:tns="http://samples.otn.com"
  xmlns:services="http://services.otn.com"
  xmlns="http://schemas.xmlsoap.org/ws/2003/03/business-process/">
  <flow name="FL" suppressJoinFailure="yes">
  <links>
    <link name="x1"/>
    <link name="x2"/>
  </links>
  <switch name="SW">
    <case>
      <invoke name="A1">
        <sources> <source linkName="x1"/> </sources>
      </invoke>
    </case>
    <otherwise>
      <invoke name="A2">
        <sources> <source linkName="x2"/> </sources>
      </invoke>
    </otherwise>
  </switch>
  <invoke name = "A3">
    <targets>
      <joinCondition>
        bpws:getLinkStatus('x1') and bpws:getLinkStatus('x2')
      </joinCondition>
      <target linkName="x1"/>
      <target linkName="x2"/>
    </targets>
  </invoke>
  </flow>
</process>
```

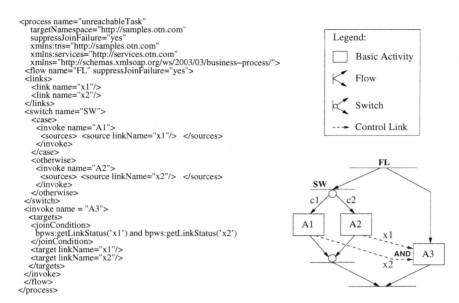

Fig. 2. Example of a BPEL process with an unreachable activity

token from the designated output place and puts a token into the designated input place. As a result, every run from the initial state to the final state will correspond to a transition invariant, and we can use transition invariants instead of relaxed soundness to get correct results. However, the results using transition invariants are not necessarily complete, because transition invariants might exist that do not correspond to runs in the Petri net. This discrepancy is due to the fact that transition invariants totally abstract from states, they more or less assume that sufficient tokens exist to have every transition executed the appropriate number of times.

A summary of the output of WofBPEL for the above example follows:

```
<net file="controlLink03PNML.xml">
  <structure ...
    <Node ... label="inv25 {name=A3}"/>
  </structure>
  <behavior ...
    <Node ... label="inv25 {name=A3}"/>
  </behavior>
  ...
</net>
```

The "structure" element contains the output of the unreachability analysis using the relaxed soundness technique, while the "behavior" element contains the output using the transition invariant technique. In this example, both techniques detect the same set of unreachable nodes in the net, one of which is labelled "inv25 name=A3" (indicating that this node is an "invoke" activity named A3 in the original BPEL process). In fact, we are not aware of any BPEL process definition where the relaxed soundness technique detects unreachable activities that are not detected by the transition invariant technique.

Competing message-consuming activities. The BPEL specification [1] states that "a business process instance MUST NOT simultaneously enable two or more *receive* activities for the same partnerLink, portType, operations and correlation set(s)."[2] In other word, activities that can consume the same type of message may not be simultaneously enabled, where a message type is identified by a combination of a partner link, a port type, an operation, and an optional correlation set. Using the state space-based technique mentioned before, we can check this requirement in a straightforward way. Activities that handle events are receive activities, pick activities, and event handlers. Fig. 3 depicts an example of a process which involves two conflicting receive activities, namely rcv1 and rcv3.

```
<process name="competingMessages01"
         targetNamespace="http://samples.otn.com"
         suppressJoinFailure="yes"
         xmlns:tns="http://samples.otn.com"
         xmlns:services="http://services.otn.com"
         xmlns="http://schemas.xmlsoap.org/ws/2003/03/business–process/">
   <flow suppressJoinFailure="yes">
   <sequence>
     <invoke name="A1" partnerLink="pl1" portType="pt1" operation="op2"/>
     <receive name="rcv1" partnerLink="pl2" portType="pt2" operation="op2"/>
   </sequence>
   <sequence>
     <receive name="rcv2" partnerLink="pl2" portType="pt2" operation="op3"/>
     <receive name="rcv3" partnerLink="pl2" portType="pt2" operation="op2"/>
   </sequence>
   </flow>
</process>
```

Fig. 3. An example of conflicting receive activities

This property can only be checked if the full state space has been generated. For this property, we could alleviate the possible state space problem by using well-known Petri net reduction rules. Except for the transitions that model the receipt of a message, we could try to reduce every place and every transition before generating the state space.

A summary of the output of WofBPEL for the above example follows:

```
<net file="competingMessages02PNML.xml">
  <structure noftransitions="0"></structure>
  <behavior noftransitions="0"></behavior>
  <error description="...">
    <events>
      <event name="rec34 {pL=pl2,pT=pt2,op=op2,name=rcv1}"/>
      <event name="rec37 {pL=pl2,pT=pt2,op=op2,name=rcv3}"/>
    </events>
    <state> ... </state>
    <path> ... </path>
  </error>
  ...
</net>
```

This XML document extract indicates that no unreachable tasks were found but two conflicting message-consuming activities were found. The document provides details of a state (i.e. a Petri net marking) in which a conflict occurs and of a path (i.e. a sequence of states) leading to the problematic state.

---

[2] For the purposes of this constraint, onMessage branches of a pick activity and event handlers are equivalent to a receive activity.

Garbage collection of queued messages. Again using the full state space, we can compute for each activity a in a BPEL process a set of message types MT_a such that a message type mt is in MT_a iff it is possible in the state space to consume mt after execution of a. In other words, each basic activity a is associated with a set of message types MT_a such that for each $mt \in MT_a$, there exists a run of the process where an activity that consumes a message of type mt is executed after a. Now, consider the situation where activity a has just been executed, a message m is present in the queue, and the type of m is *not* in MT_a. Then message m cannot be consumed anymore (by any activity). Thus, it can be removed from the queue (i.e. it can be garbage collected).

By computing this set for every activity in the BPEL process model, and piggy-backing it in the process definition that is handed over to a BPEL engine, the engine can use this information to remove redundant messages from its queue, thus optimising resource consumption. Specifically, the output of the analysis would be an annotated BPEL process where each basic activity is associated with a set of message types (identified by a partner link, a port type, an operation and optionally a correlation set). After executing an activity a, the BPEL engine could compare the set of message types (MT_a) associated to a with the current set of messages in the queue (M_q) and discard all messages in $M_q \setminus MT_a$.

About the demonstration. The demonstration will show how BPEL processes are mapped to Petri nets using a few representative examples, and will illustrate the above three types of analysis that WofBPEL can perform.

References

1. A. Arkin, S. Askary, B. Bloch, F. Curbera, Y. Goland, N. Kartha, C. K. Liu, S. Thatte, P. Yendluri, and A. Yiu, editors. *Web Services Business Process Execution Language Version 2.0*. WS-BPEL TC OASIS, May 2005. Available via http://www.oasis-open.org/committees/download.php/12791/.
2. J. Dehnert. *A Methodology for Workflow Modelling: from Business Process Modelling towards Sound Workflow Specification*. PhD thesis, Technische Universität Berlin, Berlin, Germany, August 2003.
3. B. Kiepuszewski, A.H.M. ter Hofstede, and W.M.P. van der Aalst. Fundamentals of control flow in workflows. *Acta Informatica*, 39(3):143–209, 2003.
4. A. Martens. *Verteilte Geschäftsprozesse - Modellierung und Verifikation mit Hilfe von Web Services (In German)*. PhD thesis, Institut für Informatik, Humboldt-Universität zu Berlin, Berlin, Germany, 2003.
5. C. Ouyang, H.M.W. Verbeek, W.M.P. van der Aalst, S. Breutel, M. Dumas, and A.H.M. ter Hofstede. Formal semantics and analysis of control flow in WS-BPEL. Technical Report BPM-05-15, BPMcenter.org, 2005. Available via http://www.bpmcenter.org/reports/2005/BPM-05-15.pdf.
6. C. Stahl. Transformation von BPEL4WS in Petrinetze (In German). Master's thesis, Humboldt University, Berlin, Germany, 2004.
7. H.M.W. Verbeek, T. Basten, and W.M.P. van der Aalst. Diagnozing workflow processes using Woflan. *The Computer Journal*, 44(4):246–279, 2001.

OpenWS-Transaction: Enabling Reliable Web Service Transactions

Ivan Vasquez, John Miller, Kunal Verma, and Amit Sheth

Large Scale Distributed Information Systems, Department of Computer Science,
The University of Georgia,
415 Graduate Studies Research Center, Athens, GA 30602-7404 USA
{vasquez, jam, verma, sheth}@cs.uga.edu
http://lsdis.cs.uga.edu

Abstract. OpenWS-Transaction is an open source middleware that enables
Web services to participate in a distributed transaction as prescribed by the WS-
Coordination and WS-Transaction set of specifications. Central to the framework are the Coordinator and Participant entities, which can be integrated into
existing services by introducing minimal changes to application code.
OpenWS-Transaction allows transaction members to recover their original state
in case of operational failure by leveraging techniques in logical logging and
recovery at the application level. Depending on transaction style, system recovery may involve restoring key application variables and replaying uncommitted
database activity. Transactions are assumed to be defined in the context of a
BPEL process, although other orchestration alternatives can be used.

1 Introduction

OpenWS-Transaction is a middleware framework based on WS-Coordination (WS-C)
and WS-Transaction (WS-T) that enables existing services to meet the reliability
requirements necessary to take part in a coordinated transaction. For transactions
following WS-AtomicTransaction (WS-AT), it features an innovative recovery facility that applies logical logging to restore operations on the underlying data, extending
system recovery to include uncommitted database activity. For transactions following
WS-BusinessActivity (WS-BA), it presents a straightforward scheme to automate the
invocation of user-defined compensating actions. In contrast to existing implementations, OpenWS-Transaction aims to minimize the implementation impact in existing
applications with regards to both performance and code changes.

The framework has been implemented as part of the METEOR-S project, which
deals with adding semantics to the complete lifecycle of Web services and processes
[1]. As a prototype implementation of transactional Web processes, it is particularly
focused on integrating BPEL, WS-C and WS-AT/WS-BA [2, 3], which already enjoy
wide acceptance.

The next section explains the framework's architecture. Section 3 describes an example scenario where OpenWS-Transaction enables reliable transactional business
processes. Section 4 provides implementation and evaluation details, while section 5
summarizes this demonstration.

B. Benatallah, F. Casati, and P. Traverso (Eds.): ICSOC 2005, LNCS 3826, pp. 490–494, 2005.
© Springer-Verlag Berlin Heidelberg 2005

2 Architecture

OpenWS-Transaction applies concepts from the reference specifications as well as from existing work on fault tolerant systems [4, 5]. Fig. 1 illustrates the interaction between a BPEL process, the Coordinator, and other services that benefit from the Participant framework entity. Any activities performed within the transactional scope are guaranteed to complete consistently.

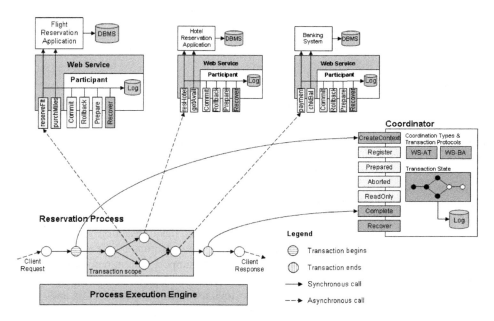

Fig. 1. Entities and their interaction in a transactional business process

Coordinators are dedicated services responsible for delineating new transactions, activating participant services and enforcing transactional behavior according to some *coordination type*. To support recovery, they also record key events throughout the transaction's lifespan using the logging schema shown in Fig. 2. Besides the operations prescribed by WS-C, WS-AT and WS-BA, the *recover* operation restores the state of pending transactions when interrupted by an operational failure.

Many services are the result of evolved applications that have defined an additional layer exposing select functionality to business partners. To take part in a distributed transaction, conventional services can use the features provided by the *Participant* framework entity. Among such features is the ability to intercept and record operation details, guaranteeing a *precommit* behavior regardless of the underlying database system. Using the schema in Fig. 3, their *recover* operation enables transaction participants to go back to the state immediately previous to a failure.

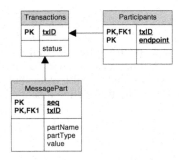

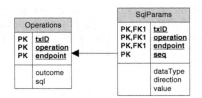

Fig. 2. Coordinator log schema   **Fig. 3.** Participant log schema

3   Example of a Transactional Process

We use a variation of the well-known travel agency use case. The process encompasses three services: A flight reservation system, a hotel reservation system and a banking system. The process is triggered from a Web application in which the user is given options for an immediate purchase (WS-AT) or a long-running process (WS-BA) that increases the chance of finding a suitable itinerary.

In the process definition, service invocations are enclosed by *beginTransaction* and *endTransaction* calls to the coordinator, which delimit the transaction's scope. Before performing any work, participants *register* with the coordinator by providing their endpoint address, which is logged to stable storage to support system recovery.

As soon as participants fulfill their part of the process, the framework logs the operation's name and outcome. For WS-AT, it also logs associated database calls and their parameters, critical to restore uncommitted activity in case of failure. Once operations are recorded, participants report their outcome to the coordinator.

Process execution continues until the *endTransaction* operation is invoked. This causes the coordinator to decide the transaction's final outcome, which depends on participant votes and current coordination type: For WS-AT, all steps of the process must succeed. For WS-BA, we assume that just reserving the flight and processing its payment is enough to consider it successful; however, because of its nature, services must supply an appropriate compensating operation for every business operation.

Following outcome determination, the coordinator updates its transaction log record and confirms or cancels each operation. Participants then forget about the transaction and the process engine communicates its outcome to the client application.

Responding to Operational Failures. Next, we modify the above scenario by introducing an operational failure (Fig. 4) after the transaction outcome has been determined. Assuming a positive outcome and WS-AT coordination type, participants are responsible to commit despite failures. However, these failures cause volatile state information to vanish and, because applications are unaware of the global process, local transactions are implicitly rolled back.

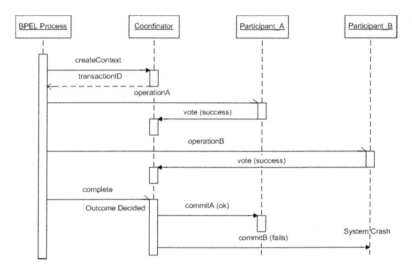

Fig. 4. A failed transactional process where one of its participants crashed

If that is the case, OpenWS-Transaction's coordinator attempts to contact the failed service for a configurable number of times and retry interval. Assuming it becomes available on time, the coordinator first invokes the participant's *recover* operation, which restores key application variables such as transaction identifier, coordination type and operation outcomes. Additionally, recovery also restores the participant's database connection and replays database activity for uncommitted operations (Fig. 5), leaving it ready to accept the final decision.

⚠	edu.uga.cs.lsdis.meteors.wstx.samples.TravelCoordinator	Beginning crash recovery of 2 transactions
⊙	edu.uga.cs.lsdis.meteors.wstx.samples.TravelCoordinator	Restored session for transactionID 192.168.0.2:1112677459590
⊙	edu.uga.cs.lsdis.meteors.wstx.samples.TravelCoordinator	Attempting recovery of http://192.168.0.2:88/axis/services/FlightService in 10 secs.
⊙	edu.uga.cs.lsdis.meteors.wstx.samples.wsat.FlightService	Registration succeeded, context created for http://schemas.xmlsoap.org/ws/2004/10/wsat
⚠	edu.uga.cs.lsdis.meteors.wstx.samples.wsat.FlightService	********* Business logic starts *********
⊘	edu.uga.cs.lsdis.meteors.wstx.util.DataAccess	Using data source 'jdbc/pgsql'
⊘	edu.uga.cs.lsdis.meteors.wstx.samples.wsat.FlightService	Restored database connection 'jdbc/pgsql'
⊘	edu.uga.cs.lsdis.meteors.wstx.samples.wsat.FlightService	Replaying procedure '{? = call reserve_flight(?, ?, ?)}'
⊘	edu.uga.cs.lsdis.meteors.wstx.samples.wsat.FlightService	stmt.registerOutParameter(1, Types.INTEGER)
⊘	edu.uga.cs.lsdis.meteors.wstx.samples.wsat.FlightService	stmt.setString(2, 'ATL')
⊘	edu.uga.cs.lsdis.meteors.wstx.samples.wsat.FlightService	stmt.setString(3, 'FRA')
⊘	edu.uga.cs.lsdis.meteors.wstx.samples.wsat.FlightService	stmt.setint(4, 3)
⊙	edu.uga.cs.lsdis.meteors.wstx.samples.TravelCoordinator	Recovery of http://192.168.0.2:88/axis/services/FlightService succeeded

Fig. 5. Participant replaying a database procedure as part of system recovery

Yet another recovery scenario is one in which the coordinator itself goes down in the middle of a process, leaving pending operations at multiple participants. Upon restart, the coordinator scans its log records forward in time, looking for unfinished transactions. State is then restored by polling registered participants on their *prepare* operation. If a participant is not available or does not seem to know about the transaction, it is asked to recover beforehand.

The framework takes into account the effects of network failures. Before performing recovery, participants check whether it is really needed by verifying the local coordination context. An additional check is done by validating participant registration at the coordinator, so recovery can not occur as the result of erroneous or malicious requests.

4 Implementation and Evaluation

The framework was implemented in Java and relies exclusively on open source projects. Web services run on Apache Axis and Tomcat. Transaction logging is based on BerkeleyDB, an embedded database system. Sample processes are deployed in ActiveBPEL. Web services access data on PostgreSQL and MySQL; other JDBC-accesible sources like Oracle and SQL Server have also been tested successfully.

Evaluating the impact on existing services, we found that the framework can be integrated into existing services by introducing changes to as few as a couple lines of code. Because protocol operations are invariably the same, developers of new applications can remain focused on their business logic.

Experimentation has shown that, even without logging optimizations, the additional overhead results in an average 7.5% increase over the operations' original execution times.

5 Conclusion

OpenWS-Transaction is a framework that facilitates the implementation of Web service-based processes requiring transactional behavior. Example scenarios demonstrate its transactional support under normal and operational failure conditions, achieved by providing the necessary protocol operations and by restoring the state of failed services.

References

1. Sivashanmugam, K., Verma, K., Sheth, A., Miller, J.: Adding Semantics to Web Services Standards. Proceedings of the 1st International Conference on Web Services (2003)
2. Tai, S., Khalaf, R., and Mikalsen, T.: Composition of Coordinated Web Services. Proceedings of the 5th ACM/IFIP/USENIX intl. conf. on Middleware (2004)
3. Papazoglou, M.: Web Services and Business Transactions. World Wide Web: Internet and Web Information Systems, Tilburg University (2003)
4. Lomet, D. and Tuttle, M.: Logical Logging to Extend Recovery to New Domains. Proc. of the 1999 ACM SIGMOD intl. conf. on Management of Data (1999)
5. Salzberg, B. and Tombroff, D.: Durable Scripts Containing Database Transactions. IEEE International Conference on Data Engineering (1996)

ASTRO: Supporting Composition and Execution of Web Services*

Michele Trainotti[1], Marco Pistore[1], Gaetano Calabrese[2], Gabriele Zacco[2], Gigi Lucchese[2], Fabio Barbon[2], Piergiorgio Bertoli[2], and Paolo Traverso[2]

[1] DIT, University of Trento, Via Sommarive 14, 38050, Trento, Italy
[2] ITC-irst, Via Sommarive 18, 38050, Trento, Italy

Abstract. Web services are rapidly emerging as the reference paradigm for the interaction and coordination of distributed business processes. In several research papers we have shown how advanced automated planning techniques can be exploited to automatically compose web services, and to synthesize monitoring components that control their execution. In this demo we show how these techniques have been implemented in the ASTRO toolset (http://www.astroproject.org), a set of tools that extend existing platforms for web service design and execution with automated composition and execution monitoring functionalities.

1 Introduction

Web services are rapidly emerging as the reference paradigm for the interaction and coordination of distributed business processes. The ability to automatically plan the composition of web services, and to monitor their execution, is therefore an essential step toward the real usage of web services.

In previous works [1, 2, 3], we have shown how automated planning techniques based on the "Planning via Model Checking" paradigm can effectively support these functionalities. More precisely, the algorithms proposed in [1, 2, 3] are based on web service specifications described in BPEL4WS, a standard language that can be used both for describing existing web services in terms of their interfaces (i.e., of the operations that are needed to interact with them) and for defining the executable code that implements composite services.

Automated web service composition starts from the description of a number of protocols defining available external services (expressed as BPEL4WS specifications), and a "business requirement" for a new composed process (i.e., the goal that should be satisfied by the new service, expressed in a proper goal language). Given this, the planner must synthesize automatically the code that implements the internal process that, exploiting the services of the external partners, achieves the business requirement. This code is then emitted as executable BPEL4WS code.

---

* This work is partially funded by the MIUR-FIRB project RBNE0195K5, "Knowledge Level Automated Software Engineering", and by the MIUR-PRIN 2004 project "Advanced Artificial Intelligence Systems for Web Services".

B. Benatallah, F. Casati, and P. Traverso (Eds.): ICSOC 2005, LNCS 3826, pp. 495–501, 2005.

The automated synthesis techniques provided by the "Planning via Model Checking" framework can be also exploited to generate process monitors, i.e., pieces of code that detect and signal whether the external partners behave consistently with the specified protocols. This is vital to detect unpredictable run-time misbehaviors (such as those that may originate by dynamic modifications of the partners' protocols), or other events in the executions of the web services that need to be reported and analyzed.

Notice that these problems require to deal with nondeterminism (since the behavior of external services cannot be foreseen a priori), partial observability (since their status is opaque to the composed service), and extended goals (since realistic business requirements specify complex expected behaviors rather than just final states). By tackling the problem of composing and monitoring web services, we have shown the capabilities of the "Planning via Model Checking" approach in realizing such a complex planning task.

In this demo we show how these techniques can extend existing commercial platforms for web service design and execution. More precisely, we describe the ASTRO toolset (http://www.astroproject.org), which implements automated composition and monitor generation functionalities as extensions of the Active WebFlow platform. Active WebFlow (http://www.activebpel.org/) is a commercial tool for designing and developing BPEL4WS processes which is based on the Eclipse platform. It also provides an open-source BPEL4WS execution engine, called Active BPEL. By implementing automated composition and monitoring within Active WebFlow, these advanced functionalities can be combined with the other "standard" functionalities provided by the platform (such as inspecting BPEL4WS code, writing or modifying business processes, deploying these processes and executing them) and become integral part of the life cycle of business process design and execution.

2   A Service Composition Scenario

The demo is based on a classical web service composition problem, namely that of the Virtual Travel Agency (VTA). It consists in providing a combined flight and hotel booking service by composing two separate, independent existing services: a Flight booking service, and a Hotel booking service.

The Hotel booking service becomes active upon a request for a room in a given location (e.g., Paris) for a given period of time. In the case the booking is not possible (i.e., there are no available rooms), this is signaled to the request applicant, and the protocol terminates with failure. Otherwise, the applicant is notified with information about the hotel (e.g., Hilton), cost of the room, etc. and the protocol stops waiting for either a positive or negative acknowledgment. In the first case, an agreement has been reached and the room is booked. In the latter case, the interaction terminates with failure.

The protocol provided by the Flight booking service is similar. It starts upon a request for flights that guarantee to stay in a given location (e.g., Paris) for a given period of time. This might not be possible, in which case the applicant is notified, and the protocol terminates failing. Otherwise, information on the flights (carrier, cost, schedule...) are computed and returned to the applicant. The protocol suspends for either a positive or negative acknowledgment, terminating (with success or failure resp.) upon its reception.

The expected protocol that the user will execute when interacting with the VTA goes as follows. The user sends a request to stay in a given location during a given period of time, and expects either a negative answer if this is not possible (in which case the protocol terminates, failing), or an offer indicating hotel, flights and cost of the trip. At this time, the user may either accept or refuse the offer, terminating its interaction in both cases.

Of course several different interaction sequences are possible with these services; e.g., in a *nominal* scenario, none of the services answers negatively to a request; in non-nominal scenarios, unavailability of suitable flights or rooms, as well as user refusals, may make it impossible to reach an agreement for the trip. Taking this into account, the business requirement for the composed service is composed of two subgoals. The "nominal" subgoal consists in reaching the agreement on flights and room. This includes enforcing that the data communicated to the various processes are mutually consistent; e.g., the number of nights booked in the hotel depends on the schedule of the selected flights. The "recovery" subgoal consists in ensuring that every partner has rolled back from previous pending requests, and must be only pursued when the nominal subgoal cannot be achieved anymore.

By automated composition of the VTA process, we mean the automated generation of the code that has to be executed on the VTA server, so that requests from the user are answered combining the Flight and Hotel services in a suitable way. This composition has to implement the two sub-goals described above. After the VTA process has been generated, its executions must be monitored, in order to detect problems in the interactions with the other partners participating to the scenario. Properties to be monitored include "correctness" checks (e.g., the partners obey the declared protocols; the flight schedules are compatible with the requests...). It is also possible to monitor "business" properties, e.g., the fact that, when an offer for a trip is sent to the user, this offer gets accepted or not.

3   The ASTRO Toolset

This section presents a general overview of the ASTRO toolset. It consists of the following tools: WS-gen, WS-mon, WS-console and WS-animator.

WS-gen is responsible for generating the automated composition. It consists in a back-end layer and a front-end layer. The back-end layer takes as input the BPEL4WS specifications of the interaction protocols that the composite service has to implement, a "choreographic" file describing the connections between the composition's partners, and a goal file defining the composition requirement. It consists of two applications (see Fig.1): BPELTranslator converts the BPEL4WS specification files and the choreography file in an intermediate (.smv) file which is adequate for representing "Planning via Model Checking" problems; WSYNTH

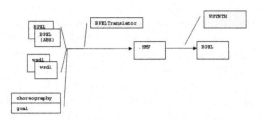

Fig. 1. WS-gen architecture

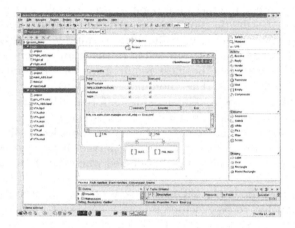

Fig. 2. WS-gen front end

takes as input the problem domain, computes the plan which fulfills the requirements, and emits the plan in BPEL4WS format. The front-end (see Fig.2) is
responsible for controlling the composition process and for managing the generated BPEL4WS specification; it has been implemented as an Eclipse plugin,
and is hence integrated in the Active WebFlow environment.

WS-mon is responsible for generats the Java code implements the monitors for
the composed process and deploying them to the monitor framework. Similar to
WS-gen, it consists in a back-end layer and a front-end layer. The back-end takes
as input BPEL4WS specifications and a "choreographic" file, while the goal file
is replaced by a file specifying the properties to by monitored. The back-end layer
consists in three applications (see Fig.3): BPELTranslator, which is in common
with WS-gen, converts the BPEL4WS specification files and the choreography
file in a .smv file which describes the problem domain; WMON takes as input the
problem domain, computes the plan which fulfills the monitoring requirements,
and emits this plan in Java format; and the DEPLOYER compiles the Java class
and deploy them to the monitor framework. The front-end (see Fig.4), which is
responsible for controlling the monitor generation process, has been implemented
as an Eclipse plugin, and is hence integrated in the Active WebFlow environment.

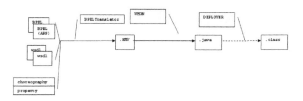

Fig. 3. WS-mon architecture

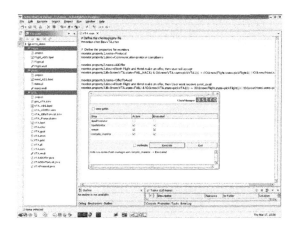

Fig. 4. WS-mon front end

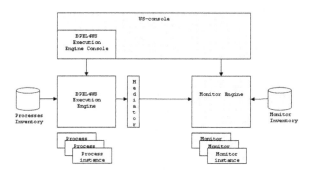

Fig. 5. Monitor framework architecture

The run-time monitor framework is responsible for executing the monitors associated to a given process every time an instance of that process is executed. It is also responsible for reporting the status of these monitors to the user in a convenient way. It consists of a back-end layer and a front-end layer (see Fig.5). The back-end layer has been implemented as an extension of the Active BPEL

Fig. 6. WS-console

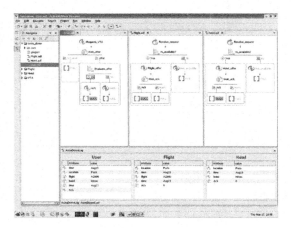

Fig. 7. WS-animator

execution engine; the main goal is to sniff the input/output messages directed to the process that has to be monitored and to forward them to the Java monitors instances. The front-end implementation, WS-console, extends the Active BPEL administration console in order to present the status of the monitors associated with each process instance. In this way, violations of the monitored properties are easy to be checked by the user (see Fig.6).

Finally, WS-animator (see Fig.7) is another Eclipse plugin, which gives the user the possibility to "execute" the composite process (in our case, the VTA). More precisely, it allows the user to play the roles of the actors interacting with the composite process, while the Active WebFlow engine executes it.

References

[1] Pistore, M.; Barbon, F.; Bertoli, P.; Shaparau. D.; and Traverso, P. 2004. Planning and Monitoring Web Service Composition. In *Proc. AIMSA'04*.
[2] Pistore, M.; Traverso, P.; and Bertoli, P. 2005. Automated Composition of Web Services by Planning in Asyncronous Domains. In *Proc. ICAPS'05*.
[3] Pistore, M.; Marconi, A.; Bertoli, P.; and Traverso, P. 2005. Automated Composition of Web Services by Planning at the Knowledge Level. In *Proc. IJCAI'05*.

Demonstrating Dynamic Configuration and Execution of Web Processes

Karthik Gomadam, Kunal Verma, Amit P. Sheth, and John A. Miller

Large Scale Distributed Information Systems Lab,
Department of Computer Science,
University of Georgia
{karthik, verma, amit, jam}@cs.uga.edu

Abstract. Web processes are next generation workflows on the web, created using Web services. In this paper we demonstrate the METEOR-S Configuration and Execution Environment (MCEE) system. It will illustrate the capabilities of the system to a) Discover partners b) Optimize partner selection using constraint analysis, c) Perform interaction protocol and data mediation. A graphical execution monitor to monitor the various phases of execution will be used to demonstrate various aspects of the system.

1 Introduction

The service oriented architecture [6] envisions a dynamic environment where software components could be integrated on the fly based on their declarative descriptions. So far, most of the work in standards of Web services (WS) has been on syntactic standards based on XML, which limits the amount dynamism possible in the such systems. METEOR-S seeks to use semantics in all aspects a Web process lifecycle, especially to support dynamic execution features. Its approach consists of comprehensive modeling and use of semantics that are divided into four types: data (such as that required for input and output message contents), functional (concerning the domain specific capabilities), non-functional (including QoS) and execution (such as that needed for exceptional handling and correctness of execution). MCEE follows the METEOR-S philosophy of using semantics at various stages during the lifecycle of Web processes and is discussed in detail in [1]. This paper demonstrates a real world scenario which is presented in [5]. The rest of the paper is organized as follows. The MCEE architecture is presented in section 2. Section 3 describes the demonstration scenario. Section 4 outlines the unique features of the system. A summary is presented in section 5.

2 MCEE Architecture

In this section, we provide a brief overview of MCEE [1]. We will present the design overview and then implementation details.

B. Benatallah, F. Casati, and P. Traverso (Eds.): ICSOC 2005, LNCS 3826, pp. 502–507, 2005.
© Springer-Verlag Berlin Heidelberg 2005

2.1 Design Overview

The architecture of our system is illustrated in Figure 1. The different components of the system are:

1. Process manager
2. Proxy
3. Configuration module
4. Execution environment

We discuss each component briefly in rest of this section.

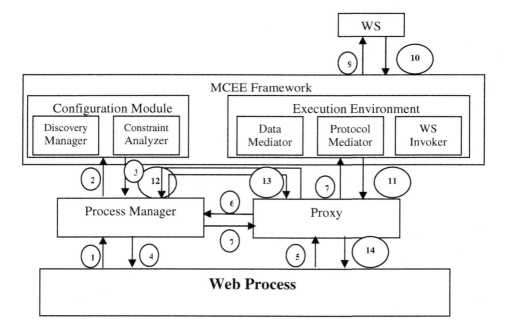

Fig. 1. Architectural overview of MCEE

The *configuration module* is responsible for process configuration. The configuration module can be called by the process manager during a) process configuration b) process reconfiguration. During both cases the configuration module performs Web service discovery and constraint analysis. Web service discovery is realized by the Discovery manager component in the configuration module. Service discovery is based on the data, functional and non-functional descriptions of the service requirements captured in the semantic template using the annotations with respect to the corresponding ontologies. The constraint analyzer component helps in creating a set of candidate Web services that satisfy the process constraints. Integer Linear programming is used for solving quantitative constraints and SWRL is used for non-quantitative constraints. A detailed discussion of our earlier work in Web service Quality of Service is presented in [3].

The *execution environment* handles the execution requests initiated by the proxy. The capabilities of the execution environment include a) Data Mediation b) Protocol mediation and c) Web service invocation. The execution environment replies to the proxy with the service output or service exception in the event of service failure. Data mediation is necessary to address issues due to data heterogeneities between the target Web service and the semantic template. WSDL-S allows for specifying data transformations using XSLT or XQuery [2]. The data mediator component is responsible for realizing these data transformations. Interaction protocol heterogeneities are handled by the interaction protocol mediator. The interaction protocol handler in framework is explained in detail in [1].

Proxies are Web services generated from the semantic templates for the partner. The proxies initiate the binding request, when they are invoked by the process. The process manager replies to the binding request by returning the service discovered for the template. The proxy then sends an execution request to the execution environment. If the service cannot be successfully executed, the proxy initiates the reconfiguration request. The execution request is illustrated in messages 8 and 9 in Figure 1.

The *process manager* is a Web service that handles three different requests a) *Configuration request,* b) *Binding request and* c) *Reconfiguration request.* *Configuration requests* are initiated by the Web process execution engine and are sent to the process manager. It forwards the configuration requests to the configuration module which configures the Web process. *Binding requests* are initiated by the proxy and are sent to the process manager, to get the binding information about the Web services discovered. *Reconfiguration requests* are initiated by the proxy and are sent to the process manager, to notify of service failure. The process manager then reconfigures the process, by halting the execution of other proxies and by forwarding the reconfiguration request to the configuration module. The reconfiguration algorithm is discussed in detail in [1]. Messages 1, 2, 3 and 4 in Figure 1 are configuration requests. Messages 6 and 7 in Figure 1 are binding requests. Messages 9 and 10 in Figure 1 are reconfiguration requests.

2.2 System Information

The system is implemented using JDK 1.4.2. Web services are written using Java and are deployed in Apache Axis 1.2RC. The discovery module is implemented using jUDDI and UDDI4J. The Web process is orchestrated using the IBM BPWS4J engine and is written in WS-BPEL. Tomcat version 4.1.29 is used for BPWS4J engine and Apache Axis. Tomcat 5.1.3 was used for jUDDI. The system uses the current WS technologies and infrastructure. This allows for interoperability between semantic Web services and Web services as they exist today.

3 Demonstration Scenario

We demonstrate a real world use case from the domain of agricultural marketing in India. The scenario is discussed in detail in [5]. The current marketing system has farmers selling their produce to either a) an Agriculture Produce Market Committee (APMC) b) merchants associated with APMCs or c) brokers associated with APMCs. In rest of the discussion, a farmer is a seller and a buyer can either be an APMC, merchant or broker. In this scenario, we demonstrate the value and utility of dynamic Web processes. This also will demonstrate the capability of the system demonstrated to support and execute such processes. Figure 2 shows an abstract process created to realize this scenario.

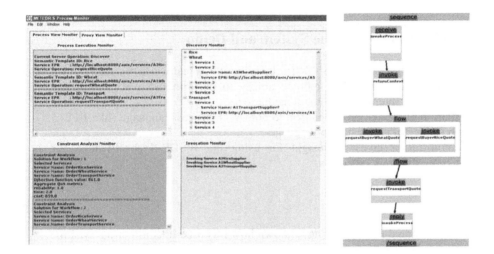

Fig. 2. Screen shot of Process Execution Monitor   **Fig. 3.** Web Process demonstration scenario

The seller captures the product(s) to be sold, the input and the output types and his constraints in a semantic template. In the demonstration example the seller wants to sell rice and wheat. Constraints on part of the seller could include a) Payment must be made on the same day as the transaction b) Payment must be in cash c) the transportation company must guarantee delivery. Proxy Web services are created from the semantic templates and a Web process with proxies and the process manager as a partner is deployed. The above three mentioned illustrative constraints will be used in the demonstration of the system.

When the Web process is executed the process sends a configuration request to the process manager. The process manager then discovers potential buyers and chooses a set of buyers who satisfy the constraints of the seller.

The constraints of a buyer must also be considered in choosing buyers. Buyer constraints may include a) Payment will be made only by check b) the transportation company will provide insurance only if shipment is greater than a certain minimum amount.

Each proxy when invoked by the Web process sends a binding request to the process manager. The process manager responds with details of the buyer corresponding to the semantic template that was used to create the proxy. The proxy then sends an execution request to the execution environment. The execution environment performs data and protocol mediations as needed before invoking the buyer Web service.

We demonstrate how adding dynamism to such a Web process helps a seller optimize his profit. This also ensures that for both the buyer and seller the most compatible business partner is chosen.

The Web process is deployed and executed with a set of ten Web services for each partner. Fig. 3 is a screen shot of the METEOR-S web process execution monitor.

4   Innovative Features in the System and Demo

1. We have demonstrated the use of MCEE by using it in a real world scenario.
2. Unique capabilities of MCEE include ability to perform discovery, constraint analysis, data and interaction protocol mediation.
3. The system implementation is agnostic to both Web process language (like BPEL) and Web service implementation language.
4. The demonstration gives an insight for using the WSDL-S specification for creating more dynamic processes.

5   Summary

We have demonstrated MCEE and have shown how it is used in configuring dynamic Web processes. While using semantics is a critical aspect of METEOR-S, we also seek to build upon existing standards related to Web services and the Service Oriented Architecture. Our aim is to preserve existing investment in Web services technology and tools; this is shown by the reuse of existing WS tools like BPEL process engine and Apache Axis to create our system. The MCEE system can be seen as layer over the current WS infrastructure, which handles the semantic information added through the extensibility capabilities. Our goal is seamless operation of WS and SWS. For this purpose, we have proposed the WSDL-S specification in collaboration with IBM, and have used it in our system as the basis of semantic annotation.

References

1. Kunal Verma, Karthik Gomadam, Amit P. Sheth, John A. Miller, Zixin Wu, The METEOR-S Approach for Configuring and Executing Dynamic Web Processes, LSDIS Technical Report, 2005.
2. R. Akkiraju, J. Farrell, J.A.Miller, M. Nagarajan, M. Schmidt, A. Sheth, K. Verma, Web Service Semantics - WSDL-S, Position Paper for the W3C Workshop on Frameworks for Semantics in Web Services, Innsbruck, Austria, 2005.
3. Rohit Aggarwal, Kunal Verma, John A. Miller, William Milnor "Constraint Driven Web Service Composition in METEOR-S", Proceedings of IEEE International Conference on Services Computing (SCC 2004), Shanghai, China, September 2004 , pp. 23-30.

4. Kaarthik Sivashanmugam, Kunal Verma, Amit P. Sheth, Discovery of Web Services in a Federated Registry Environment, Proceedings of IEEE Second International Conference on Web Services, June, 2004, pp. 270-278.
5. Vikram Sorathia, Zakir Laliwala, Sanjay Chaudhary, Towards Agricultural Marketing Reforms: Web Services Orchestration Approach, Proceedings of IEEE International Conference on Services Computing, Orlando, Florida, July 2005, pp 260-267.
6. Francisco Curbera, Rania Khalaf, Nirmal Mukhi, Stefan Tai, and Sanjiva Weerawarana, The Next Step In Web Services, Communications of the ACM, 2003

Programming and Compiling Web Services in GPSL

Dominic Cooney, Marlon Dumas, and Paul Roe

Queensland University of Technology, Australia
{d.cooney, m.dumas, p.roe}@qut.edu.au

Abstract. Implementing web services that participate in long-running, multi-lateral conversations is difficult because traditional programming languages are poor at manipulating XML data and handling concurrent and interrelated interactions. We have designed a programming language to deliberately address these problems. In this paper we describe how to use this language to consume a popular web service, and discuss the compiler, including the kinds of semantic checks it performs, and the runtime environment.

1   Introduction

Web services are used increasingly to integrate applications within and between organizations. Implementing simple request-response interactions between statically known participants using traditional middleware and programming languages is reasonably straightforward, but implementing long-running conversations among large and changing sets of participants is difficult. Web services present some serious implementation challenges: prevalent XML data, explicit boundaries, concurrent messages, and process awareness.

XML data: The data model of web services is XML InfoSet. InfoSet is an open data representation with no notion of behavior. Object-oriented programming prizes data encapsulation by marrying data and behavior. To address the mismatch object-oriented (OO) programming languages variously model InfoSet with objects, map between objects and InfoSet, or support InfoSet directly via language extensions. In all these solutions object models are indirect, mappings are incomplete, and language extensions are redundant in their OO data model.

Explicit boundaries: Unlike components in a virtual machine, or processes in an operating system, there is no supervising infrastructure between services. Because implementation technologies vary, or because organizational boundaries entail secrecy, the internal logic of other services may be completely opaque. Programming languages with global models of interacting services are useful for abstractly modeling service oriented architectures, but implementers are limited to purely local phenomena, such as messages, and can not rely on a global view.

Concurrent messages: Messages link distributed nodes, all processing concurrently. For basic scalability web services must handle concurrent messages. Implementers must be cautious of race conditions, deadlocks, and live-locks—all problems that mainstream object-oriented languages make tedious to solve.

B. Benatallah, F. Casati, and P. Traverso (Eds.): ICSOC 2005, LNCS 3826, pp. 508–513, 2005.

Process awareness: Web services often correspond to business functionality, and so are likely to be part of long-running interactions driven by explicit process models. They may engage in conversations with a dynamically changing set of partners and a large number of events that may occur in many orders.

BPEL[1] addresses some of these problems, but it turns out that coding complex multi-lateral interactions in BPEL, especially those that require partial synchronization and one-to-many correlation can be cumbersome [1].

We addressed the above issues in the design of Gardens Point Service Language (GPSL) [2] with the following features:

- **Embedded XQuery.** XQuery is a functional language for querying and synthesizing XML data [3], with a data model close to XML InfoSet. GPSL supports the manipulation of XML data via embedded XQuery expressions.
- **Services, contracts, and explicit message sending.** GPSL has explicit service and contract language elements. Lexical scoping ensures services rely on purely local data. Services exchange data by explicit message sending.
- **Join calculus-style concurrency** [4]. GPSL simplifies forking, joining, and concurrent operations with declarative rules. At a low level of abstraction these rules facilitate the manipulation of concurrent messages; at a higher level they support the modeling of complex processes with state machines.

The feature set of GPSL is unique, yet GPSL belongs to a small set of service-oriented programming languages [5, 6, 7]. In this paper we focus on writing service consumers, which is important for implementing services that aggregate other services. We also present the compiler and runtime system.

2   GPSL by Example

GPSL is primarily for developing services, and an important aspect of implementing a service is interacting with other services. In this example we describe how to use GPSL to consume the Amazon queue service. The Amazon queue service is a SOAP document/literal style service that supports inserting XML data into a queue; reading from a queue, with time-outs; and managing queues.

First we declare an XQuery XML namespace for data used by the service:

```
declare namespace sqs =
    'http://webservices.amazon.com/AWSSimpleQueueService/2005-01-01';
```

...where *sqs* is a mnemonic for *simple queue service.*

Next we write the service contract. The Amazon queue service uses a pattern where all operations have the same SOAP action and the behavior is controlled by the data in the body of the message, so the contract declaration is simply:

```
declare interface SimpleQueueService {
  declare operation SQSOp webmethod action = 'http://soap.amazon.com'
}
```

---

[1] http://www.oasis-open.org/committees/tc_home.php?wg_abbrev=wsbpel

SimpleQueueService and *SQSOp* are identifiers we use to refer to the operation.
webmethod nominates this operation as synchronous SOAP-over-HTTP. This
piece of metadata governs the behavior of the runtime system, but to the programmer *in-out* SOAP operations via a pair of asynchronous messages and synchronous *webmethod* operations appear uniformly as asynchronous operations.

Now we bind some constant values: the endpoint of the Amazon queue service,
and our subscriber ID, which we have to include in every message. We could, of
course, vary these with parameters if desired.

```
(: URI of the Amazon
Simple Queue Service :) let $sqs :=
'http://webservices.amazon.com/onca/soap?Service=AWSSimpleQueueService'in
(: Amazon Web Services subscription ID :) let $subscriptionID :=
'...' in
```

Performing an interaction, e.g. to create a queue, involves constructing a
request, sending it, and processing the response:

```
let $request :=
  element sqs:CreateQueue {
    element sqs:SubscriptionId { $subscriptionID },
      element sqs:Request {
        element sqs:CreateQueueRequest {
          element sqs:QueueName { 'My queue' },
          element sqs:ReadLockTimeoutSeconds { 10 }
        }
      }
  } in
def Process($response) { } in
$sqs: SQSOp($request, Process)
```

This sequence of element constructors produces XML like the following:

```
<sqs:CreateQueue xmlns:sqs=
  "http://webservices.amazon.com/AWSSimpleQueueService/2005-01-01">
  <sqs:SubscriptionId>...</sqs:SubscriptionId>
  <sqs:Request>
    <sqs:CreateQueueRequest>
      <sqs:QueueName>My queue</sqs:QueueName> ...
```

The *def* construct is used to introduce a new internal label, *Process*, and an
associated block to execute when a message is produced on that label. In this
example, sending a message to Process would do nothing as the block labeled
Process is empty. The line *$sqs: SQSOp($request, Process)* actually sends the
message. The prefix argument *$sqs* is the endpoint to send to. Recall that *$sqs* is
bound to the endpoint of the Amazon queue service in a previous *let* statement.
This is how GPSL supports invoking services dynamically—for example, we
could have bound *$sqs,* not to a constant value, but to data in a previous message.

SQSOp is the operation declared in the *SimpleQueueService* contract, which
provides the SOAP action and operation style (*webmethod,* in this case) metadata. The *$request* argument supplies the body of the SOAP message; this is the

fragment of XML we just constructed. Finally, the *Process* argument supplies the label to send SOAP replies to. Because *SQSOp* is declared as a *webmethod*, we must provide some way to handle replies.

This approach to message sending, though direct, is inconvenient if we need to create more than one queue. The GPSL *def* construct is very convenient for small-scale abstraction building such as the following *CreateQueue* label definition:

```
def CreateQueue($queue-name, $timeout, create-reply) {
  let $request :=
    element sqs:CreateQueue {
      element sqs:SubscriptionId { $subscriptionID },
        element sqs:Request {
          element sqs:CreateQueueRequest {
            element sqs:QueueName { $queue-name },
            element sqs:ReadLockTimeoutSeconds { $timeout }
          }
        }
      } in
  $sqs: SQSOp($request, create-reply)
} in
def Ignore($response) { } in
CreateQueue('My queue', 10, Ignore)
```

The *defs* statements can introduce nested *defs* that extract data from the response and forward the distilled result to *create-reply*:

```
 def CreateQueue($queue-name, $timeout,
create-reply) {
  let $request := (: same as above :) in
  def Unpack($response) {
    let $queue-id := $response//QueueId/text() in
    create-reply($queue-id)
  } in
  $sqs: SQSOp($request, Unpack)
} in ...
```

3   The GPSL Compiler

The GPSL compiler operates in traditional parsing, analysis, and code generation phases. The parser must handle XQuery for expressions. For our prototype we found ignoring XQuery direct constructors—the angle-brackets syntax for synthesizing XML which require special handling of whitespace—greatly simplifies parser development. Because syntactically simpler computed constructors can do the job of direct constructors, the expressive power of XQuery is unimpeded.

The analysis phase of the compiler is dominated by resolving identifiers and reporting undeclared variables or on passing too few or too many parameters. This phase includes a Hindley-Milner style type inferencer for labels. This is because we must prevent labels leaking into XML values. Syntax trivially prevents labels appearing in XQuery expressions, because variables bound to XML values are always prefixed with a $, whereas labels and variables bound to labels are not. However sending a message on a label could pass a label where an XML value was expected. The types from our inference let the compiler guarantee statically that this does not happen.

If a label could escape into a larger XML value, we would have to track the reference to that label in order to keep the closure it refers to alive; in the worst case if the label escapes from the service we must set up the SOAP messaging machinery to marshal messages into the closure. Of course, when the programmer supplies a label as the *reply-to* parameter of an operation, that label is reified as an XML value. So the determined programmer can work around the restriction by sending a SOAP message to the service itself.

The last semantic check of the analysis phase is that *in, in-out* and *webmethod* operations obey the convention of a parameter for the SOAP body and a parameter for the reply channel (in the *in-out* and *webmethod* case.) These lead to a limited set of types that are used to generate code that marshal between SOAP messages and messages on internal labels. In principle, schema validation of messages could be incorporated.

The code generator produces Microsoft Intermediate Language (MSIL), which is similar to Java byte code although differs in many details. Most of the complexity in the code generator is in creating closures and delivering messages on internal labels. For each *def* we create a class with a method for each concurrency rule, a field for each captured variable, and a method and field for each label. This field holds a queue of pending messages; the method takes a message to that label, tests whether any rules are satisfied, and if so, calls the method for the rule. We perform the rule testing on the caller thread and only spawn a thread when a rule is satisfied, which avoids spawning many threads.

We do not compile XQuery expressions because implementing an XQuery compiler is a daunting task. Instead we generate code to call an external XQuery library at runtime. One critical criterion for the programming language implementer integrating an XQuery implementation is how that XQuery implementation accepts external variables and provides results. GPSL requires access to expression results as a sequence of XQuery data model values—which is distinctly different from an XML document—to behave consistently with XQuery when those values that are used later in subsequent expressions. We use an interoperability layer over the C API of Galax[2], which has exactly the kind of interface for providing external values and examining results that we want. Our biggest complaint about Galax is that evaluating expressions must be serialized because Galax is non-reentrant.

GPSL programs also depend on the Microsoft Web Services Extensions[3] (WSE) for SOAP messaging. WSE has a low-level messaging interface which is sufficient for GPSL's needs, but it has major shortcomings too: WSE does not support SOAP RPC/encoded, and we have to include some bookkeeping to make SOAP over synchronous-HTTP work using this low-level messaging interface.

---

[2] http://www.galaxquery.org
[3] http://msdn.microsoft.com/webservices/building/wse

4   Conclusion

We have presented code samples in GPSL illustrating the use of features related to SOAP messaging and XQuery. Because of limited space we have not illustrated the join calculus-style concurrency features of GPSL, however the GPSL compiler and further examples are available online.[4]

GPSL's features for messaging, concurrency, and XML data manipulation integrate cohesively. Examples of the cohesive fit are the interplay between sending messages and spawning concurrent threads and receiving messages and synchronising threads, and the consistent treatment of inter- and intra-service messages. GPSL could be extended to address other aspects of services that are tricky to implement, such as transactions and faults. The current implementation of GPSL is also lacking in automatic resource management, expected by programmers familiar with languages such as Java or C# but complicated by the heterogeneous, distributed setting. We expect the key in these areas is to leverage the messaging/concurrency features, for example, by surfacing faults as messages or by recovering automata from concurrency patterns and reclaiming resources when a service can no longer reach a state where it can respond to certain messages.

Acknowledgment. The second author is funded by a fellowship co-sponsored by Queensland Government and SAP.

References

1. Barros, A., Dumas, M., Hofstede, A.: Service interaction patterns. In: Proceedings of the 3rd International Conference on Business Process Management, Nancy, France, Springer Verlag (2005) Extended version available at: http://www.serviceinteraction.com.
2. Cooney, D., Dumas, M., Roe, P.: A programming language for web service development. In Estivill-Castro, V., ed.: Proceedings of the 28th Australasian Computer Science Conference, Newcastle, Australia, Australian Computer Society (2005)
3. Boag, S., Chamberlin, D., Fernández, M.F., Florescu, D., Robie, J., Siméon, J.: XQuery 1.0: An XML query language. W3C Working Draft (2005)
4. Fournet, C., Gonthier, G.: The reflexive chemical abstract machine and the join calculus. In: Twenty-third ACM Symposium on Principles of Programming Languages (POPL). (1996) 372–385
5. Onose, N., Siméon, J.: XQuery at your web service. In: Thirteenth international conference on World Wide Web, New York, NY, USA, ACM Press (2004) 603–611
6. Florescu, D., Grünhagen, A., Kossmann, D.: XL: A platform for Web services. In: Conference on Innovative Data Systems Research (CIDR), Asilomar, CA, USA (2003)
7. Kistler, T., Marais, H.: WebL – A programming language for the web. In: Proceedings of the 7th International conference on World Wide Web, Amsterdam, The Netherlands, The Netherlands, Elsevier Science Publishers B. V. (1998) 259–270

---

[4] http://www.serviceorientation.com

Semantic Management of Web Services

Daniel Oberle[1], Steffen Lamparter[1], Andreas Eberhart[2], and Steffen Staab[3]

[1] Institute AIFB, University of Karlsruhe, Germany
lastname@aifb.uni-karlsruhe.de
[2] Hewlett-Packard, Waldorf, Germany
andreas.eberhart@hp.com
[3] ISWeb, University of Koblenz-Landau, Germany
staab@uni-koblenz.de

Abstract. We present *semantic management of Web Services* as a paradigm that is located between the two extremes of current Web Services standards descriptions and tools, which we abbreviate by *WS**, and Semantic Web Services. On the one hand, WS* does not have an integrated formal model incurring high costs for managing Web Services in a declarative, but mostly manual fashion. On the other hand, the latter aims at the formal modelling of Web Services such that *full automation* of Web Service discovery, composition, invocation, etc., becomes possible — thereby incurring unbearably high costs for modelling. Based on a set of use cases, we identify who benefits from what kind of semantic modelling of Web Services, when and for what purposes. We present how an ontology is used in an implemented prototype.

1   Introduction

Different Web Service standards, we refer to them as *WS**, factorize Web Service management tasks into different aspects, such as input/output signatures, workflow, or security. The advantages of WS* are multiple and have already benefited some industrial cases. WS* descriptions are exchangeable and developers may use different implementations for the same Web Service description. The disadvantages of WS*, however, are also visible, yet: Even though the different standards are complementary, they must overlap and one may produce models composed of different WS* descriptions, which are inconsistent, but do not easily reveal their inconsistencies. The reason is that there is no coherent formal model of WS* and, thus, it is impossible to ask for conclusions that come from integrating several WS* descriptions. Hence, solving such Web Service management problems or asking for other kinds of conclusions that derive from the integration of WS* descriptions remains a purely manual task of the *software developers* accompanied by little to no formal machinery.

Researchers investigating Semantic Web Services have clearly articulated these shortcomings of WS* standardizations and have been presenting interesting proposals to counter some of them [1, 2]. The core of their proposals lies in creating *semantic* standards. Their principal objective is a wide-reaching formalization that allows *full automation* of the Web Service management tasks such as discovery and composition. The potential advantage is the reduction of management efforts to a minimum; the disadvantages, however, are also apparent: Neither is it clear, what kind of powerful machinery could constitute a semantic model that would allow for full automation, including all

B. Benatallah, F. Casati, and P. Traverso (Eds.): ICSOC 2005, LNCS 3826, pp. 514–519, 2005.

aspects of all web services that might matter in some way, nor does it appear to be possible that real-world developers could specify a semantic model of Web Services that would be fine-grained enough to allow for full automation anytime soon.

Therefore, we postulate that *semantic* management of Web Services should not try to tackle full automation of *all* Web Service management tasks as its objective. We claim that the full breadth of Web Service management requires an understanding of the world that is too deep to be modelled explicitly. Instead, we foresee a more passive role for semantic management of Web Services. One that is driven by the needs of the developers who must cope with the complexity of Web Service integration and who could use valuable tools for integrating previously separated aspects.

It is the contribution of this paper to clarify what kind of objectives could and should be targeted by semantics modelling of Web Services and to present a prototype that implements this framework. The kind of objectives that are to be approached are constrained by a *trade-off* between expending efforts for managing Web Services and expending efforts for semantic modelling of Web Services. At the one end, the objective of full automation by semantic modelling will need very fine-grained, detailed modelling of all aspects of Web Services — essentially everything that an intelligent human agent must know. Thus, *modelling efforts* skyrocket at the end of fine-grained modelling. At the other end, where modelling is very coarse and little modelling facilitates management, *management efforts* of distributed systems soar as experiences have shown in the past.

In this paper we try to approach the trade-off by identifying promising use cases. The use cases demonstrate that *some* management tasks can be facilitated by a justifiable amount of semantic modelling (section 2). For each use case, we identify who benefits from what kind of semantic modelling of Web Services, when and for what purposes. In addition, the use cases allow us to derive a set of modelling requirements for an appropriate management ontology which has been presented in [5]. We describe our implemented prototype, and detail how one of the use cases is realized by this system (cf. section 3) before we conclude.

2   Use Cases

This section discusses three use cases that trade off between management and modelling efforts (an extensive survey of use cases is given in [4]). That means, they propose to facilitate *some* of the typical Web Service management tasks by a justifiable amount of *semantic* descriptions (i.e., metadata in terms of an ontology). They try to approach the trade-off point by answering the following questions:

Question 1. Who uses the semantic descriptions of Web Services?

We see two major groups of users constituted by *(i)* software developers and *(ii)* administrators. These two groups of users have the need to predict or observe how Web Services interact, (might) get into conflict, (might) behave, etc. It will be very useful for them to query a system for semantic management of Web Services that integrates aspects from multiple WS* descriptions — which has not been possible so far, but is now allowed by the approach and system we present here.

Question 2. What does he/she/it use the semantic descriptions of Web Services for?

There is a large number of use cases where the integration of semantic descriptions may help the developer or administrator. Hence, the list below is neither exhaustive nor are the individual use cases mutually exclusive. The reader may note that it is germane to semantic descriptions to state what there is and not how it is to be combined and what is its sole purpose.

Question 3. When does he/she/it use the semantic descriptions of Web Services?

We consider development time, deployment time and runtime.

Question 4. Which aspects should be formalized by our ontology?

The answers to the last questions let us derive a set of modelling requirements for a suitable ontology.

Detecting Loops in Interorganizational Workflows. Web Services based applications usually make use of asynchronous messaging, bringing upon quite complex interaction protocols between business partners. Current workflow design workbenches only visualize the local flow and leave the orchestration of messages with the business partners up to the developer. Enough information is available in machine-readable format such that a tool can assist the developer in this task. For instance, the structure of the local flow can be combined with publicly available abstract flows of the partners in order to detect loops in the invocation chain that would lead to non-termination of the system. As shown in the bioinformatics domain [3], automated composition of workflows is likely to be inappropriate in most cases. Hence, we propose to support the developers in their management tasks and not to replace them.

| *Who:* | Developer | *When:* | Development time |
| *What for:* | Code debugging | *Which aspects:* | Workflow information (plans) |

Policy Handling. Policies play an increasing role, as demonstrated by the recent WS-Policy proposal. The idea of a policy is to lay out general rules and principles for service selection. Thus, rather than deciding whether an invocation is allowed on a case by case basis at runtime, one excludes services whose policy violates the local policy at development time. The major benefit is that policies can be specified declaratively. This use case does not aim at fully automated policy matching at run time, as we think that the full generality of policy matching imposes further problems that remain to be solved. Let alone the lack of WS-Policy engines so far. Instead we propose to apply semantic modelling in order to make policy handling more convenient for the developer. As our running example, we consider a large WS-BPEL workflow where checking for external task service invocations which are associated with a policy remains a tedious and manual task.

| *Who:* | Developer, System | *What for:* | Excluding unsuitable services |
| *When:* | Development time | *Which aspects:* | Policies |

Aggregating Service Information. Services will often be implemented based on other services. A service provider publishes information about its service. This might include service level agreements indicating a guaranteed worst-case response time, the cost of the service, or average availability measures. The service requestor, in this case a composite service under development, can collect this information from the respective service providers. In turn, it offers a service and needs to publish similar measures. The semantic management must support the administrator supports the administrator by providing a first cut of this data by aggregating the data gathered from external providers. Similar to the statements given in [3], we argue that full automatic generation of such data will probably yield unwanted and inappropriate results. We see the computation results as an estimate which can be overridden manually by the administrator.

Who:	Administrator	*What for:*	Suggestion for deployment parameters
When:	Deployment time	*Which aspects:*	Quality of service

The answers to *Which aspects?* give us a clear indications of what concepts a suitable management ontology must contain. The organization of these concepts into our Core Ontology of Web Services is described in [5].

3   KAON SERVER

This section presents our prototype for semantic management of Web Services, called KAON SERVER.[1] We first discuss its architecture and demonstrate how it realizes our policy handling use case.

3.1   Overview

KAON SERVER is based on the open-source application server JBoss[2] and applies the tools of the KAON ontology toolsuite for reasoning and querying with the various aspects of Web services according to our Core Ontology of Web Services [5]. KAON SERVER obtains semantic descriptions from existing WS* descriptions, programme code, performance measurements, code reflection and modelling tools already in use. Obtaining comprises: i) parsing the XML documents, ii) extraction of relevant tags and iii) addition of the extracted information as instances to the ontology. The *Metadata Collector* component of the KAON SERVER carries out this task by taking the URLs of WS* descriptions as input. Runtime information stemming from monitoring components can be integrated, too. Another advantage of our approach is that the application logic (servlets, EJBs) may exploit the inference engine by reflection techniques in order to reflect on its own status. Finally, the developer might query the inference engine by using the admin console which is essentially an ontology browser with query interface.

3.2   Realizing the Policy Handling Use Case with the KAON SERVER

In this section we demonstrate how we have realized the policy handling use case by applying KAON SERVER. As an example for a conclusion derived from both a WS-BPEL and WS-Policy description, consider the following scenario. Let's assume a web shop realized with internal and external Web Services composed and managed by a WS-BPEL engine. After the submission of an order, we have to check the type of the

---

[1] Available at `http://kaon.semanticweb.org/server`
[2] `http://www.jboss.org`

```
...
<process name="checkAccount">                    <wsp:Policy>
 <switch ...>                                      <wsp:ExactlyOne>
  <case condition="getVariableData                  <wsse:SecurityToken>
   ('creditcard')='VISA'">                           <wsse:TokenType>
   <invoke partnerLink="toVISA"                       wsse:Kerberosv5TGT
    portType="visa:CCPortType"                       </wsse:TokenType>
    operation="checkCard"...>                        </wsse:SecurityToken>
   </invoke>                                         <wsse:SecurityToken>
  </case>                                             <wsse:TokenType>
  <case condition="getVariableData                    wsse:X509v3
   ('creditcard')='MasterCard'">                     </wsse:TokenType>
   <invoke partnerLink="toMastercard"               </wsse:SecurityToken>
    portType="mastercard:CCPortType"               </wsp:ExactlyOne>
    operation="validateCardData"...>              </wsp:Policy>
   </invoke>
...
```

Fig. 1. WS-BPEL example on the left and WS-Policy example on the right hand side

customer's credit card for validity depending on the credit card type (VISA, MasterCard etc.). We assume that credit card providers offer this functionality via Web Services. The corresponding WS-BPEL process checkAccount thus invokes one of the provider's Web Services depending on the customer's credit card. The left hand side of Figure 1 below shows a snippet of the WS-BPEL process definition.

Suppose now that the Web Service of one credit card provider, say MasterCard, only accepts authenticated invocations conforming to Kerberos or X509. It states such policies in a corresponding WS-Policy document, such as the one sketched on the right hand side in Figure 1. The invocation will fail unless the developer ensures that the policies are met.

Applying KAON SERVER, checking for the existence of external policies boils down to simply querying the inference engine (cf. [5] for the complete example). Both the WS-BPEL process and the WS-Policy document are obtained by the metadata collector of KAON SERVER. That means, the documents are retrieved, parsed, relevant tags are extracted and added as instances to the ontology. WS-BPEL information and WS-BPEL processes are represented by means of the ontology. Note that for this example it suffices to model the existence of a policy and not the policy itself.

The developer can employ a simple query to find out whether an external service requires compliance with a specific policy. Without our approach the developer would have to collect and check this information manually by analyzing WS-BPEL and WS-Policy documents.

As we may recognize from this small example, it is desirable to pose a query rather than manually checking a complex set of process definitions. Without KAON SERVER, the developer would have to check all WS-BPEL nodes for external invocations and corresponding WS-Policy documents manually at development time. We encounter more sophisticated examples where we query for particular policy constraints or where we have large indirect process cascades.

As mentioned in the policy handling use case in section 2, we do not aim at fully automated policy matching at run time, as we think that the full generality of policy matching imposes further problems that remain to be solved. In addition, there are no WS-Policy engines available so far.

Finally, Table 1 shows the benefit of our approach by comparing the effort with and without semantic management for the running example. While using the paradigm of

Table 1. Effort comparison for the running example

Effort	Without semantics	Using semantic management
Management	For each process in the WS-BPEL document: Check for external Web service invocation and check for existence of WS-Policy document	One query to retrieve external Web service processes with attached policies
Modelling	creating and maintaining the WS-BPEL and WS-Policy documents	Same as without semantics because semantic descriptions are automatically obtained

semantic management of Web Services reduces management efforts, no additional modelling efforts are required because KAON SERVER obtains the semantic descriptions automatically from WS* documents.

4   Conclusion

We have shown in this paper what *semantic management of Web Services* may contribute to Web Service management in general. We have described use cases for semantic management of Web Services that can be realized with existing technology and that provide immediate benefits to their target groups, i.e. software developers and administrators who deal with Web Services. Through the use cases we have shown that semantic descriptions may play a fruitful role supporting an integrated view onto Web Service definitions in WS*. At the basis of the integration we have put our Core Ontology of Web Services.

While we have implemented a prototype as proof-of-concept of our approach, in the long run the viability and success of semantic descriptions will only be shown in their successful use of integrated development and runtime environments. The development of the corresponding paradigm of Semantic Management of Web Services through use cases, ontologies, prototypes and examples is an important step into this direction.

Acknowledgements. This work was financed by WonderWeb, an EU IST project, by SmartWeb, a German BMBF project and by ASG (IST-004617), an EU IST project.

References

1. V. Agarwal, K. Dasgupta, N. Karnik, A. Kumar, A. Kundu, S. Mittal, and B. Srivastava. A service creation environment based on end to end composition of web services. In *Proceedings of WWW 2005*, pages 128–137. ACM, 2005.
2. R. Akkiraju, J. Farrell, J. Miller, M. Nagarajan, M.-T. Schmidt, A. Sheth, and K. Verma. Web Service Semantics - WSDL-S. Technical report, University of Georgia, Apr 2005.
3. P. Lord, S. Bechhofer, M. D. Wilkinson, G. Schiltz, D. Gessler, D. Hull, C. Goble, and L. Stein. Applying Semantic Web Services to Bioinformatics: Experiences Gained, Lessons Learnt. In *3rd Int. Semantic Web Conference*, volume 3298 of *LNCS*. Springer, 2004.
4. D. Oberle, S. Lamparter, A. Eberhart, and S. Staab. Semantic management of web services. Technical report, University of Karlsruhe, 2005.
5. D. Oberle, S. Lamparter, S. Grimm, D. Vrandecic, S. Staab, and A. Gangemi. Towards ontologies for formalizing modularization and communication in large software systems. Technical report, University of Karlsruhe, 2005.

Composition of Services with Nondeterministic Observable Behavior

Daniela Berardi[1], Diego Calvanese[2],
Giuseppe De Giacomo[1], and Massimo Mecella[1]

[1] Università di Roma "La Sapienza", Italy
lastname@dis.uniroma1.it
[2] Free University of Bozen-Bolzano, Italy
calvanese@inf.unibz.it

Abstract. In [3] we started studying an advanced form of service composition where available services were modeled as deterministic finite transition systems, describing the possible conversations they can have with clients, and where the client request was itself expressed as a (virtual) service making use of the same alphabet of actions. In [4] we extended our studies by considering the case in which the client request was loosen by allowing don't care nondeterminism in expressing the required target service. In the present paper we complete such a line of investigation, by considering the case in which the available services are only partially controllable and must be modeled as nondeterministic finite transition systems, possibly because of our lack of information on their exact behavior. Notably such services display a "devilish" form of nondeterminism, since we want to model the inability of the orchestrator to actually choose between different executions of the same action. We investigate how to automatically perform the synthesis of the composition under these circumstances.

1 Introduction

Service Oriented Computing (SOC) [1] is the computing paradigm that utilizes Web services (also called *e*-Services or, simply, services) as fundamental elements for realizing distributed applications/solutions. In particular, when no available service can satisfy client needs, (parts of) available services can be composed and orchestrated in order to satisfy such a request. In recent research [7, 8, 10, 15, 6, 9] a notion of "semantic service integration" is arising, especially to facilitate *automatic service composition* (but also discovery, etc.).

Among the various proposals, the one in [3, 4] distinguishes itself by considering also the process of the services. Specifically, the client is offered a set of virtual building blocks so that he can design complex services of interest in terms of these. The building blocks are *actions* described in an abstract and formal fashion; by making use of such virtual blocks the client can write its own service as a sort of high-level program, i.e., abstractly represented as a *deterministic finite transition system* (i.e., deterministic finite state machine)[1]. The virtual blocks are not be implemented directly, but

---

[1] Transition systems here are used to formalize the possible conversations that a service can have with its clients – including the orchestrator in the case the service is involved in a composition – describing the possible interactions of the service.

B. Benatallah, F. Casati, and P. Traverso (Eds.): ICSOC 2005, LNCS 3826, pp. 520–526, 2005.

made available through the system: the actual services that are available to the system are themselves be formally described in terms of deterministic finite transition systems built out of such virtual blocks. Such a description can be considered as a sort of mapping from the concrete service to the virtual blocks of the integration system. The idea is to exploit the reverse of such a mapping to automatically get the client service request. In [3, 4], however, available services are modeled as deterministic transition systems because it is assumed that they are fully controllable by the orchestrator through action requests: an available service, by performing an action in a state, reaches exactly a single state.

In this paper we extend the approach of [3, 4] so as to address automatic composition synthesis when available services are not not fully controllable by the orchestrator. We model such a partial controllability by associating to available services (finite) transition systems that are *nondeterministic* (in a "devilish" sense, see later). Using nondeterminism we can naturally model services in which the result of each interaction with its client can not be foreseen. Just as an example, consider a service allowing to buy items by credit card; after invoking the operation, the service can be in a state payment_OK, accepting a payment, or in a different state payment_refused, if, e.g., the credit card is not valid. Considering that the transition system of the available service is in fact a mapping that describes the real service in terms of the actions of the community, it is natural to assume that although the orchestrator does not have full control on the available services, it has full observability: after executing the operation, it can observe the status in which the service is and therefore understand which transition, among the ones that are nondeterministically possible in the previous state, has been undertaken by the service[2]. The main contribution of our work is to show how one can synthesize a composition in this setting.

2   Services with Partially Controllable Behavior

Formally, we consider each *available service* as a *nondeterministic*[3] finite transition system $S = (\Sigma, S, s_0, \delta, F)$ where Σ is a common alphabet of actions shared by all available services of a community, S is a finite set of states, $s_0 \in S$ is the single initial state, $\delta \subseteq S \times \Sigma \times S$ is the transition relation[4], and $F \subseteq S$ is the set of final states (i.e., states in which the computation may stop, but does not necessarily have to – see [3, 4]).

The client service request, as in [3], is expressed as a *target service*, which represents the service the client would like to interact with. Such a service is again modeled as finite transition system over the alphabet of the community, but this time a *deterministic* one, i.e., the transition relation is actually functional (there cannot be two distinct transi-

---

[2] The reader should observe that also the standard proposal WSDL 2.0 has a similar point of view: the same operation can have multiple output messages (the out message and various outfault messages), and the client observes how the service behaved by receiving a specific output message.

[3] Note that this kind of nondeterminism is of a *devilish* nature, so as to capture the idea that the orchestrator cannot fully control the available services.

[4] As usual, we call the Σ component of such triples, the *label of the transition*.

tions with the same starting state and action). Notice that the target service is obviously deterministic because we assume that the client has full control on how to execute the service that he/she requires[5].

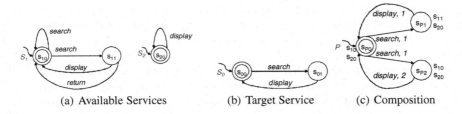

(a) Available Services   (b) Target Service   (c) Composition

Fig. 1. Composition of nondeterministic services

Example 1. Figure 1(a) shows a community of services for getting information on books. The community includes two services: S_1 that allows one to repeatedly *(i)* search the ISBN of a book given its title (search) then, *(ii)* in certain cases (e.g., if the record with cataloging data is currently accessible), it allows for displaying the cataloging data (such as editor information, year of publication, authors, copyrights, etc.) of the book with the selected ISBN (display), or *(iii)* simply returns without displaying information (return); S_2 allows for repeatedly displaying cataloging data of books given the ISBN (display), without allowing researches. Figure 1(b) shows the target service S_0: the client wants to have a service that allows him to search for a book ISBN given its title (search), and then display its cataloging data (display). Note that the client wants to display the cataloging data in any case and hence he/she can neither directly exploit S_1 nor S_2.   □

Next, we need to clarify which are the basic capabilities of the orchestrator. In [3, 4], the orchestrator had only the ability of selecting one[6] of the services, and requiring it to execute an action. Here, we equip the orchestrator with a further ability: the orchestrator can query (at runtime) the current state of each available service. Technically such a capability is called *full observability* on the states of the available services. Although other choices are possible [15, 2], full observability is the natural choice in this context, since the transition system that each available service exposes to the community is specific to the community itself (indeed it is expressed using the common alphabet of actions of the community), and hence there is no reason to make its states partially unobservable: if details have to be hidden, this can be done directly within the transition system, possibly making use of nondeterminism.

---

[5] In fact we could have a client request that is expressed as a nondeterministic transition system as in [4]. In this case, however, the nondeterminism has a *don't-care*, aka *angelic* nature.

[6] For simplicity we assume that the orchestrator selects only one service at each step, however our approach and results easily extend to the case where more services can be selected at each step.

3   Composition

We are now ready to define composition: an "orchestrator program" (indeed a skeleton specification) that the orchestrator has to execute in order to orchestrate the available services so as to offer to the client the target service. Let the available service be $S_1, \ldots, S_n$ each with $S_i = (\Sigma, S_i, s_{i0}, \delta_i, F_i)$, and the target service $S_0 = (\Sigma, S_0, s_{00}, \delta_0, F_0)$. A *history* is an alternating sequence of the form $h = (s_1^0, \ldots, s_n^0) \cdot a^1 \cdot (s_1^1, \ldots, s_n^1) \cdots a^\ell \cdot (s_1^\ell, \ldots, s_n^\ell)$ such that the following constraints hold:

- $s_i^0 = s_{i0}$ for $i \in \{1, \ldots, n\}$, i.e., all services start in their initial state;
- at each step k, for one i we have that $(s^k, a^{k+1}, s_i^{k+1}) \in \delta_i$, while for all $j \neq i$ we have that $s_j^{k+1} = s_j^k$, i.e., at each step of the history, only one of the service has made a transition (according to its transition relation), while the other ones have remained still.

An *orchestrator program* is a function $P : \mathcal{H} \times \Sigma \to \{1, \ldots, n, u\}$ that, given a history $h \in \mathcal{H}$ (where $\mathcal{H}$ is the set of all histories defined as above) and an action $a \in \Sigma$ to perform, returns the service (actually the service index) that will perform it. Observe that such a function may also return a special value u (for "undefined"). This is a technical convenience to make P a total function returning values even for histories that are not of interest or for actions that no service can perform after a given history.

Next, we define when an orchestrator program is a composition that realizes the target services. First, we observe that, since the target service is a deterministic transition system its behavior is completely characterized by the set of its traces, i.e., by the set of infinite sequences of actions that are faithful to its transitions, and of finite sequences that in addition lead to a final state[7]. Now, given a trace $t = a_1 \cdot a_2 \cdots$ of the target service, we say that an *orchestrator program P realizes the trace t* iff for each non-negative integer ℓ and for each history $h \in \mathcal{H}_t^\ell$, we have that $P(h, a_{\ell+1}) \neq u$ and $\mathcal{H}_t^{\ell+1}$ is nonempty, where the sets $\mathcal{H}_t^\ell$ are inductively defined as follows:

- $\mathcal{H}_t^0 = \{(s_{10}, \ldots, s_{n0})\}$
- $\mathcal{H}_t^{\ell+1}$ is the set of all histories such that, if $h \in \mathcal{H}_t^\ell$ and $P(h, a_{\ell+1}) = i$ (with $i \neq u$), then for all transitions $(s_i^\ell, a, s_i') \in \delta_i$ the history $h \cdot a_{\ell+1} \cdot (s_1^{\ell+1}, \ldots, s_n^{\ell+1})$, with $s_i^{\ell+1} = s_i'$, and $s_j^{\ell+1} = s_j^\ell$ for $j \neq i$, is in $\mathcal{H}_t^{\ell+1}$.

Moreover, if a trace is finite and ends after f actions, we have that all histories in $\mathcal{H}_t^f$ end with all services in a final state. Finally, we say that an *orchestrator program P realizes the target service S_0*, if it realizes all its traces.

In order to understand the above definitions, let us observe that intuitively the orchestrator program realizes a trace if it can choose at every step an available service to perform the requested action. However, since when an available service executes an action it nondeterministically chooses what transition to actually perform, the orchestrator program has to play on the safe side and require that for each of the possible resulting states of the activated service, the orchestrator is able to continue with the execution of

---

[7] Actually, the behavior captured by a transition system is typically identified with its execution tree, see [3]. However, since the target service has a deterministic transition system, the set of traces is sufficient, since one can immediately reconstruct the execution tree from it.

the next action. In addition, before ending a computation, available services need to be left in a final state, hence we have the additional requirement above for finite traces.

Example 1 (cont.) Figure 1(c) shows an orchestrator program P (in this case with finite states) for available services S_1 and S_2 in Figure 1(a), that realizes the target service S_0 in Figure 1(b). Essentially, P behaves as follows: it repeatedly delegates to S_1 the action search (notice that both transitions labeled with this actions are delegated to S_1); then it checks the resulting state of S_1 and, depending on this state, it delegates the action display to either S_1 or S_2. $\square$

Observe also that the orchestrator program has to observe the states of the available services in order to decide which service to select next (for a given action requested by the target service). This makes such orchestrator programs akin to an advanced form of conditional plans studied in AI [12]. Observe also that, in the above definition we allow orchestrator program to have infinite states in general. But obviously it is of interest to understand in what circumstances composition may be realized through an orchestrator program that has only a finite number of state.

4   Composition Synthesis

It turns out that in spite of the additional complexity of dealing with nondeterminism, one can still devise a reduction from the problem of checking the existence of a composition to satisfiability in Propositional Dynamic Logic (PDL) [5] as in [3, 4]. The reduction is much more subtle in this case but still polynomial. As a result, we have that composition synthesis can be performed in EXPTIME. Moreover from each model of the resulting PDL formula one can directly extract an orchestrator program, and, considering the finite model property of PDL, this in turns implies that an orchestrator program that has only a finite number of states exists whenever a composition exists.

Actually, it comes quite as a surprise that in dealing with partial controllability one can still use a PDL encoding instead of directly working with automata on infinite trees [13]. And this finding is particularly welcome considering that certain operations on automata on infinite trees (e.g., the notorious Safra's complementation step) have proved to be almost impossible to implement in an efficient way. PDL satisfiability, instead shares the same basic algorithms behind the success of the description logics-based reasoning system used for OWL, and hence its use is quite promising.

5   Conclusion

In this paper we studied how to synthesize a composition to realize a client service request expressed as a target service a la [3, 4], in the case where available services are only partially controllable (modeled as devilish nondeterminism) but fully observable by the orchestrator. Such an approach to deal with nondeterministic available services can be extended in several directions. As an example, by introducing a set of *variables shared among the available services and the client* that encode some basic information that is exchanged between the services, and that the client acquires while executing the target service. Once we introduce shared variables, we can use them to guard transitions in both the target and the available services.

The result can be also easily extended to the case where the client request is expressed as a nondeterministic transition system as in [4]. Note that in this case the nondeterminism has a *don't-care*, aka *angelic*, nature: the client is not fully specifying the target service he/she requires, and allows some degree of freedom to the composer in providing him/her with one, by choosing among the nondeterministic transitions which one to actually implement. Such a form of nondeterminism can be still tackled through a reduction to satisfiability in PDL.

It should be noted that our approach, in which the orchestrator at each step sends an execution request to available services and these then send back to the orchestrator their states, is a form of control that is communication intensive[8]. In fact, if communication is of concern, our model is too coarse. Indeed we should distinguish between actions that affect the state of affairs and messages for sending (either contents or control) information. Suggestions on tackling such a distinction are presented in [2].

Finally we want to stress that composition, especially in rich dynamic settings as those studied in this paper, is essentially a form of (reactive) program synthesis, and tight relationships exist with the literature on that field [11, 14, 16]. Although that literature often does not offer off-the-shelf results for composition, it certainly offers techniques and general approaches that can be profitably used to tackle subtle issues, as, for example, partial observability, which becomes an issue when the distinction between actions and messages is taken into account.

References

1. G. Alonso, F. Casati, H. Kuno, and V. Machiraju. *Web Services. Concepts, Architectures and Applications*. Springer, 2004.
2. D. Berardi, D. Calvanese, G. De Giacomo, R. Hull, and M. Mecella. Automatic composition of transition-based semantic web services with messaging. In *Proc. of VLDB 2005*, 2005.
3. D. Berardi, D. Calvanese, G. De Giacomo, M. Lenzerini, and M. Mecella. Automatic composition of e-services that export their behavior. In *Proc. of ICSOC 2003*.
4. D. Berardi, D. Calvanese, G. De Giacomo, M. Lenzerini, and M. Mecella. Synthesis of underspecified composite e-Services based on automated reasoning. In *Proc. of ICSOC 2004*.
5. D. Harel, D. Kozen, and J. Tiuryn. *Dynamic Logic*. The MIT Press, 2000.
6. R. Hull and J. Su. Tools for design of composite web services. In *Proc. of ACM SIGMOD*, pages 958–961, 2004.
7. U. Kuter, E. Sirin, D. Nau, B. Parsia, , and J. Hendler. Information gathering during planning for web service composition. In *Proc. of Workshop on Planning and Scheduling for Web and Grid Services*, 2004.
8. S. A. McIlraith and T. C. Son. Adapting Golog for composition of semantic web services. In *Proc. of KR 2002*, pages 482–496, 2002.
9. B. Medjahed, A. Bouguettaya, and A. K. Elmagarmid. Composing web services on the semantic web. *VLDB Journal*, 12(4):333–351, 2003.

---

[8] Actually we had essentially the same amount of control communication in [3, 4]: indeed even if states were not sent back to the orchestrator, at least some feedback to signaling the readiness to accept further commands should have been sent back.

10. M. Michalowski, J. L. Ambite, C. A. Knoblock, S. Minton, S. Thakkar, and R. Tuchinda. Retrieving and semantically integrating heterogeneous data from the web. *IEEE Intelligent Systems*, 19(3):72–79, 2004.
11. A. Pnueli and R. Rosner. On the synthesis of a reactive module. In *Proc. of POPL'89*, pages 179–190, 1989.
12. J. Rintanen. Complexity of planning with partial observability. In *Proc. of the 14th Int. Conf. on Automated Planning and Scheduling (ICAPS 2004)*, pages 345–354, 2004.
13. W. Thomas. Languages, automata, and logic. In *Handbook of Formal Language Theory*, volume III, pages 389–455. 1997.
14. W. Thomas. Infinite games and verification. In *Proc. of CAV 2002*, volume 2404 of *LNCS*, pages 58–64. Springer, 2002.
15. P. Traverso and M. Pistore. Automated composition of semantic web services into executable processes. In *Proc. of ISWC 2004*, volume 3298 of *LNCS*, pages 380–394. Springer, 2004.
16. M. Y. Vardi. An automata-theoretic approach to fair realizability and synthesis. In *Proc. of CAV'95*, volume 939 of *LNCS*, pages 267–292. Springer, 1995.

Efficient and Transparent Web-Services Selection

Nicolas Gibelin and Mesaac Makpangou

INRIA, Regal Project, B.P. 105, 78153 Le Chesnay Cedex, France
`firstname.lastname@inria.fr`

Abstract. Web services technology standards enable description, publication, discovery of and binding to services distributed towards the Internet. However, current standards do not address the service selection issue : how did a consumer select the service that matches its functional (e.g. operations' semantics) and non-functional (e.g. price, reputation, response time) properties ? Most projects advocate automatic selection mechanism, advising adaptation or modification of the web-services model and its entities (UDDI, WSDL, Client, Provider). These proposals also do not take advantage of distributed-systems' state of the art, mainly with respect to the collection and the dissemination of services' QoS. This paper presents an extension of the initial model that permits automatic service selection, late binding and collection of metrics that characterize the quality of service. The extension consists on a web-service access infrastructure, made of web service proxies and a peer to peer network of QoS metrics repository (the proposal does not impose modification on UDDI registries or services). The proxies interact with common UDDI registries to find suitable services for selection and to publish descriptions. They collect QoS metrics and store them on a p2p network.

1 Introduction

The World Wide Web (WWW) has been used to store, exchange and provide static data. Over the time, new emerging technologies appeared. A broader variety of resources are increasingly being made available as Web services. For instance, in E-commerce applications, the WWW enables applications to applications (a2a) connection through multiple devices without being concerned with framework or languages heterogeneity. The basis of Web services like XML and WSDL for the service's description, UDDI and SOAP for services registry, discovery and communication, contribute toward making Web services a workable and broadly adopted technology.

The basic model specifies how to describe services and its interfaces, publish and discover methods. This initial model also provides abstractions to support multiple programming languages and run-time environments. However this model presents some drawbacks. First, it doe not support automatic selection of service when more than one of them satisfy the consumer functional properties With the growing popularity of Web services, finding relevant services become an important issue. This decision is left to the consumer who will handle it

B. Benatallah, F. Casati, and P. Traverso (Eds.): ICSOC 2005, LNCS 3826, pp. 527–532, 2005.

manually. Secondly, there is no mean to capture and/or exploit non-functional properties, such as quality of service, to help select the service that best suit consumer preferences. Another important drawback is the lack of a coherency mechanism that could guarantee the accuracy of information maintained by a UDDI Registry. It is reported in [1] that 48% of the production of UDDI registry have links unusable. Though this report dated back to 2001, we believe that the problem remains.

A number of authors have already identified some of these drawbacks [2, 3, 4, 5, 6, 7]. The solutions that were proposed either introduce modifications of components of the initial model or do not address the global picture. Modifications need to be agreed and integrated by all participants, which is almost impossible to achieve. In the other hand, solving part of the problem, for instance expecting the providers to provide the QoS, is not enough. Another consideration to keep in mind is the overall performance and efficiency of the solution.

To leverage the drawbacks of the initial web service model while letting its basic components functioning unchanged, we propose to extend the initial model with a web service selection and binding infrastructure that take care of at least the following functions: (1) automatic detection of broken web services references; (2) automatic collection of quality of service metrics for consumers; (3) consumers support of functional and non-functional properties for selection.

This paper is structured as follow: Section 2 describes in detail the new web service model, while Section 3 draws some conclusions.

2   Extended Model

We propose to extend the initial web service model with a selection and binding infrastructure, while leaving the UDDI Registry unchanged. Figure 1 shows where new components are located and the way they cooperate with existing components and within one another.

The proposed binding and access mechanism is achieved thanks to the introduction of two new components : web service proxy and p2p network of QoS metrics repository. In this section, we only focus on proxy mechanism.

A web service proxy offers: (1) to services' providers an interface to publish their descriptions to the UDDI registry, (2) to services' consumers an interface

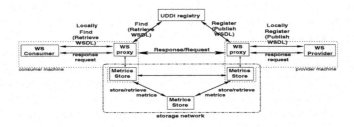

Fig. 1. Extended Web services model

to request the selection of services that best suit their functional properties and QoS requirements. With this new architecture, the requests of a consumer are forwarded to the selected service by the local proxy. The local proxy of the consumer cooperates with the local proxy of the provider to send request/response among the network. Overall, a group of cooperative web service proxies stand aside the consumers and providers and cooperate to relay (possibly modified) requests and responses to their final destinators which may be services or UDDI registries.

The set of cooperative web service proxies take advantage of their position (in between providers, registries, services and consumers) to observe ongoing activities and to collect information that can help evaluate various metrics characterizing the quality of the service offered to consumers. The collected metrics are stored in the p2p network of QoS metrics. The metrics' repository servers are in charge of the storage and the dissemination of the connected measures.

In the remaining of this section, we first specify what metrics we are considering to characterize the quality of service, as well as the means to collect these metrics. Then we discuss the main functions provided by the web service proxy. Finally, we present the selection algorithm that is implemented by web service proxies.

2.1 Quality of Service Metrics

In the extended model, we distinguish three categories of QoS metrics, depending mainly on the source of their measures. These are : service access metrics, feedback metrics, and service delivery metrics. The former class of metrics characterize the conditions for accessing the service. The metrics used by providers to characterize the conditions for accessing their services may vary from one provider to another; the measures for each service are supplied by its provider and may vary over the time. The feedback metrics measure the satisfaction or unsatisfaction of consumers. Finally, the service delivery metrics characterize the quality of the service offered by the underlying computation infrastructure. The metrics of the latter case can be computed automatically, while for metrics of the former two categories we need basics measures from end users.

Service Delivery Metrics. Unlike other extensions advocating automatic monitoring of Web Service QoS [3, 4, 8], we do not modify the provider or the consumer service. The monitoring is performed by web service proxies which can globally cooperate to obtain measurements for the following metrics: (1) service Load (average number of simultaneous; connections or requests to this service for some period of time) (2) response time (between consumer and provider); (3) service latency; (4) service throughput (average number of requests that the service can serve within a period of time); (5) service reliability (ability of a service to perform its required functions under stated conditions for a specified period of time. In our case, we monitor Mean Time between failure (MTBF) and Mean Time to Failure (MTF)).

All these metrics will be monitored and collected automatically thanks to the collaboration of web service proxies attached to providers and consumers. They intercept all exchanges between the four entities that interact within the traditional web service models: providers, consumers, UDDI Registries and services.

Extracting Service Access Metrics. To permit a provider to supply the measures of the service access metrics defined for its service, we propose an extension of the classical ("portType, message, types, binding") common Web-Service Description Language (WSDL). For instance, the provider can specify service price, service resiliation penality, maximal delay before the service stop, compensation rate . . . . This article does not provide an exhaustive list of service access metrics that the provider can use to characterize its service. Figure 2 sketches the basic language constructions used to extend WSDL in order to specify provider-supplied service access metrics. This example defines two new metrics (standard to our model). The first, *servicePrice* describes the price a consumer must pay to access the service. In more complex cases, a provider can indicate the price on a per operation basis (described in the <wsdl:operation> section of WSDL). The second access metric of the example is *serviceDelay*; it measures the maximum activity time of the service. After that delay, the consumer must pay an other slice of time, or will be denied the use of the service. This example is not a full XML description of the proposed extension (no domain name is used), however it provides the basics keywords and language constructions a provider must use to describe its metrics.

```
<qos><metric name="servicePrice">
    <metricvalue name="price" value="200" type="int"/>
    <metricvalue name="currency" value="dollar-us" type="string"/>
</metric>
<metric name="serviceDelay">
    <metricvalue name="activitydelay" value="10" type="int"/>
    <metricvalue name="unitofmeasure" value="minutes" type="string"/>
</metric></qos>
```

Fig. 2. WSDL extension example

Consumer Preference for QoS. The web-service user can specify preferences to contribute to the selection mechanism. For instance, it will be able to specify metrics like "the least expensive service which exists", "the maximum price he accepts to pay for the service", or "the maximum response time he wants the service can satisfy". For that, the user sends an extended request specifying its preferences, to the proxy which store them. The proxy parses the request to extract consumer preferences and then clean the request to forward it to the traditional UDDI registry.

2.2   Web Service Proxy

The web service proxies are located on both provider and consumer side, providing classical retrieve/publish mechanism. The proxies are UDDI compliant, thus consumers and providers never directly contact the registries. In the sections below, we depict the extended retrieve and publish mechanism.

New Retrieve Procedure. In the first step, the proxy forwards the consumer request to a public UDDI register to find all the **serviceKey** matching the request and wait for the UDDI registry response (which may contain more than one service reference)

The second really important step checks if services are available. The proxy requests the UDDI registry to retrieve the localisation of all services, and then cooperate with monitoring network to determine wheather service remain available, eliminating no longer accessible or unavailable services.

Then, the proxy retrieves the available QoS of each service, using the **serviceKey** as hash key in the store network and starts the selection algorithm for each service to compute the QoS value of services. The algorithm returns a list of matching services in the order of best-matching first. The proxy then retrieves the service WSDL description.

Finally, the proxy sends a fake localisation to the service consumer (http://localhost:port/serviceKey/). The consumer can now communicates with the distant service, but all requests are forwarded by the proxy. As we will see, with this mechanism, we can provide transparent QoS measurements.

New Publish Procedure. From the provider side the publication procedure does not really change. When the proxy receives a publication request containing the service description WSDL, it first parses the description to extract provider supplied QoS information (Figure 2); then, it requests QoS monitoring network to store the extracted metrics. With this mechanism, we can follow the evolution of the price of the services such as to enable the selection of the cheapest service. Once the analysis is carried out and the QoS information propagated in the network, the proxy forwards the publication request and the WSDL description to the UDDI registry indicated by the provider.

2.3   Selection Mechanism

The selection algorithm is used to rank services. For each potential service, the protocol compute a rank value used to sort services. We can now describe the selection algorithm applied when a consumer sends a binding request to the proxy.This mechanism comprises the steps summarised below: (1) the consumer sends a request to the proxy with its preferences; (2)the proxy extracts the preferences and forwards the request to one or more UDDI registry indicated by the consumer; (3) the UDDI registry respond with a server list of potentials matching services (4) the proxy then retrieves QoS metrics of all the listed services, (5) finally, the proxy computes the algorithm and send back the response to the consumer.

3   Conclusion and Discussion

The paper proposed an extension of the web services model to enable automatic and transparent selection and binding to services that best suit the consumers functional and non-functional requirements. This extension is built thanks to the web service proxy facility and a P2P network of QoS metric repository. Web services proxies associated with services providers and consumers offer standarized interfaces to permit them to interact with UDDI registries and Services, and take advantage of their position to collect measures for QoS metrics. Unlike most proposals that address the quality-based selection issue, the solution described in this paper does not require change on the UDDI registry or Services. It does not even require specific contribution from the services providers and consumers, but service access conditions for providers and annotations for consumers.

To access the benefits of the proposed selection and binding infrastructure, we plane to conduct a complete evaluation. Based on the results of some basic experimentation, we believe that this mechanism can improve the quality of the service experienced by the consumers. We also believe that this mechanism will help improve considerably the consistency of UDDI Registries as perceived by consumers.

References

1. Clark, M.: Uddi - the weather report.
   http://www.webservicesarchitect.com/content/articles/clark04.asp (2001)
2. Liu, Y., Ngu, A.H., Zeng, L.Z.: Qos computation and policing in dynamic web service selection. In: WWW Alt. '04: Proceedings of the 13th international World Wide Web conference on Alternate track papers & posters, New York, NY, USA, ACM Press (2004) 66–73
3. Ran, S.: A model for web services discovery with qos. SIGecom Exch. 4 (2003) 1–10
4. Day, J., Deters, R.: Selecting the best web service. In: CASCON '04: Proceedings of the 2004 conference of the Centre for Advanced Studies on Collaborative research, IBM Press (2004) 293–307
5. Mukhi, N.K., Plebani, P.: Supporting policy-driven behaviors in web services: experiences and issues. In: ICSOC '04: Proceedings of the 2nd international conference on Service oriented computing, New York, NY, USA, ACM Press (2004) 322–328
6. Maximilien, E.M., Singh, M.P.: Reputation and endorsement for web services. SIGecom Exch. 3 (2002) 24–31
7. Zeng, L., Benatallah, B., Dumas, M., Kalagnanam, J., Sheng, Q.Z.: Quality driven web services composition. In: WWW '03: Proceedings of the 12th international conference on World Wide Web, New York, NY, USA, ACM Press (2003) 411–421
8. Maximilien, E.M., Singh, M.P.: Toward autonomic web services trust and selection. In: ICSOC '04: Proceedings of the 2nd international conference on Service oriented computing, New York, NY, USA, ACM Press (2004) 212–221

An Approach to Parameterizing Web Service Flows

Dimka Karastoyanova [1], Frank Leymann [1], and Alejandro Buchmann[2]

[1] IAAS, Universität Stuttgart, Germany
{karastoyanova, leymann}@informatik.uni-stuttgart.de
[2] Computer Science Department, Technische Universität Darmstadt, Germany
buchmann@informatik.tu-darmstadt.de

Abstract. The flexibility and reusability of Web Service flows (WS-flows) are limited especially by the fact that portType and operation names are hard-coded in the process definition. In this paper we argue that through parameterization and substitution WS-flows flexibility can be improved, while reusability is enhanced. We introduce a meta-model extension to enable run time evaluation of parameter values and thus discard the need to predict any possible partner service types during process modeling. The extension enables also run time changes in portType values. We show how the approach can be mapped to BPEL. We discuss prototypical implementation for the extended functionality and present conclusions and ideas for future work.

1 Introduction

The advances of the Web Service (WS) technology facilitate platform and programming language independent application integration. The technology has matured in the last years at a great pace. In this work we concentrate on making compositions of WSs (also called Web Service Flows or WS-flows) more flexible and also more reusable. We present an approach for creating flexible WS-flows by introducing additional degree of freedom with respect to the partners' portTypes and operations, in particular to their names. It not only boosts the reusability of process models but also decreases model complexity, increases their flexibility and minimizes the process maintenance effort. The approach boils down to the concept of *parameterized processes* – essentially presenting portTypes and operations using parameters and defining run time parameter substitution policies. Parameterized processes (section 2) are flexible because process definition independence of concrete portTypes and operations is achieved. To be able to execute such process models parameters' values must be resolved at run time using an evaluation strategy that specifies what mechanism has to be executed to return parameter values (section 2). We also show how the concepts can be mapped to BPEL [2] (section 3).

Despite being viewed as very flexible, WS-flows definitions still hard code participants' types in terms of portTypes and operations (names). Hard-coding presumes precise knowledge of the naming of portTypes and operations. In fact, while it is possible in practice to agree and standardize messages sent and received, it turns out to be very difficult or impossible to agree on grouping such operations in portTypes and their naming. This implies several deficiencies of existing WS-flows.

B. Benatallah, F. Casati, and P. Traverso (Eds.): ICSOC 2005, LNCS 3826, pp. 533–538, 2005.

Process models need to accommodate the fact that types of participants in a process are identified by their portType/operation names and that equivalent functionalities can be potentially exposed under different names. Modeling alternative control flow paths reflecting alternative portTypes/participants [6], [4] is one way to tackle his issue. This *increases* the *complexity* of process models significantly. On the other hand, one needs to *make a decision* as of which concrete providers would exist at the time of process execution, which in a long-running setting is impractical and impossible. This decision must be postponed till execution time of every process instance, so that the process would be able to appreciate for unknown services.

Having a model (Fig. 1) with portType names of two suppliers of hard disk drives (HDD) fixed means the process owner has decided on the set of providers to be invoked alternatively in any of the instances of the process model; the instances of this process model invoke only instances of either of those WS types. Such decision neglects all providers that could get exposed as WSs at a later point in time (e.g. portType called WS_pT3). To involve any other WS types requires modification of the process model and redeployment, which is deemed *inflexible* for long-running processes, unless the decision on the type of participants is postponed till run time.

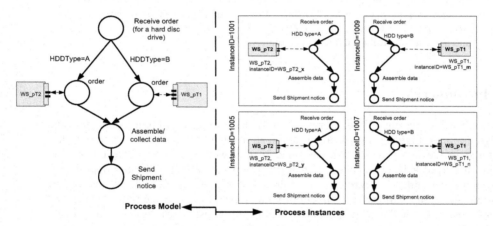

Fig. 1. State-of-the-art WS-flow

Existing WS-flows exhibit *limited reusability* because of insufficient support for loose-coupling, and hard-coding of partner WSs. Indeed there is complex, sometimes industry-specific, functionality carried out in a similar way but companies cannot always directly reuse a process model with the service providers coded, because they might need or wish to interact with providers discovered at run time.

2 Parameterized WS-Flows

We observe similarity in processes such as credit approval, payment, order placement, and so on and in some parts they differ only in the identifiers of the performing services. These processes also include alternative paths that are only there because of the differently named providers of same functionality, e.g. the scenario in Fig. 1.

To benefit from loose coupling and enable process model reusability we need to ensure that portTypes and/or operations are interchangeable from the process viewpoint and can be exchanged. Therefore we use *parameters* to substitute only *portType names and operation names* of WSs a process interacts with. It is also possible to represent other process model elements in parameterized form [3] (e.g. transition conditions, message types and parts, activity types, data manipulation activities); it is out of the scope of this work. Our approach here takes upon parameterizing portType and operation names in process activities standing for an interaction with partners (called interaction activities [7]).

Parameterized processes are defined as WS-flows having one or more interaction activities' portType and/or operation names substituted by parameters.

A parameterized WS-flow is presented in Fig. 2. Unlike the example scenario in Fig. 1 the portType and operation names of the two alternative HDD suppliers (WS_pT1 and WS_pT2) have been substituted by a parameter (WS_pT=X). We observe that when executed the parameterized process instances are not only able to involve the service types used in the initial example but rather there are also instances that could interact with other types of services (e.g. WS_pT-N) even if they were unknown at the time of process modeling. This imposes the need to compute the parameter values at run time.

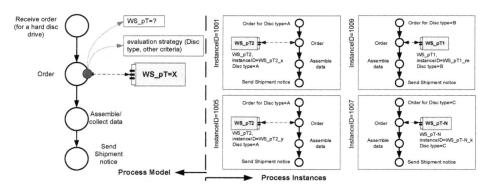

Fig. 2. Parameterized process and its instances

Run time evaluation of parameter values is performed on per process instance basis and is in general an algorithm that selects a WS type out of a set of WS types that meet a set of imposed requirements. The set of compliant service types varies from one process instance to another, because of the potentially different initial data. Once a parameter value is calculated it is substituted in the activity which then initiates an interaction with the WS. In our current work we assume that the messages constrain the choice of appropriate portType/operation values, i.e. messages are part of the search criteria.

Each parameterized activity must have the computing capability to resolve the values of the parameters; otherwise the process instances will be blocked waiting because of unknown values or result in engine faults to be repaired by an administrator.

The four major alternatives (or strategies) we specify for obtaining the value of a portType/operation parameter in an interaction activity are: (i) static provision of portTypes and operations, (ii) prompt (the user) strategy, (iii) query and (iv) from variable. These alternatives define in a declarative manner how a service is to be discovered and what is required from the service, and neglect any reference to name of the portType (and operation). Selection of a compliant service type must be followed by a step of binding to a concrete port [4], [5].

The *static* strategy specifies concrete parameters values, which can be supplied during process modeling or upon process deployment (for completeness only).

The *"prompt (the user)"* allows users to provide a process instance with parameter values. This and the rest of the strategies involve instantiation of parameterized WS-flows. Prompts can be issued to users at the time of process instantiation for all parameterized activities, or may be signaled to the user every time the execution of a process instance reaches an activity with unknown service type.

The *"query"* strategy uses in-lined or referenced query definitions which are to be executed against a WS discovery component [7]. Queries contain service type selection criteria including the messages it must accept and return, semantics, and QoS. Since it is unrealistic to obtain a single compliant portType/operation pair the result of a query is a ranked, non-empty list of compliant portTypes/operations. One of the service types returned is used in the concrete WS-flow instance.

The *"from variable"* strategy postulates that the value for a parameter is to be copied from a variable defined in the process. The values stored in this variable may be obtained from a partner in a previous message exchange.

Strategies can be combined to ensure parameter values are resolved. This can be implemented either on engine/infrastructure level or on process model level (using fault handlers).

3   Parameterized Processes in BPEL

In this section we show how parameterized processes can be defined in BPEL. The current BPEL specification [2] involves neither portType nor operation parameters. All portTypes and operations of participating WSs are coded in the activities defining interaction with WSs. In BPEL these activities are the *<invoke>*, *<receive>* and *<reply>* activities; portType and operation names are specified by activity attribute values. Since BPEL definitions are representation of a WS-flow model in text and all portTypes and operations are also strings, it is only natural to be able to substitute any attribute value with any string. Such processes that include parameterized attributes are not executable for the simple reason that there is no way to provide the process instances with these missing values. Therefore we introduce an extension to the BPEL meta-model that accommodates the needed parameter values evaluation – the one described in the previous section. For this reason we define an extension to the standard elements section of the *<invoke>* activity. The *<evaluate>* extension is the meta-model element that corresponds to the mechanism to compute parameter values. The code in Listing 1 presents an example.

The attributes of the *<evaluate>* element are as follows:

- *activated* - has the values of *"yes"* or *"no"* and states whether the evaluation is enabled; *"yes"* means that the calculation has to be performed.
- *changeType* – specifies the evaluation strategy.
- *substitute* – used for passing input/output parameter values for strategy computation mechanism.

```
<process name="Process_name"> ...
<invoke name="activity" partnerLink="partnerLink" portType="portType"
operation="operation" inputVariable="..." outputVariable="...">
    <evaluate activated="yes|no" changeType = "static |
    portType/operation | query | fromVariable" substitute="value"/>
</invoke> ...
</process>
```

Listing 1. An example representation of the *<evaluate>* extension in BPEL

A summary the mapping of the evaluation strategies on BPEL is shown in Table 1. We do not recommend the use of a static strategy directly mapped to the *changeType* attribute in BPEL. Having the evaluate element though, allows us to enforce another type of strategy at run time [4]; appropriate tooling (for process instance monitoring) is needed.

Table 1. Mapping the evaluation strategies to BPEL constructs – an overview

Strategy	activated	changeType	substitute
Static	*"no"*	Any alternative	substitute value for another alternative
	"yes"	*"static"*	Concrete portType and operation
Prompt	*"yes"*	*"portType/ operation"*	portType, operation names provided by user
Query	*"yes"*	*"query"*	Query identifier / In-line query (string)
From variable	*"yes"*	*"fromVariable"*	Expression pointing to variable containing parameter values

We have extended the open-source engine ActiveBPEL [1] to implement the *<evaluate>* extension. For each strategy type an on-purpose mechanism has been implemented. Additional data structures have been defined for each parameterized activity and get populated with parameter values at run time after a strategy has been executed. A special-purpose invocation handler has been implemented; it generates dynamically a call to one of the ports implementing the discovered portType/operation [5]. Other implementation additions are: an extended parser for BPEL processes containing the *<evaluate>* element and the strategies, data structures storing data related to each process instance and its parameterized activities, portTypes and operations names, port locations, strategy. A monitoring tool has been implemented to track the execution of all process instances. It is instrumental especially for the *"prompt"* strategy; the tool is used to prompt users to supply the required parameter values. Currently our implementation relies on a simple component for executing the query strategy because of missing standardized approach to describing WS semantics and QoS.

4   Conclusions and Future Work

Parameterized processes *aim at standardization* of process models and improve process flexibility and reusability. Flexibility by adaptation and flexibility by avoiding change [4] are supported by the proposed approach.

Parameterization simplifies WS-flow models. The simplified *control flow* (reduced number of activities and eliminated need for Dead Path Elimination [6]), yields performance improvement. *Fault handling* and *compensation* in parameterized processes require special care. *Fine tuning* of WS-flows is possible by adjusting parameter values' evaluation criteria. Missing semantic description standard and incomplete QoS models affect the search and discovery of WS types and impair a full-fledged application of the approach. It is possible to model both *synchronous* and *asynchronous communication* modes with parameterized activities. The asynchronous communication mode faces difficulties due to the insufficient capabilities to express guaranteed delivery of functionality on behalf of the partner as a combination of two one-way operations. The partner WS can return a result using the *ReplyTo* field [7] of the messages sent by the process, the operation name exposed by the process for the return call, and other correlation data.

Our future work includes experimenting with parameterizing other activity types, variables, transition conditions, and the corresponding infrastructure implementation.

References

1. Active BPEL. August 2004. http://www.activebpel.org/
2. Curbera, F. et al.: BPEL4WS Specification Version 1.1. May 2003.
3. Karastoyanova, D., Buchmann, A.: Automating the development of Web Service compositions using templates. In Proc. of GPA Workshop, Informatik2004, 2004.
4. Karastoyanova, D., Buchmann, A.: Extending Web Service Flow Models to Provide for Adaptability. In Proc. BPMSOA Workshop, OOPSLA '04, October 2004.
5. Karastoyanova, D., Leymann, F., Buchmann, A.: Extending BPEL for Run Time Adaptability. In Proc. of EDOC'05, 2005.
6. Leymann, F., Roller, D.: Production Workflow. Concepts and Techniques. Prentice Hall Inc., 2000.
7. Weerawarana, S. et al.: Web Services Platform Architecture. Prentice Hall 2005.

Dynamic Policy Management on Business Performance Management Architecture

Teruo Koyanagi[1], Mari Abe[1], Gaku Yamamoto[1], and Jun Jang Jeng[2]

[1] IBM Tokyo Research Laboratory,
Yamato-shi, Kanagawa-ken, Japan
{teruok, maria, yamamoto}@jp.ibm.com
[2] IBM T.J. Watson Research Center,
Yorktown Heights, New York, United States
jjjeng@us.ibm.com

Abstract. Business performance management (BPM) is a new approach for an enterprise to improve their capabilities for sensing and responding to business situations. In a diverse and fast-changing business environment, an enterprise needs to adapt itself to any unexpected changes. For BPM, such changes imply changes of the models and services that support BPM. This paper discusses an implementation of BPM with the focus on dynamically adapting its services. We will present the motivation, concept and architecture of the dynamic change mechanisms. First we define a set of configurations as a policy, and also define its consistency through an application context. Then we propose an architectural overview including a policy management service as an implementation of consistency management.

1 Introduction

Business performance management is a new approach for an enterprise to improve their capabilities of sensing and responding to business situations [1]. Its functionality covers data capturing, metric realization, situation detection, decision making, action rendering and business analytics. Business performance management evolves from business process management that is aimed to capture enterprise behavior in a canonical form and to automate encoded operations as much as possible. Business processes themselves are realized utilizing service based process modeling languages, such as BPEL4WS [2]. While business process management is focused on operational aspects, business *performance* management puts more emphases on improving the quality of an organization. In this paper, we use the BPM to refer business performance management. Similar to business process management systems, BPM systems can be implemented in many ways. We have found Service Oriented Architecture (SOA) [3] is particularly suitable for building management services and BPM systems.

In a diverse and fast-changing business environment, an enterprise needs to adapt itself to any unexpected changes and make corresponding adjustment in the areas such as processes, IT systems etc. For the area of BPM, such changes imply the dynamic changes of the models and services that support BPM. Consequently, BPM system is expected to cope with the changes and change itself correspondingly. The

B. Benatallah, F. Casati, and P. Traverso (Eds.): ICSOC 2005, LNCS 3826, pp. 539–544, 2005.

characteristics of SOA such as modularity and adaptivity make itself a good architectural principle upon which the BPM system can be built.

The concepts of dynamic change management are discussed in previous works [4, 5, 6, 7]. They include the idea of maintaining consistency during changes. Their concepts of consistency are considered to be guaranteed if the modified component is not included in the execution of any transaction context. Most of these works define their consistency criteria on the basis of explicit inter-component interactions, and then propose management methods of dynamic software evolution to maintain the consistencies. However, the fact that it is difficult to maintain consistency among a number of configurations within an application context hinders most efforts. Such difficulties would come from the loosely-coupled services which do not have the explicit interaction that has been defined among them although those services may have semantic relationships through the application context.

In this paper, we would like to describe the mechanism of using policies to manage BPM systems. We use the BPM as our focus area in this paper although the technology itself is generic. It can be applied to another service-oriented computing platform [8] that is aimed to maintain its consistency while changing configurations of services without stopping the system.

Firstly, we briefly introduce a dynamic reconfiguration for a BPM architecture in Section 2. Then we explain concepts of dynamic policy management in the BPM architecture in Section 3. The architectural overview of managing the consistencies of BPM services is shown in Section 4 and we conclude this paper in Section 5.

2 Dynamic Reconfiguration for a BPM Architecture

A BPM system is built as an SOA with supporting functions such as monitoring for business metrics and for detecting situations, and abilities to perform actions. All of the BPM services can be configured dynamically based on new change requirements from the business demands. Also, a lot of application contexts are generated to monitor various points of views of business situations. In this section, an example and the concept of dynamic reconfiguration of BPM applications based on policies are described.

Let us consider an order process that needs inventory management as an example, such as a PC order process from the Web. Stock for each model of PC is prepared based on how many PCs are ordered in certain interval. In this application, as shown in Fig. 1, three components of the services are used. Monitor is the component to observe the counts of the ordered items. Forecast Provider is also a key performance indicator (KPI) calculator to predict consumption for a given strategy. Inventory Manager provides an action to keep sufficient stocks to respond to the predicted consumption.

Initially, all orders from customers are considered with equal weight of service level for preparing stock. Therefore, the Monitor records all customers' orders into one set of counts, and the Forecast Provider gives one set of predictions. However, in fact, customers are categorized into two different types: the gold customers who request high-performance machines and the regular customers who request low-cost machines.

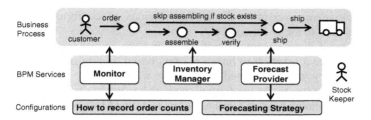

Fig. 1. An example of a BPM system: a PC order process

To respond to the gold customers' demands to be prioritized, it is necessary to change the monitoring method and the forecasting strategy to be biased for gold customers. However, the change must be applied without stopping the system, because the service should be provided 24 hours a day, 365 days a year. Additionally, even though both services are provided independently, their configurations are dependent on the application context, in which the order counts is observed and consumption is predicted based on the counts.

This is a typical case in which an external management function, called *dynamic policy management*, is required to maintain consistency among configurations.

3 Dynamic Policy Management

In the previous section, BPM applications are customized to respond to business policies. Such a customization consists of a number of configurations which are deployed into actual components of services. It implies that the BPM system is desired to support functions to handle such a configuration set dynamically.

One of the desired functions to dynamically adapt BPM applications to business policies is a runtime consistency management. For instance, it is the case of inconsistent that an event is issued after changing its producer to introduce a new format before its consumers have not changed yet for the new one. Basically, when a configuration is changed, it is necessary to avoid activating of the changed component during transition. In addition, we need to consider cases that configurations of multiple components are changed. In such case, the dependent configurations must be applied atomically for the application context which employs them.

In this section, we present a dynamic policy management function that maintains the consistency of configurations by categorizing them into three levels of a runtime application context.

A *policy* is a general rule about how to operate a BPM application in accordance with a business demand [1]. It is broken down into a set of configurations of the BPM services used in the application. It is important that the configuration set is defined externally as a policy. BPM services are provided by corresponding components in the BPM system.

A *configuration* is a component which is executed to changes a set of parameters or externalized logics of another component (called *customized component*). Configurations are identified by names which are associated with customization points of components, and they are also labeled with versions to identify them in the change history. A *consistency version set* includes versions of configurations to specify which changes need to apply consistently.

The *application context* is an execution path including the sequence of service employments which provide a function to business users based on a business policy. To be consistent with policy, the customized components which provide the services in an application context have to be configured with the same configuration set. Therefore the consistency among a set of configurations is defined by considering the ranges of the application context.

While applying configurations, the states of the customized components must be guaranteed not to be executing in any application contexts. Because changing a configuration in the middle of the context provides a chance to change the dependent artifacts of the rest of execution. It causes a malfunction behavior.

In addition, the relationships among configurations must be also guaranteed in an application context. In the BPM architecture, these relationships come from business policies. Thereby, in this paper, we categorize the consistency into three cases by the level of expansion range of the application context, as shown in Fig. 2

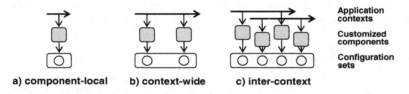

a) component-local   b) context-wide   c) inter-context

Fig. 2. Types of consistency of configuration sets

For a), *component-local-consistency* is guaranteed if a configuration transaction is completed while the configuration is not currently executing in any application context. This level of consistency is mandatory for dynamic reconfiguration, and b) and c) are the options used to preserve application semantics.

For b), context-wide-consistency is guaranteed if component-local-consistency is maintained for each configuration used in the application context, and based on it, a set of configurations which implements a policy is used together in an application context. In this case, consistency is represented by a configuration set which is provided externally. This is necessary, for example, the set of configuration which includes the Monitor's configuration and Forecasting strategy must be used together during an application context which is an interval of stock preparation described in Section 2.

For c), *inter-context-consistency* is guaranteed if context-wide-consistency is maintained for each context, and in addition, the entire application context that is running concurrently is configured with the same set of configurations. In the example of the PC order process, it is assumed that there is an interval for each model of PCs. Because the configuration change invoked by a drastic policy change, such as adding a new axis of customer type, affects all the application contexts, the changes must be applied to them synchronously.

4 Architectural Overview

As described in the previous section, a consistency version set represents a set of constrained configurations that must be applied to the components executed in the same application context. It is defined at design time, but at runtime it does not depend only on the static component structures, but also on the dynamic characteristics of the application context as described in the previous section. In this section, a framework to maintain consistency of the consistent version set within an application context is described. This can be considered as a hybrid method between dynamic relationship management in application contexts, and atomic configuration deployment that maintains the consistency of the configuration set.

The *policy management service* provides a runtime management function for configuration sets. This service consists of the following components: *session factory*, *configuration registry*, and *version coordinator*, as shown in Fig. 3.

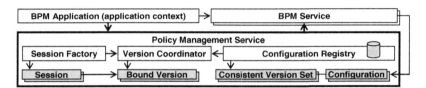

Fig. 3. Architectural overview of the dynamic policy management

The application which employs the customized components creates a *session* for each application context correspondingly. According to the sessions, the right configurations are provided to the customized components in the context.

The configuration registry maintains registered information of the consistent version sets which represent a kind of dependencies defined at design time. As a function of the configuration registry, the new configurations and consistent version sets can be registered in the registry without stopping the system. Retaining the current versions is another responsibility of the configuration registry. The configuration registry provides an administrative interface to deploy configuration sets and to specify current versions.

When a configuration is used in the session firstly, the current version of the configuration and its constrained versions are associated with the session. When the other configuration is used after that, at first it is searched from the associated versions. If it does not exist, it is requested to the configuration registry. The version coordinator maintains association between the session and versions of configurations.

5 Conclusion

In a diverse and fast-changing business environment, an enterprise needs to adapt itself to any unexpected changes. In the areas of BPM, in order to adapt already-deployed BPM applications to such business environments, it is imperative to provide dynamic reconfiguration capabilities. The BPM system is build as an SOA with supporting functions for tasks such as monitoring business metrics, detecting situations, and performing actions. Therefore an application in the BPM system is customized to adapt to a business policy by configuring each service component.

In this paper, a policy is defined as a configuration set, which is deployed into actual components. Consistency management of the configuration set is a key to realize the dynamic reconfiguration, thereby we categorized the consistency into three cases based on the level of expansion range of the application context; component-local, context-wide and inter-context. Then we proposed an architectural overview including a policy management service as an implementation of consistency management.

To allow business users to change business policies, it is necessary for BPM system not only to provide the runtime mechanisms but also to support designing and deploying business policies. In the future work, we will investigate what kind of supporting method can be provided.

References

1. Jeng, J.J., Chang, H., Bhaskaran, K.: On Architecting Business Performance Management Grid for Adaptive Enterprises. In *Proceedings of the 2005 Symposium on Applications and the Internet* (SAINT ' 05). (2005) 110–116
2. Thatte, S. et al.: *Process Execution Language for Web Services Version 1.1*. ftp://www6. software.ibm.com/software/developer/library/ws-bpel.pdf (2003)
3. Papazoglou, M.P.: Service-Oriented Computing: Concepts, Characteristics and Directions. In *Proceedings of the Fourth International Conference on Web Information Systems Engineering*, IEEE Computer Society (2003)
4. Kramer, J., Magee, J.: The Evolving Philosophers Problem: Dynamic Change Management. *IEEE Transactions on Software Engineering* 16 (1990) 1293–1306
5. Warren, I., Sommerville, I.: A Model for Dynamic reconfiguration which Preserves Application Integrity. In *Proceedings of the 3rd International Conference on Configurable Distributed Systems* (ICCDS'96), IEEE Computer Society (1996) 81–88
6. Chen, X., Simons, M.: A Component Framework for Dynamic Reconfiguration of Distributed Systems. In *Proceedings of the IFIP/ACM Working Conference on Component Deployment*. Volume 2370. (2002) 82–96
7. Truyen, E. et al.: Dynamic and Selective Combination of Extensions in Component-Based Applications. In *Proceedings of the 23rd International Conference on Software Engineering* (ICSE'01). (2001)
8. Lazovik, A., Aiello, M., Papazoglou, M.: Associating Assertions with Business Processes and Monitoring their Execution. In *Proceedings of International Conference on Service Oriented Computing* (ICSOC'04). (2004) 94–104

A Lightweight Formal Framework for Service-Oriented Applications Design

Aliaksei Yanchuk, Alexander Ivanyukovich, and Maurizio Marchese

Department of Information and Communication Technology,
University of Trento, I-38050 Povo (Tn), Italy
`aliaksei.yanchuk@gmail.com, a.ivanyukovich@dit.unitn.it,`
`maurizio.marchese@unitn.it`

Abstract. Leveraging service oriented programming paradigm would significantly affect the way people build software systems. This paper contributes to the above goal proposing a lightweight formal framework capable of capturing the essential components of service-oriented programming paradigm.

1 Introduction

The increasing complexity of the software systems has constantly led to the evolution of new programming paradigms: from functional, to object-oriented, to component-oriented, to service-oriented to name a few. Typically each successive paradigm has introduced new design approaches at an higher level of abstraction, encapsulating and sometime adjusting underlying levels. Service-oriented programming paradigm has naturally focused on the next level of abstraction over object- and component-oriented ones [1]. Established and mature paradigms are supported by well-defined analysis and design methodologies (e.g. UML notation) and supporting tools (e.g. Rational Rose). Such methodologies and tools have emerged and have become highly usable and effective due to a significant effort towards the formalization of the underlying fundamental concepts of object-oriented and component-oriented paradigms, together with an evolving and shared understanding of the abilitating technologies.

Although, some foundational concepts of service-oriented design are starting to be addressed, [2, 3, 4], proper mathematical foundations and service-oriented formalized principles and concepts are still lacking. We think that such formalization is crucial for the identification of suitable software design methodologies and supporting tools capable to meet the specific challenges of service oriented applications, e.g. composability, adaptability and platform independence.

This paper contributes to the above effort by proposing a lightweight formal framework capable of capturing the essential components of service-oriented programming paradigm. Our approach is based on the critical assessment of existing design formalization techniques, mainly in the object and component oriented programming domains. Formalization in these software paradigms covers aspects mainly related to system refinement (such as modules composition techniques,

B. Benatallah, F. Casati, and P. Traverso (Eds.): ICSOC 2005, LNCS 3826, pp. 545–551, 2005.

operations parallelism and analysis of intrinsic constraints in distributed systems. Such formalization is grounded on refinement calculus [5] through the use of refinement techniques to the most used methods for monotonic composition of programs (namely procedures), parallel composition and data encapsulation [6]. Parallel actions in software systems were modelled in [6] by their atomic representations, allowing to utilize methods originally developed for sequential systems. A mathematical foundation for object-oriented paradigm is presented in [7], where message-based automata for modelling object behavior in terms of cleanroom software engineering methodology [8] is presented. There software refinements is approached through a mathematical description of all possible transformations, capable to ensure refinement correctness with respect to other software objects.

In[9], a descriptive functional semantic for the component-oriented design is proposed and used for the definition of a formal model for the interfaces of the components. This work investigates the relationships between compositional operators for synchronous and parallel components designs and system refinement techniques. In contrast to previously referenced works, this component-oriented design approach operates with a black-box interface view on the system's components. Further research in component-based design [10] has led to precise definition of components through their behavioral characteristics as well as to the introduction of parallel composition techniques with feedbacks, enabling modelling of concurrent execution and interaction. However, functional time dependency introduced in [9, 10] does not take into account possible temporal execution of the functionality specified within the interfaces' contracts, but rather limits itself to input/output interrelations. It is important to note that the support for such temporal execution sequences is particularly important in service-oriented applications.

The present paper leverages from the above research on software design formalization approaches and aims to extend them to service-oriented programming paradigm. The structure of the paper is organized as follows. In Section 2 we briefly discuss existing approaches to Service-Oriented Architectures (SOA) and their main components. We then propose formal definitions SOA main components, namely: service, service-oriented environment,service-oriented application. Further elaboration of these models with respect to data transition properties allowed us to introduce a classification scheme for service-oriented applications in Section 3. Conclusions and future work close the paper.

2   Formal Foundation for Service-Oriented Applications Design

Service-Oriented Architectures (SOAs) [1, 11, 12] are emerging to support the specificity of service oriented applications. In a SOA, the software resources are considered "services," which are well defined, self-contained, and are independent of the state or context of other services. Services have a published interface and communicate with each other. The basic SOA defines an interaction between software agents as an exchange of messages between service requesters and service providers. This interaction involve the publishing, finding and binding of services. The essential goal of a SOA is to enable general-purpose interoperability among existing technologies and extensibility to future purposes and architectures. Simply put, an SOA is an architectural style, inspired by the Internet and the Web, for enabling extensible interoperability. In our opinion, the "basic SOA trinity" of a service, broker, and client doesn't display enough features to capture all service-orientation features . It is rather a *platform pattern*, that is used to design robust, essentially distributed applications and environments. Complimentary to the platform pattern, a service orientation *principle* may be formulated as "a set of computing capabilities of a service-oriented environment for any given moment τ, determined by the kind of the dynamically available (deployed) services". Particular set of conventions for software designed for such environment makes up particular Service-Oriented Architectures.

From the above reasoning, we propose that:

$$SOA = Principle + Platform \tag{1}$$

The importance of this statement emerges in the context of Enterprise Application Integration in large organization: in fact it is practically impossible to provide a universal platform that would strike a perfect fit for all tasks. On the other hand, the service orientation principle enables different products to be designed independently but ensuring their potential integration viability. We believe that in order to fully exploit SOA the following entities must be considered on the same importance level in a conceptual framework for service orientation: individual services, service-oriented environments, and service-oriented applications. In the next sub-sections, we provide a formal definition for the proposed entities in our conceptual framework.

2.1 Logical Service, Service-Oriented Environment and Service-Oriented Application

In our framework, a given logical service i is deployed into an environment to provide the useful functionality f_i, expressed as a programmatic interface I_i. Important feature of a service is its capability to interact dynamically, in the given environment, with other services and non-service entities (such as end users).

Logical service' implementation is thus a set of coordinated and interacting processes:

$$S_i =< P_1^i, P_2^i, \ldots, P_n^i, \Lambda >, \tag{2}$$

where S_i — logical service instance, P_k^i — k^{th} process implementing the logical service functionality f_i through the programmatic interface I_i , and Λ — network communication function between individual processes.

Service-oriented environment consists of a finite countable set of all accessible logical services implementation for the given moment of time τ:

$$Env_\tau =< S_1, S_2, \ldots, S_n >, \tag{3}$$

where n — number of logical services deployed in the environment.

Overall functionality F of a service-oriented application A is determined by the logical services involved in the provision of the application in a given environment for a given moment of time τ:

$$F_A = < S1^A, S_2^A, \ldots, S_n^A >_{Env_\tau} \tag{4}$$

Moreover, we introduce the *Application Functionality directing graph*, defined as:

$$V_A = (F_A, G) \tag{5}$$

having vertexes from the F_A set and verge set G formalizing the coordination between individual logical services of the F_A set.

Finally, the Service-Oriented application A may be formalized as the set:

$$A = < F_A, V_A > \tag{6}$$

The defined service-oriented application A is characterized by the following properties:

- to achieve computation goal, at least two logical service must be involved (otherwise SOA degrades to client-server architecture);
- services involved in the application must "coordinate" their work to solve the computational problem. Here, we mean "coordination" as any kind of interaction between involved services that aims to achieve the application goal. Coordination may be implemented by different means, including but not limited to, exchanging data, exchanging messages, service provisioning, service control, service monitoring etc.

  The presence of the coordination capability is required in a service-oriented application due to the fact that a consistent implementation of a service must be designed to be context-invariant [12]: i.e., particular service must not have knowledge about the application it participates in. In our framework, the Application Functionality directing graph, V_A, defined in equation 5, is the formalization of such capability. In concrete application, V_A may be expresses with existing implementation frameworks for capturing services processes, such as BPEL [1] and WS-Coordination. [2]

3   The Application Class Concept

In order to ground a service-oriented design methodology on our proposed framework, the following steps must be considered: first application requirements are collected to drive functionalities definition; then application's functionalities are decomposed into individual services; thus the appropriate Application Functionality graph is created; finally to realize a concrete application A, both service functionality and directing graph must be implemented.

---

[1] http://www-106.ibm.com/developerworks/library/ws-bpel/
[2] http://www-106.ibm.com/developerworks/library/ws-coor/

In the following, we introduce the concept of the service-oriented application "class" in order to capture general properties of A and to support the system architect to devise appropriate design strategies (i.e. design patterns, implementation templates, etc..).

In general, the computational task of a given service-oriented application is to process all incoming requests (tuples) from a set T_{in} in such a way that processing will comply with requirements determined by specified Quality of Service agreement set, QoS [13]. The feasibility of a given QoS requirements set depends on the implementation of the individual services involved in the service-oriented application A, on the implementation of the Application Functionality graph V_A and on the global service environment Env_τ.

In our opinion the structure as well as the access method of the application's memory plays a major role in determining the types and sub-types of a specific application. For any service-oriented application, A, there is a data space, $\hat{T}_A$, containing all data of the application

$$\hat{T}_A = M_A \cup T_A \cup \psi_A \qquad (7)$$

where M_A — tuple set capturing temporary application memory, T_A — persistent application memory, and ψ_A — virtual tuple set, encapsulating all tuples that were deleted from temporary and persistent memories. T_A includes all those tuples that were delivered to the A, except for those that left it (passed on further or discarded), *having durable state* — a state having impact on business processes. Data integrity [14] implies that, during application runtime, the incoming tuples T_{in} set is reflected on entire set $\hat{T}_A$, that is:

$$\forall t_i \in T_{in} : \hat{t}_j \in \hat{T}_A, t_i \to \hat{t}_j \qquad (8)$$

For any application A, one or more data entry and data exit[3] points may be established. To implement the specified functionality of the service-oriented application A, the following two main scenarios are possible and we use then to define the basis *classes* of a service-oriented application:

- Each tuple t_i should pass a handling path through number of services. To achieve this, it is sufficient that the service-sender would be able to pass the tuple t_i to service-recipient. These type of applications constitutes the *flow* class service-oriented application.
- Each tuple t_i is saved in a shared data space where it is simultaneously accessible to all services that would be involved in the tuple handling; in this case, the key task of such *cooperation* class service-oriented application is establishing unambiguous access sharing to the t_i tuple and mutual coordination.

Some real applications may find it necessary to combine features of both classes. With such application, *fork* and *join* points may be established in the

---

[3] Except for the cases where application is designed to retain data indefinitely — see accumulating applications as defined in [15].

Application Functionality graph. Fork point is transfer of tuple from exclusive service' memory into shared data space, and join point is tuple transfer from shared tuple space into service' exclusive memory.

4   Conclusions

In this paper we have extended the definition of SOA and we have proposed a lightweight formal framework capable of capturing SOA main components. This formalization allows us to explore the structure of a SOA and to introduce a service-oriented application classification schema. In particular tuple access methods (exclusively owned/ shared) lead to establishing two main classes of service-oriented application: the flow-class and the cooperation-class. However much more work must be done and is currently in progress. In particular, in-depth exploration of the introduced classification, class topologies patterns, QoS aspects of SOA, patterns for SOA. A more exhaustive report on current work can be found in [15].

References

1. Gustavo Alonso, Fabio Casati, Harumi Kuno, and Vijay Machiraju. *Web Services Concepts, Architectures and Applications*. Springer, 2004.
2. Mike P. Papazoglou and Jian Yang. Design methodology for web services and business processes. In *TES '02: Proceedings of the Third International Workshop on Technologies for E-Services*, pages 54–64, London, UK, 2002. Springer-Verlag.
3. R.M. Dijkman and M. Dumas. Service-oriented design: A multi-viewpoint approach. *International Journal on Cooperative Information Systems*, 13(14):338–378, December 2004.
4. Dick Quartel, Remco Dijkman, and Marten van Sinderen. Methodological support for service-oriented design with isdl. In *ICSOC '04: Proceedings of the 2nd international conference on Service oriented computing*, pages 1–10, New York, NY, USA, 2004. ACM Press.
5. R. J. R. Back. Correctness preserving program refinements: Proof theory and applications, 1980.
6. K. Sere and R. J. R. Back. From action systems to modular systems. In M. Bertran M. Naftalin, T. Denvir, editor, *FME'94: Industrial Benefit of Formal Methods*, pages 1–25. Springer-Verlag, 1994.
7. B. Rumpe and C. Klein. Automata describing object behavior, 1996.
8. D. Craigen, S. Gerhart, and Ralston T.J. An international survey of industrial applications of formal methods. Technical report, National Technical Information Service, Springfield, VA, USA, 1993.
9. Manfred Broy. Towards a mathematical concept of a component and its use. *Software - Concepts and Tools*, 18(3):137–, 1997.
10. Manfred Broy. Compositional refinement of interactive systems modelled by relations. *Lecture Notes in Computer Science*, 1536:130–149, 1998.
11. Mike P. Papazoglou. Service-oriented computing: Concepts, characteristics and directions. In *WISE '03: Proceedings of the Fourth International Conference on Web Information Systems Engineering*, page 3, Washington, DC, USA, 2003. IEEE Computer Society.

12. by Douglas K. Barry. *Web Services and Service-Oriented Architecture: The Savvy Manager's Guide*. Morgan Kaufmann Publishers, 2003.
13. James Webber Ph.D. Sandeep Chatterjee Ph.D. *Developing Enterprise Web Services: An Architect's Guide*. Prentice Hall PTR., 2003.
14. Robert W. Taylor and Randall L. Frank. Codasyl data-base management systems. *ACM Comput. Surv.*, 8(1):67–103, 1976.
15. A. Yanchuk, A. Ivanyukovich, and M. Marchese. Technical report $dit-05-059$: Towards a mathematical foundation for service-oriented applications design. Technical report, Department of Information and Communication Technology, University of Trento, http://eprints.biblio.unitn.it/, 01 July, 2005.

A MDE Approach for Power Distribution Service Development

Cristina Marin, Philippe Lalanda, and Didier Donsez

Equipe Adele, Laboratoire LSR, 220 rue de la Chimie,
Domaine Universitaire, BP 53, 38041 Grenoble Cedex 9, France
`first_name.last_name@imag.fr`

Abstract. The integration of business and operational processes is today of major importance in a wide range of industries. The challenge is to
seamlessly integrate software applications supporting business activities
and field devices belonging to the plant floor. It requires to build Internet-
scale distributed systems in complex, heterogeneous environments characterized by stringent requirements regarding security and evolution in
particular. In order to meet these requirements, distributed architectures
based on the service-oriented paradigm have been proposed. This paper
argues that the service-oriented development is too technology-driven.
We propose a reusable MDE approach for service development in power
distribution industry where the developer focuses on application logic.
The approach is currently tested for a service-platform based on the
OSGi technology.

1 Introduction

The integration of business and operational processes is today of major importance in a wide range of industries, from the manufacturing industry to the
utilities one. The challenge is to seamlessly integrate software applications that
support business activities and field devices belonging to the plant floor. The
emergence of the Internet and the proliferation of small communicating devices
permit to consider a stronger coupling between previously autonomous processes.
This is the next wave of e-business for it opens the way to creation of innovative
value-added e-services based on data regularly gathered from such devices.

This last point is strongly investigated today. Many companies are today
struggling to provide innovative e-services to their customers in order to differentiate themselves and improve their satisfaction and loyalty. For instance,
in the power management domain, electrical manufacturers are now providing
their customers with e-services for analyzing power consumption, power quality,
power devices maintenance.

However, it is clear that this goal of seamless integration is far from easy
to achieve. It requires to build Internet-scale distributed systems in complex,
heterogeneous environments characterized by stringent requirements regarding
security and evolution in particular. In order to meet these requirements, innovative distributed architectures have been recently proposed [1]. They rely on the

B. Benatallah, F. Casati, and P. Traverso (Eds.): ICSOC 2005, LNCS 3826, pp. 552–557, 2005.

notion of software services [2] used at different architectural levels and generally running on heterogeneous platforms.

Service-oriented architectures are indeed very promising: they actually provide the level of flexibility and scalability required to build industrial e-services. However, service-oriented computing is today essentially technology-driven. Most available platforms focus on the technology allowing to publish and compose services and to make them communicate. Few works have been initiated on tools and techniques supporting the design of service-oriented applications [3] [4].

This paper introduces a service development environment for the power distribution domain. The solution proposed uses a Model-Driven Engineering (MDE) approach [5] [6]. The interest is twofold. First, by applying this approach, we obtain a service design environment independent of any service-technology. Then, the MDE's model transformation techniques help to automate the service development by taking into account a target technology.

The paper is organized as follows. Section 2 introduces our motivating problems. Section 3 presents our proposition. Finally, section 4 concludes the paper and presents the perspectives of our work.

2   Industrial e-Services

The remote exploitation of industrial data embedded in smart devices represents today a major field of investigation in diverse domains like automation, building management or power distribution [7]. Manufacturers actually intend to leverage data embedded in their devices in order to provide innovative e-services to their customers and so to differentiate themselves from their competitors. This trend is made possible by two important technological evolutions. First, devices rely more and more on software and can be connected to an intranet network or to the Internet. The second major enabler is the Internet development which offers simple and inexpensive connections to most industrial sites in the world.

Industrial e-services are based on data that are regularly collected in the plant floor. Data generally supports mediation operations (aggregation, transformation, formatting operations, etc.) before being used by business-oriented applications [8] [9]. Integrating disparate information sources in a timely manner is a complex activity. In the power distribution domain, this is complicated by the environments heterogeneity (in terms of topology, network and security policies) and by their dynamic nature.

Current architectures designed to gather field devices data are organized into three tiers. The first one corresponds to field devices. The second tier is made of gateway platforms that perform device's data gathering, a first data mediation treatment. Finally, the last tier is made of powerful Internet servers. These architectures are very heterogeneous. Gateways may, for instance, run an OSGi service-platform (see www.osgi.org), especially designed for small communicating platforms. At the Internet server level we may deal with a J2EE platform with powerful treatment abilities.

Service-oriented computing turns out to be very beneficial in this context. In particular, the late-binding property of services brings the flexibility that is needed in extremely dynamic environments.

We consider that the development and administration activities for data-gathering e-services are not well supported today. For instance, current OSGi platforms provide a basic technology to describe services (usually through XML forms), publish, compose them and allow interactions [10]. But there is no tool to facilitate the use of this technology (which is arguably difficult to master) and no support regarding the design of service-oriented (OSGi-oriented in that case) applications. The result is that, as it is the case in other computing areas, applications are hard to develop, test and maintain. This paper presents a MDE approach for such service development environment.

3   SOA for Power Distribution e-Service

As previously said, service development is strongly influenced by the decision of using a given technology. In our case, this is a performance trade-off when it comes to develop rapidly e-services for the power distribution domain. Our experience in the development of such services has convinced us of the following things:

- the developer cannot handle all the technologies needed to develop the application;
- the developer should concentrate more on the application logic and not on the technologies needed to publish, discover and compose services.

We consider thus that it is important to provide developers with software tools to build and compose software services.

To do so, we have applied a Model Driven Engineering (MDE) approach to build an effective design environment. MDE is becoming a widely accepted approach for developing complex distributed applications. It advocates the use of models as the key artifacts in all phases of development, from system specification and analysis, to design and testing [11]. Thus models are no longer contemplative artifacts but really productive ones. Separation of concerns is met in the separation of the business logic from the underlying platform technology. Each model usually addresses one concern, independently from the rest of the issues involved in the construction of the system. Models transformations provide a chain that enables the automated implementation of a system right from the different models defined for it.

First, we have built a domain metamodel (figure 1) that contains the business logic for our domain of interest. It is composed of five concepts that we consider to be key concepts for the electrical domain.

The `Driver` abstracts concepts needed to interact with field devices (for instance specific interaction protocols), to receive, optimize and redirect requests to the concerned equipments. The `Device` is the simplified representation of the industrial equipment. It sends requests via the `Driver` to the actual equipment

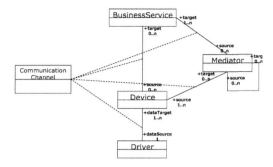

Fig. 1. Domain metamodel

from the plant floor. It also defines a data-collection strategy for acceding to the equipment that permits him to synchronize with this one. A `Mediator` is a high level concept used to transform (aggregate, integrate) data coming from one or more devices . The high level concept is the `BusinessService`. His functionality resides on device gathered data or aggregated data from mediators. For instance, in our domain a business service may be a power consumption forecast service. All these concepts interact through `Communication Channels`. For instance, a communication channel may define the data transmission protocol used to send data from one level (concept) to another.

Figure 2 illustrates the MDE process we have adopted to build the service development environment. For that, we have successively built two metamodels:

– The first one, `SOA MM` in the figure, is a general metamodel for service-oriented architectures. It contains common concepts of available service technologies. In the meantime, it is totally platform independent, thus allowing to describe a service-oriented architecture at a high level of abstraction. This metamodel does not make the object of our paper but, if interested, the reader can find additional information at (www-adele.imag.fr/SOA).

– The second one, `SOA Application MM for Power Distribution`, has been obtained by manually combining the previous metamodel describing general service-oriented architectures with the domain metamodel. It describes service-oriented architectures tailored for the electrical domain. It extends the previous SOA metamodel and specializes it to take into account the domain concepts. This former metamodel remains also platform independent but it includes now the domain business logic. Thus, we express our four basic concepts as services and integrate the communication channel as a connector concept. We have introduced three important communication channels according to domain specific interaction paradigms: the classical one corresponding to the client/server interaction (`RequestResponse-Connector`), the event communication abstracted by the `EventConnector` and the most interesting connection type - `PublishSubscribeConnector` - used to publish data from a service to another.

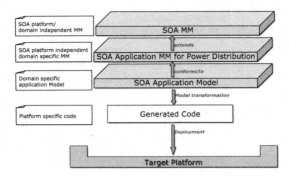

Fig. 2. MDE Approach for e-service power distribution development

The last metamodel was used as a starting point for the development of the service environment. Furthermore, it was to a large extent automatically obtained using the Eclipse's EMF project (see www.eclipse.org/emf). The so obtained environment can be used to describe a domain specific application model (SOA Application Model in our figure) using only metamodel terms. This description of an application is nevertheless abstract because we are not yet considering a specific service technology. We consider that this makes our solution reusable because even if the service technology is changed the application model will remain the same.

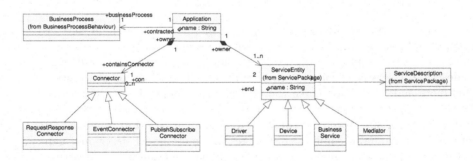

Fig. 3. Domain specific SOA metamodel

Then, the application model enters a code generation phase where a service technology is at last taken into consideration. The generated code can be then packaged and deployed on the target platform. The design environment is currently tested in real settings in the domain of power distribution for an OSGi-based e-services. The developer's job is considerably leveraged because all the OSGi-specific code is generated and he has to deal only with his application logic.

4   Conclusions and Perspectives

This paper presents an innovative approach for the development of e-services. It relies on the MDE technology that uses models to automate the code generation. The benefit we take from using the MDE approach is multiple. First, MDE permitted us to automatically obtain from a UML schema (our metamodel) a service development environment independent of any service technology. Then, another code generation phase helps us to automatically obtain the technology specific code of the described application. This leverages considerably the domain expert's work which in our vision is not necessarily a technology expert.

The approach is currently validated for OSGi based e-service development and in the future will be validated against the J2EE platform residing at the Internet server level of the presented data gathering architecture.

References

1. P. Lalanda. E-Services Infrastructure in Power Distribution. *IEEE Internet Computing*, May-June 2005.
2. M. N. Huhns and M. P. Singh. Service-Oriented Computing: Key Concepts and Principles. *IEEE Internet Computing*, 9:75–81, 2005.
3. D. Quartel et al. Methodological support for service-oriented design with ISDL. In *2st International Conference on Service-Oriented Computing*, 2004.
4. M.Tich and H. Giese. Seamless UML Support for Service-Based Software Architectures. In *FIDJI2003*, pages 128–138, 2003.
5. C. Atkinson and T. Kuhne. Model-driven Development: A Metamodeling Foundation. *IEEE Software*, pages 36–41, 2003.
6. B. Selic. The Pragramatics of Model -Driven Development. *IEEE Software*, pages 19–25, 2003.
7. I. F. Akyildiz et al. A Survey on Sensor Network Applications. *IEEE Communication Magazine*, 2002.
8. G. Wiederhold. Mediators in the architecture of future information systems. *IEEE Computer*, 25(3):3849, 1992.
9. P. Lalanda et al. An asynchronous mediation suite to integrate business and operational processes. submitted to IEEE Internet Computing, 2005.
10. H. Cervantes and R.S. Hal. Autonomous Adaptation to Dynamic Availability Using a Service-Oriented Component Model. In *Proceedings of the International Conference on Software Engineering*, 2004.
11. E. Seidewitz. What Models Mean. *IEEE Software*, pages 26–32, September 2003.

Semantic Web Services for Activity-Based Computing

E. Michael Maximilien, Alex Cozzi, and Thomas P. Moran

IBM Almaden Research Center,
650 Harry Road, San Jose, CA 95120, USA
{maxim, cozzi, tpmoran}@us.ibm.com

Abstract. Semantic Web services promise the addition of semantics annotations to Web services in a manner that enables automatic discovery, usage, and integration of services as part of every day processes. IBM's unified activity management (UAM) implements activity-centric computing concepts by representing human work in terms of activities that relate to each other using semantic information from the various contexts in which the activities are used. In this paper we explore how, using common domain-specific ontologies, we can make use of the semantic annotations added to Web services and our UAM environment, to produce dynamic and richer Web applications widgets and services.

1 Introduction

Human-based activities are best represented as informal loosely structured and semantically rich processes. Even when work activities are well-structured, for instance, using workflow systems, human realization of such workflows typically results in many variations of the different steps, while the same objectives are achieved. This is due to the executing context, which is difficult to predict or capture in workflows. Additionally, the loose realization is also simply due to human behaviors and work patterns which, unless humans are forcefully constrained, are typically loose and malleable [3].

Previous activity-based systems typically organize activities as shared tasks that can be easily modified and arranged to meet work patterns [4]. In addition to distributed task sharing capabilities, IBM's unified-activity management (UAM) [7, 8] computing environment incorporates the loose and malleable characteristics of human activities by representing activities as first-class OWL [5] instances that are interconnected using a semantic network of relationships representing the context and evolution of the activities.

As the majority of knowledge workers' activities involve some form of Web-based application, system, or services, it's easy to see that a UAM-based applications will necessarily use Web resources or be themselves completely Web-based. The addition of semantics to Web resources and Web services [2, 6] enables opportunities for creating semantically rich UAM-based applications and the ability to automate some parts of these applications (and the activities) using software agents. In this paper we investigate the initial use of semantic Web services (SWS) [6] with our UAM environment.

B. Benatallah, F. Casati, and P. Traverso (Eds.): ICSOC 2005, LNCS 3826, pp. 558–563, 2005.

2   Scenario: Use Case

To motivate how our UAM environment can benefit from SWSs we describe a use case scenario based on a simplified activity domain: reading group activities. Our domain involves a set of individual human actors (e.g., knowledge workers, researchers, or students) involved in sharing reading items. The reading items are varied; they are comprise books, book sections, articles, Web pages, and so on; they are contributed by all members of the group, which are assigned to read these items, comment on the contents, prioritize them, rate them, relate them, and make recommendations for new readings that can complement a particular reading item. An implicit goal of such reading group activities is to create new insights from the group's collaboration that otherwise would not be possible had the readings been done individually and separately.

3   Framework

IBM's UAM environment comprises a RDF datastore which keeps OWL instances for all activities, artifacts, actors, and their relationships according to the UAM upper and domain specific ontologies. To expose a services API to UAM that maintains the domain-specific semantics, we created a UAM operator ontology which allows the definition and generation of Web services representing the operations to create, add, modify, and find UAM objects.

The services parameters are typed using the domain-specific activity ontology. We maintain the semantics of the domain by creating OWL-S [9] *Profile* and partial *Process* descriptions for the generated services that are annotated with a domain ontology and a domain-specific activity ontology.

As an example, for our *Reading Group Activity* ontology we expose SWS with operations to *createReadingActity()*, *addBookReadingItem()*, *modifyReadingItem()* passing attributes such as author, description, and so on, according to ontologies for the domains *Reading Document* and *Reading Group Activity*. The generated services connect to an operator API exposed by the UAM environment which allow programmatic access and manipulation of the OWL instances in the datastore.

3.1   Activity Ontology

Figure 1 illustrates our UAM upper ontology. It constitutes the key concepts and relationships of every UAM-based application. This ontology is typically extended by domain-sepecific concepts and relationships that constitute the activities in that domain. The upper ontology defines three main concepts: (1) *uam:Activity* represents an activity—activities have subactivities, have artifacts, and involve actors; (2) *uam:Artifact* represents all non-agent (non-actor) resources—they are the passive resources that are part of activities; and (3) *uam:Actor* represents all active resources involved in an activity—these include human and software agents.

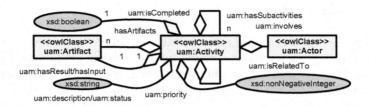

Fig. 1. UAM upper ontology

Activities have other predefined upper-level relationships to represent an activity's description, status, priority, results, and input. Further, every activity can be related to some other activity. Finally, as in real-life activities all activities have the notion of completeness and start out with this value as false. We leave it to the domain to specify when an activity transitions to the completed status state.

3.2   Operator Ontology

The UAM operator ontology specifies the necessary concepts and relationships for the definitions of the operations on the UAM environment. The operations enable external actors to operate on the UAM environment. We use the operator ontology as input to the generation of our semantic services. The operator ontology defines four primary concepts.

- *uam-op:Operator* represents a particular action on the domain's concepts. Every operator *operatesOn* a domain specific concept.
- *uam-op:Function* represents the active part of the operator. For instance a *Create* function represents operators whose actions result in newly created concept instances in the UAM datastore. Every function also associates with the necessary parameters that it requires.
- *uam-op:OperatorService* combines a series of operator instances into a service. This concept maps one-to-one to a SWS.
- *uam-op:OperatorCode* represents the procedural attachment of the code that gets executed in the UAM datastore when the operator is executed.

4   Demonstration

To demonstrate our UAM SWS, we created an application in a simple domain for which we could discover related SWS on the Web. This showed the feasibility of the system, resulted in a UAM lower ontology for the domain, and an approach to integrate SWS related to the domain. The domain in question is a simplified version of reading group activity. We discussed the primary use case scenario in Section 2.

To create our UAM lower ontology for the domain and annotate available Web services with the domain semantics, we created a *Reading Document* ontology. The main concepts of this ontology are as follows.

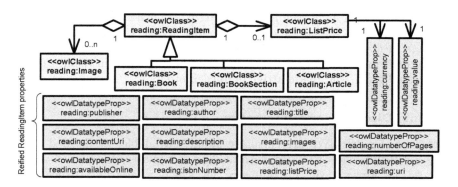

Fig. 2. Reading document ontology; showing only the concepts and reified relationships that are of concerns to *Book*-type documents

- *reading:ReadingItem* represents any physical or electronic item that can be read by human agents. This includes Web sites or Web pages as well as some printed materials, e.g., magazines.
- *reading:Book* represents a printed book. This does not include electronic versions (eBook) or audio versions of books. These could be modeled as subclasses of the generic *Book* concept.
- *reading:BookSection* represents a section of a book. This is an important concept in a reading group activity since members of the activity could agree to just read sections of a book (e.g., a page or a chapter).
- *reading:Article* represents a printed article or section of a magazine or a journal. We differentiate Web articles from articles since their properties are typically different. In particular, an article is part of a journal with a volume and issue number, has a publisher, has page numbers, has a title, and has a list of authors.
- *ListPrice* represents the price for the reading item. For a book this list price is the *value* and the *currency* that is usually listed on the back of the book.
- *Image* represents the cover art picture of the reading item (if any).

Figure 2 shows these concepts along with a reified list of the properties and their OWL types. A complete ontology of reading documents would encompass a lot more concepts and some further refinements of the current concepts. We chose to keep the ontology simple to achieve an end-to-end example since we believe the value of our demonstration is in showing how, with limited number of concepts, we can achieve value-add to our activity applications.

The next step in demonstrating our approach and following our use case scenario, is to create a simple UAM lower ontology for the domain. The intent is to define the semantics of reading group activities. Two of the main concepts and properties are: (1) *uam-reading:ReadingArtifact* which is a holder for one reading item. An artifact could be rated, have comments associated with it, relate to other artifacts, be recommended by an actor, and have a reading deadline associated with it; and (2) *uam-reading:ReadingActivity* which represents a reading activity that involves human actors and reading artifacts. A human actor can participate in many reading activities which have a title and a start date. All human actors can be assigned to a reading artifact, comment on them, rate them, recommend them, and relate artifacts to each other.

4.1 Dynamic Discovery and Integration

Since there are not many SWS are currently publicly available, we decided to overlay existing Web services that deal with reading documents with our semantics. We chose the Amazon.com E-Commerce Services (Amazon ECS) since it allows access to the contents from the book department of Amazon's Web site along with the various information collectively gathered from the Amazon community. We created simplified versions of the Amazon ECS specifically exposing capabilities related to our reading document ontology.

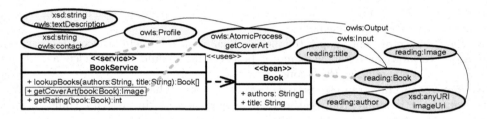

Fig. 3. Simplified *BookService* with partial OWL-S annotation. Heavy dashed gray lines show which part of the service the semantic annotation refers to. The ovals represent the OWL-S concepts and domain-specific annotations.

Figure 3 shows parts of our simplified SWS overlayed with a partial OWL-S descriptions. We only show a subset of the OWL-S *Profile* and portions of the *Process* description for one of the service's methods. The remaining methods would also be described likewise. In addition a *Grounding* instance is also attached to the *Service* instance to point to the WSDL for the service.

Similar to the simplified *BookService* SWS, the generated UAM SWS are overlaid with the appropriate OWL-S descriptions. For instance, we deploy a service to query and retrieve the *ReadingActivity* and *ReadingArtifact* instances, and these have OWL-S descriptions annotated with the *Reading Group Activity* lower ontology and the *Reading Document* ontology. The discovery process is realized by matchmaking the annotations of UAM SWSs with that of the *BookService*. We created a matchmaking agent that runs an algorithm that is similar to [10]. The algorithm looks for *Process* descriptions from SWS for which the *Input* semantically matched the *Output* from the UAM SWS.

Semantic matching either means that the *Input* class is the same as the *Output* class or that the *Output* class is subsumed by the *Input* class, e.g., the *Output* class is a subclass of the *Input* class. A concrete example is to discover that the *BookService getCoverArt* can be passed a *reading:Book* instance from the UAM SWS to generate an *Image* instance which contains the image URI for the cover art. In addition, the matchmaking also looks for cases where the discovery can take multiple *Process* method invocations. For instance, using a *reading:Book* instance *reading:authors* and *reading:title* properties the agent can determine the book's *reading:isbnNumber* which can in turn be used to retrieve the book's *rating*.

5 Future Work

We are constantly expanding the capabilities of our UAM environment. Currently our SWS generation requires the wiring of the operation definition to an existing Java class on the UAM server that operates on the datastore. We would like to eventually bypass this step by having generic Java operators that would operate on different domains and therefore not require specializations when new domains are supported. This could be achieved if the generic operators use the domain ontology as an abstract definition of the operands and the types that are passed as arguments to the operator definitions. We are also looking into using other, simpler, more lightweight SWS approaches, such as WSDL-S [1] as well as expanding our use cases to richer activity domains.

References

1. R. Akkiraju et al. Web Services Semantics: WSDL-S. http://lsdis.cs.uga.edu /library/download/WSDL-S-V1.html, Apr. 2005.
2. T. Berners-Lee, J. Hendler, and O. Lassila. The Semantic Web. *Scientific American*, 501(5):28–37, May 2001.
3. P. Dourish. Process Descriptions as Organisational Accounting Devices: The Dual Use of Workflow Technologies. In *Proc. of the ACM Conf. on Supporting Group Work*, Boulder, CO, Sept. 2001.
4. T. Kreifelts, E. Hinrichs, and G. Woetzel. Sharing To-Do Lists with a Distributed Task Manager. In *Proc. of 3rd European Conf. on Computer-Supported Cooperative Work*, Milan, Sept. 1993.
5. D. L. McGuinness and F. van Harmelen. OWL Web Ontology Language Overview. http://www.w3.org/TR/owl-features/, Feb. 2004.
6. S. A. McIlraith, T. C. Son, and H. Zeng. Semantic Web Services. *IEEE Intelligent Systems*, 16(2):46–53, Mar. 2001.
7. T. P. Moran. Activity: Analysis, Design, and Management. In *Proc. from the Symp. on the Foundations of Interaction Design*, pages 12–13, Italy, Nov. 2003.
8. T. P. Moran and A. Cozzi. Unified Activity Management: Supporting People in eBusiness. *Communications of the ACM*, Dec. 2005. To appear.
9. OWL-S. OWL-Service Ontology 1.1. http://www.daml.org/services/owl-s/1.1/, Nov. 2004.
10. K. Sycara et al. Automated Discovery, Interaction, and Composition of Semantic Web Services. *Journal on Web Semantics*, 1(1):27–46, Sept. 2003.

The Price of Services

Justin O'Sullivan, David Edmond, and Arthur H.M. ter Hofstede

Business Process Management Program,
Faculty for Information Technology,
Queensland University of Technology,
GPO Box 2434,
Brisbane QLD 4001, Australia
justin@service-description.com

Abstract. If we accept that service providers and service users all operate with autonomy in some form of market place, then a necessary prerequisite for service discovery and engagement is the description of the non-functional properties of a service. Price acts as one of the key non-functional properties used in choosing candidate services. Conventional services describe prices using several approaches (e.g. fixed price, price ranges, proportional pricing, dynamic price mechanisms). Furthermore, there are associated concepts such as price matching, price granularity, taxes and reward schemes that might need to be taken into consideration. This paper offers a discussion of the non-functional property of price. By incorporating some information about price, service descriptions will move away from the narrow distributed computing view of web services, enabling greater reasoning with respect to service descriptions.

1 Introduction

Through media such as newspapers, letterbox flyers, corporate brochures and television we are regularly confronted with descriptions for conventional services. These representations vary in the terminology utilised, the depth of the description, and the aspects of the service that are characterised. Existing service catalogues provide little relief for service requestors from the burdensome task of discovering, comparing and substituting services. Add to this environment the rapidly evolving area of web services with its associated surfeit of standards, and the result is a considerably fragmented approach to the description of services. It leaves the vision of the Semantic Web [1] somewhat clouded.

We have previously claimed that non-functional properties are an essential component of the characterisation of any service [2]. In [3] we present a discussion of many non-functional properties that can be used to improve discovery, comparison and service substitution. The non-functional properties we capture include availability (both temporal and locative), payment, price, discounts, obligations, rights, penalties, trust, security, and quality. This content has been published on the Web as a set of navigable models (http://www.service-description.com/). To develop these models we undertook a significant analysis of services from numerous domains. We have extracted hundreds

B. Benatallah, F. Casati, and P. Traverso (Eds.): ICSOC 2005, LNCS 3826, pp. 564–569, 2005.

of non-functional related properties that have been subjected to criteria before inclusion in our models. This work is an attempt to narrow the void between the functionally focused web service description standards and the non-functional description of services. It is our opinion that the semantic richness of the non-functional properties of services is not being exploited. We refer to this as "semantic myopia" [4].

The rest of the paper is structured as follows. In section 2 we provide an insight into our motivations whilst also positioning our work with respect to other research. Next, in section 3, we present a discussion of the non-functional property of price. Finally, we present our conclusions in section 4. We are unable to portray our entire formal taxonomy within the space considerations of this paper. See http://www.service-description.com/ for the complete taxonomy.

2   Motivations

Our primary motivation is to provide a necessary pre-requisite to automated service discovery, service selection and service substitution. We propose some sample questions that we put to existing web service description standards as a means of highlighting our concerns. What percentage deduction does the service provider offer when they are willing to match the price of an equivalent service from another service provider? How many reward scheme points are acquired when paying a particular price for a service? These are terms that service requestors (i.e. people, organisations) currently utilise when discovering services. Are web services so different from conventional services? Removing the "tunnel vision" of service descriptions to include both web and conventional services results in the ability to compare both types of services. We prefer not to distinguish between conventional services and web services. We are motivated to ensure that the criteria used to evaluate conventional services are also available for web services.

To achieve these benefits, a service description technique is required that is capable of expressing the functional and non-functional aspects of services. We subscribe to the notion that non-functional properties are constraints over the functionality [5]. Existing semantic web services initiatives, whilst offering the ability to capture the non-functional properties, have lacked the depth of description that we advocate. The OWL web service ontology (OWL-S) [6] offers placeholders for the description of non-functional service properties, along with a minimal number of specific non-functional properties. The Web Services Modelling Ontology (WSMO) [7] uses Dublin Core metadata and a version number as the core properties, then extends these to include web service specific categories of non-functional properties (e.g. performance, security, financial). Our approach to the description of non-functional properties is complementary to both OWL-S and WSMO. We now offer our discussion of the non-functional property of price.

3   Price

We interchangeably refer to price as cost: cost being mostly the view from a service requestor perspective, whilst price is the view from the service provider perspective. Within this paper we refer to price as the amount being charged for a service. We believe that the pricing of a service is an obligation of the service provider, one of many obligations involved with service request and provision. We refer to it as a pricing obligation since there are costs involved in supplying the service to the requestor and therefore the provider would normally attempt to recoup these costs (plus a margin).

Examples of price descriptions include:

- Carpet cleaning: a carpet dry cleaning service offers 3 rooms cleaned for $89 AUD (where the maximum room size is 13 sq m, and subject to inspection of the carpet condition). They also offer 2 rooms for $69 AUD with additional rooms $25 AUD per room. Four rooms cost $110 AUD.
- Newspaper delivery: a newsagent offers home delivery of newspapers daily for $7.20 AUD per week (i.e. 7 days for $7.20 AUD).
- Accommodation: a hotel in Surfers Paradise is offering a room for $82.50 AUD per adult twin share.

From these examples we can see that prices are complex entities. They are not always easily captured as a simple dollar value in a certain currency. Prices become quite domain specific when granularities (e.g. per room) are applied. Certain complex conditions may also surround the eligibility of a service requestor to receive the advertised price. To this end we consider that a pricing obligation can be considered to wrap the price of a service with many other important non-functional properties. These may include:

- Price validity - this provides a where and when scoping of the price's availability. Using our temporal models (defined in [3]) the temporal validity can be specified as an anchored or recurring interval, an instant or a date. We also capture the location as the pricing obligation may be specific to a limited number of the locations where a service can be requested from. For example, an online retailer may offer a priority shipping service as an alternative to standard shipping. For each region within a particular country, the retailer would be able to state the price that is available for a particular timeframe.
- Conditions - these relate to any specific requirements or restrictions to the price, or to the refund for the price paid for a service. Conditions are complex entities that require a concrete representation. We prefer to identify conditions through URL referrals. Refund conditions are common for transportation services such as plane tickets where they state that a ticket may not be refundable, or may only be refunded within a particular timeframe.
- Refund procedure - associated with the specifying of refund conditions it may also be necessary for a service provider to state a refund procedure. This procedure is used by service requestors to enact the refund process. We consider procedures to be a sequence of steps that are followed to achieve an outcome.

- Negotiability - sometimes the service provider may advertise a price but be willing to accept a lesser amount. Our model allows the provider to state that they are willing to negotiate on price.
- Price customisation - this allows the provider to explain that its service is highly customisable, and therefore the actual price cannot be expressed (e.g. a landscaping service may not be able to express the price until they have an understanding of the requestor's block of land and their objectives). This does not reduce the usefulness of the service description as the service provider is still capable of expressing the other pricing obligation related properties within this list.
- Relationship obligation - this allows the service provider to state that a relationship is required before they will commit to a price and its surrounding non-functional properties (e.g. conditions, discounts). It is possible within our model to specify an obligation that refers to the need to have a relationship with the service provider to receive the service output.
- Payee discounts - we provide an in-depth discussion of discounts in [3] but provide a link within our pricing obligation model to one specific type of discount, those related to who the payee is. This might include a person from a particular age group (e.g. the elderly), those with membership to a particular body, or even a shareholder of a company.

We consider that the pricing obligation of the service provider, in conjunction with the price, produces a new entity that we refer to as the "ServicePrice". We attach further information to this entity later in this section (e.g. tax, price granularity, price modifier). We also consider that after stating a price (e.g. 10 nights at $150 USD per night) the service provider might attach the price for additional invocations (e.g. each extra night is $100 USD per night). We assert that every price is one of the following kinds:

- Absolute price - this contains a specific amount and a currency. For example $10 AUD represents ten (10) Australian dollars.
- Proportional price - this represents a percentage value with respect to a certain item. For example, the price of entering a managed fund might be 2.5% of the value being invested into the fund.
- Ranged price - Ranged prices are further subdivided into one of two types:
  - Ranged absolute - a ranged absolute price contains a *from* and *to* value that are both absolute prices. For example, a service provider may prefer to provide a ranged price rather than a specific price (e.g. $150,000 USD - $175,000 USD).
  - Ranged proportional - a ranged proportional price contains a *from* and *to* value that are both proportional prices. For example, a service provider may state the cost of its service as a range between 1.5% and 3% of the final sale price.
- Dynamic price - this form of pricing captures mechanisms like auctions, where the price is determined by a market's natural supply and demand. We capture the type of mechanism (such as English auction, Dutch auction etc), the conditions associated with using the mechanism, the location and

temporal availability of the mechanism, and a reserve price (as either an absolute or proportional price). We provide a link to the provider of the dynamic pricing mechanism (e.g. eBay). An example of a service that could be auctioned is advertising space on web sites.

Price also includes an item granularity that is applicable to all types of prices (e.g. per person per night). The granularity of the item reflects one or more units of measure. We foresee the use of common granularities such as time (hour, minute, second, day, month, year, night, week, fortnight), weight (gram, kilogram, tonne), volume (cubic metre), area (metres squared, square metres), length (millimetre, centimetre, metre, kilometre), byte (kilobyte, megabyte, gigabyte), and person (adult, child, infant, pensioner, senior). These granularities could be extended further to support notions such as a room. This caters for services such as our carpet dry cleaning or accommodation examples.

All prices have a modifier that quantifies the price being specified. In using the term "quantify" we are referring to it in a logical sense rather than in an arithmetic sense. We have provided four example modifiers: *exact*, *limited to* (the price will not go higher than the amount specified), *inclusive* (intended for ranges of values) and *from* (the price starts at this amount and will go higher depending on how the service is configured by the requestor). Prices may include a component that is tax related. Service providers can choose to state their price as inclusive or exclusive of a tax item. If a tax item is captured, then a tax percentage is attached. For example, Australians are taxed at a rate of 10% on the majority of goods and services they purchase under the Goods and Services Tax (GST). Similar taxes include the Value Added Tax (VAT). Tax is applicable to a particular region.

Some services offer a price based on the criterion that the service requestor also requests the use of another service. An example is that the carpet cleaning service provider will offer their carpet protection service only when addition cleaning services are purchased. A service price may also provide either the service requestor or the service provider with one or more rights with respect to the service. Rights are outlined in more depth in [3]. We provide a price matching facility within our price model. Some service providers advertise that they are willing to match or better the price of another competitor. For this type of service provider we allow the attachment of a percentage which indicates what they are willing to improve competitor offers by (e.g. 5%).

Some service providers choose to reward service requestors using loyalty schemes. We attach to the price of a service the possibility of accumulating rewards under a reward scheme. Reward schemes can be provided by the service provider or by a third-party. Our model allows a service to attach a number of reward points to the invocation of the service, based on the service price that is paid (remembering that prices have a temporal and a locative availability). Reward points are only available during certain temporal intervals, or on a particular date, as well as being surrounded by some conditions. In a complementary manner we allow the service provider to state that they accept rewards scheme points as payment for a service.

4   Conclusions

Our approach seeks to offer a domain-independent method for describing the non-functional properties of both conventional and web services. Due to space limitations we have presented only part of the non-functional property of price. Our recent work [3] provides the same level of descriptive depth for other non-functional properties such as availability (temporal and locative), payment, obligations, rights, discounts, penalties, trust, security and quality. We feel that this approach is complementary to existing semantic web service initiatives such as WSMO and OWL-S.

The non-functional properties of services introduce complexity to the description of services but their inclusion is crucial to the automation of service discovery, comparison and substitution. We have stated in this paper our belief that two challenges confront the future of service description - overcoming web service tunnel vision and overcoming semantic myopia. That is, choosing to ignore both the rich history of conventional services, and the non-functional properties of services (perhaps through deferring to domain specific ontologies, or by a continued functional focus). Our work provides an opportunity for expressing the non-functional properties of services using a single technique for both conventional and web services, whilst also addressing our stated concerns.

References

1. Berners-Lee, T., Fielding, R.T., Masinter, L.: Uniform Resource Identifiers (URI): Generic Syntax (1998) Available from http://www.ietf.org/rfc/rfc2396.txt, accessed on 19-Jun-2001.
2. O'Sullivan, J., Edmond, D., Hofstede, A.t.: What's in a service?: Towards accurate description of non-functional service properties. Distributed and Parallel Databases Journal - Special Issue on E-Services **12** (2002) 117–133
3. O'Sullivan, J., Edmond, D., Hofstede, A.H.t.: Formal description of non-functional service properties. Technical FIT-TR-2005-01, Queensland University of Technology, Brisbane (2005) Available from http://www.citi.qut.edu.au/about/research_pubs/technical/non-functional.jsp, accessed on 15-Feb-2005.
4. O'Sullivan, J., Edmond, D., Hofstede, A.H.t.: Two main challenges in service description: Web service tunnel vision and Semantic myopia. In: W3C Workshop on Frameworks for Semantics in Web Services, Innsbruck, Austria (2005)
5. Chung, L.: Non-Functional Requirements for Information System Design. In Andersen, R., Bubenkor, J.A., Sølvberg, A., eds.: Proceedings of the 3rd International Conference on Advanced Information Systems Engineering - CAiSE'91. Lecture Notes in Computer Science, Trodheim, Norway, Springer-Verlag (1991) 5–30
6. OWL-S Coalition: OWL-S Web Service Ontology (2004) Available from http://www.daml.org/services/owl-s/1.1/, accessed on 21-Nov-2004.
7. Bruijn, J.d., Bussler, C., Fensel, D., Kifer, M., Kopecky, J., Lara, R., Oren, E., Polleres, A., Stollberg, M.: Web Services Modeling Ontology (WSMO) - Working Draft 21st November 2004 (2004) Available from http://www.wsmo.org/2004/d2/v1.1/20041121/, accessed on 22-Nov-2004.

Managing End-to-End Lifecycle of Global Service Policies

Daniela Rosu and Asit Dan

IBM T.J. Watson Research Center, 19, Skyline Drive, Hawthorne, NY, 10532, USA
{drosu, asit}@us.ibm.com

Abstract. Enterprise business services are often deployed over complex environments, managed by multiple service-management products. For instance, a business service may be configured as a three-tier environment with multiple services that run on different resource domains and span one or more tiers, and comprising service-management products such as workload managers, business resiliency managers, and resource arbiters. The objective policies of the enterprise business service, henceforth called Global Service Policies, determine the runtime policies used by the various management products. The lifecycle management of global service policies, including the deployment and enforcement stages, inherits the complexity of the enterprise IT environment. This paper proposes a novel framework for efficiently managing the deployment and enforcement lifecycle stages. The framework enables the complete automation of dissemination and translation of global policy for all service managers, for a low-cost, correct policy deployment. Also, the framework enables the runtime customization of resource arbitration components for using the actual business value models of the enterprise objectives global, for a high quality of policy enforcement. The proposed framework is prototyped and integrated with several IBM service-management products.

1 Introduction

In a service-oriented architecture, policies associated with business services define the business objectives under which the services are to be managed. Business objectives may be derived from Service Level Agreements (SLAs) [1, 2] established between provider and its customers. For instance, an SLA regarding a web-based application identifies the types of requests to be issued by the customer and the associated response time and availability objectives.

A typical enterprise business service consists of multiple software components, deployed over a complex environment managed by several independent service-management products. For example, a business service might be deployed as a three-tier configuration in an environment comprising web servers, application servers and data servers (see Fig. 1). Sample service-management products in this environment include i) workload managers [5] that prioritize and distribute service invocations in order to meet response time and throughput objectives, ii) business resiliency managers [4] that manage the backup nodes, and perform appropriate service reconfiguration in response to node failures such to satisfy recovery time and availability objec-

B. Benatallah, F. Casati, and P. Traverso (Eds.): ICSOC 2005, LNCS 3826, pp. 570–575, 2005.
© Springer-Verlag Berlin Heidelberg 2005

tive, iii) resource arbiters [3] that dynamically change allocation of server nodes across tiers such that the service managers can satisfy their objectives. Therefore, multiple service-management components manage the same set of services under a common set of service level objective policies, referred to as Global Service Policies.

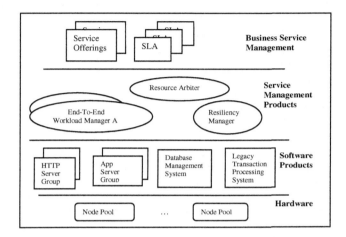

Fig. 1. Architecture of sample enterprise IT infrastructure

There are many challenges faced today in managing services in such an environment based on enterprise business objectives. Many challenges stem from the lifecycle management of Global Service Policies. The foremost challenge is the difficulty of deploying the enterprise business objectives in a consistent manner across all management components. The difficulty stems from multiple factors. First, the runtime policies used by each of these components are expressed in specific format which, most often, mixes business objectives with deployment details such as the domain in which the service is deployed, and groupings of service objectives into service classes used for management. Ensuring consistency is difficult because, many often, the conceptual elements expressed via policies do not match across these components. For example, a workload manager may manage service level objectives associated with a service endpoint, i.e., url or WSDL operation, while a resource arbiter may manage objectives associated with a node or cluster. As a result, existing solutions to policy deployment for complex SOA environments use manual, error-prone operations, involving multiple component-specific tools/GUIs.

Another challenge is the consistent enforcement of Global Service Policies across all service managers. Most prominent is the limitation of resource arbitration products to make decisions based on the actual business value model (i.e., value types and expressions) of the Global Service Policies and the related resource-allocation optimization objectives. Existing arbitration solutions use fixed value models and optimization objectives, such as a value model defined by component priority and an optimization model suitable for providing differentiated services [3]. However, many enterprises might use different value models, such as a benefit-driven model, based on service fees and penalties for objective violations. Therefore, the actual models must be translated into the arbiter's model. Most often the translation results in an approximation of the actual models, leading to inconsistent policy enforcement.

Supporting a SOA demands novel solutions for lifecycle management of global service policies, which enable complete process automation and compliance with the actual enterprise business service model. Towards this end, we propose a novel framework for global policy management. The framework comprises an infrastructure for fully automated global policy dissemination and transformation into the runtime artifacts used by the individual service-management products. The infrastructure enables runtime, low-cost updates of the service infrastructure based on separation of business service model from service deployment and implementation details. Also, the framework includes a novel infrastructure for customization of the resource arbitration process for using the actual enterprise business service value models. The infrastructure uses the novel "optimization value model" abstraction that describes the relationship between orchestration objectives and the business value models of global policies and has methods that the arbiter can invoke in its decision procedures.

A large body of research has addressed the use of SLAs for the management of complex IT environments, composed of Web Services and computational grids. A detailed discussion of related work can be found in [6]. Our proposal distinguishes from related work in several ways. First, we consider the problem of SLA dissemination in which the service and objective specifications are decoupled from the service deployment details, which is a necessity in SOA environments. Second, we address the problem of resource arbitration for a dynamic business service environment, in which both SLA and optimization objectives can change at runtime, and require immediate, fully compliant, low cost integration. In the following, we briefly present the proposed infrastructure. For an extensive presentation see [6].

2   Automated Global Policy Dissemination

Enterprise business service management components produce Global Service Policy specifications used for the configuration of all of the service-management products in the IT environment. These specifications represent customer SLAs, enterprise-specific orchestration policies, and other types of policies. Global Policy specifications are described as XML documents, e.g, WS-Agreement schema, which can include policies that relate to multiple service managers (see Appendix A). In the policy dissemination process, one has to extract the related policy specifications for each of the service managers, transform the content to manager specific runtime artifacts, and deploy them according to policy qualifying conditions.

The proposed infrastructure for automated global policy dissemination builds on the separation of the business service model from the service deployment and implementation details. Namely, a Policy Disseminator (Fig. 2) performs policy filtering and distribution to service managers based on a generic global policy model, and manager-specific Global Policy Adapters perform transformation and deployment of these specifications as service manager-specific runtime artifacts based on the deployment and implementation details.

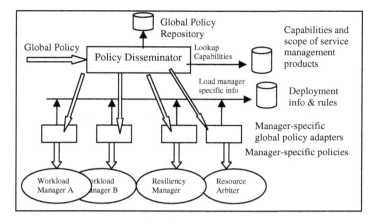

Fig. 2. Architecture for global policy dissemination

The global policy filtering is based on service manager capabilities, which are registered with the Policy Disseminator, and describe the manager's service scope and management objectives. The service scope identifies the set of enterprise services that the manager controls. The management objectives identify the type of SLO that the manager can enforce for a particular service. For filtering global policy specifications, one identifies the XML elements in the specification that define service scope and management objectives and matches them against the registered manager capabilities. For WS-Agreement specifications, these XML elements result from the content of wsag:ServiceReference and wsag:ServiceLevelObjective, respectively (see Appendix A).

The transformation of global policies into manager-specific runtime artifacts performed by Global Policy Adapters is based on (1) manager and service specific deployment information available in databases or configuration files, and (2) manager-specific rules for transformation of global policy abstractions. Adapters account for all of the global policy documents received from disseminator and for the related policy qualifying conditions, e.g., time interval when policy is applicable. Adapters handle various policy management elements, such as qualifying conditions, when the related service managers cannot handle them.

3   Customizable Resource Arbitration for Policy Enforcement

The proposed infrastructure for customizable resource arbitration is based on the novel "optimization value model" (OVM) abstraction. An OVM identifies an enterprise objective for optimization of resource allocation, such as "minimize the overall penalty value" or "maximize number of fulfilled objectives, in importance order". OVMs are defined by business service management components as orchestration policy. They are deployed at runtime to resource arbiters, which use them to customize the decision method based on actual set of active policies. Multiple OVMs may be defined concurrently, each with specific qualifying conditions. The resource arbiter determines which OVM is applicable for a decision instance and uses the associated implementation in the decision process. Fig. 3 illustrates the main OVM components.

OVM Descriptor: qualifying time and resource pool, set of metrics (business value types and service KPIs)	
OVM Method	**Function**
aggregateServiceForManager	Aggregate all objectives of a service managed by a service manager
aggregateServiceAcrossManagers	Aggregate all manager-level aggregates related to a service
aggregateAcrossServices	Aggregate all service-level aggregates related to analyzed allocation state
compareStateValue	Compare state-level aggregates

Fig. 3. OVM Model

An OVM is defined by a set of methods used by the arbiter for assessing which of the candidate allocation states is better to select for deployment, and a set of "metrics" used in this assessment, which can include global policy business value types, like penalty and importance, and arbitration-related service KPIs, such as 'distance from goal'. These methods enable the hierarchical aggregation of an allocation state "value" based on the values of the OVM "metrics" for each of the active global policy objectives in the given allocation state. The values of service objective metrics used in the aggregation of a state value are computed by the arbiter by interpreting the objective business value expressions extracted from global policy specifications, and using the service KPI values predicted by service managers or their adapters for the particular allocation state. The type of values produced by the OVM aggregation methods is specific to the OVM implementation. For instance, the value can be an array of pairs of objective importance level and maximum 'distance from goal', as needed for an optimization that maximizes objective compliance in importance order.

4   Conclusions

This paper introduces a novel framework for managing the lifecycle of global service policies in complex IT environments. The framework comprises novel architectures and techniques for performing global policy dissemination and transformation, and for enforcing global policy by enterprise-level resource arbiters. As a result, the deployment and enforcement stages of the global policy lifecycle can be fully automated while ensuring compliance with the enterprise business service objectives across changes related to the service deployment architecture, service objective business value models, and orchestration objectives. The prototype implementation integrated with IBM workload management and resource arbitration products demonstrates the feasibility of our proposals.

References

1. A. Andrieux, K. Czajkowski, A. Dan, K. Keahey, H. Ludwig, J. Pruyne, J. Rofrano, S. Tuecke, M. Xu: Web Services Agreement Specification. Version 1.1, Draft 18, submitted to the Global Grid Forum, May 14, 2004.
2. A. Sahai, A. Durante, V. Machiraju: Towards Automated SLA Management for Web Services. *Hewlett-Packard Research Report HPL-2001-310 (R.1).* Palo Alto, 2002.
3. IBM Tivoli Intelligent Orchestrator http://www-306.ibm.com/software/tivoli/products /intell-orch.
4. BMC Software:
   http://www.bmc.com/products/proddocview /0,2832,19052_19429_31452409_ 124990,00.html
5. searchdomino.com: IBM Enterprise Workload Manager: http://searchdomino.techtarget. com/whitepaperPage/0,293857,sid4_gci1012290,00.html
6. D. Rosu and A. Dan: Managing End-to-End Lifecycle of Global Service Policies, IBM Research Report RC23661, July 2005.

Appendix A: Sample WS-Agreement-Based SLA

```
<wsag:AgreementOffer …>…
  <wsag:Terms>..
  <wsag:ServiceReference wsag:Name="Service0Ref" wsag:ServiceName="Catalog">
      <wsa:EndpointReference><wsa:Address>/CatalogShopping</wsa:Address>…
  <wsag:GuaranteeTerm wsag:Name="Goal-Performance">
   <wsag:ServiceScope wsag:ServiceName="Catalog" />
   <wsag:QualifyingCondition><aspNS:PeriodName>Primetime</PeriodName>...
   <wsag:ServiceLevelObjective> <aspNS:ResponseTimeObjective>
     <TimeSecs>2.0</TimeSecs>   <Percentile>98</Percentile></aspNS:ResponseTime..>
   <wsag:BusinessValueList>
       <wsag:Penalty> …
         <wsag:ValueUnit>USD</wsag:ValueUnit>
         <wsag:ValueExpression>
           <acel:Product>
              <acel:Minus><acel:PropertySensor name="aspNS:TransactionCnt" />
                 <acel:PropertySensor name="aspNS:OnTimeTransCnt"/></acel:Minus>
              <acel:FloatConstant><Value>1.00</Value></acel:Float…>
           </acel:Product> …
       </wsag:BusinessValueList>
   </wsag:GuaranteeTerm>
  <wsag:GuaranteeTerm wsag:Name="Goal-Availability">
   <wsag:ServiceScope wsag:ServiceName="Catalog" />
   <wsag:QualifyingCondition />
   <wsag:ServiceLevelObjective> <aspNS:AvailabilityObjective>
       <AccumulationIntervalDays>365</AccumulationIn…
       <PercentageAvailability>99.99</PercentageAvailability>
       </aspNS:AvailabilityObjective></wsag:ServiceLevelObjective>
   <wsag:BusinessValueList>
       <wsag:Penalty>
         <wsag:ValueUnit>Thousand USD</wsag:ValueUnit>
         <wsag:ValueExpression>
           <acel:Product>
             <acel:Max>
                <acel:FloatConstant><Value>0</Value></acel:FloatConstant>
                <acel:Minus><acel:PropertySensor name="aspNS:Downtime" />
                   <acel:PropertySensor name= "aspNS: DowntimeObjective"/>
                 </acel:Minus></acel:Max>
             <acel:FloatConstant><Value>1000.00</Value></acel:Flo…></acel:Prod..>
       </wsag:Penalty>
       <wsag:CustomBusinessValue><aspNS:RelativeImportance>High</aspNS..
   </wsag:BusinessValueList> …
```

Applying a Web Engineering Method to Design Web Services*

Marta Ruiz, Pedro Valderas, and Vicente Pelechano

Departamento de Sistemas Informáticos y Computación,
Universidad Politécnica de Valencia,
Camí de Vera s/n, Valencia-46022, Espana
{mruiz, pvalderas, pele}@dsic.upv.es

Abstract. Probably one of the most difficult tasks in the development of a Service Oriented Architecture (SOA) is how to obtain well designed Web Services. Some Web Engineering methods provide support to introduce Web services in the software development process but do not give support to the systematic design and implementation of them. In this work, we present an extension of a Web Engineering method (called OOWS) to provide a methodological guide for designing Web Services. This allows identifying and designing the operations and arguments of Web Services following a model-driven approach, taking the OOWS conceptual models as a source. To document our approach, we apply our ideas to the design of the Amazon Web Service and compare our proposal with the solution provided by Amazon.

1 Introduction

The emerging Web Engineering discipline is being worried on how to develop well designed Web services. A web service should provide public operations with an appropriate *granularity* level in order to provide flexibility and to facilitate its connection and integration into distributed business processes over the Internet.

Some Web Engineering methods are extending their proposals to introduce Web services into their web conceptual modelling approaches (OOHDM [1], WebML [2] and UMLGuide [3]). Those approaches introduce some kind of syntactic mechanisms to include web service calls into the navigational model. However, these approaches do not give support to the design and development of Web services.

The OOWS [4] approach proposes a model driven approach to develop web applications. The OOWS method integrates navigational design with a classical OO conceptual modelling providing systematic code generation (following the strategy proposed in OO-Method [5]). The present work is an initial effort to introduce SOA and the Web services technology in the OOWS method. The main contribution of our proposal compared to other Web Engineering methods is the definition of a methodological guide that allows systematically identifying a set of functional groups that define public operations in a SOA.

---

* This work has been developed with the support of MEC under the project DESTINO TIN2004-03534 and cofinanced by FEDER.

B. Benatallah, F. Casati, and P. Traverso (Eds.): ICSOC 2005, LNCS 3826, pp. 576–581, 2005.

The structure of the paper is the following: section 2 presents an overview of the OOWS approach, introducing the steps and the models provided by the development method. Section 3 presents the methodological guide to obtain the operations that constitute the functional groups. Section 4 compares the operations that are obtained following our strategy with those published by Amazon. Finally, we present some conclusions and further work in section 5.

2 The OOWS Approach. An Overview

In this section, we present a brief overview of the OOWS method [4]. In order to build a web application OOWS introduces a development process that is divided into three main stages: *User identification, Task description* and *Conceptual modelling*.

In the **user identification** step, a *User Diagram* is defined to express which kind of users (roles) can interact with the system, providing a role-based access control (RBAC [6]).

In the **task description** step, a *Task Diagram* (see Fig. 1-A) is defined for each kind of user. In this diagram, we describe in a hierarchical way which tasks the user can achieve by interacting with the Web application.

In the **conceptual modelling** step, we define a web conceptual schema that gives support to the tasks identified above. The navigational aspects of a Web application are described in a *navigational model* [4].

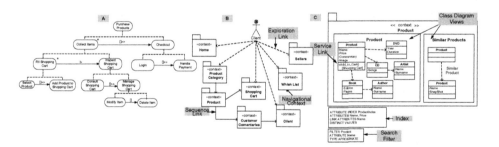

Fig. 1. OOWS models

The OOWS navigational model is defined from a set of navigational maps that describe the navigation allowed for each kind of user (specified in the user diagram). Each navigational map (see Fig. 1-B) is represented by a directed graph whose nodes are *navigational contexts* and its arcs denote *navigational links*.

A navigational context (see Fig. 1-C) (represented by an UML package stereotyped with the *«context»* keyword) defines a view on the class diagram that allows us to specify an information recovery. There are links of three kinds: (1) *Exploration links* (represented by dashed arrows) that are defined from the root of the navigational map (depicted as a user) and ends in a navigational context; (2) *Sequence links* (represented by solid arrows) that represent a reachability relationship between two contexts; (3) *Operation links* that represent the target navigational context that the user will reach after an operation execution. Furthermore, for each context, we can also define: (1) *Search filters* that allow us to filter the space of objects that retrieve the navigational context. (2) *Indexes* that provide an indexed access to the population of objects.

3   A Methodological Guide for Designing Web Services

In this section we present the main contribution of our proposal: a methodological guide that allows us to obtain the operations that implement the requirements of a Web application in a SOA. These operations are obtained in a systematic way from the OOWS models. Analyzing these models and taking into account the kind of requirements that they capture, our proposal identifies a set of functional groups (fg) that define the public operations in a SOA. We identify four fg: *User Management, Information Retrieval, Application Logic* and *Navigation Support*. These fg constitute the public interface of the designed Web service.

3.1   User Management Group

The User Management (UM) group provides the operations for the authentication, authorization and management of the potential users that interact with the application. The operations of this group can be detected using the OOWS user diagram. Afterwards, the operations of this service are detected from both the *user diagram* and the RBAC model [6] and are classified into three types: (1) Those that provide support for the user identification: `loginUser`, `logoutUser`, `obtainRol`, `changeRol` and `remindPassword`. (2) Those that give support for the generic user administration: `newUser`, `modifyUser`, `deleteUser`. (3) Those that only can be executed by an Administrator user: `newRol`, `deleteRol`, `addUserToRol`, `removeUserToRol`, `addPermission` and `removePermission` inherited from the RBAC model [6].

3.2   Information Retrieval Group

The Information Retrieval (IR) group defines operations to retrieve the information that must be shown in each navigational context (see Fig. 1-C) (a web page in the running example): (1) The `retrieve`*ViewName*`(id_sesion, [attributeID])` operation allows us to obtain the information specified in the navigational context views. The operations detected from the navigational context *Product* (see Fig. 1-C) are: `retrieveProduct` and `retrieveSimilarProducts`. (2) The `getIndexed`*IndexName* `(id_sesion, attributes)` operation gives support for the *index* mechanisms defined in a navigational context. The operation `getIndexedProductIndex` is identified from the index of the context *Product*. (3) The `search`*FilterName*`(id_sesion, attribute, value)` operation gives support to the filter mechanisms defined in a navigational context. The operation `searchProduct` is detected from the filter defined in the context *Product*.

3.3 Application Logic Group

The Application Logic (AL) group provides operations to implement functional requirements of a Web application.

The operations that constitute this group are obtained from both the *task diagram* and the *class diagram*: (1) The *task diagram* is used to determine the public operations that must be offered. For each leaf task we define an operation. In the task diagram of the Amazon example (see Fig. 1-A), we define the following public operations: *SelectProduct, AddProductShoppingCart, ConsultShoppingCart, Modify-Item, DeleteItem* and *HandlePayment*. The *Login* operation is not offered in this group because it is an operation of the *UM* group. (2) The *class diagram* is used to obtain the arguments of each operation. We detect each class that participates in an operation achievement and then its/their attributes define the operation arguments.

3.4 Navigation Support Group

The Navigation Support (NS) group provides operations to implement the navigation defined in the navigational model. The NS moves the navigational logic to the *interaction tier* facilitating both the implementation of adaptation and personalization mechanisms of web applications.   This group has three operations: (1) The explorationLink(id_sesion) operation gives support to the implementation of the exploration links. (2) The sequenceLink(id_sesion, context) gives support to the implementation of the sequence links. (3) The operationLink-(id_sesion, service) operation gives support to the implementation of the operation links.

Fig. 2 shows the implementation (Web page) of the *Product* context (see Fig. 1-C). In this figure we can see the use of some operations shown in this work.

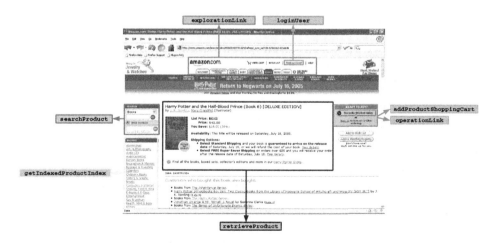

Fig. 2. Web page of the *Product* context

4 Evaluation of Our Proposal

In this section, we compare the operations that are obtained following our strategy to those published in Amazon[1]. Our intention is to identify some weak points of our proposal in order to improve our method.

Amazon web service offers 18 operations while we offer 27 operations (14 from the UM group, 4 from the IR, 6 from the AL and 3 from the NS group). Next, we show the comparative between the Amazon and our operations:

(1) `BrowseNodeLookUp`: this operation is supported by `retrieveCategory` detected from a view defined in the *Product Category* context.

(2) `Help`: it is not supported because we have not captured this requirement in our web conceptual model. This operation just provides a user manual.

(3) `CustomerContentLookup`: we implement it with `retreiveClientCo-mentaries` detected from a view defined in the *Client Commentaries* context.

(4) `CustomerContentSearch`: this operation is supported by `retreiveClient` detected from a view defined in the *Clients* context.

(5) `ItemLookup`: we support it with `retrieveProduct` detected from the *Product* view defined in the *Product* context.

(6) `ItemSearch`: This operation is supported by `searchProduct` detected from the filter defined in the *Product* context.

(7) `SimilarityLookup`: it is implemented by `retrieveSimilarProducts` detected from the *Similar Products* view defined in the *Product* context.

(8) `ListLookup`: this operation is supported by `getIndexedProductIndex` detected from the index defined in the *Product* context

(9) `ListSearch`: it is implemented by `searchWhishList` detected from a filter defined in the *Whish List* context

(10) `CartAdd`: we support it with `addProductShoppingCart` detected from the *task diagram*.

(11) `CartClear`: is not supported because in the Amazon web conceptual model, this functionality has been indirectly modelled through the task *Delete Item*. we have considered that if the user wants to clear the cart he/she must delete all the items.

(12) `CartCreate`: this operation is implicitly implemented in our `addProductShoppingCart` operation.

(13) `CartGet`: we implement it with `consultShoppingCart` detected from the *task diagram*.

(14) `CartModify`: this operation is implemented by two of our operations: `modifyItem` and `deleteItem` (detected from the *task diagram*).

(15) `SellerLookup`: this operation is supported by `retrieveSeller` detected from a view defined in the *Sellers* context.

(16) `SellerListingLookup` and (17) `SellerListingSearch`: these operations are related to the integration of Amazon with Third Party systems which is out of the scope of this work. Information about this can be found in [7].

---

[1]http://www.amazon.com/gp/browse.html/102-0679965-?%5Fencoding=UTF8&node=3435361

(18) `TransactionLookup`: it is not supported because we have not considered information about financial operation in the web conceptual model specification.

Furthermore, our approach provides additional operations that do not exist in the Amazon web service. These operations are those presented in the UM and NS groups, in addition to `handlePayment` of the AL group.

As a conclusion, we can see that our proposal provides a good enough solution that is closer to the functionality provided by Amazon and it also includes additional functionality that can be used to provide user authentication mechanisms, giving an extra control of the navigation requirements and allows to support adaptation and personalization mechanisms of web applications.

5 Conclusions and Further Work

In this work, we have presented an approach to introduce SOA and the Web services technology in the OOWS method. We have presented a methodological guide to obtain the operations that define the Web service from the OOWS models. This methodological guide can be generalized to other Web Engineering Methods, because the OOWS method shares with them the most common models and primitives taken as source to obtain the Web services.

We are working on providing mechanisms that facilitate the integration of Web applications with Third party systems (tps) at the conceptual level [7]. When tps supply us their functionality as Web services, we apply Web services composition to achieve integration.

References

[1] D. Schwabe, G. Rossi and D.J. Barbosa, "Systematic Hypermedia Application Design with OOHDM". Proc. ACM Conference on Hypertext. pp.166. 1996.
[2] S. Ceri, P. Fraternali and A. Bongio, "Web Modeling Language (WebML): a Modeling Language for Designing Web Sites". In WWW9, Vol. 33 (1-6), pp 137-157. Computer Networks, 2000
[3] P. Dolog, "Model-Driven Navigation Design for Semantic Web Applications with the UML-Guide". In Maristella Matera and Sara Comai (eds.), Engineering Advanced Web Applications. 2004
[4] J. Fons, V. Pelechano, M. Albert and O. Pastor, "Development of Web Applications from Web Enhanced Conceptual Schemas". Springer-Verlag, Lecture Notes in Computer Science. Proc. Of the International Conference on Conceptual Modelling, 22nd Edition, ER'03, pp 232-245. Chicago, EE.UU, 13 - 16 October 2003.
[5] O. Pastor, J. Gomez, E. Insfran and V. Pelechano, "The OO-Method Approach for Information Systems Modelling: From Object-Oriented Conceptual Modeling to Automated Programming". Information Systems 26, pp 507–534 (2001)
[6] ANSI. Incits 359 2004. American National Standard for Information technology. Role-Based Access Control, 2004.
[7] V. Torres, V. Pelechano, M. Ruiz, P. Valderas, "A Model Driven Approach for the Integration of External Functionality in Web Applications. The Travel Agency System". In Workshop on Model-driven Web Engineering (MDWE 2005) at ICWE July 2005, Sydney, Australia. Accepted for publication.

An Architecture for Unifying Web Services Authentication and Authorization

Robert Steele and Will Tao

Faculty of Information Technology, University of Technology, Sydney,
P.O. BOX 123 Broadway N.S.W. Australia 2007
{rsteele, wtao}@it.uts.edu.au

Abstract. Security issues are one of the major deterrents to Web Services adoption in mission critical applications and to the realization of the dynamic e-Business vision of Service Oriented Computing. Role Based Access Control (RBAC) is a common approach for authorization as it greatly simplifies complex authorization procedures in enterprise information systems. However, as most RBAC implementations rely on the manual setup of pre-defined user-ID and password combinations to identify the particular user, this makes it very hard to conduct dynamic e-Business as the service requestor and service provider must have prior knowledge of each other before the transaction. This paper proposes a new Web Services security architecture which unifies the authorization and authentication processes by extending current digital certificate technologies. It enables secure Web Service authorization decisions between parties even if previously unknown to each other and it also enhances the trustworthiness of service discovery.

1 Introduction

As a key factor in the adoption of e-Business, security is an important concern for Web Services adoption [1]. As a new computing paradigm, Web Services applications present security requirements different from those of traditional applications. The challenge in Web Services security is that Web Services applications need to provide controlled disclosure of information rather than the traditional all-or-nothing approach; the authorization procedure is more interactive and complex than the classic user-ID and password combination approach.

2 Unifying Authentication and Authorization in Web Services

2.1 Motivation

In Web Services applications, to carry out a real time, global e-Business transaction, it will be extremely valuable to have a unified architecture to allow service requestors to acquire appropriate privileges automatically and dynamically without necessarily having prior knowledge or relationship with the service provider. And it is also highly desirable that only trusted services can be retrieved in the central registry by service requestors.

B. Benatallah, F. Casati, and P. Traverso (Eds.): ICSOC 2005, LNCS 3826, pp. 582–587, 2005.
© Springer-Verlag Berlin Heidelberg 2005

A new architecture is proposed in this paper for unifying authentication and authorization in Web Services by extending certificate technologies. The architecture allows the service provider to simply define rules to group a large number of current or potential service requestors into appropriate roles, and assigns privileges to service requestors according to the role list, i.e. the architecture utilizes Role Based Access Control (RBAC) in part. Furthermore, before conducting the transaction, the service requestor can decide whether to send a request message or not by checking the service provider's business credentials.

2.2 Overview of the Proposed Architecture

There are several core elements in this new architecture to unify the authentication and authorization in Web Services applications, which are:

1. WS -Business Policy (WSBP)
2. eXtended CA (ECA)
3. eBusiness Passport (EBP)

All new elements are shown in Fig. 1 and the following sections discuss how these elements inter-operate to build a global trustworthy Web Services platform.

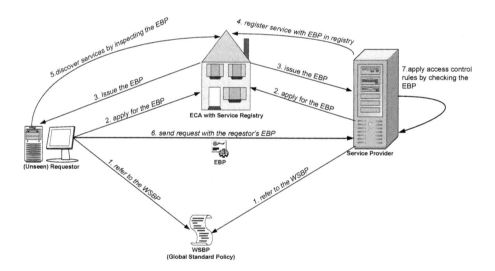

Fig. 1. Overview of Architecture

2.3 WS-Business Policy

WSBP is an important new element in the architecture. It is a standard for describing and evaluating business entities based on their backgrounds and performances. It has a rich set of criteria to enable a fine grained description and evaluation result. All evaluation data is described in XML and constrained by the WSBPXML Schema.

The WSBP has two parts, which are:

1. WS Business Policy-Common (WSBP-C)
2. WS Business Policy-Industry (WSBP-I).

WSBP-C is used to describe the common attributes of all business entities, such as registration date, number of employees and credit rating. The WSBP-I is industry sector specific evaluation criteria, where all criteria are tightly bound as evaluation criteria relevant to that particular industry.

The reasons for making WSBP into two parts are:

1. It is hard to evaluate all business entities which can be from all different locations and industries by using only common universal criteria.
2. It is not unusual that one business entity covers multiple industries. In this case, the business can be evaluated with one WSBP-C and multiple WSBP-I.

An evaluation result must have only one WSBP-C result and at least one WSBP-I. The criteria of WSBP are globally unified. The key role of WSBP is to provide a globally agreed set of criteria/ factors for evaluating business entities by a unified standard. Fig. 2 shows a potential WSBP instance - a real case might be more comprehensive and detailed.

```xml
<?xml version="1.0" encoding="UTF-8"?>
<WSBP xmlns="http://it.uts.edu.au/xml/ns/wsbp">
    <WSBP-C Name=" UTD Sydney Pty Ltd">
        <Type>Private</Type>
        <RegisteredLocation>Syd,AU</RegisteredLocation>
        <NumberOfEmployees>122</NumberOfEmployees>
        <Credit rating="8.5" rater="RoyalUnion" />
        <Certificate standard="ISO9000" />
    </WSBP-C>
    <WSBP-I Sector="Tech" Industry="ICP&amp;ISP">
        <RegisteredUsers>5033051</RegisteredUsers>
        <GooglePageRank>8</GooglePageRank>
        <PageViews>10343305</PageViews>
    </WSBP-I>
</WSBP>
```

Fig. 2. Potential WSBP Instance

By having a global standard for business evaluation (Fig. 1 Step 1) and if the results of such an evaluation can also be *authoritatively certified*, providers will be able to assign certain provider-specific roles to a requestor, even a previously unseen service requestor, based on the particular business characteristics of the requestor that have been certified. Due to the global standard, providers will be able to design mappings in advance that map requestors presenting certain certified business criteria to access roles through their knowledge of the criteria provided by WSBP.

2.4 ECA and EBP

An extended CA, the ECA does not only issue digital certificates but also evaluates business entities according to WSBP. In practical operation, the ECA's job might actually be more like a proxy as the ECA may only convert the certified paper documents into electronic form. For example, the documents may have actually been certified by a relevant government authority. After checking these stamped documents which are provided by business entities (Fig.1 Step 2), the ECA represents the evaluation results in electronic form against WSBP, along with the business entities' public key, all digitally signed by the ECA's private key. The signed evaluation results are named an e-Business Passport (EBP) (Fig.1 Step 3). The EBP is a special form of digital certificate which carries business entities activities and performance, also with their public key. As such it does not just provide authentication as a normal certificate does but also contains information to drive authorization decisions, allowing all business entities to be virtually connected. Because an EBP is digitally signed by the ECA's private key, it can be verified by the ECA's public key and no one can tamper with the data in the EBP, also, as the public key of the particular business entity has been signed in the EBP, the sender of the EBP can be easily authenticated. This ensures an EBP can not be forged and as long as the ECA is trusted, the information inside the EBP is trustworthy. An EBP will expire after a certain time to provide better trust and security and it is also renewable.

2.5 ECA and Service Providers

The ECA also allows service providers to register their services into a central registry to overcome some shortcomings in UDDI such as lack of access control and trustworthy service discovery [3] [4].

The service provider applies for an EBP based on relevant WSBP as Fig.1 Step 1 and 2 indicate. If the provided documents are qualified, the ECA will issue an EBP to the service provider (Fig.1 Step 3), and register this service provider's service into the central registry along with their EBP and all other necessary information such as WSDL (Fig.1 Step 4). If the EBP expires; the service will be removed from the central registry automatically to keep the registry a store of more current service information. A service provider can renew the EBP to prevent its expiration.

In current UDDI, there is no effective way to decide which service is reliable and trustworthy. For our architecture, only trusted services can be registered in the central registry and no longer certified and trusted services are removed immediately, allowing the central registry to always maintain fresh and trusted services.

3 Unified Authentication and Authorization

EBP is the key enabler to apply provider-side rules to achieve dynamic authorization as it carries with it certified WSBP criteria about the requestor business. However, as when a requestor carries out a transaction with a service provider, certain sensitive information may be passed in service requests, the service requestor also needs to determine whether they wish to invoke services from a particular provider. This can be achieved by requestor-side rules (Fig. 1 Step 5). The service requestor can check the provider's EBP at service discovery time and pass the provide EBP through the requestor-side rule engine. The risk in the requestor-side has been greatly decreased by pre-checking the providers' EBP. The SOAP request will only be made when the requestor finds the provider which meets the service requestor's requirements.

If the service requestor decides to conduct the transaction with a particular service provider, the service requestor will send its EBP to the provider in the SOAP header, as Fig.1 Step 6 indicates. After receiving the EBP, the service provider uses the ECA's public key to verify the EBP, the public key of the requestor inside the EBP to verify the sender and all other WSBP related information for determination of what privileges to grant. If the EBP is valid, the provider-side rule engine parses the XML document and the service requestor will be granted appropriate roles or be rejected automatically, depending on the provider's rules (Fig. 1 Step 7). After finishing the processing, the rule engine generates the highly secured tokens for maintaining the session with the requestor, encrypts the information by the requestor's public key, puts the encrypted information into the SOAP header and sends it back to the service requestor. Fig. 3 provides an example of simple pseudo-code to demonstrate provider-sides rules and how a mapping from WSBP criteria contained in the EBP to roles might work. The important point is that every service-provider will have its own specific implementation and provider-specific roles, and the implementation and roles are totally de-coupled from the service requestor. As such the service requestor does not need to know how the service provider implements its EBP rule mapping, and the rules can be very complex to meet real business requirements.

```
if (credit > 8)
    addRoles(requestor,GOLD)
else (credit between {5 to 8} && city==MY_CITY)
    addRoles(requestor,GOLD)
else
    addRoles(requestor,SILVER)
```

Fig. 3. Potential rules for mapping from WSBP criteria contained in an EBP to access roles

To accelerate the procedure of conducting real time business, service requestors are supposed to be recognized globally by only presenting their EBP. However, in the complexity of real world business transactions, exceptions will always occur. So in our architecture, the current user-ID and password based RBAC system still can be used to catch these exceptions. When the transaction can not simply use the EBP to allocate privileges, the service requestor can still be assigned the user-ID and password to get privileges manually. So the architecture will not lose any flexibility by adding the new functionalities described.

4 Related Work

There are already many standards and research activities for enhancing the security aspects in Web Services. All the standards, WS-Trust, WS-Federation, Shibboleth, SAML etc still build on the assumed token model, i.e. that the possible values inside the claim of a security token are not standardized or enumerated. To overcome this, we have proposed WSBP as a standard for even the possible "wording" of claims in our tokens, which is the EBP. This allows rules to be designed for a service in advance, referencing standard WSBP terms. Such rules can be applied to even previously unknown clients.

Smart certificates [2], is the closest research work to our proposed architecture, as it extends X.509 certificate for enabling flexible RBAC for web servers. However, as this work does not entail the proposal of a standard for the certificate contents, it doesn't enable the type of dynamic e-Business we are addressing and this work has not been extended into the Web Services domain.

5 Conclusion

The architecture utilizes and extends the digital certificate concept to introduce the idea of an e-Business Passport and a unified business policy to enable fine grained authorization for any business transaction partners where the service requestor and service provider do not necessarily need any previous negotiations before transaction. Also, it greatly enhances the trustworthiness in service look up, both for service requestors and service providers. The architecture can be used to boost trustworthiness in global dynamic e-Business. Our current ongoing research work includes finalizing a complete WSBP-C schema and implementing a prototype system.

References

1. Ciganek, A. P., Haines, M. N. & Haseman W.D.: Challenges of Adopting Web Services: Experiences from the Financial Industry, Proceedings of the 38th Annual Hawaii International Conference on System Sciences (2005)
2. Park, J.S. & Sandhu, R.S.: RBAC on the Web by Smart Certificates, Proceedings of the fourth ACM workshop on Role-based access control (1999) 1-9
3. Steele, R., Dai, J., UDDI Access Control for the Extended Enterprise: Proceedings of the International Conference on Web Information Systems and Technologies(2005)
4. Yang, S.J.H., Hsieh, J.S.F., Lan, B.C.W & Chung, J.Y,: Composition and evaluation of trustworthy Web Services, Proceedings of the IEEE EEE05 international workshop on Business services networks(2005)

Specifying Web Service Compositions on the Basis of Natural Language Requests

Alessio Bosca[1], Giuseppe Valetto[2], Roberta Maglione[2], and Fulvio Corno[1]

[1] Politecnico di Torino, Torino, Italy
{alessio.bosca, fulvio.corno}@polito.it
[2] Telecom Italia Lab, Torino, Italy
{roberta.maglione, giuseppe.valetto}@tilab.com

Abstract. The introduction of the Semantic Web techniques in Service-oriented Architectures enables explicit representation and reasoning about semantically rich descriptions of service operations. Those techniques hold promise for the automated discovery, selection, composition and binding of services. This paper describes an approach to derive formal specifications of Web Service compositions on the basis of the interpretation of informal user requests expressed in (controlled) Natural Language. Our approach leverages the semantic and ontological description of a portfolio of known service operations (called Semantic Service Catalog).

1 Introduction

The recent introduction of Semantic Web [1] ideas and results in the field of service-oriented computing has originated a vision of *Semantic Web Services* [6, 7], founded on machine understandability of the nature of operations made available as Web Services. The linguistic and ontological means for representing the properties and the capabilities of Web Services, and thus enhancing the ability to reason about the tasks they perform, seem particularly appealing for the support, based on operation semantics, of highly dynamic service selection and composition, which is an important goal of the Web Service paradigm. A major outstanding challenge to reach that goal is how to map the requirements describing a complex, composite service-oriented application (sometimes called a Value-Added Service, or VAS) to a multiplicity of simple, atomic Web Service operations, as well as to an overall service logic that coordinates their interactions.

We present an approach for the automatic generation of a high-level VAS specification (*Abstract Composition* in the remainder) on user demand, that is, starting from informal user requests. Our approach leverages semantic information about the operations exposed by a portfolio of Web Services and targets simple requests that can be expressed in (restricted) Natural Language, covering a range of workflows that can be modeled according to a set of modular *logic templates*. The Abstract Composition generated from the interpretation of a user request can be translated into an executable flow, and maps the user needs and intentions – as inferred from the original request - to known Web Service operations that can satisfy them, in a "task-oriented" way [5].

B. Benatallah, F. Casati, and P. Traverso (Eds.): ICSOC 2005, LNCS 3826, pp. 588–593, 2005.

We employ OWL-S annotations to provide a formal representation of service and operation semantics, as well as a classification of the Web Services in the portfolio.

2 Approach Overview

Our approach for the specification of service compositions at run-time has two starting points: the user request, which is processed and interpreted on the fly, to elicit functional requirements as well as a high-level view of the composition logic implied in the request; and a repertoire of well-known services that are described by rich semantic meta-data. Those two elements are, respectively, the *Request Interpreter* and the *Service Catalog,* displayed in Figure 1 together with other elements of our prototype.

This technique follows from two major assumptions: user requests are relatively simple and concise, in structure and terminology, to be expressed with a controlled subset of natural language; furthermore, a common ontological vocabulary can be established, and is consistently applied to all entries in the Service Catalog. While the latter assumption is unfeasible in a context, in which Web Services over the Internet at large and owned by multiple parties should be summoned in response to the user request, it seems reasonable and manageable in the context of a limited set of Web Services that are kept under the control of a single entity, like in the case of a provider or operator that offers value-added services to its customer base.

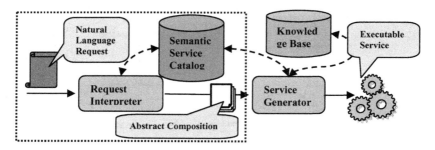

Fig. 1. System overview

Besides being used for the annotation of Web Services included in the Catalog, we exploit OWL-S also in the Request Interpreter, to support NLP techniques and our approach also includes mechanisms to transform that abstract service specification into a concrete one: the *Service Generator.* Although, functionally speaking, the role of the Service Generator – as shown in figure 1 – is simply to translate Abstract Compositions into a notation that can be executed over a service-oriented runtime of choice, its task is multifold and its structure complex, therefore a complete discussion of our solution, detailing its internal architecture, mechanisms and algorithms is not feasible here due to space limitations, and is outside the scope of this paper.

3   A Semantic Service Catalog in OWL-S

OWL-S is a framework to describe services from several perspectives: more precisely it characterizes services through a set of sub-ontologies. We have recognized the need for models and algorithms to select services on the basis of semantic annotations stored not only in their profile (as proposed for example in [2]), but also in their IO-PEs (see [3, 4]). We also propose to exploit IOPEs as a means to drive composition.

In order to enable the selection of service operations that satisfy some user requests or needs our modeling approach promotes the description of Effects in terms of the computing task that is performed by each atomic operation exposed by each service in our Catalog. To this end, we have implemented an *ad hoc ontology* called **Effects** (see bottom of Fig. 2). Additionally, we focus on I/O parameters semantics referring to a set of concepts collected in another *ad hoc ontology* called **IOtypes**. In order to reason on inputs and outputs for the automatic, semantic-based composition of operations, we extended the OWL-S model with a couple of bi-directional properties that allow us to link processes to their I/O parameters and parameter to processes that can produce or consume them (see Fig. 2).

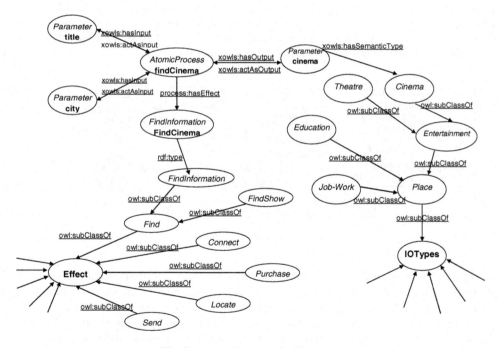

Fig. 2. Atomic Process: findCinema

4   Request Interpreter

Starting from a user request expressed in Natural Language (NL) the Request Interpreter is in charge of decomposing the sentence in order to isolate expressions that can be semantically associated to Effects listed in the Semantic Service Catalog, and hence mapped onto specific service functionality provided by atomic operations. At that end, the Request Interpreter translates the NL request into an Abstract Composition document, that is, a *formal* VAS specification. That specification includes a lattice of logic templates, describing how they relate to and can be composed with each other into the global VAS flow; moreover, it includes a list of Effects, which act as generic, semantic placeholders for operations that must be invoked along that flow.

Rather than completely parsing the sentence and interpreting each single fragment, we chose a simpler algorithmic approach that in a first step decomposes the request into fragments according to a proper logic template (if then, while do, sequence..). Then it leverages the dictionary in order to search for lexical patterns within the fragments and consequently infer the user's intention and eligible parameters.

4.1   An Instrument for Request Interpretation: The SSC Dictionary

As stated before, the dictionary contains lexical elements related to some entities within OWL-S ontology and includes pure lexical resources (as lists of verbs or preposition grouped by their role or meaning), as well as more complex ones, related to the sentence structure and its verbal governance (the *Sentence Constructions List* and the *Recognizer Catalog*).

The *Sentence Constructions List* is the main resource within the dictionary and it models the distinct expressive ways through which it is possible to request a service identified by a given *Effect* concept (see Fig. 2 for the relation between *AtomicProcesses* and *Effects*). For each *Effect* present in the SSC a set of thematic keywords and a list of eligible constructions are reported, each construction specifying a group of verbs and a set of parameters.

The *Recognizer Catalog* is the other key resource within the dictionary and models the different information the system should be able to recognize as potential parameters. It focuses on the different *IOTypes* present in the SSC and specifies for each of them a set of features which enable the isolation and recognition of a given *IOType* within a free text. Such features both concern how the data appears and which value it holds; the recognition process in fact relies on data format, on the presence of a keyword or on the candidate parameter's occurrence within a given list.

4.2   The Request Interpretation Process

This section details the various phases of the interpretation process and describes how it exploits the lexical resources within the dictionary.

The first operative step consists in recognizing the logic flow behind the request and coupling it to one of the logic templates supported in the system (if then, if then else, while do, sequence). A set of parsers properly tailored to the aforementioned templates process the request by trying to validate it against their own sentence model and if it matches, extract the distinct sentence blocks tagging them as conditions or actions. The result of this phase thus consists in the identification of the logical template and of the distinct clauses.

After this parsing procedure, we assume that different propositions have been identified and that each sentence block is constituted by only one clause with a principal verb and a set of objects. The following steps (2, 3 in Fig. 3) consist then in the interpretation of any individual action or condition retrieved in the precedent phase.

The presence within the clause of a thematic keyword (recorded in the dictionary) provides hints about the user's intention and focuses the algorithm's attention on a set of services, considered as potential solutions and therefore inserted into a list of eligible *Effects*. By taking in exam the advices contained in the *Sentence Constructions List,* the system guesses the information to look for and if a suitable verbal form is found, a search is triggered over the sentence block for values that fit the parameters reported in the dictionary. A proper recognizer is thus tuned according both to the functional features reported in the parameters' description (as the introductive prepositions) and to the semantic ones reported in the correspondent *IOType* element of the dictionary, and it accordingly tries to identify a block of text as eligible information.

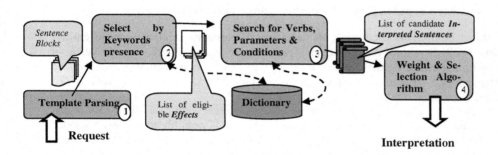

Fig. 3. Request Interpretation

If the functional information about where we expect to find the parameter and its "appearance" (the format of the data) are both verified as well as the semantic countercheck (the presence of a proper keyword in the same sentence chunk or the occurrence of the data in a list of known values), then a strong "found" is triggered, otherwise, a weak one. Once all eligible parameter values are found, the textual fragments identified as weak founds are evaluated in order to be promoted or rejected.

The analysis of each sentence block generates an *Interpreted Sentence* reporting the *Effect* id, the verbal form found, the list of the recognized parameters and the conditional expression, if present. These *Interpreted Sentences* are gathered into a list of candidate solutions and processed by a selection algorithm that constitutes the final step (phase 4) of the Request Interpretation. The algorithm works under the hypothesis that an interpretation holding more information should constitute a better solution, thus it simply assigns a score to the *Interpreted Sentences* for each element found (verbs, parameters, conditions) and then selects the ones with the highest rank.

The structural information concerning the logical flow of the request, retrieved from the template parsing (phase 1), and the distinct *Interpreted Sentences*, obtained in the followings (phases 2-4), are then unified into an *AbstractComposition* document.

5   Conclusions

We presented an approach that allows the specification of Web Services Compositions starting from user requests expressed in Natural Language. This paper shows how, under the assumptions stated in Section 2, it is possible to establish a synergy between the semantic service descriptions and the interpretation of user requests through a common ontology and consistent vocabulary. We have presently deployed a prototypal version of the system, provided with a semantic Service Catalog in OWL-S, comprising several tenths entries, and with a limited set of logic templates able to capture a range of simple workflow constructs. Our preliminary experiments with the system are encouraging, since they already enable to express and synthesize significant service compositions on demand.

We are currently working to expand the Service Catalog with a wealth of information, communication and e-commerce services in order to constitute a wider source of information, thus increasing the stress and the overall noise in the recognizing and selection procedures. At the same time, we are developing a test set of user requests that focus on our SSC servicing scope, in order to establish a validation resource for proving and tuning the algorithm.

References

1. T. Berners-Lee, J. Hendler, and O. Lassila, "The Semantic Web", *Scientific American*, 2001, 284(5): 34–43.
2. D. Mandell, and S. McIlraith, "Adapting BPEL4WS for the Semantic Web: The Bottom-Up Approach to Web Service Interoperation", *Proceedings of the Second International Semantic Web Conference*, 2003.
3. K. Sivashanmugam, K. Verna, A. Sheth and J. Miller, Adding Semantics to Web Services Standards, *Proceedings of the International Conference on Web Services*, 2003.
4. E. Sirin, B. Parsia, and J. Hendler, Composition-driven filtering and selection of semantic web services, *AAAI Spring Symposium on Semantic Web Services*, 2004.
5. Y. Ye and G. Fisher. Supporting Reuse by Delivering Task-Relevant and Personalized Information, *Proceedings of the 24th International Conference on Software Engineering*, 2002.
6. DAML-S, "Semantic Wes Services", http://www.daml.org/services/.
7. WSMO, "Web Services Modeling Ontology", http://www.wsmo.org/.

Author Index

Abbadi, Amr El   157
Abe, Mari   539
Acharya, Manoj   437
Agrawal, Divyakant   157
Aiello, Marco   424
Altunay, M.   382
Álvarez, P.   185

Bañares, J.A.   185
Barbon, Fabio   495
Baresi, Luciano   269, 478
Benbernou, Salima   353
Berardi, Daniela   520
Bertoli, Piergiorgio   495
Boote, Jeff W.   241
Bosca, Alessio   588
Bosloper, Ivor   255
Boyd, Eric L.   241
Breutel, Stephan   484
Brogi, Antonio   214
Brown, D.   382
Bruno, Marcello   87
Buchmann, Alejandro   533
Busi, Nadia   228
Byrd, G.   382

Calabrese, Gaetano   495
Calvanese, Diego   520
Canfora, Gerardo   87
Cardozo, Eleri   465
Chafle, Girish   410
Chandra, Sunil   410
Chandramouli, Badrish   366
Christie, Marcus   21
Colombo, Enzo   198
Colombo, Massimiliano   48
Cooney, Dominic   508
Corno, Fulvio   588
Cozzi, Alex   558
Curbera, Francisco   33

Dan, Asit   283, 296, 570
Dean, R.   382
De Giacomo, Giuseppe   520
de Souza, Victor A.S.M.   465

Di Nitto, Elisabetta   48
Di Penta, Massimiliano   48, 87
Distante, Damiano   48
Donsez, Didier   552
Dumas, Marlon   484, 508
Durán, Amador   170
Durand, Jérôme   241

Eberhart, Andreas   514
Edmond, David   564
Elgedawy, Islam   115
Esfandiari, Babak   101
Esposito, Gianpiero   87
Ezpeleta, J.   185

Faltings, Boi   396
Fang, Liang   21
Ferguson, Donald   33
Frankova, Ganna   424

Gannon, Dennis   21
Gerede, Cagdas E.   157
Gibelin, Nicolas   527
Gimpel, Henner   283
Goble, Carole   341
Gomadam, Karthik   502
Gómez-Pérez, Asunción   341
González-Cabero, Rafael   341
Gorrieri, Roberto   228
Guidi, Claudio   228
Guinea, Sam   269, 478

Hacid, Mohand-Said   353
Hammer, Dieter   255
Han, Jun   73
Hanemann, Andreas   241
Hasselmeyer, Peer   144
He, Xiaojun   353
Holzhauser, Roland   324
Huang, Yi   21

Ibarra, Oscar   157
Ivanyukovich, Alexander   545

Jeng, Jun Jang   539
Jensen, Scott   21
Jin, Yan   73
Jurca, Radu   396

Kandaswamy, Gopi   21
Kankar, Pankaj   410
Karastoyanova, Dimka   533
Kearney, Bob   283
Kemper, Alfons   324
Koyanagi, Teruo   539
Kudarimoti, Loukik   241
Kulkarni, Abhijit   437
Kuppili, Rajesh   437

Lalanda, Philippe   552
Lamparter, Steffen   514
Łapacz, Roman   241
Lei, Hui   366
Leymann, Frank   12, 533
Li, Zheng   73
Lin, Kwei-Jay   130
Lucchese, Gigi   495
Lucchi, Roberto   228
Ludwig, Heiko   283
Luo, Yun   101

Maglione, Roberta   588
Makpangou, Mesaac   527
Malfatti, Daniela   424
Mani, Rohit   437
Mann, Vijay   410
Marchese, Maurizio   545
Margaria, Tiziana   450
Marin, Cristina   552
Marru, Suresh   21
Martín-Díaz, Octavio   170
Mazza, Valentina   87
Maximilien, E. Michael   558
Mecella, Massimo   520
Miller, John A.   490, 502
Moran, Thomas P.   558
More, Nitin   437
Müller, Carlos   170
Mylopoulos, John   198

Nally, Martin   33
Narayanan, Srinivas   437
Nijhuis, Jos   255

Oberle, Daniel   514
Orriens, Bart   61
O'Sullivan, Justin   564
Ouyang, Chun   484

Pallickara, Sangmi Lee   21
Papazoglou, Mike   61
Patel, Parthiv   437
Pelechano, Vicente   576
Pérez-Hernández, María S.   341
Pistore, Marco   495
Plale, Beth   21
Popescu, Razvan   214

Ranganathan, Kavitha   296
Reitenspieß, Manfred   450
Roe, Paul   508
Rosu, Daniela   570
Ruiz-Cortés, Antonio   170
Ruiz, Marta   576

Sahin, Ozgur D.   157
Schuelke, Kenneth W.   437
Seltzsam, Stefan   324
Sheth, Amit P.   1, 490, 502
Shirasuna, Satoshi   21
Siljee, Johanneke   255
Simmhan, Yogesh   21
Slominski, Aleksander   21
Spoletini, Paola   198
Staab, Steffen   514
Steele, Robert   582
Steffen, Bernhard   450
Stockton, Marcia L.   33
Su, Jianwen   157
Subramanian, Subbu N.   437
Sun, Yiming   21
Swany, D. Martin   241

Tao, Will   582
Tari, Zahir   115
ter Hofstede, Arthur H.M.   484, 564
Thom, James A.   115
Trainotti, Michele   495
Traverso, Paolo   495
Trocha, Szymon   241

Valderas, Pedro   576
Valetto, Giuseppe   588
van der Aalst, Wil M.P.   484
Vasquez, Ivan   490

Verbeek, Eric   484
Verma, Kunal   1, 490, 502

Weiss, Michael   101
Wu, Qing   310
Wu, Zhaohui   310

Yamamoto, Gaku   539
Yanchuk, Aliaksei   545

Yang, Jian   61
Yu, Tao   130

Zacco, Gabriele   495
Zavattaro, Gianluigi   228
Zeng, Liangzhao   366
Zuccalà, Maurilio   48
Zurawski, Jason   241

Lecture Notes in Computer Science

For information about Vols. 1–3721

please contact your bookseller or Springer

Vol. 3837: K. Cho, P. Jacquet (Eds.), Technologies for Advanced Heterogeneous Networks. IX, 307 pages. 2005.

Vol. 3835: G. Sutcliffe, A. Voronkov (Eds.), Logic for Programming, Artificial Intelligence, and Reasoning. XIV, 744 pages. 2005. (Subseries LNAI).

Vol. 3833: K.-J. Li, C. Vangenot (Eds.), Web and Wireless Geographical Information Systems. XI, 309 pages. 2005.

Vol. 3826: B. Benatallah, F. Casati, P. Traverso (Eds.), Service-Oriented Computing - ICSOC 2005. XVIII, 597 pages. 2005.

Vol. 3824: L.T. Yang, M. Amamiya, Z. Liu, M. Guo, F.J. Rammig (Eds.), Embedded and Ubiquitous Computing. XXIII, 1204 pages. 2005.

Vol. 3823: T. Enokido, L. Yan, B. Xiao, D. Kim, Y. Dai, L.T. Yang (Eds.), Embedded and Ubiquitous Computing. XXXII, 1317 pages. 2005.

Vol. 3821: R. Ramanujam, S. Sen (Eds.), FSTTCS 2005: Foundations of Software Technology and Theoretical Computer Science. XIV, 566 pages. 2005.

Vol. 3818: S. Grumbach, L. Sui, V. Vianu (Eds.), Advances in Computer Science – ASIAN 2005. XIII, 294 pages. 2005.

Vol. 3814: M. Maybury, O. Stock, W. Wahlster (Eds.), Intelligent Technologies for Interactive Entertainment. XV, 342 pages. 2005. (Subseries LNAI).

Vol. 3810: Y.G. Desmedt, H. Wang, Y. Mu, Y. Li (Eds.), Cryptology and Network Security. XI, 349 pages. 2005.

Vol. 3809: S. Zhang, R. Jarvis (Eds.), AI 2005: Advances in Artificial Intelligence. XXVII, 1344 pages. 2005. (Subseries LNAI).

Vol. 3808: C. Bento, A. Cardoso, G. Dias (Eds.), Progress in Artificial Intelligence. XVIII, 704 pages. 2005. (Subseries LNAI).

Vol. 3807: M. Dean, Y. Guo, W. Jun, R. Kaschek, S. Krishnaswamy, Z. Pan, Q.Z. Sheng (Eds.), Web Information Systems Engineering – WISE 2005 Workshops. XV, 275 pages. 2005.

Vol. 3806: A.H. H. Ngu, M. Kitsuregawa, E.J. Neuhold, J.-Y. Chung, Q.Z. Sheng (Eds.), Web Information Systems Engineering – WISE 2005. XXI, 771 pages. 2005.

Vol. 3805: G. Subsol (Ed.), Virtual Storytelling. XII, 289 pages. 2005.

Vol. 3804: G. Bebis, R. Boyle, D. Koracin, B. Parvin (Eds.), Advances in Visual Computing. XX, 755 pages. 2005.

Vol. 3803: S. Jajodia, C. Mazumdar (Eds.), Information Systems Security. XI, 342 pages. 2005.

Vol. 3799: M. A. Rodríguez, I.F. Cruz, S. Levashkin, M.J. Egenhofer (Eds.), GeoSpatial Semantics. X, 259 pages. 2005.

Vol. 3798: A. Dearle, S. Eisenbach (Eds.), Component Deployment. X, 197 pages. 2005.

Vol. 3797: S. Maitra, C. E. V. Madhavan, R. Venkatesan (Eds.), Progress in Cryptology - INDOCRYPT 2005. XIV, 417 pages. 2005.

Vol. 3796: N.P. Smart (Ed.), Cryptography and Coding. XI, 461 pages. 2005.

Vol. 3795: H. Zhuge, G.C. Fox (Eds.), Grid and Cooperative Computing - GCC 2005. XXI, 1203 pages. 2005.

Vol. 3794: X. Jia, J. Wu, Y. He (Eds.), Mobile Ad-hoc and Sensor Networks. XX, 1136 pages. 2005.

Vol. 3793: T. Conte, N. Navarro, W.-m.W. Hwu, M. Valero, T. Ungerer (Eds.), High Performance Embedded Architectures and Compilers. XIII, 317 pages. 2005.

Vol. 3792: I. Richardson, P. Abrahamsson, R. Messnarz (Eds.), Software Process Improvement. VIII, 215 pages. 2005.

Vol. 3791: A. Adi, S. Stoutenburg, S. Tabet (Eds.), Rules and Rule Markup Languages for the Semantic Web. X, 225 pages. 2005.

Vol. 3790: G. Alonso (Ed.), Middleware 2005. XIII, 443 pages. 2005.

Vol. 3789: A. Gelbukh, Á. de Albornoz, H. Terashima-Marín (Eds.), MICAI 2005: Advances in Artificial Intelligence. XXVI, 1198 pages. 2005. (Subseries LNAI).

Vol. 3788: B. Roy (Ed.), Advances in Cryptology - ASIACRYPT 2005. XIV, 703 pages. 2005.

Vol. 3785: K.-K. Lau, R. Banach (Eds.), Formal Methods and Software Engineering. XIV, 496 pages. 2005.

Vol. 3784: J. Tao, T. Tan, R.W. Picard (Eds.), Affective Computing and Intelligent Interaction. XIX, 1008 pages. 2005.

Vol. 3781: S.Z. Li, Z. Sun, T. Tan, S. Pankanti, G. Chollet, D. Zhang (Eds.), Advances in Biometric Person Authentication. XI, 250 pages. 2005.

Vol. 3780: K. Yi (Ed.), Programming Languages and Systems. XI, 435 pages. 2005.

Vol. 3779: H. Jin, D. Reed, W. Jiang (Eds.), Network and Parallel Computing. XV, 513 pages. 2005.

Vol. 3778: C. Atkinson, C. Bunse, H.-G. Gross, C. Peper (Eds.), Component-Based Software Development for Embedded Systems. VIII, 345 pages. 2005.

Vol. 3777: O.B. Lupanov, O.M. Kasim-Zade, A.V. Chaskin, K. Steinhöfel (Eds.), Stochastic Algorithms: Foundations and Applications. VIII, 239 pages. 2005.

Vol. 3775: J. Schönwälder, J. Serrat (Eds.), Ambient Networks. XIII, 281 pages. 2005.

Vol. 3773: A. Sanfeliu, M.L. Cortés (Eds.), Progress in Pattern Recognition, Image Analysis and Applications. XX, 1094 pages. 2005.

Vol. 3772: M. Consens, G. Navarro (Eds.), String Processing and Information Retrieval. XIV, 406 pages. 2005.

Vol. 3771: J.M.T. Romijn, G.P. Smith, J. van de Pol (Eds.), Integrated Formal Methods. XI, 407 pages. 2005.

Vol. 3770: J. Akoka, S.W. Liddle, I.-Y. Song, M. Bertolotto, I. Comyn-Wattiau, W.-J. van den Heuvel, M. Kolp, J. Trujillo, C. Kop, H.C. Mayr (Eds.), Perspectives in Conceptual Modeling. XXII, 476 pages. 2005.

Vol. 3768: Y.-S. Ho, H.J. Kim (Eds.), Advances in Multimedia Information Processing - PCM 2005, Part II. XXVIII, 1088 pages. 2005.

Vol. 3767: Y.-S. Ho, H.J. Kim (Eds.), Advances in Multimedia Information Processing - PCM 2005, Part I. XXVIII, 1022 pages. 2005.

Vol. 3766: N. Sebe, M.S. Lew, T.S. Huang (Eds.), Computer Vision in Human-Computer Interaction. X, 231 pages. 2005.

Vol. 3765: Y. Liu, T. Jiang, C. Zhang (Eds.), Computer Vision for Biomedical Image Applications. X, 563 pages. 2005.

Vol. 3764: S. Tixeuil, T. Herman (Eds.), Self-Stabilizing Systems. VIII, 229 pages. 2005.

Vol. 3762: R. Meersman, Z. Tari, P. Herrero (Eds.), On the Move to Meaningful Internet Systems 2005: OTM 2005 Workshops. XXXI, 1228 pages. 2005.

Vol. 3761: R. Meersman, Z. Tari (Eds.), On the Move to Meaningful Internet Systems 2005: CoopIS, DOA, and ODBASE, Part II. XXVII, 653 pages. 2005.

Vol. 3760: R. Meersman, Z. Tari (Eds.), On the Move to Meaningful Internet Systems 2005: CoopIS, DOA, and ODBASE, Part I. XXVII, 921 pages. 2005.

Vol. 3759: G. Chen, Y. Pan, M. Guo, J. Lu (Eds.), Parallel and Distributed Processing and Applications - ISPA 2005 Workshops. XIII, 669 pages. 2005.

Vol. 3758: Y. Pan, D.-x. Chen, M. Guo, J. Cao, J.J. Dongarra (Eds.), Parallel and Distributed Processing and Applications. XXIII, 1162 pages. 2005.

Vol. 3757: A. Rangarajan, B. Vemuri, A.L. Yuille (Eds.), Energy Minimization Methods in Computer Vision and Pattern Recognition. XII, 666 pages. 2005.

Vol. 3756: J. Cao, W. Nejdl, M. Xu (Eds.), Advanced Parallel Processing Technologies. XIV, 526 pages. 2005.

Vol. 3754: J. Dalmau Royo, G. Hasegawa (Eds.), Management of Multimedia Networks and Services. XII, 384 pages. 2005.

Vol. 3753: O.F. Olsen, L.M.J. Florack, A. Kuijper (Eds.), Deep Structure, Singularities, and Computer Vision. X, 259 pages. 2005.

Vol. 3752: N. Paragios, O. Faugeras, T. Chan, C. Schnörr (Eds.), Variational, Geometric, and Level Set Methods in Computer Vision. XI, 369 pages. 2005.

Vol. 3751: T. Magedanz, E.R. M. Madeira, P. Dini (Eds.), Operations and Management in IP-Based Networks. X, 213 pages. 2005.

Vol. 3750: J.S. Duncan, G. Gerig (Eds.), Medical Image Computing and Computer-Assisted Intervention – MICCAI 2005, Part II. XL, 1018 pages. 2005.

Vol. 3749: J.S. Duncan, G. Gerig (Eds.), Medical Image Computing and Computer-Assisted Intervention – MICCAI 2005, Part I. XXXIX, 942 pages. 2005.

Vol. 3748: A. Hartman, D. Kreische (Eds.), Model Driven Architecture – Foundations and Applications. IX, 349 pages. 2005.

Vol. 3747: C.A. Maziero, J.G. Silva, A.M.S. Andrade, F.M.d. Assis Silva (Eds.), Dependable Computing. XV, 267 pages. 2005.

Vol. 3746: P. Bozanis, E.N. Houstis (Eds.), Advances in Informatics. XIX, 879 pages. 2005.

Vol. 3745: J.L. Oliveira, V. Maojo, F. Martín-Sánchez, A.S. Pereira (Eds.), Biological and Medical Data Analysis. XII, 422 pages. 2005. (Subseries LNBI).

Vol. 3744: T. Magedanz, A. Karmouch, S. Pierre, I. Venieris (Eds.), Mobility Aware Technologies and Applications. XIV, 418 pages. 2005.

Vol. 3742: J. Akiyama, M. Kano, X. Tan (Eds.), Discrete and Computational Geometry. VIII, 213 pages. 2005.

Vol. 3740: T. Srikanthan, J. Xue, C.-H. Chang (Eds.), Advances in Computer Systems Architecture. XVII, 833 pages. 2005.

Vol. 3739: W. Fan, Z.-h. Wu, J. Yang (Eds.), Advances in Web-Age Information Management. XXIV, 930 pages. 2005.

Vol. 3738: V.R. Syrotiuk, E. Chávez (Eds.), Ad-Hoc, Mobile, and Wireless Networks. XI, 360 pages. 2005.

Vol. 3735: A. Hoffmann, H. Motoda, T. Scheffer (Eds.), Discovery Science. XVI, 400 pages. 2005. (Subseries LNAI).

Vol. 3734: S. Jain, H.U. Simon, E. Tomita (Eds.), Algorithmic Learning Theory. XII, 490 pages. 2005. (Subseries LNAI).

Vol. 3733: P. Yolum, T. Güngör, F. Gürgen, C. Özturan (Eds.), Computer and Information Sciences - ISCIS 2005. XXI, 973 pages. 2005.

Vol. 3731: F. Wang (Ed.), Formal Techniques for Networked and Distributed Systems - FORTE 2005. XII, 558 pages. 2005.

Vol. 3729: Y. Gil, E. Motta, V. R. Benjamins, M.A. Musen (Eds.), The Semantic Web – ISWC 2005. XXIII, 1073 pages. 2005.

Vol. 3728: V. Paliouras, J. Vounckx, D. Verkest (Eds.), Integrated Circuit and System Design. XV, 753 pages. 2005.

Vol. 3727: M. Barni, J. Herrera Joancomartí, S. Katzenbeisser, F. Pérez-González (Eds.), Information Hiding. XII, 414 pages. 2005.

Vol. 3726: L.T. Yang, O.F. Rana, B. Di Martino, J.J. Dongarra (Eds.), High Performance Computing and Communications. XXVI, 1116 pages. 2005.

Vol. 3725: D. Borrione, W. Paul (Eds.), Correct Hardware Design and Verification Methods. XII, 412 pages. 2005.

Vol. 3724: P. Fraigniaud (Ed.), Distributed Computing. XIV, 520 pages. 2005.

Vol. 3723: W. Zhao, S. Gong, X. Tang (Eds.), Analysis and Modelling of Faces and Gestures. XI, 4234 pages. 2005.

Vol. 3722: D. Van Hung, M. Wirsing (Eds.), Theoretical Aspects of Computing – ICTAC 2005. XIV, 614 pages. 2005.